Letters of
Elizabeth Palmer Peabody

Letters of Elizabeth Palmer Peabody

American Renaissance Woman

EDITED, WITH AN INTRODUCTION, BY

Bruce A. Ronda

WESLEYAN UNIVERSITY PRESS ⬡ Middletown, Connecticut

A letter from Elizabeth Palmer Peabody to Horace Mann, Jr.,
February 1865, edited by Arlin Turner, reprinted by permission
of *The New England Quarterly.* Copyright 1975 by
The New England Quarterly.

All inquiries and permissions requests should be addressed
to the Publisher, Wesleyan University Press, 110 Mt. Vernon Street,
Middletown, Connecticut 06457.

Distributed by Harper & Row Publishers, Keystone Industrial Park,
Scranton, Pennsylvania 18512.

Endpapers: Central part of Concord village, drawn
by J. W. Barber, engraved by J. Downes. Used
by permission of Concord Free Public Library.

Library of Congress Cataloging in Publication Data

Peabody, Elizabeth Palmer, 1804–1894.
    Letters of Elizabeth Peabody, American renaissance woman.

    Bibliography: p.
    Includes index.
    1. Peabody, Elizabeth Palmer, 1804–1894.   2. Educators—
Massachusetts—Correspondence.   3. Reformers—Massachusetts—
Correspondence.   4. Intellectuals—Massachusetts—
Correspondence.   5. Massachusetts—Biography.
I. Ronda, Bruce A.   II. Title.
CT275.P484A4   1984   974.4′03   83-25986
ISBN 0-8195-5093-0 (alk. paper)

Manufactured in the United States of America

FIRST EDITION

✳ Contents

❈ Illustrations

❧ Preface

THIS VOLUME contains a representative selection of Elizabeth Palmer Peabody's vast correspondence. Doubtless some readers will want more of one kind of letter and less of another; the selection is necessarily subjective and personal. I have sought to include letters that give insight into her personality and into the various movements of which she was a part and that may be of interest to readers of the literature of the American Renaissance.

I have placed within brackets all questionable readings as well as a few editorial comments, although in most instances I have relegated comments to the footnotes. Occasionally I have placed within brackets a summary of a paragraph not quoted in the text. Words crossed out in the letters by the author herself have been placed within angle brackets. I have sought to preserve Peabody's spelling unless her mistake would distort the meaning; in these cases I have included her spelling in a note.

The location of manuscripts and other original material has been indicated by the National Union Catalogue Manuscript Code; other codes indicate whether the text came from an original manuscript or a typescript. A list of these codes can be found preceding the Introduction, together with the names of the institutions that granted permission to include their manuscripts in this edition. I am grateful to all these institutions for their willingness to cooperate in this project.

In the course of uncovering Elizabeth Peabody's letters and discovering their significance, I have incurred many debts. This kind of work, which relies so heavily on the good will and cooperation of many people, suggests to me that the old-fashioned idea of an academic community is not as tired as it sometimes seems to be. Indeed, I have been impressed again and again by the generosity of librarians, scholars, and others who have helped me during the past seven years.

I am particularly grateful to the following people and institutions:

Ellen D. Mark, Manuscripts Librarian, Essex Institute, Salem

Emily Cross Farnsworth, Brookline Public Library

Mrs. Marcia Moss, Concord Free Public Library

Bruce Thomas and Nina Myatt, Antioch College Library

the staff of the Houghton Library, Harvard

the staff of the Massachusetts Historical Society

the staff of the Bostonian Society

William Joyce and the staff of the American Antiquarian Society

Sally Pierce, Boston Athenaeum

Ellie Reichlin, Society for the Preservation of New England Antiquities

the library faculty and staff of the Lucy Scribner Library, Skidmore College, particularly Judith Reese, Gillian Lewis, Gloria Moore, Alvin Gamage, Barbara Smith, and Patricia Weller

Skidmore student assistants Pamela Fennell, Kelly Hanley, Paul Sigrist, and Sandra Rushing

typist and friend Sharon Carter

departmental secretaries Betsy McCamic and Nancy Gilchrist

the Committee on Research Grants and Faculty Lecture, Skidmore College, for its generous financial assistance for four summers

my academic colleagues and friends Mary C. Lynn, Benjamin D. Berry, and Joanna Zangrando of the Skidmore American Studies department; James Mellow, Clinton, Connecticut; Robert Saunders, Art Consultant, State of Connecticut; Edwin H. Miller, New York University.

I want to record a special debt to Margaret Neussendorfer, University of Texas, Permian Basin, who is completing work on a biography of Elizabeth Peabody. Margaret graciously provided the typescripts for letters from the Missouri Historical Society, and informed me of the addition of Peabody letters to the Gage family papers at the American Antiquarian Society. Margaret also answered several questions of mine which I posed to her during the course of assembling this edition. Margaret has been unstintingly generous in her time, energy, and knowledge, and has buoyed up my spirits several times when there seemed no end to this project. She is a colleague in the best sense of the word.

I want to acknowledge the help, encouragement, and support that Joel Myerson has given me over the past seven years. He has given out of his vast knowledge of the Transcendental movement, but perhaps more important, has encouraged and prodded at crucial moments. Joel was editor of the American Literary Manuscripts series for Twayne Publishers, in which this volume was to appear. In that capacity, Joel was of immense help in urging me on to fuller and better scholarship.

Finally, I join a "cloud of witnesses" who owe much to the encouragement and patience of Jeannette Hopkins, Director of Wesleyan University Press. It was my good fortune also to have the help of editorial interne Stephanie Oddleifson in revising and preparing the manuscript for publication. I wish to thank her for her insights and encouragement.

Naturally, I assume all responsibility for errors, omissions, and oversights.

❧ Abbreviations

CtY	Yale University, Sterling Library
DLC	Library of Congress; Bancroft-Bliss Papers
InNU	University of Notre Dame; Orestes A. Brownson Collection
MB	Boston Public Library
MCo	Concord Free Public Library
MCR-S	Schlesinger Library, Radcliffe College
MeB	Bowdoin College
MH	Harvard University, Houghton Library
MHi	Massachusetts Historical Society; Mann, Clarke, Andrew, Peabody Papers
MnHi	Minnesota Historical Society; Allen Kellogg Ford Collection
MNS	Smith College; Sophia Smith Collection
MoSHI	Missouri Historical Society; William Torrey Harris Papers
MS	manuscript in the author's hand
MSaE	Essex Institute, James Duncan Phillips Library; Peabody Papers
MS copy	manuscript in another hand
MWA	American Antiquarian Society; Miscellaneous Manuscripts
MWelC	Wellesley College Library; English Poetry Collection
MWiWC	Chapin Library; Howe Papers
NCaS	St. Lawrence University, Owen D. Young Library
NcD	Duke University, William R. Perkins Library; Mary Ann Peabody Papers
NIC	Cornell University Libraries, Department of Manuscripts and Archives; Howland, White, and Cooper Collections

NJM	Morristown National Historical Park, U.S. Department of the Interior National Park Service
NN	New York Public Library
NN-B	New York Public Library; Henry W. and Albert A. Berg Collection
NNBa	Barnard College, Overbury Collection
NNC	Columbia University, Rare Book and Manuscript Library; Moncure D. Conway Papers
NPV	Vassar College
NRU	Library of the University of Rochester; William Henry Seward Papers
NSyU	Syracuse University, George Arents Research Library for Special Collections; Gerrit Smith Collection
OFH	Rutherford B. Hayes Presidential Center, Fremont, Ohio; Luch Webb Hayes Papers
OYesA	Antioch College; Robert L. Straker Collection in Antiochiana
PHi	Historical Society of Pennsylvania
TS	typescript of the letter
TS copy	typescript of the letter prepared by another
ViU	University of Virginia, Clifton Waller Barrett Library; Elizabeth Palmer Peabody Collection and Louisa May Alcott Collection
VtMiM	Middlebury College, Abernethy Library
WHi	State Historical Society of Wisconsin

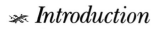 *Introduction*

LIKE THE AMERICAN REVOLUTION that catalyzed the change, the alterations in the social conditions and personal hopes of middle-class American women at the beginning of the nineteenth century may be described as a revolution of rising expectations. Reflecting the cultural belief in the worth of the individual, sensing that society as a whole seemed to place heightened value on their work as bearers and shapers of the young, benefiting from a new emphasis on companionate marriage, middle-class American women sought to widen their sphere to include social and political reforms that would affect and enhance their improved status. In defense of "woman's sphere," women became involved in religious revivalism and its concomitant tract, missionary and Sunday-school movements, in temperance crusades, and in antislavery activity, in social purity action, notably in antiprostitution efforts, in reforms of diet and dress. Only when they became involved in the women's rights movement and sought to become directly active in politics as voters did women seem to step beyond the boundaries of home, family, and children and begin to claim their identity not solely as wives and mothers but also as citizens and individuals. The profound implications of feminism began to be apparent: in the name of individualism, the central ante-bellum cultural value, some women laid claim to the privileges and responsibilities of democracy, and thereby seemed to threaten the stability of the family itself, the central social institution and supposed calm center in a turbulent age.

The lives of intellectual women of the ante-bellum period reflected this volatile conflict between a cultural ideal and a cherished social arrangement. As Susan Conrad has pointed out, women whose major focus was on the life of the mind were caught up in the same conflict as their thoughtful sisters in other areas of life: the need, under the pressure of individualism, to recognize and cultivate one's uniqueness versus the obligation to maintain the link between women and home.[1] Single women also, whether intellectuals or not, felt intense pressure to pursue domestically oriented tasks or careers, although clearly marriage was widely assumed to be the most satisfactory arrangement.

Elizabeth Palmer Peabody's career demonstrates, especially in the formative 1830s, this intense struggle between the need to cultivate the self and the ideology of domesticity. She insisted on a career, on

---

[1] Susan Conrad, *Perish the Thought: Intellectual Women in Romantic America, 1830–1860* (New York: Oxford University Press, 1976), pp. 13–14, 21–22, and, in general, the introduction and chapter 1.

private space, and emerged as an unforgettable individual, but she did not challenge the domestic, nurturing, service-oriented identity of women. While she enthusiastically accepted the intuitionism of her ante-bellum Romantic colleagues, and made frequent use of notions of dynamic organicism, she funneled those insights into the distinctive reforms of the post–Civil War period which emphasized social service and middle-class ideals rather than the primacy of the self. Because she lived so long (1804–1894) and was involved in reform on both sides of the Civil War, Peabody became an important link between two phases of nineteenth-century social and intellectual life. In more than one sense, she served as a mediator, explaining, interpreting, amending the thought of her prewar colleagues for postwar Americans who, like their parents before them, were caught up in rapid and unpredictable social change.

II

Recently, several social historians have begun to reconsider the view that pre-Revolutionary women's status was generally superior to that of their nineteenth-century female descendants. This view maintains that the labor shortage of the American colonies, the relative scarcity of women, the frontier conditions of many areas of settlement, and the Puritan emphasis on covenant as an arrangement of mutual rights and duties with limits to authority led to greater freedom and more widened opportunity for colonial American women than for their English and European counterparts. In contrast, the great changes of the early nineteenth century—westward expansion, industrial development, urban growth, the increasing separation of work and home—led to a decline in the status of women. Society struck a bargain, goes this interpretation, by which middle-class women yielded their economic importance in return for a new identity located solely within the home as wife and mother. This social arrangement, which identified the home as a refuge from the world of commerce, deprived women of meaningful adult engagement with important issues and relegated them to the condition of children, perfect companions for the little people they were meant to care for.[2]

2 "Declension" historians include Gerda Lerner, *The Woman in American History* (Reading: Addison-Wesley, 1971), and "The Lady and the Mill Girl: Changes in the Status of Women in the Age of Jackson," *Mid-Continent American Studies Journal* 10 (1969): 5–15; Barbara Berg, *The Remembered Gate: Origins of American Feminism: The Woman and the City, 1800–1860* (New York: Oxford University Press, 1978), ch. 1; and, more subtly, Barbara Epstein, *The Politics of Domesticity: Women, Evangelism, and Temperance in Nineteenth Century America* (Middletown: Wesleyan

The limitations of this approach have become apparent in recent years. Few women were engaged in commerce, law, or medicine in the colonial period. The domestic round to which women were supposedly relegated in the nineteenth century had in fact always been their assignment. Whether farm women or urban women, they faced the virtually universal tasks of home maintenance and child rearing. Equally, writes Mary Beth Norton, husbands and males in general demeaned women's work, rarely informing them of the financial situation of the household, and holding women's intellect in low regard. Women themselves, under such insistent pressure, distrusted their own mental abilities and found verbal expression difficult. Colonial women labored under two distinct but interlocking liabilities, one the largely accepted and unexamined domestic assignment, the other the very condition of being female, which, as Norton noted, was frequently examined, usually to women's disadvantage. Delicacy, modesty, and propriety were traits assigned to genteel women, while farming and urban laboring women were often stigmatized as fearful, shy, and foolish. Across the classes, women's personalities and behavior were rigidly defined by their gender, long before the industrial revolution gave rise to a cult of domesticity.[3]

The increasingly bitter quarrel with Great Britain after 1763 drew women inexorably into the public life from which they had been so insistently barred. Mob activities, passionate speeches, the furious

---

University Press, 1981). Those who prefer the "rising expectations" approach, or who see nineteenth-century women turning the materials of their culture to their own distinctive use, include Nancy Cott, *The Bonds of Womanhood: "Woman's Sphere" in New England, 1780–1835* (New Haven: Yale University Press, 1977); Katherine Kish Sklar, *Catherine Beecher: A Study in Nineteenth-Century Domesticity* (New Haven: Yale University Press, 1973); Carroll Smith-Rosenberg, "The Female World of Love and Ritual," *Signs,* 1 (1975), 1–29; Mary Beth Norton, *Liberty's Daughters: The Revolutionary Experience of American Women, 1750–1800* (Boston: Little, Brown, 1980), which contains a lucid discussion of the differences between the declension and the rising expectation approaches (xiii–xvi); Linda Kerber, *Women of the Republic: Intellect and Ideology in Revolutionary America* (Chapel Hill: University of North Carolina Press, 1980); and especially Carl Degler, *At Odds: Women and the Family in America from the Revolution to the Present* (New York: Oxford University Press, 1980), to which I am deeply indebted. Degler has sifted and synthesized the vast literature on American women and families and has provided, I think, the best analysis thus far on the place of women in American culture.

The conflict among scholars focusing on feminism and women's culture may be seen dramatically in an exchange between Ellen DuBois and Carroll Smith-Rosenberg in "Politics and Culture in Women's History: A Symposium," *Feminist Studies* 6 (Spring 1980): 26–64.

3 Norton, pp. 34–38 and, in general, chs. 1–5.

pamphlet and newspaper wars were inescapable, and women's letters and diaries reveal a growing awareness of public discord and the issues at stake. As Mary Beth Norton points out, "the activism of female patriots found particular expression in their support of the colonial boycott of tea and other items taxed by the Townshend Act of 1767" and in the general boycott of English goods in 1774. In the late 1760s, women had increased their spinning and weaving to produce more cloth for home consumption. Far from being the object of casual dismissal, women's domestic activities were emerging, under the press of the Revolution, as crucial for "the preservation and prosperity of their country."[4]

After the war, women maintained their engagement with public issues, and both men and women continued to revise their views of women's role and status. Most noticeable was the new valuation of women's domestic activities as the primary means of ensuring the nation's virtue. The shift from the demeaning of domestic work and child rearing to valuing it as central to the preservation of the nation's health was startling and rapid: "the message was unmistakable. Women had a major influence upon their children, and they should use that influence to imbue their youngsters with principles of morality and patriotism."[5]

Consequently, republican theorists sought to heighten the importance, to women, of education. Educational opportunities, writers like Benjamin Rush said, would not alter the fundamental assignment of women to domestic duties. Rush's Young Ladies' Academy in Philadelphia was designed "to allow her to prepare for the duties of life to which she may be destined." The upheaval of the Revolution, passing through the filter of domesticity, created, in the minds of writers like Rush, Judith Sargent Murray, and Susannah Rowson, the model of the Republican Mother who, in the words of Linda Kerber, "placed her learning at her family's service."[6]

Educated women comprised a social category that did not please everyone in the new republic. Some persons argued that women's intellects were unsuited to serious topics like politics, metaphysics, or mathematics, engagement with which would unsex them. To go beyond the learning appropriate for women's sphere would be to risk ridicule and rejection as a "female pedant."[7]

---

4 Norton, pp. 157, 167.
5 Norton, p. 248.
6 Kerber, p. 228.
7 Norton, p. 264.

Despite these often-repeated fears that women were invading male bastions and thus losing their identity, educational possibilities did increase in the 1780s and 90s with the opening of elementary education to girls and the founding of private academies for young women. The curricula of these academies included traditional academic subjects such as grammar, history, languages, and philosophy, as well as pursuits like dancing and music designed to improve feminine social poise. Emma Willard wrote her own history and geography texts (as would Elizabeth Peabody in the early 1830s) and encouraged active student involvement in learning. Many of the female academies eliminated the classics from their curricula, a reform springing directly from republican ideology, at least for Benjamin Rush, for whom the classics were a reminder of aristocracy and pretentiousness. The discrepancy between male and female education was narrowing, and the very fact of becoming literate drew women irresistibly into modern society. Still, the rationale and goal of female education remained firmly linked to domesticity.[8]

The intense political discussions, the Revolutionary activism, the postwar maintenance of a new awareness among women, the growth of educational opportunities, all point toward the emergence of women, under the impact of the Revolution, from a demeaned and ridiculed position in society to one of recognition and importance. Motherhood became a political, not just a personal, role, and the defense of the republic was seen to rest squarely on the shoulders of America's Republican mothers. But, as Norton observed, this decision to validate the domestic arena made moving beyond it difficult. Only those who, like teachers and missionaries, were able to define their work as extensions of or substitutions for motherhood were able to exist in extradomestic circumstances, and even those roles were seen as temporary employments. Nonetheless, even by such small measures did women's social status and self-regard improve by century's end.[9]

III

Elizabeth Palmer and her sister Mary were two such late eighteenth-century young women, who saw in schoolteaching not simply an excuse to get away from home or a chance to earn one's own wage, poor as it was, but as a job that was increasingly socially acceptable for young women before marriage. As Carl Degler points out, before 1860

8 Kerber, pp. 192–93, 198, 200–201, 215, 218; Norton, p. 256.
9 Norton, p. 298.

perhaps as many as twenty percent of Massachusetts women taught at some point in their lives. In 1793 a New Hampshire farmer inquired if Mary Palmer was qualified to teach his and his neighbor's children, and when Mary gave up teaching to marry Royall Tyler, she wrote that Betsy "made up her mind to become a teacher in some female academy as soon as possible."[10]

Elizabeth (Betsy) Palmer, mother of Elizabeth Palmer Peabody, was born in 1781. As a child she read widely in the library of her grandfather General Joseph Palmer (1718–1788), a member of the Continental Congress and commander in 1777 of the Massachusetts militia. This voracious reading in English literature, geography, and classical literature and history laid the foundation for her later teaching career and her writings and translations. After the General's financial failure and death, his son Joseph, a schoolmaster, moved to Vermont with his wife and family. He died in 1797. After a few interim ventures, his daughter Elizabeth was invited in 1798 to enter the boarding household of the Reverend Stephen Peabody in Atkinson, New Hampshire; Mr. Peabody's wife was the sister of a Mrs. Cranch, a Palmer family friend. Elizabeth Palmer's position in the Peabody household was somewhat "anomalous," as her daughter later described it—she was "in some respects on the same social footing as the family . . . in others on a level with the kitchen servant."[11] Elizabeth strove unsuccessfully to get along with the kitchen servant, Lydia: "I am sensible that she feels hurt and dissatisfied with the attentions I receive from those who pay not the same to her." Elizabeth's own domestic tasks were rigorous: she prepared meals, scrubbed floors, washed, ironed, and mended clothes, never feeling that this was done to Lydia's satisfaction.

Her daughter wrote that, among the boarders, her mother "went by the name of the 'walking dictionary' because her extensive reading enabled her to answer all the questions asked." In Elizabeth Palmer's own words, her "laborious employments" in domestic chores were often interrupted by the boarders, students at Stephen Peabody's academy. " 'Miss Betsey [sic], do write my piece off, do compose me a poem to speak next Saturday, do write me a letter to carry into school today, do correct my composition, do look over my figures in rhetoric, or

10 Norton, pp. 291–92; Degler, p. 379.
11 This description of Elizabeth Palmer's life at the Reverend Peabody's and of her relationship with Nathaniel Peabody, including all quoted material, comes from Elizabeth Palmer Peabody, "Mrs. Elizabeth Palmer Peabody," *Boston Daily Advertiser*, 10 February 1879 (TS Copy, OYesA).

make me some, and pray hear me say my lesson in geography.' All these requests I must comply with, or they will think me unkind." Elizabeth Palmer Peabody concluded, after reviewing her mother's story, that because of the contact with both teachers and pupils, "she became really both a pupil and a teacher, although nominally neither." On the other hand, too much self-assertion outside the boundaries of "maid of all work" and informal tutor to the boarders apparently led to censure. As Elizabeth Palmer wrote, "I mean to do all I can to keep peace, and have determined never to write anything again, excepting letters, and as few of them as possible; never to touch a book, except upon the Sabbath, and to devote every moment to work of some kind. I am convinced that my attempts to write poetry have gained me more ill will than any actions of my life. It is a received opinion that a poet is good for nothing else; and a person may throw five hours away at the toilet and yet be loved and admired, when she would be condemned if she spent one hour at the pen."

Thus, in several ways, the experience of Elizabeth Palmer illustrates the Revolutionary and the post-Revolutionary condition of women. Betsy's war hero grandfather encouraged her to read widely in his library. Her schoolmaster father modeled for his daughters the socially acceptable employment of teaching. Her educational accomplishments increased her stature in the eyes of the male students and her social position in the eyes of her caretakers, and her teaching and intellectual interests became lifelong commitments, not frivolous or temporary pastimes. On the other hand, she encountered criticism when she sought to assert too much independence of mind in writing poetry. The editor of the *Boston Daily Advertiser* wrote in his summary of Elizabeth Palmer's life: "it was not so much her literary tastes which subjected her to unfavorable criticism as her determination to be independent and self-supporting."

Teaching at Stephen Peabody's academy in Atkinson was a Dartmouth student from a New Hampshire farm family, Nathaniel Peabody, no relation to Stephen. Mrs. Stephen Peabody and Mrs. Cranch opposed the friendship and the ensuing engagement between Nathaniel Peabody and Elizabeth Palmer on the grounds "that the social position and family rank of the young man were not regarded . . . as sufficiently high to entitle him to aspire to the hand of their 'poor relation'." Nonetheless, Peabody and Palmer were married on November 3, 1802, and moved to Andover, Massachusetts, where Nathaniel served as preceptor and Elizabeth as preceptress at the North Andover Free School. Of that experience, daughter Elizabeth wrote, "her school was *sui generis,* and had some features which were more cultivating to the individual genius than the present cramming process, her aim being to give that love of literature which was the solace of her own hard life."

In 1804, they moved to Billerica, Massachusetts, where Elizabeth Palmer Peabody was born on 16 May. Mrs. Peabody opened a boarding school for girls, but her ambition for her husband to practice medicine prompted a move in 1806 to Cambridgeport, because Nathaniel could attend lectures in medicine at Harvard College. In 1808, the growing family, now including Mary Tyler, moved to Summer Street in Salem. There Mrs. Peabody set up a school, based on the principle of educating children to the very limit of their capacity. Her mother's school, which she attended, and private lessons were Elizabeth's introduction to literature, history, philosophy, and theology. Her father, now practicing dentistry rather than medicine, much to his wife's chagrin, taught Elizabeth Latin, and inspired her eventually to learn ten other languages.[12]

IV

In the first years of the nineteenth century, Mrs. Elizabeth Peabody was participating in the fuller role society allowed women. Her daughter Elizabeth became the heir of the new value placed on domesticity and the greater interest in women's education. She was also a part of the theological and ecclesiastical quarrel between two wings of the churches of the Standing Order in Massachusetts. Thus the shifts in both social relations and systems of belief served as influences on Elizabeth Palmer Peabody.

The orthodox Calvinist position on the major doctrinal questions, developed in the course of the sixteenth century and transmitted to America by Puritan settlers, included beliefs in the sovereignty and inscrutability of God, the Trinity, the authoritativeness of Scriptures, the election of a few for salvation and the deserved damnation of the many, and the vicarious sacrifice and atonement of Jesus Christ, who was fully human and fully divine. The movement on the part of some Anglo-Americans away from these beliefs in the mid- and late 1600s was gradual and complex, involving many changes in practice and doctrine within the colonies as well as the importation of new theological and philosophical ideas from abroad. By the end of the 1740s, the Great Awakening had divided colonists between those who cham-

12 Charles H. Foster, "Elizabeth Palmer Peabody," *Notable American Women,* ed. Edward T. James *et al.* (Cambridge: Harvard University Press, 1971), 3, pp. 31–32.

pioned the mysterious and arbitrary acts of God as the source of faith and of life itself and those who insisted on judging the enthusiasm of the revival by the rules of Scripture and reason. Although at the time of the Awakening the faithful divided over the issue of revivalism, eventually some of the antirevivalists became Arminians, asserting human ability to choose for sin or for righteousness.

Rejection of the doctrine of the Trinity became associated during the eighteenth century with English liberalism, whereas "supernatural rationalism" quickly became a characteristic feature of New England Arminians. As students of Isaac Newton, the liberals preferred to think of the cosmos as law-bound and predictable rather than upheld by the hand of an unpredictable God. Such a view of creation mirrored the social and economic position of many of the liberals, who had come to exert considerable control over the worlds of politics and commerce, and saw no reason not to think of all creation in similar terms. Such a law-bound universe overseen by a beneficent God led an increasing number of colonists to echo their European and English cousins in arguing that ethics can be discerned from a rational study of nature, and that ethical behavior was in fact the essence of the religious life.[13]

While the impact of the Enlightenment on religion led some English liberals to become deists and question the need for belief in supernatural or miraculous interventions in the natural order, most American liberals refused such a drastic conclusion. They believed that while nature provides a coherent revelation of the existence of God, and suggests the quality of our duty to each other, it must be supplemented by the supernatural revelation attested to in Scripture, hence the label "supernatural rationalism." As Conrad Wright has noted, an insistence on the historicity of the miracles of Jesus Christ as proofs of His message can be seen among liberals as far back as Charles Chauncy in the 1740s and became the bedrock of Andrews Norton's Biblical hermeneutics in the 1820s and 30s.[14] Such an insistence derived in part from the enormous influence of John Locke on the

[13] The development of "liberal religion" in the American colonies as part of the Enlightenment has been described by many writers. I have relied principally on Sydney Ahlstrom, *A Religious History of the American People* (New Haven: Yale University Press, 1972), ch. 22; Daniel Walker Howe, *The Unitarian Conscience* (Cambridge: Harvard University Press, 1970); Joseph Haroutunian, *Piety versus Moralism: The Passing of the New England Theology* (1932) (Hamden: Archon Press, 1964); and Conrad Wright, *The Beginnings of Unitarianism in America* (Beacon Press, 1955) (Hamden: Archon Press, 1976).

[14] Wright, pp. 142, 146, 155.

American and English Enlightenment. Locke had propounded a psychology in which data from outside the self are combined to form simple, then complex ideas, an insight that had tremendous implications for the religious life.[15] Faith for the Puritan or revival figure was an inner, heartfelt response to the gift of grace. Faith, says Wright, for the Arminian was "an assent of the mind to any truth or matter of fact, upon testimony. . . . If it is a man who testifies, then our faith is human faith; if it is Christ or his apostles whose word we are willing to accept, the result is Christian faith."[16] Miracles thus become, for the liberal, granted their divine source, both objectively true and reliable as touchstones of faith.

In addition to the influence of Newton and Locke, English writers like Bishop Joseph Butler and Archdeacon Thomas Paley together with the Scottish Commonsense philosophers helped shape the American liberal outlook. Butler's *Analogy of Religion, Natural and Revealed, to the Constitution of Nature* (1736) provided a buttress for supernatural rationalism, while Paley's *Christian Evidences* (1794) and *Natural Theology* (1802) demonstrated the reasonableness of the Biblical witness and the reliability of the natural order as a revelation of God's character and intentions. The Scottish group, including Thomas Reid, Dugald Stewart, and James Beattie, became increasingly influential by the end of the eighteenth and well into the nineteenth century. Their influence stemmed from their attempts to retain Lockean empiricism while refuting the skeptical and subjectivist implications that some, like David Hume, drew from Locke. Locke argued that our knowledge of the world outside the self depended on our "ideas" of that reality, "ideas" formed out of sense impressions. He claimed that such "ideas" did conform to the objective world, but Hume insisted that we have no evidence that this is so; we cannot really know something is objectively true without assuming some truth in advance. For Thomas Reid and his disciples such a conclusion was troubling, since it put the empirical method, which was becoming the preferred approach in so much eighteenth-century thinking, at odds with the metaphysical assumption that genuine truth could be determined rationally and conclusively. In refuting Hume's skepticism and justifying "the common sense and reason of mankind," Reid argued that knowing begins with the structure of the mind, which is characterized by "perceptions" through which sensations are sorted and put in context prior

15 Ahlstrom, pp. 352–53.
16 Wright, p. 159.

to the operation of reason. Such perceptions are part of our very being, the basis, as much as sense data, upon which ideas are built. Much as with Kant and his followers, or, later, Darwin and his, Reid's disciples seemed to go beyond their master's careful work in their haste to establish exactly what these perceptions are, and included such propositions as the intuitive acknowledgment of mathematical axioms and the intuitive acknowledgment of the existence of God.

Reid and the other Scots also addressed the question of morality, and proposed that the self is governed by conscience or "moral sense," the operation of which is natural, providing more "perceptions," more intuitive frameworks for the subsequent function of reason. Further, the human conscience does not imagine or create moral truth; we grasp the morality that exists objectively, and do this intuitively, prior to reasoning. Moral claims, then, are both intuitive and objective, an ingenious solution to the skepticism that Locke's psychology seemed to introduce.[17]

The instruction in epistemology and moral theory that one was likely to get in American colleges did not rely wholly on Scottish Common Sense philosophers; English and eventually German approaches were also present. But, as Daniel Howe has pointed out, the Scots provided, especially for the Unitarian community, a useful synthesis of objective truth and psychological method, all tending to cement a solid social order. The Unitarians of William Ellery Channing's generation thus found the Scots most appealing philosophical companions.[18]

The liberal party had been maturing throughout the eighteenth century. It had emerged into the light of public controversy when King's Chapel in Boston, formerly an Anglican church, in 1787 ordained James Freeman as its clergyman. Freeman, a liberal, had been serving as the Chapel's lay reader since 1782, and since 1785 had been introducing such changes in the Book of Common Prayer that the Anglican bishops of Connecticut and New York both refused to recog-

17 Ahlstrom, pp. 254–55.
18 Howe, pp. 80–81. Other useful authorities on the Commonsense philosophy include Herbert Hovenkamp, *Science and Religion in America, 1800–1860* (Philadelphia: University of Pennsylvania Press, 1978), chs. 1–6; Henry May, *The Enlightenment in America* (New York: Oxford University Press, 1976), pp. 346–58; Terence Martin, *The Instructed Vision: Scottish Common Sense Philosophy and the Origins of American Fiction* (Bloomington: Indiana University Press, 1961); and, particularly, Donald H. Meyer, *The Instructed Conscience* (Philadelphia: University of Pennsylvania Press, 1972), pp. 35–42, whose lucid discussion of Thomas Reid informs the substance of this section. See also Sydney Ahlstrom, "The Scottish Philosophy and American Theology," *Church History* 24 (1955): 257–72.

nize King's as Anglican. The decisive break began in 1805, however, with the election of Henry Ware to the post of Hollis Professor of Divinity at Harvard College, over the strenuous objections of Charlestown minister Jedidiah Morse. The election of John Thornton Kirkland as Harvard's president in 1810 placed the college firmly in liberal hands. Angered by what he considered the betrayal of orthodoxy into the hands of heresy, Morse published in 1805 a pamphlet attacking the choice for the Hollis post. In the same year he founded the orthodox journal the *Panoplist,* and was instrumental in establishing an orthodox seminary at Andover in 1808.

In 1815, Morse moved closer to precipitating a crisis in the Standing Order when he attempted to link the American liberals' outlook with that of the more aggressive English Unitarians. The response to this came from the pastor of Federal Street Church, Boston, William Ellery Channing, first in some exchanges with Samuel Worcester, and then more fully in his 1819 ordination sermon for Jared Sparks, "Unitarian Christianity." Devoted to a discussion of the principles of Biblical interpretation and the doctrines that emerge from interpretation, Channing's sermon was marked by a strong claim for human ability, dignity, and righteousness.[19] Channing assumed that virtuous people possess enough reason to interpret Scripture and draw out those beliefs which seem most to conform to common sense.[20] Equally, the loving and morally perfect God whom we discern in Scripture cannot and does not behave whimsically; for Channing, God as vengeful judge has been replaced by God as loving Father. Hence, Channing linked humanity's capacity for good with Christianity as an ethical religion, encouraging people, through the inspiration of the virtue of God, to be virtuous themselves.[21]

After the publication of this sermon, Moses Stuart, professor of Biblical Studies at Andover, attacked Channing's Biblical hermeneutics, while Henry Ware and Andover professor Leonard Woods stormed at each other over the issue of human nature and infant damnation. Giving great impetus to the growing denominational conflict was the Massachusetts Supreme Court's Dedham case in 1820. In the conflict between orthodox believers who left the local church but still

---

[19] Ahlstrom, *Religious History,* pp. 393–95; Haroutunian, p. 205.

[20] See Jerry Wayne Brown, *The Rise of Biblical Criticism in America, 1800–1810: The New England Scholars* (Middletown: Wesleyan University Press, 1969), p. 72, and William Hutchison, *The Transcendentalist Ministers: Church Reform in the New England Renaissance* (New Haven: Yale University Press, 1959), pp. 12–15.

[21] Haroutunian, p. 205; Hutchison, pp. 4–5.

claimed to be the church, and liberals who remained connected with the parish, the Court decided that the bond between church and parish was sufficiently strong that those who remained constituted the church, with their representatives entitled to administer the church property. Thus many New England churches passed into the hands of Unitarians. With the founding of the *Christian Examiner* in 1824, to join the *North American Review* (1815) and the *Christian Register* (1821) as the leading Unitarian journals, and the establishment of the American Unitarian Association in 1825, the emergence of a distinctive denomination was virtually complete.[22]

The Peabody family, caught up in this conflict, experienced its divisiveness intimately. Like other New England families, they divided along orthodox-liberal lines, with Mrs. Peabody adhering to the liberal cause and several of her sisters remaining Calvinists. Elizabeth recalled her own instinctive tendency to claim the liberal cause: "it seemed personally original with me to reject Calvinism, and I early clearly felt the moral argument against it." Even at age ten, she remembered, she had the teacher's instinct to protect as well as to instruct, and became her sister Sophia's religious guardian. Sophia seemed such an innocent child that Elizabeth was "determined she should never hear of any of the terrible doctrines" of Calvinism.[23]

Peabody's preference for liberal religion may have had as its primary cause the powerful influence of her mother, who had chosen the liberal side in the argument. Mrs. Peabody's influence over her daughter may also have been strengthened by the unassertiveness of father Nathaniel, a largely silent figure in this story, a disappointment to his wife and possibly to himself. The three Peabody sons, Nathaniel, Wellington, and George, were all personal and professional failures. By contrast, Mrs. Peabody appeared to be a rock of strength and stability, a model for her daughter of both strength of character and maternal, self-sacrificial spirit.

Much later in life, Peabody recalled an incident from her childhood that illustrates a shift from reverence for distant disinterested authority to respect for intimate benevolent authority, a shift simultaneously personal, social, ecclesiastical, and theological.[24] She remem-

22 Ahlstrom, *Religious History,* pp. 397–98.
23 These reminiscences were written by Peabody for her nephew Julian Hawthorne and are published in Norman Holmes Pearson, "Elizabeth Peabody on Hawthorne," *Essex Institute Historical Collections* 94 (1958): 270.
24 For a discussion of the implications of these shifts in attitude, see Ann Douglas, *The Feminization of American Culture* (New York: Alfred Knopf, 1977).

bered being asked by a young woman, "Who made you?" "I remember my pleased surprise at the question, that I feel very sure had never been addressed to my consciousness before. At once a Face arose to my imagination,—only a Face and head,—close to me, and looking upon me with the most benignant smile, in which the kindness rather predominated over the intelligence; but it looked at me as if meaning, 'Yes, I made you, as you know very well.' I was so thoroughly satisfied, that I replied to the question decisively. 'A man.'" This response prompted great ridicule, and Elizabeth stormed off to get her mother's opinion. Caught off guard and probably embarrassed that the four-year-old eldest child could not answer such a basic question, Mrs. Peabody responded in a way that seemed, in her daughter's recollection, "a little out of character." Her answer summoned up in the mind of the young child "another image of God . . . conveying not half so much of the truth as did that kind Face, close up to mine, and seeming to be so wholly occupied with His creature. The new image was of an old man, sitting away up on the clouds, dressed in a black silk gown and cocked hat, the costume of our old Puritan minister. He was looking down upon the earth, and spying round among the children to see who was doing wrong, in order to punish the offenders by touching them with a long rod he held in his hand, thus exposing them to everybody's censure."[25] How much of this story is the product of the intervening years cannot be measured, but it does form a striking personal parallel to the more general liberal redefinition of God, beginning at least in the 1740s, along rationalist and sentimental lines, a redefinition given most fully in Channing's "Likeness to God."

Nine years after her youthful request to take her sister under her wing, Elizabeth Peabody wrote Sophia, on March 31, 1823, one of many hortatory letters, this one a classic restatement of Unitarian rationalism. She provided Sophia with a list of books to read, cautioned her against excessive curiosity, and suggested an interpretive method for reading the New Testament: Do the passages conform to common sense? The reading list revealed that combination of English liberals, like Paley (together with the bolder theologian Joseph Priestley), and Scottish philosophers so appealing to Unitarians.[26] In her 1880 remi-

25 Elizabeth Peabody, *Lectures in the Training Schools for Kindergartners* (Boston: D. C. Heath, 1888), pp. 70–72.
26 See below, p. 59 ". . . that summer I wrote to Sophia half-a-dozen letters of advice in regard to her self-education in religion, and the morals of daily life; to which she wrote enthusiastic letters of acceptance. That was in 1822 when she was 13 years old. . . ." Pearson, p. 271.

niscence of Channing, Peabody recalled her reading of the Scottish writers in the early 1820s, and there are several references to these writers in letters to Horace Mann.[27] More broadly, the Scots' union of intuitionism and empiricism appealed to Peabody, who strained at the boundaries of Unitarianism but never admired or aspired to the private and interior visions of those who had decisively broken through those boundaries.

In 1820, at age sixteen, Peabody established her own school in Lancaster, Massachusetts, with her sisters Mary and Sophia among her few students: "I taught History as a chief study,—the History of the United States, not in textbooks for schools, but Miss Hannah Adams History of New England, which might have been entitled, 'The Providence of God in New England,'—& Rollins' Ancient History, and Plutarch's Lives." In 1822 she left Lancaster for Boston "in a high heroic mood, intending to get money to educate at College my brothers."[28]

In many ways, Peabody's experiences as a young single teacher duplicated and extended her mother's. Like Elizabeth Palmer, Elizabeth Peabody was welcomed in society and admired for her intellectual abilities. The society in which she began to move, sometimes rather dazed at how far she had traveled socially, was the intellectual and social elite of Unitarian Boston and Cambridge. Part of the reason for the success of Unitarianism in so rapidly dominating institutions and periodicals in eastern New England came from the close-knit quality of the group. As members of clubs and societies, alumni of Harvard, business or professional associates, men of letters or faculty colleagues, male liberals together with their wives projected a sense of tolerance of new ideas and a commitment to social harmony under their direction.[29] While Peabody would soon find out how superficial this tolerance was, she never lost this early impression of a community ethically advanced, intellectually vital, and committed to social welfare.

Probably no influence more firmly located Peabody "in the bosom

27 Elizabeth Peabody, *Reminiscences of the Reverend William E. Channing* (Boston: Roberts Brothers, 1880), pp. 74–75, 123, 127–28.

28 Pearson, pp. 270–71.

29 Descriptions of the Unitarian elite and their leadership role in Boston may be found in Martin Green, *The Problem of Boston* (New York: W. W. Norton, 1966), pp. 41–59; Oscar Handlin, *Boston's Immigrants* (1941) (New York: Atheneum Press, 1972), pp. 1–24; Howe, pp. 7–12; David Levin, *History as Romantic Art* (Stanford: Stanford University Press, 1959), p. 4; and Anne Rose, *Transcendentalism as a Social Movement, 1830–1850* (New Haven: Yale University Press, 1981), pp. 1–37.

of Unitarianism" than that of William Ellery Channing.[30] Peabody
first saw Channing at age eight or nine, when he preached at Salem's
Second Church. She was much struck with his ascetic appearance,
which she connected to his closeness to God.[31] She saw him again in
1817, during a visit to Boston, and in 1820, when he came to Salem to
preach at John Emery Abbot's ordination. Two years later Channing
returned to Salem to deliver the funeral sermon for Abbot.[32]

In May 1825, when Elizabeth and Mary moved to Brookline to
open a girls' school, Elizabeth's contact with Channing increased. The
following year she moved to Boston to begin a school there, and one
day appeared in Channing's study to announce that she was going to
copy out his sermons so that they could be printed and have a wider
circulation. She overrode all his objections, including his fear that she
would skimp on her own reading by devoting so much time to copying. When she proved her intellectual ability by copying a sermon
while listening to Plato's *Timaeus* and then answering questions on
that work, Channing was convinced, and agreed to allow her to serve
as his unpaid personal secretary. By 1828 she was spending most of her
evenings at the Channings' home.

A gentle and irenic man, disinclined to combat, Channing was
essentially a teacher and nurturer rather than a polemicist for a new
denomination.[33] The task of organizing the new body fell to his assistant at Federal Street Church, Ezra Stiles Gannet, and that of chief
defender of the faith to Andrews Norton. Channing was most comfortable with his Sunday-school classes and with discussion groups of
Sunday-school teachers.[34] Peabody was impressed with his manner toward the young and sought to model her style after his. In her *Reminiscences* she quoted an 1825 journal of hers in which she described
Channing with his own children: "He treats children with the greatest
consideration, and evidently enjoys their conversation, and studies it
to see what it indicates of the yet unfallen nature. He will never tire,
I see, of that observation of children of which I am so fond, and does

---

30 The phrase comes from a letter, ca. 1840, to Orestes Brownson (MS, InND).
31 Peabody, *Reminiscences,* pp. 12–13, 15.
32 Peabody, *Reminiscences,* p. 19.
33 Biographical information on Channing may be found in William Henry
Channing, *The Life of William Ellery Channing* (Boston: American Unitarian Association, 1880); John W. Chadwick, *William Ellery Channing* (Boston: Houghton
Mifflin, 1903); Arthur W. Brown, *Always Young for Liberty* (Syracuse: Syracuse University Press, 1956); and Madeline Hooke Rice, *Federal Street Pastor* (New York:
Bookman Associates, 1961).
34 Conrad, pp. 209–10.

not accuse me of being visionary when I tell him of my divination."[35]

Channing encouraged and legitimated the tendencies already evident in Peabody. He seems never to have inquired about her marriage prospects and treated her as a highly intelligent apprentice teacher. He included her, as her "Cuba Journal" letters to sister Mary reveal, in some rarefied theological discussions, counseled her about her own career, and confided his own views of other people's personal dilemmas.[36] He gave a quasi-paternal blessing and encouragement to this young intellectual; she repaid his early and crucial encouragement in her graceful and laudatory reminiscence of his life. The sense of warmth and gratitude she felt is evident in other ways as well: when she introduced the philosophy of German kindergarten theorist Friedrich Froebel in the 1870s, New England mothers responded, she reported happily, " 'But this is nothing new; more than fifty years ago Dr. Channing taught us to live with our children and to look upon them as capable of the life of Christ'."[37] Channing hovered over her major postwar reform, the kindergarten, as much as he did above her prewar teaching. And, although she long planned to write her own reminiscence, her book on Channing was the closest she ever approached this goal.

Like William Henry Channing, in his *Memoir* of his uncle, she saw him as a closet Transcendentalist; Channing, however, belongs squarely in the camp of Christian Unitarians and was, in Sydney Ahlstrom's words, its "representative man."[38] Personally gentler and more tolerant than Andrews Norton, on doctrinal matters he stood as one with the Harvard professor. Channing's influence had the effect of centering Peabody quite firmly in the Unitarian fold. That she was able to absorb more radical ideas in religion and philosophy after such a heavy dose of liberalism attests to her hunger for new ideas, her willingness to change, and to the greater personal freedom offered her in the Transcendental circle.[39]

Channing's theology, given classic statement in "Unitarian Christianity" and "Likeness to God" may also be discerned by examining his differences with Andover Seminary's Moses Stuart. Orthodox practitioners tried to attack Channing on Biblical bases, and Stuart led this assault. For Stuart the Bible was divinely inspired; the subse-

---

[35] Peabody, *Reminiscences,* p. 81.
[36] See below, p. 145.
[37] Peabody, *Reminiscences,* p. 92.
[38] Howe, pp. 18–19; Ahlstrom, p. 398.
[39] Rose, pp. 52–56, 176–78.

quent task of the scholar was to discern the content of its doctrines. Without major internal contradiction and validated by miracles, fulfilled prophecy, and its ethical superiority, the Bible was to be accepted as truth, even if beyond comprehension. Channing, Jerry Wayne Brown writes, also accepted the Bible as the touchstone for the Christian life, but there he began to diverge. His insistence that the Bible be seen in its changing historical context echoed the liberal hermeneutics practiced first in this country by Joseph Buckminster and was based on the textual and linguistic work of seventeenth- and eighteenth-century European, and especially German, scholars. Following their work, Channing elevated human reason in its ability to discover the living logos from the historical vehicle in which it was carried. As Brown summarizes, "Reason must be used to select the proper meaning of a scriptural text within the context of the proper understanding of the writer's situation."[40] Channing insisted on the power of human rationality as the way to discern the core spiritual truth, distrusting spontaneity and ecstasy as means of revelation. He disapproved of Emerson's Divinity School Address and was disturbed by Theodore Parker's "Discourse on the Transient and Permanent in Christianity" because of their emphasis on the nonrational dimension.[41]

As Channing instructed, organized, and disciplined Peabody's mind, encouraging her interests in translation and her vocation for teaching, and conversing with her about religion, art, education, feminism, and a myriad other topics, he was essentially training her to think historically.[42] He believed in the centrality of history in education and the importance of history in Biblical interpretation. Her review of Herder for the *Christian Examiner* stressed the need to establish historically accurate texts.[43] In that same year, and periodically throughout the 1830s, she held Historical Conversations, or Conferences, mostly on classical history and literature, for women in the Boston and Salem areas. She also wrote several texts, including *Key to History, Part I, First Steps to the Study of History* (1832), *Key to History, Part II, The Hebrews* (1833), and *Key to History, Part III, The Greeks* (1833). All these courses and writings stress respect for the wisdom of the past, the authority of tradition, and the need for historical continuity as well as respect for human ability to discern and judge. Like Channing, Peabody threw herself on the side of the social and

---

[40] Brown, pp. 57, 62, 65–66; Haroutunian, p. 201.
[41] Howe, p. 19.
[42] Conrad, pp. 187, 207–208.
[43] *Christian Examiner,* 60 (May 1834), 174–75.

historical shaping of human life rather than on the side of those, like Bronson Alcott and the Salem poet Jones Very, who stressed the primacy of private judgments.[44] Even when she was most taken up with Transcendentalist thinking, in her work with Alcott at Temple School, she criticized his allegorical reading of the Bible, preferring a historical one, and took exception to his denial of the shaping power of society over the human character.[45]

V

In the early 1840s, Elizabeth Peabody wrote to Orestes Brownson about his publishing her essays on the Hebrew Scriptures. She described herself as one raised "in the bosom of Unitarianism" and as having gained those "principles of philosophizing" characteristic of Transcendentalism in the decade of the 1830s.[46] This shift, to an elaboration and refinement of the Unitarian heritage, was simultaneously personal and intellectual, affecting Peabody's self-image and her status as a single professional woman, as well as affecting her thought and expression.

Like other young adults in her time, and ours, Peabody was absorbing information and theory at an amazing rate. Her March 1823 letter to her sister Sophia demonstrates all the traits of a precocious young person proud of new learning. Her emotional maturity, however, lagged behind. In the early 1830s, Peabody experienced a series of personal crises for which she was quite unprepared: the New Bedford incident of the winter of 1830, in which she tried to intervene on behalf of some of her pupils and ended up alienating several of her supporters because of her intrusiveness; the triangle with Horace Mann and her sister Mary, who later married Mann; her sometimes deeply bitter arguments with Mary over issues of discretion and propriety. Elizabeth Peabody was groping toward recognition of levels of living beyond the mental. These crisis moments may well have combined with a growing realization on her part that her life was not going to conform to the accepted pattern of courtship and marriage prescribed for young women. A torrent of strong feeling, clearly evident in the letters of the early 1830s, gave her personality more distinctiveness and set her off from the more reserved wives and daugh-

44 John B. Wilson, "Elizabeth Peabody and Other Transcendentalists on History and Historians," *The Historian* 30 (November 1967): 72–86.

45 Bruce A. Ronda, "Elizabeth Peabody's Changing Views of the Child," *ESQ* (1977): 109–110.

46 Peabody to Brownson, [ca. 1840] (MS, InND).

ters in her circle. On the other hand, she never plunged through to the conviction of her brother-in-law Nathaniel Hawthorne or that of Herman Melville that will and rationality are in the service of that which is more fundamental, one's passions and psychic inclinations.

Other men and women of her time shared a similar experience of emotional upheaval, which helped Peabody break through the reserve of the social and intellectual elites of her day and acknowledge the often impressive power of her emotions. Even if they never embraced Transcendentalism or read Romantic writers, many Americans in the early and mid-nineteenth century felt the surge of the new currents of thought and expression. Women wrote passionately to each other both before and after marriage, and men and women corresponded and spoke in more passion-laden terms than they had in the pre-Revolutionary decades.[47] The loosening of Calvinism's grip and the strengthening of family ties based on affection rather than authority contributed to the emergence of public expression of feeling. Even in those families where orthodoxy was supreme, the revolt against it assumed a passionate character, as in this passage from a letter by Harriet Beecher:

But in America feeling vehement and absorbing . . . become still more deep, morbid, and impassioned by the constant habits of self-government which the rigid forms of society demand . . . It seems to me that the intensity with which my mind has thought and felt on every subject presented to it has had this effect. . . . All that is enthusiastic, all that is impassioned in the admiration of nature, or writing, or character, in devotional thought and emotions, or in the emotions of affection, I have felt with vehement and absorbing intensity,—felt till my mind is exhausted, and seems to be sinking into deadness.[48]

The great cultural movement of Romanticism toward which Peabody was drawn in the early 1830s manifested itself in New England substantially in the form of Transcendentalism, although there had been important precursors, including the artist Washington Allston. The advance of protest against Unitarian theology and practice began among a handful of young men and women in the Boston area who

47 Carroll Smith-Rosenberg, "The Female World of Love and Ritual," in Degler, pp. 35–51.
48 Harriet Beecher (Stowe) to Georgianna May, May 1833, quoted in Charles H. Foster, *The Rungless Ladder. Harriet Beecher Stowe and New England Puritanism* (Durham: Duke University Press, 1954), pp. 7–8.

had become dissatisfied with the theistic rationalism of their elders.[49] The particular focus of attention was the heavy reliance on Locke both in Biblical hermeneutics and more generally in Unitarian epistemology. For Unitarian Biblical scholars, Locke had transferred Scripture into a source of external stimuli which the senses absorbed and the mind arranged as ideas, rather than a source of inner awakening. In general, the accepted approach to knowledge, in the eyes of the disaffected, seemed cool, detached, hyper-rational, too given to deference to authority, too prone to consider its own advances the last word in modern thought.[50]

The influx of books and ideas from England and the Continent in the first decades of the nineteenth century provided one kind of encouragement for people growing impatient with Unitarian attempts to harmonize rationality and the miraculous, enlightenment and Christianity. A large audience, not just the disobedient young, was coming into contact with new books stocked by the Boston Athenaeum and appearing in private libraries—those by Wordsworth, Coleridge, Carlyle, Schiller, Goethe, Herder, and the brothers Grimm—or reviewed in journals.[51] Some New England intellectuals, like George Bancroft and George Ticknor, traveled across the Atlantic to study, while others, like Emerson, went to recuperate or sightsee. New modes of thought returned with them.

Perry Miller has pointed out that the Transcendentalist phase of Romanticism, however stimulated by foreign impulses, grew on native soil.[52] In its insistence on the ability of the individual consciousness to intuit divinity, in its stress on the powerful, emotional, and unmediated link between self and universal truth, Transcendentalism recalled the

[49] I have relied in my discussion and understanding of Transcendentalism on Ahlstrom, *Religious History*, pp. 388–402, 583–614; Paul F. Boller, Jr., *American Transcendentalism, 1830–1860: An Intellectual History* (New York: G. P. Putnam's Sons, 1974): O. B. Frothingham, *Transcendentalism in New England* (1876) (Philadelphia: University of Pennsylvania Press, 1972); George Hochfield, "Transcendentalism," in Brian Barbour, ed., *American Transcendentalism: An Anthology of Criticism* (Notre Dame: Notre Dame University Press, 1973), pp. 35–51; Alexander Kern, "The Rise of Transcendentalism," in Harry Hayden Clark, ed., *Transitions in American Literary History* (Durham: Duke University Press, 1953), pp. 245–314; Donald Koster, *Transcendentalism in America* (Boston: Twayne Publishers, 1975); Perry Miller, ed., *The Transcendentalists, an Anthology* (Cambridge: Harvard University Press, 1950), "Introduction"; and Rose, pp. 38–108.

[50] Wright, pp. 158–59.

[51] Levin, pp. 6–7.

[52] Miller, *The Transcendentalists*, p. 8; Miller, "From Edwards to Emerson," in *Errand into the Wilderness* (1956) (New York: Harper Torchbooks, 1964), pp. 184–203.

original Puritan revolutionary impulse, particularly that of dissenters like Roger Williams and Anne Hutchinson, as well as its later manifestation in Jonathan Edwards, who described the gift to the regenerate of a divine and supernatural light, which allowed them to apprehend holiness, a "sense" they had not possessed before. If Transcendentalism was linked backward to the mystic potential in dissenting Puritanism, it was linked forward to the cultural aspirations of individualism and democracy. The existence of Reason, Coleridge's term for the power to apprehend truth directly, depended on neither class, gender, nor education, and thus suggested a profound egalitarianism. For the Transcendentalists, freedom became the key to the spread and exercise of Reason, the intuitive grasp of truth, resulting socially in the perfection of human institutions.[53]

The burgeoning hostility toward Christian Unitarian rationalists was not only an intellectual tempest or generational dispute; it had social and institutional implications as well. In their protest against Calvinism, Unitarians had charged their opponents with setting limits on free speech and free inquiry. The limits that some Unitarians themselves felt obliged to erect became clear in the 1830s. Anne Rose has provided several examples of the social situation against which Transcendentalists reacted. As members of a generally elite segment of society, Unitarians viewed with alarm the rise of labor movements, which appeared to threaten the social harmony upheld by the liberal hegemony. As Rose says, "by insisting on their rights, liberties, and duties as citizens, workingmen adhered to the tradition of the secular Enlightenment and American Revolution . . . liberal religion was seen as a tool of class oppression."[54] The trial and imprisonment of Abner Kneeland, viewed with satisfaction by many Unitarian Bostonians, on the charge of blasphemy revealed the contradiction between professions of tolerance and the response to threats that seemed to shake the social order. The state is required, said Massachusetts Chief Justice Lemuel Shaw, to protect its citizens against "an intended design to calumniate and disparage the Supreme Being, and to destroy the veneration due to him."[55] Transcendentalists, still members of the social elite themselves, never fully identified their movement with working-class movements. Their protest against the thought of their day was theological and aesthetic, but it led them, like the laborers, to rethink social arrangements

---

53 Hochfield, p. 41.
54 Rose, p. 26.
55 Shaw, quoted in Rose, p. 28.

and experiment with alternatives. They hoped for friendships that would be intense, supportive, and nurturing; they sought to make spouses full partners in the movement; they established havens of conversation and exchange of ideas in an increasingly suspicious environment; and they erected alternative communities, like Brook Farm and Fruitlands, to try to live out their desire for full human development and for more rewarding interpersonal relations.[56]

But, most of all, Transcendentalism must be seen against the broadest background—the development of the Romantic movement, which had gestated throughout the eighteenth century and was born in the wake of the American and French revolutions. Despite the enormous hostility of the American Transcendentalists toward Locke and other figures of the Enlightenment, many of the greatest thinkers of the eighteenth century provided compelling ideas, especially with regard to the creative power of the imagination, that would be put to use by the artists and intellectuals of the new era.[57] For English Romantics, the French Revolution was the great catalyzing event that seemed to draw together the divergent mental and emotional streams of the age: anger at tyranny, fear of industrial growth, belief in individual creative power and the power of the nonrational. The possibility of genuine individual and social renewal now seemed within reach. The American Revolution, for that matter, had provided an early signal of the dawn of a new age. Joseph Priestley, the Unitarian clergyman and scientist who had fled to Pennsylvania from persecution in England, saw the two cataclysmic events as "the inauguration of the state of universal happiness and peace distinctly and repeatedly foretold in many prophecies, delivered more than two thousand years ago."[58]

Romantics saw their work as a means of clarifying and transforming the events of their age, not often through direct commentary, but through symbolic, prophetic utterance. Romantics tried, in M. H. Abrams' words, to fuse "history, politics, philosophy, and religion into one grand design": the emergence of a renewed humanity in a restored world.[59]

[56] Rose, pp. 109–61.

[57] See, for example, the highly original and stimulating book by James Engell, *The Creative Imagination: Enlightenment to Romanticism* (Cambridge: Harvard University Press, 1981).

[58] M. H. Abrams, "English Romanticism: The Spirit of the Age," in *Romanticism and Consciousness,* ed. Harold Bloom (New York: W. W. Norton, 1970), pp. 95–97. See also Abrams, *Natural Supernaturalism: Tradition and Revolution in Romantic Literature* (New York: W. W. Norton, 1971).

[59] Abrams, "English Romanticism," pp. 101–103.

The Romantic world view and aesthetic outlook flowed from such a transforming zeal. The model of the universe described by Archdeacon Paley in the late eighteenth century featured a static mechanism, a perfect and motionless reflection of the mind of God, running smoothly and eternally. Revolutionary politics, economic transformation, and the development of the idea of the imagination's inherent creativity gave rise to a different metaphor—life as organism, growing, relating, interacting. A new set of preferred values and behavior followed: "change becomes a positive value . . . it is not man's punishment, it is his opportunity . . . we have a universe of emergents." The central aesthetic principle that follows from such an outlook, says Morse Peckham, is "dynamic organicism." And that is the second major principle for New England Transcendentalists, the first being a belief in the efficacy of Reason.[60]

As clearly as American Transcendentalism is a branch of the Romantic tree, there is more to Romanticism than the New England rebels imagined or admitted. Transcendentalists used Reason to distinguish the eternal elements of religion from its one-time manifestation, "historical Christianity." But, not surprisingly, the tenets of the Transcendental faith looked remarkably like those of the generation of Channing. Neither the liberals nor their radical offspring could quite imagine a movement of consciousness that led to secular humanism. Likewise, the Transcendentalists insisted that the created order mirrors the divine law and the promptings of the human heart, but could not follow Melville or Dickinson up the Romantic tree to the point where the self projects all the meaning there is.[61]

In the fall of 1832 Mary and Elizabeth Peabody moved into Mrs. Rebecca Clarke's boardinghouse in Boston. Mrs. Clarke's son, James Freeman Clarke, and her daughter, Sarah Clarke, were both to become deeply engaged with the Transcendentalist movement during the

[60] Morse Peckham, "Toward a Theory of Romanticism," in *The Triumph of Romanticism* (Columbia: University of South Carolina Press, 1970), pp. 10, 12; Hochfield, pp. 41, 42.

[61] Emerson suggested such a radical possibility in *Nature* (1836) but more often relied on the analogy argument, that humanity mirrors the spiritual essence of the cosmos. Harold Bloom, "The Internalization of the Quest Romance," in *Ringers in the Tower* (Chicago: University of Chicago Press, 1971), pp. 13–35, and Robert Langbaum, *The Poetry of Experience: The Dramatic Monologue in Modern Literary Tradition* (New York: W. W. Norton, 1957), pp. 11–12, 19–37, point to the ways in which more advanced Romantics reenter the world of experience to formulate and test values that the self projects onto the world.

1830s.[62] The arrival at Mrs. Clarke's of Dedham lawyer Horace Mann, in despair over the death of his wife, Charlotte, prompted in the Peabody sisters a sympathetic outpouring of feeling. Eilzabeth, in particular, whether out of curiosity, sense of challenge, or covert affection, engaged Mann over the issue of his intense grieving. She agreed with him that the inexplicable death of the young and pious Charlotte made absolutely intolerable the theology of Mann's childhood minister, Nathanael Emmons, for whom suffering and loss were part of the will of an inscrutable God. The Unitarian consolation was hardly more soothing. How could one say this was a well-modulated universe when such cruel irrationality occurred? Ultimately, Peabody urged Mann to accept creation as empowered by the spirit of love and to feel God's love and acceptance within himself. Mann's comfort, Peabody was saying, would follow from the exercise of his Reason as he intuited the nurturing care of a parental God.

Peabody's validation of her feelings and her willingness to push at the limits of the liberal outlook made her favorably inclined toward the educational reforms of Amos Bronson Alcott. In 1834 she agreed to serve as Alcott's assistant at Temple School, a private academy held at the Masonic Temple on Tremont Street in Boston. She also began boarding with the Alcotts. At first, as her letters and journal entries indicate, she was in full agreement with the reformer. Alcott's desire to bring out the "spiritual existence" of children echoed the educational philosophy of her mother: "it seems to me that the self-activity of the mind was cultivated by my mother's method in her school . . . Not so much was poured in—more was brought out"—and of Channing.[63] Because she had already come to believe in the existence of innate knowledge in children, Peabody had no trouble approving of Alcott's desire to explore the child's mind, highlighting its essentially spiritual character, primarily through the techniques of conversation and of journal-keeping. Alcott worked "to bring out clearly in the children's consciousness, the perception of their spiritual existence, as being the most real and permanent."[64] Under his guidance, Peabody moved closer to the central Romantic view of the child as morally and spiritually advanced, as a lucid transmitter of divine wisdom. This was

[62] Joel Myerson, " 'A True & High-Minded Person': Transcendentalist Sarah Clarke," *Southwest Review* 59 (Spring 1974): 163–72.
[63] Elizabeth Peabody, "Female Education in Massachusetts: Reminiscences of Subjects and Methods of Teaching," quoted in Conrad, p. 203.
[64] Peabody, MS Journal, 29 December 1834 (MS: NNB)

certainly Alcott's view at Temple, and while Peabody had growing reservations about his pedagogy, especially the sometimes painful introspection which the pupils' assignment of keeping journals involved, she did agree that children were more in touch with the organic essence of all life than adults were. Another Romantic principle was that of the creative force of the imagination, to which Alcott gave a standard formulation. Peabody recorded this exchange of teacher with pupils at Temple: "Can you understand this definition: imagination is the power that represents, re-presents spirit? Yes. Imagination represents spirit, soul, mind, the outward world, and God. . . . What is imagination? Imagination is the power whereby you picture out thoughts that never were realized in the world."[65] Influenced by her work at Temple, Peabody could give a similar definition: "It is the concentration of profound feeling, reason, of the perception of outward nature into one act of the mind, that prepares the soul for vigorous effort in all the various departments of its activity."[66]

The aspect of her work at Temple that particularly shaped her understanding of the imagination was an investigation of children's speech. She began her 1834 review of Herder's *The Spirit of Hebrew Poetry* in good rationalist fashion, but then moved in a distinctly Transcendental direction. Beyond the historicity of the Biblical texts lay their poetry, "the expression of abstract and spiritual truths by sensible objects, by the forms, colors, sounds, changes, and combinations of external nature."[67] The imagination, she implied, invested those inner and eternal truths with imagery drawn from the outer world. But the full creative power of the imagination remained limited for her, since the human mind and the natural order were reflections of the same divine originator, a point Archdeacon Paley would not disown.[68]

By late 1836, Peabody had stepped into another debate that served to separate Christian Unitarians from their radical dissenters. In her November 23 letter to Mary, she described the controversy about miracles

[65] Elizabeth Peabody, *Record of a School: Exemplifying the General Principles of Spiritual Culture* (Boston: James Munroe, 1835), p. 166. For a discussion of Alcott's philosophy of education, see Bruce A. Ronda, "Genesis and Genealogy: Bronson Alcott's Changing Views of the Child," *The New England Historical and Genealogical Register* 135 (October 1981): 259–73.

[66] Peabody, *Record of a School*, 3rd ed., quoted in Conrad, p. 205.

[67] Peabody, "The Spirit of Hebrew Poetry," 175

[68] See Philip Gura, "Elizabeth Peabody and the Philosophy of Language," *ESQ* (1977): 155.

between Andrews Norton and George Ripley, and demonstrated a vigorous and accurate grasp of the intellectual issues at stake. She also recognized the social dimension of the conflict, noting Andrews Norton's denunciation of the Transcendental movement as appealing to women. That she was present at a meeting of the *Christian Examiner*'s editorial board speaks of the enlarged opportunities for discussion of important issues open to her. And, in the last years of the decade, Peabody herself became a kind of mentor for the emerging talents of Jones Very and Nathaniel Hawthorne.

Thus, by the close of the 1830s, Peabody had become fully engaged with the Transcendental phase of Romanticism. She had felt personally the need for recognizing and honoring intense emotion as a valid source of insight, connecting that recognition to the Romantic doctrine of Reason. She saw in the child a model of moral and spiritual wholeness. She saw imagination as the crucial creative act of the mind. She developed, in Susan Conrad's words, a "romantic strategy of investigating history . . . for the spiritual truths it might reveal."[69] Although her historical awareness led her to advocate restraint of the more ecstatic flights of her peers, as in the case of Jones Very, history could be for her nonetheless a means to regenerate human culture, certainly a central Romantic desire.

Elizabeth Peabody did not, however, fully conform to the Romantic ethos and aesthetic. She shaped a distinctive version of the Transcendental code, combining Romantic impulses, a concern with history, a commitment to her vocation of teaching, and consciousness of her gender and status as a woman. She discovered in the kindergarten movement the perfect vehicle for what became her conservative idealism. Kindergarten reform became all the more relevant in a postwar reform world anxious to define the role of the reformer in ambitious terms.

Already in the 1830s Peabody had begun to distance herself from some of the more wide-eyed Transcendentalists. While her enthusiasm for Alcott's goals at Temple School remained strong, she began to doubt his method. She wondered, for example, whether some physical stimulation was not crucial in early education, besides the education of the mind and encouragement of the moral life. She worried that Alcott manipulated his students' discussions, rather than allowing genuine expression. She was annoyed that he had so little sense of his-

69 Conrad, p. 216.

torical and cultural particularities and seemed to subsume all experience under grand and sweeping generalizations.[70]

The rift between Peabody and Alcott was a complex affair made up of theoretical and pedagogical issues, seasoned with personal and emotional clashes. Peabody felt increasingly vulnerable as a single woman boarding with the Alcotts, where her privacy, especially of her mail, seemed to be threatened. She connected her own sense of defenselessness in the face of possibly hostile public opinion toward Temple School with Alcott's probing and revealing of his young students' feelings. There were certain insights and intimations in a child's inner life that were better left unexplored and unexpressed, she thought: "the instinctive delicacy with which children veil their deepest thoughts of love and tenderness for relatives, and their reasonable self-gratulations should not be violated . . . in order to gain knowledge."[71] When Alcott was preparing to publish his *Conversations with Children on the Gospels,* Peabody wrote to implore him to suppress some passages: "Why did Prophets and apostles veil this subject in fables and emblems if there was not a reason for avoiding physiological inquiries &c? This is worth thinking of. However you as a man can say anything, but I am a woman, and have feelings that I dare not distrust, however little I can understand them, or give an account of them."[72] Peabody's fears that her association with Alcott would unsettle her own professional status, which had already been shaken in the controversy over her New Bedford students, were not unfounded. After publication of the first volume of *Conversations* in December 1836, she could not find work in Boston and had to rejoin her family in Salem.

The poet Jones Very provided another opportunity for Peabody's tempering of the Romantic afflatus. As her letters to Emerson indicate, Very believed he was the embodiment of the Second Coming; he had announced his mission one day when he was alone with her. She had an almost desperate desire to calm him, derived apparently in part from disagreement with such a messianic possibility, from her awareness of the impropriety of his presence, and perhaps out of fear of his sudden frenzy.[73]

Peabody provided the fullest prewar expression of her versions of

70 Ronda, "Peabody's Changing Views," 108–110.

71 Elizabeth Peabody, *Record of a School,* 2nd ed. (Boston: Russell, Shattuck, 1836), viii.

72 Peabody to Bronson Alcott, 7 August 1836 (MS, copy, MH), in Bronson Alcott's MS "Memoir 1878."

73 Peabody to Emerson, 20 October 1838, 3 December 1838 (MS, MSaE).

idealism, reform, and religion in her 1858 essay "Egotheism, the Atheism of Today," in two essays on Brook Farm, and in "The Dorian
Measure," an essay in her *Aesthetic Papers.* In "A Glimpse of Christ's
Idea of Society," she argued that Jesus encouraged His followers to see
the kingdom of God and the Church as identical, and proclaimed that
the kingdom would not come until Christ's influence is spread to all
corners of the earth. This gradual, organic unfolding of the kingdom
may come about in various ways, she noted. Even the apparently secular revolutionary movements are part of the transformation of society.
The great danger in such movements is that the individual is lost sight
of, and she offered in contrast the example of Jesus, who combined
self-sacrificial love of others with a perfect sense of his own person-
hood. Self and society together must unfold organically. "The final
cause of human society is the unfolding of the individual man into
every form of perfection, without let or hindrance, according to the
inward nature of each." Education provides, of course, the principal
aid to such unfolding.[74]

In "Egotheism," Peabody outlined the consequences of failing to
maintain this self-society balance. People caught up in their inner,
subjective versions of reality "deify their own conceptions; that is, they
say that their conception of God is all that men can ever know of God.
In short faith commits suicide . . . and the next step to this is necessarily EGOTHEISM . . . not recognizing that there is, beyond our conception, inconceivable Power, Wisdom, and Love—of the immanence
of whose substantial being within us our best conception is but a transient form . . . we find this 'latest form of infidelity', as the understanding has rather blindly denominated it . . . for man proves but
a melancholy God."[75] Although she names no names, one can feel her
criticism of Alcott, Very, and, in an ambiguous fashion, of Emerson as
well.

In "The Dorian Measure," Peabody gave further shape to her
views. She identified, in early Greek culture, a love of moderation and
balance. The Dorian view of the state was not simply that it was a
negative influence, as modern society and her Transcendental colleagues saw it, but that it was a means of collective identity, making
each citizen "a living member of the body of the state." The Dorian
educational system, featuring music, dance, and gymnastics, led to in-

[74] Elizabeth Peabody, "A Glimpse of Christ's Idea of Society," *Dial* 2 (1841): 226.
[75] Elizabeth Peabody, "Egotheism, the Atheism of Today" (1858), reprinted in
Last Evening with Allston and Other Papers (Boston: D. Lothrop, 1886), p. 245.

dividual cultivation and group participation. She hoped that by adopting some of the Greek practices in a Christian context, we would ensure that the United States would be a truly Christian nation. We were already divinely sanctioned: "Never before the birth of our political constitution, which was not made by men, but grew up from the instincts of Christian men who had brooked no control of their relations with God, was there any nation on earth, within which the life eternal could unfold its proportions."[76] The notion of America's providential history was widely held both during the Revolutionary period and well into the nineteenth century. Peabody recalled that Channing's Unitarianism seemed to her a direct consequence of the Puritan migration, and both part of the inevitable march of God's history:

The moral character of the Unitarian movement did not originate with Dr. Channing, of course; but was the logical evolution of the Pilgrim emigration,— for that was a mighty deed, and lifted the first doers of it from the ground of the Calvinist speculations, from which doubtless they started, into that superiority to scholastic abstractions which Robinson evinced, when he said that more light was to break out from the written word than Luther or Calvin had seen; and which Roger Williams practically demonstrated, even before the first pilgrims were dead, by founding the first community in Christendom—if not on earth— that separated Church and State. . . . The American and French revolutions were further exertions of human power to realize the freedom and dignity of man, and had helped to give a new method of religious as well as political thinking.[77]

Although the organic metaphor was part of the Romantic critique against mechanistic philosophy and elitist politics, Peabody used the metaphor to express her more conservative social thinking. Society-as-organism was a harmonious-sounding concept, but one increasingly out of phase with social changes. Labor leaders, including Orestes Brownson and Thomas Skidmore, rejected the organic version of society as a ploy to maintain feudal distinctions of inferior and superior. Unitarian elites embraced the metaphor, but found, as in the cases of

[76] Elizabeth Peabody, "The Dorian Measure," in *Aesthetic Papers* (Boston: E. P. Peabody, 1849), p. 99.
[77] Peabody, *Reminiscences*, pp. 27–28. For discussions of the providential view of American history, see Sacvan Bercovich, *The Puritan Origins of the American Self* (New Haven: Yale University Press, 1975), Levin, *History as Romantic Art*, pp. 24–40; and Ernest Lee Tuveson, *Redeemer Nation* (Chicago: University of Chicago Press, 1968).

such disturbers of the peace as Abner Kneeland and Bronson Alcott, that maintenance of that harmony required the law or public opinion to silence dissent, or, as in the case of the return of fugitive slaves, the presence of military force. Class, ethnic, racial, and geographical divisions developed rapidly in the 1840s and 50s, making Peabody's vision of a harmonious Christian society ever more untenable.[78]

The conservative implications of her organicism for the condition of women and families are apparent in "The Philosophy of History in the Education of Republican Men and Women," which appeared in the February 1855 issue of *The Una*. Peabody claimed that a knowledge of history would deepen women's understanding of the dynamics of the family, which, not surprisingly, she saw as an organism and a microcosm of the larger organism that is society. The oppression of women and children, and particularly the practice of polygamy, was widespread in the Asian world and could be seen among Mormons, she charged. American women should know the past in order to prevent such tyranny from upsetting the living organism of the family.[79] If Mormons and Asians represented the sexual free-for-all, the polymorphously perverse, end of the spectrum, then stark individualism, or egotheism, represented the other. That end of the spectrum, she appeared to believe, was occupied by people like Caroline Dall. In her books and lectures, Dall argued that women were discriminated against economically, legally, and educationally, and required fair treatment as citizens, not as wives and mothers. "We have not laid a secure foundation for any statement on this subject, unless we have made it clear that 'woman's rights' are identical with 'human rights'; that no father, brother, or husband can have all the privileges ordained for him of God, till mother and sister and wife are set free to secure them according to instinctive individual bias."[80] To Peabody, this insistence on individual rights violated the organic and family-centered definition of woman. Dall's willingness to make such statements publicly, insistently, and sensationally prompted Peabody's sharp response. Horace Mann had a far more satisfactory view of women's role, she felt: "He thinks a woman is doing a *higher* & nobler & finer duty when she is educating her own children than when she is

[78] Daniel Howe provides a brief but cogent description of the Unitarian view of society as organism, which appears to lie behind Peabody's social thought, in *The Unitarian Conscience,* pp. 125–31.

[79] Peabody, quoted in Conrad, pp. 214–16.

[80] Caroline Dall, quoted in Degler, p. 343.

addressing public audiences; when her left hand does not know what her right hand is doing—and in this I recognize a high ideal of woman—The *inward* scope is the *highest* scope of human action."[81]

VI

In the post–Civil War period, Elizabeth Peabody was taken up in many causes: freedman's education, Indian rights, memorials for dead writers. The list of friends and correspondents she had acquired by the end of her life is impressive:

Wordsworth, De Geranda [o], Carlyle, Mazzini, Kossuth and his sister, Harriet Martineau, Mary Somerville, Mary Howitt, Fredrika Bremer, F. W. Maurice . . . Wilberforce, William W. Story, Robert Browning, Sir Edwin Arnold, William Henry Channing, Tom Hughes, Canon Farrar, Dean Stanley . . . William Ellery Channing, Ralph Waldo Emerson, Washington Allston, Margaret Fuller, Lucretia Mott, Lydia Maria Child, Wm. Lloyd Garrison, Catherine Sedgwick, Fanny Kemble, Charles Sumner, Agassiz, E. P. Whipple, Theodore Parker, Whittier, Charlotte Cushman, Henry James, Harriet Beecher Stowe, Bronson Alcott, Thoreau, Longfellow, Dr. Holmes, and many others.[82]

But the kindergarten movement was clearly her great postwar cause and the one that linked her most securely with her prewar endeavors.

In 1859, Peabody met the daughter of Carl and Margarethe Schurz. Margarethe had operated a German-speaking kindergarten in Wisconsin in 1856, following the methods of German educational reformer Friedrich Froebel, and Agathe had been in her mother's class. Peabody was charmed and impressed by the girl.

It was her remarkable behavior that so impressed E. P. that she remarked to Mrs. Schurz, "that little girl of yours is a miracle, so childlike and unconscious, and yet so wise and able, attracting and ruling the children, who seem nothing short of enchanted."

Said Mrs. Schurz, "No miracle, but only brought up in a kindergarten."

"A kindergarten?" asked Miss Peabody. "What is that?"

"A garden whose plants are human. Did you never hear of Froebel?" asked Mrs. Schurz.[83]

---

[81] Peabody to Caroline Dall, 21 February 1859 (MS, MHi).

[82] Maria S. Porter, "Elizabeth Palmer Peabody," *The Bostonian* 3 (January 1896): 341.

[83] Peabody, "Origin and Growth of the Kindergarten" (1882), quoted in Agnes Snyder, *Dauntless Women in Childhood Education, 1856–1931* (Washington, D.C.: Association for Childhood Education International, 1972), p. 31.

Margarethe Meyer Schurz (1833–1876) began her kindergarten with her own children as pupils. In his *Mother Play* and other volumes, Froebel described the need for sense-training, using colors, shapes, and textures. To this, he counseled, should be added music and cooperative games. Pervading his pedagogy was a sense of the unity of God, humanity, and nature, on which early childhood education should be based and which kindergarten teachers should seek to stimulate in children. Froebel pursued his reforms in the period of intense nationalism following the Napoleonic wars. Patriotic Germans were stimulated by the idealist philosophies of Fichte, Schelling, and Hegel. The Hegelian dialectic influenced Froebel's educational theories dramatically: the eternal law in all things is manifested in nature and in the spirit, and comes together in the eternal Unity, which is God. All things are destined "to unfold their essence . . . to reveal God in their external and transient being . . . education consists in leading man, as a thinking, intelligent being, growing into self-consciousness, to a pure and unsullied, conscious and free representation of the inner law of Divine Unity, and in teaching him ways and means thereto."[84]

In 1848 Froebel traveled to Hamburg to give a course on the kindergarten. Hamburg was the home of Heinrich Christian Meyer, a liberal manufacturer, whose oldest daughter, Berthe, helped arrange Froebel's visit, and whose children all attended the educator's lectures. Berthe, with her fiancé, Johannes Ronge, moved to England after the failure of the 1848 Revolution. Margarethe went with her sister and met the German exile Carl Schurz there in 1851. The following year they were married and emigrated to the United States. Eventually settling in Wisconsin, Schurz was swept into abolitionist politics, and in this domestic void Margarethe determined to recall and re-create the liberal educational ideas of Froebel for her children.

Stimulated by her contact with the Schurzes, Elizabeth Peabody established a kindergarten, the first English-speaking one in America, on Pinckney Street in Boston in 1860. By 1861 there were thirty pupils, two assistants, a French teacher, and a teacher of gymnastics, in addition to Elizabeth and her sister Mary, who joined her after the death of her husband, Horace Mann, in 1859. By 1867, however, Pea-

---

84 Friedrich Froebel, *The Education of Man,* quoted in Snyder, p. 24. Biographical details and lengthy discussions of Froebel's philosophy of education may be found in *Kindergarten and Child Culture Papers: Papers on Froebel's Kindergarten . . . Republished from the American Journal of Education,* rev. ed. (Syracuse: C. W. Bardeen, 1890), pp. 17–48, 69–124, 181–89.

body was dissatisfied with the results of her work and journeyed to Europe to learn about kindergartens firsthand. Upon her return fifteen months later, she plunged vigorously into the movement that dominated her life for the next quarter-century—kindergartens along genuinely Froebelian lines.[85] The kindergarten movement caught up all the threads of Peabody's life and career: her mother's influence, her early work as teacher and tutor, the seminal effect of Channing and his Unitarianism, the Romantic and Transcendentalist revolt, her acceptance within those dissident circles, her passion for history, and her conservative idealism.

The focus on the education of young children was virtually a leitmotif for Peabody. It grew out of her mother's tutelage and developed in the spacious quarters of Temple School. The Romantic celebration of the child, as in Wordsworth's "Intimations" ode, lifted up the young as those closest to virtue and divinity, and meshed with the heightened attention paid to children throughout the nineteenth century. As Carl Degler has written, children were beginning to be seen as different from adults, as occupying a period of life worthy of recognition, care, even extension. "Simply because children were being seen for the first time as special, the family's reason for being, its justification as it were, was increasingly related to the proper rearing of children."[86]

Such rearing, many nineteenth-century people agreed, was women's special task. In the two previous centuries, fathers were the central parental figures, or else, as the child-rearing literature advised, parents divided the tasks of nurture. But in the early nineteenth century, women alone were emerging as the primary care-givers, at a time when industrial and institutional changes were altering many of the premodern functions of the family. Women now concentrated their efforts on their children, and to that end a considerable advice literature became available. Literature for children flourished throughout the century, accentuating the interest in and concern for the young.[87]

The kindergarten movement represented the taking up of this domestic concern for children to the national level, making it a national reform. The manner in which Elizabeth Peabody, as leader of the nationalization of early-childhood education, carried out this reform was consistent with the tendencies of her thought from the pre-

[85] Snyder, pp. 48–56.
[86] Degler, p. 66. See also Bernard Wishy, *The Child and the Republic* (Philadelphia: University of Pennsylvania Press, 1968), chs. 3, 5.
[87] Epstein, pp. 21–22; Degler, pp. 68–69, 75.

war years. The Froebelian kindergarten would be based on the organic metaphor, on "mother love," on systemization and rationalization, and on the development of public-minded citizens.

The uses to which Peabody put the notion of organicism were seen in her essay on Brook Farm and in "The Dorian Measure." The kindergarten pupil should be encouraged to grow organically, both physically, through play, and spiritually, through music and art. Indeed, said Peabody, Froebel saw the two dimensions as one: "True education shall lead out the imprisoned spirit, growingly conscious of individuality, by means of the symbolism of the prison house itself, which is that correlation of necessary forces we call the material universe."[88]

The ante-bellum use of organicism had a spiritual and aesthetic quality. Development was through the material but into the spiritual. In post-1865 America, however, reformers increasingly applied the metaphor in terms limited to the body and the natural order. Anxious to reconstruct the war-ravaged land, eager to use new discoveries in biology, chemistry, and geology, middle-class reformers portrayed society as analogous to the structure of the human body. Biology, as William Leach has observed, was at the heart of their angle of vision. The kindergarten, in such an outlook, became a preventive reform as well as a means to the new society.[89] Shaped by *the human providence of education,* children will adopt "the laws of order, by which God creates the universe," and avoid unorganic and anti-social behavior.[90] The image of society as a healthy body was linked with Froebel's stress on physical activity as well as with Peabody's own delight with Dorian culture and its music, dance, and gymnastics.[91] On the other hand, Froebelianism insisted on the presence of divinity in all life, seeing the growing child as aspiring to express that divinity. Other, more materialist, approaches to education—those that stressed psychology, testing, measurement—preferred to treat the child as an entirely physical entity. By the end of the century, the conflict between these two approaches in the circles of early childhood educators was in full tilt.

Kindergartens as extensions of "mother love" were consistent with Peabody's prewar acceptance of the family-centered identity for women. Indeed, describing the kindergarten as a home away from home may

88 Peabody, *Lectures,* p. 93.
89 William Leach, *True Love and Perfect Union* (New York: Basic Books, 1980), p. 324.
90 Peabody, *Lectures,* p. 14.
91 Peabody, *Lectures,* p. 78.

have soothed the worries of mothers reluctant to give up their charges. And while all mothers may desire to love their children, the fact is, wrote Mary Mann, "that the actual parents of the majority of the human race have a very inadequate sense of their duty to their children." Kindergartens may become, not just centers for young children, but also training schools for mothers. This might come about by requiring a course in early-childhood education, along Froebel's lines, in every public school. Mary Mann also claimed that kindergarten education had a positive effect on the parents and families of the participants: "Men stay at home from the grog-shops to hear their four-year-old babes sing! and teach the older ones the pretty plays." Kindergarten teachers will never replace parents, of course: "The kindergarteners are the educators to be consulted by mothers rather than wise men who exercise their brains about school curriculums. . . ." But kindergarten advocates left the strong impression that while they base their program on the interactions typical of mother and child, their goal was a systematic, predictable, and repeatable curriculum not tied to the mysterious whims of individual parents.[92]

Hence a third mark of the kindergarten movement was its systematic and rationalized character. In his annual Reports on the condition of Massachusetts public schools and in his assault on the sectarian nature of public education, Horace Mann was an early exponent of regularized institutional education.[93] But much schooling, and particularly much of the most innovative schooling, in ante-bellum America was private or tutorial. Alcott's Temple School, Roundhill School, George Bancroft's and Joseph Cogswell's academy in Northampton, Miss Pierce's School for young women in Litchfield, Connecticut, are but the best-known examples of superior private education. Like other reforms, education came under the spell of organization after the war.

The Civil War itself contributed to a new mood of impersonal collectivism, the need to subsume the cranky and unpredictable individual in the needs of the community.[94] The post-war feminist movement provides a useful illustration of this shift. Many leaders of the movement, including Elizabeth Cady Stanton and Mary Putnam Jacobi, were readers of Comte, who argued that positivism, the mark of

[92] Mary Peabody Mann, "Kindergarten and Homes," in *Kindergarten and Child Culture Papers,* pp. 654, 657, 661; see also Wishy, ch. 11.

[93] See Michael Katz, *The Irony of Early School Reform* (Boston: Beacon Press, 1970), pp. 139-53.

[94] See George Fredrickson, *The Inner Civil War* (New York: Harper and Row, 1965), especially chs. 7, 9, 11, 12.

true science, characterized the highest level of human civilization. The new age, Stanton and Jacobi agreed, was to be fulfilled only through organization and centralization, but also needed to be rid of the male element of destructive individualism and replaced by the love element, the essential female quality.[95]

The kindergarten spread systematically, through training schools, British and American Froebel Unions, college departments for educating kindergartners, as at New York City (later Hunter) College in 1874, and through ceaseless floods of pamphlets and books. Most of all, the reform spread through the attachment of kindergartens to public-school systems, beginning in St. Louis in 1873. Along with the national spread of the movement came the challenge of rival approaches. In describing the formation of the American Froebel Union, Peabody wrote to Henry Barnard that "the Union was formed primarily to protect the *name of Kindergarten* from being confounded with methods of infant-training inconsistent with Froebel's idea and system, and which was assumed, without sincerity, as a cover of quite another thing, which calls itself 'the American Kindergarten,' and claimed Froebel's authority expressly for its *own* devices."[96]

Finally, the kindergarten movement aimed to produce public-minded citizens, equipped to participate in the new group-oriented middle-class life of industrial and urban America. Early-childhood education was intended to be the first in a series of measures to wean people away from individual, inner, nonrational preoccupations and toward an essentially public existence. Mary Putnam Jacobi's cry "live in the open air" was a late-century echo of Elizabeth Peabody's anxiety about revealing secrets and invading privacy. Although she recognized and expressed strong feeling, which provided a strong inner spur toward the Romantic position in the early 1830s, Peabody restricted this by her acceptance of the ideology of woman's sphere and by her desire not to probe others' privacy or allow such investigation to occur to her unwanted. Part of this impulse toward discretion may have originated in her awareness of her precarious position as a single woman. But her unwillingness to probe the hidden heart came from a philosophical position as well. Her organicism, as expressed in her prewar essays, was based on analogies between the law of the heart, the law of society, and the law of nature. All these together constitute the

95 Leach, p. 140.
96 Elizabeth Peabody, "Development of the Kindergarten," in *Kindergarten and Child Culture Papers*, p. 13.

unity of God. To stress the individual too extensively represents a disruption of the unity, an idolatry of the self. To explore the inner life, or to be known too intimately, might result in the unleashing of passion, and, as she warned in "The Dorian Measure," "the chief danger to a nation and to a man is from within, that the passion and the will may be too strong for the uncultured intelligence."[97]

Many postwar reformers saw individualism and Romanticism as their chief obstacles in achieving a more systematized and harmonious body politic. An oppressive and tyrannical arrangement, romantic love was based on private passionate moments, thrilled to conflict and tumultuous reunions, and throve on fantasy. In consequence, many suffrage advocates argued, women were the slaves of love and of masterful men and regularly became pregnant both in and out of marriage.[98] The solution was two-fold. First, as a part of the Social Purity movement and its assault on prostitution, women were encouraged to minimize their own sexuality, and to bend men to their standard of infrequent intercourse. This effort, as Carl Degler notes, was meant to improve the condition of women within marriage, to reduce male prerogative, and to redefine a biological drive as a cultural one, and therefore treat it as a public and discussable phenomenon.[99] Second, human relations in general and affectionate relations particularly were to become more rational, subject to scrutiny, debate, even the advice of others.[100]

This image of the self as a public figure, progressively being freed from the grip of irrational desire and impulse through education, corresponds to the purposes of Peabody and other kindergartners. The goal of early-childhood education was to bend the child away from egotism and isolation and toward group activity. In a letter to William Torrey Harris, Peabody called the child alone "a depraved being," while Mary Jacobi called the unsocialized child a "neuropathic individual." For many reformers, the kindergarten was a clinic for the bearers of potentially social pathologies, whose individualistic behavior was a form of mental illness.[101]

97 Peabody, "The Dorian Measure," in *Aesthetic Papers,* p. 98.
98 Leach, p. 106.
99 Degler, pp. 271–72, 280–81.
100 Leach, pp. 101–28.
101 Peabody to William Torrey Harris, 28 August 1870 (MS, MoSHi); Leach, pp. 331–32.

VII

In February 1885, the first installment of Henry James' *The Bostonians* appeared in *Century Magazine*. The portrait of the indefatigable reformer Miss Birdseye, humorously though affectionately drawn, created a minor tempest. His aunt Kate Walsh, his brother William, and James Russell Lowell all criticized James for lampooning Elizabeth Peabody, by then a venerable institution of reform, indeed, "the Grandmother of Boston." James rejected the parallel vigorously: "I absolutely had no shadow of such an intention," he wrote to William. "Miss Birdseye was evolved entirely from my moral consciousness, like every other person I have ever drawn." But then James went on to indicate what he was trying to portray, and the extent to which Elizabeth Peabody had impressed herself on the consciousness of at least some of the cultivated community became apparent. "[The character] originated in my desire to make a figure who should embody in a sympathetic, pathetic, picturesque, and at the same time grotesque way, the humanity and ci-devant transcendental tendencies." If this happened to look like Miss Peabody, James went on, so be it. He insisted that he had no jest in mind, and that indeed his Miss Birdseye is an honorable figure. "She is treated with respect throughout, and every virtue of heroism and disinterestedness is attributed to her. She is represented as the embodiment of pure, and purest philanthropy."[102]

In short, Henry James had portrayed Elizabeth Palmer Peabody in his novel. He had reversed only the physical size of the real and fictional reformers, and had kept true to the weight of her impact.[103]

---

[102] *The Letters of Henry James,* ed. Percy Lubbock (New York: Charles Scribner's Sons, 1920), 1, pp. 115–17.

[103] Regarding his Aunt Elizabeth's size, Julian Hawthorne tells this anecdote: "We had a cat, and the cat had had kittens a day or two before. Aunt Lizzie came into the nursery, where Una and I were building houses of blocks, and sat down in the big easy-chair. The cat was in the room, and she immediately came up to my aunt and began to mew and to pluck at her dress with her claws. Such attentions were rare on pussy's part, and my aunt noticed them with pleasure, and caressed the animal, which still continued to devote its entire attention to her. But there was something odd in the sound of her mewing and in the intent regard of her yellow eyes. 'Can anything be the matter with pussy?' speculated my aunt. At that moment my father entered the room, and my aunt rose to greet him. Then the massacre was revealed, for she had been sitting upon the kittens. Their poor mother pounced upon them with a yowl, but it was too late. My dear aunt was rather a heavy woman, and she had been sitting there fifteen minutes. We all stood appalled in the presence of the great mystery." Julian Hawthorne, *Hawthorne and His Circle* (New York: Harper and Brothers, 1903) pp. 17–18.

Further, despite his protests of innocence, it is likely that the novelist
was encouraged in his portrait by his family's amused but not condescending attitude toward Peabody, as witnessed in an anecdote provided by Edward Emerson. He was present one evening at the Jameses'
when William came home and described an encounter with Peabody,
whom Emerson disguised in his story as "Jane Smith." It appeared
that Jane Smith "beset" William with news of the art lectures of William Rimmer. At this, Henry, Sr. exclaimed, "The man's a fraud! It's
impossible he should be anything else if Jane Smith believes in him!
Wh-wh-why! Jane Smith—she's one of the most d-d-dissolute old creatures that walks the earth!" The James family "shouted with joy," recalled Emerson, "though knowing well the saintly, if too optimistic
character of the lady, at the Jamesian felicity of the adjective. For they
saw, in memory, the gray hair falling down under the bonnet askew,
the spectacles slipping down with resulting upturned radiant face, the
nondescript garments and general dissolving effect, symbolizing the
loose reasoning and the charity falling all abroad—yes, in a sense a dis-
solute personality."[104]

Henry James wished to highlight the gap between prewar and
postwar reform in the character of Miss Birdseye. But James was
wrong, or at least too simple. There are impressive continuities in
Elizabeth Peabody's vocational and intellectual life which link her
early and late years. Vocationally, of course, teaching provided the major continuity, as did her interest in history, her work as a mentor and
encourager of others, and her efforts as chronicler of her age and her
contemporaries. Self, society, and cosmos as living and interwoven organisms, reflecting divine origin and divine aspiration, unfolding according to universal law, constituted the most crucial belief that
spanned her many years.

There were, to be sure, differences between the young and the
older Peabody. In her late twenties, she was concerned to carve out
and defend her professional status at the same time as she allowed herself to experience deep feeling and to recognize her intuition as a
legitimate source of truth. By the late 1860s, she had achieved her
status as an intellectual woman, and was increasingly channeling her
emotional life through the sluices of middle-class reform activity.

But the continuities seem more impressive. Despite her personal
eccentricities and her associations with known radicals like Parker and

104 Mark de Wolfe Howe, *The Later Years of the Saturday Club, 1870–1920* (Boston: Houghton Mifflin, 1927), pp. 156–57.

crackpots like Jones Very, Elizabeth Peabody did not, as William Lloyd Garrison and Margaret Fuller did, see American culture as fundamentally flawed; rather, she accepted the ruling conventions, seeking to liberalize and humanize society within those conventions.

Ironically, much as Peabody fit impressively into the organic and systematic nature of reform in post–Civil War America, by the end of her life the theories of childhood education were changing again, and made her outlook appear old-fashioned. Susan Blow, her disciple and an ardent Froebelian, began to encounter individuals who ridiculed the emphasis on unfolding the divine essence and who preferred to rely on data from psychology and physiology in designing curricula. By 1905 Blow was giving courses at Columbia Teachers College in conjunction with Patty Smith Hill, a defender of the new scientific, secular approach that came to inform the Progressive education movement.[105]

Thus, the conventional division of intellectual and reform life at the time of the Civil War may not explain the richness and continuity of a person like Elizabeth Peabody. It was not until near the end of the nineteenth century that the steady assault of secular and scientific thinking and the preoccupation with the ambiguities of urban and industrial life began seriously to wash away the religious foundations of a considerable number of thoughtful Americans. In the new century, Americans began to return to private pleasures and to lose their zeal for public service. Simultaneously, modernism began to champion the artist-hero alienated from a stifling bourgeois society.

What has often prevented historians in the past from treating Elizabeth Palmer Peabody as a serious figure in social and intellectual history is that her concerns centered on children and on women, both single and married, rather than on politics or economics. Even more, she has evaded our understanding because she was not an alienated self. We find Thoreau, Emerson, and the early Brownson, certainly Melville, Poe, Dickinson, and Fuller more appealing and contemporary because they assaulted and threatened their culture; they assumed a kind of lonely Romantic splendor on the edge of society. It was not so for Peabody. She was a profound optimist. She cared about neither status nor possessions, but was passionately involved in causes, believing that change was possible, indeed inevitable. Her sister Sophia once paid her this tribute: "As I sit and look on these mountains, so grand and flowing and the illimitable aerial blue, beyond and over, I seem

[105] Snyder, pp. 70–79.

to realize with peculiar force that bountiful, fathomless heart of Elizabeth, forever disappointed, but forever believing; sorely rebuffed, yet never bitter; robbed day by day, yet giving again, from endless store; more sweet, more tender, more serene, as the hours pass over her, though they may drop gall instead of flowers upon this unguarded heart."[106] Our post-Freudian, nuclear age is deeply aware and perhaps paralyzed by an awareness of forces within and without that terrify and oppress us. We feel a kinship with Margaret Fuller when she confessed, "I have no belief in beautiful lives; we were born to be mutilated: Life is basically unjust."[107] And we may likewise feel that Peabody was naïve in her boundless enthusiasms, in her cosmic optimism. We feel a great gulf between ourselves and a person who could say:

I cannot understand unhappy people. . . . Those people who say that life is not worth living, find it so because they do not go to work to make it worth living. Why does sadness overpower them? Is it so much harder for them than for others to see sin and suffering? What right have they to add their weight to the world's burdens? Is it a sign of intellect to be cowardly? And do these people not dream that the spiritual power which makes an intellectual condition impossible is vastly superior to any power that the intellect alone can attain?[108]

Or is it possible, on the one hand, to acknowledge the insights of Augustine, Pascal, and Kierkegaard concerning the deviousness of the heart, the life of the demonic that is part of the human condition, and yet, on the other hand, acknowledge Elizabeth Peabody's resilient core of faith, which sustained her?

Although obviously Peabody was at times not at all loving, she believed in the dynamic, reconciling power of love. This belief allowed her to enter vicariously into the lives of the people whose causes she espoused. As Sarah Clarke recalled:

While most mortals instinctively take care of number one, she alone totally neglected that important numeral, and spent all her life, all her strength, her marvellous enthusiasm, her generous fiery ardor in the cause of others. She was no longer herself Elizabeth Peabody, she was a company of exiled Poles, of destitute Germans, banished Frenchmen, expatriated Italians or Hungarians,

106 Sophia Hawthorne to Mrs. Elizabeth Peabody, 29 September-10 October 1850 (MS, NN-B).
107 Fuller, quoted in Barbara Welter, "Mystical Feminist," in *Dimity Convictions* (Athens: Ohio University Press, 1976), p. 174.
108 Springfield (Mass.) *Kindergarten News* 4 (February 1894): 45.

all of whom must be helped, must be put on their feet, must be made known to those able and willing to help them.[109]

Although Peabody stressed self-sacrifice throughout her life, and Sarah Clarke illustrated the way in which she threw herself into the lives and causes of others, these impulses sprang neither from ego-diffusion nor weak will nor "self-annihilation," as she would put it, but, rather, from a self-assurance that allowed her to expand herself sympathetically into the lives of others. She had as a young woman experienced, through the intervention of Channing, a reorientation of self, a conversion she herself described as a "rebirth."

In thinking of the moral orientation toward life that her letters reveal, it might be useful to compare Peabody with that strong woman of the same period Margaret Fuller. Both were intellectuals, both reform-minded, and both caused raised eyebrows because of their unorthodox behavior and appearance. Despite the distress, amusement, or anger they caused their community, both also conformed to the ideals of nineteenth-century middle-class womanhood. Fuller agreed with the notion that women are incomplete without men, and felt herself fulfilled only when she took Ossoli as lover and husband. Peabody was particularly concerned about sexual fidelity and propriety, although she herself remained celibate and single. For Fuller, however, liberation was always self-awareness, which led to a progressively greater sense of alienation from American culture, such that personal fulfillment could be achieved only through exile. For Peabody, liberation was achieved only by an awareness of a moral, guided universe, powered by the dynamic and personal force of love and by an understanding that true maturity is achieved by seeing that same universal power operating within the self and others.

Like many other women of the nineteenth century, Elizabeth Peabody worked to confer on women the same privileges and duties that men enjoyed. For her specifically it was enhanced educational opportunities, but through her example, she doubtless encouraged others to study history, read widely, engage in reforms, and agitate for social change. Building on the efforts of the Revolutionary and immediate post-Revolutionary generations of women, which included Peabody's mother, nineteenth-century women worked steadily to enhance their role in society while simultaneously linking with each other both for-

109 Sarah Clarke, "This comes saluting the friends of Elizabeth Peabody—" (MS, MB).

mally and informally in supportive ways. But to think of women like Peabody and Fuller or Peabody and Caroline Dall as engaged in similar work of women's social and cultural advancement invites doubt as to the depth of their similarity.

Gerda Lerner has suggested that a distinction be made between efforts for women's rights, which involve access to society's privileges and opportunities equal to that of men, and efforts for women's emancipation, which imply, in her words, "a radical transformation of existing institutions, values, and theories."[110] Both efforts qualify, in Lerner's eyes, as "feminist," although the first is reformist and the second is the more challenging and advanced, the more radical, position. Catherine Beecher, champion of women's education and of domesticity, qualifies as a feminist in the first category; Elizabeth Cady Stanton is clearly an emancipationist. Assigning both the descriptive term "feminist" may stretch the word more than is warranted, but Lerner's intent is clear, and helps locate Elizabeth Peabody in the cultural geography of the nineteenth century. In her own rigorous education and in the equally rigorous classes and discussions she conducted for women, in her desire to be fully a part of the Transcendentalist movement, including running a bookstore and helping issue the *Dial,* in her tireless reforming, Peabody was a living demand for equal access to at least some of society's institutions. She was, in Lerner's terms, a champion of women's rights. Comparing her with Margaret Fuller, who had a vision of the human intellect as androgynous and who felt stifled by the narrowness and conventionality of American society, or with Caroline Dall, whose willingness to mention female menses in a public lecture violated even Peabody's sense of decorum, is instructive. In her acceptance of some of society's deepest cultural assumptions—the sanctity of the family, the nurturing role of women, the unique connection of women to children's education—Elizabeth Peabody was, despite all her fears to the contrary, a decorous and tactful nineteenth-century woman.

[110] Gerda Lerner, contribution to symposium "Politics and Culture in Women's History: A Symposium," *Feminist Studies* 6, #1 (Spring 1980): 50–51.

Profiles of the Peabody family, November 8, 1835: (*top row, left to right*) Mrs. Elizabeth Peabody, 57; Dr. Nathaniel Peabody, 61; Elizabeth, 31; Nathaniel Jr., 24; (*bottom row*) George, 22; Sophia, 26; Mary 29; and Wellington, 20.
(*Courtesy Essex Institute, Salem, Mass.*)

Portrait of Sophia Amelia Peabody, sister of
Elizabeth Peabody, probably painted by Harding
in 1830.
(From *The Peabody Sisters of Salem*)

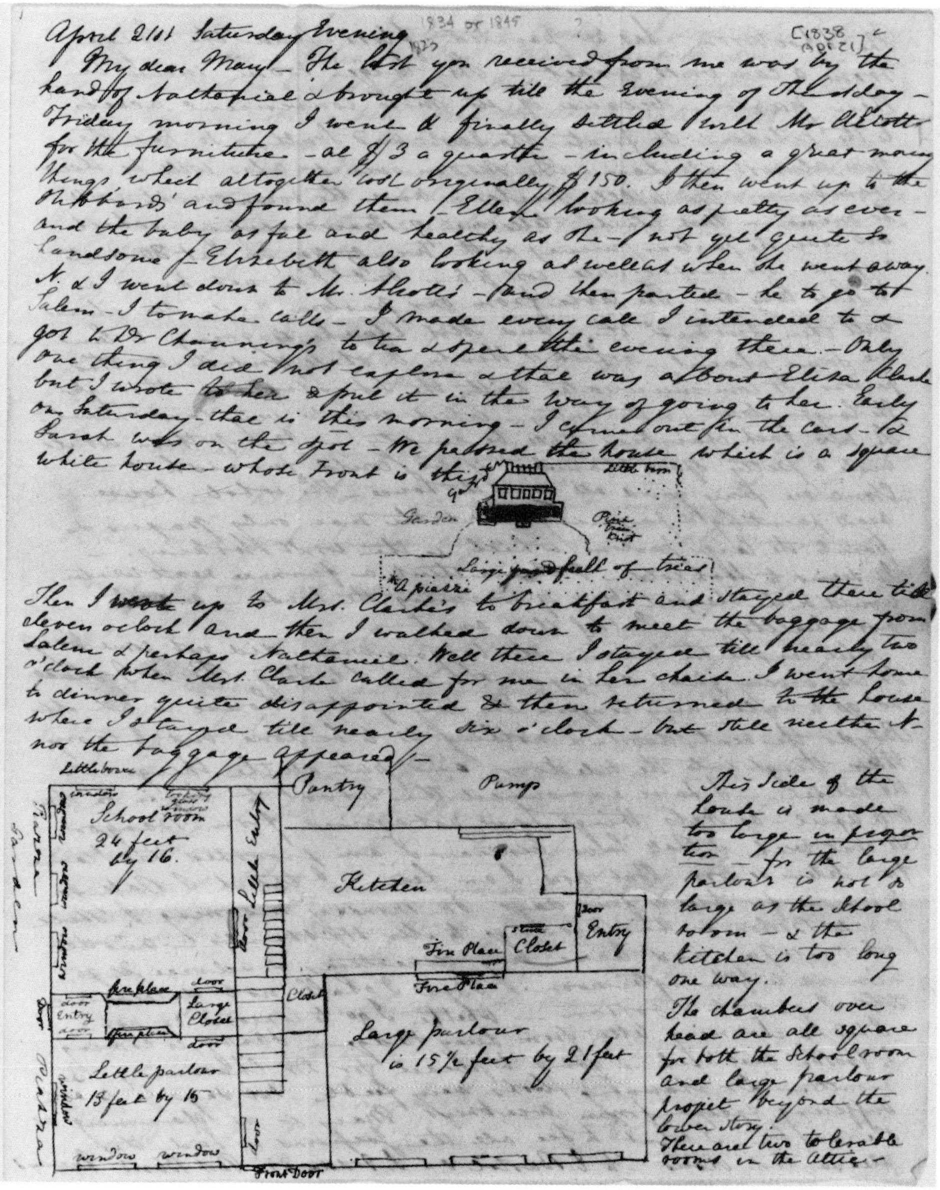

April 21st Saturday Evening

My dear Mary — The last you received from me was by the hand of Nathaniel & brought up till the evening of Thursday — Friday morning I went & finally settled with Mr Alcott for the furniture — at $73 a quarter — including a great many things which altogether cost originally $150. I then went up to the Hubbard's and found them — Ellen looking as pretty as ever — and the baby as fat and healthy as she — not yet quite so handsome — Elizabeth also looking as well as when she went away. N & I went down to Mr Alcott's — and there parted — he to go to Salem — I to make calls — I made every call I intended to & got to Dr Channing's to tea & spent the evening there — Only one thing I did not explain & that was about Eliza Clark but I wrote to her & put it in the way of going to her. Early on Saturday that is this morning — I found out from the cart-he Sarah was on the spot — We passed the house which is a square white house — whose front is this

Garden   Green house
[sketch of house]   Ellen Hn.
Large yard full of trees
& a piazza

Then I went up to Mrs. Clarke's to breakfast and stayed there till eleven o'clock and then I walked down to meet the baggage from Salem & perhaps Nathaniel. Well there I stayed till nearly two o'clock when Mrs. Clark called for me in her chaise. I went home to dinner quite disappointed & then returned to the house where I stayed till nearly six o'clock — but still neither N nor the baggage appeared —

[floor plan diagram with labels:]
Little room
School room
24 feet by 16.
Pantry   Pump
Kitchen
Fire Place   Closet   Entry
Fire Place   Large   Closet
Little parlour
13 feet by 15
Large parlour
is 15½ feet by 21 feet
Front Door

This side of the house is made too large in proportion — for the large parlour is not so large as the School room — & the kitchen is too long one way.
The chambers over head are all square for both the School room and large parlour project beyond the lower story.
There are two tolerable rooms in the attic —

Letter written by Elizabeth Palmer Peabody,
dated April 21, 1838.
(*Courtesy Massachusetts Historical Society*)

Sophia Amelia Peabody
Hawthorne, wife of Nathaniel
Hawthorne, from an etching by
S. A. Schoff.
*(Courtesy Essex Institute,
Salem, Mass.)*

Nathaniel Hawthorne
*(Sophia Smith Collection,
Smith College)*

The Wayside, Concord home of Sophia and Nathaniel
Hawthorne, who appear in the left foreground. They were
married in 1842.
(*Concord Free Public Library*)

Mary Peabody Mann, wife of Horace Mann. They were married in 1843 and lived in West Newton, Massachusetts, until Mann's appointment as president of Antioch College.
(*Courtesy Massachusetts Historical Society*)

Horace Mann, Sr.
(*Antioch College*)

Left to right: Horace Mann, Jr., George Combe Mann, and Benjamin Pickman Mann, as children.
(Courtesy Olive Kettering Library, Antioch College)

Horace Mann, Jr. *(Concord Free Public Library)*

Mary Peabody Mann
(*Courtesy Olive Kettering Library, Antioch College*)

⚹ I
1820s

Education for "Woman's Function"

ELIZABETH PALMER PEABODY's early education reflected her mother's belief that women were capable of intellectual mastery. To Mrs. Elizabeth Peabody, the mental and moral life of society depended on educated women. Her daughter Elizabeth wrote in 1882, "When I was yet quite young my mother gave me to read an article in the old *Portfolio* upon woman's function in America, in which it was shown that in this earlier period of our history, when our national resources were to be developed, and an unlimited career of activity in this was open upon men, the higher interests of society must be cared for by women; that is, literature, art, and all the virtues and graces that make society progressive spiritually, morally, and intellectually."[1]

In pursuit of such an education, Elizabeth Peabody was taught solely by her parents. Mrs. Peabody's school in Salem, Massachusetts, which she conducted from 1809 to 1818, was the principal site of Elizabeth's education. The curriculum was rigorous: "The aim was History and Literature, beginning with the English, but extending backwards, to the history and translated literature of Greece and Rome. The qualification for entrance was to *read English intelligibly;* and her youngest scholars were eight and ten years of age."[2] Pupils learned grammar, arithmetic, geography, and elementary science, and Mrs. Peabody read aloud examples of wit and style from the *Spectator,* the *Rambler,* the *Edinburgh Review,* and the *Quarterly Review.* Nathaniel Peabody, then practicing dentistry in Salem, also took responsibility for his eldest daughter's education. Elizabeth Peabody recalled that her mother "sent me an hour or two every day out of school, into my father's study to learn Latin of him."[3]

In 1820, the Peabodys moved from Salem to Lancaster, where at age sixteen Elizabeth began her own teaching career. Her sisters Mary and Sophia were "among my few scholars. They never went to any other school." Her pupils came from both the uneducated and educated families of the Lancaster area: "the daughters of the farmers and traders of Lancaster; also the minister's daughter." Her formal assignment was the teaching of history, both ancient and American, but she saw her real subject as "human life." Much as would Bronson Alcott later, Peabody suggested to her pupils that they seek to estab-

---

1 Elizabeth Palmer Peabody, "Letter from Miss. E. P. Peabody," *American Journal of Education* (Barnard) 32 (May 1882): 742.
2 Ibid., 739.
3 Ibid., 741.

lish connections between words as indications of external reality and of the inner reality they point to. "What are words?" she would ask. "They are the signs of our thoughts and feelings in all their minutest shades and variations."[4] Her instruction in 1820 thus prefigured her philosophical idealism of the 1830s and later.

Peabody did not teach, as other teachers did, by requiring memorization of rules, but by identification of the function of words in relation to other words. A skeptical father who witnessed this exercise in her school in Brookline later recalled selecting a passage for the students to analyze. "I told the class," Peabody wrote, "to tell all they could find out of the meaning of the words, each one in turn taking a sentence in order. They did so, first naming the sensible objects and telling by what senses they cognized each, whether it expressed one or more things, whether it was spoken of or spoken to or expressed a speaker." They discussed words that expressed qualities, and "whether these were appreciated by the senses or by the abstracting powers of the mind." At the end of the hour, the father was convinced. For Peabody, the lesson was clear: "to understand and use language adequately, touches into life the whole spiritual nature."[5] Peabody remembered her year in Lancaster as one of the happiest in her life and her family's life.

To her nephew Julian, she wrote, "I left Lancaster at age eighteen to keep school in Boston,—in a high heroic mood, intending to get money to educate at [Harvard] College my brother [Nathaniel]."[6] The money proved unattainable, but she did pursue self-education; she listened to Mrs. Edward Tyrell Channing read the lectures of George Ticknor on modern literature and history; she wrote long didactic letters to her sister Sophia filled with references to her own intensive reading—from Madame de Staël's *Corinne* and *Ten Years in Exile* to novels by Walter Scott and James Fenimore Cooper, and much journal literature; and she took Greek lessons from a nineteen-year-old divinity student, Waldo Emerson.

But cosmopolitan Boston was not to be her home for long. In the fall of 1823, Peabody accepted a position as tutor for the family of Benjamin Vaughan in Hallowell, Maine. Vaughan was willing to share with her the riches of his large library of ten thousand volumes.[7]

4 Pearson, "Peabody on Hawthorne," 270; Elizabeth Peabody, "Principles and Methods of Education," *American Journal of Education* (Barnard) 32 (May 1882): 722.

5 Peabody, "Principles and Methods of Education," 724–25.

6 Pearson, "Peabody on Hawthorne," 270–71.

7 Peabody, "Letter from Miss Peabody," 739.

Her mother similarly had found in the library of her grandfather Joseph Palmer an invaluable encouragement—"I remember her telling me that she never remembered the time when she did not read Shakespeare, and I have a vivid picture of her as she described herself lying on her stomach on the floor of her grandfather's study in Germantown [a neighborhood of Braintree, now Quincy], reading from the old *Folio* aloud to her grandmother when she was four years old."[8] In March 1824, Peabody moved to Oaklands, the estate of Robert Hallowell Gardiner, sixteen miles from the Vaughans, to become tutor there, and she sent for Mary to replace her at the Vaughans. "It puts me in a very panic of delight," she wrote her sister, "the *very idea* of you coming so soon."[9] A year later, Peabody decided to leave Maine, and in May 1825 she and Mary opened a private school in Brookline, a fashionable country suburb west of Boston.[10]

In the fall of 1826, Elizabeth and Mary Peabody moved from Brookline to Boston to open a school on Colonnade Row on Beacon Hill. They enrolled children of prominent Bostonians like Nathan Appleton, one of the founders of the Lowell mills. Two years later, the entire Peabody family moved into the rented house on Colonnade Row.

Seeking a prominent name to promote their school, the Peabody sisters arranged a collaboration with educator and elocutionist William Russell, but the union collapsed when Russell departed abruptly for Philadelphia in 1830, leaving the sisters with large debts. Nonetheless, it had been a successful decade for Elizabeth Peabody. A flourishing school was in operation, her acquaintance with William Ellery Channing, the Unitarian clergyman and author, had evolved into a close mentor-student relationship, and she had gained a growing feeling of participation in a vibrant intellectual milieu.

Elizabeth Peabody's correspondence during the 1820s consists primarily of letters she wrote to members of her family—to her mother describing her social contacts, to her sisters giving advice on reading and study, to her brothers describing scientific lectures she had heard and giving moral advice. To Maria Chase, her Quaker Salem friend, Peabody wrote cheerful, teasing letters full of talk about books and ideas. To Sarah Russell Sullivan, a friend from Brookline, she wrote many letters during the 1820s, a number of them summaries of Chan-

8 Pearson, "Peabody on Hawthorne," 271.
9 Elizabeth Peabody to Mary Peabody, 18 March 1824, MS, MNS.
10 Pearson, "Peabody on Hawthorne," 271.

ning's sermons, others responding to Mrs. Sullivan's concern that Peabody was indiscreet and impulsive.

William Ellery Channing's almost magnetic appeal is apparent in this powerfully descriptive letter.

❧ To Maria Chase   *(excerpt)*

April 1820

Another celebrated person whom I have seen is the Rev. Dr. Channing[1] concerning whom we had some conversation almost the last time we met. I have been to hear this celebrated and justly admired preacher three times since I was in Boston.—I have heard it said that strangers were generally not prepossessed in favour of him from his manner—especially when they came with their expectations very highly raised as is generally the case. It is true there *is* nothing remarkably graceful in his manner—it is possible if used by another person they might appear awkward—neither when he begins are you struck by his manner—it is perhaps cold—certainly it is not striking or remarkably pleasant particularly in prayer during the first five minutes. His person too I find is generally considered unprepossessing. He is very small in his stature—rather stooping from extreme ill health—very pallid—dark complexion and black hair—perhaps his eyes are rather sunken and he looks as if just arisen from the bed of death—but his eyes are black and *perfectly beautiful* and just before

[1] William Ellery Channing graduated from Harvard College in 1798 and served as tutor to a Virginia family for a year and a half. Exhausted by a self-imposed regimen of study, Channing returned to his family's home in Newport, Rhode Island, in 1802, and was soon appointed to a minor teaching post at Harvard. The following year he was ordained to the ministry and installed as pastor to the Federal Street Church in Boston, which he served until his death in 1842. In 1814, he married his cousin Ruth Gibbs.

Despite his weak health and reclusive nature, Channing found himself the spiritual head of the liberal revolt against religious orthodoxy in the early nineteenth century. He believed that he and his fellow Unitarians (as they reluctantly agreed to be called, although not relishing the association with the more radical English Unitarians) had full claim to the name Christian and that the distinctive Calvinist doctrines had no bases in scripture. Channing particularly opposed the Calvinist denigration of the nature of humanity. His personal and philosophical traits led him to advocate reforms which involved individual betterment, such as temperance, education, and the peace movement.

he shuts them when he prays he looks up with the divinest expression I ever saw in my life—and again when he says "Amen." You will naturally suppose after all this—that there is something beside that irresistible personal attraction that has given Mr. Channing that irresistible and almost unrivaled power over the minds of almost every audience that he has addressed—that has long given him undisputed preeminence among his brethren *in eloquence.* It *is* something else—for his voice which I remarked to you as remarkably sweet has no great compass naturally and what little it originally had is weakened and narrow'd by consumptive complaints until it has no great power of expressing anything but pathos and persuasion for which it is perfectly adapted. The power of his eloquence consists in the greatest degree—in the power of the sentiments he expresses—he never preaches a sermon which can be called ordinary;—every word that drops from his lips is replete with wisdom and he is always attended to—and his words always come *recommended*—since they come from lips that never utter words merely for effect or for the sake of appearing brilliant or eloquent—or for the sake of overpowering the feelings of his audience and being called irresistable:—they come recommended because his life in every delicate shade in which it is known is perfectly consistent—because slander and envy and jealousy and hatred cannot *imagine* a spot upon his character—measuring it by a very high standard too. Because—when he gets interested his voice is attuned by his feelings to that peculiar tone which has a corresponding chord in every human breast—because his motions are dictated by his heart and nature speaks in every one of them—because there is something so transcendently beautiful in the expression of his fine eyes which seem instinctively to look upon heaven as their native home—because he is *sincere* and "God has set a mark upon sincerity and ordained that the language of the heart should never fall chill and cold upon the ear."—In his prayers too—after the first five minutes you forget that first impression of coldness in his manner for his words begin to flow with an ease peculiar to himself and as his own feelings become warmed by his subject the feelings of his audience are excited—I can only compare it to a strain of soft but irresistibly persuasive music which even before you are aware it affects you has carried captive all your feelings—and what more particularly marks his excellence is this—that you do not think of him who is speaking but your whole soul is absorbed in what is said. What is the grand cause of Mr. Channing's power in the devotional part of his exercises is not his addressing his *prayers to the audience* but to Heaven and indeed that habit he has of looking up to Heaven so continually is the charm of his manner. You feel that he is indeed a man "whose thoughts are not of this world"—and you almost fancy that full dark eye can extend its powerful glance beyond the ordinary reach of human ken. You will naturally suppose that I want to see this wonderful man in every situation possible—consequently you will not be surprised to hear that I followed him into the Sunday school. This school is divided into classes which are attended to by several gentlemen and ladies of the society. Mr. Chandler formerly of Salem and the celebrated Prof. Ticknor have each a class and Mr. Channing merely goes in after the recitations and makes some remarks to the children and sometimes converses with them. There was no room for the latter the day I attended, but he was peculiarly happy I thought in his manner of doing the former. Mr. Chandler said to me after meeting that he had never seen Dr. Channing appear more *truly great* than sometimes at these meetings among these children. Another exercise of his is meeting during the winter months once a fortnight the ladies of his congregation to expound scripture, the New Testament particularly—chapter by chapter—the method of which I will tell you when I see you. These meetings are very interesting and Miss Townsend says Dr. Channing never appears better out of the pulpit than when attending them. I attended once and was very much delighted. There is a sweet expression in Mr. Channing's mouth when he speaks—but I have heard people say they could not feel at ease when conversing with him. Not because he is stern—or austere—or unconversible—or taciturn but they say there is an *indescribable something* about him—I do not believe I should feel so—but you know I have a vast deal of *impudence* to bear me out. I expect he will call here this week, however, and then I can better tell.

MS, MNS

On her spring 1821 visit to Boston and Cambridge, Elizabeth Peabody is impressed by the sophistication and high seriousness of the Unitarian elite.

✄ To Maria Chase   *(excerpt)*

[May 1821]
[A detailed description of architecture and society in Boston, and a discussion of the faculty of Harvard and their wives, including the following.]

The superior intelligence and the uncommon variety and weight of talent in the Professors of Cambridge and their wives is not the most striking characteristics of the society. The President and Drs. Ware and Norton and Frisbie[1] being minds of a superior order whose fine powers are principally bent to the extension and diffusion of liberal and enlighten'd principles of religion and the most refined morality—being themselves more remarkable for the purity of their manners and conversation than even for talents—give a tone of seriousness and truth to the society which without taking in the least from its vivacity or elegance precludes every thing like *levity*. You will not find any ladies there whose business is dress and visiting—all have some serious pursuit all engaged in some pursuit or other which is engrossing—and although they are not ceremonious they are always visiting one another—and their husbands brothers and friends all being engaged in the same pursuits there is no restraint about talking and improving by their conversation. There is indeed a constant stimulus to improvement. You seem to be moving all the time for every thing about you is in a state of progressive improvement and if you stand still—bye and bye they will forget you were ever "one of

[1] Levi Frisbie, professor of Latin and Alford Professor of Natural Religion, Moral Philosophy, and Civil Polity at Harvard College, was known for his conservative views of ethics and literature; John Thornton Kirkland, president of Harvard from 1810 to 1828, transformed the college into a university, increased the standards of teaching, and improved the quality of faculty; Henry Ware who became Hollis Professor of Divinity in 1805, signaling the ascendency of liberal views of Congregationalism at Harvard, was respected for his modesty, serenity, and fairness; Andrews Norton, Dexter Professor of Sacred Literature at Harvard Divinity School, whose most important work was *Evidences of the Genuineness of the Gospels* (Boston: J. B. Russell, 1837–44), was an early critical student of the Bible and was actively involved in the theological controversies of the time, espousing the position of conservative Unitarianism.

them." There is no pedantry in their conversation they never think of showing off—and why? because every body is as wise as they think they are and every body knows something and there is a constant exertion to keep upon level and you are sure that even if you do know to-day more than some others they may sit up all night and put you down tomorrow. But there is nothing of this—they all study and improve not for the purpose of display—or to astonish their neighbors but they pursue learning as a Christian Disciple writer said of Col. Pickman "for the purity it gives to manners for the pleasure it bestows on its possessors and their friends for the aid it affords to religion and the light it adds to moral philosophy"—with them knowledge is not an abstract phantom but a real person who is the arbiter of their destiny—for what avails any thing we possess if it is merely to be the inmate of an evening? The Cambridge people know that life is not given them to trifle away and while they would adorn and beautify it with every thing beautiful in art or literature—they recollect that all these things are subservient to a higher aim. In all the brilliancy of the society of Cambridge this feeling is never lost that every thing is given for the single purpose of making men *good* as well as *happy*—and this keeps up that zest for improvement which would unavoidably sometimes go down if it had not such an object in view. The person who is to take this letter has been standing by all the time I have written this last page and I am in a desperate hurry and got *so much to say now* I think I shall write again this week. Yrs ever Elizabeth

MS, MNS

Peabody heard William Ellery Channing deliver a farewell sermon to his Federal Street congregation in Boston before leaving for a European tour.

✎ To Mrs. Elizabeth Peabody

My dear Mother   Boston, May [26] 1822
    I have just returned from hearing Dr. Channing's farewell sermon, and I do not know when I shall feel a greater impulse to write.[1]

1 This sermon was delivered on May 26, 1822. The Channings returned from England and Europe in August 1823.

Yet I do not mean to describe or to narrate, for it is out of my power. I wish you, who can so deeply feel, could have seen and heard him; for if there is anything sublime on earth, it is the sight of a good and pious man, at a moment of deepest agitation, resting calmly upon the goodness of God, while breaking the tenderest ties of nature and social life. If anyone then present should hereafter trifle with religion he must first erase from remembrance, the steadfast eye of that sainted form and the deep tones of feeling in which he told them, that he had spent strength and perhaps life itself in search of truth; but that he was satisfied and blessed God for the exchange. If any there present should think themselves too greatly afflicted, I trust they will remember the confiding air, the pious resignation, the joy, yet the calmness and depth of feeling with which he committed himself and his people to God, without the shadow of a doubt. He made no exclamations; he did not flourish, he had no long sentences; nor a single trick to make people cry. But he poured out his spirit as he expressed it, with the freedom of a long known friend. He spoke of himself and of his reasons for leaving; of the duties he had done and of those he had left undone; of the opinions he had propagated, and of his continued belief in them. He thanked the people for their kindness, for their attention to his preaching, for their outward morality of conduct; but he told them they had not answered his hopes; they did not let religion have a sufficiently powerful sway over their hearts; for he is too good a man to flatter, and when warmed most by tender feelings does not desert his duty, which is to make men better. His last passage was all love and tenderness; and in it he surveyed the probable changes of the society before his return, if indeed he should live to return. If that were the last time he spoke he wished them to remember his last words. He then summed all most valuable in one short passage, which he spoke with a voice low, tender, deep and sweetly toned, and his eyes were fixed on heaven every moment, as if to call a spirit down to sanctify his words, and as if he called God to witness the intenseness of his sincerity. I do not believe there was a heart untouched, an eye that did not moisten at that moment. But a spirit from on high seemed to sustain him and I felt no fear of his sinking under the trial. He bade his people farewell, perhaps forever, imploring their prayers, not as a matter of form he said, but from a *conviction* of the efficacy of prayer. He stated what he wished them to pray for in his behalf, and blessed God that he might unite his spirit with theirs, although wandering in distant lands or tossing on the stormy ocean. I intend to remember the calm beauty of holiness that dwelt on his countenance as he said things, which convulsed every one else with sorrow, and as long as I remember it I fear not that my spirit will sink how ever great may be my trials.

I walked in from Cambridge this morning, or was lead [led] in, for I was blinded. My eyes have not yet recovered but are getting well. I spent the past week at Mr. Dana's and had a doctor twice a day, was blinded and placed in a rocking chair and all the family were so kind and entertained me so continually, either with company, conversation or reading that I felt perfectly happy.[2] I passed one evening at Professor Farer's with not a large party.[3] I enjoyed myself entirely. Mrs. F. is out of health, but looked tranquil. She is gentle and unassuming. I had no opportunity of conversing with Olivia, but May charmed me. She is very handsome, very animated, very natural, very frank, very witty and has a perpetual flow of spirits. Mr. Emerson, who formerly kept the Academy in Le. [Lancaster] was there. He looked like a shepard and I should be delighted to see him with a crook.[4] I danced with him on the carpet to Mary Buckminster's playing. Last Sunday morning Miss E. Dana, Sophia Dana, Mr. Buckminster and I walked in to hear Dr. C.[5] The morning was fine and Mr. Allston, the painter, says the esplanade is not so fine as the prospect of Boston over the water from Cambridge.[6] The water was smooth as glass and the whole city was reflected in softened beauty on the smooth margin, while the richly cultivated line of hills that swept the opposite side of the horizon formed a most delightful contrast. After tea we walked back to C., having exchanged Mr. B. for Professor Channing, who carried us in at the rate of four miles an hour.[7] When on the bridge we witnessed a glorious sunset. We there met Mr. Allston who is engaged to Miss E. Dana. Give my love to Mary. I hope Sophia has

2 Elizabeth Peabody's sight had rapidly deteriorated in these years, and by 1825 she was wearing glasses. Richard Henry Dana was a poet, essayist, and editor of *The Idle Man* (1821–22).

3 John Farrar (not Farer) was a mathematician, physicist, astronomer and Hollis Professor of Mathematics and Natural Philosophy at Harvard. His wife, Eliza Ware Rotch Farrar, author of advice books for young women, was known for her hospitality. Later Peabody would encounter her sarcasm and hostility.

4 George B. Emerson was a leading educator of the early national period, presiding over academies in Boston and Lancaster, Massachusetts, and later was a prominent leader in freedmen's education.

5 Elizabeth and Sophia Dana were Richard Dana's daughters.

6 Washington Allston, writer and artist, was a landscape and genre painter whose technique and choice of subjects greatly impressed the Transcendentalist circle.

7 Edward Tyrell Channing, Boylston Professor of Rhetoric and Oratory at Harvard, was an important influence on style and expression in his day.

begun to study—let me know how all the boys lessons go on. I shall not write any more till I commence my school.

ELIZABETH

TS copy, OYesA

One of a series of didactic letters to her sister Sophia, a clear statement of Elizabeth Peabody's commitment to Unitarian theology and Common Sense philosophy, and an indication of her own reading.

✹ To Sophia Peabody

Boston March 31st 1823

Theology, my dear Sophia, is a science of all others the most interesting, the most absorbing, and the most important. I have recommended to you the cultivation of your intellect, your taste, and your heart, by literature & science, by the fine arts, and by those habits of pious meditation, charitable judgement, benevolent feeling and severe self examination which taken together constitute religion. You cannot but feel that were there but one world, all I have said would apply and that to be happy in it, you could steer no course so likely to ensure your wished for issue, as the one you have perceived me to point out. But there is more than one world and you must feel anxious above all other things to make yourself acquainted with that science which points out the evidences of a future state. You may be thrown among unbelievers, and you should be able to attack their strong holds, and be prepared to meet them however insidiously they may attack you. Children may come to you for reasons, when they are about being confounded with the sophistry of vice, and you should, by previous meditation upon the subject, be prepared to give them clear and ready answers. There is much false religion and many speculative subtlities, & nice points which have taken place of what is more important. Gloomy minds have cast dark hues over the Christian system, speculative minds have discovered what was never there,—light minds have given it an air of fanciful speculation to it;—small minds have narrow'd it—and it is necessary you should be able to look at religion in all these ways that afterward you may be the more likely to see it as it is.

You now have no system;—but have undoubtedly a strong bias toward Unitarianism. I hope I shall be impartial enough to advise you to counteract even this *bias,* which of all others, (it would be affectation to deny it) I think the most happy. The course I think the best to pursue I shall now point out. When the Christian revelation was first imparted to men the world was under the influence of a system of philosophy, a compound of all the ancient systems by Animonius Sacca—and the finest & most speculative minds were imbued with it.[1] It continued in vogue even long after many, if not most of these men were converted to the Christian religion. It is barely probable, to say the least, that if they continued philosophers after professing being Christians, they should endeavour to make their philosophical opinions & Christian doctrines agree. From this source Unitarians think all the corruptions of the Christian doctrines spring.—Your first course after reading Paley: Natural Theology & Evidences of Christianity then should be to make yourself acquainted with this system of philosophy.[2]—For this purpose it would be well to read Enfield's History of Philosophy[3]—and you will then perceive in what state the world was as to speculative opinions when Christ first came upon Earth. While the recollection of this is fresh in your memory I should wish you to read Dr. Priestley's History of the Corruptions of Christianity with great attention[4]—and with *critical scepticism*—and then you can form a fair judgement whether it is not possible that what he considers as corruptions *may* not have been derived possibly—from those systems. For it is an important point, to account for such strange opinions (as *I* & you must consider many of them) ever getting abroad—and if you can trace them up to these

[1] "There can of course be no question of Plotinus's having influenced Origen who was his elder by twenty years. The resemblances between them ought perhaps to be explained by positing a common influence from the teachings of Ammonius Saccas, who was the master of both, but it must be admitted that in the last analysis we know next to nothing about Ammonius's thought" (Jean Danielou, *Gospel Message and Hellenistic Culture,* vol. 1 of *A History of Early Christian Doctrine* [Philadelphia: Westminster Press, 1973], 424).

[2] William Paley, often-quoted advocate of natural theology, was the author of *Natural Theology* (1802) and *Evidences of Christianity* (1794).

[3] William Enfield, English Presbyterian clergyman, was the author of *History of Philosophy* (1791).

[4] Author of hundreds of works in science, philosophy, political science, and theology, including *History of the Corruptions of Christianity* (1782), Joseph Priestley had several vocations. He was an English Unitarian clergyman, theologian, scientist, and radical political theorist. During the period of suppression of political dissent in England following the French Revolution, Priestley came under increasing attack. In 1794 he emigrated with his family to the United States.

fanciful systems a great deal is attained—But having done this do not consider your work finished. The new-Testament must after all be your test. Take each one of these doctrines, by Unitarians, called corruptions, & read the Testament thro' in relation to each of these doctrines *separately*—and write down all you are in favor of it—Having done so you must endeavour to explain the apparent contridictions by your own reflections upon the gradual change in the meanings of terms, &c & if it is impossible to do so to your own satisfaction— you must write them down and ask an explanation of your doubts of some person your judgement approves as wise and candid and learned. If the new Testament authorizes our belief of them you must reconcile the apparent inconsistency of their being known before—in the best manner you are able—and believe without hesitancy what ever you think the N. Testament authorizes. If after making this trial, which will necessarily require much time & individual attention—your result is—that these doctrines are corruptions—it will be of service & a pleasure to you to read Dr. Priestley's Institutes of Natural & Revealed Religion.[5] Perhaps you may not think exactly as he does upon all the subjects—but you undoubtedly will on many. And thus having possess'd yourselves of the reasons which Unitarians think they have for believing as they do, I would introduce you into the region of Controversy. The word is a bug bear to many—but you will not be frightened by words. Controversy is now carried on in a more candid and liberal spirit than formerly—and a controversial pamphlet is generally written with more scrupulous attention in the writers not to commit themselves by making assertions which they cannot support, than any other theological papers are. Mr. Stewarts second Edition of letters to Dr. Channing & Mr. Norton's review of it is the first I would recommend because it takes up the important doctrines of the Unity or Trinity of God[6]—and after that the whole controversy between Dr. Wood and Dr. Ware.—[7]

5 Joseph Priestley, *Institutes of Natural and Revealed Religion* (1774).

6 Moses Stuart (attributed author), *Letter to Rev. William E. Channing: In Favor of the Doctrine of the Trinity* (Boston: J. Loring, 1819).

7 In response to William Ellery Channing's "Unitarian Christianity" (1819), his Baltimore ordination sermon for Jared Sparks in which Channing developed the concepts of a benevolent God, the essential goodness of humanity, and the harmony of all creation, Leonard Woods, professor of divinity at Andover Seminary, argued (in *Letters to Unitarians Occasioned by the Sermon of the Reverend William E. Channing at the Ordination of the Reverend J. Sparks* [Andover: Flagg and Gould, 1820]), that Calvinists as well as Unitarians see God as Father, but where Unitarians insist only on God's mercy, Calvinists also assert his justice, especially with regard to human sinfulness. Woods argued as well that children are prone to evil and require

After reading the above your opinions will be pretty much formed one way or the other I would then advise you to read Middleton's Letter from Rome[8] which will show you how quickly the common people corrupted Christianity by the Pagan rites—while the more speculative part of the community were corrupting its doctrines with the Philosophical fancies of the time. At the close I wish you to read Mr. Spark's letters to Episcopalians[9]—and if it is answered—as undoubtedly it will be—if there is any Episcopalian in the country who thinks himself equal to it—read the answer too—The course then I have pointed out is—

1. Enfields History of Philosophy
2. Priestley's History of Philosophy
3. Middleton's Letter from Rome
5. Priestley's Institutes of Reveal'd Religion
6. Stewart & Norton's Controversy
7. Wood & Ware's Controversy
x4. Sparks' letters to Episcopalians—

---

instruction and restraint. In *Letters Addressed to Trinitarians and Calvinists Occasioned by Dr. Woods' Letters to Unitarians* (Cambridge: Hilliard and Metcalf, 1820), Henry Ware, Hollis Professor of Divinity at Harvard Divinity School, responded that humanity comes into the world "innocent and pure" (p. 20) until through exercise of choice, we form our own characters. In his second contribution, *A Reply to Dr. Ware's Letters to Trinitarians and Calvinists* (Andover: Flagg and Gould, 1821), Woods argued that we must go beyond the attractive features of children and inquire of their moral characteristics. We will then conclude that children manifest the same fallen moral sense as do adults. In *Answer to Dr. Woods' Reply in a Second Series of Letters Addressed to Trinitarians and Calvinists* (Cambrige: Hilliard and Metcalf, 1822), Ware reasserted that children have a mixed and innocent nature and are not inclined to evil from birth. Woods's final response (*Remarks on Dr. Ware's Answer* [Andover: Mark Newman, 1822]) opened with an attack on Ware's use of the term "innocent," pointing out that Ware cannot describe children's moral nature both as "mixed" and as "innocent," that is, free from moral taint. In contrast, Woods reiterated his allegiance to the doctrine of total depravity. In his final contribution to the debate, Ware restated his belief that humans are born free of all moral corruption and of any sin imputed to us from another (*A Postscript to the Second Series of Letters Addressed to Trinitarians and Calvinists in Reply to the Remarks of Dr. Woods on Those Letters* [Cambridge: Hilliard and Metcalf, 1823]).

8 Conyers Middleton, English clergyman and author of *Letter from Rome Showing Exact Conformity between Popery and Paganism* (1729).

9 Jared Sparks, *Letters on the Ministry, Rituals, and Doctrines of the Protestant Episcopal Church* (1819).

There are many—very many more books which I have perused in relation to this controversy that I know would be instructive but I must
limit my advice to a few. A long string of books would frighten you
from beginning this course— After having read the above—which
gives a general idea of the state of the Question with great attention—
I doubt not you will have excited an enthusiasm for the study which
will not easily be satisfied—and books enough will come in your way—

After the remarks I have made in my former letters respecting
the temper of mind which should be habitual to you—and the feelings of piety you should cherish—I need not warn you from becoming so speculative as to become *cold*. There will I think be no danger
of it. I could make one more restriction upon you. Do not, at least,
until you have read & reflected a great deal—be prone to discuss this
subject in conversation. You can think more impartially & more candidly alone—when you cannot feel the wish to shine in argument,
which may involuntarily creep in, if you are talking, & make you use
sophistry. Hear all you can—& ponder it well—but I would not, were
I you, talk of it much.

Theology, as you must perceive, involves the science of human
nature deeply—and to be able, when you differ from the wise the
learned & the good, to regard them with respect & love—and believe
them as pious as those who think as you do—may seem a difficult task.
But observation & reflection will show you that this can be done. You
should not; however rely upon your own observations and reflections
unassisted by method. The science of the human mind will undoubtedly attract your attention—and I cannot refrain from directing
you a little in this.—Read Tucker's Light of Nature[10]—Brown's Philosophy—and you will be possessed of the opinions of great men—and
in the last of a man who seems to be equally a favourite with the
Orthodox & the Liberal & those philosophy many bring together the
jarring sects—at last.

I will not tell you after all this—to think for yourself. I think
your mind is too independant & bold *not* to think for itself—but you
must recollect it is much more uninformed—& inferior to those, many
of whom you will differ from but comfort yourself in this with the
reflection that while you think independantly and perhaps in some
respect *peculiarly,* you are sincere & GOD does not require *correctness*

10 Abraham Tucker, *Light of Nature Pursued* (1765).

of opinion but a disposition to obtain it—not success in your enquiry—but effort & industry.

You will see from the penmanship of this—how hurriedly I have
written it.—I might perhaps at another time write better & give you
more cogent reasons—but today I determined to delay it no longer.

It is not necessary you should begin this enquiry now—Wait till
you have time and feel like it—for it should absorb your whole soul
as it did *mine* when I pursued it—Goodbye—and may GOD grant that
your results whatever they be may give you as bright & cheering a view
of GOD's government as my results have given me—And then you can
endure life however calamitous & hail the approach of Death—however sudden & seemingly unopportunely it may present itself.

—————ELIZABETH

MS, MN-B

---

*Tutoring the family and neighbors of Benjamin Vaughan, Peabody
writes a cheerful but homesick letter.*

✸ To Mrs. Elizabeth Peabody

Hallowell [Maine]

[September 1823]

I expected to hear from you before this. Why do you not write?
I continue contented, am treated with every attention and kindness.
The society here is fine. Mr. Merrick is a very intelligent agreeable
man, his wife a first rate woman.[1] His daughters are highly cultivated
in mind and their manners are perfect. Mr. C. Vaughn reminds me
perpetually of Dr. Thayer as to his character and his treatment of me.
Mrs. C. Vaughn I should have known anywhere for a Boston woman.
Her manners are retiring but she improved upon acquaintance very
much. Her friends think her faultless, and indeed she appears so;
there is not one disproportionate feeling in her mind. She always does
right, is always quiet, and must be sought to be appreciated.[2] Harriet

---

[1] John Merrick was a prominent citizen in the Hallowell area, known for his
education, practical judgment, good sense, and civic responsibility. He and his wife
Rebecca Vaughan Merrick had six children.

[2] Charles Vaughan, not Vaughn, was a merchant prominent in developing the
Kennebec Purchase. After bankruptcy, he settled in 1798 at Hallowell and devoted

is very pleasant. Charles Upham said of her, "she is the flower of the Eastern state[s]."³ This family are christians, every feeling is subject to christian principles, every word and apparently every thought is regulated by christian rules. They love one another entirely. Mr. C. V. says "every good thing that belongs to our children is from Mrs. Vaughn." He is a charming old man, and has all the fresh feelings of youth about him. He cannot speak of his mother *now* without emotion, and sometimes quotes her authority though she has been dead thirty years. Mr. B. V. is all the scholar and not a little of the enthusiast but he is very aged and infirm.⁴ Mrs. B. V. is as full of life and spirit as if only 24 years of age. There are many others here very pleasant. At Mr. Gardiner's there is always company.⁵ I have spent a day and two nights there and was much pleased. Mr. G. looks and speaks like George Emerson. He is highly respected and admired.

I have 22 scholars, three others are engaged. They seem to think me pledged to receive but 25. If I can obtain a dozen more I will send for Sophia, therefore I wish her to study French diligently. Do you not think a master could be procured for her, to whom she could recite Latin and under whom she could write her exercises? I will be responsible for the expense. If Sophia can begin the second part of the Latin tutor and then write through a book [of] Elegantic Latin, recommended to me by George E. and keep her corrected exercises they will be very serviceable to her here. I shall not want her till December. I want her to keep all her French exercises.

ELIZABETH

TS copy, OYesA

---

himself to improving agriculture. He married Frances Western Apthorp in 1790. Nathaniel Thayer was Lancaster's Unitarian clergyman.

3 Harriet was Charles Vaughan's daughter. Charles Upham, a clergyman at Salem's Unitarian First Church, was noted as a learned champion of Unitarianism.

4 Benjamin Vaughan, English economist, agriculturalist, and defender of the American Revolution, emigrated to the United States in 1796. He became a member of many scientific and literary societies and maintained an extensive correspondence. He married Sarah Manning in 1781.

5 Robert Hallowell Gardiner, greatly interested in innovative agriculture, founded the Gardiner Lyceum in 1821 for technical training and was a leader in the local Episcopal church, called "Old South" church.

Peabody exchanges boasts of intellectual attainment with Maria Chase and tries to maintain a properly Unitarian perspective on so scandalous a novel as Samuel Richardson's Clarissa.

✣ To Maria Chase

My dear Maria—   Jan 23rd [1824]
    I do not wait for a bright moment, but am determined to immediately answer your letter. I am quite *'numplish'd'*[1] at your great doings in science.—We have nothing to compare it with here:—Prof. Cleveland has not come as was proposed.[2] I should think you would enjoy the Chemical Lectures particularly—I know little of the science—but enough to have the impression that it is the most interesting of the physical sciences.
    My french will lag till Mary's arrival. There is no kind of an instructor here.—I have begun German—and have the assistance and counsel of one of the most charming old bachelors and elegant scholars in N. England—yclept Dr. Tappan—of Augusta.[3]— If I make any marvellous attainments I will report progress to you.— I am studying Livy in Latin—and Homer in Greek—besides the Greek Testament which is the only scripture I read at present.—
    I think the effect of those scenes of vice in Clarissa so questionable[4] that I should hardly dare to recommend the book generally— but I disagree with Lydia in her judgement. I think no mind capable of appreciating Clarissa's character could receive injury from Lovelace, and no one capable of appreciating her character could read the book without benefit. There is more female rakishness in society than

    1 "Numplish'd" is underlined twice in the text.
    2 Parker Cleaveland, not Cleveland, was Professor of Mathematics and Natural Philosophy at Bowdoin College and an important early geologist and chemist. He was invited to lecture many places, and did lecture at Hallowell, Portland, and Portsmouth, Maine, but refused to leave Bowdoin after 1820.
    3 Benjamin Tappan, a graduate of Harvard College and Divinity School and tutor at Bowdoin College, was invited on June 3, 1811 to become the pastor of Augusta's South Parish Church. Tappan was a strict Calvinist. In 1825, James Walker, a Unitarian clergyman and later president of Harvard College, was invited to preach in Augusta by several liberal members of South Parish. Tappan's refusal to allow Walker to preach in the parish church caused a split in the church and the founding of East Parish, later called All Souls Church (Unitarian). I am grateful to Shirley Thayer, Librarian for Maine Materials, Maine State Library, for information on Cleaveland and Thayer.
    4 Samuel Richardson, *Clarissa Harlowe* (1751).

persons, educated as we have been, are aware of, until having been for some time conversant with the world.—I do not mean *in conduct* so much as in sentiment.—If it were not for the character of Clarissa— it is true that the vividness and truth of Lovelace's character would be a presumptive evidence against the virtue of the mind that conceived it. But no one who was not thoroughly good could picture a character so beautifully consistent as Richardson's Clarissa.—Lovelace *may* have been drawn from real life.—I think with you respecting that furious Anna Howe.[5]

I read nothing but the divine Brown—Oh Maria—what a treasure is that book! I think I take more pleasure in the exercise of my most common faculties—now that I have better defined the proper objects of investigation and inquiry—and Brown certainly shows us plainly enough what we ought not to speculate upon—or what it is useless to attempt.[6]

I *pity* you for the loss of citizens—the glory of Salem is departing most truly. As to Mary—she *must come in* the spring and I do not think I shall go west—*at least* till Commencement.

I do not know as I should call that thing about Caroline which you refer to—*naivete*.—I have seen it, however, in the American character, altho' I cannot, at this moment, recall an instance we mutually know. If I can get Griscomb's Europe I will read it[7]—by the way— that reminds me—did you ever read The political state of Europe at present—by a citizen of the United States—(Alexander Everett)?—If you have not you will find it a very delightful work—and it is not long.[8]—

I have nothing interesting to tell you. In my last letter to you I described the people.—I have left the reading Society, however, and all company whatever and am very studious.—The description of a month ago is the description of today—write very soon to your E.P.P.

MS, MNS

5 "That furious Anna Howe" is a character in *Clarissa Harlowe*.
6 Thomas Brown was a Scottish Commonsense philosopher, whose *Philosophy of the Human Mind* was popular at Harvard and among Unitarians in the early 1820s. Like other works of Commonsense philosophy, Brown's book provided a systematic classification of the various powers of the mind. Such an outlook, Daniel Howe notes, encouraged Unitarians in a fundamental mind-body dualism (Howe, *The Unitarian Conscience*, 42).
7 John Griscom, not Griscomb, *A Year in Europe* (1823).
8 Alexander Everett, *Europe* (1822).

Peabody's Boston Unitarianism encouraged her to observe the limits of orthodox Christian behavior and observance, as is clear from this rather astonishing letter to her mother, a reminder of the mother's duties to her sons.

✹ To Mrs. Elizabeth Peabody

February 2, 1825

I was much obliged to you, dear Mother, for your good letters, giving an account of Mr. Shepherd's lecture.[1] I wish I had his simple apparatus, perhaps Pa's ingenuity might contrive it for me. Miss Edgeworth's book on education is not to be considered as a system, but there is a vast deal of truth in it. Mr. Edgeworth's chapters betray his infidelity and you will not approve any more than I do his idea of not making any difference between the Sabbath and other days.[2] I wish my brothers to be impressed strongly with veneration for the Sabbath. I always thought it the most important of Christian ordinances. Religion is infinitely the most important thing to be impressed on the boys. It was ever to me a thought before which every other thought shrunk into insignificance. Friendship, literature and elegant society have bestowed and are bestowing upon me much, but without religion they would not weigh a feather against the evils of life even such as I have known and felt. Your account of Mr. Brazer's sermons delighted me.[3] Last Saturday night, I received all your letters by Mr. V just as I was setting off for Gardiners. I was not well, but as the weather was fine, and Mr. G. had a double sleigh I thought I should feel better for the visit. When we arrived we found them just feasting upon a packet from Boston. Emma and I went upstairs where she always has a fire and she read me some of her sister Ann's letters and a tragedy of Ravenswood by a blue stocking of Gardiners.[4] It was tolerable but not to be compared with the novel. Then we had some delightful though serious conversation which held us through half

---

[1] Charles Upham Shepard, not Shepherd, was graduated from Amherst in 1824, moved to Cambridge, and later became a prominent mineralogist.
[2] Maria and Richard Edgeworth, *Practical Education* (1798).
[3] John Brazer became pastor of the Unitarian North Church in Salem in 1820. Peabody would later encounter him in 1838 in the controversy over the poet Jones Very.
[4] Unidentified.

the night. The next morning we found a raging storm, and I concluded not to venture to church, so took my pen and began my analysis of Brown's philosophy. When Emma came home we went down and talked a while and as the storm was too high to venture out Mr. Gardiner went through the afternoon service at home. He read prayers, the scriptures and one of Jebb's admirable sermons.[5] He is a fine reader and I scarcely heard any thing that pleased me more. Mr. Gardiner is a rare combination of public spirit and every domestic excellence, of the perfect gentleman and the humble Christian. After the service we dined at five o'clock and then Emma and I retreated to our chamber and Mrs. G. joined us and we had a delightful evening. I read her my analysis and she said it was very correct. At six o'clock I was awakened by Mr. W.[illiam] V.[aughn] who had just arrived, having cut down through the snow drifts. This is just like W. V. who, without the least parade or sentimentality, is one of the most warm hearted excellent friends I ever had. He knew if I was blocked up I should not venture to Gardiner again.

ELIZABETH

TS copy, OYesA

5 A reference to either John Jebb, English theological and political writer who also practiced medicine, or his son John Jebb, bishop of Limerick and pioneer in the Oxford movement.

One of several Peabody accounts of Lafayette's visit to the United States in 1824–25.

✳ To Maria Chase

My dear Maria,   June 28 1825
    I have no words to express my contrition for my unpardonable neglect of your delightful letter—some time since—and it was almost with a *pang* that I opened your dear little note.—
    My excuse is—that I had nothing to say until the 17th &c—and it was necessary to write all about *that*—home.[1] I presumed you would

1 In 1824, President James Monroe invited Lafayette to visit the United States. He arrived in New York on August 16, 1824, and after a tumultuous welcome in New York, toured New England, various cities on the way to Washington, D.C., and

feel interest enough to enquire and hear about it all—from our family—

Even about these I have nothing new to say. Every day and hour of recollection will indeed deepen the impression they have made on my soul—"as streams their channels deeper wear"[2] But I can *not say* anything new about them.—

I have not heard of the 'blessed Lafayette' since he departed from Boston. I must not neglect however to tell you a few little anecdotes that may not have reached your ear—which displays the high finish of his character—his annihilation of self—

When Madame Scott was Madame Hancock—the wife of Governor Hancock[3]—Lafayette was in the habit of visiting there—When he returned to this country at this time—he enquired for her and found that she had laid aside the glorious name of Hancock—the only thing that could make her interesting to anybody now (for she was always a dowdy) and was now the widow of a schoolmaster—Moreover—he found her in a different part of Boston from where he had

---

then to Monticello to visit Thomas Jefferson. After visiting sites of western Revolutionary War conflicts, he returned to Boston in time for the fiftieth anniversary celebration of the Battle of Bunker Hill. Elizabeth Peabody was in the crowd that attended this celebration, which she described in another letter to Maria Chase. The Rev. Joseph Thaxter, who had prayed on the day of battle, gave the invocation, and the crowd then sang John Pierpont's hymn to the tune of "Old Hundred." She was struck that at the moment of receiving Daniel Webster's most effusive praise, Lafayette looked as if "it was no longer *pleasure* . . . to receive these tributes. . . . There seemed a great— *great*—weight on his breast" (MS, MNS).

Elizabeth's program from this celebration is in the library of the Morristown National Historical Park. At the top is "Elizabeth P. Peabody received on Bunker hill June 17th 1825." In the right margin, alongside "Services on Bunker Hill, for 17 June, 1825" she wrote "*Shook hands with LaFayette* with the gloves on herein enclosed—." In the right margin opposite the text of Pierpont's hymn is "While this hymn was sung a Revolutionary soldier—while the tears rolled down his cheeks exclaimed "Good God! this is too much for mortal man to bear!" In the left margin alongside Pierpont's hymn is "To be preserved till June 17th 1875 and to be carried upon that spot again at that time." Alongside "ADDRESS by the President of the Association" Peabody wrote "Daniel Webster—overwhelming." Next to "CONCLUDING PRAYER by Rev. James Walker" she wrote "sublime! but spoken so low as to be heard but by few." At the bottom of the program Peabody wrote, "As the survivors passed me—one said 'take your last look of us!' All looked happy and animated—most of them decrepit with old age—many maimed from battle." In the left margin she wrote "*Postscript* On June 17th 1875 I alone who was the oldest of the party in 1825 went again to Bunker Hill at the Centennial celebration. All the rest were dead [word illegible] my sister Mary Mann & Mr Charles Vaughan, both too infirm to go from Cambridge while I was well & [word illegible] my nephew Ben. Mann went with me—"

2 "As streams their channels deeper wear" is unidentified.

3 John Hancock married Dorothy Quincy in 1775.

left her—for not having a spark of sentiment she had abandoned the house—where she once received the heroes of the revolution—He went to see her—looking disturbed and took her into another room—and with a voice trembling with emotion—said "My dear Madam—how is this?—Why do I not find you in the stone house on the hill—is there any change of circumstances?—I am your husband's friend!" Dolly replies—"Oh no indeed sir—it was a mere family arrangement and mere matter of convenience—leaving the stone house"—He was instantly relieved—and returned to the company as light hearted as usual—

Matthew Carey of Philadelphia—now rich and receiving Lafayette at his house—went to him a destitute Irish youth—and received five hundred dollars to begin his fortune with—[4]

When the South End of Boston was burnt down—Mr. Breck received under injunction of secrecy 300 guineas for the sufferers from Lafayette.

—But I cannot stop to tell you any more for I want to tell you how I hope you will prosecute your plan of coming to see me—Come through Saugus and Cambridge. You can easily enquire the way—and avoid Boston—Start at ½ past four *in the morning* from Salem—and calculate to stay all night—which you can do perfectly conveniently—and if you will allow me to *set a time*—why cannot you come on the 6th of July? You and Sophia was the party—was it not?

You will find me *very, very, very* happy to see you—and instead of my own stupidity—I will put Brookline walks—and Lafayette stories foremost—Why do I not hear from Lydia—and where is your expedition to the White Mountains gone?—

I charge you not to come on the fourth of July—as I shall not be at home—

Ever your affectionately
ELIZABETH

To Miss Maria Chase
    in
        The realms of Peace

MS, MNS

4 Matthew Carey was an essayist, journalist, and publisher.

Peabody's gifts of observation and description are evident in this account of Channing's Sunday-school classes.

✴ To Mrs. Elizabeth Peabody

Dear Mother,   June 1826

I saw today at Dr. Channing's Sunday School Miss S. Savage, who told me she was going on the morrow to Salem.[1] So I write a few lines to express to you my admiration of Dr. C. After meeting I went into the Sunday school. There are half a dozen classes of 20 or 18 each, sometimes more. The girls are instructed by ladies, the boys by gentlemen, and Mr. Chandler and Mr. Ticknor had each a class.[2] All the classes had short lessons in the Bible, which were given them by Dr. C. to repeat. The manner of Professor Ticknor in questioning was very familiar and happy and the children appeared pleased. The recitations were soon over and Dr. C. came in and opened their lessons in the Bible and read the first verse, "In God we live and move and have our being." He then closed the book and enlarged in a familiar manner upon this truth, endeavouring to make the children feel as well as repeat it, telling them they were to apply it to their every day conduct. His manner and even his voice is so affectionate and insinuating that he seems peculiarly adapted to this office. Mr. Chandler, who walked home with us, said, that he had never seen Dr. C. when he appeared more truly great than among these children. In the afternoon he preached and I carried my glasses to see him. He does not look as I thought he did, but he looks extremely interesting and his eyes are very fine. The first few minutes of his prayer is not striking. He has not that peculiar manner of beginning that Mr. Brazer has which strikes down every feeling prostrate at the first clause. Yet as he goes on, and his own devotional feelings enkindle, he becomes touching, overpowering. As Everet said, I believe of Cooper, he has the gift of an angel in prayer.[3] His sermon was upon the glori-

---

[1] Miss Savage was apparently a friend of the family who carried this letter with her to Salem.

[2] George Ticknor, educator and author, traveled extensively in Europe before returning to teach modern languages and literature at Harvard College.

[3] C. C. Everett (not Everet) was the first Unitarian minister in Hallowell, Maine, ordained there in 1824 and presiding over a church increasing in numbers and influence.

ous designs of God in creating us as we are. The most part of it was only applicable to the advanced Christian yet could be understood and would not I think have been called mystical or enthusiastic by the indifferent—*indifferent*, I cannot conceive of anybody's being indifferent after hearing such a sermon. He was so animated that his voice had none of that tone which some accuse him of and which was brought on by sickness, and his fine eyes had an expression I cannot describe. The brightest ray of light that illumines Mr. Everet's features is yet human, and we should never be in danger of mistaking it, but the ineffable light that beams from Dr. C.'s eyes as he looks upward "is light from heaven."

ELIZABETH

TS copy, OYesA

To reformer and teacher Dorothea Dix, Peabody suggests a theme that is surfacing with increasing intensity in the late 1820s: beneath the controlled and self-effacing exterior lies a self filled with feelings waiting to be expressed.

✎ To Dorothea Dix[1]

[Newport]
My dear Miss Dix—   July 8th 1827
    Yours of June 21st—came a day or two since   Had I known that I could send to you by private hand yesterday I should have written— but I did not know it till I learnt it from Charles today—And I will not wait till next Saturday lest it prove a bad omen upon our opening correspondence.

---

1 The product of an unhappy childhood, Dorothea Dix opened her first school in Boston in 1821. Until 1824, Dix taught and pursued a course of self-education through intensive reading and attendance at public lectures. Exhaustion and the symptoms of tuberculosis forced her to curb her activities; she spent several summers at Narragansett Bay as governess for the family of William Ellery Channing and the winter of 1830–31 with the Channings in the Virgin Islands.

Dix's most famous reform activity, the treatment of the mentally ill, began in 1841, and until the Civil War she traveled throughout the United States and, in the 1850s, Europe, investigating conditions, writing reports, and lobbying legislatures for change. In 1861, she became superintendent of army nurses, a task requiring more tact and patience than Dix possessed. After the war, Dix took on a number of causes, including raising funds for the completion of the Washington Monument. She died in 1885.

I thank you very much for your letter—and I hope I shall continue to hear of the children—they are exceedingly interesting to me for their own sake—for their parents' sake—and for my favorite ideas' sake—being educated more nearly according to what I consider the true principles of education than any children I know—I look with intense interest at the result—& I think I may gain many ideas from the *phenomena* they exhibit!—(*what phraseology,* you may say!)

I am delighted with your account of the *external woman* (as my landlady may say). I hope Miss Gibbs[2] will keep you "reading, walking &c" all summer & give you uninterrupted opportunity of enjoying

"Spontaneous wisdom—breath'd from health
Truth breathed from cheerfulness"—[3]

I hope you will not consider it a loss that you will "do less than ever before in the same space of time"—

"Thinkst thou midst this mighty Sum
Of things forever speaking—
That nothing of itself will come
But we must still be seeking?—"[4]

(Hear what comfortable words our exalted Wordsworth says)
You ask me a momentous question when you ask how far *friendship* warrants us to go in faultfinding—Friday—13th—I have not had a *second* since writing the above to peruse the deep subject started in the last sentence. It is one which has engaged my deepest reflections a great deal.—I have had the fortune or misfortune (as you may deem it) of experiencing in my own person that effects of most liberal tho' in most instances most kindly meant faultfindings.—Whether I should myself—without this I cannot pretend to say—But of one evil I think it is inevitably the cause—*egotism*—not talking about one's self so much as *feeling one's self* always—a degrading sense of being bound by a chain of adamant to the meanest of Nature's works—"He whose eye is ever on himself—Beholds the least of Nature's works" Wordsworth[5] There is another evil felt by one *whose duties* are a great draught upon spirit—*depression—discouragement*—Could I

2 Sarah Gibbs, called Aunt Sarah because she had not married, was the sister of Ruth Gibbs, wife of William Ellery Channing, and mistress of the family estate, Oaklands, in Newport until her death at age ninety-one.
3 William Wordsworth, "Tables Turned," lines 19–20.
4 William Wordsworth, "Expostulation and Reply," lines 25–28.
5 William Wordsworth, "The Yew Tree," lines 24–25.

open to you the mental experience of my past life—you would shudder *as I do*—at the Spectacle of an independant spirit hovering on the brink of degradation—becoming a slave to fallible beings like itself.— But I must not even refer to this subject.—It is my rule never to find fault with an individual for whom I do not feel a personal & very warm & tender interest—be it child or grown person.—And never to find fault unless I can clearly see a method of removing the fault which I can point out:—& moreover never to find fault unless circumstances will allow me to be near & watch the result:—And I have always determined to whenever it resulted in evil, that *mine* was the fault (of *judgment* if not of heart).—I have done it with my scholars— with my sisters—my friends—and I never yet failed to make them take the same views as I did—of their present condition & their capacities— But few have been in such a school as I have been—to learn to find fault.—Every way in which it *ought not to be done*—has left its burning trace upon my soul—which writhes even to remember it.—a friend of mine who has seen me under these operations a great deal said to me the other day that she often doubted whether I understood what was meant—I bore it philosophically—these were not her words but her idea & she meant it in no unkindness—She thought my philosophy arose from a consciousness that it was not deserved which she thought I had strength of mind to pursue even in the face of reproof.—I do not know why it was—but my mind instantly ran over the past with the thought of "how little has my manner represented what was passing within" and all seemed to concentrate into one agonizing sensation which before I was aware exhibited itself in that language which before is understood by all human hearts altho' there are no articulate sounds.—It is actually the fact that it took me more than a week to recover from that *one* unregulated movement of Memory—I could not speak without crying—every pulse in my body fluttered at every look— a dim sense of pain accompanied circulation—my intellect seemed to have a dun cloud over it—& my heart was oppressed—*tho' not penetrated* as the reality of what I remembered had penetrated it.—Two years determinate turning away from the bitter sense of disappointment I always occasion to people who take an interest in me—& a determinate cultivation of those glorious views of human nature which *"our beloved & revered"*[6] has opened to my mind since my return from the East ward—. has soothed my heart & made it in a degree strong to resist the dagger of reproach from without.—

6 "Our beloved and revered" is a reference to William Ellery Channing.

The proper way of improving others is not directly to find fault but to awaken moral sensibility & to render these moral views & sentiments practical subjects—& by discussing their influence or proper influence upon other characters than the individual in question— "When the Spirit gives its own illumination & the conscience is tender—then is man's heart wont to tell him more than the watchers on the high tower." I have no more time—but my most affectionate & respectful remembrances to our valued friends—I am yours affectionately   E. P. Peabody

Eliza Cabot returned on Wednesday—well & bright—I hope my next letter will be better—it is unfortunate for you that I pitched upon a subject too agitating to me to allow me the free play of my true powers—

MS, MH

One of many letters written to Sarah Sullivan. Here Peabody explains in a kind of foreshadowing of her later Romanticism, that "love is the end & destiny of the human soul" and comments on the pride of intellect.

✾ To Sarah Russell Sullivan

[November 1827][1]

I am sure I must have expressed myself very clumsily, my dear Mrs. Sullivan to have produced by my letter—just such a note as lies

---

[1] The date for this letter is taken from the existence of several such letters to Sullivan, all written in the late 1820s, and from one in particular, dated November 1827 and incomplete, which bears a great resemblance to the letter above. In the November 1827 letter, Peabody writes: "There have been moments in my life when existence was felt as a burden—altho' my principles would not let me acknowledge it as one—and at these times—a kind note—or word—or smile has indeed gone to my heart—but in the happiest hours of my life—my heart was also *full* as *sensible* to a kind word—or smile or look—There may be some days—when you seem to yourself to do nothing for your fellow creatures—because you may have a cold in your head— & rheumatism in your hand—& can neither instruct—entertain—or do—but if you have *sent your love to me*—above all if you have written a note of half a dozen words—do not say you have done no good—you have sent a summer feeling thro' one human being's heart & given a new impulse to every principle of goodness." (TS copy, incomplete, OYesA)

before me.[2] It is perhaps always dangerous to enter too minutely into one's own peculiarities—at least I should judge so by finding how ill I succeeded in explaining mine—but then on the other hand I find no difficulty in understanding others who are very different from me—& the pleasure I experience in following this kind of investigation makes me hesitate to pronounce it a general rule to refrain from such confidential communications. But you did not take my meaning. Because I told you I valued the love of the meanest above the *intellect* of the highest—you think I make no discrimination of interest to correspond to the different minds from which I receive affection. I do think there is a difference in *love* & I value that of any person in proportion as I think their minds are clear & capable of entering into individual character. I did not say or mean that I received as much pleasure from the love of the uncultivated as the love of the cultivated, when the latter were unsophisticated enough to dare to love generously. En passant I would remark that there is a besetting sin to the cultivated of our imperfect age of the world—which breaks & scatters & palsies this noble energy of heart which is encouraged on every page of Scripture as the perfection of human nature;—& that is—the spirit of criticism—not of discrimination—but of criticism. A perfectly uncultivated mind will love naturally & freely & generously—from an internal feeling that love is *the end & destiny* of the human soul. But when the pride of intellect is once excited—there does not come any more generous love till it is humbled—& when it is obliged to yield in individual instances—yet it is rare to find it yield universally. If I have a right idea of Mr. Sullivan—he is a case in point. It seems to me his general sentiment towards human beings is the right one. If he were captious in his conversation—setting out people's foibles—always holding up before him *the scales* wherewith to weigh every word & random action—if every glance of his eye had in it the expression of a reviewer—society could be very excited by him & perhaps think him a very much greater man. But he is great enough to dare to be kind— he is not afraid of being thought indiscriminate & tame—& his benevolence is not cold good will. The consciousness of intellect is enough for a really strong mind. The acknowledgement of it from others is necessary to one, half developed & weak from its unbalanced conditions.

2 Sarah Russell Sullivan was the wife of Richard Sullivan, who was a lawyer, politician, original subscriber to the Massachusetts General Hospital, and longtime resident of Brookline. He and Sarah Russell were married in 1804; she died in 1831.

All these things I have felt very much in my intercourse with society. I always instinctively look for affection—some peculiarity of constitution either bodily or mental made it my first subject of reflection. Had I been born where the light of Christianity had not beamed—& still constituted as I was—I should have discovered that love was the principle of virtue. The pride of intellect was the first thing that ever excited my ridicule;—& I never have been able to tolerate it since—when it obscured to the mind of the possessor—what alone is divine in human nature—its power of being interested to tenderness in others. I hope you understand me now—& because I tell you I would rather be loved by you than entertained by you—not think I am insensible to the improvement to be derived from your views of things. Your notes seemed to express your regret that you simply had not time to entertain me. You sometimes [part of sheet torn] meaning correspond with what I have here written—And believe me still with grateful affection

Yrs
ELIZABETH PEABODY

TS copy, OYesA

In 1825, Elizabeth Peabody returned from a two-year stint as governess to the Vaughan family in Maine and opened a school in Brookline, Massachusetts. Mary Peabody taught with her sister, and in the first year they attracted thirty students, many from leading Boston families like the Appletons. In 1827, the school moved to Franklin Square, Boston.

✎ To [Nathan Appleton][1]

Dear Sir,   [1827]
You ask me what have been my intentions respecting Fanny's studies this winter.

[1] The staff of the Houghton Library, Harvard, has identified this letter as addressed to Henry Wadsworth Longfellow. It may, in fact, be addressed to Nathan Appleton, banker, manufacturer, politician, and one of the founders of the city of Lowell, Massachusetts. Appleton's daughter Fanny, who later became Longfellow's wife, attended the Peabody school in 1827. On February 20, 1827, Fanny Appleton wrote to her brother Thomas: "I now go to Miss Peabody's school, and I like her

The first hour of every day, except Monday, is employed by the whole school in writing. Tardiness is merely punished by the obvious consequence of the thing itself—losing some of the time devoted to writing of which they are all fond, and we have thought Fanny was gaining a very pretty style of penmanship.

The succeeding two hours—on Monday—Wednesday—& Friday—have been given to the Latin Lesson, which has consisted this winter in studying the Grammar and immediately applying what was learnt in it to the translated lesson—Fanny did not learn the Latin Grammar thoroughly at first, and after she had studied some months last winter I was sorry I had not put her to studying it over again. In the summer being absent[2]—she lost what slight hold she had got of it last winter, and therefore this winter I determined to begin with her from the beginning. I have let the class construe literally and with the latin arrangement (that they might learn to think in the latin arrangement of words), and then inflect the nouns—and adjectives—and verbs;—and then I have allowed them to throw the sentence into good English;—and asked questions and made explanations with the view to illustrate the comparative syntax of the two languages.—Fanny is exceedingly careless and rather indolent—but she has not fallen out of the class. In all that required quick perception and judgement I found her quite on a par with the best in school—but in application she is indifferent.—These three lessons in latin every week is the general rule of the school. In some instances, when they have been particularly reluctant to study it—I have omitted it for a lesson in geography;—and have sometimes omitted the *writing* for a lesson in geography which is the study which always fills up the *odd time* when any accident prevents the going on of a class.—The three alternate days are given to French. The class to which Fanny belongs have nearly finished Telemaque.[3] The lesson is five pages to translate—and then the parsing of every verb.—After this a lesson in the exercises—which

---

very well, though I have to walk in the cold, a great way, as it is in Franklin Place" (Edward Wagenknecht, ed., *Mrs. Longfellow: Selected Letters and Journals of Fanny Appleton Longfellow, 1817–1861* [New York: Longmans, Green and Co., 1956], 4).

2 "Being absent" is keyed with an asterisk for insertion in the text.

3 *Télémaque* was a didactic romance written by French theologian and cleric Fénelon for the edification of one of his pupils. Secretly published in 1699, *Télémaque* contains a long treatise on government and on conduct befitting rulers. In his assertion that the law is higher than a ruler's will and that suspects ought to be held innocent until proven guilty, Fénelon incurred the disfavor of the court of Louis XIV and was deprived of his archbishopric.

have been *read* in a class—and they have read as far as through the pronouns—and the next quarter they are to *write* from the beginning as it will be necessary for them to go over again.

A great deal of ground cannot be gone over in either Latin or french—when only six hours of the week are devoted to each. And it is our object that what the children learn about be taught thoroughly. But they must learn and recite all within this time for you will perceive that it is a large proportion of the time which is given to it—& more could not be spared from English studies.

An hour every day is given (to each class) for reading and composition both under the care of Mr. Russell—[4]who also takes the charge of spelling, and defining words.

The hour which is left—is given alternately to arithmetic and History.—As a stepping stone from Colburn's First Lessons to his Sequel (and one is needed) I have given my pupils Lovell's Arithmetic.[5] Fanny is very averse to this study—and fell behind her class from inattention at the time when I examined them in arithmetic, which I do every day, by requiring them to sit round in a class and tell me how they do the sums—& following their directions with a piece of chalk upon a black board, so that every error can be made manifest to the whole class, who have the privilege of correcting each other. Nothing can be more easy than this method of learning to work out operations in figures,—but it requires *attention* and here Fanny failed. I stopped the whole class that she might have time to go over the Compound Rules—and allowed the rest to study Geography at that hour—but she went over them so rapidly I fear she did not get well acquainted with them, and I have anticipated putting her back with the class below the next quarter.—She has not seemed averse to

[4] William Russell, first editor of the *American Journal of Education*, was a partner with Mary and Elizabeth Peabody in their Franklin Square school in 1827.

[5] Warren Colburn, *Colburn's First Lessons: Intellectual Arithmetic, upon the Inductive Method of Instruction* (Boston: William J. Reynolds, 1821). It is possible that Peabody assigned another edition of this text, entitled *First Lessons in Arithmetic on the Plan of Pestalozzi, with Some Improvements*, 2d ed. (Boston: Cummings and Hilliard, 1822). Two more editions of this text came out in 1823 and 1825. The sequel to which she refers could have been one of six texts then in print: *Arithmetic: Being a Sequel to First Lessons in Arithmetic* (Boston: Cummings and Hilliard, 1822), a second (1824) or third (1826) edition of that text, *Arithmetic upon the Inductive Method of Instruction, Being a Sequel to Intellectual Arithmetic* (Boston: Samuel F. Nichols, 1826), an 1826 edition with that same title (Boston: Bazin and Ellsworth), or an 1827 edition with the same title (Boston: Hilliard, Gray, Little, and Wilkins). The Lovell text to which she refers is John Espy Lovell, *Introductory Arithmetic Prepared for the Pupils of the Lancasterian School, New Haven . . . Part First* (New Haven: S. Wadsworth, 1827).

Geography—and I do not know but she is pretty well versed in it,—but in general what taxes her memory without attracting her taste passes away from her mind as rapidly as it goes into it—and she learns lessons very quick.—By dint of repetition I hope this will be impressed on her mind—and when she has more time I wish her to draw maps.—

One of my principal objects this winter has been the History lesson. More of what cultivates the mind can be drawn out of this lesson than any other. In order to have one connected story up to the time of Christ, I began with the Sacred History (disconnected as much as was desirable from *religion*). My method has been to read from the Old Testament of Josephus about an hour—taking up a certain portion of the narrative and making observations and explanations in order to assist the imagination in realising the state of the times: the next day employing the hour in asking questions concerning the lesson of the day before. They wrote these questions—and as often as once a week I went back over the whole ground asking the questions—Fanny took great interest in this excercise. I hope she could answer the questions to you.

After having gone over this history—I divided it into centuries, marking each by the most interesting person who lived in it.—They learned these by writing them down; as they know the story and were interested in the individuals.—This is to serve as a foundation to Chronology. I ask them when Theseus lived—for instance—they tell me in the time of Abimelech (Judges) & they know *his* time (as respects the Christian Era).—I have just begun Plutarch which I am about to read in Chronological order of the lives,—And shall let them write questions & review as I have done in Sacred History. These history lessons come at least four times a week.

I believe this is *my*[6] plan—at least as far as regards the class to which Fanny belongs.

You must decide whether Fanny receives advantage from the plan. She has natural talent in abundance. She reads the best in her class—is quick in discriminating synonyms—and in all exercises which require ingenuity—and is *beautiful* in whatever requires *taste*.—But she dislikes hard study—is too willing to be assisted, and often when *we* would throw her upon her own resources, she obtains assistance from her schoolfellows.—

We have but one punishment in our school which is that when there is neglect and carelessness in schoolhouse—there should be study

6 "My" has been underlined twice in the manuscript.

at home an extra lesson.—This serves as a stimulus to attention and industry. But Fanny has the privilege from home—of never studying at home. I cannot therefore enforce this rule upon *her* & being out of its reach, she has no mechanical stimulus to industry. If you could think it consistent with the health of her body—for me to apply this rule to her—it would prove much to the health of her mind.

You will excuse my delaying this answer and now writing it so hastily—for I am *moving* today—Respectfully Elizabeth P. Peabody

MS, MH

Peabody encourages Dorothea Dix to take a teaching post in Lancaster, Massachusetts. Despite her obvious enjoyment of life in Boston, Peabody described with wistful longing the town in which she had lived and first taught.

✴ To Dorothea Dix

My dear Miss Dix,   January 24th, 1828

Your note is lying before me & reproaching me for its being unanswered, for I know that you must yearn for the sight of a letter from N. England.

As to my doings they are pretty much confined to my school, for some of the exercises of which I am obliged to prepare out of school hours. I began to read the History of Literature of the South of Europe (Sismondis)[1] of which you know I spoke to you the beginning of this month—& have actually got half thro' it—but I do not believe I should have read so far—had not I read it to Fanny Jackson—who cannot read on account of her eyes—& for whose sake I have made great exertions. In the society line, my greatest enjoyment is in visits to Dr. Channing—especially on the appointed evenings.—Our Sunday School meeting in his study have been peculiarly interesting this winter—there is more general conversation than there ever was before—and the *education party* is most interesting & instructive—Mr. Phillips' mind seems only to move by the law of Relative Suggestion (if I may borrow the technicks of Brown); it is absolutely delivered

[1] Jean Charles Leonard Simonde de Sismondi, *Historical View of the Literature of the South of Europe* (New York: J. and J. Harper, 1818).

from the Suggestions of time & place. There is nothing factitious about the mind of Dr. Follen either—& you know the rest of the party! No book ever gave me such a treat as these conversations. But I will not venture to give you any account of them in a letter.—I suppose you know our beloved & revered has been quite ill lately.—But he preached last Sunday—Speaking of sermons I never read Smiths' but shall endeavour to procure them.[2]

"What interests (me) most?"—Why there is nothing more interesting than that dear delightful little trio of celestials which you bequeathed to me from your Sunday class. Miss Hunt really grows more beautiful every week—It would seem from the development of her own sweet Spirit—for it is nothing less than pure *moral beauty*. I teach them on Thursday afternoons—& have finished all I had to say to them (or rather all I could take time to say to them) about the Old Testament & am again upon the Gospels. They enquire for you & desire me to remember them to you.

Do you know Mr. Bailey of the High School? The High School is broken up—*because it succeeded* so well. People thought there would be no domestics—it is said. Mr. Bailey proposed a private school—at the price of 15$ to 20$ a scholar—& he had *seventy five applications*. He received them all—but it was entirely unexpected & he had no assistance. He obtained one person temporarily but he must have more & better—he says. The ages vary from six years to twenty years of age. He is himself in school four hours in the morning—during which he teaches in all his departments.—He has the school room open to all of his scholars that please to come in the afternoon—to write & sew—& draw for all which departments he has instructors—& is not himself present in the afternoon. presume he must need & have assistance, however, in his own department in the morning.—

Perhaps you would like to take a department in this school—& I should think it would be the wiser course for you—not to take individually the responsibility of a school which you could not always leave at a day's warning,—But I know of another School which I should think you would very much prefer—which would be more independent & yet from its size not so [word blotted out] laborious? I mean the female department of [illegible] school in the sweet [Auburn?] valley of beautiful Lancaster.

Miss Lewis is engaged to be married and I do not believe will

[2] Peabody's reference may be to Puritan preacher Henry Smith, called "silver-tongued Smith," active in London at the end of the sixteenth century.

very long continue there. I kept school there one blissful year—and could you enjoy & improve in any proportion to what I enjoyed & learnt—you would feel you had wherewithal to draw upon as counterbalance for all the evils of life. The place in its external aspect is the paradise of the land—Dr. Thayer[3] is the presiding spirit of truth & goodness—& tho' it is not exempt from the evils of a *terrestrial* paradise—yet if any place has *a guard angelic* over it from many who constitute its society & from its external [illegible] Lancaster is that place. This is no answer at all to your note—which tho' short is comprehensive. But, I am actually driven out of my very ideas by this multiplicity of things to do. I have a thousand things to-day—but if I should begin to answer your questions about the comparative advantages of a city & country life—or *discuss* the reasonableness or unreasonableness of your conscience of which you give me so interesting an account—I should write you & myself quite into a state of exhaustion. I have been a *lengthy* letter writer in my day—but life is too interesting to me now to afford me time to *cultivate expression* or even to indulge it.—In respect to a city & country life—I should think you would find the latter much preferable on the score of health. Why cannot you tell me how the Lancaster plan strikes you. The Guilds could assist you in obtaining that place. Forgive this dull letter. I know you have many better correspondents— (Lancaster would be a good place too for yr brother who might be in Mr. Carter's department of the institution & there finish his education.) Goodbye & believe me yours affectionately E. P. Peabody

MS, MH

3 Dr. Nathaniel Thayer was the Unitarian minister in Lancaster, Massachusetts.

⚹2
1830s

Schoolteacher and Romantic

FOR ELIZABETH PEABODY, as for many of her contemporaries, the 1830s were years of transition—minds were changed, vocations shaped, influential writings composed, and causes joined. For Ralph Waldo Emerson, for Amos Bronson Alcott, whose life intersected Elizabeth Peabody's so jarringly during this decade, for Margaret Fuller, Nathaniel Hawthorne, Jones Very, George Ripley, and Orestes Brownson—the thirties were watershed years.

The decade opened inauspiciously for Peabody, however. William Russell's unpaid debts had forced her to close the Beacon Hill school, and there were other anxieties to be faced. She wrote later to her nephew Julian, "Just at this time, in 1831, or 1832 [actually the winter of 1830–31] I had been greatly tired by intense sympathy with a great tragedy in a circle of my friends; and mother's health broke down; and some other domestic services quite broke me down, on whom too great responsibility rested; and I felt I could not do my duty to my scholars without a change."[1] The tragedy to which she referred was likely the consequences of her intervention in the affairs of some of her students from New Bedford. The themes of indiscretion and tactlessness mentioned in her letters and conversations of succeeding years stemmed from that episode. The details of the affair are vague, but the outline is this: Peabody had gone to New Bedford in the winter of 1830–31 apparently to thwart what seemed to her a conspiracy by relatives of several of her pupils to usurp the students' property. She was rebuffed by the relatives she accused, with damage to her reputation. Mrs. Eliza Farrar, wife of Harvard professor John Farrar and author of advice books for the young, became particularly pointed in her hostility toward Peabody. Peabody, in the aftermath, lost several good friends, including Sarah Russell Sullivan of Brookline, whose goodwill she later regained. She experienced for the first time, but certainly not the last, a conflict between her own persistence, curiosity, and outraged sense of justice, and the cultural limits of tact, reticence, and propriety society placed on women, and especially single women, of her era. Energetic intrusiveness, she was beginning to discover, was not always appreciated. She returned to Boston, brooding over the weakness of humanity.

In 1832, Elizabeth and Mary Peabody rented rooms for living and teaching at the Somerset Court boardinghouse owned by the gossipy Mrs. Rebecca Clarke, mother of James Freeman Clarke and

<hr />

[1] Pearson, "Peabody on Hawthorne," 274.

Sarah Clarke, longtime friends of the Peabodys.[2] In the fall, concluding that teaching was not bringing in enough income, Elizabeth Peabody opened an "historical school," a reading and discussion seminar on ancient history and the Greek tragedians that met twice a week for six months, and yielded fifty dollars.[3]

Mary Peabody was steady, quiet, withdrawn, and supremely conventional. Elizabeth, to the contrary, was occasionally tactless, energetic, and unconventional. Their contrasting personalities began to lead to irritation, and Elizabeth's letters in these years reflect an ambivalence toward her sister that would peak after Mary Peabody's return from her post as governess to an American family in Cuba, but simmer beneath the surface through the later years until Mary's death in 1887.

Also, during the fall of 1832 Horace Mann moved into Mrs. Clarke's boardinghouse, precipitating the second crisis of the decade for Elizabeth Peabody. The story of the tangled and intense relationships among Elizabeth and Mary Peabody and Horace Mann is best told in Jonathan Messerli's biography, *Horace Mann* (New York: Alfred Knopf, 1972). Devastated by the death of his twenty-three-year-old wife Charlotte Messer, Mann had fled to Boston to attend to some investments and try to assuage his grief. As the first anniversary of his wife's death approached, he abandoned the boardinghouse to mourn in solitude. Elizabeth Peabody, provoked by his unassuaged grief, took on his case with enthusiasm, and attempted to reason him out of his depression. To Peabody, Mann may have become more than a cause. She combed his hair, held his hand and head, and received him as a visitor at least once a week. She must have seen in him the perfect combination of good cause and appealing vulnerability, the sort of person who was to attract her, although not romantically, several other times in her life. In a conversation with Caroline Dall, Mrs. Clarke noted that the forward but naïve Miss Peabody caused concern and amusement around her boardinghouse dinner table: "Everybody thought Miss Elizabeth was dead set on Horace Mann. He wouldn't come out of his chamber for a week after his first wife died, and I had to send his dinner up. One day Elizabeth Peabody wanted to take it. 'No,' said I, 'it isn't proper Miss Peabody. I don't want you to.' 'Oh but I must' said she 'I've got something to say to Mr. Mann.' Then

[2] Elizabeth Peabody to Mary Peabody, 10 February 1835, "Cuba Journal," MS, NN-B.
[3] Peabody discussed her historical conversations in detail in "Principles and Methods of Education," 736–37.

they all began to talk about Mr. Mann's marrying again. Elizabeth declared indignantly that he'd never be married again. 'In your presence,' said Mr. Fairbanks, laying his hand on his heart, 'In *your* presence Miss Elizabeth I think he will.' Great fool! He really seemed to think he'd said the right thing."[4] Realizing by the summer of 1834 the depth of her attachment, Mann explained that their relationship could only be that of a brother and sister.

At the end of 1833, Mrs. Richard Cleveland of Lancaster, who had introduced her earlier in Boston and Cambridge circles, suggested that Mary Peabody go to Cuba as governess to the children of her friends the Morrells. Her younger sister Sophia might accompany her. The arrangements were quickly made, and the sisters left in November 1833. To her absent sisters, particularly to Mary, Elizabeth wrote long and detailed letters, collectively called the "Cuba Journal." One letter suggested that Mary and Sophia stay on in Cuba indefinitely rather than return to the precarious economic situation in Boston. Mary, whose feelings of affection for Horace Mann had been nurtured in secret, did not want to leave him to her competitive and flamboyant sister, and she returned home, along with Sophia, on May 30, 1835.

Elizabeth Peabody had organized a reading class, a second historical class, and moved out of Mrs. Clarke's boardinghouse to live with the Rices on Bedford Street. In 1834, with the arrival in Boston of Bronson Alcott and family, Peabody was launched into her third crisis of the decade. She agreed to be Alcott's assistant at his new school. With thirty pupils, including the Rice and Lee children she had been teaching and others she rounded up, most of them under ten, Alcott and Peabody opened Temple School on September 22, 1834. She described the school's progress in her book, *Record of a School*, published in 1835, staying up some nights until one in the morning to write it. By the time Mary and Sophia returned from Cuba, a growing estrangement had arisen between teacher and assistant. Peabody disliked Alcott's method of instruction, believing that it encouraged far too much introspection. She was living with the Alcotts, too, and felt personally at odds with them. When in 1836 Alcott published *Conversations with Children on the Gospels*, Peabody was horrified by the frank disclosures of conversations of hers he had chosen to include. But the damage was done. Peabody feared that people would associate her with the indiscretions Alcott's book revealed, and,

4 Caroline Dall, "Studies Toward the Life of a 'Business Woman' Being Conversations with Mrs. R. P. Clarke," MS, MCR-S.

at least for a time, a school in Boston was out of the question for her.

Fortunately, Peabody's role at Temple School and her book describing it had attracted the attention of Emerson. His invitation in late 1837 to attend a meeting of the Transcendental Club was her fourth watershed event of the decade. He introduced her to the literary-theological-philosophical group of which he was, vaguely, the head, and through them to a larger world of ideas, writing, and influence.

In the fall of 1837, Peabody was back in Salem nursing the chronically ill Sophia and her mother. She visited the Hathornes, who had lived near them twenty-four years earlier in Salem. She was convinced that some short stories, appearing anonymously in S. G. Goodrich's *New England Magazine,* had been written by the eldest daughter of the family, Elizabeth, but to her astonishment, discovered that they had in fact been written by Nathaniel. In November, the Hathornes— now Hawthorne, the new spelling invented by Nathaniel—returned the call.[5] Peabody encouraged Hawthorne to give up his anonymity and seclusion, a role of which she became justifiably proud.

Peabody was somewhat more ambivalent about another eccentric literary figure in Salem, the poet and essayist Jones Very. In the fall of 1838, after a spring and summer in West Newton living and working with her brother Nathaniel who was trying his hand at teaching, Peabody had returned to Salem, where she encountered Very. Very one day appeared at her house to announce that he was the Second Coming of Christ. Frightened by his orphic intensity, she sent Very to Emerson, hoping that he could channel Very's divine madness into creative effort. Very ended up in the Somerville asylum for the insane.

By the end of the decade, Peabody was fully engaged in the Romantic movement. She was reading *Levance,* a treatise on education by German poet and essayist Johann Paul Friedrich Richter, Thomas Carlyle's *French Revolution,* and Madame de Staël's *Revolution.* She had been moved by Emerson's "Divinity School Address" of 1838 (although less so by his book *Nature*). She witnessed the tempest in the editorial offices of the *Christian Examiner* over George Ripley's criticism of the Unitarian defense of miracles. She befriended Theodore Parker, the Unitarian minister who would soon rock the intellectual

[5] Peabody told this story in several places, including her [1885] letter to Francis Lee and in her reminiscences written for her nephew Julian and published in Pearson, "Peabody on Hawthorne," 261–68.

and religious community with sermons that threatened to shatter the still-young liberal denomination.

Peabody's correspondence during the 1830s was as rich and varied as her experiences. In the first two years (1830–31) she continued her letters to Sarah Sullivan, often exploring the themes of discretion and tact, impulse and spontaneity which were so much on her mind. When Horace Mann entered her life, she wrote him many lengthy letters, devoted primarily to arguments and exhortations on the subject of his grief.

In sheer numbers, the "Cuba Journal," of which samples appear here, dominated the decade's correspondence. This diary-like account, to which Elizabeth Peabody added every week or less, provides intimate details of daily life, her rounds of visiting, and lists of reading, as well as valuable descriptions of Alcott's Temple School and her developing relationship with Mann. Letters to and about Emerson, a description of Hawthorne in a letter to Mann, and two letters to Elizabeth Bliss Bancroft regarding a political appointment for Hawthorne, mark this decade, as do several letters to Orestes Brownson. At the end of this extraordinary period, Peabody wrote several vivid letters to Emerson describing the temporary insanity of Jones Very.

Peabody describes the wedding of her former student Lydia Sears to Samuel Foster Haven, who would become known as a New England historian and antiquarian.

✦ To Sarah Russell Sullivan

My dear Mrs. Sullivan—   May 17th 1830

As I had a delightfully calm leisure day yesterday, I employed myself in the evening with recollecting Mr. Greenwood's sermon of the morning, which I send you enclosed.[1] Mary tells me that among the other great pleasures of her visit, she also numbered hearing Mr. Palfrey.[2]

---

[1] Francis William Pitt Greenwood was a Boston Unitarian clergyman, editor of the *Unitarian Miscellany,* and associate editor of the *Christian Examiner.*

[2] John Gorham Palfrey, Boston Unitarian clergyman and historian, wrote the *History of New England* (1858–75).

I intended to close my day by writing to you—but I fell into a reverie in the latter part of the evening, which ran away with the rest of my time. It was my birth day—the anniversary also, of my first going to Brookline which I did on the day I came of age four years ago. I have always remarked that all the great changes that have come over my dream of life, have commenced on my birth day. I could not but feel that not an unimportant one was taking place now—though not so obvious. Within the last week—I have parted with the Benjamins & Lydia—& our family was reduced to that of my own immediate connections.

With Lydia, the day before, I had heard a long & interesting conversation as she passed through town after her journey, on her way to her own home. The wedding of the week before was a most exquisite hour to me, & I was glad to find her own mind was dwelling on it with the most sacred feeling of homefelt delight. I had seen many marriages but never knew before what a minister might make of it. I was prepared for Mr. Channing's being interesting, but I hardly was aware of all that a human voice could do.

No one was here but the two families—I mean the two households. Not even a relation was invited beyond the immediate family. I brought down a tumbler of flowers and put it on the table after Mr. Channing came & took my seat. The bride & bridegroom came in, with their attendants, and without sitting down,—Mr. Hilliard gave Mr. Channing the certificate,—& he commenced with a prayer. I wish you could have heard the tones of his voice. Lydia told me, yesterday, that as soon as they touched her ear—every flutter was composed. She saw no one—she felt only in the presence of God & his voice seemed to utter every thing that she felt. When it was over I looked at her, and saw that the deep flush which had been in her cheeks all day had subsided & she stood perfectly calm looking down "not like a trembling girl but like a being breathing thoughtful breath" while in thrilling tones of the deepest solemnity, he spoke to Mr. Haven. When he spoke to her, she raised her eyes, over which a thin veil seemed to have fallen, which quenched their brightness, but I never saw such an expression of sweet seriousness, & earnest attention, on a human countenance as in hers as she continued to look at him till he had finished—& he pronounced them husband & wife with the usual form. The tone of his voice as he had spoken to her, was perceptibly softer & more tender than before. And in the prayer that followed, there is no describing the tenderness & delicacy in which he touched upon their future duties to each other & to heaven. When it was over—no one was in a situation to speak—tears were in their eyes—but more in the eyes of every one else. Mr. Channing first broke the silence & going to her—took her hand—& said "I wish you every happiness"— then my Mother & Mr. Haven's went & kissed her—& we all followed—not a word was spoken—and she said she would not have had a word spoken for the world. She sat down—& she said every thing seemed full. She felt as if there was a consecration shed over the spot—she dreaded to have it *end*. The cake & wine was brought in—& Mrs. Haven taking up the flowers—said "how beautiful are these flowers." Mr. Channing then spoke to all of us—& then went to her again—& shook hands with her. He asked her where she was going—& spoke of the beauty of the season—& of the route—to Mr. Haven. Then having shaken hands with her the third time he left us. We still sat round in silence—some growing more composed & some less so—& *she* smiling through her tears. She said to me yesterday—that it all seemed to her just as it should be;—tears were the only adequate expression,—a sort of holy spirit—had passed by—& it seemed as if we ought to be hushed with silence. She could not conceive of feeling awkward or embarrassed. Her only desire was to keep forever in her heart all she was feeling at that moment. And ever since—she said Mr. Channing's voice pronouncing those vows—& snatches of recollections of his prayers—have been floating over her like angels wings—there never was any thing so beautiful—so sacred. She felt she should be better forever for it. In an hour they were off on their journey & nothing broke the spell.

You may think, my dear Mrs. Sullivan, how delightful it was to me—to see this pure & innocent creature, so happy and so rightminded;—& to feel that my love had been to her the asylum where she had preserved so entirely the innocence & the tenderness of her spirit, unharmed. When she came to me—she was just as innocent—& just as rightminded—but there was a cloud over her spirit—she had never been sympathized with, or encouraged to trust in her own feelings;—& pain, embarrassment, & gloomy presentiments filled her being & imagination. Under the wing of friendship—she had put forth her beautiful nature & learned to trust herself—though indeed she ever must be peculiarly feminine. I do not know that she could stand alone—but at least she is now not dependent on circumstances—&

Heaven has given to her a steadfast friend. I am sure you will be interested & therefore I will not apologize for this narrative.

Ever yours
E. P. P.

TS copy, OYesA

A brief but powerful notice of the tension between the cultural ideal of womanhood, "the lady and the Christian," and Peabody's desire to nourish "a real legitimate independence."

✼ To Elizabeth Davis Bliss[1]

My dear Mrs Bliss—   Boston July 8th [1830]
    You asked me for the french of De Gerando's letters[2]—I doubt whether you will be able to make them out—but if you cannot—you can wait until I come out—which will be I think this week.—My friend Fanny Searle also wished to see them—
    I thought with some trouble of mind on some subjects with which I conversed with you.—I am no great philosopher—dear Mrs. B—though I do *smile* upon the vexations of life—And to be misunderstood is a great vexation. But I cannot consent to be coldhearted and selfish in order to be thought prudent—though I do think discretion is a beautiful quality. But there are satisfactions which we cannot sacrifice—for the speech of people who do not look beneath the surface & can only read *the large letters* (to use your own figure.)— I feel that I grow in independence.—I have suffered intensely from contact with society all my life—for I chose to keep myself *unsheathed*—through fear of being selfdeceived—and I would never consent to shield myself from suffering by any expedients I thought it was better to suffer it out—of all things not *to defy* the world—⟨and⟩ or to defend myself;—but when by the progress of the individual mind a real legitimate independence was acquired—to enjoy it.—I

1 Elizabeth Davis married Alexander Bliss in 1825. He died in 1827. In August 1838 she married George Bancroft, historian, Secretary of the Navy, and ambassador to England and Germany.
2 Peabody refers to the publication "this week" of her translation of Baron Joseph Marie de Gerando, *Self-Education: Or the Means and Art of Moral Progress* (Boston: Carter and Hendee, 1830).

cannot boast that this has come—perhaps it is too much to ask for it before the evening of life—but it is certainly *coming*—and though I cannot prevent the weak tears from falling when I feel that the beautiful ideal which is before me of the lady & the Christian does not shine forth to allure & to guide those I love & those it is my duty to guide—into the right path—yet I feel that I can rise over this weakness nothing doubting that the germ of that is within—& that *half* the difficulty at least is that *the eyes* which look are defective—or see through a false medium.

But I should do myself injustice were I to intimate that random remarks can ever call a tear.—No—their immediate effect is as small as it deserves to be—but when I think of the *suffering*—whose sufferings must be increased by the idea that these random remarks have some foundation—I am not so unmoved. I know that even this however is weak. I doubt that I am too anxious to have my sympathy felt.—Indeed indeed—it is not pleasure you will allow for me to think that Mr A— believes in me whom he must warn—when I feel that I should be considered a comforter—(if there *can* be one on earth)—were I known—But there may be some good end in it. Excuse this long letter—I am yours—truly—E. P. Peabody

There is one thing I said to you—which conveyed *more* than my words strictly expressed. I thought at the moment I would let it go.—But my conscience has troubled me ever since. What I told you I did not *do*[3]—I *had done*. Now pray do not *tell*[4]—for I *do not now*—the occasion having passed away. But you should not *all* but have *asked me*—dear Mrs. B—I do not think I ever had such a temptation to tell a lie—and in fact I yielded so far that it terrified me, for all but *told* one. Your sincere friend E. P. Peabody.

MS, DLC

3 "*Do*" is underlined three times.
4 "*Tell*" is underlined twice.

The influence of Channing and the memories of Elizabeth Peabody's first teaching post are described in this warm letter to Channing's wife Ruth.

✖ To Ruth Gibbs Channing

My dear Mrs. Channing,   Boston, August 31st [1830][1]
    I have two letters to send which I wrote in Brookline. The one to Mr. Channing is particularly dull—as usual;—but still there is some matter in it I wish to communicate, & so I will send it.—I began my school today with twenty five scholars full of spirit—and I feel as if I were going to be more successful than usual—but this feeling often comes upon me—& perhaps it is more brilliant than substantial. Yet it is one of my blessings—for unless I felt a new creation within now & then, I shall grow dispirited. I was heartily tired of vacation though I had a sweet visit in most beautiful Lancaster—where I feel as if I understood life and its purpose better than any where else.—I suppose it is, that I view it in the light of youth when energy and not despondency answered to every stroke upon the nervous system—when nearer "being's height" (as Wordsworth calls absolute Infancy,)[2] the widest cloud was yet skirted all round with light—the light that fills the eternal spaces beyond our immediate atmosphere. I wish it had in addition to its surpassing beauty, the air of Rhode Island—&· then I could almost hope the bright genius that inspires Mr. Channing would breathe upon me—for *I love* nature—I thought *better* than any one else—till I saw Mr. Channing last summer—but I must yield to him in sensibility.—
    I thought a great deal of you in Lancaster—as you were associated with my last enjoyment of the country—and many times I attempted to write—but when I came to put my thoughts on paper I found them unwrittenable—and in general I think that is the case with all

1 The year 1830 is derived from Peabody's reference to Lydia Sears's "new tie," her wedding in May 1830 to Haven.
2 Thou little Child, yet glorious in the might
    Of heaven-born freedom on thy Being's height,
    Why with such earnest pains doest thou provoke
    The years to bring the inevitable yoke,
    Thus blindly with thy blessedness at strife?
(William Wordsworth, "Ode: Intimations of Immortality," viii, lines 121–25.)

thoughts that are worth expressing. But *some* have the gift of tongues. I have it in a degree to communicate with my inferiors—but in the ratio of my desire to interest those who are above me—I feel my power of doing so fail.

The way that I am going to instruct in reading for the future—is to have the children every day select something to read at home—& read it in the morning—as well as they can. If they neglect to bring it in the morning [one word illegible]—the penalty must be to come in the afternoon & read it. I think this will give it an importance— and an interest—which is the main thing—in order to produce pleas- ant reading.—The spelling I shall attend to constantly & perhaps by these means I may myself learn how to read & pronounce my native tongue!

Last week I attended Commencement & William acquitted him- self beautifully. I do not know on what principle they gave him so low a part. He made it the first part decidedly, I think.—Storrow was tame. There was little brilliancy on the whole & very little absolutely uninteresting on the other hand.—Susan Channing does not speak audibly, & I believe there is a good deal of anxiety felt about her.—I have not seen her myself, since she returned from the island where she gained much—& enjoyed a great deal more—I understand.

The people have not done failing. The Leasly [?] failure inter- ested us the most—but they have escaped with honour & good name unscathed—& are going on. Tom was obliged to sell a perfect jewel of a library—most German books.

I have a class in Natural Science in School. I suppose Mary will want to join it. I am glad you are better. I hope you will be able this winter to peep into the School—I think you will find it improved.—

Did you hear Mr. S. Ward had shot off his hand? He was sporting on Phillips beach—his *life* has been despaired of—but he probably will recover now—since he has lived so long.[3]

I am glad to hear you are to return in October.—If you have de- cided which week—I beg you will let Molly send me word—for there

[3] The family of Samuel Ward, Sr., in New York City was probably the one known to both Peabody and the Channings. Ward's children included Julia, who later married Samuel Gridley Howe, the reformer and political activist, and Sam, who later became famous as an investor and philanthropist. Sam, who was seventeen in 1830, had returned home from Round Hill School in Northampton to attend Columbia, and would go to Europe in 1832 to pursue his education. Sam was just the kind of dashing and flamboyant figure to get into such mischief as Peabody here de- scribes; unfortunately, this appears to be just a rumor, since no such mishap befell Sam Ward.

is an event of no small importance to those concerning, waiting Mr. Channing's return. My little friend Lydia feels so sadly at leaving Mr. Channing's pastoral care—that it will require all the cheering influences of a blessing on the new tie—with his own voice—she says—to make her feel it *right*.

Yours affectionately E. P. PEABODY

MS, MH

Elizabeth Peabody instructs a young student in the real meaning of patriotic festivities.

✖ To Elizabeth Lee

[Boston]

My dear Elizabeth,   [1830]

I hope you did not quite forget,—in looking at the skyrockets,—the Catherine's wheel,—the procession, etc.—What was the event which was so carefully commemorated. I know there was nothing very appropriate in the commemoration. Except the flag on which was written 1630—there was nothing historical in the parade.—I think it would have been a good plan to have had some kind of a ceremony which would have impressed the memory—the emigration of the English Colony—

It was not the hundred and one Plymouth Pilgrims—you know,—It was a separate set of pilgrims—fifteen hundred in number—who with Mr. Winthrop as their head—& charter of privileges in their hands—& hearts full of religion & resolution—that came out to plant a separate colony from the Plymouth colony—namely a *Massachusetts Colony*.—They intended to find a place to settle in and call it Boston. But when they arrived at Salem which had been settled some years before, there was some difficulty about provisions, and they were hurried into setting down upon the peninsula between Charles and Mystick rivers—which had already been named Charlestown—There they remained some time—but the weather grew hot and the climate there seemed unhealthy;—besides they could not find any clear good water—(which is very curious for there is good water enough in Charlestown now.)—Therefore they began to think of removing. & in full sight of them on the other side of Charles River was this fine peninsula, called by the Indians Shawmut, & by themselves Trimountain[1]—(do you know why these names were given to the peninsula?—tell me in your letter)   There was not any settlement here then—but only one cottage on the west side where Mr. Blackstone lived[2]—& he considered himself the owner of the peninsula. The agreement was made with Mr. Johnson[3]—but on what terms is not now known. About three years afterwards (according to the records) a portion of land—fifty acres—was set off near his house—to belong to him and his heirs forever. Mr. Blackstone sold this however afterwards & removed to Providence. He was quite an independant man—and he would not join any of the churches. He said he left England because he would not submit to the Lord Bishops—& in America he did not intend to submit to the *Lord Brethren*. You can hardly take the wit of this perhaps, but you will understand it one of these days—

Your affectionate friend
E. P. PEABODY

MS, MNS

[1] Trimountain was the name originally given to the Boston area by Puritan settlers in 1630 before they renamed it Boston in honor of the English town of the same name.

[2] William Blackstone had already settled near Boston when John Winthrop's contingent arrived in 1630. Blackstone disliked the Puritans' self-righteous arrogance and ascetic discipline, and they disapproved of (and probably envied) his easy self-assurance and evident prosperity. He resettled in Rhode Island in 1634, to be followed shortly by Roger Williams and other dissidents from Massachusetts Bay.

[3] Edward Johnson was a New England official and historian, author of *Johnson's Wonder-Working Providence of Zion's Savior in New England* (1654).

Elizabeth Peabody's bruising encounter with "unmeasured evil" in the New Bedford experience left her exhausted but instructed, as she describes in this letter to Sarah Sullivan.

✖ To Sarah Russell Sullivan

My dearest Mrs. Sullivan   Boston March 18th 1831
    It went to my very heart to see your dear handwriting again. I assure you I should have written you often this winter if I had thought it would have been agreeable to you—but I knew you always knew

that I was ready—& Eliza or Sarah would say so—if they thought it was best.

It is true I have suffered deeply this winter[1]—but there is nothing sent on us by God—which has not—(if ever so dark)—a *glorious reverse*. *Theoretically* I had admitted the idea of evil which was all but infinite—& knew that Christianity outmeasured even this. But it has so happened that until now I never *saw the struggle*—for in the cases where there was this unmeasured evil—(& I *have* seen such—I *have* seen people in whom the whole moral being was touched with evil—in whom the moral life was absolutely extinguished for this world)—there has been no attempt at repentance.

But *repentance* has not been all that has consoled me this winter. Indeed *such consolation* would have well nigh overpowered poor human nature—since it is a great effort of mind to keep one's eye on the *result*—while imagination is outdone by the *spectacle of the suffering process*. *But*[2] I have seen *virtue*—unsullied—unfailing—triumphant—which would have convinced me of immorality & Christianity & a God—had I never known it before. When you return, my dear friend (with the flowers & sunshine of June, as you intimate that you may—) you will be able to listen perhaps to some things I can tell you—which will make you understand what I mean—when I tell you—that I have had much to enjoy—this winter—much to confirm my faith in the real existence of moral truth & beauty embodied. I do not mean to imply that I have had only *one* such picture to look at. I have seen a *great deal* of noble—pure—& elevated character which has made me think better of my species—but there has been one picture which is a study for an angel—& of which one of the witnesses not exaggeratedly said "it requires the pen of a seraph to do it justice"—& yet all this is so simple & natural that you only wonder all the world is not *just so*—so *humble & self-watching* you feel it would be cruelty to *express admiration* even if you did not before feel it were profanation to *admire*.

But *words* do not give ideas—I wonder that I use them—on such a subject.

I thank you for your 'lecture' as you call it. It would prove me

---

[1] "I have suffered deeply this winter" refers to the New Bedford affair, Peabody's attempt during the winter of 1830–31 to intervene in the financial affairs of several of her pupils and their families. She alienated several of her friends, including, for a time, Mrs. Sullivan, although this letter suggests that that relationship had mended.

[2] "*But*" is underlined twice in the text.

needing one if I said I did not need it. I have been & am aware of these dangers—& I have endeavoured to watch over my mind & keep it natural—under the effect of such uncommon circumstances. And I do not see that I have less sensibility to the *little affairs* of other people—& is not *a gain* that my *own personal trials* have faded away & it seems to me I shall not be liable to have my heart sink at the loss of a smile that I expected—& that conscious of possessing the will to do right I feel I shall not agonize so much in the future as I have done in the past for mistakes & wrongdoing which perhaps had their *origin* in a *too troubled spirit*. I have less animal spirits but nature demands something—in compensation for so great gifts to the intellectual & spiritual man. I take all measures which seem to me proper for having happy & innocent sensations of pleasure—& never felt more interested—nay *so much* interested in every detail of my school. I have had a little class of fine girls just beginning to form their views of life—to read & lecture to—& they have been as gay as larks under my instruction—& does not this tell well for me?—& if I do not lose my sympathy with the young—the innocent—the good—& the happy—have I not a right—that is—may I not think it right & innocent—nay even my duty save it is the *deep—deep* impulse—I might almost say *necessity* of my nature—to weep & pray for the guilty—in the hours of solitude & silent watching—that he may not fail in what I believe his sincere purpose. [Eleven lines crossed out.]

You will excuse this great blot—but I have scratched it out because it is not well to dwell on this painful subject. [Eight lines crossed out.]

Where are you going?—& shall I write to you? I trust to have much to say of a general nature—for my thoughts seem to have broken through all the bounds of time—& circumstance. I will tell you of a book if you are well enough to read French which will interest you deeply—Benjamin Constant's History of Religion.[3] Dr. Follen has quoted from it in his lectures—& said every body ought to read it—& Mr. Channing used to read me passages out of it of surpassing interest & eloquence. I have had one long sweet letter from him this winter.

My sister Sophia has been well enough to paint—& we have all been *transferring* this winter—but for a week or two she has sunk entirely—though her picture (the second one she has attempted) is but half done. She revived at the flowers as usual—& is still as bright

3 Benjamin Constant, *De la religion considérée dans sa source, ses formes et ses developpment* (1824–31).

& cheerful & happy as ever. I have been very egotistical but I wished that you should go away with the recollection of me as *quiet & happy*— even tho' clouds are about me.

I still have some of my letters which I find I did not return to you that contain some of the best recollections—but they had better rest here till you return.[4]

I wish you would lend me while you are gone those or *that* extract book you once lent me—containing extracts from Jeremy Taylor,[5] Fenelon, Miss Lowell,[6] Dr. Channing, and others?

Very affectionately yours

E.P.P.

TS copy, OYesA

[4] Peabody may be referring here to recollections of the Sullivans' daughter Mary, who was a pupil of Peabody's and who, as this letter suggests, had died the previous winter.

[5] Jeremy Taylor was a seventeenth-century Anglican clergyman known for his eloquent and imaginative preaching.

[6] Rebecca Amory Lowell, daughter of John and Rebecca Lowell, known in her family as Amory, was a favorite cousin of the poet James Russell Lowell.

✀ To Dorothea Dix

Boston,

8 August 1831

My dear Miss Dix,—

I was very sorry to hear from the [Misses?] Swains that you were not well—but glad again to hear that you were as well as usual.—by Charles' letter to Miss Loring.—I write now in behalf of another friend—a mutual friend—Mrs. Rice.—You know perhaps something of her daughter Anna—& that most unhappy *Set of nerves* on which she is *suspended*—and the unfortunate state of mental and perhaps I may add moral weakness—which has resulted—partly however from injudicious treatment.—Mr. Emerson has advised her to leave school— & to suspend all study.—It is difficult to know what to do with her. But it is felt that if you will let her come & stay with you the rest of your time on the island (—it will be at least six weeks will it not) and, will give her any thing to do which you think proper—or *nothing* if you think proper keeping her under your influence & having in view to help her character—& communicate to it some of your characteristic selfreliance & energy—it would prepare the way for her continuing at your school—after your return to Boston to her great advantage.

I am very anxious you should undertake this—for Ann's sake.—It seems to me that the girl will be *utterly ruined*—become dissarayed or imbecile—unless she finds an anchor for her soul—At present—she does not say—nay—dares not *feel* that her Soul is her own.—Were it possible for me to take her—that is—in the first place—would they think it worth while—I am sure I could do something for her.—But as a *day scholar* without some previous tutoring—I feel I could do nothing for her—& even if I felt otherwise—of course *I* could not propose *myself*— I spent yesterday with Mrs. Rice—& she thought it would be the *greatest blessing* if you would take her. And she asked me to write you.—The plan is for her to be subjected entirely to your discretion—& if you conclude to take her—I wish you would answer me *immediately*—so that Mrs. Rice may know by Saturday.—I will then write you all my ideas about her from my observations during [illegible] years & it will help you with those you have yourself made—to understand the difficulties—& remedy them.

And now to fly to another piece of business. My friend Miss Lewis that was (who married Mr. Joseph Williams of Lancaster—a very aggreeable sensible gentleman whom I have long known—wishes to take one or two boarders—She asked me if I knew of any body—& I told her of *the Benjamins* and they wish to go to her—and she thinks of taking a house.—Well yesterday I heard Mrs. Hathorne was going to leave your Grandmother's house & that another person was wanted there—immediately thought—that it would be pleasant for my friends to take that house & have your Grandmother for their boarder than any thing else. But before I proposed it to them—I thought I would ask you—as you probably know all about it.—I do not know what is the rent of the house. If it is high—your grandmother's board would not be sufficient perhaps—& they could have the Benjamins beside—But Mr. & Mrs. W do not wish to keep a *boarding house strictly* so called—but to have one or two boarders—*who desire a private boarding place*—

Will you drop me a line by the mail—& with love to the several Miss. Swain whom I hope you see often—and to my friend Molly—need I say to the *beloved & revered*—her parents—believe me very affectionately yours—

E. P. Peabody

This letter is not for Mrs. Rice's eyes of course—and Mrs. Williams does not know of it but the latter asked me to do what I could for her—& I know believes that I will

MS, MH

Samuel Foster Haven's jealousy of his wife's relationship with her old teacher is the subject of Elizabeth Peabody's postscript to a letter written by Mary Peabody.

❧ To Lydia Sears Haven

October 23, 1832

My dear Lyd—Mary has left me some paper which I improve though I wrote so lately. The truth is that I am determined if possible not to get out of the habit of communicating with you—now that I have *proved* I *think* to your gude man by my long cessation of intercourse—that it is no part of my plan of loving—to endeavour to *govern* my scholars—especially when they are married. The truth is—my darling—I love you too truly—too *purely*—to express any particular jealousy of Sam's opinion of me. I *know* that there *are* such things as love of power which does not respect any *relations of life* & therefore he may have felt a little (which I fancied or thought I saw that he did) that I would be liable to abuse your affection for me but there are exceptions to all that dishonour human nature, though the dishonour be ever so common. And I believe that I do not deceive myself when I think I *am one* in this respect at least,—and I think that by this time he does feel *convinced* that I am not *disposed* to endeavour to 'work you up to *any* thing' even if it were in my power.

MS, NN-B

Peabody's postscript to her sister Mary's letter of November 8–11, 1832 comments on the death of Caspar Spurzheim on November 11.[1] Her advice is directed, it appears, at her student, whose health was already in decline.

To Lydia Sears Haven

November 8–11, 1832

My dear Lyd—I have nothing to add—but yet feel a desire to communicate—I have of course nothing to say about Dr. Spurzheim's death—as it was the will of God—& *as far* as it was. That it was in a degree the consequences of his own *enthusiasm*—is to me exquisitely painful for that was a neglect of duty & the only kind of wrong. One so good had a temptation to do—but though so wise he was but a man—& has paid a bitter penalty—for he did not wish to die away from his home—& has left a great work unfinished (if phrenology is true)—which no one can take up where he left it—If his death but teaches us the duty of taking care of our health conscientiously—he may be consoled in heaven for what else is left undone.

MS, NN-B

1 Johann Caspar Spurzheim was a student of Franz-Joseph Gall, the originator of phrenology. After Gall was banned from lecturing about his new approach in Vienna in 1802, he and Spurzheim lectured throughout Europe. In 1832, Spurzheim came to the United States. In 1862 Nathaniel Bowditch recalled that "the course of lectures was attended by a more brilliant company than have listened here to any other lecturer upon any subject whatever" (Bowditch quoted in Gilbert Seldes, *The Stammering Century* [1928; reprint, New York: Harper & Row, 1965], 307).

Peabody provides a description of her historical conversation on Greek history and art.

To Sarah Hale[1]

My dear Mrs. Hale— [April 1833][2]

I have had this winter a reading party—to meet twice a week—which is half a school—and in which I undertook to read all the

1 Sarah Preston Everett Hale was the sister of Edward Everett and wife of journalist and editor Nathan Hale.

2 "April 1833" is written at the top of the MS in another hand.

beautiful things I could find about Greek literature & antiquities and especially Greek art—& have read the translations of Eschylus—& Sophocles—&c—We have been lamenting that we could not have heard Mr. E. Everett's lectures of olden time[3]—& at last the daring thought took flight—that perhaps you could graciously lend them to us—provided [MS torn] would be very freemasonryish.

Something has been already said to him by one of my party—but he did not accede quite—yet I thought from what was said that had *you* been the requestor—it would have presented itself a little differently.—I know it is a great favour to ask—but it is not an *unheard of* impertinence—for I once belonged to a secret little party—to whom Mr. Ticknor lent *his lectures*—[4]

Yours truly with respect
ELIZ. P. PEABODY

P.S.—I have—dear Mrs. Hale—concluded to *give up* in regard to my price—& take children under ten years of age for fifteen dollars (but they must know how to read)—& those over ten years of age for twenty—will not [they do better?]—Please let one of the children take this note to Mr Emerson when they next go—

MS, MNS

3 Peabody refers to Edward Everett's Boston public lecture "Antiquities," delivered December 26, 1822. Everett was one of the most prominent figures of the nineteenth century. A Unitarian minister, scholar, politician, and preeminent orator, Everett completed his M.A. at Harvard Divinity School and was installed as pastor at the Brattle Street Church when he was not yet twenty years old. From there, less than a year later, he became professor of Greek literature at Harvard College. His further studies earned him the first Ph.D. granted to an American; his was from Göttingen University in 1817. Everett's professional duties sharpened his oratorical skill, and he became a public and political figure. He served as Congressman from Middlesex from 1825 to 1835.

In 1841 Everett became Ambassador to the Court of St. James's, and served briefly as Secretary of State. His instinct during the years of sectional tension was toward compromise and conservatism; he deprecated the agitation of the slavery question. When war broke out, however, he used his oratorical gifts for the Union cause. His most famous address was the two-hour speech at the dedication of the national cemetery at Gettysburg on November 19, 1863. His speech, however, has been overshadowed in reputation by Lincoln's two-minute "Gettysburg Address." Exhausted by a strenuous round of speech-making, Everett died on January 15, 1865.

4 For Peabody's knowledge of Ticknor's lectures, see her letter to Maria Chase, June 12, 1822.

A fuller account of Peabody's historical seminar, detailing costs and curriculum.

✄ To Maria Chase

My dear Maria,—   [April 1833][1]
        You know what I said to you when I was in Salem about a class
there for history and literature—on the plan of my Boston class.—I
desire very much to go to Salem in May to stay three months with
Mother in her *bereavement*[2]—and have been thinking quite seriously
of doing something about it. I have had quite an agreeable encouragement here lately, which is the spontaneous forming of a class that will
last just till the first of May.—Some ladies—six married ones! & fourteen unmarried—most intelligent & well informed ladies—made a
party supplying themselves with tickets of admission at a certain fee—
& proposing to me to read to them any regular course I might choose—
historical or literary. They meet the alternate days with my other historical school.—We employed six days in reading various beautiful
things about ⟨Plato⟩ Socrates—including some manuscript translations
I have of Plato—& now we are reading Herder on the Spirit of Hebrew
Poetry—which is an exquisite book.[3]—
        The plan I propose for Salem—is—to have the admission tickets
$5 My historical school in Boston is $10—a piece;—to meet three times
a week at the hour agreed upon as most convenient; to remain as long
as they think they can bear—i.e. from 1½ to 3 hours—(My classes here
are for two hours—the ladies generally stay longer—one day we read
& talked for three hours).—The course to be—Some articles on the
Poetry &c of the Heroic ages from several sources; Herodotus' History;—Schlegel on Dramatic Literature[4] as far as it is applicable to

        1 In her [April 1833] letter to Sarah Hale, Peabody refers to her "reading party"
that is studying Greek literature and art. This letter to Maria Chase cannot be later
than May since Peabody says her class will end the first of May.
        2 This reference is unclear. It could be that Mrs. Peabody grieved over the de-
parture of all her children from the parental home. *See* Mrs. Elizabeth Peabody, Journal, 5 July 1832, MS, MHi.
        3 Johann Gottfied von Herder, *The Spirit of Hebrew Poetry*, 2 vols., trans.
James Marsh (Burlington: Edward Smith, 1833). First published in *Biblical Reposi-
tory* 2 (1826): 327–47, 506–45; 3: 429–44.
        4 Probably August Wilhelm von Schlegel, *Über dramatische Kunst und Littera-
tur*, 1809–11.

Greece; & the times of Socrates.—We can accomplish this I think in three months if we meet regularly.—Another course which would be very interesting would be—Herder's exquisite book on the "Spirit of Hebrew Poetry"—Parts of Michaelis upon the Jewish law[5]—The old Testament history—and I had thought it possible there might be a separate class for this course at a dollar a ticket to meet once a week— Many would be interested in *that*—that would not be in Grecian Literature—& vice versa.

You can show this to Mary White and ask her about it—for it is not worth while for me to write another letter. She is to be out of town all summer I know—still it may be in her power to help it on— by speaking of the plan at the Dorcas Society & at other places. Of course I would have nobody *urged* to join it—but some may *desire* to—of their own accord—as it certainly would be a great intellectual pleasure to go through these books. Dr. Channing thinks it is important for ladies to do such things—He rejoiced greatly at the formation of my second reading party—and said he wondered how women ever got the notion that there was a period when intellectual cultivation on a regular system was to be laid aside—he was sure it was peculiar to them—for men never thought so—even though they considered themselves as the stronger minds—

For Mary White's satisfaction I will tell the names of my 2nd reading party—Mrs. Bliss, Mrs Fleming, Mrs Wendall Davis, Mrs. Train, Mrs. J. K. Mills, Mrs. John A Lowell, the two Miss Lowells (John)—two Miss Russells (N. P.), two Miss Sturgises (Wm), two Miss Benjamins, Miss Codman, Miss E. Davis, Miss Hayward, Miss Goddard, Miss Belknap.[6]—This is independent of the historical school which goes on with diminished numbers, however.

It seems to me the scientific—Lyceum-going town of Salem might furnish out these two classes in moderate numbers—when *that* closes?

But goodbye—Thine am I— E.P.P.

P.S. I have been a little *worried* at your not answering my last letter Why did you not—dear?—Was it wrong?

MS, MNS

[5] Johann David Michaelis was a Christian orientalist and author of early critical treatments of Jewish history, including *Das Mosaische Recht,* 1770–75.

[6] Among the members of this reading party were Mrs. Elizabeth Davis Bliss, Mrs. John A. Lowell (wife of John Lowell, a politician and writer), her daughters Rebecca Amory and Anna Cabot Lowell, and Ellen and Caroline Sturgis, both Transcendental poets.

*Peabody's efforts as a teacher of history led her to write her own text-
books and to plan an accompanying book of illustrations.*

✖ To Sarah Hale

My dear Mrs. Hale   [May 15, 1833]
    The plan of my book of illustrations is this: as my key to History[1]
will lead my students over Hesiod—Homer—The Tragedians and
Pindar—preparatory to their reading the political history—I intend
to have the illustrations of Flaxman[2]—lithographed—and wish to add
to them any outlines that I can procure of ancient statuary—basre-
liefs &c—illustrating Ancient Story—historical and mythological—My
question is—is there any work of this kind already in existence—Mr.
Ticknor mentioned Visconti's Iconography[3]—but he does not own it—
and it is not in the Atheneum or College library—He also mentioned
a German book of *Hirt* on archeology &c[4]—Perhaps Mr. Everett has
one or both of these—or perhaps he could tell me of some other books
which I could procure. I can have any thing copied on stone & beautifully too by my sister Sophia—
    I have seen the Elgin marbles in outlines—Have they ever been
done—with *restorations*—do you know?—
    My object is solely Grecian—& not Roman mythology & history—
I should like to have the stories of Pindar illustrated and the tragedies
of Sophocles—& any beautiful *gems*—I should put in besides—but I
know where I can procure Dagley's gems[5]—Perhaps Mr. Everett knows
of some others—And, will you ask him if there is an English translation of the orphic hymns—of the hymns of Callimachus[6]—Here is a
quantity of *requests*—but if I succeed in ever getting my book done
according to my plan—I do trust there will not be such ignorance
prevailing among the young damsels—as that they shall be driven like

1 *Key to History: Part I, First Steps in the Study of History* (Boston: Hilliard,
Gray, 1832).
    2 John Flaxman was an English sculptor and illustrator, known for his illus-
trations of the *Iliad* and *Odyssey* (1793) and of the *Divine Comedy* (1802).
    3 Ennio Quirino Visconti, *Iconografia Greca* (1823–25).
    4 Possibly Aloys Ludwig Hirt, *Bilderbuch für Mythologie, Archeologie und
Kunst* (1805–16).
    5 Richard Dagley, *Gems, Principally from the Antique, Drawn and Etched by
Richard Dagley* (1822).
    6 Callimachus was a Greek sculptor of the late fifth century B.C. He is tradition-
ally credited with the invention of the Corinthian capital.

me to torment such good friends as you—and gentlemen that they do not know—besides—with the questions of *helpless ignorance.*

Yours with regards as ever
& gratitude
E. P. PEABODY

May 16th [1833?][7]

I found that edition of Flaxman sold for *68 dollars—today!* My illustrations will not cost a third as much—& should you not think therefore that I might easily get a subscription for it?—

MS, MNS

7 "1833?" is written here in another hand.

Another example of Peabody's voluminous correspondence with Horace Mann; here she attempts to rouse him from his grief over the death of his first wife Charlotte by reminding him of his civic responsibilities.

✄ To Horace Mann

Dear friend—   [August 1833][1]

I believe you went away a little displeased. Something was wounded in the idea perhaps that anybody speculated upon your whereabouts, as if it were impertinent, indelicate, or something.[2]

But I could not pardon myself to let such a false delusion exist for a moment. You entirely and wholly misapprehended the whole form and substance of the feeling which has led your friends to remark to each other upon the circumstances with which you have chosen to surround yourself.

1 Horace Mann was raised in a strenuously Calvinist family under the spiritual direction of "new divinity" advocate Nathaniel Emmons. Graduating from Brown University in 1819, Mann entered Tapping Reeve's law school in Litchfield, Connecticut, the following year. In the late 1820s, Mann practiced law for several important businesses and rose rapidly in his profession. He married Charlotte Messer in September 1830, despite her declining health from tuberculosis. Less than two years later, in August 1832, she died, plunging Mann into a grief that Elizabeth Peabody was powerless to counteract. As an antidote to grief, Mann reluctantly entered politics, and was elected to the Massachusetts State Senate in 1835. In 1837, he became

Let me tell you then that at the time you went to Madame C[larke]'s there was a feeling among your *gentlemen friends* universally, that there was *no hope* of your improvement in health or spirits any more. I heard a great many things through the Clarkes and Helen Loring, which the Curtis and Loring gentlemen said   At that time, they considered that you were wrapping yourself up in despair and courting death, as it was lamentable beyond expression that any one should do, who was so signally gifted to benefit others. I remember too how J. Willard's countenance fell when he found you had gone and how strongly he expressed himself in regret.[3] *Many other gentlemen* whom I happened to hear considered it as a sort of death warrant. When Mr. Mills first spoke of it to me, he seemed to think there never was anything so dismal.[4] The idea of all seemed to be that a more cheerful and cheering place of abode *was necessary* to the health of one whose want of health sprung chiefly from an ever present sense of

---

Secretary of the Massachusetts Board of Education, and traveled the stae working for free public education. Mann married Mary Peabody in 1843 and continued his studies and reports on education, but in 1848 turned again to politics, serving in the U.S. House of Representatives until 1852. In that year he agreed to become the first president of the new Antioch College. Mann died in Yellow Springs, Ohio, in 1859.

After Charlotte Mann's death on August 1, 1832, Mann's friends tried to help him reconstruct his life. Edward Loring, Mann's classmate in Litchfield, suggested that he move to Boston from Dedham, form a partnership with his cousin Charles Loring, and board there as well. Instead, Mann moved into the boardinghouse of Mrs. Rebecca Clarke on Somerset Place. As the first anniversary of Charlotte's death approached, Mann grew more and more moody, abandoned the boardinghouse, and moved his living quarters to his office on the third floor of a building at 4 Court Street.

2 At Mrs. Clarke's boardinghouse, Mann increasingly confided in Elizabeth and Mary Peabody, who became, as Jonathan Messerli puts it, "the self-appointed custodians of his welfare" (Messerli, *Horace Mann*, 167). His abrupt departure from Somerset Place made the sisters feel they had offended him, but Mann wrote to assure them that this was not the case. "The change I contemplate has had no connection with the causes you suggest. To part with my friends (if I may call them so) at the house, was long an insuperable obstacle to the adoption of another mode of living. When I first went to the house where we are, I had hopes, that the intellectual and refined society of its inmates would do something towards filling up the void in my life. But . . . I only found so much of that which I mourned, as to be a perpetual remembrance of it. . . . At this time, too, the anniversary of that fatal day, when all the foundations of earthly happiness sunk beneath me, was approaching and drawing me into its vortex, I will not attempt to describe to you the power of imagination where memory supplied it wtih such materials, I saw the necessity of effort; and in the hope of being able to break the spell that bound me, I resolved upon the proposed change" ([1833]; MS, MHi).

3 Joseph Willard was a lawyer and historian, and an incorporator of the New England Historic Genealogical Society.

4 James K. Mills was a Boston businessman and supporter of public schools.

bereavement and calamity. It was not that you might not have everything which *money could buy*, there, but that there were to be expected but "cold charities" there, and you needed the constant appliance of cheerful, social intercourse.

I did not entirely sympathize with all this. I had seen so much of
your suffering from the accidents of common discourse. I had so often
felt that even friendship and an unforgetting sympathy were not sufficient defenses against such accidents, and I have so much confidence
in one's own *instinct* that I felt entirely that it was worth the experiment. And I felt too that outward appliances were but of little consequence, that comfort or even tranquil endurance and especially a
lively resignation and a *acceptance of life again* must come from
something further inward. I think *much* of the good influence of solitude, when there is sufficient health for health of mind. But I believe
I am the only one of your friends who have *really acquiesced* in your
living as you do. Even Mr. H. Lee[5] whose interest in you (until within
six weeks) was *altogether* his interest in the good of society has frequently expressed the greatest regret that you should give yourself as
he said "so little chance to get better of grief." And he must have
learnt the circumstances and taken the impression from some one—it
was certainly not from *me*.

Nor do I think one particle of all this feeling and expression had
a cast of impertinence or meddling spirit in it. With your most intimate friends, it was the most affectionate friendship joined with (what
it was *purely* in many to whom I refer) *public spirit*. I never heard
you mentioned for your private value alone, even by those who feel it
most, but because you have a head and heart such as may not be
replaced—*for society*. I speak of a simple matter of fact, and can even
you be insensible to such kind of appreciation? If it cannot make life
valuable, does it not make it a little more *tolerable*? And supposing
it to be the unexaggerated truth—as it appears to *us*, for I will include myself—can you be *hurt* or *feel annoyed* at this *anxiety*?

No one, however, would presume to interfere with your arrangements. No one probably has. But now you have been sick, and this
seemed to bring out a new expression of the feeling. Each one seemed
to think the other might have influenced to draw you from your
solitude, to save you in some degree from the action of overhanging

---

[5] Henry Lee was a Boston merchant, scholar, and advocate of free trade. Willard,
Mills, and Lee were Boston acquaintances of Mann's, much interested, as Peabody
suggested, in his mental and emotional recovery from the death of his wife.

calamity, and to feed this valuable life whose mainspring is in the cheerful heart. Not a word has been said, not an idea has been suggested that the most irritable pride or the most lofty spirit could be touched by. I do no more than justice to your friends when I say that *not one* seems ever to have conceived himself to be in any relation *to you* (whatever might be accepted) save that of the *obliged party*. Nor would any spectator, therefore, conceive of it in any other way. The only idea is, can this precious life be preserved for *general interests* which are suffering for those who can comprehend them. And even if it cannot, can we catch some of the elixir while it is exhaling for our own heart treasury? If *the former* is enthusiasm, it is shared by many not deemed enthusiastic generally; if it is benevolence, who is the object of it—certainly not yourself? *And as to the latter feeling,* it cannot be helped while human hearts are what they are, precious gifts of the Giver of all good, by whose transmuting power the very voice of virtuous suffering becomes something inexpressibly dearer than pleasure. There is one simple sentence—"We do not know ourselves, Miss Peabody, till we have been tried," one of the first on which I heard your voice falter, whose cadence woke me up for months at a certain hour of the night (as well as coming often in the day) and claimed the tears your presence always sends back to my heart, which I would not *give up,* I don't know why. But you understand or at least have perceived and cannot, will not deny any of the mysteries of feeling. We would not have our friends sick or in suffering in order to express our affection. But when *it is so,* there is a blessing to the heart received. There are therefore two aspects in which the same things are to be looked at as they come from *friends* or the *indifferent,* and they are to be answered accordingly. What may be deemed due to selfrespect with the latter would be cruel to the former. Then it becomes generosity to surrender one's self to friends and to let them take the place of that instinct of self-preservation which calamity deadens. The most careful friendship may not accomplish the desired end, but what consolation there is over the grave of ill-spared excellence to feel that all that human strength and attention could do was done. Then the event is *only* God's, and must be right.

Do not think, however, that I love you so little as to wish for a second that you should live for the purpose of giving my heart food for its immortalizing powers. I *know* it is *for my race* only that I feel a pang at the thought of your leaving it. But *while you live,* I would fain have my little share of all those tones that come up from the deep unfathomable sea, which suffering alone moves *deepest* on earth, but which heaven's happiness alone can sound. How deep will that happiness be which goes deeper than sorrow! It will discover and open out new regions of being! It will awaken tones that shall in their turn awaken emotions "too deep for tears."

And how will that happiness first come upon you? While affectionate friendship watches over the death-dimmed eye and listens with craving heart for the last tones of the beloved voice *to treasure up*—there shall steal over the fleeting spirit "the voice sweeter than all the harmonies of nature" and "sober certainty of waking bliss" will possess and heal you wholly, and *we* shall not therefore entirely grieve.

I have written this not to urge you farther on the point which I have it yet in my heart to drive for, Mr. M—, but because I would defend myself and others to whom I have alluded from your displeasure and misapprehension. When your own want of "self-esteem" involves the natural expressions of your friends' affection in a cloud, it is *a defect*! It is necessary, if Lavater's aphorism is adopted at all, that it should be *all round,* and indeed it is a better rule than to "treat your friend as if he were to become an enemy tomorrow."—

"Your best friend must needs be better than you know"
Morning—Two vessels from Havanna! this morning. I shall surely have letters.

TS copy, OYesA

In a dream the night before, Peabody reports, she attained what has been missing so far in her relationship with Mann: complete honesty and a genuine sense of communion. She traces this dream to her viewing of a statue of Horatio Greenough's representing Love.

✷ To Horace Mann

My dear Sir,—   Friday night, 12 o'clock [1833]
    I have promised my children here that I will take them to the Blind Asylum, and now I understand tickets must be procured from the trustees, and I wish that within a week, if it lies in the way of any of your walks, you would procure them for me.[1] I have intended to ask

1 In March 1830, Massachusetts governor Levi Lincoln appointed Mann to be head of a commission to oversee the construction of an asylum for the mentally ill and

you the two last times I saw you, but forgot it, and shall next time doubtless, and so I write.

I have Miss Edgeworth's *new novel, "Helen"*.[2] It was given to me for my sister M—but I do not yet know of an opportunity to send it. Should you not like to read it? If so, do send your little boy for it. It is, I think, a noble book, for it breathes a high generous spirit, tho' its scene is laid in that English society which seems to me the very *barbarism* of civilization. There are very beautiful characters in it, and the story has a powerful dramatic interest which grows very strong in the second volume. I think it would *rest* you from your labours to get interested in it. I hope I shall have my visit from you on Sunday evening, though I fear I did not entertain you much last Sunday evening. But *it seems to me* as if I had about got thro' with my egotism now, though I begin to doubt appearances in that particular, for

> In the lowest deep—a lower deep
> Still yawning to devour me
> Opens wide.[3]

I still and constantly find myself useful—what can reasonable woman ask beside? But I do get *so tired,* before that part of the day comes in which I have a second at my command, that many a thought dies unwritten, with which my Molly[4]—and also yourself—might be *edified,* or which you might *suffer* (as the case may be). I hope and trust you have not been so *tired* this week, as you have been in those previous. It is certainly one of the mysteries that you should be thus tried with hard work beyond your strength, and so made intensely conscious of this weary world, that it is so desirable you should forget, altogether.

But I am too weary tonight to say a great many things which I

---

in mid-1833 appointed him a trustee of the New England Institution for the Education of the Blind. In a letter to Mann, the director of the institute, Dr. Samuel Gridley Howe, referred to a visit Mann made, accompanied by Mary and Elizabeth Peabody (4 October 1833; ME, MHi).

2 Maria Edgeworth, *Helen, A Tale* (1834).

3 Me miserable! Which way shall I fly
  Infinite wrath, and infinite despair?
  Which way I fly is Hell; myself am Hell;
  And in the lowest deep a lower deep
  Still threatening to devour me opens wide,
  To which the Hell I suffer seems a Heaven.
Milton, *Paradise Lost,* book 4, lines 73–78.

4 Molly was a frequently used nickname for Mary Peabody.

have thought, my dear friend, since I received your last note. You ask much, in asking to be *as conscious* of the heavenly world, and what passes there, as of this. Yet it is true that you have many facilities that few possess on this height and far flight, for you have given all your soul to one of its inhabitants, and that for *such reasons* as must make it a cherished duty of the purified spirit to watch over your heavy struggle with life. Last night I dreamed of having a long talk with you. We were speaking, I thought, on this very subject, and as I often do in my *day* dreams, I said every thing I thought in the happiest manner; and you were drawn into the freest communication and told me many circumstances which has especially aggravated the calamity from which you were suffering, and seemed to be relieved by having told them and by what I said, and by the thoughts that arose in consequence in your own mind. I felt a severe disappointment when I awoke and felt it was all a dream, and that the calm, sweet and far searching look with which you had said some things had not yet come up from your troubled heart.

I could trace my dream to a visit I had made to Greenough's last work which is a bust representing Love, and to my eye infinitely beyond any of his other works.[5] No *earthly* passion mingles with the expression and yet it is *human* not as we are accustomed to fancy the angelic (which, by the way, is hardly *above* humanity but *below* or *wide off*). Its calmness shows that not a discord is in all the far chords of its soul, and that *that* is the reason why it is calm. The repose is not the repose of indolence, for the thought that is present evidently stretches to the farthest bound of existence and *makes it near*. The soul is gone forth to embrace its object, with such complete self-forgetfulness that you feel that long ages might intervene before it can make the circuit and get back to itself, and with such complete power that there is no *sense of reaching or of want, for it has succeeded already and forever*. It is human nature in its divinest form,

---

[5] Horatio Greenough was the first American to become a professional sculptor. His reflections on the organic nature of art made him an acquaintance of several of the literary Transcendentalists, most notably Emerson. Greenough's most famous work is the controversial statue of George Washington. In a letter from Greenough to Robert Gilmor dated February 25, 1829 the sculptor wrote, "I was induced by several considerations to make some stay in Carrara—I had several busts to execute." The editor of the Greenough letters, Nathalia Wright, comments that these included busts of Josiah Quincy, John Adams, John Quincy Adams, Mrs. Gilmor, "and possibly the ideal 'Genius of Love' and portraits of Washington, John Marshall, and Andrews Norton" (Nathalia Wright, ed., *Letters of Horatio Greenough, American Sculptor* ([Madison: University of Wisconsin Press, 1972], 24, 26).

where nothing human is lost but all is *consecrated* forever. Some one present said it should be called Piety, not Love. There certainly could be no happier representation of Piety, unless indeed the sentiment which was raising the soul to the contemplation of a higher nature would necessarily have an expression of awe in it, and rapurous adoration. *This* expresses the perfect comprehension of a kindred nature, and entirely satisfactorily moral, intellectual and social companionship, where there was perfect self-respect to start from. The soul has gone forth as completely as in worship, but it is in companionship only, yet such *sacred* companionship as probably there is not, actually developed, this side of heaven. I thought of you, and wondered if I should ever be so blest as to see that expression mingle with yours, as it might, were all *circumstantial associations* removed. I then thought of that other, *the complement of your being* (as you once called her), and felt, **Even** so might she look, from her pure abode, upon her beloved husband, bereft though he be of every form of happiness but *virtue,* that only form of if which bears the tests of celestial vision! With that same still, serious, yet deeply founded serenity of look may she look *through* the agony of his nerves, to the unconquered unconquerable sweetness of spirit that never ceased to flow forth wherever there is pain to be relieved, or want mental or physical to be supplied. *So* sublimely acquiescent *her* far reaching spirit grasps the yet unattained good of a reciprocally conscious presence. Could *you* realize this, would not a kindred calm spread over these long tried nerves, from the consoled and tranquillized spirit? My thoughts did not get so far at that time, but when I was asleep, and free from all circumstantial associations, they went even so far, and hence my dream.

As ever, yours

E.P.P.

TS copy, OYesA

This highly charged account of a conversation between Mann and Peabody on their familiar topic of his inability to feel consolation for his grief is part of Peabody's "Cuba Journal."

✎ To Mary Peabody   *(excerpt)*

December 21, 1833

But I promised to write about Mr. M— which is the most interesting thing I have to say. Last Saturday night I told you he came for the first time after you went away, for there was a *tremendous* storm the Sunday after you went away when he intended to come and then I was obliged to write him a little note and tell him not to come till Saturday, for I had engaged myself for every evening, expecting to be sure to see him either on the Friday, Saturday or Sunday night after you went. Well, I *expected* him until a *quarter of nine* and then gave him up, horribly disappointed, and then most unexpectedly he came and said he had been very busy, and was going to Dedham the next week to advocate ten causes. I made a violent effort not to seem disappointed at not seeing him before and at seeing him so late, but so I rather overshot my mark, and I do not know what I should have done but for the quietus of the knitting work. However, I had a pretty pleasant time for about three quarters of an hour, telling him things and answering his questions, and showing him the profile which seemed to amuse him exceedingly, and whose expression puzzled him, he said, for he could not catch its meaning, and he declared Sophia had given him a great deal more expression than he had. We **found** the shape of the head wrong on the back of it, and the coat and the neck were not right. After this was over, I read him Ann Mason's message and we talked a little about her, and he asked me why I had not written to him so long. I told him I had several times—but had burned my letters, because they were rather reliefs to myself than any thing that would be interesting in themselves and the end was accomplished in their being written. He said, I am sorry you did not send them, for I have needed them this last month. This he said in that accent which you know, and whose effect, *repetition* seems not to diminish. I then said very seriously and earnestly that it gave me the greatest pleasure to write, but that I never sent a letter without immediately having a revulsion of feeling and repenting of it. But why should you feel so, said he, you do not think me sincere, for I have always told you that they always instructed. I told him I always believed him sincere and I believed him when he thanked me for them but I knew he would thank me for the motive. I did not aspire to instruct but only to soothe and interest, and I *might* do *just the contrary,* and this I always felt after I had sent my letter and the excitement of the impulse in which I had written it was passed, and I needed assurance. But I have given you this assurance, said he. No, said I, that you never did; you have never said any thing but what was too *general* to apply to the letters in particular, but a very little will satisfy me. If you are always glad to receive them, it is enough. I could not hope or expect that they would never give you pain. Well, said he, I always am glad to have had them, and I need them. He bit his lips, and you know how he always looks when he does that. You have not been so well lately, said I. He shook his head, and in a minute or two moved to go. I was sorry to have him go in this condition of mind, but I was in no state of mind to meet it, and so I did not oppose his going, but said I would write as often as I could while he was in Dedham. When he was gone, I could not but feel that I was sorry I should not have been in a better state and that if I was in a right state I should not be so blank when occasion occurred. I thought of the influence I had had in former days upon some minds—much inferior to his indeed—but I was sure that if I was in my full strength I should not be so impotent even in the contest with his. This led to a consideration of myself and of subjects in relation to myself which was a strengthening process, and I felt as if I should not be so caught again. . . .

I had written Mr. M— a note in the morning telling him of [Channing's] preaching and I told him I was sorry I had not been the evening before in a better state of mind. I felt it must seem strange to him that when he had plainly intimated that he had been suffering peculiarly, I had not drawn forth some detail of what it might have been a relief to express, that I wished he could spare me another evening which might be better worth remembering while he was away. He came immediately after tea and had hardly seated himself before he said, Did you think he (Dr. Channing) answered the objections he stated? I said *no*. And how should you answer it, said he. On which I began to *orate* upon the social system which led into a long and interesting conversation upon the want of present perfection in this. . . . On this subject, as usual, he stopped short, and referred to all his horrible associations with the divinity. I protested very earnestly against his allowing them to govern him and begged him to make his present need the occasion for fixing his mind on that which would alone meet it. He asked me how love of God could be born amidst such suffering. . . . In another place he said he had the past to look back upon and the future to look forward to, but the *present* was an *eternity of woe*; he never heard of a person's death without a pang of envy. I asked him if the present had not *an object* in the counsels of Eternal Wisdom, which he acknowledged. He said, yes, and he knew he had no right to cease to live—and did not. I asked him if *mere life,* merely not dying, was all that was implied in the duty of living, if it did not imply progressive intellectual and moral power, and if this was the case, if there were no means of this intellectual and moral progress about him, and so much *to do* internally that there was little time for this passive endurance which he prescribed to himself. He said nothing, and I referred to the stimulus he had had, and which had convinced him through painful duties heretofore, and how he might recover this, by exerting his mind on whatever would make another life real, and its connection with this—*felt.* He said he did not know whether it would help him to believe there was this *nearness* combined with the wall of separation. There was for a moment a pause. Do you think, said he, I could sleep tonight if I thought my wife was in the room? You never should have doubted it, and then it would have supported you. He was silent again. If it were so, said he, I think she could not but have overstepped the boundary line. If she were in full communion with God, I answered, as you believe, and he is wise, as you believe, her tenderness for you without growing less may be *another reason* to her to concur with His plan for you. He was silent for a long while and intensely still. At last he said, in a hardly audible whisper, This thought of nearness overwhelms me. I did not reply, but immediately felt that it must needs do so, *if it was new,* and more especially if he doubted the special providence of God, his heart must be expanded by the consciousness of God's love, and strengthened, so as to be able to *bear* these revelations of Christianity concerning the future life. There was something almost fearful in seeing how deeply this idea of nearness affected him, when he had fairly brought it before his mind. I saw it was a truth that could not stand alone in a mind of such sensibility, that it required as a *frame* the more general truth of the Absolute presence of God in love, which he had not. In a few minutes he shook his head mournfully as if it could not be, and arose. I said I fear you have been excited to no purpose, my dear friend. *No,* said he, and he stood

still leaning upon me as I also arose, and fixing his eyes with an inward look of calm still endurance upon my features. Could you but
trust, said I. I do trust, said he. But it is not the trust of love? *No,
no, no,*[1] said he. I should not be so importunate, said I, upon this
subject, but that I believe in my soul that you must come to this. Can
the trust of love spring out of misery? It *has,* in the souls of thousands,
said I; nobody ever *bore* your sufferings, except by means of it, I mean,
retaining all their powers to act; but to those who have had it, such
trials have added new powers to act and bless. He answered only by
a most affectionate pressure, and then moving to go, explained his
movements during his fortnight's absence, and inquired into mine,
with reference to the passage of letters. He said among other things
he was going to give up his trusteeship at Worcester. I expressed regret. He said he made the law which rules him out, and it would be a
relief. Why it was a pleasant duty? Oh no, said he, very painful; it
always made me sick to go; I could not but feel how necessary the
trust of love was to the sympathetic and benevolent, as well as to the
impress[ion]able[?], but I said nothing, reserving that for a letter.

When he had gone, I felt *spent,* and lay down on the sofa and
went to sleep.

(Next day)   I have written four letters to him this week, each a
sheet, which *I think* are as good as any thing I have ever written; they
have not involved the afterhorrors as usual. . . . It is Sunday, and I
have written another letter to Mr. M—, for it is a rainstorm upon
the snow which makes going to meeting impossible. . . . Mary White
came to see me last night . . . it was a delightful rouser to see her.
Mother wants to write some in this. [Peabody ends with:] It is the
last day of the year—the most unsatisfactory year I have ever passed,
yet I have made two most valuable *acquaintances* in it, the friendship
of Mr. Mann and of Sarah Clarke.[2]

MS, NN-B

1 The third "no" is underlined twice.
2 Sarah Clarke was the daughter of Mrs. Rebecca Clarke, at whose boardinghouse Elizabeth and Mary Peabody and Horace Mann were staying. Clarke formed
close friendships with the Peabody sisters and with Sophia Peabody as well, with
whom she shared talent for and love of painting. Through Sophia, Sarah Clarke came
to know Hawthorne and attended Sophia's and Nathaniel's wedding in 1842, at which
her brother James Freeman Clarke officiated. Sarah Clarke studied painting with
Washington Allston in 1832. She was a supporter of Bronson Alcott's Temple School,
enrolling her younger brother Thomas there and teaching as an unpaid art instructor
in 1835. An account of Clarke's involvement with some of the major literary figures
of her day is Joel Myerson, " 'A True and High Minded Person': Transcendentalist
Sarah Clarke," *Southwest Review,* 59 (Spring 1974), 163–172.

An excerpt from Peabody's "Cuba Journal"; Mann, she reports, does not believe in divine revelation or Christ's resurrection from the dead.

✄ To Mary Peabody   *(excerpt)*

January 8–24, 1834

It stormed in the evening (Jan. 11th) and prevented me from having a visit from Mr. M—. But yesterday evening, which was Sunday (12th), he came, and was very agreeable indeed, only we had a long talk about Christianity, and the truth is he does not believe in revelation at all; he does not believe that Jesus Christ rose from the dead, nor any of those things. But he thinks him the most extraordinary person that ever existed and his instructions as the finest and most worthy of consideration, and that his life was providential. But he had no unreserved committal of his mind to his guidance, as if he believed as we do. The conversation did not become personal, and he was quite merry some of the time, and the visit was very pleasant and cheering.

MS, NN-B

James Freeman Clarke, a Unitarian minister, was graduated from Harvard Divinity School in 1833. He pastored the Unitarian church in Louisville, Kentucky and served as editor of the *Western Messenger,* a Transcendentalist journal. In 1840, back in Boston, he organized the Church of the Disciples and was its minister until his death in 1888. Clarke was involved in many of the reform movements of his time, particularly the anti-slavery crusade, and brought to each his characteristically transcendental outlook.

An excerpt from "Cuba Journal." Peabody tries to explain to a sister who possessed, in Elizabeth's words, great "rectitude of soul," that is, supreme conventionality, the rhythm in her own life between the need for solitude and the energetic desire to engage with other people.

To Mary Peabody   *(excerpt)*

February 8, 1834

I am so poor. I have paid last quarter's board, and for my wood and lights for all winter. Historical school will give fifty dollars the next quarter. I do not know how much the reading party will give, but I hope fifty, and I have saved some money from last quarter which will, altogether, pay in April for this quarter. My present prospect is to go home in May pennyless and prospectless, except for what I may hope from the Christian Examiner. I cannot but rejoice that you and Sophia are so well provided for, during these dreadful times. If Mr. [George] Emerson should offer me a place in his school, I would take it for three hundred dollars. Do not think I am low-spirited. I have not been once. I find it perfectly easy to command my spirits and to be happy when alone. And when I say this, you must not misunderstand me and think you are not as dear, as highly thought of, as precious to me as ever you were in your life. It is my chief happiness to think of you and Sophia, how I love you both, you are both beyond the sphere of my irritable nerves and overstrained mental, moral and physical system, to which constant human contact had become agony unspeakable—I cannot tell why. If I felt it more with you yourself than with any other, it was not because I loved you less, but *more* than others, and because I felt that I constantly gave to you the withering pain of feeling that I was elevated and good than you had believed. I found (it is true) within the last few months that I had exaggerated your dissatisfaction with my moral condition, in some particulars, but I had only exaggerated—I had not *created* it. Now if I felt that you had some ground for your disappointments, this made it only the more painful to me. The less I blamed you, the more I must needs blame myself. I wish I could convey to you exactly what I mean. I never have been able to do it. I wish I could let you see how I feel that you can not understand me,—while I do not impeach your judgment but very little, your affections not at all, your rectitude of soul least of all.

I am like Sophia in the charmed [chained?] sea   (though I never disliked or felt a particle of aversion, but on the contrary have doated
[doted] on those with whom I could not live without being in inevitable pain), *in disease.* But it is only temporary: and I do not like to
be treated like a chronic patient. For the present I need the intercourse of new friends, who will love and value me for what I am and
give me that affection I can *win* at this present *and rest from feeling*
about those who have felt for me so much, and who *I feel* have felt
for me so much, that I feel when I see them as if I were a burden
and a blight upon their path. Sarah Clarke has written me some
divine letters, since she has been gone, which have done me a world
of good, for she speaks as if I had been to her a creative and enlarging and softening influence, from first to last, and Mr. M— spreads
sunshine round my heart by his brotherly tenderness, his stimulating
approbation, and by expressing that I interest his mind and beguile
his sorrows, and this exquisite Mrs. Davis is another delightful influence, for she shows me that I can yet make new friends and inspire
new confidence. Thus I feel I am improving all the time, and my
greatest pleasure in this is that when you come home you will find
I am improved, that I shall not be to you a perpetual burden, that
your estimation of my moral character will restore my mental movements to that respect in your eyes which they would doubtless always
have demanded and received had I not proved unworthy the trust my
Creator had given me. I do not feel as if I had said just what I wanted
to. If I did say just what I meant, you would feel that it was a tribute
to yourself, that I could not be happy with you when I felt I did not
secure your respect *to the last degree,* and would not be wounded by
it. That you love me as well as you do Sophia I do not doubt. But
is it possible for me to believe that I give you the moral satisfaction
and pleasure that Sophia does? Yet nothing less could satisfy my
heart or *conscience,* and it is in vain to think of making me happy
without it. But this must be attained as you know partly by my own
silent energy, and therefore I would be alone for all our sakes. You
know what DeGerando says about the necessary alternation of solitude
and society. You can have solitude in society, because reserve is a part
of your character—*I cannot* for I *must* communicate wherever there
is a human being presented to my senses. My solitude must therefore
be circumstantial also. I have always felt this, but I feared it would
not be understood and so have done violence to my nature. I felt
from the time I went to Colonnade Row that a chamber to myself
would have been a greater blessing than anything else. But I thought

if I should take one you would be wounded—you would think I wanted to conceal something—you would never imagine the real truth, that it was merely a physical, nervous distress that wanted every impression of the senses to be removed, while I was perfectly willing that you should know every thing in my mind and heart—the same feeling, nothing more, that Sophia used to have when she did not wish to hear a voice. Only the cause of *my* distress was mental weariness or moral excitement, and especially that greatest of all moral excitements, the feeling of inward discords and disproportions which every one must feel more or less in the course of their development, and which I have a keener perception of than those who have by nature a less deep and wide view of human nature and its relations within its own sphere of social action and to its Creator. Now I do not want you to think that there has been any fault or omission on your part, because you have not been to me the friend I needed, by not always understanding me or my wants. It is no wonder you have not been able to understand and foresee, for I myself have been equally ignorant. At every turn of my life I have been astonished at myself. And I feel that not yet has my imagination measured the extent of my own sensibility. This I hope to regulate—not by *repression* but by *employment* of it, which is the only regulation. In the meantime *do you* enjoy your self as much as possible, and tell me all you enjoy and suffer in simplicity and truth, and I shall keep up my journal of events and incidents. For the rest trust me to God and my allegiance to him. And do not talk to Mr. Mann or any other of my friends as if I was an enigma in your eyes, for in truth I am very simple, more *simple* than people in general, which is the very reason I am so often misunderstood.

Yours ever, most simply and entirely
EPP

MS, NN-B

An intensely felt letter about an emotional meeting with Horace Mann, describing an unconventional relationship.

✸ To Mary Peabody   *(excerpt)*

February 12, 1834

I had my tea brought up to me and then had the room nicely cleared away, and to be sure he came. First*

No, first he asked me if I had had another letter from you. I told him yes, and that I had one written to Mrs. Bulfinch and one to Harriet Guild.[1] "Oh, pray read them all—those letters last Saturday night were so bright and beautiful, I felt as if I had been in a *beautiful dream* all the next day. They were a perfect gallery of enchanted moving scenes." So I read the letters and he rejoiced in all that was beautiful and bright in them.[2]

we talked about Jefferson, then Jackson, then politics. Then he referred to my letter and thanked me for it and said he wished he had *that sentiment* (piety) which I described—he needed it enough, for he was perfectly unsupported in heart; but he did not have it, nor anything of which it could be compared or from which it would grow, for not only was the theology of his childhood all horror and gloom, but his life had been a chain of suffering and disappointment, and every body he loved was in misery, suffering from calamities they were irresponsible for. He had never seen happiness but in one— there every thing was indeed concentrated—but to be consumed! He made much more words in this speech than I have made, and said it with so much desperation, that I involuntarily moved up to him and took his hand with my left hand and put my right over his shoulder, and said, "not consumed, but *translated*." He laid his head upon my shoulder and pressed my hand and said, "I trust so. But it is not your trust or Miss Martineau's. Last night I finished her book on the Jews; the first part seemed to me illogical and untrue, looser than anything she has written, but the last was a fervor of faith that was very eloquent.[3] When I laid it down I could not but weep long and bitterly

---

[1] Harriet Guild was a Salem friend of the Peabodys; Mrs. Bulfinch's identity is unknown.

[2] "No . . . in them" is written in the bottom third of the letter and keyed for insertion here.

[3] Harriet Martineau, sister of the respected English Unitarian theologian James Martineau, was a noted writer on political and economic topics. She won a

that I could never feel so, and the motion of my heart was changed for *hours*." "But why should you think," said I, "that any thing you have not got you never can get?" "How can I feel gratitude," said he, "when I suffer and every body I love suffers? I have not the elements of this faith. I have toiled for the means of enjoyment and of doing good and they have failed when I am too weak to do the work over again. I once set a value on life and *for life's best objects* and life is desecrated to me. Those I love suffer without fault of their own and I cannot relieve them. Nor do they find any more compensation than I do in submission for *they* submit *as I do,* though you would tell me it is not submission for there is no love or hope in it—that is true—*I* have the energy of a desperado, which makes me try to bear up like a man, while I *must live*. I look forward to life *with clenched teeth* and say, *Come,* come and do your worst—the worst is done—let come what may."

To all this eloquence of woe, uttered in a deep, low tone and with a look that seemed to me on the verge on insanity, I listened in profound silence, and in *profound calmness too, if you will believe it* (so much has my mind recovered its tone). In truth I did not want to appear shocked, which I thought would check a flow which I was sure would do him good, since the fountain was within him. I reflected what I should answer; at last I said: "Your experience has indeed been singularly dark, but, my dear friend, there must be a particular *transaction* between the creature and creator in order to enter into that divine friendship which I believe in. I do not know whether you understand precisely what I mean by this friendship, but yet I think you must from my last letter." "Yes, I know what you mean—you were very clear—it was very rational and very expanded—very unlike the selfish devotion which you reprobate as much as I do—but I do not see how a finite creature can enter into such relations with the Supreme Being." "I was going to say," said I, "that there was a particular transaction to which he calls us, and the price of which is a sense of communion with him. I cannot better express it than to say it is an act of magnanimity, by which we are required to abstract ourselves from our own lives and do justice to the greatness and wisdom of the laws by which we suffer, but which are the source of all the happiness and excellence there is in the world." "Show me *that* and I am satis-

---

prize in 1830 from the English Central Unitarian Association for three essays on converting Catholics, Jews, and Moslems. In 1832, the association published *Providence Manifested through Israel,* which is likely the book referred to.

fied." "It can easily be reasoned out but it would not help you to *feel* perhaps, without you would in the first place put your mind into the attitude of confidence by this moral act of magnanimity." "Magnanimity in the creature towards the creator? How is that possible?" "It is just as possible as the *opposite,* which you feel—the holding back of trust; and both are possible from the fact that the creator is conceived as a finite being necessarily, from the finiteness of our minds, and presents himself to be judged to his creatures. Circumstances have given him such a finiteness to your mind that his nature is not only in miniature (as to all of us) but *distorted,* and so your moral nature has pronounced judgment against him—this judgment makes an impression on your imagination just in proportion to the strength of your moral nature, and the general correctness of its decisions."

At this instant, hearing someone coming, he started from his position and moved to the other end of the sofa. George [Peabody] came in, enquiring for a book which when he found, he went down stairs again where he was sitting as usual. Mr. M. spoke to him as usual and very naturally. As soon as he was gone, he returned to his former position and in the gentlest, sincerest tone said: "Show me how my personal sufferings and those of my friends have arisen out of the laws which bless and educate mankind in general and my heart will be satisfied."

As I was not prepared to enter into such an immense subject I told him I had rather write than attempt to speak that demonstration. "Well, do write," he says, "if you have time to spare for it—your letters give me a great deal of pleasure as well as instruction, and when they give me pain, it is such pain as a man *would not be without."* "But after all," said I, "I cannot think for you as you can think for yourself. It is the eye of faith that must trace the footsteps of the divinity amid the disturbing forces of this world, and as the most powerful agencies of the physical world are the most secret, so are those of the moral world. Animal nature takes no cognizance of the great agencies of attraction, and intellectual nature unless it cultivates the moral will be also insensible to moral agencies. You do not doubt of virture and disinterestedness because you have the key in your heart and are sure there are such things and therefore find them everywhere like golden threads connecting society together. But there are those, who selfish and sordid themselves, see only the selfish masses of society, and whom no argument could convince, and to whom no demonstration could be made of these real things. Nothing is so hardly cultivated as the sense of the moral presence of God, and if the habits of childhood have not set it going, it indeed requires a great effort to begin it—and if you have suffered a great effort of magnanimity to be willing to do it."

He pressed my hand again and again, and the expression of anguish with which he had begun to talk passed from his countenance. But from the first to the last there were no tears—as there generally are—There was then a long silence, till he heard somebody come again, and started up. He had brought up his hat and cloak, and as I supposed he would go, when Mary Jane came in, I told her I would be ready for her in a quarter of an hour. When she had gone out he said, "Oh, I have stayed too long"—it was after ten. I could not but laugh at my incivility at turning him out so and begged his pardon. He smiled too, and after a few words of no consequence he went.

I suppose I have not given you but little of a conversation that lasted an hour and a half or more, for it was just before nine that he introduced the subject, but I know you are more interested to hear it than any thing else, and I should like to give it all to you and every look and motion too, if I could, just as I like to hear things.

MS, NN-B

In this excerpt of a letter to her sister, Elizabeth Peabody offers a brief but classic description of the Unitarian attempt to identify miracles as literal fact and thus ground Christianity in observable reality. This letter is part of her "Cuba Journal."

✖ To Mary Peabody

April 3 [really 4] 1834

But Dr Channing's sermon had carried it [her soul] into the highest heaven of Christian hope—He began with referring to the fact of its being Easter Sunday—and said that the resurrection of Christ answered the greatest difficulty in the way of christian faith[.] For that difficulty arose from the senses & the imagination—He then described the effect of seeing the body of the dead—and the circumstances of the grave—and how Imagination was stimulated by it to represent to itself everything discouraging and appalling—But the resurrection (he said) addressed the senses—it showed the very body that was disfigured & mutilated & committed in utter hopelessness to the grave rising with new beauty & life & power—and ascending to the region where Imagination was called to follow. He proposed to make such a use of it—now when excellent beings whom we had known & loved had gone there—He said that Nature prompted us—& Scripture presentations aided us—& there was no danger of substituting fancy for reality if we grounded all we said on those ⟨everlasting laws of the soul⟩ essential principles of the soul which were everlasting—& on which the discovery of every new law throws light—

MS, NN-B

In a sermon entitled "The Evidences of the Spiritual World," James Walker[1] argues that religion is grounded in the inner reality, in intuitions. Peabody reports on the differing responses of Channing and Horace Mann to this notion.

✎ To Mary Peabody   (*excerpt*)

April 10–13, 1834

When it was over Dr. Channing said it was excellent as far as it went—(establishing that we had spiritual impressions & perceptions—which could not be resolved into sensations—that the development of these spiritual perceptions &c which constituted religion in the soul was necessary to the complete development of the man—& that this part of man's development involved by an original intuition of our nature the actual objective existence of a spiritual world, just as the development of the senses involved the existence of a material world—both resting on this intuition as the evidence of their respective existence. But Mr. Channing said he was not willing to call every development of the spiritual nature of man *religion*—that it was the moral nature alone whose consciousness involved the idea (even to the demanding) of a being of infinite excellence;—which was alone re-

[1] James Walker, then pastor of the Unitarian Charlestown Church, became president of Harvard College in 1853. As editor of the *Christian Examiner* (1831–39), he provided to Ripley, Hedge, and Brownson a forum for their views. He himself remained a Unitarian champion of the Scottish Commonsense philosophy.

ligion. . . . I said to him that I thought there were persons of high moral development in whom Religion did not take form—

He replied—yes & that *that* fact did present a difficulty—How there could be a deep sense & any development of moral excellence without a spiritual world rising up correlative—& especially without a Supreme Being—presented to him a perplexing problem—He did not understant that mind

Mr Mann said—that there was one peculiarity in moral impression & feelings—that they could not be experienced without involving a conviction of *laws*—& that these laws were the spiritual world—

Dr C said—*yes*—*The sense of obligation* was certainly felt & here there was a striking difference between the ⟨class of⟩ moral sentiments—& the love of beauty—which belongs to the intellect—But you do not mean that the mind can rest in these laws—*abstract* laws—

Mr M said—of course laws involved the necessity of a lawgiver—I asked (recurring to what had been admitted—respecting existence of moral development without the sense of a Supreme Being as a moral object) whether there was not always a belief in the perfection holy of human beings in such cases—if circumstances had prevented the belief of God—

This was admitted. . . .

Sunday 13th April.——My dear Mary—I laid my pen aside & wrote a letter to Mr M— and this morning I awoke to a perfectly exquisite day And sat down to a long meditation upon the light & happiness that have come over my mind since my last Wednesday's conversation with Dr C—recorded above.—I feel that I have found my way again—which I have darkly felt that I had lost—

MS, NN-B

Peabody takes note, in her "Cuba Journal," of the growing concern among Horace Mann's friends that his fixed grief will soon carry him off.

✳ To Mary Peabody   (*excerpt*)

[July 31–August 3, 1834]

Mr Mills talked about Mr M—introducing the subject. . . . He says that Edward despairs of Mr M's ever getting up from this calamity[1]—that for months he has not referred to it—That he considers Mr M—as more & more depressed and overcome—that he does not hope that he will live long.—Mr Mills seemed to think it was an irreparable loss—he said if he would be nominated for any public duty—it would be carried without a doubt—that he was profoundly respected on all sides—he was singleminded clearheaded & beyond suspicion of selfish aims—by those even who only knew him in public—He thought too that he had most extraordinary talents—It is evident that his gentlemen friends think his case even more desperate than we do.—

MS, NN-B

[1] In the early 1820s, Edward G. Loring studied with Mann at Tapping Reeve's law school in Litchfield, Connecticut and helped involve him in the world of Boston lawyers and Whig politicians.

In her "Cuba Journal," Peabody chides her sister Mary, who was acting as Sophia's chaperone while both were in Cuba. There had been a brief flirtation involving Sophia, and Elizabeth worried about her youngest sister's reputation.

✄ To Mary Peabody   *(excerpt)*

31 July [in another hand]   [August 8–10, 1834]

I was very glad to get an adequate explanation of your tribulations—& Now I can hope it will have no recurrence. But that is a *dark* affair *on J. B.'s account.*[1] He *knew better* than to expose S to be

[1] On the voyage to Cuba, Sophia Peabody met James Burroughs, a forty-year-old agent for sugar planters and brother-in-law of Elizabeth Peabody's Boston landlord Mr. Rice. Sophia reported his attentions, but Elizabeth became alarmed when Sophia wrote to Burroughs and accepted gifts from him. Burroughs apparently proposed marriage. Without telling Mary, Sophia agreed to maintain a sisterly relationship with Burroughs, and they continued to correspond. Burroughs discussed the relationship publicly, even reading one of Sophia's letters aloud in his Havana boardinghouse. As this excerpt indicates, Elizabeth was critical of Mary's guardianship. Mrs. Richard Cleveland, wife of the American vice-consul in Havana and mistress of the school in Lancaster where Mary and Elizabeth taught, discussed the affair openly in Boston and Salem. Reference to the Burroughs affair recurs several more times in Peabody family letters. When Burroughs moved to New Orleans, Elizabeth wrote to Mary that she was grateful that Burroughs returned all of Sophia's letters ("Cuba Journal," [20 September–6 October 1834], MS, NN-B).

talked about for he knows the country—& I do not believe he is a person who *ought* to talk sentiment to any lady.—If he *did* do it I cannot doubt he was *refused.*—But you ought to have insisted on seeing & knowing the whole—I should have done so—or have quarrelled outright—& even at the expense of being called a highhanded tyrant,—for the relation of sister—& the situation of guardian has a *divine right* of certain prerogatives—& do not wonder you felt in an agony—I should have told her that if she intended to have secrets—she had better go straight home—for you could take the responsibility—unless you shared the confidence.—I think it was the particular blessing of Heaven that sent Mrs. Cleveland to your relief—Why did you not *tell me*? I did not read (without being provoked) your remark that *I* should "lose my reputation in a week in such a country"—But you are so full of such random things to me—I have learnt to try to believe that they mean nothing.

MS, NN-B

In another "Cuba Journal" letter, Elizabeth Peabody finds herself on the receiving end of criticism about her own impropriety.

✕ To Mary Peabody   *(excerpt)*

August 18 [1834]

Your private letter of July 27th excited again all my wrath against J. B.—I have already expressed it in my letters that are on the way to you. I hope I said nothing to wound poor dear Sophia's feelings—but I remember I was shocked somewhat to find that she did not in all things consult your sense of propriety—& was a little provoked besides to be quoted as authority on the wrong side of propriety.—But James B— is a very rascal—for he knew better—& as Mrs Cleveland said boasted of his letters at the boarding house—I do not know whose words you quote in calling you "prudish" "squeamish" &c—surely not mine—

MS, NN-B

Peabody provides her sister Mary with descriptions of Temple School.

✄ To Mary Peabody (excerpt)

September 14–19, 1834
We went up to Parkers & thence to the schoolroom. That table all repaired of mine is put before the gothic window in the schoolroom opposite to another table of this shape [here she included a drawing] where Mr Alcott is to sit. Very pretty desks all round the room—with pretty chairs on for the scholars—Plato on a pedestal in one corner—Socrates on a pedestal in the other. Christ in bas relief larger than life over Mr Alcott's head   Behind him a rare handsome piece of furniture serving for books, etc—carpet on the floor—large stove—flower pots on a green table behind the stove—

✄ To Mary Peabody (excerpt)

September 20–October 6, 1834
When School begins they take their chairs & sit in a large semi-circle before Mr Alcott—& he talks to them—reads to them—hears them read—and Spell—and define words—these exercises take up all the time until recess—After recess I take them and give them Latin lessons—Arithmetic—& Geography lessons—thus you see I am not obliged to go there until eleven oclock—but at present I prefer to go—because it is very entertaining to me to hear Mr Alcott talk. . . . Sept. 21st . . . I will tell you now a little about the schoolroom. It is about 10 feet [word illegible] with the upper part of the Gothic window to light it & two of those little holes thus [here she included a drawing] which gives a crisscrossed light. Just before the Window stands one long table at which I sit—Opposite the Window is the appearance of a door—the same shape as the window—& Mr Alcott is going to have a piece of furniture including closet library shelves & Blackboard there—with a bust on the top.

MS, NN-B

*This letter to Mann on nearness to God recalls Peabody's conversation
with him described in her February 12, 1834 letter to Mary. How very
much Peabody wanted Mann to feel the consoling presence of God is
indicated in the variety of rhetorical strategies she uses and the intensity of the language.*

✹ To Horace Mann

My dear friend,   Tuesday—[1834][1]
    I think I never saw a mind in the probation of suffering without
either first or last coming to the feeling that the most *general* truths
were the most adapted to console it.—To myself—there is one short
sentence *"God is happy"* which has quieted me and consoled me when
all lesser truths, and nearer means have failed. But these words would
be cold—aye ferocious—to the soul that did not ⟨love Him and⟩ feel
without a shadow of doubt that He loved it—& that his concern for
its well being & enjoyment *transcended* even the selflove with which
He endowed it, for ⟨its⟩ the purposes of self preservation,—⟨&⟩ as well
as the affection ⟨it would have⟩ which he gave it the power to awaken
in its fellow beings. To ⟨such⟩ a soul so believing it would contain all
consolation, for it would imply that all occasions of suffering, were
so—only in their relation with our ignorance, & that there was a
glorious reverse to even the blackest cloud over the earthly path.—
Can your deducting mind see any fallacy in deriving this as a corollary
from the two above propositions?—But you will say perhaps—"and it
is *cold* as a mathematical corollary & as little fitted to meet the wants
of a heart"—Separated from its source I grant this—but let us consider—*these general* moral *truths*—tho' mathematically deducted what
are they but the breathings of the Infinite Intelligence—the elements
of that soul which he created? & ⟨therefore⟩ if so—why are they not
the conversation of God with the individual—and if they are this
conversation—the effect upon the heart will be according as we view
his motives or *purposes* in communicating.—If there is any kindly
purpose—in this instance of the above truth, it is that of winning the
soul of man—into a simple trustful conversation of heart & mind with
Him,—into love & its consequences.—

1 "1834" is written in another hand next to "Tuesday."

"Can ⟨we have⟩ love ⟨of God⟩ spring from the bosom of suffering?" You asked me this last Sunday night. *Yes*[2]—and you have experienced it.—For *me*—my dear friend—you have expressed a very affectionate friendship.—Before you did it in words, you did it by the most confidential manner.—And yet—if I do not mistake—the *very words of mine* that attracted you—sent each of them a pang through your bosom—I touched the very chord whose slightest vibration was pain—Not one word that I said of comfort did you believe— not *one view* that I presented did you take into your mind—and consequently every word might have given you pain and increased the sense of your desolation.—When what I had said broke down the bulwarks of your self control & your "distressed manhood fled shrinking to your harmless infancy for aid," & "you wept in unrefrained loud bitterness, indeed like a child"—*even then* you laid your poor suffering head upon my bosom—and pressed *the inflicter of pain* to your breaking heart—*and why was this?* It was because you believed that sympathy and tenderness dictated my painful words—and stimulated the very ideas—that were "dry as summer dust" to your apprehension. You saw & could not doubt the simplicity & sincerity of my friendliness—and you could [word illegible] not reject any expression however painful of the *presence* of that *friendliness*. So love acts in its faintest form.—

And so if you believed in God's love—you could take pain—& love him better [several words illegible] every time you thought of him—though his presence was manifested by a pang—If you would begin by endeavouring to conceive of him as *loving* you even so much as you then thought I loved you—that is—as regarding you with tenderness and sympathy—*every event* of his providence would insensibly lose its sharpest sting—your *justice* would be enlisted to explain his dealings with yourself and to realize—that however it might *seem*—*it was not what it seemed*—but something better—something worthy of Himself—

"But even then what could I do more than *endure?*—& I *endure* even now."—*Hardly*—my friend;—from your own account of yourself (which indeed is exaggerated—but it is doubtless the exaggeration of a *real fact*) *not half of you* endures—the spark of life still continues to burn—but your whole physical nature is in a state of faintness—the kindly affections still burn with a brightness that throws into the shade the faint flames of innumerable unwounded hearts but they are [one

---

2 "Yes" is underlined twice.

line illegible] so much less energetic than they were that they only seem [one line illegible] to "return to you sorrowing" [several words illegible] (I quote your own words)—& even your intellect (you say) is weakened & made ineffective.—*This is not life*—and if you live at such expense it is desirable that you *live wholly*—that you have all the powers of action you ever had—& that they are in progress—nothing less could vindicate the moral purpose of God.—

The Love of God!—to this you are now called—I cannot but think. No other blessing—no lesser good—can be to you a *good* now—till your soul is *consciously* anchored on this Rock—the Rock of Ages.—You need this as a condition. Your sensibility needs it as a shield—This came to me with overwhelming force on Sunday evening—when your nature seemed to sink under the weight of thought of *nearness*—and you said it "overwhelms me." I felt that if your soul ⟨had⟩ would stretch⟨ed⟩ itself to realize the presence of the Ineffable God as *a friend* and make him *real* in his very Invisibleness—you could bear ⟨even⟩ that *nearness* [several words illegible] (being consciously sustained by the arm of your God) without associating with it that withering sense of *absence*,—⟨being sustained by the arm of God consciously⟩

I say *consciously*—the heart cannot be sustained *uncons*ciously—it only *exists* in action—it is only another name for the *acts of affection*—its support is in the reality of the objects of affection & their presence. A heart to be *supported* must have a [word illegible] present friend in order never to lose its support—it must have an *omnipresent friend consciously*—(& be in the act of loving right [?]) But as the plainest truth in mathematics cannot be put into a⟨nother⟩ mind which will not put itself into the attitude of inquiry—so the vastest & noblest and sweetest object of affection cannot find entrance into the *heart.*—that will not put itself into the attitude of *loving* toward it—As omnipotence itself cannot create a ⟨valley⟩ hill without at the same time creating valleys—so the Creator cannot give a faculty of loving—without involving a liberty of being indifferent with the gift—and making *desire* a condition of reception.

Am I painful in my earnestness?—Yes I know I am—but it is a pain you will *bear* & not love me the less for inflicting it—because [several words illegible] all love—even the faintest friendship—is generous—& surrenders itself to suffering in order to prove itself free from every form of selfseeking—& in order to show its faith in the others essential desire to save its object from the slightest pain that *may be escaped.* [Two lines illegible]   Nor would God allow you to be in suffering—did he not see that it was necessary for you to enter into his higher plans now—in order that the happiness—which was daily growing more refined & elevated—should grow yet more refined and take in a wider sphere.—I would not be so importunate if I did not believe.—(and how can I believe otherwise?) that the *circumstance of death* and [word illegible] passive *presence* would fail to give you what you want—without your *mind* was prepared by the reception of this truth to take the wider—deeper range which this acquaintanceship of God—would give it. As there was a time in your life when the most elevated part of the communion you ⟨once⟩ enjoyed with your wife would have been lost to you—from your own undeveloped condition of mind—so *now* you need new development perhaps in order to be prepared to enjoy what is in reserve. But this is but one of the inferences from that truth of God's love—which you must see by an ultimate act of your own mind.—And which is the first thing: *the frame truth* of all other truths. My *friend*—how *can* you live without it.—*You are not living* You are dying—and this suffering is the dissolution of body and mind—Turn unto me, said the Lord, for why will ye [refuse?] and this is the voice of Reason as well as the poetry of Revelation.—Now do not let any commonplace false association enter it to do away the effects of *my words*—*every one* of which comes fresh & original from my heart.—Your ever faithful friend E—

MS, MHi

To the direct question Mann has said he finds nothing masculine or unorthodox in Peabody's behavior she reports in her "Cuba Journal."

⚡ To Mary Peabody   (*excerpt*)

January 6–7, 1835

We talked of human life & suffering—And of my character. He said he would answer me any questions I [would?] ask him about myself—And as he had been telling me that he did not believe any deeper fault had ever been found with me than of manner & of neglect of some outward matters—I asked him if—had he never heard anything he should have observed me—*he personally* should ever have remarked any thing outre in my person as manners—He said—*No*—

I then asked him if he thought that thro' earnestness—enthusiasm—or any other innocent cause even—I was ever betrayed into an overbearing—intrusive—masculine manner—

He said—*No*—*indeed* [two words illegible] it was remarkably the other way—and that I gave every mind a chance—and [was] remarkably free from taking advantage of my superior gifts of mind!

MS, NN-B

Peabody wishes Mann would know only her thought—not her behavior. In her favorite topic of consolation, her argument turns more and more to nature, intuition, and experience.

✖ To Horace Mann

My dear friend   March 2nd 1835
I wish I had not been so stupid-tired last evening. It was only my body that *was*. My mind was full of thoughts, if I could but have got hold of them. I do not know when I have had such a *thinking time* as the last few weeks. Waldo Emerson's lectures have *inspired* me,[1] and encouraged my heart, and made me think better of myself than I have ever done before,—of which you had perhaps a ludicrous   . exhibition last evening. I have very little *art*, or perhaps I should not have told you outright that I thought I had perhaps made on you too strong an impression of my weaknesses and that I wanted you to think my judgement worth something. I know you think highly of me in many respects. You have said many times in many ways that you thought I was gifted, but then you and I know there are many people who have some *gifts* who have no *wisdom*, and whose *influence* one would deprecate over one's mind, and whom one cannot think of without feeling *faint* with regret. And you have always thought highly enough of me for my *personal gratification;* for I am quite contented and very much delighted to have you like me at all, and to feel that my "welfare will always be dear" to you—which is

---

[1] Peabody's reference is probably to Ralph Waldo Emerson's series of public lectures on biography, delivered at the Masonic Temple, Boston, which began January 20, 1835 and ended on March 5, 1835. He discoursed on Michelangelo, Luther, Milton, Fox, and Burke.

part of a precious sentence that I have under your own dear hand and seal. As I think of this precious friendship from one who never falters, I am astonished and infinitely more than satisfied to know *it is mine*. It is entirely for a disinterested reason (!!) that I have been lately wishing that you knew me only in theory and not in practice or rather not in sensibility (for my practice I do think is wiser than are the exercises of feeling that accompany them). If you only knew me as a *philosopher*! I think my philosophy would interest your thoughts, because (as I think) it is the *lifegiving*. And when I consider what this same philosophy has enabled people to become and to do, I feel as if I had never lost my *practical* faith in it (my theoretic faith I never did lose). I should never have had so many dark times. I should have borne all my inward crosses. And it grieves me to think I have not borne my testimony to it in this way. Perhaps the next mistake was to *tell* all my failures, even those that were not palpable to sense or observation. I think there has been some *self-indulgence* in this last with respect to you. But thoughts and processes of feelings are *events* with me. I do not have a conversation with you, for instance, even if it is all on one side, and come out of it just as I was before. I am a very different person from what I was one year ago. I am a different person from what I was six weeks ago. I never for all the rest of my life shall be as I should have been had I not heard some particular sermon or some particular lecture, or gone through some particular meditation. When I tell you how I feel on a particular occasion, and the truth or falsehood of the feeling is discussed and it is proved false, I trust I am delivered forever from that. In short, my dear friend, I have not in my practice any more than in my theory, that idea of yours, that a person of decided character must be the same, and cannot change, and cannot turn their thoughts. The organ of *firmness* I do not think is intended to perpetuate any particular state or conjunction of states of mind, but to give *tone* to the tide of progress that sweeps onward ever deepening and widening towards the *ocean*, which we ever approach without arriving at it—for why? The Creator forever creates, and the universe ever expands, so that the emanating stream which constitutes our particular being, finds the field which it traverses forever expanding, and even could it circle back to the point from which it sets out, it would not then be in God for he is himself where he was not. But this is perhaps too daring a speculation. Yet it is *lifegiving* to think of those things. Brown's greatest mistake was in limiting the field of philosophy to the phenomena of mind and rigidly excluding the mind itself from all inquiry.[2] By what right did he undertake to stifle that intent desire of the human spirit to inquire into its own nature which all nations that have had any cultivation have manifested? I do think that of all ways of smothering life that have been devised, none could be more effectual than that of considering the immaterial spirit as if it were a physical object. Why should it be considered *as if* it were what *it is not*?

But you originated Brown's philosophy before you read it, you say. Was it not his *ethics*? Those are beautiful and *true*. And do you not think your moral delight in them might have thrown a halo round the metaphysical part: I am sure it was so for me for a while. I thought I believed in Brown's metaphysics during the dark night of my Gardner life, and I clung to it as if it were my last link with light and goodness, and never was Christianity so *inoperative*. But *that leaven* leavened the whole lump. I believed that Jesus spoke in the name of the human soul, and that every thing he said of himself, we ought to be able to say of ourselves, and metaphysically we *could* say of ourselves, even, "I and my Father are one," and "for this cause was I sanctified and sent into the world," and all those things. *I* do not understand from Christ's words that he was *consciously* pre-existent in another world, but that he felt he was a portion of that eternal spirit which when it finds a human organization begins to *know itself*, a career that never ends *because* the eternal spirit can not be comprehended short of *Eternity*,—consequently I could not forever rest within the limitations of enquiry that Brown proposes. This *feeling* which he forbids intelligence to pry into [is] the only thing worthy the enquiry of intelligence. Are all the tender relations of life but the accidental adjacency of clods of the valley? Will the accidents of time and place account for those sentiments which create a new heaven and a new earth, invisible to all eyes, incomprehensible to all hearts, except those in which they are developed. If you were a consistent Brownist, my friend, by this time you would be erecting, like the mourning mother he describes, a monument to *Time the Comforter*. But how far is this state in which you are from such a consummation! If I had no argument from within, if I had never known any other human soul, what I have known *of you* would be enough to convince me that Brown's philosophy was *superficial*. How little it explains of

2 Thomas Brown stressed the invariable sequence of cause and effect, argued for intuitive understanding that the same cause will produce the same effect, inferred the existence of God as cause of an orderly universe, and otherwise shared the views of his fellow Scottish Commonsense philosophers.

your sufferings! You feel it yourself. You say how vain is all argument before *feeling.* Your own soul is a wonder and an amazement to you. You see the mourner lay aside his weeds with the feeling that you must be different from all others—whether the regerminating love of life in them has sprung from having risen over calamity and entered into a spiritual communion so much more intense that it makes up for absence from the senses (of which I believe there are some instances) or it is the more common case that the waves of time and circumstance have worn away—I can hardly call it the *rock* of remembrance! With you, however, remembrance *is* a rock, and vainly may earthly states of mind dash upon it. Your intense *sensitiveness* makes every wave an agony, yet it wears not away. There is no hope for its peace but that the storm of Time should give place to the calm of Eternity—which *includes* the life here if we so *will.* When the sun comes forth in heaven, the clouds will turn into glory, the waves will settle down into smoothness, and the Rock of Remembrance, that *consciousness* of yours which is *one* with the remembrance of the pure, the tender, the disinterested, the devoted (nay, have you not said yourself?) the *devout,* will *rise up,* the chief object to the eye, *calm,* strong, receiving and radiating light. "And what has all that you have been saying to do with the coming forth of that sun?" perhaps you will say; "I acknowledge that I *need* Religion." True, but you cannot admit that your philosophy may be wrong, and what can Religion be in an intelligent soul like your own but the perfection of human reason, and what can be the road to it but *philosophy,* by which I mean a true idea of what is the *very subject* to all knowledge, and what is the method to all knowledge, and what is the method of pursuing it. You have tried *one way,* and (tho' it has given you much for it has certainly left you as pure and good as it found you which false philosophy does not often) it has still failed to give you *strength to bear* your own burden—the end of life is unattained—*circumstances* have carried away from you the happiness which was so boundless in enjoyment that you thought it would be unlimited and *uninterrupted* in duration. You have been prostrated and you cannot rise again. Why not cast behind you all the speculations of the past? Forget that you ever had a theory of mind? Surrender your spirit even as an experiment to the guidance of another who, *you do believe,* has most *carefully* and thoughtfully, and with all the tenderness of that friendship which is the bond by which the Creator intended *all his children should be linked into brotherhood,* entered into your feelings and thoughts, and meditated day and night upon them for two whole years *with reverence* for their character and the most unbounded *faith* in *their object.* I think you might trust me as well as you could trust your own *selflove,* supposing you have any. I would say, look at Nature *yourself,* and not by the help of modern metaphysical writers. You have power to see and to reason from what you see, and your own experience is *richer* than you can conceive other men's to be. You have ever had the *phenomena* of your own soul before you, through an early habit of reflection; you have ever been intensely susceptible to all the vicissitudes of the natural and social world around you; the philosophy and religion of others has made the deepest impression on your soul, and yet your soul so kept its own that it *threw off* the chains of opinion and sought truth for itself. You have loved as few men love, and it was answered as still fewer have it answered, not only with tenderness and devotion to yourself, but with a revelation of moral beauty and spiritual presence that outdid the hopes of passion. You have preserved consciousness and power to reflect and feel yourself *alive* after the most terrific visitation which Death can make to a human being, thus have you looked on the world in the plenitude of hope and the desolation of despair, and in *each state* has your undying social sentiment, originally stronger and purer than usual, brought near to you the interests of all human beings. What an experience, should you question it yourself, having for the time veiled all "the idols of the mind" that Bacon tells of as being set up from time to time by the ever absolutely narrow though intently enlarging understanding. I do believe there is not an hour of this experience but would tell you of God, and at last you would wonder at yourself as Jesus did at Philip, who *asked* him to *show the Father. Out of God* you certainly came, as every star told your evidently most *spiritual childhood,* moving you to the sphere you took so *naturally,* and what was that Ideal which made the Calvinists' God look so terrible and so wicked to your noble and sympathising heart, *but the Father's face,* which Jesus declares the angel spirits of children *do behold?* You had no part and lot with *spirits of evil* such as wicked imaginations had conceived as going about doing evil and giving pain just to gratify a depraved nature: and so *orphaned* as you were of spirit creating forms of beauty with which true education would have surrounded your imagination—you suffered and struggled for *you* could not be enslaved, till the painful fever of your heart was forgotten for a time in the newfound *activity* of a stimulated brain. Then you created

Brown's philosophy you say, and it was indeed a fair creation and worthy of its author, but it did not *exhaust the subject or fathom eternity,* and why should the manhood of your mind limit itself to the *robe* which was indeed a wonderful selfwrought garment for the boy. I have no objection to Brown's philosophy *for that time.* It made you perfectly happy and kept you good, and its mission was accomplished. But God would not have you rest *there.* He intended you should know more of Nature, including himself, than Brown's philosophy could teach. And so He sent you a happiness that no metaphysics could analyze. Another stream from his overflowing fountain, which had dawned into consciousness in far different circumstances from your own spirit, which in its progress thus far had appropriated to itself with unerring instinct all that was sweet and beautiful, was to meet yours, and reveal what the destiny of human spirits is in the eternal world. Can any circumstances of her previous life *explain* to you the character of her spirit? She has sisters, and you have told me they were singularly united;—but "that divine manifestation of her feelings when anything was done for the amelioration of suffering and the improvement of humanity," all that was *characteristic of her,* that indefinable charm that was *herself* and discriminated her from all others, which was something in beauty *above* beauty, *did not that come from God?* Can any thing satisfy you so well as to say and to feel it is *felt* by another, that she "came forth from God," beaming with a light and power that earth could not darken or impede;—but which only clothed itself with earth, and its thoughts and feelings with earthly images in order to find and bless your soul with a happiness not of this world. Will you say she was not conscious of the heaven from which she came, that she could not remember it? It was not so—you know she was conscious of much that was unutterable, much that she could not realize in her imagination. Her looks and her tears spoke volumes, her silence was often a *revelation* of the world within in its appropriateness and its espressiveness. And you could no more *understand* the cause of your own immeasurable feelings as you gazed upon the miracle of her love for you than you could the *cause* of that love, and vice versa.

When you one day said to me that if I could imagine my sentiment toward God suddenly interrupted, I might imagine your bereavement. I felt there was no *irreverence* in the comparison. I doubt whether, in the highest flight of that sentiment, I have seen and felt more of God, than I do literally think *you have seen and known* when you thought yourself looking only upon your wife—she *being* what you described her to be in that letter to Mary,[3] which I still think the divinest apotheosis a mortal woman ever had, not even excepting Dante's immortalization of Beatrice, or Michael Angelo's of Vittoria Colonna—nor am *I* alone. I never shall forget the tone and manner with which Dr. Channing took it from my hand, when I read it to him (by your permission). "Give that to me. Can I not have it? It is very remarkable." "I believe it *is true*, sir," said I, "by others' testimony." "*It is plain that it is true*," said he, after he had read it to himself again, "and can a man who has seen such truth be hopelessly *miserable*?" When I would have taken it from him, he drew it back. I said, "I do not feel at liberty to give a copy of it." "Let me keep it a few days," said he. "I would not have it seen" said I; "it was the expression of the most confidential friendship, in answer to a sympathy he was impelled to requite as he could." "*It shall be sacred*," said he. But I cannot describe to you his manner—it was *so inward*. I never saw him so strongly moved on any occasion.

About a week after I was there and he detained me till we were alone. He then gave it to me. "That woman," said he, "fulfilled her mission. Cannot your friend understand how she *must* look back upon him? Cannot he conceive that in understanding her and being influenced by her, he had given to her spirit an element of happiness than which the universe can afford nothing in comparison?"

He has often referred to it since, and always expressing this intense feeling in regard to her character. His interest went beyond her (personally); he has thought about her family, her father, and told me little circumstances and impressions he had gathered from enquiry of people who had known *him*. He seems to be impressed with the idea that a character so perfected at so early an age and leaving such an impression uppermost in the mind of a bereaved husband, was a kind of miracle. Once when you were very unwell and low, I said to him that I thought you would die, and almost wished it. "No," said he, "he must not *die* till he is more comforted, or *death will be no comfort*. He has received more than most men, but he has yet to learn *what it means. If he knew himself,* he would cease to be so unhappy. Wish *this* for him, not the circumstance of death."[4]

3 Peabody refers to Mann's eulogy of Charlotte Mann in his letter to Mary Peabody, August 26, 1833 (MS, MHi): "She purified my conceptions of purity and beautified the ideal of every excellence. I never knew her to express a selfish or an envious thought, nor do I believe that the type of one was ever admitted to disturb the peacefulness of her bosom."
4 Mann's grief was beyond Peabody's therapeutic abilities, and, therefore, she

And such seems to be the language of Providence. You have gained what the outward world may teach. Its highest moral lessons are impressed on your heart. You embody order, benevolence, duty. So completely are you trained to act according to moral antecedent and sequence that you feel no liberty to do wrong. You cannot but discharge every duty of social life that presents itself to your mind, You are so perfect a *Brother man* that you have nothing to require of yourself, except to keep on and I do not know as you feel *that* so much of an effort, as to be conscious of this requisition. What is all this superabundant feeling which "goes forth like the dove and finds no rest and returns to you sorrowing?" This part of yourself you do not yet *know,* this which the loved and translated called forth and which time only gives you opportunity of measuring without meting, is the *Son of God,* who has not yet found his home in his Father's bosom, and who wanders in his father's house as a stranger, not knowing that it is all his own, even that mansion where dwells his best beloved companion spirit. The outward world, this present framework of society as you have viewed it, you have outgrown, and God has clothed it with pain to drive you inward. The social duties have given you much—there is a relation of yourself and of those you love to God and to another framework of society on a wider plan and with less vicissitudes and darkness that you are now to learn. There are doubtless great advantages in studying the spiritual philosophy in this world, looking through the *glass darkly,* or you would not be bound to the stake of life for that purpose. You bid me once think of my feeling towards God, in order to understand your devotion and self-annihilation in the thought of your wife. I will ask you to think of that sentiment of confidence she inspired in you in order to understand the nature and character of my faith in God. And then you will

---

sought the help of William Ellery Channing. In conversations with Channing and Peabody, Mann revealed that he had replaced the Calvinism of his childhood clergyman, Nathaniel Emmons, who had argued that acquiescence in the divine will was humanity's duty, with a rationalist view of the universe as operating according to divine law, in which violations of physical or natural law invariably resulted in retribution. But such a view had no room for undeserved suffering, indeed, no room for death, and the death of his wife called Mann's enlightenment model into question. The more he rejected a belief in a beneficent God as a cynical deception, the more he elevated Charlotte in his estimation and the more he blamed himself for not living up to her standards of purity. Because of this crisis, Mann came to reject his former love of stylish dress and entertainment and became prim, censorious, and moralistic, seeing in propriety the only fit way to honor Charlotte's memory. I depend for these reflections on Messerli, *Horace Mann,* 173–75.

comprehend how *intimately* I feel *desirous* that *a beloved brother like yourself* should not *hold back* in doubt and scepticism, but should enter into the whole, eagerly seizing every light which may be offered and not stopping short in despair when there is a treasure of love before him, which only requires a voluntary activity, for you to enjoy it. Despair is the only fatal error. Yet if you feel it, tell me of it, *constantly*; let me see and hear all its phases. *I cannot despair* of seeing the light kindle in your faded features, *even upon this subject.* Can you conceive that I hope to see the look of *peace and joy* in your countenance, even with the name of the blessed departed on your lips? When you are a real disciple of the Great Spiritual Philosopher and Exemplification, you will conceive of it and realize it, I do trust and believe. God hasten the time! Alas He cannot, but only you yourself.

TS, copy, OYesA

Peabody meets Lydia Jackson and reports to Elizabeth Bliss on her suitability as Emerson's fiancée.

✼ To Elizabeth Davis Bliss

Boston
[March 4, 1835?]

My dear Mrs. B—

Coming into town yesterday from Lowell—upon a little business—I heard Miss J was in town—& went immediately to see her—& received your letter.[1] I could not but smile at your trouble of mind. I wish you would dismiss all fears—I am so much inclined to admire your friend & have so many sympathies with her—there is really no fear of not doing justice to her—You may have surmised from my letter to her—that I felt some of the anxiety you expressed—& I con-

---

[1] Peabody's description of Lydia Jackson as possessing "the rare characteristic of genius—inexhausible originality" comes from a meeting with Jackson at the home of Mrs. Bliss, described in her letter of February 25, 1835 to Mary Peabody (MS, NN-B). Since *this* letter is to Mrs. Bliss, and since we may presume Mrs. Bliss attended the gathering at her own home, this cannot be the February 25 meeting described here. Ralph Rusk notes that Jackson attended Emerson's lecture on Edmund Burke, which was delivered March 5, 1835. This presents a possible date for the letter, that is, the day before, since enough time would have elapsed for Mrs. Bliss to develop the doubts about Jackson to which Peabody refers.

fess I did—I wanted to know much whether she thought & felt in such a way as that the natural & beautiful contrast of her character & Waldo's[2] was to be productive of a more perfect union—or of disunion—And her answer—which you saw—entirely settled my mind at peace on that point.[3] Her theory of family union is perfect—& the sensibility she displayed lest any thing she might say would by its absurdity if it had any wound that friend—for whose sake she wished to be prudent—is the "guest angelic" I have no doubts now.—Besides—I had an hour's full communication with her this morning—in which she told me much of her exercises in connexion with her brother-in-law's crime & I can entirely understand & sympathize with all that—& *know* just how it was—for I felt in sympathy with Mrs. R—just so.—[4] And unless I had had that experience I could not have understood her feelings—nor do I think any one can imagine or follow with imaginary experience such a state of mind.—Few persons are called to look into such depths of grace—if you will allow me such a technicality.—

I am only in town for a few days & am fortunate enough to find

---

Sarah Clarke had also attended that February gathering at Mrs. Bliss's home, and in a letter to her brother James she described Lydia Jackson as "a singular looking person, and to my thinking, very handsome. Her eyes are somewhat like lamps, and the expression of her face is that of a beaming soul, shining through. . . . Her movements are free and graceful; she is a soaring transcendentalist; she is full of sensibility, yet as independent in her mind as—who shall I say? Margaret Fuller." Sarah Clarke's letter also contains this exchange between Lydia Jackson and Elizabeth Peabody. With regard to honoring the Unitarian heritage, Jackson said, " 'I respect Unitarianism, for without it we should never have had Transcendentalism. That was a foothold.' 'It was terra firma,' said Miss Peabody, 'And nothing else,' said Miss Jackson, 'cold and hard, with scarceful a firmament above it' " (Sarah Clarke to James Freeman Clarke, 28 February 1835, in Ellen Tucker Emerson, *The Life of Lidian Jackson Emerson,* ed. Dolores Bird Carpenter [Boston: Twayne, 1980], 49, n. 222).

2 Lydia Jackson had been engaged to Emerson since January 30, 1835. Emerson disliked the sound of "Lydia Emerson" and in his correspondence to his fiancée in the early months of 1835 began addressing her as "Queen" and "Lidian." After their marriage on September 14, 1835, she was addressed by all as Lidian. This was Emerson's second marriage; his first, to Ellen Tucker, lasted only sixteen months and ended with her death from tuberculosis in February 1831.

3 As a young woman of twenty-three, Lydia Jackson had an intense spiritual experience. Like her fiancé, she was a seeker after religious truth and was open to insights from unconventional sources. She remained a Unitarian all her life but because of her unusual beliefs and her familiarity with continental literature she was accused of being a Swedenborgian. Apparently Peabody questioned Jackson on this point and, as this letter suggests, on more personal matters of compatibility with Emerson as well. This was not simply nosiness or possessiveness on the part of Peabody or the other Transcendentalists. They realized the profound effect marriage would have on Emerson's unfolding career; for the sake of all he represented to them,

here Lydia—Waldo Emerson who lectures tomorrow[5]—Furness who also lectures[6]—James Clarke just from the West—& here boarding in this very house in this nest of Abolitionists Gurley the Colonization agent—over whose life of Ashmun I had been weeping with enthusiasm & love.—[7] to think there was martyrdom even now inhibited with humility—& for the blacks—& in the Colonization Society—of which I think more highly the more I know of it. I expect to learn much of Gurley—It is a comfort to see a man who does not get into a passion on the subject—but it would be horrid to see want of self government in one who was privileged to acquaintance with Ashmun in his day of [word illegible] in Africa—and who [MS torn] saw his dying moments.—I am on fire with enthusiasm about this hero—statesman—martyr—who even under the horrors of Calvinism pursued the *"splendours of holiness"*—

I want to mention that next house to Mr. Haven's in Lowell is a family of Warrens—where I have seen several Plymouth people—& have been delighted with a great many chance remarks about Miss J—especially those dwelling on her sweet temper—but I fear Mrs. B will be a thorn in the rose of happiness from all I hear of her—

Good bye—I am yours truly E.P.P.—And should be very glad of another letter from you.

MS, DLC

---

they wanted a compatible spouse. In July 1835, Jackson wrote Peabody, "not that I am a Swedenborgian—or expect to become one—yet repeated experience of this kind, affords, to me at least, a strong presumption in favour of what the N[ew] J[erusalem] Church Christians [that is, the Swedenborgians] assert of their faith" (Lydia Jackson, quoted in Ralph Rusk, *The Life of Ralph Waldo Emerson* [New York: Charles Scribner's Sons, 1949], 220).

4 In 1835, Lydia Jackson's brother-in-law Charles Brown experienced a financial setback and, in its aftermath, he abandoned his family and fled the country. "Mrs. R" is probably a reference to Mrs. William Russell, wife of the educator who had similarly abandoned his family, departing Boston in 1828 and leaving the Peabody sisters with a considerable number of unpaid bills from their joint private-school venture.

5 As I suggested above, this may be a reference to Emerson's March 5, 1835, lecture on Edmund Burke, number six in his series on biography delivered to the Society for the Diffusion of Useful Knowledge at the Masonic Temple, Boston.

6 William Henry Furness was Emerson's classmate and lifelong friend. Furness had a long career as minister to the Unitarian church in Philadelphia and was active in antislavery reform.

7 Ralph Randolph Gurley, New England agent of the American Colonization Society, was frequently described as a serene and guileless person utterly devoted to the cause of colonization. Jehudi Ashmun, general agent of the colonization society on Cape Verde Island, was the subject of Gurley's *Life of Jehudi Ashmun: Late Colonial Agent in Liberia* (1835).

Peabody presses her case with Mrs. Bliss to keep her son William in Bronson Alcott's Temple School and describes its curriculum and Alcott's method of instruction.

✖ To Elizabeth Davis Bliss

My dear Mrs. Bliss,   [before August 1, 1835][1]

I believe I ought to ask your pardon for my *brusqueness* yesterday—It is certainly a great responsibility for a mother to direct the education of two boys; & her misgivings ought to be attended to with the most respectful consideration. And in most cases I find no difficulty in this. With persons who cannot or who do not theorize I can talk forever to make them take an idea & explain to them the connections of a practice which is not often faithfully carried out from the principles of a spiritual philosophy—that almost all *Christians* virtually acknowledge. But with you of course I could not think of arguing with any idea of giving information—and perhaps I was unduly disappointed to find that *even you* were not able to keep that practical faith in the spiritual philosophy—& the methods which flow from it, which is the evidence of a *living faith*. It was a horror and consternation to my mind to think of William Bliss being put into any Latin school for a considerable time, and especially into one of those mentioned. I take the liberty to send you Milton's & Locke's treatises on education,[2] for you to see what they say about sacrificing years to the acquisition of what may be easily learnt as Milton says in a year.— Doubling the time he gives, however, I am sure that such a boy as William Bliss or one much inferior can be fitted for college in all the branches in which boys are examined there, *in two years*—even if he does go to Mr Leverett's school; & certainly in Mr Cleveland's[3]—and how early do you wish him to go to College? It is a misfortune for a young man to graduate before he is eighteen.

[1] This letter is dated from Peabody's reference to the publication of *Record of a School* on the first of August.

[2] John Milton, "Of Education," 1644; John Locke, "Some Thoughts Concerning Education," 1690. Peabody might have had access to *Some Thoughts Concerning Education, by John Locke; and A Treatise of Education, by John Milton; With an Appendix Containing Locke's Memorabilia on Study* (Boston: Gray and Bowen, 1830).

[3] Mr. Leverett's and Mr. Cleveland's schools were probably private academies in Boston that prepared boys for entry into Harvard. I am unable to identify them further.

If he leaves Mr Alcott's school in the fall—he will not have gone thro' much of his course. He will not have been taught Geography; Arithmetic; the Art of Writing; facility in Composition;—English Grammar; all of which things it is very desirable to learn before entering a Latin School. Neither will he [two words illegible] have come into the first class of Latin. I have a class, eleven, twelve, & thirteen years old in Viri Roma & Latin Exercises, which it will take William a year to get up to, unless he neglects what I think necessary English Studies, to give a disproportionate quantity of time to Latin. He can also learn Plane & Solid Geometry with me before he leaves us, and if I were you I would not think of his removal yet. I am more & more convinced that Mr Alcott's school is not understood, even by those who are most interested in it; and long for the first of August to come, when my Record of a School will be published.[4] When people, *knowing what the school is,* take away their children, I shall have nothing to say—but it distresses me when I am sure they know not what they are doing.

I asked Mr. Alcott yesterday afternoon—to say to the children—that he thought of giving up conversation about mind—and soul—& spirit and conscience—& such things;—and teach them exclusively about rocks—and trees—and mountains—&c &c and machines & engines.—Now, said he, very pleasantly & easily—how many of you will be glad of that—for you are tired of thinking so much about thought & feelings—& right & wrong—I wish you could have *seen* the *silence* & seriousness this thing occasioned—"too bad"—began to be said all round—Now tell me how many would be glad, for *I know who would be glad*—& shall be very much pleased to see them know themselves.— One boy got up.—Oh *he is so lazy* he cannot even play—said ever so many. Several more joined—perhaps six—one of them saying—you did not say you shouldn't teach us about words—Some words perhaps, but not many said Mr A—for you know we cannot talk about words without thinking what the words mean—& you know ⟨almost⟩ most of our talk is about the spiritual thoughts which words represent.— Several who had got up went back. *Oh it too bad—too bad—too bad*—said the rest & they looked at those standing up saying pooh— and shan't you read in Pilgrim's Progress—& Spencer—& Krummacher oh no—said Mr. Alcott—that is all about the mind—& feelings & conscience—*Every one* then went back to their seats—

Well, said Mr A. who had rather the school would be as it is—

4 Elizabeth Peabody, *Record of a School* (Boston: James Munroe, 1835).

full of thoughts & feelings about conscience, God, the mind, the soul—with ⟨its⟩ all my punishments & all my disagreeable fault finding &⟨its⟩ the necessity of self-control & selfknowledge &c &c &c—They all rose *with acclamation.* Among those that had stood up at first, John Davis was *not,* but only some *lately entered* scholars & two little boys five yrs old—& S.C.—Each one separately came to Mr A—before he left the schoolroom, & said he had changed his mind.

Yours truly
ELIZABETH P PEABODY

I have put in a mark at the place of Locke—where I want you to begin & read perhaps to the end—& have marked the sentences of Milton which it is worthwhile to meditate on.—Milton you know was an elegant classical scholar & Locke a very excellent one.

MS, DLC

Peabody pens an early criticism of Alcott, which contains several of the reservations she would develop more fully in the following year.

✄ To Bronson Alcott   (*excerpt*)

October 8, 1835

I think you are liable to injure the modesty and unconsciousness of good children by making them reflect too much upon their actual superiority to others. . . . I think the injury would be the greatest, not with the most ideal, but with the most sentimental. A collateral disadvantage, however, to both classes is that of being talked about by the whole city. . . . the other point of difference . . . goes deeper into the philosophy of things. . . . I wanted to see if you did not change my opinions, and have expected that you would. But a year's observation of your practice has not convinced me, and my own opinion and feeling have only grown more strong.

I do not think that Evil should be clothed in *forms* by the imaginations: I think every effort should be made to strip it of all individuality, all shaping, and all coloring. And the reason is, that Evil has in truth no substantial existence, that it acquires the existence it has from want of faith and soul-cultivation, and that this is sufficient reason why all cultivation should be directed to give positiveness, coloring, shape, etc., to all kinds of good,—God alone being eternal truth.

From Franklin B. Sanborn and William Torrey Harris, *A. Bronson Alcott: His Life and Philosophy*, 2 vols. (Boston: Roberts Brothers, 1893), 1:189–90.

As was true of her other letters to Alcott, Peabody composed a criticism that touches on reputation, method, and philosophy. She disliked having the pupils talked about and might have worried about her own reputation as well; and she disapproved of the intense introspection of the journal method. Philosophically, her argument seems a combination of the Unitarian view with something much deeper. She might simply have been saying to Alcott that the task of education is to bring out humanity's moral nature, hence giving shape or reality to evil is confusing to children who need to be encouraged to think positively about their own unfolding natures. Or, Peabody might have been echoing the longer-standing tradition that runs from St. Augustine through Martin Luther—that while sin has a kind of reality, it is only a negative reality, not an independent existence. Suffering and evil obviously appear in human life, but only in the absence of good, and not as ultimates. Hence, says Augustine, God is neither the author of evil, nor are there two gods, one evil and one good. Emerson reflects this Augustinian thinking in his book Nature *(1836). See Newton Arvin, "The House of Pain: Emerson and the Tragic Sense," in* American Pantheon *(New York: Delacorte Press, 1966), 23–31, for a discussion of the problem of evil in Emerson's thought.*

Peabody passes on some comments of Allston's that were flattering to Sophia but do not reflect well on Allston's assessments of his contemporaries.

✖ To Sophia Peabody   (excerpt)

Somerset Place, Boston
My dear Sophia,   [ca. 1835]
     I went last night to see Mr. Allston—& after we had been there a little while he came in—and before he sat down—enquired most particularly after your health—prospects—employments—&c—& expressed great interest in your little ladyship.—

He said a hundred fine things. He entirely agreed with me about Goethe—& said about him of his own accord just what I think. He thinks the Goethe-worship ridiculous nonsense—and says he knows *nothing at all* about *Art*—of that he *is certain*.—He thinks nothing in Wilhelm Meister worth anything—excepting some detached sentences—& the critique about Hamlet—that he looks at every thing as an artisan not as an artist.—He saves him, however as a poet—which he says *he may be* notwithstanding he is so hard a philosopher—& he doubts not that he is—as he never could have had so great a reputation if he had not been great in some department—He saw no greatness in his Autobiography—of any kind—his admiration of Hackett proves him incapable of understanding art—for Hackett had not a particle of genius—[1]

MS, NN-B

[1] Philipp Hackert, not Hackett, was a landscape painter and one of several artists Goethe encountered on his travels through Italy in the late 1780s. Goethe took lessons from Hackert in Rome in 1786 and later in Naples, and felt he owed much to Hackert, who emphasized accuracy and discipline in drawing. Perhaps it was this stress on skill rather than on intuition that so irritated Washington Allston. For Goethe's impression of Hackert, see *Italian Journey*, trans. by W. H. Auden and Elizabeth Mayer (New York: Schocken Books, 1968), 197–98.

Peabody discusses the sale of some of Sophia's paintings and then castigates her for false impressions of Horace Mann.

✷ To Sophia Peabody

	Saturday night
My dearest Sophia	[February 21, 1836][1]

I certainly think you have a right to give that picture to the fair—especially if you can get paid for the expense of it—& by giving it *so*—you can have the luxury of contributing all that it sells for— above what is given to you. As to Theodore [several words illegible] more likely I think to buy the *Flight into Egypt*—when you have finished that—& you can have in the course of time another picture for Mrs. Philbrick.[2] I only hope Theodore or Mr Philbrick will not

[1] This letter, dispatched to Salem, is postmarked February 21.

[2] Theodore Parks and the Philbricks were apparently Salem friends of the Peabody family, although there are no listings for Philbricks in the early Salem direc-

happen in upon that fair—& get their pictures there instead of buying them outright from you. I have no doubt it will be a great advantage to you to have the pictures seen. As to the Salvator Rosa & Flight into Egypt—I hope to see them in the Athenaeum Exhibition—& I think Mrs. Rodman will like the Salvator Rosa—if you do not get Florimel.[3] What has little Robert said to the picture you sent him? Has he written to you? I wish you would send back that manuscript Mary sent you which has Goethe's Brother and Sister in it[4]; for we think that it will be a good plan to have that copied in little manuscripts & sold—do not you?—Caroline Harding and Ophelia think of both copying it—and putting it into nice covers with something drawn on them perhaps. I wish you would send me your extract books also. Perhaps they would afford contents for other books. Those extracts from Wilhelm Meister—might be written off—as beauties of Goethe. You see we are to have a *blind fair* here as well as in Salem.—

I do not know whether Mary sent you a note I wrote & which was forgotten in one of the trunks—in which I answered what you said about Mr. Mann.—I had concluded not to send it—as I did not feel able that evening to do justice to my subject. But I assure you all your impressions are a wicked lie. If Mr. Mann is not one of Nature's noblemen—then there are no such persons. I beg you to entirely suspend your judgement about him—till I have time to sit down by you—& show you the truth. He is too wretched—or it would be a pure delight to see & hear him every day. But I really should not wonder if he should not live.[5] He is one of the few who might die

---

tories. By 1828, when the Peabody family moved to Colonnade Row, Boston, to board in the same house where Mary and Elizabeth were conducting school, Sophia had become a sheltered hypochrondriac and invalid. Under the ministrations of Dr. Walter Channing, William Ellery's brother, Sophia improved enough to listen to the lectures of Francis Graeter, who taught art at the school. Sophia also took lessons from landscape artist Thomas Doughty and portraitist Chester Harding. Washington Allston encouraged her art, which had turned primarily to copying. By the end of the decade, Sophia had a studio with a friend Mary Newhall, while Elizabeth, as this letter suggests, was at work selling her copies.

3 Salvator Rosa was an Italian painter noted for his wild landscape scenes and regarded as a forerunner of Romanticism in art. Sophia Peabody copied several of his paintings. *Flight into Egypt* was one of Sophia's original works; *Florimel* is a work painted by Washington Allston.

4 "Goethe's Brother and Sister" may be a reference to Johann Conrad Seekatz's work, *The Goethe Family in Pastoral Costumes.*

5 This passage from a ca. 1836 letter of Mary to Elizabeth Peabody suggests that Horace Mann's unrelieved and continuous suffering gave Mary the same exquisite frisson of delight that it gave Elizabeth: "What you say of Mr. M is most sad—does it not make you *not love* (I do not like the word *hate*) the world, to think that the ways

for love because one of the few who knew how to love. But all the harm grief can do him is to kill him—it has not checked his energetic benevolence—or chilled his fine enthusiasm—or dulled his keen perception of truth & justice—and to give the least pleasure to another draws him for the moment—& as long as he can do any thing about it—from his own incurable grief—The expression of benevolence & personal happiness is so identical—that it is not always easy to tell of the happy how benevolent they are. But when a man feels that personal enjoyment is shadowed forever— (the forever of this world— but which looks *so long* as to make the other world seem *a star* in coldness & distance)—and yet there is nothing but benevolence & excellence comes out—it is surely because there is nothing but goodness within. Whatever may have been the doubts respecting him— (but I should much question the *quality* of that spirit which did not by instinct recognize the fine quality of his)—I guess the most sceptical could not stand the exhibition of such true virtue—as this trial has exhibited—because it has left it without external stimulus—For my own part my mind is torn between the desire that he may die as *he* wants to do—& my interest in that general good of society—which he is one of the few who can really promote.

Do not you tell your Salem folks about those *books* which I have mentioned—because we wish them to have all the advantages of novelty at our fair. Your fair will be splendid *without doubt*—but there are so many fairs here—that we are *put to it*.

Do not forget to put that manuscript in the Trunk. Give my love to dear Molly Newhall—and tell her I wish she could do something for the blind—but that I look forward to the impulse she will derive to cultivate her constructiveness—so that she may be more potential in the future.—Will not the Marblehead girls work for your fair?—

Ever yours with love to Mother & all

ELIZ. P. PEABODY

MS, NN-B

---

of it & the fear of its ways should cut him off so completely from the sympathy that he needs—for it is not enough that he knows it exists for him in a few who must guard every expression of it—he needs it every morning & noon & evening—a thousand of his social sympathies might be fed & bring forth for himself happy fruits if he could be situated in a family that could understand & appreciate him & his circumstances—the thought of him gives me a perfect *aversion* to happiness—if you can conceive of such a feeling—I feel as if nobody ought to have it if he does not—and what a state of being is that when even love can wound!" (Mary Peabody to Elizabeth Peabody, [ca. 1836], MS, MHi)

*A vivid letter detailing the bitterness and estrangement between Eliza-
beth Peabody and the Alcotts, a conflict both personal and philosophical that would surface again in the early 1870s.*

✄ To Mary Peabody

My dear Mary—   [April 1836][1]
    Don't you think that Mrs. Alcott came into my room & looked
over my letters from you & found your last letter to me & the one to
Sophia & carried it to Mr. Alcott—& *they have read them*——You
may conceive the state of mind that Mrs. Alcott is in.—Mrs. Alcott
predicted to me "eternal" damnation for what she calls the "greatest
crime" she ever knew of—that is—the existence of a correspondence
of this sort.—They take it for granted that all *you* think—I think—&
moreover that I have made you think what you do. They will not allow that you formed your views from yr own observation   Moreover
they think that I have talked of all Mr A's private affairs to every
body. Mrs Alcott says your letter proves to a demonstration that I
have talked to Mr M[ann] about them & she has no doubt I have to
all the rest of my acquaintances. She says she finds herself at the mercy
of two unprincipled people—& so forth and so on.—Words cannot
describe just how tremendous it all is.[2]

    [1] While this manuscript bears no date, it seems likely that it was written in
April 1836 along with the two letters that follow and with the Peabody Holograph
Journal of April 11–April 15, 1836.
    [2] The relationship between Peabody and the Alcotts began a year and a half
earlier on much more amicable footing. Enthusiastic about Alcott's Temple School
experiment, Peabody encouraged her friends to send their children there (to Elizabeth Davis Bliss, before August 1, 1835; p. 150), taught half days, and kept a journal
of the school which she published in 1835 as *Record of a School* (Boston: James
Munroe). Alcott was pleased to have a person so widely connected working at his
school: "Miss P— is now present every day, and keeps a journal of the *operations*
and *Spirit* of the *Instruction*. . . . I deem the opportunity of being observed and
interpreted by her, during my *professional* life, as propitious in every respect" ("Life,
Speculative and Actual, 1835," January 5–6, p. 21, MS, MH). As if to seal this relationship, Peabody lived in the same boardinghouses as did the Alcotts—on Somerset
Court, which was behind Park Street Church, and on Bedford Street and Beach
Street, in residential neighborhoods south of Boston Common—and moved in with
them when the Alcotts rented a house of their own on Front Street, also south of the
Common.
    In 1836, however, tensions between the Alcotts and Peabody surfaced. During
the spring, Alcott led his pupils through a discussion of the Gospels, and his heavy-
handed direction of the conversations to conclusions acceptable to him offended her.
Such conflict may be seen in the acerbic exchange between Alcott and "Recorder"

Mr Alcott came into my room yesterday after dinner & opened the subject without telling me he had read these letters—& attacked me about my & your views—&c—I did not know what he was at—for a long time—until he quoted a paragraph from your letter—as a part of a conversation you had with Mrs. A last winter (—*that* about "poor men's bills.—") I told him I had indeed received that expression in a letter from you within a week—"Then she repeated it" said he.—This I thought not likely & could not help suspecting that Mrs. A had seen the letters & told him what was in them—& he had taken the idea that you had said it last winter. We were interrupted in our conversation by a desire on my part to go out on an engagement—& when I came home I found the enclosed note on my table—Sarah Clarke came in while I was thinking about it & with no introduction I showed it to her—and she agreed with me that it was impossible to

---

[Peabody] over the connection between individual illness and individual morality, in *Conversations with Children on the Gospels* (Boston: James Munroe, 1836–37), 2:144–45.

Sylvester Graham's lecture series on physiology and health provided another opportunity for conflict. Alcott heard Graham on February 18, 1836, at the Swedenborgian chapel and was impressed with Graham's idealistic interpretation of physiology as a scientific approach to the study of spirit. On March 1 the Alcotts both attended the first of Graham's series, "The Science of Human Life," which ran until May 4, with Alcott apparently attending them all ("Bronson Alcott's 'Journal for 1836,'" ed. Joel Myerson, in *Studies in the American Renaissance* [Boston: Twayne Publishers, 1978], 18–19, 54). With her characteristic bluntness, Peabody managed to criticize a figure who was the latest influence on the impressionable Alcott: "At dinner I mentioned in answer to Mr Alcott's question, how Mr Graham was regarded in Salem, that he was unfortunate in beginning with a lecture on the possible protraction of human life to two centuries—with pictures of the patriarchs that would be,—which suggestion did not prove very agreeable—implying very strongly that *I* should deem it no desirable thing to live so long but rather a misfortune;—for which I proceeded to give my reasons, and Mr Alcott replied that if analyzed this reluctance to live another century would prove to be a *suicidal statement*. . . . I remarked that ⟨his⟩ Mr Graham's class in Salem consisted of physicians principally—whereupon his abuse of physicians *as a class* was brought upon the carpet. . . . Mr A said he never abused physicians as a class—to which I replied that I had heard him say they fed like vampyres on the community for the sake of money—& I had also read in his articles—expressions of a like kind." After more exchange of this kind, Peabody went to her room, feeling "very uncomfortably." Reflecting on her own part in the conversation and finding herself blameless, she concluded, "I am quite sure that he has planted himself on dangerous ground—for his own humility & selfestimation without a doubt of having the key that unlocks all wisdom—in his own metaphysical system—he subjects every thing to the test of his talismanic words—and as they answer to them in his predisposed ear—they take their places—" (Elizabeth Peabody, 11–15 April 1836, MS, NN-B). For more on Peabody's philosophical and pedagogical conflicts with Alcott, see John B. Wilson, "A Transcendental Minority Report," *New England Quarterly*, 29 (June 1956): 147–58, and Bruce Ronda, "Elizabeth Palmer Peabody's Views of the Child," *ESQ* 23 (1977): 106–13.

live in the house with people who would do such things. She stayed with me all night—& in the morning I wrote to Mr Alcott that our relations were at an end—grounding my decision on this last act— Sarah read the letter—& thought nothing less could be done. After breakfast I gave it to Mr. A—In a little while he came up & talked a long while—I did not intend to say a word—but as he went on saying what I thought & had said & had done about him—Sarah urged me to speak & tell him that I did not think nor had I said & done such things. This induced me to reply but it was to little purpose—except that it gave him new grounds of animadversion respecting my tones &c. Sarah said I did not speak as she wished.—In all this matter Sophia has of course taken Mr Alcott's part—& Mrs. Alcott's—& they have talked the matter over for a day or two.—Mr Alcott was talking this morning of my *letter to you*—& I told him he did not know what was in my letter to you.—He said Sophia said it was a letter that would make any body think he was "a thief & a murderer!"[3]—Sophia had called Sarah Clarke into her room in the morning to warn her against taking my views of Mr A—&c—& Sarah said Sophia was to be taken care of just like an insane person.—However Sarah understands Sophia's goodness entirely—& indeed understands all round beautifully. I think it was a special providence all round that she came. I do not think it impossible she may come back—She was obliged to go to Newton—on account of her class this afternoon.

If you ask me how I feel—after all—I can only say that I feel more calm than I ever did under any of my commotions. I know I have felt & acted righteously with regard to Mr A—And all this matter has arisen out of this breach of honour on their part though Mr & Mrs A say that I must not speak *the word honour*—when I have done things so much worse—as if that made any difference—even though I had acted dishonourably—which I *have not*—I have endeavoured to say to them both that we have been independently confided in by both parties—& conversed with one another about the facts subjected to our consideration—in a sacred confidence that would have harmed no one—if it had remained where it ought to have remained—and that they are responsible for what they have brought on themselves.

I cannot tell you half till I see you—And I do desire—my dear Mary—that you would do nothing & say nothing of this matter—till

[3] It is possible that Peabody is referring to one of the following two letters in this edition, but neither letter would cause Alcott to think she believed him "a thief & a murderer."

I see you—By all your affection for me—I conjure you to write nothing & say nothing till we see one another. I hope you have retained all
the letters.—

And do not be worried about Sophia. She will be protected by
Heaven I verily believe—in her purity & innocence of intention—&
will return on Monday morning—or on Tuesday—according as I can
arrange matters. You may be sure I will take the tenderest care of
her.—I would not have her know—especially now—how much she has
contributed to bring about the present crisis.—

But I do not regret the crisis. It is better we should separate.—I
do not think I shall explain the separation to a single person. I would
not for the world have Mr M— know Mrs. Alcott looked at my letters—because he would think she would be guilty of every other outrage—& be alarmed lest she should speak of *him*—which I verily believe she would not do. Mrs A & I had a little talk about that matter
after you left—& I do not believe there is the slightest danger—But he
would judge by circumstantial evidence of course.—I shall let him
know merely that I separate from Mr Alcott—because we could not
agree in adjusting our mutual duties—to our mutual satisfaction. I
shall ask him to ask me no questions—& trust the matter to his generous judgement—nor shall I suggest any thing in regard to Mr &
Mrs. A—. He thinks—I have thought every thing good of them—& he
will continue to think so.—I shall see him Sunday Evening—perhaps
for *the last time*!

I have had some opportunity to observe how I can do—with respect to other people. Mrs Bliss called to day—& I told her I should
not engage another year with Mr Alcott. She was more sorry than I
could have believed—We talked a great deal about it—assuming &
carrying on the Idea that we separated in mutual amity—& from ex-
trinsic considerations altogether.—Then the Havens came & the same
thing appeared with them. No explanation *can* be required or *will*
be.—I told Mrs Bliss I should be glad to do something which would
enable me to *pay up* about the Records, and should look out for it.
This is true—& it seemed to occupy her attention.—You need not tell
any body in Salem till I come—unless you should be asked.—And then
you can say I promised to tell you why I came to the conclusion—after
my return—& what my future plans were.—As Sophia will keep up her
acquaintance & friendship here—the world need not know of estrangement—& we shall not be compelled to tell of Mrs A's breach of honour—probably—. I think she & Mr A will keep their own secret—
probably—I never knew a case in which I felt less disposed to do any

thing overt. I have done & said nothing I repent of.—But I do wish I could have *appeared* always just as free from unkindness as I felt.— But that manner is the entailment of former errors. You know some people think Alcott [?]—"ferocious"!—No wonder they should think I am! You have no idea of what a quantity Mr & Mrs A have both said about what they expect to happen from our representations.—To all this I have not vouchsafed a word of reply—nor shall I—Is this pride? But every word I say about the Past—is treated with contempt—and they will not hear me say that they have got a very exaggerated idea of your views as well as my own—And I cannot condescend to make *any promises*—to be insulted about *them*. Indeed I say as little as I possibly can—for not a single word is said—that I do not wish unsaid the next moment—So it is taken—both by Mr & Mrs A—

I was sorry for your last letter to Mrs A about Abolition. It made her very angry—& she showed it to Mrs. Chapman[4] & spoke quite sharply about it—though I did not hear all she said—

One of my sins has been punished signally. I have been conscious always with regard to you & Sophia of a perverseness in regard to some things.—that is—if you found fault with me *unjustly* about any particular thing—& suggested to me something a good deal worse than ever entered my head—as I must say you both of you often do—to defend it whether I have done it or not—& even suggest some worse thing as my motive. A great many such unexplained matters have gone into the Past—Some of these Sophia has brought up—& detailed. She told Sarah Clarke that I was in the habit of doing such things as Mrs. Alcott has done. That I defended it in principle & practice. She has mentioned names & circumstances—of which I have not the most dreamy recollection. She told her (all this was before me) that you & she had often talked over with sorrow & amazement these deviations from principle *&c &c.*[5]—Now I am sorry for this—though I think Sarah trusts me through. At any rate I left it to her good judgement— merely saying that if I looked into S. Hathaway's letter—it was because she gave me general or particular leave to do so—And if either of you had remonstrated—I should be very apt to say—that I did it because I liked to do wrong—or because it was dishonourable—or because I wanted to see when she did not know it.—With respect to defending Sir Harry Vane—too—she has shown me up—as she appre-

4 Maria Weston Chapman was an abolitionist, one of the founders of the Boston Female Anti-Slavery Society in 1832, leader in the Massachusetts Anti-Slavery Society, and assistant to William Lloyd Garrison in editing the *Liberator*.

5 "&c &c" is underlined twice in the MS.

hended it.—I do not complain of this.—I am responsible for her view of me—And yet I can not for the life of me help being a little pleased to feel that I am better than I am thought. It is, however, an abominably selfish pleasure. But then now Sophia is compensated for any pain of thinking ill of me—by being able to keep up her adoration of Mr Alcott—

⟨I wonder whether⟩

Ten oclock

The above, my dear Mary, I have written at intervals with a raging headache. I am now relieved a little & will close. I have seen Frederica & she is in the same old sixpence. She said Mrs A— entirely misunderstood her about that matter of Dr C's kitchen, that it was Mr Tuckerman who made the report—& she wanted you & me to contradict it. Mr Conwell has written in a ⟨preface⟩ blankleaf to your edition of the Love of Jesus[6]—that there is not but one mistake—that on the 73rd page—& Frederica believes he is right—& that Mr Stone was wrong—She was perfectly delighted with Mr Douglas' letter & especially the seal. She sends her love. I told Mr Brownson last night all about the two translations. He has seen her—& believes in her—& is a very just man.—But he said that there was not the slightest reason why you should pay for that edition—& tomorrow I will tell it all to Mr M— In the meantime pray make no promises—Frederica says Miss Dodge did all the mischief about the letters,—concerning which she was so angry with *me*.

I feel very happy tonight!—I do not feel any resentment towards any body. I think there are certain things which from their excess became amusing—One of these was to hear Sophia this evening talk about the Alcotts—She says she has unbounded trust that they never looked into a letter before—nor ever will again—not on account of the bad consequences to themselves—but because they are *so good*. She thinks I am exceedingly uncharitable because I do not agree with this view. As to her—she is a sweet creature—& I wish she could be content with my thinking so—without requiring that I should think she judges rightly about matters & things of an external nature.—I am

[6] The passage about Dr. C's kitchen and Mr. Tuckerman is unclear, and I could discover no book of the 1830s called *The Love of Jesus*. Since Peabody later refers to translations, it is possible she mistranslates D. F. Strauss, *Das Leben Jesu*, which, Jerry Wayne Brown says, first entered the United States in 1836 or 1837 (Brown, *The Rise of Biblical Criticism in America*, 149). For a treatment of the impact of Strauss's book on the Transcendentalist movement, see Brown, *Rise of Biblical Criticism in America*, 140–52.

glad she feels as she does—because that will be a bond of union in the families—And pray do not let either Mother or Father know any thing about this. I hope you have not before.—Mrs. Alcott brought up this charge against *you*.—I told her I did not think you had—and I should not have done it—Nevertheless—if you had—I presumed it was because you had a right—I should not apologize for or condemn it. At least until I heard from you Now—my dear—write me any thing you choose about this.—And do not be distressed.—If possible I will finish a letter—with which I intend to leave the house & send it to you.—I want you to return it—*in that large box*[7] on Monday morning—which I need to pack up my things. I shall leave my furniture here. You must tell the stageman to *surely* bring it on Monday.

Mrs. A let out one thing I had almost forgotten. She says that one day last summer—at Mrs. Beache's—you took five dollars from her—to go & buy some things—little things—they did not cost a dollar—It was the last five dollars she had—You brought back the things—but not the money—She was very much distressed for it for [MS torn] days—And one day she asked you if you could lend her a quarter of a dollar—You left the room as if to look for it & never returned—She said she never had told of this!—I asked her why she did not ask you for it—She said she *could not*! Now—my dearest—you must get five dollars if you borrow it from Miss Rawlins—I *think* I shall have enough money to get along—but I should doat [dote] upon ten dollars—if you feel perfectly willing to borrow as much as that of her—But do not—unless you had just as lives [lief?] as not.—Do not tell—write—or think anything—if you can help it—till I see you except to me.—I wish you would not tell Mother even—quite yet. Will you copy my letter to Mrs A—if I do enclose it—

Perhaps you had better send up my letters to you—about this.

MS, MHi

7 "In the large box" is underlined twice in the MS.

*This letter is principally about the death of Emerson's brother Charles,
who died May 9, 1836, of tuberculosis.*

✵ To Mary Peabody

15th of May

Dear Mary—If Cornelia[1] goes on Monday I shall send the Cabinet of
Fine Arts—two volumes—which M. A. D.[2] says she may keep until
July—& which gives a great deal of Anatomy—as much perhaps as an
artist wants for practical purposes—Perhaps by study & copying she
can keep what is important to her.

After dinner to day I went to see Lydian. She was alone—but she
told me Waldo had arrived & was with his mother & Elizabeth at Miss
Haskins & they all were going to Concord in an hour.[3] She said he was
suffering more than even she was prepared for. And showed me a letter
from him written just after Charles's funeral—which she ought to
have received yesterday. It was a wonderful letter for the idea it gave
of a friendship—He feels his life *wrecked* completely[4]—The expres-

1 That is, Cornelia (Mrs. Thomas B.) Park.

2 Mary Ann, or Marianne, Dwight was an art teacher in Boston, friend of Sophia
Peabody, and member of the Brook Farm community.

3 Emerson was returning from Charles's funeral in New York City and had apparently stopped at his aunts' home in Boston together with his mother Ruth Haskins
Emerson and Elizabeth Hoar, daughter of Judge Samuel Hoar and fiancée of Charles.
Mrs. Emerson's sisters Ann, Elizabeth, and Fanny probably all lived at the same address, 13 Front Street.

4 Emerson felt the death of his brother intensely. To Lidian he wrote, "I can
never bring you back my noble friend who was my ornament my wisdom & my pride"
(12 May 1836, in *The Letters of Ralph Waldo Emerson*, 6 vols., ed. Ralph Rusk [New
York: Columbia University Press, 1939], 2:20). Privately, Emerson wrote, "Who can
ever supply his place to me? None. I may live long. I may, (tho' 'tis improbable) see
many cultivated persons, but his elegance, his wit, his sense, his worship of principles,
I shall not find united—I shall not find them separate" (*Journals and Miscellaneous
Notebooks*, 10 vols., ed. William Gilman et al. (Cambridge: Harvard University Press,
1960–), 5:152.
The Emerson family's grief was shared by other members of their circle. Mary
Peabody wrote Elizabeth that "It is too melancholy, the whole of it, and I suppose
you like us can think of nothing else but the bereaved. . . . I dread to think of Elizabeth H.—I feel that Waldo is based upon a Rock—I am not *afraid* for him, but my
heart almost stops beating when I think of her" ([1836] MS, MHi). Sarah Clarke noted
that when she met Emerson after Charles's death, "I looked away. I could not help it,
for it seemed like intruding on his sacred sorrow to demand so much as a look of
recognition—but I could not help seeing that the seraphic smile was quenched—Ah
Mary—when such a bright planet shoots from the horizon, how dark it leaves us!—
and how uncertain & shadowy become the things of time & sense!—" (Sarah Clarke
to Mary Peabody, 15 May [1836], MS, MH).

sions were like Mr M's—only not despairing—not general—but as if this was a peculiar case—he characterized Charles—he had said before he went away that he should never be any thing to the world or to any body—if Charles Emerson died.—He seemed to think he was annihilated now.—He *thanked* his wife for knowing Charles—& said he could not have forgiven her for not knowing him—henceforth he could make no new ties—for with no one could he commune who had not the Idea of Charles which no words could give.—He said Elizabeth exhibited the power of truth.—that his mother comforted them all—You must not tell even Mary White that I have seen these letters. I have given you no idea of this letter. It was a wild heap of beautiful ruins—Its paragraphs were each a unit. But there was a wild conceit in their expressions.—Broken melodies—beautiful even in ruins seemed his shattered soul.—He went to see Sarah Hoare[5]—When he went in he said "Elizabeth is well—and Charles—is well—" & that was all. Sarah had already had a letter from Eilzabeth who had promised to write to her at any rate.—It was this: "dear Sarah—we did not find him—but lifeless—He fainted on Monday after a ride & did not recover—I am well & came comfortably—and Strength is given me to bear it now—& I have not all the weight at once—it will come in every day of the future when I do not see him. I am well—you need not be anxious for me—my darling sister."[6] Sarah went back to Concord with them.—She found Elizabeth more composed than she hoped—when she went up to see her to go—When I left Mrs Emerson—I went down to Mrs Dwights—to see Mrs Alcott's landscape which I never yet had seen—what an exquisite thing it is!—Mrs Dwight was extremely interesting. She asked me to go & ride with her & I did—and wondered— for the hundredth time—why I did not see her more—she is so interesting—and she is wonderfully improved too—has made a great advance. She knows how to feel about art. She was speaking of pictures— and said it irritated her to have a great picture thought of as an article of furniture—it was making a *secondary* object of it—a room should be made for a picture—not a picture for a room—& so she would have it.—After that I went to see Belinda who told me all I have told you about E. & S. Hoare—they are very intimate you know—& entirely absorbed.—But really I tremble less for E—now—than I do for Waldo. She seems more herself than Waldo does *himself*. Then I went

---

[5] Sarah was Elizabeth Hoar's sister. Peabody frequently added an "e" to their last name.

[6] Quotation marks begin each line of this passage: "dear Sarah . . . my darling sister."

to see Sally Gardiner & Miss Jackson. We talked of Charles all the time. Sally carried the *roll* after all—& Edward has it. The packet went through the Thwings. Sally will be in Beverly in three weeks and will stay there a good while—She expects to see you while there a good many times.

Sunday—Today I went out early in the morning—& have been out all day which is unusual. First I went to Mary Benjamin's —& saw her & Park[7] who seems really desirous to help along Margaret Fuller[8] & me—in making our thoughts known—I then went to hear Mr Greenwood & heard—Mr Colman![9]—I went home to the Lee's[10] to dinner; & had a beautiful time with Miss J—& Sally—who I shall not see again till October—& Mrs Lee & all are going away in about a week for the summer! I had a beautiful time. Afterwards I called at Mrs. Bliss's on my way to hear Mr. Stetson[11]—& she said she would take off her things & stay home if I would—& so we did—& we mourned over the Emersons—& that factitious trouble Mrs Brown.[12] She said a great deal about the manner Sophia had been brought up.[13] She said Sophia had noble traits of character—& overcame her mother's coldheartedness & hardheartedness toward her—for moments—but Mrs. Brown was too thoroughly selfish even to love her children—She said her heart ached for Sophia time without number—and when I told her how it was in Concord—she said that was not half so bad as

7 Mary Elizabeth Benjamin, sister of Park Benjamin, married the historian John Lathrop Motley in 1837. Park Benjamin was a journalist, and editor of the *New England Magazine,* 1831–35, the *American Monthly Magazine,* 1836–39, and the *New World,* 1839–45.

8 In the year of Charles's death, Fuller had not yet begun the conversations that would bring her such fame in Boston. In 1835, she had been working on review-essays, studying Goethe, and forming a friendship with the English writer and reformer Harriet Martineau. Both Fuller and Peabody, as this letter suggests, were looking for sympathetic publishers for their work. Fuller was editor of the *Dial* from 1840 to 1842.

9 Henry Colman was a graduate of Dartmouth College and a Unitarian minister. He vigorously upheld the conservative Unitarian side in controversies with Transcendentalists. Attempts to install him in the Unitarian South Church in Salem caused a great furor, and his followers formed a separate congregation, which Colman served from 1825–31. After 1833, he wrote voluminously on agricultural topics.

10 This probably is Mrs. Henry Lee, wife of the prominent Boston financier, whose bankruptcy in 1837 as part of the panic of that year caused similar failure among his creditors.

11 Caleb Stetson was a Unitarian minister in Medford and member of the Transcendental Club.

12 Mrs. Brown was the mother of Charles Brown, husband of Lidian Emerson's sister Lucy. Brown was infamous for his abandonment of Lucy and their children in 1835 after a financial disaster.

13 Sophia Brown was the daughter of Charles and Lucy Jackson Brown.

she had known it.—Sophia's chief characteristic now is her complete silence & reserve. No wonder. I do not think Sophia's [Peabody] or your comfort or leisure are to be compromised at all for her—but I hope you will think out a way by which you can have her—I have thought that perhaps as Sophia cannot sleep in that room next to Pa's—Sophia B. *might* have her bed *there*—if you did not feel like having her in your room—as you might not—I do not like to hear you say you are confined by Foster—If you make a case of him—he must come here the sooner—but any body might put him to bed.[14] I should think *Mrs Lee wants her ornithology. Now don't forget it next trunk—nor the American monthlys—especially the last—nor that Lithographic outline head*—and I wish Sophia would write the directions for that Lithographic outlining for Sarah Clarke. Did Sophia say she had a stone?—I wish she could but draw St George on the Lithographic Stone—at least with the red ochre tracing it from her ⟨copy⟩ drawing as she did Flaxman.

Father has just come—and has gone over to South Boston—& Mr M does not come and so I will finish my letter. I will first finish my day. I called at Lydian's brother's Dr Charles Jackson's[15]—on an errand for her. He said he had seen Mr Emerson—"and he bears his grief" said he "like a philosopher—calm, even smiling"—I absolutely *shuddered*. And when I came home I found a letter from Waterston[16] who was in New York and at the funeral.—He said he stood at the grave with Waldo & that when he turned away from it—compressed nature found its way *in a laugh*—and an ejaculation "dear boy."—He saw he approached him & Waldo took his arm—"When one has never had but little society—and *all that society* is taken away—what is there worth living for?" said he. Waterston only offered silent sympathy I should think—Today Mr Dewey[17] preached at Chauncy Place—where he could naturally speak of Charles Emerson—as it was his father's church—& he paid him a most beautiful tribute—As Sally Gardner & Ellen Sturgis—who heard it—say—

[14] Foster Haven was the son of Lydia Sears and Samuel Foster Haven. The Peabody sisters looked after Foster during the last months of his mother's life; she died in August 1836 of tuberculosis.

[15] Charles Thomas Jackson was Lidian's brother, later noted for his discovery of ether's anesthetic qualities.

[16] Robert Cassie Waterston was a minister, writer, and public speaker. Ordained in 1839, Waterston served several churches in the Boston area and was prominent in benevolent work.

[17] Orville Dewey, Unitarian minister in the Boston area, was deeply concerned about social reform—particularly aid for the poor and antislavery.

And now for your letter. This matter of Sophia B—this is decisive. You certainly ought not to be troubled with any thing more. I am sorry about Foster. When Sam comes down to Salem you must tell him when your vacation will be—& ask him to let Foster take that week for his visit in Lowell—if possible—because you *must come* to Boston the last week in June.—Sam will not put him here before the fall—but perhaps he will take him to Dedham in September—*During August I will be ⟨there⟩ in Salem* & can see to him.— You must constantly speak to him & to Sam—as if he were to come to Boston in the winter, as if Sam thinks he is no trouble—he may think it is as well to let him stay. I hope Sophia puts down all he says[18]—especially about his mother. Those memoranda I suggested to you might be made by either however—& be dated—Pray do let it be done—

I hope he is never to learn that heaven *is far off*—which you suggest is the *lesson of Time*!!

What you say of Eliza Dwight is beautiful—I wish I could see her—I do not know but I shall come down some Friday—before she goes—I thought she was a beautiful mother & very much of one the last time I saw her—Is not Foster with Willie a good deal?

I guess I shall send you down my letter to Mr A.—I am quite astonished to find that you think Mr *A* is the person hardly dealt with! *He cried an hour* Mrs A said.—I had cried *whole nights* again & again—that first winter—when I could not find him out.—I accused him of what he had formerly confessed to me—that he considered himself as a thinker superior to all other people—mentioning Dr. C—He had accused me of what I considered littleness in the extreme—*& has never taken it back*—for he expressly told me—after I came here—that I misunderstood him when I understood from that note of his—that he meant to say that he had seen any reason to alter his opinion—except (as far as I could see)—for the worse.

MS, MHi

[18] Sophia Peabody wrote back, "I *have* begun the memorandum of Foster. I am going to try to paint him next week—Don't tell Sam" (Sophia Peabody to Elizabeth Peabody, 3 June 1836, MS, NN-B).

Elizabeth Peabody's impatience wtih her sister Mary's conventionality and deference to others bursts forth in this apologia.

⚡ To Mary Peabody

[Boston]

My dear Mary—   [week of May 16, 1836][1]

I am already provoked that I have been obliged to defer so long answering your excellent letter of Saturday[2] which—considering on what grounds it starts—is quite a masterpiece—But I have had no time—& now may not get this done for Mrs. Swain—I shall reply to you passage by passage—

You begin by saying that no one who would love you as you want to be loved—would find what they want in you.—Now I should like to know *how you want to be loved* & wherein my love of you has failed—if it has failed—You say you have not satisfied my intellect when you have satisfied my moral sense—I will reply that you have always satisfied my intellect—when you have done justice to your own—& never disappointed me in that way except when you have stopped short—through some whim—on a course of thought. There is a class of Ideas which I do not think you *originate.*—But there are no Ideas that you are not fully able to take—reflect upon—& actuate. I have sometimes been provoked to find that because you could not *perceive* for yourself some Ideas—you would not *receive* them—& that you would go upon the notion that they were not intended for you—

1 This letter refers to the "Cabinet of Fine Arts" Cornelia will carry back to Boston, and so was most likely written in the week following May 15, the date of the previous letter mentioning the cabinet.

2 Mary's letter, which Elizabeth paraphrases here, has not been located. In another ca. 1836 letter in which she agrees with Elizabeth's decision to leave the Alcotts's house, Mary writes: "I know you would not be happy at home where [?] we should be very happy to have you. You know Nath—& Welly are going very soon to South Boston So those sources of vexation would be withdrawn and here you might write tranquilly—But I don't think you would be so happy here at present. You and I had better live apart for a time, at least. But of all things I want you to come away from the Alcotts—If you do not, I think I shall give you up to your devices, or never give you any more advice about any thing. If you will go to a new place, and lay down that rule I suggested about speaking or writing of your self even for *one* year, I think the health of your mind will improve—I do not think it is quite a sound one now— " (MS, MHi). Mary's "rule," in the context of her advice to Elizabeth not to keep a journal, seems to recommend a minimum of introspection.

& you were responsible upon them.—I do not say you have not Perception & Embodiment of *much*—In the article of Embodiment I think you surpass me in proportion to your Perception—very much—Your fancy is beautiful—& your grace of execution very great—I am aware that there is a class of Ideas—those which concern the Moral & Intellectual Absolute in which I am more highly gifted as far as Original Perception goes.[3] But I cannot see why that should make any difference between us—since you are abundantly able to receive every view which I can take—& are more felicitous in embodying it.—

You say you believe confidence depends as much on *circumstances* as upon anything else. Here I think you make the mistake. Confidence depends on *Will*.—And when circumstances have united two individuals in the same family—chosen them alone out of the family for a common duty—given them the same education & the *same friends*—it requires but a small exertion of Will—to make the confidence perfect. I do not think *circumstances* always or perhaps often help the confidence of husband & wife *so much* as circumstances have helped ours.— Even in that relation—a *will* controlling circumstances—is absolutely necessary always to keep up confidence. How few instances—give a perfect image of confidence in that relation.—

But you come to the confession in your next sentence. It is not *Circumstances* that prevent confidence on your part towards me. You acknowledge what I have said a thousand times & what you would not admit—& thought me most *unreasonable* to believe—that it was *something in me* which prevented your confidence.—You say "When the question is of discretion, I must say that I should not choose you for my confessor." Now this is the beauty of your letter & why I like it— that you tell the simple unvarnished truth.—I hope you never will desert this point again—but that you will always acknowledge to yourself & to me whenever this subject is up—that *you do not confide in me because you do not think I have discretion.*—

Now as I think *I have discretion* & as I think *discretion is an entirely essential thing*—Your coming to this decision—& acting upon it—as it has ever been perfectly plain that you have—with the most entire confidence that your impressions in regard to my *indiscretion* are correct—& without ⟨allowing⟩ making me either explain the cases away—or acknowledge their character—*is & ever has been the wound that I have felt perpetually irritated between us.*

---

3 "Original" is smudged in the MS, and it is not clear whether Peabody wished to cancel it.

Discretion as a sentiment implies sensibility to the feelings of others—when these feelings are consistent with their *well-being*—and a thoughtful sensibility of heart makes *recklessness* impossible. Indiscretion as a sentiment implies *recklessness*.

If you believe I am by sentiment and principle indiscreet—you have no moral right to love me at all—and it is *wicked* in you to ever express any respect or esteem for my character.—Indiscretion is a trait of character that cannot exist ⟨alone⟩ without other evils. It cannot exist alone.

Discretion as an overt act—has to do with particular cases always—A friend who has any opportunity for free intercourse fails in the first duty of friendship—who allows another friend to commit an act of indiscretion—without being made sensible of it.—

But you say that I *cannot bear* being told of my faults. Here is a point on which you have always done me injustice. You have, for instance, when you have thought or fancied or got the impression that I have done a mistaken action—an indiscretion for instance—accused me of being in sentiment utterly reckless—undervaluing the virtue itself which I have failed to represent—& then expected that I was to be perfectly quiet within & without accepting the charge! Worse than this—not seldom you have not even told me anything—but only *acted on the ground for a long while,* that I not only had not this virtue—but never would could or wanted to have it,—and therefore you have arranged your life under this category with respect to me—making its whole cast one continual insult to my powers of improvement in action—& my actual sentiments.—

If I am indiscreet in sentiment—if I have this gulf in my character—*who but you has ever been in a situation to cure me of it? Where did you get your immunity from the duty of working at it—till it was cured? & till my* conscience was awakened to it? ⟨I do⟩ And[4] supposing you do not think it *is all that*—but that my indiscretions are single acts.—what kind of friendship is that which would let me go on doing injustice to my own character—without doing your best to make me see the *individual case*—in some other way than merely referring to it—when the time is past & all the circumstances—forgotten—& the matter quite irremediable.—

---

4 "Do" is smudged in the MS, and Peabody might have been attempting to cancel it. "And" clearly begins with a capital, so it is likely she neglected to cancel "I do" more definitely.

There is, however, one palliation of this *offence* or this *failure in the duty of friendship*—which you *do have*—I will not admit that I am impracticable—but I will allow that I have not been a very easy person to deal with—that I have been a very agitated person ever since you came into personal relations with me—that the first year after we came from the East ward[5]—I was too diseased & irritable to be dealt with comfortably—& that I did not help you at all to do your duty to me—But I made what you called satisfactory reparation in confession & gratitude to you afterwards—& we began again & went on very well for a good while & during my first winter in Boston—my summer with Mrs. Prescott—& my year with Mr. Russell I am sure I acted with as much conscientiousness & deliberation as you could wish—& we had union & confidence—with very little shadow.

I am very well aware—that when the family came to Boston—& things went so contrary to what I thought right—especially after I got to Tremont Place—that I became a trial again through my extreme irritability and more especially after the N. Bedford affair took place.—There I was accused of Indiscretion (when I was not indiscreet) by those for whose comfort I deliberately sacrificed the sympathy of almost all my former friends—my reputation became the victim of Mrs. Farrar's cold hearted selfishness—Perhaps there was never a purer disinterestedness in any body's heart in all respects—than there was in mine—when I began that terrible winter of 1830.—I am willing to allow the trial was too great for me—I was *overcome with Evil*—What with the call on feeling & intellect—in sympathy with Anna;—the labour on those children—Frank—ER [?]—the Gannets—& Hathaways;—the loss of accustomed sympathy especially from Mrs. Sullivan—Mrs. Guild—& Sally Gardiner;—the failure of the school;—the condition of the boys prospects; the injustice from N. Bedford; & the naturally withering effect of all the moral deformity included in all these things;—& Dr. C away at the time of trial[6]—I feel that the *stimulus failed*—& Life lost its character of Moral *Beauty*

5 In 1825, Elizabeth Peabody returned from Maine, which is probably what she means by "the East ward." The following year she moved to Boston. William Russell began teaching at Elizabeth and Mary's school in 1827. In 1828, the Peabody family moved to Boston.

6 "The terrible winter of 1830" and indeed this entire section in the letter refers to the previously mentioned intervention by Peabody on behalf of some of her students who, she thought, were being cheated of their inheritance. As a result of her spirited involvement, Peabody's reputation suffered, as she says, at the hands of Mrs. Eliza Farrar. "Frank . . . Sally Gardiner" were children, their parents, and Peabody's friends at the time of the New Bedford incident.

even to *my hopes*. But when you returned from Rhode Island I had a
good deal risen—I know I was too violently affected by Dr. Spurzheim's death just at the moment when I thought I might possibly
gain from him the resurrection & the life—& I know that I felt too
painfully the sequestration from Dr. Channing—but I think that from
the time you returned from Rhode Island—*your want of confidence*[7]
was the most galling—as well as most unnecessary—& most disastrous
to me.—I do not think that ever before you so completely matured a
plan of treating me in a selfdefending—& to me heart withering manner.—In your mind was perpetually the fact that I *was* what the New
Bedford affair tended indeed to *make me*.—I do not know what would
have become of me—if Mr. M— had not fallen like an Angel of comfort & sustaining friendship on my path—received my confidence—&
mended my heart with his essential approbation—& unshadowed sympathy.—He restored to me the Idea of my Character—& was almost a
Lethe & quite a Eunoe to my Soul.[8]—I *did hope* no bitterness would
ever mingle with this new stream of friendship—where we both could
drink without visitations from the demon peopled Past—I did feel
that he drew us together in becoming a common object of affection to
us—& in respecting us both *equally* as it were—and I cannot conceive
what you can mean when you say *you* were "never conscious of separation" when you say in other parts of your letter that we were so very
[one word illegible] always ever since we have been together—which is
much stronger than I should state it—for I think we have always enjoyed a great deal from each other—although we have always been
separated—or at least always were till then—

As I said before—I do not know whether I shall ever say any thing
to Mr. M— on this subject. That I never can feel that happy union
which for a time I enjoyed with you & him—in thinking that here was
a part of our mutual experience that was as transparent as Heaven's
intercourse will be—until this matter is explained is true.[9] But I feel

7 "Your want of confidence" is underlined twice in the MS.
8 Elizabeth Peabody's proper but passionate relationship with Horace Mann
has already been discussed; here she compares his influence to that of Lethe, the river
of forgetfulness, and Eunomia, daughter of Zeus associated with order and the season of summer.
9 Mary Peabody saw things differently. Several years later, she wrote these bitter
lines to her sister: "My own opinion is that he [Mann] thinks you have lorded it over
me in a certain way & that has always made him indignant—as long ago as when we
were at Mrs. Clarke's he used to express indignation about it to Sarah [Clarke] for
she told me of it then. . . . I think you not only do but *never have* seen my husband
exactly as he is. . . . There are chords in me that you have severed [?] that vibrate

that I can bear this without its destroying my character—In the place of a pure enjoyment—I shall have *much pleasure* but united with a degree of *endurance*—which I hope I may endure as a Christian. I have little hope I shall ever come *so near* Happiness again—in human circumstances.—But life is not everlastingly *hemmed in* by circumstances that grow opake [opaque] in the absence of the will to control them & make them transparent.—Should I ever say anything to Mr. M— it would be of this sort—I should acknowledge that I *cannot feel* confidence in the Human Affections beyond their manifestion by circumstances—or in spite of an everlasting contradictory circumstance, any more than he can *feel* confidence in the Divine Love—when he does not *understand the action*—& shall confess to him that the dropping of that veil *before me* which was raised *to you—makes me—feel as if there was something very peculiar in me which can make the difference*—& I shall ask him if he cannot say *something* that will make me feel differently—

You speak of its being constantly expressed to you that I have no discretion &c—& you think I have lost the best opportunities any body ever had for the kind of confidence I desire—

This means that I have thought it right to act sometimes differently from what other people think right—Mrs. Prescott doubtless thinks I am indiscreet—& Mrs. Cleveland—& whoever has been annoyed by my action—But I never have done or said any thing which affected another—in recklessness of their feelings—& without having a good reason for it—I certainly never did anything that would trouble another—or was at all likely to—unless absolute sense of duty compelled me. But it is much easier for people—when they do not like a thing—to say another did it recklessly or from selfish ends—than to seek & find out the principle—even when the way is so simple—as *to ask the agent.* I am not surprised in this—except it comes from one who has had a chance to know my character.

One word more—

In looking back on my life—with respect to you—and the rest of our family—and with respect to Mr. Alcott—since the middle of last summer—I perceived that I have not adjusted the virtue of *forbear-*

---

only with agony—It might cease to be so from this day if you could only *practically* realize that you are sometimes in the wrong in your intercourse with people" ([1843?], MS, NN-B).

ance correctly with that of *frankness*—Feeling that forbearance was always a concession to human weakness,—where I have wished to *respect most*—I have felt as if forbearance was more of an insult than it was any thing else.—As I have in the course of time—dwelt on the advantages of *truth & transparency*—& felt that there was to be in the Soul developed a *Love* that would preclude offences—I have more & more ceased to practice *forbearance.*—Here is my sin—& I shall try to *sin no more* in this way. That I am capable of forbearance when I see that *that* is the instrument—*past* time may show. Was I not forbearing with Mr. Russell from first to last & through some disappointment?—Was I not forbearing with Mrs. Prescott?—to F. Hill—Blakes—& Cabots?—With the Benjamins? & indeed in *what instance* that I thought *clearly saw* that this was the way—have I not kept in it? I never thought it was the way to deal at home—& I must say that with all the evil my want of forbearance has done—it is a question with me still whether in some instances—it was not more needful to impress the *truth* in all its naked ugliness—

You advise me not to keep a journal—& not to think of myself for three years.—I have found that the study of myself the last two years—has produced none but good effects—that I am calmer—clearer—wiser—stronger—I am sorry to find that you do not see the advantage of it—& that your advice finds no echo of suitableness in my mind.—

Forgetfulness of one's self in some active duty—having sole & absorbing reference to others—is some times a specific for temporary evils & diseases—But I think I have received all the benefit which *such* appliance can bring—& at *thirty two years* of age & about *commencing a life of study*—I hardly see what can be your imagination of the possibility of such a thing—& still less what advantage you think can be gathered?—*It is the only thing* I have never done yet—my own peculiar Intellectual Life has been *sacrificed—consciously sacrificed* my whole life—from the time I left Lancaster—The best year that has occurred since—was that year I kept a journal in Brookline—the next best was that comparatively solitary year that you were in Cuba—I mean for intellectual cultivation—& the recovery of moral dignity.—But in saying this last I do not mean to exclude *your influence*—for while you were in Cuba—all your virtues acted on me with more force from being unmixed with the pettiness of those things growing out of your want of confidence— (which are always annihilated with me—except when they are actually occurring & acting on me.)—

And here I suppose I may as well end this discussion.—That there is a better world you believe as well as I.—I believe it is nearer than you do—even *at hand*—& *within*.—You think it is above the region of Circumstance, & thus thinking you can never find it till beyond the grave.—Whatever may be the circumstances.—We certainly cannot *enter it together*—Till we be agreed concerning this possibility.—

I have just heard that Cornelia is to call on her way to Salem—& I believe I have done—so I will close up this letter. Mrs. Swain—with whom I passed last evening very pleasantly indeed at Rose's—will carry Sophia the Cabinet of Fine Arts today.—Goodbye I hope you will not find any "cruelty" in this letter.   E.

I wish you would return that letter ⟨of⟩ to Mr. Alcott by Mrs. Swain if she returns Thursday—And ask her to leave it at Rose's. If I do not see her I will call for it.

Bennet says there are opportunities to John [?] quite often this season. They heard yesterday that he was well.—*Why* does Wellington go to South Boston at present?—I should think it would be a *real loss to him*. Why cannot he wait at least till the lecture time—& let Nat *go alone*? Tell me if you send the Sartor to George—[10]

MS, MHi

[10] That is, Thomas Carlyle's *Sartor Resartus*.

To the eye of faith, Peabody says to Mann, creation itself speaks of God's redemptive love. For him, however, existence is still "a living grave."

✣ To Horace Mann

Lowell, Saturday night
My dear friend   [August 1, 1836]
There can be nothing more beautiful to appearance than this evening, with the darkling moon in the black sky—black from its deep clearness. But what is tranquil dark sky for a spirit that enquires and can gain no assurance into the state of an absent suffering friend?

This anniversary night[1]—how fares it with the unconsoled mourner?—this is the question that keeps my heart awake and restless, although all nature and man seem to have wrapt themselves in midnight's stillness. I have wished that I was in Boston tonight, not that I could be sure that you would come, and tell the tale of sorrow to my aching ear and heart, but that I should feel that if you *did not,* it was from *your choice,* from your feeling that it was better to be alone. I know that solitude is sometimes more for our peace in sorrow than in the tenderest friendship, but solitude must be a choice, not a necessity, *to do us good.* The soul of man should always feel that it has adequate sympathy at its command, that if it inclines to speak there is an ear ready to listen, that there is a heart of friendship strong enough to bear our burden if we but lay it down. Let this be a conviction and then perhaps there is often relief in choosing solitude, We are alone without feeling abandoned.

That note of yours, which closed with speaking of yourself as buried in a living grave (an image containing much truth and some consolation to such a heart as yours, as it implies the conception of the loved one, *in life*) had in it a sweet assurance. It is much to know *there is a plectrum* which may strike a sound of joy from the long silent strings that have once discoursed such music of happiness, and of late such *dirges of woe.* It seemed to me as if I should be able sometimes to use that hoarded wealth of your memory, whose very utterance would *react* in consolation. How gladly would I listen to words which such a theme and such a feeling as it excites would bring forth, and I am sure you would be relieved to make any heart the depository of what overflows from yours, and yet leaved no void.

I hoped to see you again in Boston, and had a letter from your friend C[2]—which would have compensated you for coming, for it was full of her friendship for you—and of those you are never weary. She spares, however, some space to speak of her affection to me, and as you know how I have always estimated her, you may be sure that you have conferred no slight good upon me when you have given the occasion

---

[1] Charlotte Mann died on August 1, 1832; in 1836, August 1 fell on a Saturday. Hence the speculation as to month and year.

[2] Catherine Haven was the daughter of Dedham judge Samuel Haven and sister of Lydia Sears's husband Samuel Foster Haven. During the time Mann practiced law in Dedham in the late 1820s, a friendship developed between them, until Judge Haven felt Mann was blocking Catherine's genuine suitors and obliged him to sever their relationship.

of this. She tells me very distinctly, however, that though she should love me for the fact of *your* having found in me a friend when you were in sorrow, and of *her* having gained through my means a means of communication with you, yet not for that *alone* does she love me, but for myself. But I have good reason to believe that had it not been for you, she never would have found out that there was any thing in me deserving of being loved for itself alone. Do you suppose that I mention this as a reason for not valuing this late reciprocation of a regard and admiration I have always felt? By no means. It is all the dearer to me that it has this association with you. I love to trace as many *other* blessings as I can to the same dear friend that I know has done more than any other person to restore to me *the birthright* of my being—self-confidence.

It is Sunday morning, the morning of *the resurrection*. I hope you admit its delightful associations into your mind, that you realize your own rising from this "living grave" to that light which shall not have any evening. For my part, I should find evidence (were all other wanting) that I myself was a part of the all-loving, all-embracing, all-blessing spirit, who is our Cause and our Father, our friend, and final comforter, in my Infinite Faith in my power to comfort the sorrowing. Though baffled and for the time impotent as I generally feel that I am, yet the hope from the cloud of tears, and mortal sorrow will put on the immortality of spiritual joy. The truth is, that there *is* in the Universe this all-loving Spirit, and that I see it with my most inward faculty. I sometimes ask myself what is the reason you are not allowed to die, and enjoy again the free exercise of all your faculties of which you are so sure you are so nearly bereft here below? What is wanting to complete your character as a fellow-worker with angels, and the purified just! What action of your spirit does your dearest friend wait to see burst into life, that she may whisper to your soul, "It is finished. Come thou blessed of my father to the rest prepared for you." And *I do see* one thing wanting, without which heaven would not be a perfect heaven, and you could not enter into *every feeling* of the *angel*. You are not *as sure* of the love of God for you as you were of your wife's love. You could not commit your destiny into his hands with the same boundless confidence—there is a secret sense that you know better than He does what is good for you. I feel as if you would not be permitted to die until this sentiment has filled your heart. For as a *kind parent* would restrain his child from contemplation even of those animate, unless he had first felt through filial affection that these very duties were the *gift of love*. So God would keep the veil drawn over his holy of holies until the child who I am sure is his *well-beloved* shall have surrendered himself in the rapture of gratitude for the past *to be guided,* whithersoever the Father will, whether by an earthly path or not. At that moment the guided and the Guide will look at each other face to face *as friends.* What a friendship! *And why does it not exist?* What could be done to the vineyard, that has not been done to it?

Had you not *had all* which earth can offer (for its *quality* made up for its limited duration), it might be hoped that a *new blessing* would elicit the unbounded faith in God which God deserves from the heart which he created and which that heart could not withhold if it was quite true to itself. But blessing had done its utmost. *Passively* you have received everything that Omnipotence can bestow. One great last action is called for you in you—the supreme act of disinterestedness and magnanimity—"Father, *not as I will,* but as thou wilt." The last eight words are involved in the utterance of the first. Could I hear it on your lips in such a *heart tone* as I have heard you pronounce *some words,* could I see it in your countenance, was it once uttered by your whole being—it seems to me I should not feel sure of your mortal life another hour; it seems to me I should be able with my own hand to close your eyes with thankfulness and joy. And though I could not think of the *bereaved race* without tears there would be no discord, but that grand bass-tone in all the echoes of my heart.

I find myself in a melancholy scene. *This* poor child's[3] faith stops very far short of yours, and her understanding comes to an end so long before yours does that it leaves much less scope for the exercise of the moral nature, which is the only source of faith. I doubt if we ever move from this spot. The Dr. commissioned me to quench her husband's last hope yesterday, and it was more painful to do then if I had been able to show him that were the finite joy ended, the *infinite* certainly commenced for him. The moral world is as much nought for him as you *imagine* for the sphere of your disembodied friend to be to you. But it is different to watch the entrance of a friend into the gate of heaven, the last gate, and to see them hovering without even knocking at the gate of Brotherly Love. *It is painful* to see an inferiority to ourselves in virtue, but there is a sense of sublimnity in seeing one superior to ourselves in virtue yet *not so happy in knowledge.* That sense of subliminity you give to your friend.

Elizabeth

3 Lydia Sears Haven died of tuberculosis in the summer of 1836.

P.S. Let me know of your *whereabouts* all this month—it is an anxious season for your friends. It was the last part of this month last season which made you sick. Let me know if you are sick. I want to know. Send for George and tell him if you are too sick to let me know yourself. Where do you live?

TS copy, OYesA

Peabody severs her ties with Alcott, and begs him to reconsider publication of Conversations with Children on the Gospels *for her reputation's sake, his own apparently already far gone.*

✄ To Amos Bronson Alcott

Dear Sir: August 7th 1836

The very day after my letter to you I received a communication from a friend; by which I learn that much more extensive than either you or I were aware of is the discussion of such subjects as it is known were discussed in connection with the birth of Christ censured even by friends of your system and of yourself, and that something of an impression was gratuitously taken up that I left the School on that account—an impression for which I can in no ways account, except it was thought I ought to leave it. For I have been *very wary* what I said about it—generally leading off from the subject when it was mentioned, but turning attention upon your purity of association being so much like that of children. For I always wanted the plan to succeed in this particular of it especially, so sure I am that it is impossible to keep children ignorant and that it is better to lead their imaginations than to leave them to be directed by idle curiosity. And yet I do not think I should ever have ventured so far myself. And a great many questions I thought were quite superfluous, and what was to be gained by them was not worth the risk of having them repeated and misunderstood abroad. A great deal is repeated, I find, and many persons, liking the school in every other respect, think it is decisive against putting female children to it especially.

I have told you this in the spirit of friendship, and hope you will not despise it. I am conscious of the effect of a few week's freedom from the excitement of being a part of the School, or taking down that exaggerated feeling which made every detail of it seem so very important to the great course of Spiritual Culture; and I never was under half the illusion in this respect that you were.

But with respect to the Record: whatever may be said of the wisdom of pursuing your plan as you have hitherto done in the school-room, where you always command the spirits of those around you (only subject to the risk of having your mere words repeated or mis-interpreted) I feel more and more that these questionable parts ought not to go into the printed book, at least that they must be entirely disconnected with *me*.

In the first place, in all these conversations where I have spoken, I should like to have that part of the conversation omitted, so that it may be felt that I was entirely passive. And I would go a little farther: there is a remark of Josiah Quincy's about the formation of the body out of *"the naughtiness of other people"* which is very remarkable. Please to correct that in my record. But if you wish to retain it, you can add a note in the margin saying: "the Recorder omitted Josiah's answer in this place, which was &c. &c."—putting Josiah's answer in your note.

There are many places where this might be done, and thus the whole responsibility rest upon you. I should like, too, to have the remarks I made on the Circumcision omitted. I do not wish to appear as an interlocutor in that conversation either. Besides this, I must desire you to put a preface of your own before mine, and express in it, in so many words, that on you rests all the responsibility of introducing the subjects, and that your Recorder did not entirely sympathize or agree with you with respect to the course taken, adding (for I have not the slightest objection), that this disagreement or want of sympathy often prevented your views from being done full justice to, as she herself freely acknowledges. In this matter yourself also is concerned.

Why did prophets and apostles veil this subject in fables and emblems if there was not a reason for avoiding physiological inquiries &c? This is worth thinking of. However, you as a man can say anything; but I am a woman, and have feelings that I dare not distrust, however little I can *understand them* or give an account of them.

Yours, etc.

E. P. Peabody

MS copy, MH. This letter is found, copied in Bronson Alcott's hand, in his MS volume "Memoir, 1878."

Elizabeth Peabody's pedagogical and personal conflicts with Alcott, revealed so powerfully in her 1836 letters, intersected with a larger criticism of Alcott's school and teaching method. She correctly noted that the discussions of birth and circumcision in a school of girls and boys was causing horror and outrage among the students' parents and in the larger community. After the publication of these conversations, the attack on Alcott's morals and propriety was nearly universal. The editor of the Courier, *Joseph Tinker Buckingham, labeled Alcott "either insane or half-witted," "an ignorant and presuming charlatan." The* Recorder *printed the conclusion of a local clergyman that Alcott's "filthy and godless jargon" was simply an example of the poison of Transcendentalism (quoted in Madelon Bedell,* The Alcotts *[New York: Clarkson Potter, 1980], 130–31).*

Alcott's general teaching methods at Temple School were a target of growing public criticism. Harriet Martineau severely criticized Alcott's relegation of the body to the status of symbol for the spirit, exclaiming, "such outrageous absurdities might be left to contempt, but for the consequences in practice. . . . His system can be beneficial to none, and must be ruinous to many. If he should retain any pupils long enough to make a full trial of his methods upon them, those who survive the neglect of bodily exercise and over-excitement of the brain, will be found the first to throw off moral restraint" (Society in America, 2 vols. [New York: Saunders and Otley, 1837], 2: 277–78). *Nathan Hale, editor of the* Boston Daily Advertiser and Patriot, *indicted Alcott's experiment in progressive education for unnatural stimulation of curiosity, lack of exercise, and moral laxity. "The essence of the system appears to be, to select the most solemn of all subjects—the fundamental truths of religion as recorded in the gospels of our Saviour,—and after reading a chapter, instead of offering any illustration of what is there recorded, to invite the pupils to express, without discrimination or reserve, all their crude and undigested thoughts upon it—and especially on those points which are most difficult to be understood and not excepting those upon which inquisitiveness is useless, and often improper and mischievous."* (Boston Daily Advertiser and Patriot, 21 March 1837)

Elizabeth Peabody shared these pedagogical concerns, and this letter clearly indicates that she feared for her already somewhat shaky reputation. She was also concerned about Sophia's reputation; her youngest sister served as recorder while Elizabeth had been away. Peabody's attempts to distance herself from the text in which these excesses appeared as well as from Alcott himself may be seen in the "Re-

corder's Preface" to the first volume of Conversations with Children on the Gospels. *Here she announced the theme of the text—the presentation of a new type of evidence for the truth of Christianity in the intuition of children.* Conversations *would show the startling affinity of the child for the character and teachings of Jesus. However, what is said here is not to be taken as necessarily representative of Alcott's views; "still less are they to be regarded as any intimation of the recorder's; who, though occasionally an interlocutor, was, in general, a passive instrument, and especially when she felt that she differed from Mr. Alcott, on the subject in hand, as was sometimes the case"* ("Recorder's Preface," in Conversations with Children on the Gospels, 2 *vols. [Boston: James Munroe, 1836–37], 1: iv).*

This letter of August 7, 1836, represents Elizabeth Peabody's final break with Alcott as colleague and boarder. However, she was still able to see much that was worthy in his experiment. In early 1837, she wrote a long and penetrating analysis and defense of Alcott's method for the Register and Observer, *in which she commented that Alcott's lack of rigorous logic in his conversations was of positive benefit to the children: "Their young brains ought not to be exercised in chopping logic. Their pure imaginations should wander free into the eternal reason"* (undated clipping in Alcott, "Autobiographical Collections," *1834–39, MS, MH).*

A description of George Ripley's clash with Andrews Norton over publication of the view that belief in the historicity of miracles is not required of Christians.

✼ To Mary Peabody

My dear Mary—   [November 23, 1836][1]

I have written to Sophia a long letter[2] about my journey & arrival—but have reserved for you all I learnt about the Ripley affair.[3]—It seems that all the Ministers, (Mr. Young & Mr. Palfrey ex-

[1] "Concord Nov. 23" is written at the top of the first MS sheet in another hand; the date is also part of the address. Peabody often stayed at the Emersons when she visited Concord in the late 1830s.

[2] This letter has not been located.

[3] George Ripley graduated form Harvard Divinity School in 1826 and was installed as minister in the new Purchase Street Church in Boston, a Unitarian congre-

cepted)[4] entirely approve of the course Ripley has taken—altho' they do not generally *believe* with him in regard to the question of *Inspiration*. Mr. Young has openly preached against the article.—Mr. Palfrey thanked God in his next Sunday's ⟨sermon⟩ prayer for the evidence of miracles—implying in the same ungenerous spirit as Mr. Norton has done—that Mr. Ripley attacked miracles!—But the theological students almost to a man have come to see Mr. Ripley—& are extremely interested in his views—& the courses of study & thought that have led him to this view of Inspiration. For to them it is a matter of great interest—since Mr. Norton's influence in denying the doctrine of Inspiration—has been thought for a long while to have originated the palsy that lay so long on the Theological school—& from which it has only begun to rise since he left it.—The laity have taken the false idea from Mr. Norton's letter—that Ripley does not allow the miracles— or takes away their use;—but even that has done good—for it has revealed the fact hitherto unknown to the ministers—that the bulk of the thinking laity do not believe in miracles—& that their *incredulity* on this point affects the soundness of their belief in Christianity—& thus that they need to have the foundation in Inspiration clearly brought out—& the miracles also placed on their true foundation—Mr Ripley says that even the false impressions that have gone forth from Mr. Norton's letter are valuable—for it has roused attention to the

---

gation. Ripley immediately plunged into a study of German literature and theology, particularly the work of Schleiermacher. In the November 1836 issue of the *Christian Examiner*, Ripley reviewed James Martineau's *Rationale of Religious Inquiry*, an attempt to use scientific principles to determine the truths of religion. At the end of the review, Ripley raised the question of miracles, asserting that acceptance of them has never been a test of Christian faithfulness and that Jesus' miracles could not be seen as the sole confirmation of his divinity. In an angry rebuttal published in the Boston *Daily Advertiser* (November 5, 1836) Andrews Norton restated his position that miracles are the sole and incontrovertible evidence that Jesus' words are to be taken as divine truth. Norton also proposed that in the future those who challenge the views of authorities should be sure of their ability to do so and should submit their writing to others before publishing (Hutchison, *Transcendentalist Ministers*, 58–60).

After this controversy, Ripley edited *Specimens of Foreign Standard Literature*, a series of translations of European Romantic texts. He was one of the original members of the Transcendental Club, a contributor to the *Dial*, and together with his wife, Sophia, the organizer and leader of Brook Farm. In 1849, Ripley succeeded Margaret Fuller as literary critic for the New York *Tribune*, gradually arriving at a position of prestige and security, eventually having great influence on the development of American literature in the decades following the Civil War. He died in 1880.

[4] Unitarian clergyman Alexander Young served South Church in Boston for nearly thirty years.

subject & created an *audience* on *several subjects*. He is not in the least alarmed about Mr. Norton's suggesting that he does not believe in miracles because he says—he is sure of his ground—he *does* believe in them—and he knows *why*—& he knows or has a clear view of *what they were intended for*—In this *Review of James Martineau* he has undertaken to say that they *are* not—& were not intended as—*proofs of Inspiration*—for Inspiration has a more interior—& more mental proof.—And this is a very important point to have established.—If *Inspiration* is to rest for its evidence on *miracles*—which are themselves to be established by *historical evidence*—then all Christianity rests on *history*—& Jesus Christ is not the same yesterday today & forever—The ministers—although they defend Mr. Ripley in saying his say—are not generally of his opinion in regard to the place of miracles, but Dr. Channing told Mr. Ripley he was astonished to find how *general* among the intelligent laity was the doubt as to miracles. He said Mr. Mann was at his house then—and expressed his opinion very fully & said that unless the clergy changed their ground & addressed the nature of man to find the evidences of Christianity founded therein they would find themselves entirely behind the age.—Dr. Channing's ground is different in point of doctrine from either Mr. Norton's or Mr. Ripley's. He believes that Inspiration has one evidence—& miracles another—as Mr. Ripley does—But he thinks that miracles were intended for a different purpose than that which Mr. Ripley does—& he *did think,* (he says,) that they constituted the evidence of Christianity *with people*—while now he begins to suspect that the contrary is the case—And Mr. Norton has been so long engaged in demolishing Inspiration—that it has left Christianity without effective evidence in the Unitarian community. Dr. C. is full of animation on the subject—and says that the effect will be to produce a *revival* in the dead churches: and at the meeting of the Christian Examiner proprietors at his house—it was decided that *free discussion* should be carried on in the Examiner—& since Mr. Walker resigned as soon as Mr. Norton came out in this way—a new Editor is to be chose who will carry it on. As soon as this was discovered by Mr. Norton & Mr. Palfrey *they withdrew*—& so I suppose Mr. Walker will be persuaded to resume.—It seems that Mr N attacked Mr W about this article in a very uncivil way—and after a long talk Mr W said that *he being the Editor*—If he were again to receive the article he should put it in—& that a meeting had better be called & a general principle adopted—free discussion or sectarianism. When it was called—Mr Walker—like a king—resigned the Editorship (for Mr Norton had come out in the interval with his letter), & then simply as one of the number proposed that the question should be put. Mr Norton said the question was whether the Christian Examiner was to contain truth or *every opinion* that might be broached!—Mr Walker corrected him with saying that the question was whether the Christian Examiner should contain Mr. Norton's views—or whether the questions that were in the minds of the contributors & the public should be *discussed*.—Mr Norton doubted whether there was any *question* of this nature among sensible men! Mr. Walker said—& other gentlemen joined him—that it was *the* question at present among thinking people. Mr. N—asked if he really believed when he put that article in that any person would agree with it. Mr. W—said that he himself did not exactly agree with it—but that he *knew* it would meet & satisfy a large class of minds & that it was the view of a portion of the association of Ministers.—No, said Mr Norton—only of *women & very young women*!!—Mr Walker reminded him that if no controverted topic was admitted into the Examiner— his articles—denying the inspiration of St Paul—& that article of Mr Noyes's[5]—which Mr Norton forced into the Examiner—& which a meeting of Unitarians in Boston thought it necessary for them publicly to disown—in which the Inspiration of the Prophecies was denied—[two words illegible]—been excluded—Mr Norton then changed his ground & said the good of the public should be consulted. Another replied that the question was exactly this—whether the good of the public did not require *free discussion*. *Dr. Parkman*[6] said—that he did not think the public could be so much injured by the article in question, whatever might be the decision respecting it—as by the manner in which the subject had been bro't before the public. Was not that *brave* for Fanny?—The truth is Mr Norton got *black and white* all round—& it is so much the more valuable—because the Company did not agree with Mr Ripley—but thus decided on the *general principle*. They adjourned to Dr C's study—& there it was finally determined that the Examiner should go on. For one plan was to give it up—& the Liberal party including Dr C—Mr Walker— (all indeed but Mr N & Palfrey) to start a new one.—But the opinion was unanimous that this would kill the Christian Examiner—for there is no sympathy with Mr

[5] George R. Noyes, "Whether the Deity of the Messiah be a Doctrine of the Old Testament," *Christian Examiner*, 3rd ser., 3 (January 1836), 273–302.

[6] Francis Parkman, father of the historian by the same name, was a Unitarian minister who studied theology under William Ellery Channing and at Edinburgh University. Active in the affairs of the Ministerial Association, Parkman served New North Church in Boston from 1813 to 1849. He died in 1852.

Norton in the community—His disbelief in Inspiration being even a greater sin than it would be even to give up the miracles—which the Inspiration party do not mean to do.—It is said in [MS torn] that Mr Brazer & Mr Upham[7] have written to [MS torn] express their thanks at the course he has taken. I am afraid that I have given a very confused account—but I have been interrupted every minute—& have not told you half the good things that have been said all round. Ripley published today four or five sermons that he preached a year or two ago on this subject.[8] And how fortunately Furness's book on the real character & use of the miracles arrives in just now.[9]

MS, NN-B

7 John Brazer was minister at North Church in Salem; Charles Wentworth Upham, influential member of the Salem community and friend of Andrews Norton, was minister at Salem's First Church. Both of these were Unitarian congregations. If the defaced manuscript says they thanked Norton for his stand, this would be consistent with their general hostility toward Transcendentalism, most notably expressed in their harassment of Jones Very in 1838.

8 Peabody's reference is to Ripley's *Discourses on the Philosophy of Religion* (Boston: James Munroe, 1836).

9 That is, William Henry Furness, *Remarks on the Four Gospels* (Philadelphia: Cary, Lee, and Blanchard, 1836).

Peabody tries to recruit John Sullivan Dwight as a contributor for her proposed journal of education; it never materialized.

✖ To John Sullivan Dwight

Mr. J. S. Dwight,—[2]
    Dear Sir,   [1836][1]
    Mr. Theodore Parker told me last winter, that he spoke to you of a plan of mine, of writing, in the course of several years,—a manual of Education; for which I should need the assistance of other minds

1 After Peabody left Temple School, she tried her hand at various projects, including founding a journal. In a letter of August 23, 1836, to Sophia Peabody, Bronson Alcott refers to "Elizabeth's paper." "I hope she will carry her purpose into execution. Such a periodical is extensively wanted" (*The Letters of A. Bronson Alcott*, ed. Richard L. Herrnstadt [Ames: Iowa State University Press, 1969], 29). The University of Rochester has dated this letter 1837; it seems more likely to be 1836, since it appears to refer to the same journal, which never got off the ground.

2 John Sullivan Dwight, music critic, editor, Unitarian clergyman, received sev-

than my own: and that you replied that you would gladly furnish an article upon Music. Every time I have seen you since, I have wished to have a talk with you upon this subject, but have been prevented by the many persons present, and therefore I have concluded to write upon it,—and trust you will excuse the liberty I take in addressing you first.

My Manual is to be general in its character, but leaning toward the subject of female education. The first article is to be from my own pen, upon the Idea or final Cause of the institution of the Family, & the effect of its various relations in unfolding & cultivating the human being.—I wish to show that as it is the ⟨most⟩ only Universal Institution, so it is the most effective, having a bearing upon the whole nature of man. The second article is to be on the Religious view of Nature, as the second means of Education in order; & in this I shall recommend Drawing & Music as accomplishments that should be put at the command of every child, early enough to meet any genius that may exist, for expressing themselves by "simple severe lines" or by *sounds harmonious.* Mr. Graeter[3] has promised me an Article upon drawing to come next, of which he has already shown me the analysis; and I wish that you would give me one on Music. The next Article is to be upon the Use to be made of the Gospels in Education. And Mr. R. W. Emerson has given me his lecture on the Aims & Uses of Biography— for the *last.* I shall be glad if I can get all this finished in time to publish thus much—this winter—in one volume. But I cannot depend on Mr. Graeter for any particular *time.* I did wish to have it early enough for New Year—but this I think will be impossible now. My second volume is to be on the use to be made of the Moral Poetry of England in Education:—with commentaries on Bunyan, Spenser, Shakespeare, Milton, Coleridge, & Wordsworth,—showing young persons how they may make these authors assist them in the Science of Selfknowledge. I have also other volumes in contemplation, of which the plan is also laid out; but I will not trouble you with any farther account at present. I should like very much to have a long talk with you about it all—&

---

eral letters from Peabody in 1840–41, when he was removed from his first and only pulpit, the Northampton Unitarian Society, which he had filled for a single year. Peabody writes this letter to him in the period between his graduation from Harvard Divinity School in 1836 and his installation in Northampton in 1840.

3 Francis Graeter was the art teacher at Elizabeth and Mary Peabody's Colonnade Row school in Boston in the late 1820s.

wish you may come to Salem soon. Shall you not come and preach this winter?—

    With great respect & regard—

                Yr's Elizabeth P. Peabody.

P S. I have made no plans about the publication—but should like to know to what member of the American Stationer's Company—I ought to apply.—Can you tell me;—& whether you know any thing about the predilections of that company?—I hope you will write me a good long letter in answer and tell me something about the article on Music you shall write—if you conclude to do this—& I trust you will—for you are the only person I know who would be the least likely to write such an Article as I want.—

MS, NRU

Rusticated in Salem after the collapse of Temple School, Peabody reads and longs for the stimulation of Boston society.

✄ To Elizabeth Davis Bliss

                                             Salem,

My dear Mrs. Bliss,—   December 23rd 1836

    I return to you a manuscript which I have had a long time. I have read the original with it—& finding it not perfectly translated—have made another translation—which is more literal—but I guess it is correct. It is very hard—as every thing of John Paul's is[1]—but I think I had a different edition of the original—as my original is not quite so elaborately expressed and some few passages are omitted.

    I wish I were in your class at Miss Fuller's. I should enjoy reading with so fine a scholar. I made quite easy progress in Schiller—but find Goethe harder;—and really sigh for the speeding of a master or mistress.

    I meant to have called & had an hour or two with you on my return from Concord—for I thought I should then be full of interest to

---

[1] John Paul was the pen name of Johann Paul Friedrich Richter, German Romantic novelist and humorist.

you—But my time slipped out of my fingers—I hardly knew how.

Only think of my not hearing the Lectures![2] But I do not despair of having them in Salem.—This is a grand place for study—and reflection. I do nothing in the world by way of helping in the world save teach a Sunday School—& *act the nurse* occasionally to my invalid sister—who is very miserably this winter *(bodily)* —The rest of the time I read German & write letters—& occasionally write in a Common book. It seems another world than Boston. You cannot imagine how different it is.—But it has its peculiar pleasures.—

Have you read Mr. Furness's book—and Mr. Ripley's—& Mr. Brownson's—[3] I have—but nobody else in Salem I believe. The people here care about nothing stirring—& read every species & form of transcendentalism as if it were Evil Lore—one learns what one's self is made of in such a *Space;* how much & how *little.* But I enjoy it very much.

You know something of what my plans have been. As my paper has not obtained an adequate subscription I have been negotiating with a publisher to offer me some thing to write *a book* of the same name—to contain all my odd ends on education. And that scheme will assure me till it is frustrated. In the mean time I like to hear from Boston folks—do they ever keep up foreign correspondences?

Yours truly

E. P. PEABODY

MS, DLC

2 Peabody is probably referring to Emerson's lecture series, "The Philosophy of History," delivered at the Boston Masonic Temple from December 8, 1836 to March 2, 1837.
3 The books she mentions are William Henry Furness, *Remarks on the Four Gospels* (Philadelphia: Carey, Lea, and Blanchard, 1836); George Ripley, *Discourses on the Philosophy of Religion Addressed to Doubters Who Wish to Believe* (Boston: James Munroe, 1836); and Orestes Brownson, *New Views of Christianity, Society, and the Church* (Boston: James Munroe, 1836).

Peabody tries to explain her doctrine of decline from primordial harmony and her psychological interpretation of Paradise Lost; *she defends her method of rearing young Foster Haven.*

✎ To Horace Mann

My dear friend   January 11th, 1838
      I am so glad that you are going to lecture on any subject that will stir up your imagination and make you exert any artistic power (whose exertion is always so grateful in its influence on the feelings) that I do not delay to answer your letter, which I received a few hours since, even *one day.*
      It amuses me to think that your thoughts are taking the same direction as mine—but with characteristical difference of aim. I am also going back in my imagination to the primitive times, but it is my object to prove that all things began in a Paradasiacal harmony, from which man has strayed, but to which he must return. And *you* wish to prove that all things began in Chaos and still in Chaos are. *Of Chaos* you can find much [?] particular account in Milton's Paradise Lost, since he believed in the Eternity of Matter, and as a consequence I should say, in God's being but *half omnipotent.* By the way, I have been reading Milton this winter to a class of thoughtful young women, and out of it have lectured on mental and moral philosophy, and have found I think the ideal foundation of that wondrous poem as it existed in Milton's mind. The fall of the angels from Heaven into Hell is but an image of the fall of the powers of the inward nature of man from the peacefulness and happiness of Innocence into the fiery misery of Evil—a process which must take place before any outward evil action can be done. Satan in the heavenly state was self-respect, that sentiment which governs all the other powers. And the duty of feeling filial towards God is the only *higher* virtue to Self-respect. But the selfrespecting mind returns upon itself, instead of filially obeying. This is represented in the cause assigned for Satan's rebellion—which is God's exaltation of the Son (the filial spirit) to be *the first powers,* until all things are absorbed again in Himself. Self-respect falls in refusing to be filial and becomes Pride, which is the adversary of the Son and Father and of all peace and harmony. The host that followed Satan is all the powers of the mind, each evil angel being but a good power

wrongly bent and still half glorious with its spiritual origin. The armies of Satan and of Michael (which very name means Likeness to God), their encounter, represent the struggle of the good and evil of our natures. When Messiah comes to the rescue of his own, it represents the all controlling influence of the filial spirit, in purifying the mind. The punishment of the evil angels represents the nature of such evil in itself. Man placed in the midst of Chaos, in a garden, represents man innocent, but *free to do evil. Liberty* is imaged by Chaos on one side for man to range in, if he does not prefer the duty of worship and obedience, Chaos is the representative of man's liberty—in other words *the matter* in which we are immersed.

As to the ancient idea of Chaos, it seems to me to be a tradition of the Deluge. So far I agree with Bryant in his whimsical theory. His book, "The Analysis of Ancient Mythology,"[1] would perhaps give you the information you want, but as to pointing to pages and volumes, I should think as soon as giving you landmarks though Chaos itself is a fine exhibition of Chaos. It is in the Atheneum.

Instead I will send you herewith, and shall *I* be so bold as to add three lectures, which I wrote this winter for my classes? You can read them all in one evening for they do not require any study. This will show you my views of the old time, *somewhat.*

I have a little treatise planned, to be called "The Primitive World," or "The Fall of Man" (I have not concluded which). I want to speak of the Fall of Man as a universal tradition, pointing to a great historical fact. That fact is that Man was created and set into life in physical perfection, in harmony with the external world, &c., traditions of which time have come down to us in the story of Paradise and the Golden Age—that for aught we know generations of men are included in the two words of Adam and Eve.

But as men were made of two elements, the spiritual and material, and the former worked one way (by activity) and the other worked the other way (toward passiveness)—the very heights of present good to which men attained became a snare *so* that men were materialized— in other words lost the predominating activity of the spiritual principle, and sensual indulgence, false philosophy, political ruin were the consequences, and this change is the fall of man, a fall not of the spiritual principle itself as the Calvinists think, but of *the race as a race.*

[1] Jacob Bryant, *A New System; or, An Analysis of Ancient Mythology* (London: T. Payne, 1774–1776).

This is to be my first part. The second will be on *the Recovering principle* which has been ever since at work, but does not sufficiently understand its end, even when it thinks itself taught by Christ, its great Apostle. What do you think of my plan?

I think your plan is very good. You might make a fine poem, and Poetry is the true teacher of the people, and is not supposed to be *fiction* if it does not come in rhyme. It is indeed the only *truth*. I hope you will let me see your lectures—and you will, I think—to show me that you were not affronted at my criticizing *the others*. How many lectures shall you make?

In looking over your letter again, I find I have not answered your question. I do not think I know of any description of Chaos in old poets save Ovid's, but Lucretius probably had one. His philosophy—poor man—began and ended in Chaos.

And now with respect to what you say of my memoir of Foster.[2] I am much obliged to you for saying exactly what you differ in, thus far, because so I can get an opportunity of answering you. I only wish you had said all you thought. I meant to have asked you to sit by pen, ink and paper when you read it and write down what you thought was false.

I had no idea of implanting any error in Foster, by and bye to be rooted out. What I said to him I believed myself.

You say it is a capital error to say that *God put thoughts* into him? but pray tell me whence thought comes, if not from God. Of course I do not mean *words,* for they come from the outward world—but the power of thought, the ever-breathing Life of the Soul—is not that God's constant gift?

Now here is the *very root* of the matter, the very turning point of the difference between the Materialist and the Spiritualist. The latter believes God *is* and not *was* the Creator, that God forever and ever

2 Unfortunately, it is not clear how much the memoir she sent to Mann resembles "A Psychological Observation" published in *Lectures in the Training Schools for Kindergartners* (Boston: D. C. Heath, 1888). A later reflection told how Foster Haven's mother Lydia had been so tormented as a child by the thought of an angry God responsible for death and grief that she vowed to keep her own child ignorant of the fact of death and the name of God until he was old enough to understand. When Lydia herself was dying, Elizabeth Peabody was sent for. Lydia confided that she felt she had failed in raising the boy because he was so totally without affect. Peabody, on meeting Foster, realized that he had not been emotionally nurtured because of Lydia's fear that he would suffer when inevitable loss occurred, but Peabody encouraged him to respond to the world around him and to his inner experience. She gradually introduced the theme of a loving God, and eventually reconciled the boy to the impending death of his mother.

strives within us finite beings, and indeed that it is the circumscription of matter alone which makes us finite. When matter presses on us most powerfully we have but animal life. Even there, however, the life from God is powerful enough to organize a moving mass of clay and make it feel itself *one* with the living spirit within. But not all our spirit is embodied, for matter organizes our investigations into it, and all our intellect is clothed with material forms—*we think in pictures*. Yet still there is a degree of our spirit less subjected to matter and more god-like still—this is *Affection* and *Moral Sentiment*—the clearest presence of God we have. Now nothing short of a belief in God like this seems to me of any avail. Because you have a dry image, an Idol of the Intellect as Bacon says, which you call God, your theism is so inefficient in supporting your mind. I have endeavoured to tell you that God was just where you do not look for him—in your own moral sentiment, so all-controlling and irresistable that to your own consciousness your will seems to have no liberty. Because your will serves the true God which is Ideal Good (in the theist's view not an abstraction but a self-conscious active Being) with your whole heart and mind and strength and power, you feel as if you had no liberty. Nor can you conceive how the Image you call God (a combination of philosophical abstraction and early impression on your imagination) can have any power.

I told Foster that God put thoughts of good into him, when he tried to keep from being naughty. This is childish language but wisest philosophy. It means that good thoughts grow if we strive to keep pure and trust in the omnipotent, omniscient God who is ever present *creating* the Soul in all its powers.

I told him also that *naughty* was not from a source of power, but was the absence of the mind's unconsciousness of God, and *so it is*. Surely you think so. You do not believe in any evil spirit—you will allow that a wrong state of mind always arises from taking a partial view—a view which leaves out *the good*. Thus I should analyze to him his desire for his mother's good things. He must call for good thoughts and try to see that it was right not to have that which would deprive his mother of what was necessary for her health. As soon as he thought of that, he would be *willing* to go without. So it always proved when he wanted her fruit. I would say, "Would you have it, and leave poor sick mother without any, when she cannot eat meat and bread and butter that you can?"—and immediately he was perfectly willing to give it up. By addressing the affections through the reasoning intellect thus, so much of God as ever is present in affection awoke. You ask me if I had not better keep such subjects away from a child till he was older and could reason. I answer it is impossible. All children begin to ask on such subjects, at least if they are required to act right, and whenever they go into the subject they meet the same difficulties. I resolved questions for Foster which were in my own mind for years unsolved to the peril of my moral character—nay, to its corruption in many points. I gave him my own theory of evil and my own theory of good *as it is now*. I try to keep naughty out, in order that the good within me may expand, and in time of temptation I virtually beg of God that I may realize so much of *himself and his views of the matter* as to have no such temptation, and so temptation is conquered when it is conquered.

I wish you would not dismiss my views of evil so lightly. I should think it a crime to take advantage of a feeble mind as you suggest. But I do not think evil an entity. How curious it is that you should deny that good is an entity, as you always seem to do, and stickle for evil as an entity. Now I think good is entity, the only pure entity, and *evil is a state,* a partial consciousness of good. When partial good calls itself *entity,* and acts in its own partial state, then evil exists first moral, then natural, but always finite in its nature and limited in time—yes, limited even though its consequences stretch out of human vision.

But this is enough now, especially as you have my letter by Mary.

Mr. Foote will probably carry this bundle. He is an excellent fellow, who by pure merit and with a shrinking from all office-seeking as nice as your own, has been put into that place of Governor's counsel most unexpectedly to himself. They go to Susan's [?] to board *half* and more than half for the moral and intellectual advantage of *your* society. Mary (his wife) tells me that Mr. Foote has set his heart upon being in the same house with you, because he shall so value your views on all subjects. So see the advantage of your going about lecturing. You obtained this worthy disciple in your Salem sojourn. They are so intimate with Susan that it will not disturb the family circle. I am glad to find they all love you so dearly, and admire you so much. I hope you will be *condescending*. They have so much delicacy and *real feelings,* and comprehension of your case that you need not fear they will ever draw you into any embarrassments. Every subject over which you would draw a veil will be sacred to them without your being at the trouble of intimating it yourself. I do not know people with whom your wounded heart could be *safer* than with Mrs. C. and Susan and even with Lucy whose faults are many but not, I should think, of that sort. Mary thinks they value your society very much and understand you better probably than you can imagine.

Mary wants me to send up the letter I received from Sarah Clarke for you to read as you wanted to read it, she said. If I do, you must be sure and send it back by Mary next Wednesday.

Affectionately yours
Elizabeth P. Peabody

TS copy, OYesA

An invitation to a young clergyman to be part of a lecture series in Salem, and a reflection on the spread of Transcendentalist thought and expression.

✖ To Robert Waterston

My dear Robert—   Salem February 26th 1838

Your letter caused me some disappointment—but you certainly justify your refusal—and it cannot be gainsayed. Can you think of anybody who would do it well? I thought of Henry Bowditch[1]—who would be an object of great interest in Salem—But I hear his father is very ill—If he gets well & you know H. B. & should happen to meet him—why cannot you sound him on the subject. I have thought of Fox of Newburyport—but we should prefer not to have a clergyman. There are some objections to asking Mr. Taylor I think—the principal one is that he probably would refuse—and he is less appreciated in Salem than elsewhere I think.[2] However we may ask him—Besides he refused when asked once before.

I mean to try to get more of those biographical lectures from Mr. Emerson when I make my visit—But when you see Mr. Very tell him I am not *sure* of any but the one on Biography which is in my possession.[3] I have just been writing to Mary Channing a long letter about Mr. Emerson's idea of God   —I think he will convince you when he answers your letters—that altho' he denies personality to God—that is to say—any thing corresponding to our sense of personality that he

[1] Henry Bowditch was a Boston physician and abolitionist.
[2] Edward Taylor of Boston was one of the models for Melville's Father Mapple in *Moby-Dick*.
[3] As noted earlier, Emerson delivered a course of six biographical lectures in 1835 at the Masonic Temple. In 1836, he gave a private lecture course on English biography and literature in Salem.

saves the Selfconsciousness of Being. At least he startled me once in the same manner—& then cleared me up—so far.

Mr. Walker is to come to the Lyceum tomorrow night & I hope he will bring his lecture on Transcendentalism[4]—I always admire him & Mary heard & liked that lecture & did not think it contradicted anything important in Mr. E's transcendentalism. Will not Dr. C print his lecture on Peace?[5]

It seems rather ungrateful for your pleasant three pages to close so quickly—but I am rather dry of interesting matter—Sophia has had a month's severe illness—but now is getting better—and my brother George is sick in his chamber & nearly helpless with so strange a disease as paralysis & we feel rather dismal here.—[6]

When you wish to send to me—by giving a letter to William Howes—or William White (the former is the most direct) you can always send it to me—for they send every week—they are undergraduates—I do not know which class

Yours very truly

ELIZABETH P. PEABODY

Tuesday evening

I had just hear Mr. Walker's Lecture which is grand—Only I cannot understand why he refuses to name the transcendental facts he affirms to exist—*innate ideas* and I am afraid he made some backhanded thrusts at Carlyle & Mr. Emerson—But I shall see him tomorrow and will enquire into it.

MS, MSaE

4 This could be "Philosophy of Man's Spiritual Nature in Regard to the Foundations of Faith," 1834, a tract widely thought to be a defense of Transcendentalism but in fact a restatement of Scottish Commonsense philosophy.

5 Peabody's reference is to "Lecture on War" (1838), in which Channing outlines his case for selective conscientious objection (*The Works of William E. Channing* [Boston: American Unitarian Society, 1882], 664–79).

6 George Peabody was dying of spinal meningitis.

*A justly famous letter announcing her "discovery" of Nathaniel Haw-
thorne, although in response Mann was flatly unimpressed.*

✧ To Horace Mann

My dear friend,—   March 3rd [1838]¹

You may think that I do not feel very bright if a letters of yours
could lie in my portfolio a week unanswered.—And it is true that for
seven years at least—no calamity has ever oppressed me like this condition of George's—worse than death to him for it has not like death a
glorious reverse—in which the heart can repose—Next to vice—to be
a hopeless cripple is the most terrific thing—especially if the sufferer
is an energetic young man.—The heroism of his quiet & even cheerful
endurance heightens the pathos to me—of the case.—

And then I am meditating going to live in Baltimore myself—for
the sake of a *little* money. This is almost an intolerable sacrifice.—

So your report & letter have been unacknowledged²—I have thought
however I would give much for the sight of you—An hour or two of
your affectionate brotherly presence—such as I have had at some moments when I less needed them—would have been a real comfort. Now
that is impossible—or even a letter—in your present press of engagements.—And how can I write in this style to you—who are so full of
duties—so weary I know—& require so different a tone? Forgive my
selfishness!—

1 "1838," written after "March 3rd" in another hand, but is the appropriate
year for the content of this letter. In "Sometimes Things Just Don't Work Out: Hawthorne's Income from *Twice-told Tales* (1837) and Another 'Good Thing' for Hawthorne," *Nathaniel Hawthorne Journal* (1975): 11–26, Wayne Allen Jones transcribes
the text of this letter in full, correctly and conclusively attributing it to Elizabeth
Peabody and placing it properly in its context. Mann at this time, Jones notes, was
seeking authors for a series of books meant for the Massachusetts district school libraries, and Peabody recommended Hawthorne. In his article, Jones also provides a
transcript of Mann's reply of March 10, 1838. Regarding Hawthorne's stories, Mann
wrote, "I have read several of the 'Twice Told Tales.' They are written beautifully—
'*fine*' is the true word. But we want something nearer home to duty & business. . . .
such a story as the 'Wedding Knell,' wherefore is it, & to what does it tend?" (MS,
MHi).

2 Peabody refers to Mann's *First Annual Report of the Massachusetts-Board of
Education, Together with the First Annual Report of the Secretary of the Board*
(Boston, 1838).

After writing the above sentence I took up the pamphlet & read through both Reports—which are most animating—because they show that something is to be done now—and yours is very interesting as well as wise. But it seems to me you think school committee men more important than *the teachers.* You will smile if I say you speak of teachers as if they were the school boys in comparison. You speak of the legislature & school committee men as choosing books—A convention of *teachers* for that purpose—where books might be discussed—& then each book decided on *by vote* would be infinitely better. Teachers are the best judge of books. I should like to see an analytic table of contents for that book on morals you want to have written.—The moral class book of Mr. Sullivan is a stupid book for the young.[3] And this reminds me of something—which I wonder I had not thought of before.—

There is a young man in this town—not so very young either— (he is between thirty & forty years old)—of whom you have heard—the Author of the "Twice told Tales."[4] He is I think a man of first rate genius.—To my mind he [two words illegible] surpasses *Irving* even— in the picturesque beauty of his style—& certainly in the purity—elevation—and justness of his conscience—An extreme shyness of disposition—and a passionate love of nature—together with some peculiar circumstances have made him live a life of extraordinary seclusion. When he left college he did not fancy one of the three professions— but preferred that the literary part of his life should be ⟨in⟩*voluntary.*—In study and thought many years have passed—and occasionally he has dropped a gem into the passing periodicals—some of which are gathered into the above named volume ⟨periodical⟩. His time of study however has a length passed—and he is now turning his attention to taking up some serious business for his life—Authorship does not seem to offer a means of living—He has not thriven with the booksellers. His

[3] That is, an often-reprinted and widely used conservative textbook by William Sullivan, *The Moral Class Book, or the Law of Morals Derived from the Created Universe, and from Revealed Religion* (Boston: Richardson, Lord, and Holbrook, 1831).

[4] Nathaniel Hawthorne became, along with Mann, Jones Very, Emerson, and many refugee intellectuals, one of Peabody's "causes." As this letter suggests, she was concerned both with securing a livelihood for Hawthorne and enlarging his literary reputation. The first she accomplished through several interventions, resulting in Hawthorne's appointment as measurer at the Port of Boston, the second through letters such as this and through her unsigned review of *Twice-told Tales,* which appeared in the March 24, 1838, issue of Park Benjamin's *The New Yorker,* praising Hawthorne's "genius."

book which sold so quick has yielded him nothing by the delay & at length failure of the stationers company.[5] But he had in his mind one great moral enterprise as I think it & you will agree—to make an attempt at creating a new literature for the young—as he has a deep dislike to the character of the shoals of books poured out from the press—If you will take the trouble to read "The Gentle boy"—& "little Annie's Ramble" & "The Gray Champion" & "the Maypole of Merry Mount" you will I think see indications of a genius for such an enterprise that could not fail to make a *fortune* at last that would satisfy so very moderate desires as his—He told me of this scheme only to say he thought he should be obliged to give it up—But I think he has no genius for negotiation with booksellers—& moreover [one word illegible] he seemed inclined to *reconsider* when he found that I too thought this reform necessary & feasible.—He has deep views—thinks society in this country is only to be controlled in its *fountain of youth*—has a natural religion that overflows in silent worship—& the delicacy of his morality is I think beautifully indicated in "Fancy's Showbox—" another of those "Twice told Tales" which were not written for the young—but have merely been the amusement of his leisure hours.—He says that were he embarked in this undertaking he should feel as if he had a right to live—he desired no higher vocation—he considered it the highest.—Now you will agree with me in thinking this indicates a pure & noble mind—for he has political friends who have been offering him government offices & every temptation had he any low ambition—

I am quite acquainted with a sister of his[6]—a remarkable person—who has a great influence over him—when she pleases to exert it—And I see him a good deal myself & find him deeply interested in ⟨what⟩ such things as interest my mind—& you know what they are—Now I wish you would say something in your next about this—Whether you do not believe that *hereafter* such labours will be more appreciated than at present—Capen is a bookseller of *principle*—the only man I know in that line capable of being liberal.—If you have leisure—I

[5] The American Stationers' Company published *Twice-told Tales* on March 6, 1837. Out of the first thousand printed, only six to seven hundred were sold, and Hawthorne's return of 10 percent per volume sold (at $1.00 each) did not amount to much; early in 1838, the Stationers' Company folded, another victim of the Panic of 1837.

[6] As Peabody later wrote (to Francis Henry Lee, ca. 1885), Elizabeth Manning Hawthorne had played a memorable role in her life when they were children. In 1836, when Peabody had returned to Salem, she at first believed Elizabeth Hawthorne had written the anonymous stories in the *New-England Magazine*.

think a suggestion from you to *Capen*—who thinks every thing of you—to endeavour to enlist Hawthorne by good offers to write for the young—would perhaps secure him to this work—But it should be done soon—

I hear your lecture at the Temple was very great.[7] I trust I shall hear it or read it.—I believe I will enclose Sarah Clarke's letter to show you that *others* beside me—are blown skyhigh by the breath of your mouth—Be sure to return it—

Sunday. Mr. [Caleb] Foote has brought the manuscript & thinks there never was such a lecture as yours.—Mary is writing to you—I thank you for *feeling* that I had better not go to Baltimore. She is on that side of the question—She sees many advantages in my going & thinks I shall write &c.—If I go I shall endeavour to be true to my transcendentalism & make it turn to account. The *separations of life*— these are real—for they are on both sides. "tis Lethe's gloom without its quiet—the pain without the peace of death"[8]   —Is nothing to be done here—think you—[9]

MS, MHi

> [7] Mann's lecture on education was delivered on March 2, 1838, at the Masonic Temple.
> [8] Absence! is not the soul torn by it
>   From more than light, or life, or breath?
>   'Tis Lethe's gloom, but not its quiet,—
>   The pain without the peace of death.
>   (Thomas Campbell, "Absence")
> [9] At the bottom of the last MS sheet is this postscript: "My dear friend—Mr. Foote advises us to tease you for your lecture till we prevail upon you to do us the charity to lend it—*do* let us have it—all in your own good time—Yr friend Mary." "Do" is underlined twice.

Peabody makes her final break with the Alcotts and moves to West Newton to help her brother Nathaniel at his school. Her ties with Boston are still strong, as this letter reveals.

✂ To Mary Peabody

April 21st [1838][1] Saturday Evening
My dear Mary—The last you received from me was by the hand of Nathaniel & brought up till the evening of Thursday. Friday morn-

ing I went & finally settled with Mr. Alcott for the furniture—at $3 a quarter—including a great many things which altogether cost originally $150. I then went up to the Hibbards' and found them—Ellen looking as pretty as ever—and the baby as fat and healthy as she—not yet quite so handsome—Elizabeth also looking as well as when she went away. N. & I went down to Mr. Alcott's—and then parted—he to go to Salem—I to make calls. I made every call I intended to & got to Dr. Channing's to tea & spent the evening there. Only one thing I did not explore & that was about Eliza Clark but I wrote to her & put it in the way of going to her. Early on Saturday—that is *this* morning— I came out in the cars, & Sarah was on the spot—We passed the house which is a square white house—whose front is this: [Peabody drew an elevation of the house here].

Then I went up to Mrs. Clarke's to breakfast and stayed till eleven o'clock and then I walked down to meet the baggage from Salem & perhaps Nathaniel. Well there I stayed till nearly two o'clock when Mrs. Clarke called for me in her chaise. I went home to dinner quite disappointed & then returned to the house where I stayed till nearly six o'clock—but neither N—nor the baggage appeared.

[Another drawing of the house appears here.] This side of the house is made too large *in proportion*—for the large parlour is not so large as the schoolroom—& the kitchen is too long one way.

The chambers overhead are all square for both the schoolroom and the large parlour project beyond the lower story. There are two tolerable rooms in the attic.

The schoolroom has a painted floor, and the large room a canvass carpet. The large room must be in their parlour because of its more convenient access to the kitchen. It fronts the East and South & so has the sun almost all day. The room over it also will be their chamber. The little parlour and the room over it will be mine. Mrs. Clarke tells me of strawcarpeting which will cover the parlour (mine) with twenty yards at 30 cents a yard. The carpet will cost $6—but I do not know as I shall buy one. The table from our parlour and six chairs will then furnish it. And Mrs. Clarke is going to lend me some chairs, which I think I shall put in to this parlour. It communicates with the schoolroom, through the large closet, & the entry—which will be very convenient. The two back chambers will be empty. One of them would make a pretty spare chamber if we could furnish it. Closets are very

1 Elizabeth Peabody's move to Newton to help her brother Nathaniel with his school there dates this letter as 1838.

good all over the house. The whole house needs painting & papering, But the man only papers & paints the large parlour which is the worst looking. It seems to look cold. I should think a furnace next winter would be the cheapest way of warming the house—and the most healthy.—But of that anon.

What can be the reason the baggagewagon did not come today? It was a very great disappointment to me. But I shall not go to watch any longer. The key of the house is to Mr. Boyd's the next door, & nothing is to be done but to carry the things into the side door and put all the things into the kitchen. I have announced the school to begin on the 30th April—as Nat's things have not arrived from Bangor. So next week I shall have leisure. I am provoked that I came from Salem so soon. But now I am here, I think I shall go to Concord for three or four days. On Monday morning I shall go in to Boston in the cars, & go to Mr. Hibbard's, and see what is to pay and leave my directions & advice & go to Concord in the afternoon. But I shall not determine till I get to Boston, whether to go to Concord or not. I had a charming letter from Lucy Hedge. Harry is coming to Boston next week, & going to preach for Dr. Channing a month.[2] Dr. Channing looks very feeble, but says he is not suffering except from weakness. Mary is as charming as she can be. I went to see all the Jacksons & had the pleasantest visits—to E. Bartol's—L. Goddard's—Mrs. Bliss's— Quincy's and some places where I only left cards. I wrote notes to Cornelia & Catherine Parker—Sophia Ripley & Mary Elizabeth were sick with colds. I did not go to Mrs. Mills', but to Mrs. Dwight's & Sue's—&c. I can tell you nothing new about the school until next week when we shall have begun. I am excessively tired after having walked about that Hunnewell place all day.

Sarah says she has something to say—so here goes. Give my love to dear George. If I go to Concord I shall write from *there* to *him*. I trust Sophia has begun her journal.

My dearest Mary—You are an enigma with your notes about flowers with names all too heavenly—'immortelle'! what can it mean—Is it metaphor or fact. I hope it is a beautiful fact. If not in Newton we

2 Frederick Henry Hedge, son of Harvard professor Levi Hedge, studied in German gymnasia and graduated from Harvard Divinity School in 1828. He served the Congregational church in Bangor, Maine from 1835 to 1850, later becoming professor of church history at the Divinity School, editor of the *Christian Examiner,* and professor of German languages and literatures at Harvard College. Hedge was an early defender of German philosophy, founding, along with Ripley and Emerson, the Transcendental Club and contributing a few items to the *Dial.*

will sit under the Immortelle in a yet fairer region with all our loved ones about us, weaving amaranthine garlands for their angel locks and talking over old times & earthly trials—not that I really believe in any such idle Paradise but it is necessary to a substantial Idea of a World or a Life that there should be gardens & groves therein—at least I find it so—and talking of that, in summer's heats how cool & sweet will be those pine groves in Elizabeth's new home—I call it hers for she took possession of it yesterday & walked all day among the trees—waiting for Nathaniel & waiting in vain & taking cold I fear throughout the day. The cold is still latent, but it must be there, Thank George for the scroll he sent me & for its antique form & choice casket. I will answer it soon.

Yours ever
SARAH[3]

Sunday morning. I am not sick—have no cold—shall not go to Concord tomorrow, perhaps not at all. At least shall wait till *afternoon here*. E.P.P. I mean to write today to Susan Howes & Elizabeth Peabody.[4]

MS, MHi

3 "My dearest Mary . . . Yours ever Sarah" is a postscript to this letter and is written in Sarah Clarke's hand.
4 "Sunday morning . . . Elizabeth Peabody" appears to be in Peabody's hand.

The artistic Sophia Peabody had as hard a time as her sister Mary in understanding Elizabeth. This letter points to some of the difficulties in Sophia and Elizabeth's relationship, one which would become stormy in the 1850s.

✳ To Sophia Peabody

July 31st 1838

My dear Sophia—I must answer your letter immediately—for I am sure you have greatly misunderstood my words—or given them a breadth of interpretation that I had no idea of—When I said I had seen new meaning in the words "The gods prefer integrity to charity"—I did not mean to say that I did not always think *veracity* the first thing—far less did I mean to express that I was conscious of any want of veracity—and I assure you I do not *now*—and if you think so—I at least do not agree with you—and cannot conceive what you found it on—However I do not mean to take you up for that—only it explains to me some things that have often wounded me—and among other things some in your last letter but one.—When I said Sarah Clarke thought Mr. A— no more *divine* than I did—I did not mean that she did not *say* he was divine—but that *I* could say and often did say—he was *divine* in the *same sense*—and that this—in neither case included the absolutely thinking that every social action he did was right—The words I quoted of Mr. Emerson's—were also his own words—but I did not interpret them as broadly as you do—nor did I think them at all contradictory to his other often expressed opinion that Mr. A— is an entirely *devout* man—You asked me not to reply to this—but I have—because it will illustrate what I mean by this "wounding."—I have often been completely puzzled by your way of receiving things I said—& your way of insisting on *words of your own*—& particular forms of expression—& sometimes interrupting my remarks with corrections calculated to give other people the idea that I was not veracious—but I did not really entertain the idea that you did not think me so—or thought me indifferent to the subject—An exaggeration in words sometimes conveys an idea much more completely than literal exactness—But conversation is hacked down to concentrated mediocrity when the want of a generous confidence in the hearer—or of a generous interpretation—makes all these happy exaggerations—& sharp concentrations of magnum in parvo—lies.—"I always tell lies," is a common remark of Mrs Guild—because she is conscious of onesided views for the time being.—But do you on account of her saying this—not believe her?—It is merely a key she gives you—to interpret her by—

I do not mean however to say as much as Mrs. Guild does—I do not tell lies—*but the truth*—and few people are so transparent—I always speak the truth as it appears to me—and with no regard to consistency.—I can easily believe that any one who doubted my truth— could find abundant means of confirming themselves in the idea—and I have no doubt—that you have tormented yourself needlessly about it.—I write this to prevent if possible future torture of this sort although you will find *me* going on just the same as ever—

Now do not distress yourself about my thinking that you do me injustice &c—I am very glad to have had this opportunity of preventing a future misunderstanding—which would have arisen had you not written just as you did—Exercise a little of your generous imagination in this department & you will find that I am all the truer for all my exaggerations—I do not mean to refer to this subject again— nor await you to do it—because that will be agitating—It is for your sake—that is, to make you comfortable about me—if possible—that I write on it now.—What I did mean by the new light I had had was this—I feel as I never felt before that to be true to one's self is the first thing—that to sacrifice the perfect culture of my mind to social duties is not the thing—that what we call disinterestedness of action is often disobedience to one's *daimon*—that one's inward instinct is one's best guide—that selfdenial may encroach on the region of the spiritual—I am sure that during the years I lived in Boston my desire to set an example (of not claiming any thing merely because I wanted it) to the boys—was wrong—& that had I had a room to myself—which I did not like to ask for—as it would have been a manifest inconvenience— has in the end resulted badly for all concerned—& so forth—Something must be allowed to one's self for the infirmities of nature & it is better to be called selfish and oldmaidish than to lose one's own soul— It is only in the Millennium when love can be "an unerring light."— Though still this whole view would be very much abused I know by a selfish disposition.—I do not mean to say or imply that I have always been guided by disinterestedness—& that I have not had *almost* all the advantages of *selfishness*—I know I have—and I have acknowledged much of the truth of Socrates' aphorism instinctively—I have often & often acted selfishly—because I knew I could not act disinterestedly in the instance without a certain falseness—But this was always painful to me—because it argued a great infirmity to be selfish in order to be true—But I see now that to the *imperfect* this must be—the duties will clash—& if we act selfishly on a high principle—it becomes a different thing. I hope you understand me.

I was delighted with all your letters and your desire to have me come home—I shall go to Concord next Saturday as I have a chance to go without expense & return in a week with Mr. E—who comes to preach for Mr. Francis—& then go straight home—& bring E & the baby—but do you think I had better bring Ellen—she will take your head off with her screaming—as she cries after every thing now—Is it necessary to bring home my mattress?—they seem really to need it. Tell G[eorge Peabody] to send along his letter to Sarah Clarke—if he cannot write on the subjects that are most interesting to him—to tell

her that very thing—and ask her to do so.—The expression of *want* is
the best way to get a letter—on any particular subject—I shall write
to him from Concord.—I have no words to express my sorrow about
Eliza Curtis—but shall be wary of what I say till I see how it is with
herself. If it is real love on her part—perhaps it is a provision for his
salvation—But *her* life will be one of trial—that is certain—and what
a treasure she would be to a man who knew how to value the best and
holiest of women—

I shall part with N[athaniel Peabody]—very pleasantly—there
were some developments the last day I was in school—which convinced him of the value of my moral lessons—& my going away after
I had set him a going—seems to open his eyes to the fact that I did not
come merely to gratify my own wilfulness but to set him up in life.
This is the first fruit of my acting according to my own selfishness
you see—And now goodbye—I am ever yours with the greatest affection—which is & ever has been entirely undisturbed by whatever has
occurred—whatever jars may have occurred—I have never missunder-
stood your *virtue*—or felt any diminution of confidence in your principals—Even when I have differed in *views* I have seen clearly that
the light which I thought made you err was light from heaven—

By the way I did not mean you should not put down your visitations of truth in your letters to me—But now it is not much matter
since I am coming home—

Tell E Hawthorne that if she will write to me—I will at least
burn up that letter that she first writes—we will made a bargain about
the last of the correspondence—I want to get one letter from her before I come home.—So say you can send it & get it before you tell her
of my return—& put it in the Post——I have written to Miss Burley
and she will answer to Mary. Sarah Clarke will buy the things except
what can be got in *Lynn* (first page)—Send me word—& keep the
money till I come—I will bring them if Miss B[urley] sends the money
to Mary P[eabody]—as I asked her to do.

MS, NN-B

Peabody's version of Jones Very's "insanity," reporting the hostility shown him. She then gives a summary of her readings, a virtual catalogue of Transcendental texts.

✄ To Ralph Waldo Emerson

[Concord]

My dear Mr Emerson—   September 24th 1838

The very day poor *Very* was carried to the Insane Hospital[1]— (for you have doubtless heard of his misfortune); he came to see me, to deliver to me his Revelation;—& he told me he had sent to you his Essay on Shakespeare.[2]—I suppose this was written in his yet sane hours—& I wish only to say that it was written *for me*—and is to come to me when you are done with it.—I have been in hopes to hear ever since he went to Charlestown that he was sick of a brain fever—which would prove his insanity but a temporary delirium but I have not—& so I suppose it is water on the brain—It was probably produced by intense application. He was superintending the Greek class—out of wh. he has got a vast deal of studying—& he has the idea of a great moral responsibility—which arose I suppose from his success in awakening the sentiment of duty in others.—Besides he has been a year or more in his divinity studies, & writing besides.—I have feared insanity before.—I thought (at the time) that the visit to Groton showed it.— *These impulses* from above I think are never sound minded—the insanity of Quakers— (which is very frequent under my observation) always grows out of it—or rather begins in it.—I wonder whether some thing might not be written by a believer in the doctrine of Spiritual-

1 Jones Very, poet, essayist, Unitarian clergyman, attracted the attention of Elizabeth Peabody with his lecture "Why There Cannot Be Another Epic Poem." She encouraged Emerson to invite him to deliver his address at the Concord Lyceum, and Emerson did so on April 4, 1838. Very returned to his work as freshman tutor in Greek at Harvard, but soon became the focus of controversy with his mystic utterances in class and his belief that he was one embodiment of the Second Coming. Salem clergymen Charles Upham and John Brazer were instrumental in having Very committed to McLean Asylum for a month, beginning September 17, 1838.

2 Very's "Shakespeare" was published in *Essays and Poems by Jones Very* (Boston: Little and Brown, 1839). He completed it in 1838 just before he was sent to McLean. This difficult, brilliant and original essay contrasts the man of genius, Shakespeare, with the man of virtue, Christ. Shakespeare's genius is the product of his own insight and will, whereas the virtuous one achieves higher status through total self-abnegation, a state Very saw as his goal.

ity—which would show the difference between trusting the Soul &
giving up one's mind to these *individual illuminations.*

I have been a little provoked & a good deal amused to hear some
old womanly talk from Mr. Brazer & others about Very.[3] They evidently impute to his transcendental ideas—this misfortune—considering that his notions grow straight out of the idea that the evidence of
Revelation is a more inward one than *miracles.* Mr. B was ninny
enough to ask this poor crazy youth for the *miracles* that tested mission. ⟨He⟩ Very said "this revelation would not have miracles."
"Then" said Mr. B "I must say to you—you are laboring under hallu-
cination! &c" as if the best proof of his having no mission was not that
he had no *idea* to communicate:—for his whole Revelation consisted
in reading the 24th chapter of Matthew & explaining its figures rather
[word illegible]—but—not absurdly—& then thinking he had communicated something very important & praying to God his auditor
might have witness of the Holy Ghost.[4] He went thro this ceremony
with me.—He was so gentle & harmless and happy in his hallucina-
tion—that one almost forget how wretched it was—that such a beautiful light had gone down in darkness. He spoke of going to you &
telling you his discovery & when he went to the Hospital—his greatest
grief seemed to be that he was so persecuted he could not give you his
revelation. He was promised that you should be informed he was there.
He also wanted to enlighten Mr. Francis. He used Christ's words all
the time & in the whimsical manner an insane person might. But the
thought which has pressed itself on my mind *most* is—how some people have taken it all—as nothing but *transcendentalism*—which shows
how very entirely they do *not* apprehend *the ground* of a *real belief* in
Inspiration.—What a frightful shallowness of thought in the community—that sees no difference between the evidence of the most mani-

3 Salem Unitarian clergyman John Brazer's hostility toward Very has already
been noted. Emerson's friend Samuel Gray Ward was puzzled by Very's elliptical sayings; Gray recorded one such conversation, "Samuel Gray Ward's Account of a Visit
from Jones Very in 1839" (L.H. Butterfield, "Come with Me to the Feast; or, Transcendentalism in Action," *M.H.S. Miscellany,* 6 [December 1960]: 1–5). Richard Henry
Dana, Jr. was more definite in his opinion of Very, connecting Very's aberrations with
the unorthodox union of the Transcendentalists: "He is quite intimate with Emerson
and the Other Spiritualists or Supernaturalists, or whatever they are called, or may
be pleased to call themselves; and his insanity has taken that shape accordingly. I am
told that some of them are absurd enough to say that he is not insane—but that the
world does not understand him. Would their insanity were no worse than his;—but
'madness is in their *hearts*' " (Butterfield, "Come with Me to the Feast," 5).

4 In Matthew, chapter 24, Jesus provided a vision of the Eschaton in which the
faithful will be persecuted, false messiahs will arise, and natural disasters will occur.

fest insanity & the Ideas of Reason!—I wish you would give us a course of lectures on the *art of thinking*—If you will not—I think I shall try to stimulate H. Hedge to do it. Nothing do we need so much. You might append it to your Goethe Lectures on the art of Studying—indeed it is an identical subject.—⁵

I have just reread Carlyle's Revolution⁶—& am reading in connection Mad. de Stael's Revolution.⁷ What a wonderful woman! Have you read it lately?—I think what she says of Mirabeau—gives you the greatest confidence in her impartiality—since his playing cross with her father must have awakened as much prejudice as she was capable of feeling. The chapter of Mirabeau's death—struck me particularly. But what a picture of Buonaparte!—don't you think you are getting too much in favour of Buonaparte. Can Buonaparte's own story be trusted? Dr. Channing thinks—the Las Casas Journal was a part of Napoleons great scheme of Egotism.⁸ Dr. Channing's idea of Buonaparte does not seem too strong besides Mad. de Staels account.—I know she was too near to judge best.—but she loved truth & was not easily prejudiced—what a multitude of fine intuitions there is—in this book of hers— (It tells well for her that she shows great beside Carlyle—whose work seems to me more & more marvellous as I read it more.—And yet in the impossibility of differing from him I almost fear the *enchantment* of individual genius.—I have not been able to look into the book since I read it last winter—before now. I have shrunk from taking the burden of the great subject upon me. I felt on reading the book so much as if I had been there—that I shrank from going through it again. Just as one would shrink from going thro the experience again. What a proof this is of Carlyle's complete success in the painting. And now *this time* I am comforted & composed by his explanation of things. I heard his song of reconciliation before but did not appreciate it fully.

I have got a book of Jean Paul's—or rather it is Miss Burley's—

5 Emerson did not deliver a lecture on Goethe until the "Representative Men" series in 1855. It is possible that Peabody refers to his "Introductory Lecture on the Study of Uses of Biography" delivered March 18, 1835 at the Concord Lyceum.

6 Peabody's reference is to Thomas Carlyle, *The French Revolution, A History* (Boston: Little and Brown, 1837).

7 Anna Louise Germaine Necker, Baronne de Staël-Holstein, *Considerations on the Primeval Events of the French Revolution* (1818).

8 Las Casas, Napoleon's chamberlain, accompanied him into exile on St. Helena and acted as his secretary in compiling what was later called *Mémoriàl at Sainte-Hélenè* (1823).

On Education—called "Levance"[9] should you like to read it for you own sake & Waldinos.[10] It is too hard for my young German—& Miss B would gladly lend it to you. Wm Howes is now in the Law school[11]— & sends a carpet bag home every week & we can send to you through the same—if you have a regular communication with the Cambridge bookstore—do you?—Miss B—has many curious & new books.—Wm. Silsbee did not go to Concord I suppose. On reading your Cambridge address[12] he said he understood it *all* & liked it *all*—& so there was no excuse to go.—But sometime when it was *natural* he should like to talk with you on those subjects & should like to exchange with Mr. Frost.[13] He is gone to Bellows Falls to preach three months. I heard him preach here delightfully. He is a holy & just minded apostle— with the voice of wisdom itself—earnest & pure toned. I measure souls with my *ear*—some what as you do with the *eye*—& his tone is a true one I am sure. James Clarke also swallowed the whole address & felt it digest as strong food for men—but Judge Fay of Cambridge says in great wrath that you ought "to be *indicted* & *forbidden* to preach—a man who also holds the doctrine that *felt self-interest* is the only efficient motive of human action.[14] Mr. Bellows[15]—a warm hearted & very successful young preacher—lately having collected a society in the West & done other efficient things—but still quite youthful in his mind—was at Newport when the address arrived.—A gentleman carried it down to *horrify* the Dr. with it. So he selected passage after pas-

9 Jean Paul was Johann Paul Richter, whose treatise on education, *Levana* (1807), was widely read in educational and reform circles.

10 Emerson's first child, Waldo, had been born in 1836.

11 William Howes and William Silsbee were Salem residents and 1838 graduates of Harvard College.

12 Some members of the Harvard Divinity School class of 1838 asked Emerson to address the class, and his remarks of July 15 have become justly famous among his works. Years later, Elizabeth Peabody recalled for James Cabot the circumstances surrounding the Divinity School Address and the fierce controversy it prompted (June 30, 1879; see below, p. 385).

13 Barzaillai Frost, Dr. Ezra Ripley's assistant at Concord Church, had been Emerson's classmate at Harvard Divinity School.

14 Judge Samuel Fay of Cambridge was a close friend of John White Webster, a professor at Harvard Medical School accused in 1849 of murdering his colleague George Parkman, also of the Medical School. Webster asked Fay to defend him; Fay refused but remained Webster's friend up to Webster's execution.

15 Henry Whitney Bellows was educated at Round Hill Academy and Harvard College and Divinity School, graduating from the latter in 1837. In 1839, he assumed the pastorate of First Unitarian Church in New York City. Bellows became prominent in the public life of New York, and soon his church had to build larger quarters,

sage of horrors as he thought them—& read them the Dr saying—
"Well! that is pure Christianity"—"That is noble thought"—if that
shocks I not know how they have borne me—"I am afraid I not said
[?] what I meant to do—if that is [word illegible]"—& such things. I
understand he rejoices that your serenity is not disturbed by such
"*outrageous* illiberality"—as you have received.—The more I think &
hear the more I am rejoiced that the address is fairly [word illegible]
& could only wish the one word *Teacher* and *teacher* because in fact
the latter is what you *meant*. But I forgot I had "said too much of the
address" already—

I am resuming the Greek studies I left off with you!16—& in a fortnight have almost recovered what I once knew—I am enjoying myself
very much again—Idleness & freedom from responsibility is a necessary condition both of acquirement & thought with me—is not this
rather an exception to the general rule?—My brother George grows
weaker. He has just reread Carlyle & Mad de Stael—He says nothing
new on spiritual subject—I think he is not well enough to think
hard—He talks little but likes to hear other talk among themselves.——

There is one thing that I wish—and that is—that you would leave
me *in your will*—all your sermons—to keep for two years giving me
leave to make extracts according to my judgement & *print them*. This
is perhaps a premature request—as you may outlive me—& I hope
will live at least 40 years longer at any rate. But [?] & *use them* in sick
rooms & to prepare people occasionally for your more concentrated
compositions.—What should you think of trusting my judgement?
Love to Lidian.   EPP.17

MS, MSaE

---

which became the Church of All Souls. Among his many objects of concern was
Antioch College. Bellows organized and administered the U.S. Sanitary Commission
during the Civil War, and afterward devoted himself to Civil Service Reform. He died
in 1882.

16 In 1822, Peabody took Greek lessons from Emerson. Both were painfully shy,
never raised their eyes from their books, and were "too much afraid of each other to
venture any other conversation" than that concerning the lesson. Emerson refused to
take money for the lessons, for, as Peabody recalled, "he found he could teach me
nothing" (Elizabeth Peabody, "Emerson as Preacher," in *The Genius and Character
of Emerson*, ed. F. B. Sanborn [Boston: Osgood, 1885], 150–51).

17 Under the address, written vertically in the center of the sheet is found:
"When you have entirely done lending Pericles & Aspasia—please remember us."
"[N]ew edition of the Growth of the Mind—the Swedenborgians—especially all the

ladies among them—who think" is written vertically in the left margin on the first
MS sheet. Protective tape obscures several words. "[Y]ou quite prepared for the light—
would you but become a little child.—If you should ask why I have written this letter
perhaps you could not answer the question—It is to say that that manuscript of Very's
belongs to me" is written vertically in the left margin of the second MS sheet. "I wish
you would tell Lidian I have had a letter from Mr. Gräter who gives a very good
account of himself—except that he declares his wife is *not* deranged—She adds a postscript in excellent spirits. I still hope to get his book out of him before he dies" is
written in the left margin of the third MS sheet.

*Peabody describes her attempts to get a political appointment for
Nathaniel Hawthorne.*

✎ To Elizabeth Hawthorne

My dear Elizabeth   Friday [October 19, 1838][1]
    A little while after I sent my note last evening—I has a packet
from Mr. Brownson enclosing a note in answer to my congratulations
on his office[2]—In my note I [had] said—that the Government's doing
this good thing for him would cover a multitude of sins in my eyes
even if they were sharp enough to discern them—& that now I wanted
it to do another good thing—& that is—give to my townsman Hawthorne an office like his—requiring very little time & work—& having
abundant leisure & liberty—& in or about Boston—for I was afraid
New England wld otherwise lose him.—So I said—what can you do
about this? Has not Mr. Bancroft just such an office *in his gift* and
does he know his writings & claims?[3]—I know he has influential
friends at Washington who would fain get him there—&c &c
    Well—this was a mere venture—I had no idea that anybody but
the president had offices in their *gift*—But see what Mr. Brownson
writes "There will be no difficulty in getting a place for Mr. Hawthorne—providing he will accept one."—Mr. Bancroft assures me he

[1] "Oct. 19, 1838" is written in another hand in upper left corner of first MS sheet.
[2] George Bancroft, appointed collector of the Port of Boston by the new president of the United States, Martin Van Buren, in turn offered Orestes Brownson a
patronage post, the stewardship of the United States Marine Hospital in Chelsea.
Brownson accepted and held this post until the Whigs came to power with the election of Harrison in 1840.
[3] Peabody's direct appeal to Bancroft is documented in her letter of November 6,
1838 to Mrs. Bancroft.

should be delighted to give him a place, but he had supposed he was a sort of man who would by no means accept one. Mr. Bancroft has a high opinion of him—loves his writings. Pray tell me what kind of a place he will accept—and I doubt not it may be done for him"—[4]

So much for the sovereign people!—But for the life of me whatever is the political aristocracy of it I cannot help being glad. It would be better for him to be in Boston than here.—I am afraid he never will be happy here. And he might have a more agreeable office than a Post office. Besides—he can come & see us on the Railroad—& we will make him enter into some engagement to that effect—will we not?—I sent word *forthwith*—because he said he was going to Boston & may like to know before he goes—But I do hope I shall see him first—And will be very glad indeed to write to Mr. [Bancroft] Brownson another letter telling all the *immunities* the office must have—& I suppose he will show it or tell it to Bancroft.—

In my hurry last evening I forgot to say that Mr. Silsbee is downstairs—I asked the Dr. if she was ready to see company[5]—& the Dr. said she hardly feels like it I guess but nevertheless I guess your brother would not be refused if he were to send in his name—and very like it would be a pleasure that would help on her recovery—especially if he contradicts her all the time in the *piquante* manner of an accomplished conquette.

Father had a more uncomfortable night the last—but the rest of us had a better one—for he did not call us up—& George slept all night—poor child—what a *grey day*!—But I feel quite sunshiny about this same office—Yrs truly E. P. Peabody[6]

MS, MSaE

4 This note to which Peabody refers is not in the Brownson papers at Notre Dame University.

5 The she referred to here is most likely Sophia Peabody.

6 Beneath the address on the first MS sheet is written "Please give this to E *immediately*."

Peabody warns Emerson that Very is linking his own outlook to that of the Concord writer.

To Ralph Waldo Emerson

Dear Mr. Emerson,   October 20th 1838

I suppose you have heard of Jones Very's insanity—and very like in an insulting way—for Satan seems to be let loose upon you—and all the people gone rabid— (I mean the people who have a hold of the press)—I think I can see the Great Reason send its humorous witness over your features now & then—presently checked however by the benevolent regret which that heart of yours (which you are pleased now & then to blaspheme) throws over the "sweet fun"—that is somewhat too angelic for this world of sin & woe—& which also *loves* darkness better than light—

But Jones Very is my theme.—I had the honour of receiving the poor fellow's revelation—baptism of the Holy Ghost and all—before he went to Charlestown at all—Dr. Bell says his digestive system is entirely out of order—& he thought he had done so much for him as to cure him of the revelation—& then advised that he should go home & be watched over there. He came home as I understand freed from the delusion of being a prophet extraordinary—& to do as he pleased—& go where he pleases.—but I think he is as crazy as ever—

So it seems he is going to see you—next Monday—& deliver his revelation—He thinks you quite *prepared* but not yet quite arrived at the Father's mansion.—He has been here to day—talking an hour. He says he was intoxicated with the Holy Ghost when he came to see me before but now he is sobered. He is however manifestly insane.—Yet I cannot think him beyond the reach of influences & I thought I would take the liberty of suggesting to you what I think so that his interview may possibly be of some advantage.—He is much more amenable to me than to any body else—& I think it is because I treat him simply— I let him say his say—& then just tell him now & then—that what truth he utters & he does say much not inconsistent with truth—except perhaps in its exaggeration—is no revelation to me & that I do not on a general principle expect *personal* prophets—or regard God as dealing *personally*—He assents to me on the whole—tho' immediately after he begins.—I tell him that he should take medicine—& obey his friends—because if it is truth he utters—medicine will not purge it away—& that Jesus always acted on the "proximate motive"—&c—I give him no false sympathy.—His mother who is a coarse materialist pretends to believe him & to think that he is not sick &c—which is foolish.—& Mr. Brazer (the doubly distilled old woman)—goes & talks to him about working miracles to prove his mission or yielding the point that he is insane.—Since he has come home he has been telling him that *you* (from whom Mr. B ⟨he⟩ affects to believe all the thing comes) are now universally acknowledged to be & denounced as an atheist—& measures are taking!! to prevent you from having any more audience to corrupt—& ever so much more nonsense of whose malice or whose utter philisterei as the Germans say—I do not know which is the greatest.[1]

But the result is—that Mr. Very thinks you *and he* are perse-cuted—& he goes expecting full sympathy.—He is very harmless—& when gently dealt with will allow the other party to *say* his *say*—and I think that you may assume an *authority* which I cannot—and at least try that experiment once. But I would not—if I were you—stretch your charity so far as to invite him to stay in the house—or if he comes late & you have to—in charity—limit your invitation—else you may not easily get rid of him.

I will not apologise for the liberty I take in making this sugges-tion—for I am sure your kindness will agree with me—that it is worth while for you to take advantage of the association of Ideas—which you have in your favour in his mind—to govern it a little. You are the only individual who has the slightest chance of doing him this service. What I write for is just to give you possession of the data.

—I have [word illegible] a letter half written to Lidian, which I shall send by Very—when he goes. He is going to carry you his article on Hamlet[2]—which I am going to read now [?]   Miss Burley & I spent an hour or two together the other day chiefly talking of you—& our sympathies moral intellectual & religious with you—which the more

[1] "Philisterei" is from the German student slang "philister," one of the Philis-tines.

[2] On October 17, 1838, Very left McLean Asylum, where he had been under the care of Dr. Bell, and called upon Elizabeth Peabody. After he departed Peabody recorded her impressions for Emerson.

In "Hamlet," an essay mostly written while Very was at McLean, Very observed that the Dane's madness was only apparent; in fact, his quest for meaning was pro-found sanity in a world of superficiality. As in the essay "Shakespeare," Very con-trasted the tortured and self-doubting hero with the man of faith who, through self-emptying and being filled with the Holy Spirit, confidently awaits the final revelation.

we understand you the more we feel;—& rejoicing to hear that you had said "none of the dirt thrown upon you sticks to you"—for even *you* cannot make your friends quite so *sublime* as not to feel some degree of tenderness for the *man* of flesh & blood & part of "that *tissue*" so mysteriously called the Human heart.—

To go down to small things—please read in the next [?] Democratick—your old pupil's attempt at the Beautiful Arts[3]—& where you think it is very silly believe it is misprint—for there are *12*! [word illegible] shockingly plausible—but all excruciating to me.—And in some idle hour if you ever have one give me some *criticism* if it is worth the honour.—They [several words illegible] (which would not be true democracy it seems) & give it to the State Legislatures—*connected with* colleges. This is bad—but it was all printed before my voice was heard.—Yrs ever, EP.P

MS, MSaE

3 That is, "Claims of the Beautiful Arts," *United States Magazine and Democratic Review* 3 (November 1838): 253–68.

An intercession with the new Mrs. Bancroft on behalf of a job for Hawthorne.

✖ To Elizabeth Davis Bliss Bancroft

My dear Mrs. Bancroft,   Nov 6th 1838

After I was left alone with Mr. Bancroft—the day I called to see you—we had some conversation about my friend Hawthorne so desultory &c that I have felt somewhat troubled about it since.[1]—I find that he is by no means indifferent to the possibility of getting an office in the Custom house.—I told him Mr. Bancroft mentioned the Inspector of Customs as if that was yet to be disposed of—& that he spoke of writing to him. This evening I saw him & he remarked Mr. Bancroft had not written yet. He also said he did not doubt he should write

1 Since the new collector of the Port of Boston, George Bancroft, had just married Elizabeth Bliss, Peabody's friend, Peabody felt she had an opening to Bancroft for a post for Hawthorne. An initial interview with Bancroft did not go particularly well, as this letter suggests, but dauntless, Peabody wrote to Mrs. Bancroft. Bancroft offered Hawthorne a choice of positions and he chose that of measurer.

more—After he had an office that would narrow his leisure—and spoke with much earnestness of the necessity of action among men—as a means of healthiness.—I have been so strongly impressed with the fact that he was capable of extraordinary things; and I was myself so sorry to have him leave the quiet of nature which has done so much for his genius to go into the coarse arena of public life where no character seems to secure a man from outrageous abuse—that I did not say as clearly perhaps as I ought to have done—that there is nothing about him in any way to unfit him for acting an ordinary part in life. He is upright, faithful, and intelligent.

I said to Mr. Bancroft that he would not like a master.—But he says he should, of course, expect to be under the direction of the Collector—if employed in the Custom House.—He merely meant he did not wish to be a clerk.—Mr. Bancroft asked me if he was "interested in politics" & I thought looked disappointed when I said I thought not—and you know I talked to you about his ignorance on such subjects. Nevertheless, as a matter of *Sentiment* as well as *habit*—he is certainly on the administration side of the question. All I have a right to say is—that the cast of his mind determining him to imaginative literature & thinking—he has little interest & takes no personal part in electioneering and local subjects of party division which would require investigation unsuited to his taste.—Yet were it a matter of duty—he would doubtless make these investigations, & do his part.

TS copy, DLC.

A conversation with Very, a question about printing Very's sonnets, and a conversation between Hawthorne and Very, which Peabody witnessed.

✳ To Ralph Waldo Emerson

My dear Sir—   Salem December 3rd 1838
I received your packet with gratitude and Mr. Very to whom I delivered *his* ticket says he shall go to Boston on Wednesday and will take to you this letter.[1]—I suspect that there is no fear of *abduction*

[1] On December 5, 1838, Very came to Boston to hear Emerson lecture on "The Doctrine of the Soul" and to attend a meeting of the Transcendental Club. Before the

now—and as Mrs. Very stands guard over his liberty & tranquillity, I doubt if he is further assuaged by Dr. Brazer—on whom Mr. Very has ceased to call. I went to see Mrs. Very on Saturday—and I think it will be the last time—though she considers me a friend & asked me to come again—but it is painful to see such a tiger of a woman—She is almost a maniac from the simple vehemence of passion—She has been long at war with the world for Atheism's sake—and now has adapted the other view—identifying her son with the God in whom she at last believes.—There is something very strange in it all. There is a brother who seems a lovely & rational young man. I wish I could see *him* alone.

Last evening Very [word illegible] was here—talking like an angel—and endeavouring to promote the new birth in me—Mrs. Foote & her sister were present   He was very charming and when he explained & explained in answer to my questions and self-analyses—it seemed to me as if I thought & believed exactly so—though I did not acknowledge it quite—that is—I contended for a less violent & more compromised expression of the same ideas—He says, however, that there is no such thing as physical evil—that Sophia's resignation & acceptance of pain for instance is below the mark—that perfect yielding of wilfulness would produce freedom from the sensation of pain itself—that Jesus had no bodily pain on the cross—but only mental for the sins of others—which were in opposition to the Father's will.—I cannot receive this—can Lidian? Otherwise—it seems to me I do—I think I see & accept what he calls the sacrifices of the love of beauty, love of truth, &c & as this is the main point, I intend the next time I see him to tell him that I believe I do stand spiritually speaking—where he does—his answer will determine me [?] whether I understand

---

lecture he met with William Ellery Channing, who had expressed a desire to talk with him. Present with Channing were Wendell Phillips and James Freeman Clarke. Clarke, now editor of the *Western Messenger* in Louisville, Kentucky, was impressed with the spiritual depth of the young poet. In his sympathetic and insightful introduction to a selection of Very's poems, published in the *Messenger,* Clarke connected Very to the radical wing of Christianity that claimed direct guidance by inner light and intuitive knowledge of God's will (*Western Messenger* 6 [March 1839]: 309–11). Very's poems appeared in 6 (March 1839): 311–14; 7 (April 1839): 366–73; 8 (May 1840): 43; (January 1841): 424; (February 1841): 449, 462, 467, 472; (April 1841): 549–52.

In June 1839, Very decided to allow Emerson to edit his poems, and from an enormous sheet containing four double columns of sonnets Emerson selected sixty-six. Very resisted any revisions, since he claimed the verses were not his but messages from the Holy Spirit. Nonetheless, Emerson managed to wrest editorial power from the author, and, in September 1839, Little and Brown published Very's *Essays and Poems.* A full account of the preparation of the manuscript is found in Peabody's letter to William P. Andrews, 12 November 1880, MS, MWelC.

him or not—Perhaps the apprehension of a real sympathy in his views will take away from him the isolated feeling that produces this violence of expression—

But Miss Burley feels very differently from me about him—She says he has always appeared to her extremely *good*—& with great powers of apprehension on *points*—but naturally excessively conceited—putting the most inordinate value in all his own thoughts—& not capable of complete *views all round subjects*   When he goes there he talks a great deal more violently—they argue with him very gently—but he seems driven into extremes that he never uses at our house—they say too that he expresses deep gloom—& looks gloomy & tells them they are wicked—& truth itself is a poison to them—He speaks of the misery of being with people he cannot esteem—& says to them there has been no good man since the apostles until himself—

I can account for this different expression there and at our house—on the theory that it is absolutely insane—for then he would be acted upon by the slight difference of their way with him—Miss Burley apprehends & deals with him as Mrs. Sam. Ripley would[2]—only more calmly—he does not *frighten* her—but she says his conversation torments her—& affects her dreams at night—

He wants to print his sonnets I find—How marvelously they flow from him—impromptu—one or two a day.—And don't you think they have great artistical merit? Why should they not be printed—& the Shakespeare's too—and why should he not introduce the whole with an account of his states—a psychological autobiography?—I wish you would think of this & put him up to it—

He has expressed a wish lately to go to the West—& James Clarke (I understand) is so interested in him that he is coming to Salem to see him. He wants to preach & thinks he might find a pulpit there—as probably he might—Would not the journey do him good?—and might it not be useful to him to deal with such unmystical & yet free & liberally disposed people as the westerns?—Miss Burley thinks he is getting exasperated *here* with the words "hate" &c that he used so freely. Action would perhaps scatter this concentration—

Does Lidian receive his dicta about there being no physical evil? He says *she* received more of his mission than you did.—My sister Sophia receives all—except that about *the pain*—& she says she *doubts* about that—not feeling that she is sure she surrenders her will.—What

---

[2] Sarah Bradford Ripley, wife of Samuel Ripley and sister of George Bradford, was famous for her knowledge of botany, Greek, and differential calculus.

seems to me the most harmful portion of his discourse is his doing away with that meaning of the [word illegible] that answers to the understanding [several words illegible]   This is a step beyond Swedenborg—who lets the obvious sense remain, though he puts two other senses on beside.

Did Elizabeth Hoare tell you that I was present when he delivered his mission to Mr. Hawthorne? It was very curious—Hawthorne received it in the loveliest manner—with the same abandonment with which it was given—for he has that confidence in truth—which delivers him from all mean fears—& it was curious to see the respect of Very for *him*—and the reverence with which he treated his genius.— There is a petulance about Hawthorne generally—when truth is taken out of the forms of nature—that reminds me of your brother Charles though the happiest & healthiest physical nature tempers it—so that it only expresses itself—on that one occasion.—But in this instance he repressed it & talked with him beautifully—He says Very was always *vain* in his eyes—though it always was an innocent vanity—arising greatly from want of sense of the ludicrous & sanctified by his real piety & goodness. He says he had better remain as he is—however— one organ in the world of the impersonal Spirit—at least as long as he can write such good sonnets—I meant to have written you a castigation by the way for your obstinate blindness to this real *Poet*—I remember you once said in a sermon that if you found you could not discover the Milton & Plato of yr own day you should feel that you probably had no real apprehension of them at all—Perhaps "out of yr own mouth &c!!"

Did you read Mr. Peabody's (Andrew's) review in the Chr. Ex?[3]— Miss Burley says "he did not touch on Mr. Hawthorne's highest merit— *The highest merit of any writer*—the unconscious but complete anatomy of the soul—as discoverable in the Gentle Boy—or the analysis of the imagination—as seen in his other tales generally."—I am trying to persuade him to go & hear your lecture on some Wednesday. He declares no human voice can command his *attention*.—but I defy him—not to listen to you without woolgathering beauty—& if your eye is as unerring as you think—my further arguments will be superfluous—Love to dear Lidian—I am yours EPP

MS, MSaE

3 Andrew Peabody's review of *Twice-told Tales* appeared in the *Christian Examiner*, 3rd ser., 20 (November 1838): 182–90.

Very lists the besetting sins for several members of Peabody's circle.

⚓ To Lidian Emerson

My dear Lidian   December 1838
    The enclosed letter Mr. Very forgot to take last week—and so I will send it to you with a little greeting—[1]
    I write in my father's sick chamber—where I have dwelt night & day for more than two months—with the interval of about a fortnight—Mary has received an anonymous present of a course of railroad fare tickets together with a ticket to the Lectures[2]—& so goes to Boston every Wednesday night—to be *rapt* inspired—& made whole—and I on the hope of another visit next summer & another reading.— Last Wednesday George had so wretched a turn of agony that she did not feel able to leave him—but he is excessively anxious she should go—We have had delightful accounts of both the lecture & the Audience of last Wednesday. I suppose I am not to hope for the rest of that letter from Mr. E—which broke off so ludicrously—just as he began on the interesting subject of Dr. C—Dr. C (Very said) listened to him in the most docile manner for three hours—His difficulty is—he says— *the love of rectitude*—You know your husband's is the *love of thought*— mine is the *love of truth*—& Very's own was *love of beauty*—*Angelic sins* are they not? I wish I had time to write more—I am sure he *is crazy* on one point—thinking that he alone is accessible as a matter of fact to the Spirit—He does not distrust his own *love of obedience*— which is also a [word illegible] if the loves are—& his sticking to this notion is as wilful as Dr. C's *love of rectitude*.
                      But there is no more time
    Mr. Emerson *ought to lend* Mary the first lecture—but far be it from me to solicit for her—or anybody else in poor old Salem—Give Him ever so many thanks for the ticket.

MS, MSaE

    1 "The enclosed letter" has not been located.
    2 Emerson delivered a private series of ten lectures on "Human Life," beginning December 5, 1838, at Boston's Masonic Temple.

After having "discovered" Nathaniel Hawthorne, Peabody was concerned that he lapse back into seclusion and inaction.

✸ To Elizabeth Hawthorne   *(excerpt)*

My Dear Miss Hawthorne,   [ca. 1838]
    I saw how much your brother was suffering on Thursday evening, and am glad you think it was not a trial, but rather the contrary, to hear my loquaciousness. I talked because I thought it was better than to seem to claim entertainment from him, whose thoughts must be wandering to the so frightfully bereaved. There seems so little for hope and memory to dwell on in such a case (though I hope everything always from the Revelation of Death), that I thought perhaps it would be better if he could divert himself with the German. . . . Even your brother, studying the *Pattern Student of the World,* may be enabled to take such a view of a literary life as will fill his desire of action, and connect him with society more widely than any particular office under Government could do. If, as you say, he has been so long uneasy— however, perhaps he had better go; only, may he not bind himself long, only be free to return to freedom. In general, I think it is better for a man to be harnessed to a draycart to do his part in transporting "the commodity of the world"; for man is weak, and needs labor to tame his passions and train his mind to order and method. But the most perilous season is past for him. If, in the first ten years after leaving college, a man has followed his own fancies, without being driven by the iron whip of duty, and yet has not lost his moral or intellectual dignity, but rather consolidated them, there is good reason for believing that he is one of Nature's ordained priests, who is consecrated to her higher biddings. I see that you both think me rather enthusiastic; but I believe I say the truth when I say that I do not often overrate, and I feel sure that this brother of yours has been gifted and kept so choice in her secret places by Nature thus far, that he may do a great thing for his country. And let me tell him what a wise man said to me once (that Mr. J. Phillips of whom I once spoke to you): "The perilous time for the most highly gifted is not youth. The holy sensibilities of genius—for all the sensibilities of genius are holy—keep their possessor essentially unhurt as long as animal spirits and the idea of being young last; but the perilous season is middle age, when a false wisdom tempts them to doubt the divine origin of the dreams of their

youth; when the world comes to them, not with the song of the siren, against which all books warn us, but as a wise old man counselling acquiescence in what is below them." I have no idea that any such temptation has come by your brother yet; but no being of a social nature can be entirely beyond the tendency to fall to the level of his associates. And I have felt more melancholy still at the thought of his owing anything to the patronage of men of such thoughtless character as has lately been made notorious. And it seems to me they live in too gross a region of selfishness to appreciate the ambrosial moral aura which floats around our ARIEL,—the breath that he respires. I, too, would have him help govern this great people; but I would have him go to the fountains of greatness and power,—the unsoiled souls,—and weave for them his "golden web" as Miss Burley calls it,—it may be the web of destiny for this country. In every country some one man has done what has saved it. It was one Homer that made Greece, one Numa that made Rome, and one Wordsworth that has created the Poetry of Reflection. How my pen runs on,—but I can write better than I can speak.

Julian Hawthorne, *Nathaniel Hawthorne and His Wife*, 2 vols. (Boston: Houghton Mifflin, 1884), 1: 165–67.

A calm, even wistful note—Very is quiet, Peabody's school is closed, and she is about to go away.

✒ To Ralph Waldo Emerson

My dear Mr Emerson—   June 1839
    Mr. Very's brother brought this packet for you—and wants me to send it—which I shall do to the care of Mr. Abel Adams.
    Mr. Very has kept his chamber for more than two months, being not able, and still less inclined to leave it. Do you know that he said when he went into this state that he should come out of it in a year? His brother says he has remarked this nine months of the time has passed—and his brother thinks that he will return to the ways of men in a year as he said. The brother is a nice young man fitting for college. He says he thinks his brother is somewhat morbidly excited. And he does not agree with him at all in his extreme views but still is not sure that he is deranged—and cannot give up the hope & expectation

that he will again become like other people.—He thinks he has been benefited by being kept so quietly at home lately.

My school closes and I go to Boston the 24th of June, where I intend to remain a little while & look at the Allston gallery some more. Then I have it in mind to make visits to Spring Street—Brookline—Newton—& Concord—and it is no matter in what order—so that if you can have me at any time I should like to know when.—I suppose you received my answer to your last—in which I said I should not be able to go the 15th as you so kindly & hospitably planned. I write in great haste & can only send my love to all your beloved household.

Truly yrs—

Eliz. P. Peabody

MS, MSaE

In this heady atmosphere of Emerson, Hawthorne, Very, and Allston, it is not surprising that Peabody should say she had "been awake for about two months!"

✎ To Sophia Peabody

Concord, Mass., June 23, 1839

Here I am on the Mount of Transfiguration, but very much in the condition of the disciples when they were prostrate in the dust. I got terribly tired in Boston. I went to the Athenaeum Gallery on Monday morning, and in the evening Hawthorne came and said that he went to the Allston gallery on Saturday afternoon. I went to Allston's on Tuesday evening. He was in delightful spirits, but soft as a summer evening. He seemed transported with delight on hearing of your freedom from pain, and was eager to know what you were going to paint. I said you had several things a-going, but did not like to tell of your plans. He said, then you would be more likely to execute them, and that it was a good thing to have several paintings at once, because that would save time, as you could rest yourself by change. I carried to him a volume of "Twice-Told Tales," to exchange for mine. He said he thirsted for imaginative writing, and all the family had read the book with great delight. I am really provoked that I did not bring "The Token" with me, so as to have "The Mermaid" and "The Haunted Mind" to read to people. I was hardly seated here, after tea yesterday, before Mr. Emerson asked me what I had to say of Hawthorne, and told me that Mr. Bancroft said that Hawthorne was the most efficient and best of the Custom House officers. Pray tell that down in Herbert Street. Mr. Emerson seemed all congenial about him, but has not yet read his writings. He is in a good mood to do so, however, and I intend to bring him to his knees in a day or two, so that he will read the book, and all that Hawthorne has written. He is in a delightful state of mind; not yet rested from last winter's undue labors, but keenly industrious. He has uttered no heresies about Mr. Allston, but only beautiful things,—dwelling, however, on his highest merits least. He says Very forbids all correcting of his verses; but nevertheless he [Emerson] selects and combines with sovereign will, "and shall," he says, "make out quite a little gem of a volume." "But," says he, [Very] is always vain. I find I cannot forget that dictum which you repeated; but it is continually confirmed by himself, amidst all his sublimities." And then he repeated some of Very's speeches, and told how he dealt with him. I am very stupid. I have been awake for about two months! Mr. Emerson is very luminous, and wiser than ever. Oh, he is beautiful, and good, and great!

Your sister,   E.

Rose Hawthorne Lathrop, *Memories of Hawthorne* (1897; reprint, Boston: Houghton Mifflin, 1923), 28–30.

In Hawthorne and His Circle (*New York: Harper and Brothers, 1903*), *Julian Hawthorne recalled that "my father read Emerson with enjoyment; though more and more, as he advanced in life, he was disposed to question the expediency of stating truth in a disembodied form; he preferred it incarnate, as it appeared in life and in story. But he could not talk to Emerson; his pleasure in his company did not express itself in that form. Emerson, on the other hand, assiduously cultivated my father's company, and, contrary to his general habit, talked to him continuously; but he could not read his romances; he admitted that he had never been able to finish one of them" (p. 68).*

Orestes Brownson has labeled Horace Mann an infidel. Elizabeth Peabody is shocked to hear that he gave as his source of information Peabody herself.

✎ To Orestes Brownson

Mr Brownson—

Dear Sir—   July 6th 1839

I understood a few days since that you asserted that my highly respected friend Mr Mann was an infidel & founded thereon a judgement that he was unfit to be entrusted with the office he now holds— and that you adduced as evidence the testimony of a lady, who, you said, had requested you to endeavour to convert him—& this lady was understood to be *me*.[1]

I felt grieved & shocked & had not my conscience been pretty clear, should have felt grievously selfreproached to find that any language of mine had been so unguardedly used, as to convey to your mind this impression.—I have some recollection of saying to you at the time Mr Mann called on you in Boston that I wished you could communicate some of your Ideas to him, as, like the bulk of the community, I

[1] The work of the Massachusetts Board of Education under Horace Mann's leadership invited the attacks of both Calvinist clergy and educators because Mann had insisted on keeping sectarian tracts and other influences out of public schools. Democratic politicians also were hostile to the board because of its Whiggish origins. Because Brownson, then editor of the *Boston Quarterly Review,* had criticized the centralizing effects of the board, it was expected that he would join the general criticism. Fearing that her voluble conversation might have added fuel to his views, Peabody wrote this letter of explanation. She had written Brownson before, July 14, 1837, assuring him that *he* was not an infidel in her eyes at least.

Brownson did criticize Mann (in *Boston Quarterly Review* 2 [October 1839]: 393–434), but not for indifference or hostility toward religion. It was that impression that Peabody wished to dispel, and in that was apparently successful. As Arthur Bestor has pointed out, "the effect of this letter is difficult to determine," since by 1844, Brownson had completed his pilgrimage from Unitarianism to Catholicism and proceeded to charge Mann with all Elizabeth Peabody had feared he would, and more. "Mr. Mann knows nothing of the philosophy of education, for he knows nothing of the philosophy of human nature, and nothing of Christian morals and theology. His theory is derived from German quacks, and can only rear up generations of infidels" (*Brownson's Quarterly Review* 1 [October 1844]: 547).

This Peabody letter and a fine commentary are found in Arthur Bestor, "Horace Mann, Elizabeth P. Peabody, and Orestes Brownson: An Unpublished Letter, with Commentary," *Proceedings of the Middle States Association of History and Social Science Teachers,* 38, no. 1 (1940–41): 47–53.

thought him to have inadequate ideas of Christianity, properly so called, & I wished this earnestly because as he is a peculiar & profound sufferer from the domestic misfortune of his life—and an ardent philanthropist at the same time. I thought that some different Ideas might soothe the anguish of the former, & give new hope & joy to his action as the latter.

But although I wanted his faith to be quickened & clarified, I did not mean & am sorry that you understood that he was an *infidel*. Few Christians I think know so much of Christianity as he, & have that I know of *actualized so much*. The kingdom of God being what you represent it in your last number of the Boston Quarterly I hardly know a man who I think stands so high in it—& although I do not agree with him exactly, & think I *see* some ⟨things⟩ truths which he does not—I feel as if I were more of an infidel than he.

Yet I can imagine very well how my words might imply what you understood. But dear sir *you* could not think that I meant to convey the impression, that our stupid public takes from the word *infidel*. Mr Mann sees through humbug—but you & I would call that *faith* & not *infidelity*.—He believes in the infinity of moral good, the law of moral cause & effect, & acts in the love that died on the Cross.—Nevertheless he generalizes in a different manner from you & me. We do however do ourselves wrong in forbidding him to work miracles & cast out devils merely because he does not use our "open sesame." He that is not against us is for us. If the devils are cast out, we should acknowledge the presence of the God.

No man in this world has deepened my faith in the substantiality of God over all blessed for ever, nor the life of any man more deeply illustrated the spirit of Jesus Christ to me than Mr. Mann—I cannot rest in the thought that through me, & my onesided blundering way of expressing myself, he should be called *infidel*. Pray dear Sir, dismiss this word from your lips & this idea from your mind. It is making me the instrument of a gross wrong.

.

Yours, very truly
with respect
ELIZ. P. PEABODY

It happens that there is a *religionist party* against Mr M's operations, which makes it [im]portant that those who see & feel his religion, should bear testimony *for* & not against him—& so would I. The want of truth that I think he has, I only feel as falling short of the wants of so great and beautiful a nature as his own, but the truths he possesses are nevertheless enough to newly enliven the dead world around us, & are strictly Christian—& he calls them so.

MS, InNU

A brief but provocative note to her brother George, suggesting both her devotion to home in the conventional sense and her quest for a more authentic sense of self not dependent upon the shifting opinions of others.

✎ To George Peabody   *(excerpt)*

August 8 [1839]

I find Mr Emerson preparing his sermon & his Dartmouth Address for the press, & I have begun to read the lectures. . . . this sermon at Cambridge has excited a great deal of opposition even to the degree of astonishing himself—but he does not waver—on the contrary is more bold—He finds that a superstition has taken the place of real Christianity—& he is determined to stand true to his convictions & speak. . . .

I begin to grow independent. Wherever I can be myself and *act* if not speak my soul, is my home. Mr Emerson says *our home* is not this or town, or even a particular body. It is the *unity of our character*. I not only am coming to the *place* home, but to the *being* home. Such a combination of *homes* cannot but succeed. I have come to the conclusion that disinterestedness is a maggot of the brain, and the only virtue is to be indifferent to these phenomena we call men & women. Among these phenomena, however, I reckon E. P. Peabody

MS, NN-B

≉3
1840s

From the School to the World

IN CONTRAST to the achievements and adventures of the Peabody sisters, only disappointment and sorrow seemed to befall the Peabody boys. The youngest, Wellington, had been thrown out of Harvard, joined a ship's crew, and in 1837 landed in New Orleans, only to die there of yellow fever. George had died in November 1839 a painful death from spinal meningitis. After that blow, Elizabeth Peabody proposed that the remaining family—Mary, Sophia, Nathaniel, and their parents—move back to Boston from Salem. She had herself moved, in her intellectual life, from teacher of the young to teacher of adults, through her contacts with Transcendentalists. She now decided to educate a wider public.

Peabody had conceived of a plan to open a bookshop, and in July 1840 her West Street bookshop and library was open for business at 13 West Street, a narrow block between Tremont and Washington streets. She sold domestic and foreign books and magazines, or lent them at small fees. She stocked her father's homeopathic medicines, of which Nathaniel became the dispenser and, at the suggestion of Washington Allston, sold art supplies. The bookshop was perhaps her most successful business venture.

As an intellectual center, the bookshop attracted the leading reformers and writers of Boston and its surroundings. James Freeman Clarke was pleased to find that she stocked German, English, and French periodicals.[1] For Thomas Wentworth Higginson, the bookshop provided volumes of French eclectic philosophers—Victor Cousin, Theodore Jouffroy, Benjamin Constant—and also "Schubert's 'Geschichte der Seele' and many of the German balladists who were beginning to enthrall me. There was also," Higginson wrote, "Miss Peabody herself, desultory, dreamy, but insatiable in her love for knowledge and for helping others to it. James Freeman Clarke said of her that she was always engaged in supplying some want that had first to be created."[2] It was widely recognized that the availability of foreign literature made the bookshop indispensable in Boston's cultural life. Peabody wrote that "about 1840 I came to Boston and opened the business of importing and publishing foreign books, a thing not then attempted by any one. I had also a foreign library of new French

1 Edward Everett Hale, ed., *Autobiography, Diary, and Correspondence of James Freeman Clarke* (Boston: Houghton, Mifflin, 1891), 144.
2 Thomas Wentworth Higginson, *Cheerful Yesterdays* (1895; reprint, New York: Arno Press, 1968), 86.

and German books."[3] This foreign circulating library, whose books "stood on shelves in brown-paper covers," as Edward Everett Hale described them, was represented by a catalogue of 1,161 items.[4]

The Transcendentalist journal the *Dial* was published at the shop during 1842 and 1843, and meetings led by George Ripley to design the utopian community that would become Brook Farm were held there in the winter of 1840–41. The bookshop and library was also the meeting place for several of Margaret Fuller's conversations. Fuller had come to Boston from Providence, Rhode Island in December 1838, her intellectual abilities and powers of conversation already well established. Bronson Alcott called her "the most brilliant talker of the day." Beginning November 6, 1839, Fuller gathered a group of about twenty-five women and, meeting in the West Street shop (apparently then not yet open for business), she conducted a thirteen-week series on Greek mythology. A second series of conversations on the subject of fine arts, in November 1840, was apparently also held at the bookshop. Fuller held a third series, on Greek mythology, for nine sessions, March 1 to May 6, 1841, at George and Sophia Ripley's house, and once at West Street.[5]

Peabody's letters to the young Unitarian minister and later music critic John Sullivan Dwight show her active and sympathetic interest in the Roxbury experiment, Brook Farm. Her steadily widening circle of interests involved her in the arguments over Theodore Parker and his refusal to leave the Unitarian fold despite his ultraist views. Peabody attended several meetings of the Transcendental Club, and described two of these meetings in an 1840 letter to Dwight. In 1842, she attended the Convention of the Friends of Universal Reform, a collection of advocates of the most advanced causes, assembled by William Lloyd Garrison; and she brought into the West Street vortex advocates of communitarianism, vegetarianism, hydropathy, phrenology, clairvoyance, and mesmerism. In 1843, she attended the Boston

---

[3] Peabody quoted in George Willis Cooke, *An Historical and Biographical Introduction to the "Dial"* (New York: Russell and Russell, 1961) 1: 148.

[4] Edward Everett Hale, *A New England Boyhood* (Boston: Little Brown, 1920), 248. The catalogue has been published with an introductory essay by Madeleine Stern in "Elizabeth Peabody's Foreign Library," *American Transcendental Quarterly* 20, supplement (1973): 5–12.

[5] Joel Myerson, "Mrs. Dall Edits Miss Fuller: The Story of Margaret and Her Friends" *Papers of the Bibliographical Society of America*, 2d quarter, 72 (1978): 189–92.

Convention on Fourierism, and subsequently wrote an essay on that movement for the *Dial*.[6]

In the 1840s, the Peabody family went separate ways. Sophia Peabody and Nathaniel Hawthorne were married on June 9, 1842, Mary Peabody and Horace Mann on May 1, 1843. But not until the next decade would the Hawthornes and Manns leave Massachusetts. Nathaniel and Sophia settled at first in Concord; for three years, until Hawthorne's appointment as surveyor at the Salem Custom House, their financial situation was precarious. Sophia and children often visited Mary Mann, who had settled in West Newton while her husband Horace pursued his work as secretary of the Massachusetts Board of Education.

At the bookshop, Elizabeth Peabody continued to attract both conventional customers and those who had been caught up, emotionally or intellectually, in the cultural crosscurrents of the age. One such person was William Batchelder Greene, who, at twenty-two, had come to the Boston area in 1841 to recover his health after serving as an army officer in the campaign against the Seminoles in Florida. Attracted first to Orestes Brownson, whose combative spirit he admired, he lived briefly at Brook Farm, and entered Peabody's orbit when he inquired at her bookshop after an English translation of Kant. Peabody introduced Greene to her circle. They found him even more opinionated than she did. Greene approved of Emerson, who, he said, understood the objective nature of the Oversoul, but the other Transcendentalists were much too subjective to suit him. He was especially critical of Theodore Parker, as Peabody noted in an undated letter evidently written in this period. Parker had criticized Greene's view of divinity, and Greene took the remarks to mean that Parker was critical of conventional morals as well. Greene was, in general, Peabody concluded, ill-disposed toward Transcendentalism, "lumping together the errors of pure mind—with the bad passions of *modern french novels* and the moral indifference of Goethism." All this Peabody found confusing and distressing. She had thought that Greene attributed to Transcendentalism "a *certain coldness* with respect to individual relations; that people approached one another for purely intellectual purposes." That was certainly how he treated *her*. From his constant commentary on her "various intellectual, religious,—& even *moral* deficiencies," Peabody concluded that Greene thought she had "no feelings to be

6 Elizabeth Peabody, "Fourierism," *Dial* 4 (April 1844): 473–83.

wounded, and no *respectability!*"[7] Whether Greene did think that Transcendentalism bordered on libertinism or coldness of feeling, it was evident that Greene and Peabody were unable to balance a personal relationship with intellectual discourse. Greene believed that Peabody expected too much from him; he told Orestes Brownson that "she is a strange character—entirely too hard for me."[8]

The store's customers declined in the second half of the decade, and in 1845 Peabody began to teach again, this time in a school for boys conducted by the Hungarian linguist and political refugee Charles Kraitsir. Kraitsir had come to America in 1833 and became a professor of modern languages at the University of Virginia in 1840. His antislavery convictions prompted a move to Boston, where he lectured on his philological theories. He believed that the original sounds of human language, the actual root sounds in their physical production, sprang directly from intuitive human consciousness in response to the external environment. This fusion of inner reality and physical nature was crucial to Peabody and other Transcendentalists, who wished, as Philip Gura has said, "to perceive, or provide, a philosophical unity to a world which by 1840 seemed badly fragmented."[9]

After Kraitsir returned to Hungary in 1848 in the midst of the abortive revolution, Peabody turned her primary efforts toward the publication of *Aesthetic Papers,* which she hoped would become a periodical. Emerson, Hawthorne, Dwight, and Thoreau were among her contributors. In April 1849, Thoreau had written to her, "I will send you the article in question before the end of the next week," adding in a postscript, "I offer the paper to your *first* volume only."[10] Contemplating writing a review for James Russell Lowell's *The Pioneer,* critic Thomas W. Parsons wrote, "Now I have looked into these Aesthetic Papers and amid many things that I dislike I find others which I consider too excellent to be dismissed with a sneer. . . . I cannot write a *puff* and you must ask me to. But if you will give me the permission I will say what I candidly think of this affair, premising that I cannot compliment some of the *verses.*" In a postscript, he added, "I think that Mr. Thoreau has got into better company than

7 Elizabeth Peabody to Orestes Brownson [1842], MS, InNU.

8 William Greene to Orestes Brownson, 24 August [1842], MS, InNU.

9 Philip F. Gura, "Elizabeth Peabody and the Philosophy of Language," *ESQ* 23 (1977): 160. This section on Peabody and Kraitsir is drawn from Gura's article and from his book *The Wisdom of Words: Language, Theology, and Literature in the New England Renaissance* (Middletown: Wesleyan University Press, 1981), esp. chap. 4.

10 Henry David Thoreau to Elizabeth Peabody, 5 April 1849, MS, PHi.

he deserves and doubt if there is much in him." The essay in question was Thoreau's "Resistance to Civil Government."[11] Unfortunately, *Aesthetic Papers* gained few subscribers, and its first issue, in May 1849, was also its last.

[11] Zoltan Haraszti, "Letters of T. W. Parsons," *More Books: Bulletin of the Boston Public Library* 13 (October 1938): 357–58.

A note of sympathy on the death of her correspondent's father.

✂ To Rebecca Amory Lowell

Salem

My dear Miss Lowell—   May 1, 1840

I went to call on you yesterday and was much disappointed not to see you again—it is so long since! this winter I have intended it—and once I went & you were not at home—I then put it off—and when your father died[1] I could not immediately intrude upon you feeling as I did so deep a sympathy in an affliction which had so many depths—in a case like yours—where his character added so much to the usual feelings of a child and your retirement of life made the loss of so deeply loved a relative so irreparable to every day—I should have gone out to Roxbury yesterday had I not thought that perhaps there your grief would be reawakened—among the long loved scenes associated with him.—And yet perhaps I am wrong.—Death too has its happy side—and sometimes we accept it for a friend with a peculiar sense of *rest*.—You have sympathized with his sufferings so much that perhaps you rejoice even now in his security forever from all touch of pain—Perhaps reviving nature in this outward spring is a perpetual lyric in which your mind can hear the beloved spirit clothing itself in new forms—and pluming itself for a new flight—I think Nature is ever a frame to whatever human action is worthy of it—and when the cold snows of winter break up and pass away—and Beauty comes forth so fitfully—with such sweet promise—is it not an emblem of the soul bursting the cerements of old age—and responding in its own native *life* to the call of its Maker?—

I have now closed my visit to Boston and do not know that I shall

[1] Rebecca Amory Lowell's father, John Lowell, called "the Rebel" because of his unswerving opposition to the War of 1812, died March 12, 1840.

again leave Salem till next winter—I shall not be able therefore to go and see you & tell you about the conversations as you desire me to do—& indeed I could do no justice to them in a letter—But they were very successful—The tone of the whole class was so modest and docile—& refined—& dignified—& everything was so elegant about Miss Fuller. Some foolish reports have been made of things said—never said—&c—as is usual in our society—but much more prejudice has been disarmed than strengthened. I am confident. —and I feel as if there were no member of it who does not feel with more sensibility than when they began—all the motives for a noble & aesthetic life—without any extravgance or desire to change any thing but *the Spirit* with which we live into something continually more disinterested, beautiful—and serious. But these are vain words—unless you know particulars & these cannot be written in a letter.—

There is one thing I want to speak about, however, for which I hope I have room—I understand from a lady of my acquaintance (Miss Burley) that your brother Mr. J. A. L.[2]—is a german scholar who was at one time deeply interested in German literature & I wish you would tell him of a thing that has come into my head (for no one else is responsible for or privy to the thought)—There is a son of Prof. Hedge of Cambridge who was educated in Germany.[3] He went there at 12 years of age & received his classical education & the first development of his mind there. —When he returned here he passed a year or two in our college—studied divinity & settled here as a minister. For the last few years he has been in Bangor. Perhaps your brother knows all about him. He has the singular advantage of being brought up in both literatures—and a man of genius & taste—being *au fait* in both. One of the best proofs of his powerful mind is—that although he can write & even think in German with as much ease as in English—his English is so easy & idiomatic that it bears no mark of foreign admixture—& his turn of thought is decidedly English—as well as his taste. Several years ago I heard him say he has a mind to deliver in Boston some courses of lectures on German literature—taking up all the great artists in succession giving biographical sketches—criticisms—& accounts of their words—& then perhaps giving the history of their philosophy in the same way. —He then thought however that there was not quite enough curiosity awakened & besides there was some risk in

2 Rebecca Amory Lowell's brother was John Amory Lowell, who became a prominent Boston businessman and philanthropist.
3 That is, Frederick Henry Hedge.

abandoning his profession for it. —I heard yesterday that he was here—and about leaving Bangor (although the people there are very inviting) for indispensable reasons—& was probably about to look for a new parish. It struck me that here might be an *interregnum* as it were in his clerical life—& now curiosity is so completely awake concerning German literature & philosophy—that it would be a good time for these same lectures—and I could not but wish that your brother know all about it. Of course I do not expect that my opinion will weigh any thing on the subject with your brother who is a perfect stranger to me & my capacities for judging. But I wish he would think of it himself—He might read his review of the Life of Schiller in a Christian Examiner of some years since to see a little into his way of viewing subjects[4]—& Dr Mather of Cambridge—Dr. Channing of Boston[5]—& more especially Mr. Hedge himself who is here for a week or two as I understand would be good sources of information to apply to. He gave a series of popular lectures on literature at Bangor last winter which were very sucessful. & he printed a lecture at the opening of the Lyceum the year before which was very superior. Indeed He is *I* think & those who know him— (Dr Francis of Watertown for instance think so) a person of first rate mind who is passing his life much less usefully for the world than he should—because he is not forthputting and has not personal charms.—He is not merely a person of uncommon & rare attainments—but a man of genius—a poet—& a *logician*—most rare union.

This last part of my letter dear Miss Lowell which I intended to have very clear and good has been interrupted several times & I must hope I have made myself intelligible. The word *German* stands in our community as such a bugbear—that it seems to me nothing can be done for the people which would relieve more suffering than to have the literature analyzed—Truly your friend—

Elizabeth P. Peabody

MS, VtMiM

4 Hedge's essay, "Schiller," appeared in the *Christian Examiner* 16 (July 1834): 365–92.
5 This is probably William Ellery Channing, but which Dr. Mather is referred to is unclear.

Advice to a young minister on balancing spontaneity and preparation, and an interesting comment on the limitations of expression that comes solely from the heart.

✖ To John Sullivan Dwight

[May 20, 1840]

My dear friend—Perhaps you are hardly prepared for this warm address—but I trust you will be able to respond to it—for it impresses my sentiments toward you—& besides I must use it to justify some things I am going to say in this letter—but which if they are too intensive—you shall not answer it—& yet I will hold myself forgiven for my boldness—which I know you will forgive for this once—

Today is your Ordination day[1]—& altho' you do not probably recognise any toto caelo difference between the Layman & Minister, you doubtless are full of feeling at the thought of receiving a human sanction to the relation & what grows therefrom of a Christian to his fellow men. The rest of us hardly have our Christian priveleges in our state of society—The ordained minister alone has them & can without seeming arrogance assemble his fellow pilgrims in the road to truth Good & Beauty & discourse as the word is given to him on the most interesting themes—

What I am going to say respects some part of your services. A certain want of fluency in prayer—has been the real cause of your want of outward success—more than any other thing—& even in the place

---

1 John Sullivan Dwight was graduated from Harvard Divinity School in 1836, but was without a pulpit until the Northampton, Mass. Unitarian society called him in February 1840. Dwight's friends were worried that his vagueness, lack of confidence, and dreaminess would make it hard for him to find and hold a pulpit. Theodore Parker wrote him in 1837, "you surround yourself with the perfumed clouds of music. You mingle the same perfume and melody in your sermons, but you carry all the vagueness of musical clouds where clearness and precision are virtues. . . . Duty, not dreaming, is for men. You must get a place in the real world before you can walk into the ideal like a gentleman." Henry Bellows wrote Dwight in 1836 that "a good many of your friends who admire your genius fear, I think, whether it is destined to have a full manifestation" (George Willis Cooke, *John Sullivan Dwight: Brook-Farmer, Editor, and Critic of Music* [Boston: Small, Maynard, and Company, 1898], 11–13, 16). In 1838 Dwight became permanent supply preacher for the Unitarian society of East Lexington, and in 1840 moved to Northampton. He was ordained May 20; George Ripley preached the ordination sermon and William Ellery Channing delivered the charge to the minister.

where you are—it is *felt* although overlooked in the estimation of your many high & beautiful gifts. Now it has always seemed to me as if a few hints from *another* would remedy this deficiency—but I felt there was a difficulty in giving them while you were yet a candidate—because there would be something painfully embarrassing to a mind noble and delicate as yours—in the consciousness of *praying* with reference to the criticisms of an audience—But now the case is different—Now you are settled in spite of this defect and you will feel it a duty to make every exercise of your public service such as to minister to your audience's edification. And may I not feel my sense of friendship (founded on & quickened by my gratitude for spiritual benefit received in my acquaintance with your most apprehensive mind) a guarantee of my being privileged to give you my poor thoughts on the point?—

I suppose the evil has originated in your idea of being *spontaneous*—You have thought there was falsehood perhaps in making an exercise of this kind a subject of premeditation & composition—You have heard so much formal praying that you shrunk from it as the only evil—But in your case it was hardly to be feared—You might premeditate & even write—& still there be no danger of your *losing sight* of God—or losing *feeling*——However I think that even on your own plan if you would be *very short*—& as soon as you felt yourself hesitate should close—you would outgrow it—especially as *now* you will find yourself much more at ease than when you were ministering to a congregation of whose individuals you knew nothing. —I remember Mr. E[merson] said that once you had a theory about preaching of the same kind—and did not put enough intellectual labour into the composition of a sermon—but you had got over that—& hence I infer that you may change your idea about prayer. Is it not an intellectual exercise as well as an overflow of the heart? Does it not imply a comparison of the actual state of the Soul with its ideal in order for the subject of petition? Is it not something more than what Fenelon describes it? I think so—even when we speak of secret prayer—But public prayer is to a larger portion of a congregation the most important part of the service—There is so little voluntary thought with those not intellectually disciplined that it is their best religious meditation. If it touches the springs of attention it carries their minds through an intellectual expression of devout feeling, which makes these devout feelings of some value to the soul—when otherwise they would pass away without fructifying it.—If I had a larger sheet of paper I should doubtless say a great deal more in this head but it is perhaps fortunate that I have not—I wish I knew your ideas about it—& about the public expression of religion generally. Will you not write to me? I could guess the rest if you would say but little & I suppose you feel pressed at present with your new duties—

It is right for me to say that when I heard you preach last—*I* felt nothing but pleasure in the prayer—Which seemed to me full—free & rich—and should have supposed that the difficulty was completely outgrown—but that I have heard what is said about it at Northampton & elsewhere—I certainly know no one else in such a state of *palpable growth* as yourself—save & excepting—Mr E[merson]—I was charmed & interested by your first sermons but felt your next movement in practical talent to be very great. The last years of your life in which you have borne an apparent failure with such courage—dignity—and beauty has done for you palpably—what no outward success could have done—It has turned you visibly from a child into a *man* in *bearing*—& in hoping for you now a continued prosperity I can hope for nothing more than that you should advance as you have advanced already and should adversity come again—I should feel you again would—"give us beauty for ashes" &c   My drawings missed you in Boston—I hope they reached you untroubled   Yours very truly

Eliz. P. Peabody

MS, NPV

More on Dwight's inability to conduct public prayer fluently and confidently. Preparation, Peabody says, does not suggest lack of faith, but faith in thought as a vehicle for the divine.

✖ To John Sullivan Dwight

June 18th 1840

My dear Mr. Dwight—I have already answered your letter once—and a curious adventure happened to my letter. It went up to Boston in the cars by my sister Mary who was to give it to Miss Cochrane—I suppose she dropped it—At any rate it came back to *me* by the baggage-carman—opened & resealed—the "Northampton" scratched out & "Salem" written instead! At first I was too much chagrined to think of writing another—but believe I will not let it operate so seriously.—

What a beautiful song you give me for my "severe simple lines"—you are certainly the prince of translators—and I should like much to send you more.—What do you want most of all out of Flaxman—& how can I get anything to you if I want to?—I like to *hear* the music my pencil draws—

Your apologies for not writing make so pleasant a paragraph of your letter that I am glad you made them—although they were unnecessary. I had no thought of being neglected—for I had imagination enough to picture out all the circumstances of leaving Boston—being ordained & meeting this gorgeous summer in so favourite a haunt of his—I was only a little worried lest my letter had seemed in its subject an "intrusion into the Sanctuary only the holy should enter."—Your reason for not making a preparation beforehand for your Sunday devotions is certainly cogent—& if it stands—may not be set aside.—But such preparation as I meant seems to me no "want of faith"—*but faith* in the *principle* of *thought.* "Is not all prayer a sally into the unfound infinite"—by *thought? We* certainly do not confine thought to the operations of the understanding but make it cover the spontaneity of Reason—whose condition is the calmness of solitude—but which can be remembered & repeated in the congregation—for it cannot sally with time. "It is the same yesterday, to day, & forever."—But I am so much inclined to think your hesitation is purely nervous that I have an equal confidence that the other plan—which you seem to like better—of *stopping* quakerlike when the Spirit ceases to blow in a stream—would be sufficient. It is a common remark that you are much longer than people in general—Perhaps too—to feel at home in a congregation—& to know what is in the hearts of many—& what are their *wants* & *needs*—will do the work. Nothing can be more unnatural & disagreeable & restraining than the position of a *candidate.* It is a false position; and yet I do not see how it is to be avoided for the people must choose their minister in the present organization of the Church.—I understand Mr. Ripley is making a move towards a new organization[1]—& I am to hear by a letter from him tomorrow all about it. I have no objections to new organisation—only let us retain Jesus as the root of the Church—for as yet we have not exhausted the "unsearchable riches" of *his* gospel—hardly begun to explore them.—

But to turn to your pleasant letter which lies before me—I am

[1] George Ripley's new organization was the communitarian experiment at Brook Farm, the leadership of which he assumed on March 19, 1841, the day he preached his farewell sermon to his Purchase Street Unitarian congregation.

astonished that *mine* sounded so flattering—I had such a sense of my adventuresomeness in assuming without leave the place of counsellor on any point—that I felt bound to express my gratitude for what I had gained from you—& it was due to myself to show you that I had some sensibility to your merits—I did not think to make you "tremble"—my confidence in you is founded in your humility or rather is justified by it—if I may dare to approach that fairest tenderest lowliest flower—Do you know of a little yellow star oh very minute whose four or five radiating lines make a circlet not larger than the pupil of the eye? I do not know its name—but have found it in September fields.—It is so very fine that it refuses to be plucked from the bosom of its mother earth where it gleams—an emblem of the richness—the latent light below.—It may not ornament a mortal bouquet—but withers if it is gathered with ever so much love—I thought when I saw it—of humility—that most intimate grace—that irremoveable flower of a deep rich [word illegible] soul—

I am delighted with your intimation of more letters forthcoming. I shall rejoice to hear of your plans & doings—your successes & failures.—It is beautiful to me that you feel "in a warm world" & that "GOD and *nature* never fail." When I first saw you in Salem Streets with Miss Hedges—I felt an involuntary sensation of pain—you looked to me so *unsheathed* in a world which has at least cold winds & dreary seasons—& chilling northeast storms—I have had greatest pleasure in seeing you gradually wrapped in the mantle of manhood—& it is a new joy to know that the robes of childhood were not rudely *sent* away—that you can lay aside your mantle at will as you sit at your "still window" or otherwise go out of your hut—again the child of the German Story.—I trust you will not have to be taught by any experiences *like mine*—since you have escaped so long.—But *I* may be *wrong* in having experienced *chills*—I doubt not it is the warm spirit makes the warm world. *One* faith, however, I have *kept*—and that is that *"coldness* is *negative"* and all evil *finite*—in the presence of the protoplastic soul—Even the evil of losing one's faith for a Season! How mysterious is this faith that underlies despair itself and sustains us through the darkness of doubt!

I shall accept from you gladly something less than "oracles & angelic sentences"—so do not wait for *great hours* to write to me. And still do not feel obliged to write unless it gives you pleasure—I remember you said your pen was not your plectrum though I have found it so—for *me*. Very truly yr friend

ELIZ P. PEABODY

But the mystery of the letter is unexplained. It was not unsealed but Mary sealed it with sealing wax before sending it to the Post Office as it was too late for Miss Cochrane & the man carried it to the Salem Rail-Road—but no matter for the particular—since it was not read.

MS, NPV

A vivid description of two meetings of the Transcendental Club, one at Theodore Parker's house and another at Peabodys' West Street address.

✄ To John Sullivan Dwight

Boston Sept. 20th 1840

My dear friend, Do you think I am a grave deceiver that I have not written?—It was an old formula of mine that I could only [word illegible] the wicked & unhappy—and I still think so—in so far as my scribblings to the good and happy are always much less good than my homilies & attempts at consolation—Now then can I write to you?—As well might I address an Angel in Paradise—

Is the falling leaf only another tone of the music of life—another hue of the beauty you always see?— Does the Spirit still put into your mouth what you must say every Sunday without writhing and anguish?—I hope so even though it deprives me of all chance of writing you a letter—& may the roses you gather have no thorns—the sweet no bitter—& your life be an amarinthine flower—

If there had not been so much to tell you about the two meetings at Parker's & here—I should have written as I promised—but how could I—It would have taken a dozen sheets of paper—At both places it was the same subject—& Mr Ripley said his say—very admirably too—& making no small impression of the reality of the evils he deplores—the key of which is—that the ministers & church are upheld in order to uphold a ⟨church⟩ society vicious in its foundations—but which the multitude desire should continue in its present conditions.—Mr Hedge on the other side eloquently defended the Church—which (as Catholics) has given a true culture to the Imagination in creating Gothic architecture in all its varieties—& *painting.*—the whole circle of whose subjects he went over with a beautiful criticism;—& which (as Protestants) was educating the Reason—but he yielded to Mr Ripley that the Social Principle was yet to be educated—the church of Humanity yet to grow—but as another branch from the same trunk—& not on the ruins—

Margaret Fuller gave her idea of a true man in describing Jesus Christ—W. H. Channing described the union of man with God—as the true church—Robert Bartlett said the church was founded on sin—that the gentlemen were talking of a church for angels—& he described an angel as "aboriginal of heaven" & contrasted him with man—the mixture of mortal & immortal—forever requiring regeneration & redemption.[1]—Now & then Theodore Parkers deep organ-like voice came in with a sentence in aid of this or that speaker—

Mr Emerson was not present here but was at Parker's—& said "To distrust that the Divine Soul would find its own organs—was the essence of atheism" & that we should "let what would die only ourselves *live* ⟨ing⟩ & trust ⟨ing⟩." Also he wrote me a good letter when he sent me word he could not come to the meeting here—which I will show you when you come & also tell you more—

Today I heard Parker preach the second time that sermon which is to appear in the October dial—[2] & again the deep music of his earnest voice *moved* me as I am seldom moved. He is really inspired—& this afternoon he preached another sermon which was like the lament of Jeremiah—only *greater*—if I may dare to say it—At least it proved that that old Hebrew had not drunk up the River of God—but left some of its deep murmur still to sound in our living ears—I want you to hear Parker preach *now*—He has got on fire with the velocity of his spirits speed—& the elements melt ⟨with⟩ in the fervant [?] heat of his word—He proves that the "organization" yet admits a living spirit—& that God yet visits his church—I felt this afternoon after I came out as if I had heard some great piece of music—I wanted to hear "more & more & forever"—Even now it is an effort to write down in words even the outskirts of the feeling which he awakened   [W]hat was it?—why it was a picture of what man is actually—& what society is—& the whole riddle of the Sphinx—with a mystic solution running

1 William Henry Channing was William Ellery Channing's nephew. A graduate of Harvard Divinity School in 1833, he served Unitarian churches in New York City and Cincinnati, and in 1854 went to Liverpool to take a prominent Unitarian church there. He returned to England after the American Civil War and service with the Sanitary Commission.

2 Parker's sermon was "A Lesson for the Day; or the Christianity of Christ, of the Church, and of Society," *Dial* 1 (October 1840): 196–216.

all through—not expressed to the understanding in words—but intimated to the Soul—in the *very tone* in which he stated the enigma—
He said himself afterwards "there was nothing in it"—but it implied
every thing—& put you in mind of everything—You felt that that man
had the solution—& that it could not be told—*it must be lived*—

He is a son of Thunder—If your people get frivolous—send for
him to give you a labour of love—& you too can sprinkle your honey-
dew over his people to their edification—for *all* need *all* influences—&
there are different manifestations but one spirit—I have just been
writing to William Silsbee—from whom I heard yesterday—& who has
been suffering lately from anxiety for the life of his child but it is
better.—He has greatly enjoyed a visit from H. Bellows—whom he
seems to love & admire.—He seems to be very happily married—& that
reminds me that when I heard of Anna Barker's engagement to Mr
Ward—I was most happy for Mr Ward—whom I do not know—but
then any body must be so *blest* at having won Miss Anna Barker!
Well—that night I dreamed it was you not *Mr Ward* & you were so
happy I almost died of joy by way of sympathy—& for a week after I
kept continually thinking of you as I had seen you in my dream *so
blest*—that I could hope it may prove a veritable prophecy of some
equal good [one word illegible] for you.[3] I cannot realize that that
happiness was only a dream—Truly affectionately your friend—

E. P. Peabody

MS, MB

[3] Samuel Gray Ward, a wealthy Bostonian and classmate of Jones Very, was an
occasional contributor of poetry and criticism to the *Dial.* In autumn 1839 he became engaged to Anna Hazard Barker, a lovely young New Orleans woman, angering
Margaret Fuller, with whom Ward had also been cultivating a relationship. He and
Barker were married October 3, 1840.

A request that Brownson publish in his Quarterly Review *the rest of her series on Hebrew Scriptures, three of which appeared in 1834 in the* Christian Examiner, *and a glimpse into Peabody's own view of her movement away from Unitarianism toward "The Newness."*

✹ To Orestes Brownson

Dear Mr Brownson—   [ca. 1840][1]
   I have heard you express so many of the ⟨se idea⟩ views—though in a different form—of the manuscript which I enclose to you—that I am tempted to give it to you—and let it take its chance in your Review—It is No 4 of those articles on the Hebrew Scriptures—published in the Christian Examiner in 1834—but *written* in 1826 (the first year of my intellectual life properly speaking)[2]—I wrote them with no view of ever being an author but copied them off 10 years after with some improvements especially in this last article—Yet as you remember even then the questions that have since been so warmly discussed as to inspiration miracles &c had not been brought up in our community—& the word *transcendentalism* I never had seen except in Coleridge's friend.[3] Had not Mr Norton cut off untimely my little series which consisted of six numbers, it would have ⟨been⟩ recorded quite a little historical fact, there in the bosom of Unitarianism, an unlearned girl, with only the help of those principles of philosophizing she gathered from the perusal of Coleridge's friend, & ⟨relying on a single method of interpretation⟩ relying simply on her own poetical apprehension, as a principle of exegesis, should have seen just what is here expressed, concerning the *socialism* of true Religion & the divinity of Christ. [?]— When a thing is true—it is true many ways—& has many sides of evidence—& so I should think there might be an interest to you in seeing that there was evident to a simple seeker in these ancient Records that

---

   [1] In *Orestes Brownson's Life,* (Detroit: Henry Brownson, 1898–1900) Brownson prints this letter along with other documents from around 1840, when Brownson was still thinking "transcendentally" and had not yet converted to Catholicism.
   [2] The three essays published in the *Christian Examiner* were: "Spirit of the Hebrew Scriptures, the Creation," new ser. 11, 16 (May 1834): 174–202; "Spirit of the Hebrew Scriptures, Temptation, Sin, and Punishment," new ser. 11, 16 (July 1834): 305–20; and "Spirit of the Hebrew Scriptures, Public Worship: Social Crime and Retribution," new ser. 12, 17 (September 1834): 78–90.
   [3] Samuel Taylor Coleridge's *The Friend* was a periodical, published from June 1, 1809 to March 15, 1810.

characteristic of Religion which has come to you through an experience so intense of the social evils of this present world:—

Perhaps it would be well for you or me to write *a note* introductory of this article, stating its date &c—I should rather *you* would write it—And if you do will you please let me see it. I believe I told you the circumstances of its being rejected from the Xtn Ex. I had the satisfaction of having at the time Mr Walker's good word. He said he liked the article best of all the four—& he had put in the other three freely & expressed his liking of them—Indeed had it not been for this I should never have thought of presenting them. Mr Greenwood saw by accident the article on *the Creation*—which one of my friends had in manuscript & asked me to print it—& this gave me my *first idea* of printing any thing—

Yours respectfully
E.P.P.

MS, InN

Peabody, a warm supporter of the Brook Farm experiment,[1] describes some of the people who are gathering there.

✄ To John Sullivan Dwight

April 26 [1841]

Dear Mr Dwight—Your sister tells me that you do not get letters & that she is about to send to you—& so I will send you a little note of passing events. The Ripleys have been three weeks yesterday at their place: that is George—with occasional visits of two or three days from Sophia—Frank Farley—William Allen & Eliza Barker went the first fortnight & they cleaned the stable arranged the house ploughed & planted—going through the hardest & most disagreeable work they

---

1 Peabody wrote two essays describing and endorsing Brook Farm, "A Glimpse of Christ's Idea of Society" in the *Dial* for October 1841 and "A Plan of the West Roxbury Community" in the January 1842 *Dial*. Peabody's letters to Dwight describing Brook Farm and other correspondence, along with a narrative description, are found in Zolton Haraszti, *The Idyll of Brook Farm, As Revealed by Unpublished Letters in the Boston Public Library* (Boston: Trustees of the Public Library, n.d.), reprinted from *More Books,* February and March, 1937.

will ever have to do.—They also every day milk their cows—and such is the effect of regular feeding that already they give more milk than at first.—In a fortnight Hawthorne & Mr. Warren Burton joined them and Hawthorne has taken hold with the greatest spirit—& proves a fine workman—but Frank Farley is the crown etc—He knows how to do every species of work—from cooking & other kinds of domestic labor & through all the processes of farming & dealing with livestock—and solaces his leisure hours with the fine arts—for he draws—& reads aloud with *histrionic* beauty.—

Thus far—dear Mr Dwight—I wrote some day last week—and now (yesterday) I received your letter by Judge Lyman with its many questions. You will see by the above answers to some of them. Sophia Ripley cannot go for a continuancy until the last of May—but she spends three or four days in the week with her husband. While they are so few—& the community plan is not in full operation it is unavoidable that they must work very hard—but they do it with great spirit—& their health & courage rises to meet the case.—Wm Channing is I believe to join them in June as well as George Bradford—they have young Newcomb from Providence—Margaret Fuller's Brother Lloyd—fitting for college & one or two more children—who also help. Mr. Ripley keeps her tour school in the country next house to them for the summer—[2]

But what is altogether desirable *is*—that they buy the farm & go to build—& get all their hands & heads assembled. Ripley still retreats from printing even a prospectus—but has determined on the 11th of

[2] Frank Farley was an experienced farmer from the Midwest. William Allen was one of the original shareholders. Of James Lloyd Fuller, Margaret's youngest brother, Lindsay Swift writes: "[He] had no intention of remaining a neglected genius, and it is recorded of him that he kept a diary which it would be absurd to call private, since it was his habit to tear out pages and leave them about so that the objects of his displeasure could not well avoid finding them" (Swift, *Brook Farm* [1900; reprinted, New York: Corinth Books, 1961], 73). Other members Peabody refers to are Warren Burton, who was graduated from Harvard Divinity School in 1826 and served three Unitarian pulpits briefly, in 1837 becoming a minister-at-large, occupying himself in educational and social reforms; and George Partridge Bradford, instructed in his youth by Sarah Alden Bradford Ripley, a woman of prodigious learning and a sympathizer with Transcendentalism. In 1828 Bradford was graduated from the Divinity School; after a preaching engagement, Andrews Norton informed him, "Your discourse, Mr. Bradford, is marked by the absence of every qualification which a good sermon ought to have" (Swift, *Brook Farm*, 189). Bradford took up teaching, but was unable or unwilling to stay at any single appointment very long. He was an enthusiastic member of Brook Farm and a willing laborer, but left when the community turned to Fourierism; and Charles King Newcomb, a graduate of Brown University, an occasional writer, and devotee of the Roman Catholic church's sensibility (though not of its doctrine).

May to have a meeting which will be holden at our house on account of our large parlor to which is invited a company of persons—combining supposable interest in the plan with solid cash in their purses or influence over the purses of others—& to these it is to be shown— *what this school is* its moral—intellectual—practical aspect—Its relation to the life of its professors— & then it is to be shown that without ten thousand dollars capital can be raised in addition to what money the associates bring—this same school can not go into immediate operation. By an article which operates as a bonus for those who *take a share* as well as send pupil—they think they can raise this in such a way as that while it benefits the community it benefits the other party too—they hope to raise this 10 or 12 thousand dollars instanter & proceed to build—so all gather together in the fall—

Very truly yrs—
E. P. Peabody

I close so abruptly because I may be obliged to send this right off but if I have more time I will write you a little better.—E.P.P. April 26th

MS, MB

Dwight has resigned from his Northampton church. To let him know that persecution for unpopular ideas is not uncommon, Peabody writes him about Theodore Parker's situation in Boston.

✎ To John Sullivan Dwight

[June 10, 1841][1]

My dear friend—I have been intending to write to you every day since I heard last Friday of your being in trouble with your people but have wished to learn something more definite that what Agnes (Mrs Higginson) told me—which was—that you "had been treated abominably & had given them their six months warning."[2]—I am sure you must

[1] Peabody referred to the "Puritan of today" as that of June 10, [1841].

[2] On the first anniversary of his ordination in Northampton, Dwight preached a sermon reviewing the year, saying that criticism of his preaching came from worldly people who did not want to hear the truth. Discontent among his parishioners grew. On June 22, 1841 Dwight wrote, "From all that I have discovered of the character of the individuals of whom my society is composed, I feel more and more con-

have been treated abominably to have come to so sudden & severe a resolution & I am grieved to think that your hopes of happiness should be so cruelly blighted even for a season—But my dear friend I am not surprised—Every day convinces me more and more that Christ is yet a *sword* & not yet *peace*—The whole head is wrong & the whole heart is sick.—Truth will not be swallowed—& people are in the A b c of the art of Spiritual life.—I hope & trust & am quite sure that you must have some sympathy in individuals who have eyes to see & hearts to understand—but still with your gentle temper & tender heart I can imagine that a difficulty will be something very painful to you. I wish I knew something more definite about it and how you feel about it exactly but I know no so short way as to write & ask you.—

What shall I tell you of things here?—Ripley's Society have concluded not to invite Parker there I believe.[3] There are some too timid to dare so bold a Spirit—& the impression is very strong that he will not remain if he should come more than a year or two—Ripley had frequently said this & it is what he thinks—Parker is not disappointed though he thinks he should have been asked. James Clarke's church increases—but perhaps you heard what was not exactly true that there had been an opposition to Parker's preaching in his pulpit.—A question *was* raised by one or two of the Society—and James Clarke introduced the subject after church—the day P— was to come in the evening & showed in a very luminous speech that it was a deathblow to the principle on which their church was organized—This caused an immediate revulsion of feeling in the few who did not want him to come—The *cause* was that P— had preached a sermon in South Boston on the subject of what was the transient & what the permanent of Christianity so called which was reported by some to be a denial of Jesus Christ & the Bible—& some of our church supposed that this would crush the little flock—But Clarke showed that to be unwilling to have him come would be to excommunicate him without a hearing for opinions—which they did not pretend to judge—consistently with their platform—The beauty of it is that a large part of the Church

---

vinced that the relation between us never could have been lasting." A few days later he wrote, "I am free! I heard nothing of the doings of the parish meeting till three days after. It was very thinly attended, and most of my friends were absent" (Dwight quoted in Cooke, *John Sullivan Dwight*, 44–48).

3 Partly to console Dwight for his loss, Peabody described the controversy surrounding Theodore Parker's sermon "A Discourse on the Transient and Permanent in Christianity," preached as an ordination sermon for Charles Shackford, May 19, 1841.

prefer him to any other preacher, some of them even to Clarke himself—& of those in the city who are thinking to join Clarke—very
many want to see if Parker after all may not be invited in—Parker
preached unconscious of the talk and on human sympathy "a very
beautiful but not in its nature a disputable sermon" & charmed all
the people. When however he heard the circumstances—he was a good
deal moved—especially as he heard of it in rather an exaggerated
form—and wrote the church a letter saying if he had known it he
should not have preached. This was read in a social meeting & called
forth a warm talk—in which was said a great deal to gratify P— & his
friends—and nothing to wound[4]—But the whole thing shows what a
baby the public is—how little the [word illegible] ardent of them
know about [word illegible] & liberality—how conservative they are—
&c &c. James C— was not so much surprised as some of the church
were—to find this ignorance and stupidity & quick loss of idea in the
interests of organisation—but he said it would be much harder to educate our church than it was to collect it together—But he is equal to
his work mild—wise—& ideal—though so formative—To prove to you
this I will tell you that he has bro't about one revolution. When we
began & lay preaching was proposed—there was great horror &
speeches & voting against it—but at the last Social meeting *it was
voted* unanamously that he should call upon his laybrethren at his discretion.

    I could fill you a page about Parker—who goes on with the rapid-
ity of an Angel—improving and unfolding and making a prodigious
impression on people in spite of clerical opposition in the meanest
tricks.—One of James Clarke's society said to me the other evening
that he was to be requested to come into the city & deliver a course of
lectures—on Christ—Duty—&c—& would have an overflowing audience. I go to hear him preach—& it is always good—better than
others: & sometimes—frequently—*very great*. But I cannot speak of
him in the end of a letter.—He grows deeper and tenderer as he grows
bolder & more radical—and it seems to me that he looks more and
more like the pictures of the old Saints—I hardly know so affecting a
sight as he is in prayer,—Sophia Ripley said the other day that one
felt how much he suffered whenever he poured himself in prayer—It
is a living evidence of living communion & always produces a great im-

---

4 Peabody refers to the controversy occasioned by the invitation extended to
Theodore Parker to preach at James Freeman Clarke's Church of the Disciples. This
dispute is the subject of the two following letters.

pression.—His sermon at South Boston was a consuming fire—I heard it—and even Lathrop & the other Philistines that blasphemed it were compelled to bear testimony to its surpassing eloquence. But it is palpable to every body how many of the ministers dread his coming—while the common people "hear him gladly." His people at Spring Street are very faithful—& they are constantly gratified & supported by the evidences of interest in him in the country round—I think you had better get him to exchange with you two or three Sundays while you have the command of your pulpit & see what he can do with his battle axe among your hard knots—& come yourself to Spring Street and get refreshed in the neighborhood of the Community where you will I do not doubt in the end set up your nest—Lydia is going to New Jersey to make a visit of some weeks & perhaps he would go—if you have a quiet study & he can carry *his work* to do—in the mean time.— I should think the change of scene would do him good as well as yourself—If you come back again here there is still East Lexington left for you—as yet unsupplied—and now preached to by Mr. Barton [?] of whom they are probably very tired—It would be delightful to you to be so near Emerson—

You know about Wm. Channing, I suppose[5]—He has a rough path to walk—what with the revilings &c with which his confession is met with. His friends say some that he is mad & others that he is wicked. Fortunately *you* have no wife & children so you will be accused not of murdering innocents &c. but only of suicide—

Thursday—I have just returned from Thursday lecture and heard Theodore preach a most "inoffensive sermon" as he called it—on doing to others as you would have others do to you—which was indeed very sweet only I wished that he had taken the opportunity to have given them a *shaking* on some more disputable subject—Since I have returned I have found a paper the Puritan of today—the 10th of June— in which is in the first place a letter from Mr. Folsom minister of Haverhill in answer to a demand on the Unitarian clergy made in the orthodox papers of last week—a demand to have the Unitarian clergy come out & say whether they sanctioned this [word illegible] Dei &c— Mr Folsom disowns Mr Parker's sentiments for himself & for the Unitarian ministers generally and Mr. Shackford's Society in particular— There followed a commentary on Mr Folsom's letter such as you

[5] William Henry Channing, nephew of William Ellery Channing, resigned his Unitarian pastorate in Cincinnati in 1841 when he announced his beliefs that Christianity was not a divine institution and the Bible not an inspired document.

would expect—and further there is another article proposing to indict Mr Parker for blasphemy before the Grand Jury under the Revised Statutes page 761—Section 85th—

So you see my dear friend—you are persecuted in good company—Heaven grant you may "bate no jot of heart nor hope"—& do write to me and tell me how you think & feel about all these matters—

I am truly your affectionate friend

Elizabeth P. Peabody

The meanness of Mr. Folsom's letter surpasses anything—not one word is said to express indignation at the garbled extract but he delivers Parker over to the *dogs*!

MS, NPV

In this and the following undated letters, Elizabeth Peabody provides her version of a dispute in the Church of the Disciples over opening the pulpit to Theodore Parker. Clarke, Peabody suggests, has been glossing over his dubious role in this argument, and the record needs to be set straight.

✣ To James Freeman Clarke   *(incomplete)*

[1841]

correction of the matter.—Then, my dear friend, I *know* you did not see Parker between the writing of his letter & the reading of it to your church—& that you did *not* ask him to withdraw his letter though you may have imagined that this letter I put into your hand the other day, would make him do so.—At the meeting you said what impressed his friends with the idea that you were as earnest as they that the whole thing would be explained in a manner satisfactory to Mr Parker.— And in truth I believe that it was not until after all this—& when you from further reading of the letter detected what you thought was an *intention at sarcasm* that your feelings took the direction they have now—The writing of that letter you shew me reacted upon yourself— I did not suppose (from you saying when you showed me that letter with a laugh, "You would not have me sent *that*—would you?") that you had ever for a moment thought of sending it.—I felt when I read Parker's letter that it was *human*—or would be if it was sent—& could not see the same excuse for your irritability at a *possible sarcasm* (which as he said was not *his* but made of the obvious relations of the case as they lay in nature) as for *his* excitement at what was— (or would have been had it been as he supposed) a public & grave denial of his honesty as a man and denying that he was a *Christian minister.* The courier had said that "It was to be seen whether the Unitarian Clergymen would receive him longer as a Christian ministers, into their pulpits" What you said to Mr Bracklett about Mr Parker requiring to have every body say they like him &c—struck him as absurdly as it did me. He could not conceive that any person should believe such a thing of a rational creature & that you *could not*—unless you were very much prejudiced against Mr P individually to interpret his letter, or even find in it, what nobody else found in it, viz. *a refusal to preach for us*—But Mr Brackett thought that you were entirely disposed [several words illegible] I do not wish to seem to be at variance with you about facts—I told him I would see you today & put you right about dates

Yrs. truly E P P

MS, NNBa (incomplete)

In a letter of May 29, 1841, to Theodore Parker (MS copy, MHi), Clarke reported his version of the controversy over Parker's preaching at his church. Two parishioners had come to Clarke to report dissatisfaction among some in the church over the invitation because of Parker's extreme views. They feared that Parker's presence would give the church a bad name. Clarke told them that the invitation could not be rescinded. On Sunday, he requested that the church members remain after the entire congregation was dismissed; he discussed the matter and all who spoke agreed that the exchange should go on and that they would attend.

In these two letters to Clarke, Peabody disputed the version he presented to Parker. Although he did not mention this to Parker, Clarke was offended by what he took to be sarcasm in Parker's letter in which Parker said he would not have preached had he known of the opposition. Peabody saw no such sarcasm, she wrote, and further criticized Clarke's response to Parker as irritable and inhuman. Further, Clarke apparently thought he had asked Parker to withdraw the letter referred to above (saying he would not have preached), but Peabody disputed that as well. What seemed to be an unresolved confusion is whether the congregational meeting took place before Parker's sermon, as Clarke's letter says, or after, as Peabody's says.

✖ To James Freeman Clarke

My dear James,—   [1841]
    I have *written* my "ipse dixit" because, as the next meeting may prove one of controversy, & I should be the only woman who would probably have any thing to say, I should prefer my communication should be *read,* & my name not mentioned.
    I sent out to Parker for the letters you wrote him & find that I *did* remember more correctly than yourself on one point.—you *do not ask* him in your letter to withdraw *his*—but express cheerfully your willingness to lay it before the church—& he never took the idea that in sending it he was doing any thing you did not fully concur in & approve. I have also made inquiries of several persons—& I find I am right as to my recollection of the general impression of the meeting, so far at least as Parker's friends (not acquaintance). They all supposed that you accepted the appointment to write the letter, because you approved of the vote—& that you would take the earliest opportunity to follow it up with a proposition of exchange.*

Truly your friend, E.P.P.

* otherwise they would have debated more at the time.

MS, NNBa

Peabody rejoices that Dwight is no longer captive to the spiteful congregation at Northampton; now he can minister "in a truly transcendental way to a true church of friends."

✖ To John Sullivan Dwight

My dear friend—   June 24th 1841
    Mr. Nichols came and brought your letter which I was very glad to get—Sophia R— told me a little about your letter to them & now I shall endeavour to see it as well as show them mine—but I think you

give a very conceivable rational and philosophical account of matters. I have lived & observed enough to understand it precisely—"The atmosphere & your nature" are at odds.—I know your nature is *divine* & a hundred years hence you will be all the sweeter angel—that you did not even *see*[1] *the Shades* where opinionatedness & all the other forms of Selfism [?], pusillanimity &c dwell—"making night hideous"—I do not go quite so far as Margaret Fuller (in her theories) does you know she thinks the Brahma transmigration is the only true way of becoming divine (at least with my *heart*) but feel as if there was an ignorance which *is moral* bliss—& that it is worthwhile to forego the honors of Ulysses heroism in the cimmerian land—for Ganyemede's finer fate—

The Ravens shall feed thee—and I am rejoiced to learn from Mr Nichols that you will not be obliged to leave Northamptons beauties when you "shed the [word illegible]" It looks *regal* to stay on the spot—and minister in a truly transcendental way to a true church of friends without aid of surplice—pulpit—sermon—or ordinance—without money & without price—celebrating the communion of the Lord at the social feaste [?] "in spirit & in truth" without sanctimonious form—& enacting instead of preaching Ideals of Home &c— I depend upon you my friend to be a worthy minister in the new administration—which is beginning in one way or another all about—I rejoice to remember your gentle temper—your freedom from all petulance—your dislike to dwelling upon your own individualities & claims—& your freedom of the empyrean—& can afford very well as your friend to dispense with certain *tacts* & *know*ledges—that are always deformities unless sanctified by souls of flame—that find these the hardest things to sanctify—If I had the command of a Northampton paper I should like to put in it an article—headed

J.S.D.—versus the "River people"

& insert underneath an extract from "Story without an end" beginning page 109th on to the end of that section—I quote from the American Edition—But as you say—no matter about *ourselves.* You will like to hear that Parker's sermon has gone off like wildfire—the first edition ⟨has⟩ is almost all sold—He has his audience—enthusiastic—satisfied— The several ministers of our city have given out (except Mr Pierpont & Mr Clarke) that they shall not exchange with him—they do not consider him a Christian minister—or that they *should not*—if they consider themselves so—if they thought as he does!—This has made the

---

1 "See" is underlined twice.

people so wrothy—that they say to one another—why not do the thing ourselves, & so there has been a very handsome letter writen him by some individuals—merchants— (all excepting one—*not* personal acquaintances of his) requesting him to come into the city and deliver a course of lectures (5) at the Temple in September & October—upon the Permanent Christianity &c &c—as he shall like—Is it not a new proof of the stupidity of the party of the Past—thus to give *point d'appui* for the party of the Future to act with advantage?—It is so natural that this should be done—when it is seen that he is not to be heard in the regular way—through their suicidal fears—"Nature is the most brilliant of wits."—2

With respect to the Community—I do not see how it is to step out of its swaddling clothes—unless Mr Ripley makes known in some regular way or allows some friend to do so the plan in detail & in connection with the Ideal.—He enjoys the *"work"* so much that he does not clearly see that his plan is not in the ways of being demonstrated any farther than that it is being made evident—that gentlemen if they will work as many hours as boors will succeed even better in cultivating a farm.—But I trust something will be done soon of a magnetic character—to find the steel which is scattered in the great heap of leads which make up our Society. I am more & more interested in it—as I see the evils arising out of the present corrupt—or petrified—organization. W. H. Channing has left Cincinnati & his mother expects him home soon to spend the summer with her—in Cambridge—

I have just been interrupted by some people who have come from the Thursday lecture where Ellis has been preaching—they say—a really spiteful sermon which of course has *spited* nobody but himself— He said *young men* who were *selfeducated* & consequently partially educated had always done all the mischief there has been done in the world &c &c &c !!—3 Do you know Mr. [?] Pratt [?]—He says in a note to me speaking of Parker's sermon—"I will not attempt to express my sense of the beauty of the discourse—Its sunlike brilliance—its celestial spirituality, its holy & earnest tone of piety, its truthfulness &c &c &c are admirable—" J. F. Clarke in a note to me also says "Parkers sermon blazes with fire from the Bush—It is the best defense of true Christianity I have ever seen—It is the only answer to those infidels who

2 In 1842, Parker was persuaded by a group of Boston citizens to give five lectures, which he combined into *A Discourse of Matters Pertaining to Religion* (1842).

3 George Edward Ellis, Unitarian clergyman and historian of New England, was ordained to the Harvard Unitarian church in Charlestown in May 1840, a pulpit he served for twenty-nine years.

expose the absurdities of theology & think they have put down religion"—Stetson said he took a pen to criticize and could only fill the
margin of the discourse with notes of admiration—I only want *two
words* altered in the discourse—for me to say—it is as good as I can
imagine for the thing—I do not like to have him say that Christ's character &c has not exhausted the fullness of God—because it always suggests the idea that his imagination has exhausted Christ's character—
in spite of his assertion to the contrary—& while society & men are not
yet in sight of that degree of perfection I do not think it is worth while
to talk about its limitations. Our poor apprehension *limits* it sufficiently. And if he must say that the New Testament has parts which
revolt the moral sense—I want him to *point them out* because these
are so few places that most people do not even notice them. I sometimes wish he had a little larger bump of masculineness in his phrenology—but he is a *hero saint*—& every day looks more & more like an
old picture of one of the Masters—Yours affectionately E. P. Peabody

Have you seen the New Edition of Dr [?] Channing's [?] works?[4] The
Introduction is *new* and *most beautiful*—serene wisdom all alive with
the dignity of the Soul—Liberty —& the sweetest humanity. And many
other things I never saw before re-published here—among others the
charge to you about which I am writing him a letter—in answer to a
sweet one from him that came yesterday

MS, MB

4 *Works of William E. Channing, D.D.* (Boston: James Munroe, 1841).

Peabody's position as publisher of the Dial *is suggested here; she appears to have had no further association with Thoreau.*

✲ To Henry David Thoreau

My dear Sir   Feb. 26th 1843
    I understand you have begun to print The Dial and I am very
glad of it on one account[1]—viz—that if it gets out early enough to go

1 In January 1843, Emerson read a series of lectures on New England to audiences
in Baltimore and Philadelphia, and in February gave nine lectures in New York City.

to England by the steamer of the 1st of the month—it does not have to wait *another month*—as was the case with the last number—

But I meant to have had as a first article a letter to the "Friends of the Dial" somewhat like the rough draft I enclose and was waiting Mr. Emerson's arrival to consult him about the manner of it.[2] I have now written him at New York on the subject & told him my *whys* and *wherefores*. The regular income of the Dial does not pay the cost of its printing & paper—& there are readers enough of it to support it if they would only subscribe & they will *only* subscribe if they are convinced that only by doing so can they secure its continuance—He will probably write you on the subject—

I want to ask a favour of you—It is to procure me a small phial of that black lead *dust* which is to be found as Dr C. T. Jackson tells me at a certain leadpencil manufactory in Concord[3]—& send it to me by the first opportunity—I want lead in this *fine dust* to use in a chemical experiment—

Respectfully yrs

E. P. Peabody

He left Thoreau in charge of the *Dial,* giving him the power to send directly to the printer anything he thought would be acceptable.

Peabody submitted other material to the *Dial* in addition to her two articles on Brook Farm. But Emerson thought the religious topic of one manuscript too ponderous "for our slight modern purpose," as he expressed it to Margaret Fuller. He had already told Peabody that her style in his view was too studded with superlative expressions: "You would think that she dwelt in a museum where all things were extremes & extraordinary" (*Letters,* 2: 350; *Journals and Miscellaneous Notebooks,* 5: 262). For her part, Fuller was determined to keep Peabody out of the *Dial: "I never saw anything like her for impossibility of being clear and accurate in a brief sense"* (Fuller to Emerson, April 1842, MS copy, MB).

Anxiety about publishing Peabody was not limited to Transcendental circles. Before her "A Vision" appeared in the March 1843 issue of James Russell Lowell's *The Pioneer,* his sister Mary Lowell Putnam wrote: "I feel very anxious about the next number of the Pioneer. I cannot help writing you a few lines on the subject— I am afraid Carter is too *easy* and that his good nature will induce him to admit articles not worthy to appear in your magazine. I hear that the first article in the next number is to be a *Vision* by E. P. Peabody. Now with all my regard for Miss Peabody, I cannot think that her abilities qualify her to write a leading article for *any* periodical. Her name alone would be an injury to any work to which she should be a contributor—and her vision should be something very *transcendent* indeed to enable it to make head against this prejudice." (Quoted in Sculley Bradley, "Lowell, Emerson, and *The Pioneer," American Literature* 19 [November 1947]: 237)

2 Such a letter never appeared.

3 Dr. Charles Jackson was Emerson's brother-in-law.

P.S. I hope you have got your money from Bradbury & Norton.—I have done all I could about it. Will you drop the enclosed letter for Mrs. Hawthorne into the Post Office—

MS, ViU

Mary Peabody and Horace Mann's wedding is the subject of this brief but surcharged note, with its revealing postscript.

✄ To Rawlins Pickman[1]

Dear Miss Pickman—   [May 1, 1843]
      I enclose you some geranium leaves which garnished the wedding thinking you might like to press them—Mary was dressed in the beautiful grasscloth—& handkerchief that Mrs. John Forbes gave her. With the gold band around her head that Mr. Mann gave her & no other ornament—though she had many given to her that were beautiful—The illuminated countenance of Mr. Mann, so full of joy & tenderness was the ornament you would have most enjoyed; as I did.—We waited the ceremony for you till your messenger arrived & were all most disappointed that you could not come. I shall soon go to Salem I think—& there shall see you.

      Truly yrs—with love to Aunt & Mary—Elizabeth P. P.

P.S. I went with them down to the steamer & saw their stateroom as they intended you should also do[2]—We parted with smiles—not tears—& when I saw the great monster creep away with her there was no discord in my heart.

MS, MHi

1 Love Rawlins Pickman was the daughter of Benjamin and Mary Tappan Pickman. Her brother Thomas married Sophia Palmer, Elizabeth's aunt. I am grateful to Ellen D. Mark, manuscript librarian at the Essex Institute, for this information.
      2 A rainstorm prevented all the guests from attending Mary and Horace's wedding; only Elizabeth, the Peabody parents, and James Freeman Clarke, the officiating minister, were present in the Peabody parlor at 13 West Street. After the ceremony, the Manns boarded the *Britannia* for their honeymoon voyage, which took them to England, Germany, the Netherlands, Belgium, France, and Ireland. They returned to the United States in November 1843.

This letter to John Sullivan Dwight reflects Peabody's respect for his knowledge of German.

To John Sullivan Dwight

To/Mr. J. S. Dwight

Dear Mr Dwight— Thursday the 23rd [May, 1843]

I thought you were coming into the city Saturday to spend Sunday & had the NibelungenLied already for you—And wanted you to look it over & if you saw a place that inspired you put into my hands some translations of it—For the engravers think that if it is a popular poem it would be easy for them to do the illustrations—but none of them had German. If they do it—I do not doubt you might make a very good bargain with them.—

Truly yr friend
EPP

The poem will be here all this week—will you not come in at least as early as next Saturday?

TS copy, Fruitlands Museum, Harvard Massachusetts; copy from Margaret Neussendorfer.

In a letter to Emerson's feisty aunt, Peabody explains her reliance on Kraitsir's philological theories; she makes some startling statements about organicism, which put her more in the company of Jonathan Edwards and Horace Bushnell than of orthodox Calvinists, Unitarians, or Transcendentalists.

To Mary Moody Emerson[1]

My dear Miss Emerson,— [ca. 1843]

I received your letter by your young minister—Alfred E—but he could not stay for me to get acquainted with him.

1 Ralph Waldo Emerson's aunt, Mary Moody Emerson, born in 1774, stayed on with the Emerson family after the death of Waldo's father, William, in 1811. A sharp-

264 1840s
You spoke of my understanding him and he me—as you and I might not understand one another. I have been trying to think out *into words* that change in my opinions and creed which makes me feel that I have *changed*—without having lost that aspect of truth either, or that truth which Unitarians as a body have gained over the Orthodox as a body.

This change I have been reluctant to attempt to put into words, because I have not an understanding sufficiently practiced—a logical expression equal to the height of my thought. I have had an instinct of this from the first and when occasionally I have ventured out of that magic circle of Silence which seems to be an Eternity enclosing absolute truth, I find clouds arise, and myself lose the vision. Since I knew Dr. Kraitsir I have seen a little into the reason why we puzzle ourselves so much and perpetually lose the truths which the great God gives us whereby to live. We have lost the key to language, that great instrument by means of which the finite mind is to compensate itself, for its being fixed to a point in space and compelled to the limitations of the succession we call time. We use words that are no longer symbols but counters—Our logomacy does not coincide with the eternal logos, and yet we are so constituted that words affect us according to their nature in some degree, and talking about one thing while we are thinking about another, and inextricable confusions arise! I have literally begun at my a b c and I mean to understand the languages of those men who have made some advance, and enter into their labors. Moreover Kraitsir is not merely a Philologist, but a mathematician, and one who studies and teaches mathematics as these lie behind and independent of words. I intend to put myself under his tuition in this also, and in the course of a *year or two*, I think I may possibly get weaponed to contend with the great Silence adequately and win from her the expression of what God has graciously pleaded to say to *me* individually.

But before I get ready you may be in "Kingdom come." And so I

---

tongued, intelligent, and independent-minded person, Mary Moody devoted herself during the following years to assisting in the rearing of the Emerson children (sometimes to the frustration and despair of Waldo's mother, Ruth), writing a spiritual diary, reading religion and philosophy, and quarreling with her relatives. Although her nephew Waldo Emerson disagreed with her religious views—Mary denied it, but both her theology and her extreme personal asceticism were markedly Calvinist—he appreciated the rigor of her mind and the quality of her instruction during his youth. She died in 1863.

will just try to shadow out with vocables of confusion, knowledge that I know will be "darkened by words *without* knowledge."

When I use the word Orthodox, you must cast out of your mind all thought of all Orthodox persons you know, and think of St. Paul or St. John, and of those very intelligently!

My change consists in having got some notion of life on the one hand and of sin on the other. I have discriminated life at once from the creative essence, and from dead existence. Perhaps I may say with the Germans—It is a becoming—and yet I cannot *exactly*, for there is an objective as well as a subjective condition of life, and neither of the conditions are *the life*.

But with regard to sin. In actual transgression all believe. Most intensely Dr. Channing, the great champion of the dignity of human nature—believed it. Nay, even Theodore Parker, whose philosophy, if he has one, may be said to deny the possibility of going counter to the will of God, believes in transgression, and inveighs against it, with an eloquence of moral sensibility which makes him—maugre all his errors of philosophy and theology, a very excellent preacher to a certain audience, whom few preachers reach. But the orthodox would penetrate to the principle of Sin. Sin with them is a fact of their very life, while with the Arians, Unitarians, etc., it is to be predicated only of the manifestation. I find it difficult to express myself exactly here. The Unitarian refers sin to Circumstance. He may be sorry some wrong thing is done—some wrong feeling felt, some error has been pressed on him, and may repudiate the action, even to the point of not repeating it. But he does not see in it anything to make him mistrust his essential self— his organic self, I may express it perhaps. The orthodox man looks upon the wrong thing done as a comparatively trifling matter when compared with that fault of his organic self whence this wrong thing came, and which makes all his action, when he looks to it narrowly, have some wrong tinge or bias in it.

Now I think I understand and know that these two opposite views make the dividing principle between Unitarians and Orthodox—because I retained the superficial theory of the former after it was revealed clearly in my own experience that the principle of sin is organic in man. Those words "total depravity" are very ambiguous—because we do not make proper distinction. *Arrest a man at any moment* and observe him arrested—cut him off—and he will revolve forever in a vicious circle—or cease to revolve—and die like a plant or animal of longer or shorter date. This is the idea I mean to express in that

"Vision" which you have, and which seriously, in my religious experience, cast forth to seek the individual visible church, to which I belong. But the Unitarian cries out: is not this implicating God, and making him the author of Sin? Perhaps it does make him the author of sin—in that last analysis. Perhaps sin is his minister, introducing us into deep secrets of the Divine nature, and it may be that those expressions of the apostles—which *misinterpreted*—have crushed the race into hell—morally and physically too—were but attempts of minds (teeming with truths too great for the *word-symbolization* of a degenerated race to reflect) to express central truths. *Jesus Christ* is not looked at *symbolically* by those who read the New Testament—Even Waldo is bent out of his perpendicular and whereas all things else are symbolical to him—he is deceived and his eyes blinded—by the impertinence (not of Jesus—as he thinks) but of his own notion of the apostles above Jesus. We think—or we talk as if we thought we solved the problem of physical evil—and so are willing to consider *that* as a minister of God—but *Sin* we do not see round, and so we question whether that is a minister of God—And it is a wonderful Minister indeed! I speak however of the abstract *Sinfulness*—not of *concrete sins*—when I make the bold proposition that as far as I can understand myself—*Sinfulness* has been the greatest Angel to me.

God has not created in the race of man a duplicate but at best an image of himself—Even the *Uncreated* cannot [have] created the *Uncreated*. *Absolute cause may* produce effect which may be a relative cause. But Absolute Cause cannot produce Absolute cause. When God creates a man—he creates a creature—and the creature [text incomplete].

MS, MWA

An example of Peabody's critical ability in her comment on a favorite book.

✣ To Phoebe Gage

Sept—1846

These two leaves—in a [word illegible] copy of vol. 1 of Herder[1]
To Miss Phoebe Gage
    with the regards of
        E. P. Peabody
This was all that Herder published.—Mr. Marsh translated also the posthumous papers with which Herder was about to make a second volume.—And which I cannot obtain to accompany this—

It is because this is a favorite book of mine that I send it to you—& not for its outward show—as you perceive. But I think it is a key that unlocks a hidden world within the world of the Old Testament Or is the poetical world which Herder's criticism makes visible, even to the eyes of New England pastors [?], the *outward* world of the Old Testament, within which lies the spiritual world of Old Palestine—This I think would be the truer statement. Herder was a greater poet than theologian—but the poetry he develops is *truth*, on the perception of which is conditioned the apprehension of the more Universal Truth—the prophecy that binds the world's history into a rounded whole.—

MS, PHi

1 This note refers to Johann Gottfried von Herder, *The Spirit of Hebrew Poetry*, 2 vols., trans. James Marsh (Burlington: Edward Smith, 1833).

As the West Street bookshop's profits declined, Peabody began taking on boarders and students, including Caroline Dall's sister Anne, who had been studying with Peabody, in the barely controlled chaos of the Peabody household.

✄ To Caroline Healey Dall[1]

My dear Mrs. Dall,—   [March 20, 1848][2]

Your father said if I had anything to say about your sister to communicate with you. And it seems to me I ought to write.—Soon a new quarter will begin & I do not feel I am doing my duty to let it appear I am satisfied. She left the impression in Mrs. Lowell's *School* (as has come to me from the scholars) (she was never mentioned between Mrs Lowell & myself) as being incorrigibly stupid as well as selfish—But my observation has brought me to the conclusion that she has perfectly good faculties & can learn any thing & that the whole difficulty lies in an entire want of *moral principle upon the subject*. I do not mean that she is positively wicked in any principle or feeling—but she is simply *negative*. She apparently thinks not only of nothing but herself—but with respect to herself—she thinks only of the present moment—This passion for reading is simply selfindulgence   It is with no plan or purpose & seems to have no love of knowledge in any sense—or sense of superiority in any body—no openness to instruction—She is gentle— she has no resentful passions as I see—And if it were possible to put any thing *into her* which could awaken an aspiration, a benevolence, or any principle of Life directly or indirectly religious—I think she

---

1 Caroline Healey was raised in a prosperous Boston family, but forced to support herself after her father's bankruptcy in 1842. Healey was a devoted follower of Theodore Parker and attended Margaret Fuller's Conversations, where she first encountered Elizabeth Peabody. Teaching at private academies provided a meager income for her until her marriage to the Reverend Charles Dall in 1844. Dall's missionary assignments took him away from his home for longer and longer periods of time until he left for India in 1855, where he stayed until his death in 1886. Caroline Dall turned, after his departure, increasingly to writing and lecturing on the topics of women's economic and legal rights.

Dall and Peabody agreed that women's finer natures would elevate and redeem society from its male baseness, but Dall insisted on popularizing and publicizing the cause of women, while Peabody saw women working within society's institutions to improve them.

2 "Mar. 20, 1848" is written in the upper right of the first MS sheet in another hand.

might be made a new creature of—If not she will sink down, in no long time, into a perfectly narrow, insignificant, disagreeable, selfish, *old maid*—in the worst sense of that term—whom every body will dislike.

In some respects *this* house is not good for her. There are no young people & no sacrifices are *indispensible* here. She pursues her own way entirely—never asking—never seeming to think whether or not she may do or leave undone any thing for any body—I do not mean that we want anything of her for our sakes—but for her own it would be well if she were somewhere where her selfish habits would produce a little more *obvious commotion*—so she should recognize them.

The dissatisfaction I have with her as a scholar is this—She does not seem to feel any responsibility about using her faculties.—She writes very badly—I tell her she ought to write copies &c—"No she cannot write—she never could—she never can—it does no good to try"— There is no idea apparently that she has no moral right to settle down into this—She has begun to study French German & Italian—she has never shown the slightest *willingness* to enter into my ways of viewing these languages which is necessary in order to do the thing well— Whatever is *new* or a method she rejects—apparently thinking I can *make her know*—when of course I can only give her the means of knowing—not even those unless with her steady cooperation—There is nothing like an open willing mind—Dr Kraitsir has given a course of french lessons—a course of German lessons—& two courses of Italian lessons this winter in my schoolroom in the afternoons—I gave her leave free of expense to attend these (which *I* never omit)—& she would not—This shows the state of mind—She could not help seeming interested in the only one she did attend—But instead of this she buries herself in a book in the bookroom—My opinion or feeling about any thing she never seems to consider any more than if it was not given—& it is not my nature to volunteer these undescried—She does *least well* of the class in every thing she studies except the translation of french—& I give her lessons to learn out of school—But they are *never* faithfully done—She gives all her *best* hours to reading & takes the sleepy end of an evening when she ought to be in bed for her lessons—& in the morning reads again till schooltime—I gave her with all the rest, an exercise to write of German verbs—Most of the others who study Latin & draw—besides (she does neither—) did theirs in one week—She has been five or six & has not done them yet—one little girl two or three years younger than she did them   My mother heard her say at the beginning that she never intended to do them. They were of no use—& thus without an *open* rebellion to me—there is a *real one.* I told her a few weeks ago—She must not read out of school till she had caught up to her class in all in which she was behind.— *She continues to read,* and this thing is not done

Now under these circumstances is it worth while for your father to pay me nearly 75 dollars a quarter for her—Is it not better that she should be sent to some *man* who can make her work by such motives or means as I have no taste for employing—or else go home & let this money be given to the poor?

There is yet a fortnight before the quarter is out—& I want you to write to her & tell her that I feel unwilling to *keep her* unless she will entirely change her whole plan—and voluntarily & heartily give me the disposal of *all her time* in school & out as I think best—It should do her real good to go *out of herself three months* & give herself up to another.—It might transform her—You can show her this letter if you think best—I think it would be a good plan for you to send her to come & spend a Sunday with you—& talk with her & show her this letter—or write to her yourself—& reserve this letter if that fails.—I have been *plain* though I know it must be disagreeable because it seems to me that duty & honour require this—After all I have only touched outlines.—

Yours very truly E. P. PEABODY

MS, MHi

William Ellery Channing, 31,
Unitarian minister and mentor
of Elizabeth Peabody, from
painting by Washington
Allston, 1811.
(*Sophia Smith Collection,
Smith College*)

Channing as an older man.
(*Concord Free Public Library*)

The original Masonic
Temple, site of A. Bronson
Alcott's Temple School,
corner of Tremont
Street at Temple Place,
Boston.
(*Boston Public Library*)

A. Bronson Alcott's School of Human Culture, by Francis Graeter,
the school's drawing master.
(*By permission of the Houghton Library, Harvard University*)

A. Bronson Alcott
at the Concord School of Philosophy.
(*Concord Free Public Library*)

Ralph Waldo Emerson,
photograph by Black.
(*Concord Free Public Library*)

Lidian, Emerson's second
wife, with their son Waldo.
(Frontispiece to R. W.
Emerson, *Journals*, 4
[1836–38] [Cambridge:
Houghton Mifflin, 1910])

LOUISA MAY ALCOTT.

Louisa May Alcott
(*Concord Free Public Library*)

Central part of Concord village, drawn by J. W. Barber,
engraved by J. Downes. The Unitarian church is at the right.
(*Concord Free Public Library*)

Henry David Thoreau,
drawing by Edward W. Emerson.
(*Concord Free Public Library*)

Elizabeth Palmer Peabody, photograph by Gutekunst.
(*Concord Free Public Library*)

4
1850s

After West Street—The Search for a New Cause

IN JULY 1849, Nathaniel Hawthorne's mother, Elizabeth Manning Hawthorne, now living with her son and his family on Mall Street in Salem, became seriously ill. On July 29, two days before his mother's death, Hawthorne visited her and recorded in his journal: "For a long time I knelt there [at her bedside], holding her hand; and surely it is the darkest hour I ever lived. Afterwards, I stood by the open window, and looked through the crevice of the curtain. The shouts, laughter, and cries of the two children had come up into the chamber, from the open air, making a strange contrast to the death-bed scene. . . . Oh, what a mockery, if what I saw were all."[1] But, he concluded, God provides comfort through His assurance of a better state to come.

After Mrs. Hawthorne's death, first Hawthorne, then the children in turn became ill, and Elizabeth Peabody was called from Boston in March 1850 to help her exhausted sister Sophia nurse them. In November Peabody closed her bookshop for good, although her brother Nathaniel continued to live there, dispense homeopathic medicines, and take in boarders. Among his boarders was Mary Caroline Hinckley; her untidy habits so disturbed the fastidious Nathaniel that Elizabeth Peabody was prompted to fire off a series of scathing letters to the offending Miss Hinckley. The worst of it was, Peabody charged, that her brother seemed to think Mary Caroline's sloppiness the product of her Transcendentalism! Mary Hinckley soon moved out, uncowed by Peabody's verbal onslaught. On the bottom of the last letter from Peabody, Hinckley wrote, "What misrepresentations this wicked letter contains! It is more base than her undisguised abuse of me. It is adapted to deceive even the very elect."[2]

The decade of the 1850s was for Elizabeth Peabody diffuse and shapeless. She was concerned about emigrés. Her manuscripts, for example, contain a lengthy series of letters to Gerrit Smith, Samuel Gridley Howe, and others on plans to resettle Emilie Kossuth, sister of the Hungarian revolutionary. She was deeply troubled by the growing sectional controversy, reflecting on it in a series of letters about the plight of Kentucky plantation owner and antislavery writer Mattie Griffith. She continued her voracious reading and held historical conversations. She became interested in spiritualism, a movement that already had wide popularity. Perhaps the most notorious examples illus-

1 Nathaniel Hawthorne, *The American Notebooks* (Columbus: Ohio State University Press, 1972), vol. 8, *The Centenary Edition of the Works of Nathaniel Hawthorne,* ed. William Charvat et al., 428.
2 Mary Caroline Hinckley, postscript to Elizabeth Peabody to Eugene Hinckley, 30 August 1851, TS copy, OYesA.

trating spiritualism's commercial and entertainment potential were the Fox sisters of Hydesville, New York, who claimed to communicate with the spirits of the dead through rapping. They signed up with showman P. T. Barnum in 1849, creating a tremendous sensation; they spawned hundreds of imitators in their wake—magicians, mediums, seance holders. Although later shown up as a hoax, the episode pointed to a deep common hunger for communication with the dead and confirmation of human immortality in a time when the advance of technology and scientific thinking made many doubt their religious faith. The formation of spiritualist societies throughout the country and the countless informal attempts at communication with the dead attests to the desire on the part of many to believe that life was not simply material and ephemeral. By 1870, Sydney Ahlstrom has estimated, perhaps eleven million Americans claimed some sort of belief in spiritualism.[3]

For Elizabeth Peabody, spiritualism paralleled her belief in the power of intuition to apprehend truth directly and confirmed her sense that creation is an organism vitalized by an intelligent and loving God. Her conviction that humanity is essentially spiritual rather than material made her an obvious recruit and she tried to get other members of her family involved, as well. Experiencing seances in Boston, she became convinced that her niece Una possessed the potential to be a medium. Hawthorne refused to allow his daughter to participate. "But should it ever come of itself," she wrote Sophia, "the purity of the medium would be a fine chance to take an observation, and I should treat it to Una as if it were not at all *strange*—only rather curious. Then it will not agitate her."[4]

But nothing seemed to rivet and organize her attention in the 1850s as had the constellation of religious and reform issues of the 1830s or as the kindergarten movement would in the 1870s and beyond. When she did choose a cause in the early 1850s, it was one that seemed particularly farfetched and doomed to failure: the use of chronological charts to teach history. Her advocacy sprang from her commitment to teaching history, particularly to women, and from her frustration at the time needed to cover chronology. As a solution to the problem of a clear and rapid presentation of vast amounts of historical time, she turned to the charts of Josef Bem, an exiled Polish general who had devised a system of squares and colors to represent sequences of events. Bem had introduced his system into France in the mid-1830s, and a

3 Ahlstrom, *Religious History,* 488–90.
4 Elizabeth Peabody to Sophia Hawthorne, 23 March 1851, MS, NN-B.

Polish emigré Podbielski brought it to America in 1845. His system seemed to teach relationship as well as sequence, and even revealed the divine hand behind events. "Details show the activity of the finite mind, and the action of second causes; outlines mark the decisions of the Divine Mind interpreting events, and the working of the Divine will controlling them."[5] She encouraged other educators to try this system, carried the charts to school committees during a tour of the Northeast beginning in November 1850, and published a guide to Bem's system, *The Polish-American System of Chronology* (Boston: E. P. Peabody, 1850). But the method never caught on, and indeed suggests the backwaters into which Peabody's gusty enthusiasm sometimes carried her.

Peabody was recalled from her tour in January 1851 to come to West Newton to care for Mrs. Peabody, at sixty-three aging and ill. Hawthorne, who seemed to have disliked the town, moved his family to Concord, and Elizabeth and Mary nursed their mother in her last days. Mary was preoccupied with the illness of her own children. Her husband Horace Mann was in Washington serving as congressman. Elizabeth Peabody wrote: "When Mr. Mann is at home, & the children are well—about once a week—Mary will come in & take my place & I shall get rest from care for a night."[6] Their mother died two years later, on January 11, 1853.

The 1848 election of Zachary Taylor as president of the United States and other Whigs to public office had promised the accession of their appointees to patronage posts and the speedy removal of Democrats. Hawthorne claimed that the position he had held since 1846 as surveyor at the Salem Custom House was not a political reward, but he was dismissed nevertheless early in 1849. In the summer of 1849 local Salem Whigs and Democrats, and some national politicians, battled over Hawthorne's political fate, making and refuting charges of corruption. The dismissal was upheld. During that summer when his job was in the balance and his mother lay dying, Hawthorne wrote *The Scarlet Letter,* which was published the following year. In the summer of 1850, the Hawthornes moved to Lenox to a cottage rented from William and Caroline Tappan, friends of Sophia. During that summer Hawthorne wrote *The House of the Seven Gables;* it appeared in April 1851. *The Blithedale Romance* followed in May 1852 after

---

5 Elizabeth Peabody to Mr. Woolworth, State Normal School, Albany, New York, *The Free Presbyterian,* 4 April 1885, 90 (TS copy, OYesA); Peabody, "Principles and Methods of Education," 732–33.
6 Elizabeth Peabody to Sophia Hawthorne, 6 April [1851], MS, NN-B.

the Hawthornes had returned to West Newton. Again caught up in political issues, Hawthorne wrote a campaign biography for his Bowdoin College classmate Franklin Pierce, the Democratic nominee for President. His election in November 1852 raised Hawthorne's hopes for a political appointment, rewarded by the post of United States consul in Liverpool. The Hawthornes left for England in July 1853.

Horace Mann had served in the House of Representatives as a Whig from 1848 to 1852. In 1853, he had been drawn back into the educational world when he was approached to serve as first president of the new Antioch College in Yellow Springs, Ohio. In September, he and his family departed for Ohio.

Probably feeling somewhat abandoned, Elizabeth Peabody moved with her father to Eagleswood, New Jersey. Eagleswood, near Perth Amboy, was the site of the Raritan Bay Union, a cooperative society established in 1853 by Marcus and Rebecca Spring, wealthy New York City philanthropists. Spring asked Theodore Dwight Weld, the antislavery leader, to establish a school at Eagleswood, and Weld agreed. His wife Angelina Grimké Weld taught history, her sister Sarah taught French, and Elizabeth Peabody served as Weld's "principal assistant."[7]

In the fall of 1854, Hawthorne began to send money from England to help support Dr. Nathaniel Peabody, whose health had begun to decline. He died at Eagleswood in January 1855 and was buried in Eagleswood's private cemetery. Hawthorne intercepted many of Elizabeth's letters to Sophia describing their father's illness and death. In the spring of 1855, Hawthorne announced that he had kept a letter of hers from Sophia. Furthermore, he was irritated by her accusations that Sophia had neglected her father and family. Peabody had no understanding of "conjugal relations" and it was impertinent for her to lecture the Hawthornes on such a subject. On a financial matter, he wrote, "You *did* make the suggestion about my borrowing money to set your brother up in life! *What* a memory! Perhaps you write in your sleep?"[8] Sophia too expressed impatience with her sister. Commenting on Peabody's lectures on the slavery crisis, she wrote, "your letters to me would be far more appropriate to a slaveholder." Peabody's graphic description of a slave auction in a letter to their daugh-

[7] Maude Greene, "Raritan Bay Union, Eagleswood, New Jersey," *Proceedings of the New Jersey Historical Society* 68 (January 1950): 9–10.

[8] Nathaniel Hawthorne to Elizabeth Peabody, 19 January 1855 and 20 April 1855, quoted in James Mellow, *Nathaniel Hawthorne in His Times* (Boston: Houghton Mifflin, 1980), 457.

ter Una Hawthorne prompted a protective response like that Sophia later exercised in heavily editing her husband's journals: "For the consequence is," Sophia wrote, "I have to suppress your letters to her and she is disappointed. What is the virtue or use of forcing the subject upon the poor child?"[9]

Elizabeth Peabody's sympathies were fixed immediately and instinctively on the antislavery cause. She later regretted not having been more deeply involved earlier in this crusade. Like so many other New Englanders, she was aroused by the example of John Brown. When the opportunity arose to plead for the life of Aaron Dwight Stevens, one of two Harpers Ferry raiders still alive, Peabody went to Richmond to meet with Virginia governor John Letcher. Letcher refused to pardon Stevens, who was hanged.

Peabody attended several antislavery rallies. In a January 1861 rally addressed by the fiery abolitionist Wendell Phillips, a riot broke out in the hall. The speakers struggled through their texts to the mounting roar of hostile demonstrators. At the end of the tumultuous meeting, Peabody found herself being escorted home by several of her former pupils, armed against possible proslavery violence. The war had indeed come home; the hall where Phillips spoke was the same Masonic Temple where she and Alcott had conducted Temple School.[10]

[9] Sophia Hawthorne to Elizabeth Peabody, 7 August 1857, quoted in Mellow, *Nathaniel Hawthorne*, 468.

[10] This story is told in Louise Hall Tharp, *The Peabody Sisters of Salem* (Boston: Little Brown), 289–90.

Mrs. Elizabeth Peabody's death, described to Sophia, who was living with her husband, Nathaniel Hawthorne, and their family near Lenox, Massachusetts.

✹ To Sophia Peabody Hawthorne   (excerpt)

Tuesday Night.
[12 January 1853]

So very quietly she passed at last, that it was a quarter of an hour we were in doubt; but she had labored so for breath for eighteen hours, that I have no feeling yet but thankfulness that she went without access

of suffering, and that she is above and beyond all suffering, forever
and ever. Doubt not she is with you, more intimately than ever; for
the spirit must be where the heart's affections are. Her last words about
you were when I asked her if you should come again. "Oh, no; don't
let her come—don't let her come—oh, no; don't let her come and leave
that poor baby!" So characteristic! That was yesterday, and I wrote
you last evening. Last night we put her to bed at ten o'clock; and I,
as usual, lay down at the head of the bed, and, till two o'clock, she slept
more peacefully than for a long while. Then she roused and got up
for a short time, but soon wanted the bed; and then she lay in my arms
two or three hours, during which time I thought she would go; but at
five she wanted to get up, and we put her in the lolling-chair. When she
was settled there, and the table and pillow put before her, and she had
gone to sleep, father came in, and I left him and Mary with her, and
lay down and slept soundly three hours. It was ten o'clock before we
put her to bed again; and then Mary or father or Margaret or I had
her in our arms all day, till she went. She was strong enough to raise
her body and hold up her head till the last; and we changed her position, as she indicated, all the time. At the last moment, Mary was lying
at the head of the bed, supporting her, with the intervention of some
pillows. I was on the other side of the bed, and father in the rocking-
chair. So long a time passed without a sound, that father rose and
went to look, and then I; and (as I said) it was quarter of an hour.
She breathed very gently the first part of the time. We all felt so thankful when it seemed that she had indeed fled without a sign, when we
had been dreading a final struggle between her tenacious life and the
death angel. But, no; her life went out into the free spaces, and here
she lies, for I am sitting by her bedside, this first night. Mary has gone
home; father has gone to bed. We are all at peace—peace—peace. This
sentiment in me shuts out all realization that the only being in the
wide world whose affection for me knew no limit, has gone out of it.
It seems to me that I never shall feel separated. She scarcely spoke but
in monosyllables; but these showed she was perfectly sensible. Several
times she wanted me to "go to bed," and did not seem to realize that
it was the daytime. I think she was perfectly conscious, but I am not
sure that she knew that she was dying. I was not sure myself, though I
knew she could not live long. I read to her one of David's Psalms of
Thanksgiving in the afternoon; I thought it might awaken sweet
echoes of association.

My dear Sophia, I hope your heart too will rest in peace upon the thought of the ascended one,—ascended, and yet, I dare say, hovering over the beloved ones.

From your affectionate,
ELIZABETH

Julian Hawthorne, *Nathaniel Hawthorne and His Wife*, 2 vols. (Boston: Houghton Mifflin, 1884), 1:485–87.

Despite her own youthful independence and insistence on education for women, Mrs. Peabody was highly protective of her daughters. She often indulged in speculating on the worst possibilities, particularly with regard to Sophia and Mary. Because of Sophia's real and imagined illnesses, her mother was sure she could never marry, or, if married, never have children, and was stunned when Sophia announced her intention to marry Nathaniel Hawthorne in June 1841. Mrs. Peabody continued to offer her warnings and admonitions. In May 1843, Mary Peabody and Horace Mann were married, and Mrs. Peabody poured out her anxieties to Mary in turn, particularly when the Manns traveled to Ohio in 1852, where her son-in-law became president of Antioch College.

As for relations between Elizabeth Peabody and her brothers-in-law, they were often strained and always complicated, for several reasons. Hawthorne was, as Louise Tharp put it, "hers by right of discovery, a literary rarity brought to light" (Peabody Sisters of Salem, 207). But Hawthorne resented her interference in his life, and wrote her angry letters, especially when he and Sophia were abroad, insisting that she not meddle in his domestic life. As for Peabody's relationship with Horace Mann, it was even more complex. Mann had confided some of his deepest feelings to her during the two years following the death of his first wife, Charlotte Messer. But Mary Mann would not tolerate talk of the past, and insisted that even in the 1830s Mann had only barely tolerated Elizabeth's attempt to expose and heal his psychic wounds.

A frantic, complicated, name-scattering letter, urging support for a farm purchase to settle Emilie Kossuth, sister of the Hungarian revolutionary.

✖ To Samuel Gridley Howe

New York City
My dear Dr—   30 April 1856
    I thank you for the kind expressions & appreciation of your note.—
I think I was *but just* in putting little weight on certain things.[1] I enclose or send accompanying this letter the advertisement of the *place* which we *have bought*: a fruit farm in New Jersey—planted by a superior Hungarian Agriculturist or rather *Horticulturist*. He came here among the first immigrants & he & *Mezeros* (War Minister of Hungary) bought & planted this farm & built a house—they had a thousand trees & vines besides of the best kinds on their cellar—But a fire broke out in their house & burnt it down—& all those things in the cellar which was quite discouraging.—Then Kotona's friends in Transylvania sent him word that if he would send him 2000 florins a years, & being discouraged at the fire he went off & Mezeros could not work the farm himself—so he sold it for $2400 & went to teaching—The present owner has built this pretty house whose light rooms will enable her to keep summer boarders till the fruit is mature for the market. But it is not what it would have been for good husbandry—the present owner has business in the city & has neglected it—the access by a steamboat & railroad to the city enables persons residing there to be in the city at 8 oclock in the morning & to leave it at 5 or 6 in the evening—so that Emil can board with her & be at the metropolitan bank every day—which is a great comfort to her—The place *cost* 2600 dollars—1200 to be paid down & the rest to be on mortgage. When your & Mr. Stearn's money comes (which is $500 I believe) we shall have $2000 $200 is one mortgage to be paid this year & 600 is neces-

---

1 Emilie Kossuth, Madame Zulawski, had married and divorced a Polish nobleman, who pursued her to the United States. Peabody was anxious to get Kossuth safely settled. In 1856, Peabody wrote a eulogy upon the death of Kossuth's sister Madame Meszlenyi, which stimulated interest and financial support for the Kossuth family. But by October 1856, the fruit-farm scheme described here had fallen through, as had a second attempt to settle the family on another farm. By the end of 1856, Emilie Kossuth seems to have drifted away from Peabody's orbit.

sary in order to buy a cow & horse & support her boarders of which she has one engaged already—Another mortgage of $600 is due to a rich gentleman in the West—to whom I am going to write & try to make him *give it in*—And by all ways & means I am going to try to get the $600—that will make my sum complete to $2600—We have as I say full $2000 now—Zsega lay at the point of death some weeks ago & she is detained in town with him now going to a friend's house *tomorrow* when she has to give up the one she is in   But a Hungarian friend Dac who knew all about the farm has gone down to see to it—till she comes. The Dr. wants him longer under his own eye for there is trouble yet in his lung or side—though he is recovered wonderfully—He is not yet up except to have his bed made—Had he died I think she would have died too. He is made very happy by this prospect—& if you had heard her hearty & tearful 'God bless you' you would have said, I ought to be satisfied. I wrote to Bennet Forbes to help me when I was deliberating about this farm—but he says he cannot & he did not want to ask any body—I have a great mind to ask Mr Cushing—wish you would mail to him one of those copies of Mad. Meszlenyi—for that has been the spell by which I have conjured hitherto—& also send one to Mrs Wm W. Twain New Bedford & one to Benjamin Rodman New Bedford   I have not got any more here—& I do not know whether any are left at my brother's. Have you asked Stephen C Phillips or Charles Francis Adams—I believe the latter is stingy—I shall write to those persons in New Bedford & perhaps to Mrs Cushing. Do you know that Mrs. Bryant—Mrs George Lee's daughter? but I will write to Mrs George Lee—I enclose you a note I have received from my Physiological friend. You see she has the fullest instincts of a lady. I think Mrs Burrill might like to have her board there for taking her scholars into her class—If she should go to South Boston—she would be called upon by ladies in Roxbury—& so have two classes. It would be rather late for Boston. I was sorry not to call on Mrs. Howe & so was Madame but she could not leave the bedside of Zsiga & I was completely in the hands of "devils" all the time. I met Miss Sedgewick coming out of 180 [illegible] Street yesterday & she has been worried too at Mad's inconsiderate speech of me—a good deal—but she said "she *is*[2] a noble woman—she meets your Ideal of a [word illegible] exile—& she has known her intimately enough every thing.

Your friend, E. P. Peabody

MS, MWiWC

2 "Is" is underlined twice in the text.

Another cause of this decade was Mattie Griffith, white author of a fictional slave autobiography. As this letter suggests, Griffith's situation was a dramatic one—she was a wealthy Southern woman who, when awakened to the moral dilemma posed by slavery, was threatened by neighbors and fled North to poverty and obscurity, relying on her newfound Northern friends for support.

✎ To Frances Adeline Seward[1]

Mrs. Seward—
My dear Madam—   May 22, 1857

I have seen a letter to Mr. Furness of Philadelphia from your husband, touching the "Autobiography of a Female Slave" & its author[2] which emboldened me to write to you to ask you if you will not like to aid in a project which is on foot to assist that very noble young girl—in her great purposes—

She is as perhaps you know from Mr. Furness an orphan with an only sister—& *all* her property is *in slaves*—whom it is the first desire of her heart to make free—But the sister with three small children & very delicate health—is dependent on her—For she was so unfortunate as to have been married for her beauty & wealth when very young to an Irish Catholic physician—who with brutal neglect of *her* all the while—*sold* all her property consisting also solely of negroes and then—because her sister Mattie (the authoress) would not yield to him *her negroes* to be sold (which she would not do because she felt obliged to set them free) threw his wife & children upon her—just as she was coming to the north in the hope of gaining a means of subsistence for herself—So that instead of earning income for herself only, she had to earn it for *five persons*—& hitherto & for a year to come it is necessary for her to hire & support a nurse for her sister's younger child.—The sister is a noble mind & heart but nearly broken hearted & broken in health. Still she looks forward to assisting her sister bye & bye in gaining income—by some kind of labour—They are very highly & widely connected with aristocratic families of Kentucky Virginia & Maryland—a few of whom are Catholics.—Mattie has been

---

1 Frances Adeline Miller Seward was the wife of Republican politician William Henry Seward and a woman of liberal sympathies and humanitarian views.
2 Martha (Mattie) Griffith, *Autobiography of a Female Slave* (New York, 1857).

known from childhood among her friends as opposed to slavery—but
they never have appreciated the depth & entireness of her soul's ab-
horrence of it—& treated it as an *eccentricity*—Nevertheless they have
in some degree humoured her in the disposition of her negroes while
she has been under age—& shielded her from the operation of the
law—when she & also her agent have been at two several times presented to the Grand Jury for violating the laws of the state in the
privileges given to her negroes—The known conservatism of these families on the slavery question has been her protection.—But as soon as
she was of age she determined to make them free—and as she had had
some distinguished success in the literary line from childhood—her
thoughts turned to authorship—& she was sanguine that a conscientious & faithful picture of slavery *from a slaveholder* would *initiate*
at least a literary life in the North—by which she could support herself and family—& be able *to return* to her poor people the money
they had earned for her—to establish themselves in freedom—

But her way is beset with difficulties—As soon as the book was
published her whole connection in the south was outraged in their
own opinion—to the last degree—& have denounced her—not however without holding out to her every temptation to return provided
she will publish in all newspapers that she *did not write the book* &
renounce her plans of emancipation—As they have found her proof
against every thing of this kind—they have within the last few months
taken another tack—and her Catholic relations—& even the Protestant ones have combined to induce the husband of her sister to claim
those children (there are three under seven years of age) in order as
they say "to bring them up in the Catholic Church"—

Mattie & her sister have both repudiated the Catholic Church
(Mattie has done it publicly) *because* they were advised by Mattie's
confessor to refrain from Emancipation on account of its being preju-
dicial to the interests of the Catholic church—an advice which opened
their eyes to the yawning chasm between the interests of this terrible
ecclesiasticism & those of *humanity*—the true Church of Christ.—The
object of this persecution—of which the bad husband is made the instrument by *bribery*—is to torment *Mattie* into returning.—But she
has thrown her sister under the protection of the laws of Pennsylvania
so favourable to mothers—& hopes to have her legally free from her
tormentor in September—but meanwhile they are obliged to be on the
qui vive against *kidnapping*—& this prevents them from being so eco-
nomical in their arrangements as they would like to be—

Meanwhile "the Autobiography" has not sold well.—She found

it almost impossible to get a publisher—& at last Redfield took it almost against his will—and on the bargain of not giving her ten percent on the retail until after having sold 2000 copies—(which he says
are not yet sold)—& he told her he should not advertise it much—&
he has not advertised it except in the AntiSlavery Standard—Liberator—& such points[?]—& did not print Mr. Sewards letter even in the
Tribune but only in the AntiSlavery Standard. He *says* he has distributed 200 volumes among AntiSlavery leaders—& does not pretend
to have done any thing out of that precinct—where it is least necessary
to have done any thing! I am pretty sure that he does not wish to peril
his Southern market by advertising it in papers which go South at
all—He did not send a copy even to the National Era.—Her hope was
not merely in the sale of the book—but in its giving her some reputation by which she thought she might write in newspapers & periodicals
& for booksellers—but not a thing of the kind has presented itself—&
she is brought to a standstill.—

She is a woman of such dignity delicacy and want of knowledge
of the world in a certain sense—that although Antislavery people have
come round her with expressions of sympathy . . . to work for antislavery *gratis*—I said to her that as an antislavery agent I thought she
might earn a thousand dollars a year—& I found it was an acute
pain—to her—to be supported pecuniarily "to do her duty" as she
said—But at last I convinced her she had no right to refuse employment at their *hands* when the alternative was to receive her income
from her slaves & *that* argument she yielded to—especially when I
showed her that she could be doing an indefinite amount of good to
the cause by her pen meanwhile—

She is thoroughly noble entirely unexacting & I shall not like to
have her know till the year has passed—that I ask so few ladies to subscribe—& that there is exactly a *subscription solicited*—I want to have
to come to her in another point of view—To her the instrument of
one's labour is "a harp of thousand strings" it is necessary to be careful not to untune it—This weight of sensibility—and the intense activity of her mind which now is consciously [word illegible] are at
most too much for a delicate organisation—& the wise physician under
whose care she is—says it is infinitely important to her health that her
energies have free play towards the end she has in view—

She has made her will which is in the hands of Passmore Williams
& if she does die—the slaves will be free—& her sister & her three children penniless & unsupported by her sustaining sympathy & set her
slaves free with what they have earned this summer to start with in a

free state—Make herself known as a writer—Give an impulse to the
sale of the Autobiography—and be able to start fair another year to
support herself—her sister then probably being able to assist her in
some way—

I mentioned my plan to Mr Furness & one or two persons—who
have promptly met it—& I am encouraged to go on & get the whole
subscription made up & then it must be presented to her as the *payment* for value *to be received*—as it is at all events a great trial to her
to come upon the antislavery friends for payment of labour even—as
she had hoped to with the general expression of sympathy—she has
not hitherto made any revelations of her pecuniary position—or any
claims—& it is only within three weeks that I have won from her the
whole story.—I called on her because I had read her book—& heard
that she wished to liberate the slaves on whose labour she had always
lived—& by conversation with her I found a person more profoundly
alive on the subject of human rights—& the sin & spiritual suicide of
slaveholding—& who gave me a more terrible impression of the sum
of human agonies that slavery is—than any thing I every had seen or
heard or imagined   She told me the birth of the sentiment & thought
in herself at five years old—and I saw the possibility of an Eva[3]—because here was an Eva who had grown up—& who had out gone our
wisest ones in the depths of her observations & the profoundless of her
deductions—If ever one got an impression of a mind taught by the
Spirit of Truth—I got one from my first conversation with her. Neither Christian saint or political philosopher can teach her for she
knows. I saw she was profoundly sad—& I divined pretty much the
whole situation & to this divining sympathy she poured out—throwing
away all reserves—She showed me her letters from Kentucky she told
me all about the persecutions of the Catholics & her proslavery
friends—& that she & her sister & the children must still be eating the
bread earned by her slaves or *starve*—unless they could get work—&
they would take "the humblest so it were honest" for they "would play
lady no longer—"

I cannot in a letter more than hint at what has occupied whole
days to reveal to me of all the bearings of all things she has told me

But I have made a plan—& that is that 20 ladies should subscribe
or be responsible for $50 a piece to be paid to her as a salary for the
ensuing year beginning if possible the first of July—to be paid *quar-*

[3] That is, the heroine of Harriet Beecher Stowe's novel *Uncle Tom's Cabin*,
which appeared serially in the *National Era* in 1851–52 and in book form in 1852.

terly—& engaging her to *write* tales & whatever else she desires to write & can get published by *giving it gratis* to periodicals & newspapers.— In this way the present distress can be met—she can support her family & herself *this year*—go to Kentucky in October as she wishes to do

If you will be one of the twenty ladies—my dear Madame—will you be so kind as to let me know—& also at which quarter of the year you will prefer to pay it. I am the sister of Mrs Horace Mann—& living for the present summer at Darby Delaware Co—Pennsylvania

Yours respectfully
Elizabeth P. Peabody

MS, NRU

A report of Peabody's encounter with spiritualism, which so vexed Hawthorne.

⚹ To William Logan Fisher[1]

July 4th My direction until October is
Curson's Mills, Newburyport *Mass*
My dear Sir   July 4 [1858][2]

You did not ask me to write in reply to your letter, but my heart prompts me to do it. I had not heard of the death of your son Charles William; for my Philadelphia friends never write, nor Mrs Pugh. I felt, when I saw you last, that this calamity was hanging over you; and now you say you should be consoled, if you believed in Modern Spiritualism, of which you *lack the evidence*. I never had any single thing which ⟨was⟩ had such evidence to prove the communication of the disembodied with the embodied, as the apparent communication of your son Lindley to you & his mother, by that letter & speech which came by Hannah Leedom [?]; *except* the manifestations made at Mrs. Pugh's, about a fortnight after, through the same medium; the most remarkable of which *to me* was the apparent conversation with me of Dr Channing, & which was cut off short by the words—"I cannot say

---

1 William Fisher was a member of the influential Fisher family of Philadelphia, which suggests that spiritualism was not limited to less-educated members of society, but also embraced by prosperous and influential individuals.

2 The date of this letter was provided by the Pennsylvania Historical Society.

any thing more on this subject now, because this medium is inadequate. It is like pouring water into a vase; the water must take the shape of the vase; seek another medium." Did I not tell you this? and how, some weeks after, in New York, I was present with another trance medium, at a private circle; & without my saying a word, the medium addressed me, beginning just where the other medium broke off—& went on talking on the same subject, which was—the condition of the mind of man with respect to nature before any succession of generations had complicated moral or natural circumstances ⟨relations⟩—in fact the interior condition of *the first man*—The two mediums, *both* private persons—not known to the public as mediums—had never heard of each other. Neither persons got any clue from *me*—for I did not speak to either, but only formed my ⟨thoughts⟩ questions in my own mind. What was said was good; & had no self-contradiction in it [I]t was tersely said also; and I never had heard it said or read it elsewhere.—The view was in accordance with those I had thought of—& even maintained in an unpublished written essay of mine, viz. that man at first had an open eye & understanding of visible nature—or natural science,—until by indolence & selfindulgence he became blind & weak—& therefore yielded to passions which deteriorated the organs of intelligence, that have to be laboriously exercised *now*—in order to obtain a moiety of what was at first gained without labour;—*but,* in compensation for this loss of open vision, he has developed moral energies, which, in the end, shall restore the race to their pristine clairvoyance, ⟨several words illegible⟩ including a vision of the disembodied, (as we call those who have laid off the grosser forms of matter which confine us to this globe).

There seemed to me in this manifestation what I had never seen, & what but few manifestations that we hear about *have,* viz. an *internal evidence* in the manifestation. What came through Hannah L— was not any thing she had ever thought. But about a year ago, I had a *continuation* of that very conversation of Dr. Channing's very unexpectedly, and without trying after it with another medium. For having been taken by a friend to see a very spiritual minded woman, who never went into a trance, but had, as she believed, spiritual impression which oftentimes were referred, by involuntary writing & otherwise, to particular individuals, I began to talk with her about it by asking her how *she knew* these were impressions from spirits & not her own productions—& while she was telling me the history of its development, in her case, she all at once began to describe the way in which the soul began to live in this world, & the relations it never ceased to have with heavenly companions, although, when the earthly companionship was not harmonious she said this intercourse was confined to the seasons of dreamless sleep when we always are *in heaven*— (& hence sleep is so recreative)—She then began to talk about external nature & its origin & became very interesting; & I soon found she was talking about what Dr C— had apparently been speaking of *to me* by the other mediums & this made me remember—what I had entirely forgotten—that she was a medium.—When I stopped her suddenly & said,—"Are you speaking from your own mind?" She replied—"no— *from Dr Channing's*." I said—"From Dr Channings? Why should he speak to me?" "I do not know," said she, "but as soon as you came in Dr Channing seemed to say to me—'I shall have something to say to this person'—& it is he who has answered your questions. He often talks to those he did not know when on Earth. He did not know me." She probably thought I was *not acquainted* with him—as I meant she should suspect—when I asked "why should he speak to me?" and in fact I was a stranger to he—& she did not know I had ever known *him*.

Now I should not hesitate to take *the comfort* of a consciousness of having talked with a disembodied spirit—if I needed such.—And I do not know why you, or Mrs. Fisher, should doubt the impression that *you certainly had*—of having communicated with your son Lindley.—Do you, in fact, need the evidence *for yourself* so much as for others? Is it not that you want to convince Elizabeth who doubts & others of it rather than to convince yourself? But Elizabeth does not doubt at all, as she said that day, *of immortality;* nor feel the *need* the personal intercourse that you crave, and so *had* (if you can *trust* to *your senses* then—)   She rather *shrank* from it—*& consequently*—for according to the theory on which we acted that day—the medium is not the clairvoyant's imponderable fluid (or spiritual body) *only*— but the union of *two or more* spiritual bodies so as to form *one organ*. I think at this moment of Jesus Christ's words—"Where two or three are gathered together in my name, there am I in the midst of ⟨you⟩ them." Perhaps these words reveal *a law of spiritual existence* that is universal—& wherever two or three are gathered in an intense spiritual concentration on any ⟨individual⟩ disembodied spirit—*he can be there in the midst of them.*—I am sure *that condition was made*—that day that the Leedoms & I & your wife & yourself sat down together; for doubtless each one of us was not only in harmony of feeling, but in harmony of *thought,* and *that thought* was intensely *your son.*[3] And

3 "Son" underlined twice.

did he not seem to rush upon the scene, & say to you just what you wished to hear—namely—that he was *"supremely happy?"*

I know that a doubt is naturally thrown over a satisfactory scene like this, by reading of so many miserable manifestations. But if it is a *law of nature* that spirits should manifest themselves to men *under certain conditions,*—it is no reason to doubt satisfactory manifestations, that there are irregular & disgusting ones, when the conditions are not what they should be. Not only wise & good spirits are disembodied; but foolish & bad spirits ⟨are⟩ also; and a mixed company, or a weak or wicked state of mind, may give them access to us, just as bad taste and weakness lead us into the bad company of the *embodied* & attract *them* to us. I remember a beautiful story that was told to me by a reader of Swedenborg, who said Swedenborg somewhere in his writings related his being in spiritual vision of a group of disembodied spirits who seemed to be conversing on a certain subject *(which he named)*—& he said he observed a person with thoughtful brow & folded arms appearing among them & walking round as if listening to them & then disappearing; & he asked one of the group about him *who it was* & received for reply, that this was "a *spirit yet embodied,* who, in high seasons *of meditation* [several words illegible] *became visible to them."*—But this spirit was not probably conscious of the persons of this group of angels; but only conscious of *their thoughts* which perhaps he thought were his own production—This ⟨story⟩ fact seemed to me a happy illustration of the law of Spiritual nearness— which is not like bodily nearness of *place*—but exact *sympathy of spirit.* May not a good deal of that spiritual impression we receive in *seasons of silence,* be the association with *angels* as well as with the heavenly Father?—and in those moments, when, in silent meditation, you feel happiest & most peaceful, why is it not *reasonable* to believe that your sons come to you?—The sensuous impression *once* received through a medium *is valuable* if it will strengthen that very reasonable view of the subject. I say *very reasonable*—for independant of all mediumship & long before I ever heard of it—I was convinced by reasonings of Dr Channings See his sermon on the future state in his works & Mr. Henry Ware's see his sermon on the *Intercession of Jesus* in his office of Christ as well as by the exercise of my own reason—that the dead never deserted the living—whom they loved—although they could not approach them thro *their senses*—or in any way but by *kindred thinking & feeling*—and if the embodied will not do their part by exercising their faith in the possibility of this intercourse—in vain do they love us & hover over us—perhaps—and it may be a *pain to them* that we doubt. It is a fact that *among the manifesta-tions,* there is often one of pleasure on the part of the spirits, at the facility with which some persons accept them. I know that the dead children of Mrs. Gray of New York (the physicians wife—a lady of great sweetness & truth—who *believes* without a shadow of doubt) often express gratitude that she will watch & wait for them as she does with whatever medium she can get hold of—whom she is willing to associate with—for she has had choice of mediums!

Jesus prophesied greater things than any of the wonders he per-formed—*if only his disciples would grow in faith* which is itself the evidence of things unseen—It seems to me that it was the great object of all he did & said, to make his disciples of that & of all time realise that the bounds of *their senses* ⟨not⟩ were not the bounds of possibil-ity, but, that according to the *desires of the mind* [several words illeg-ible] acting in *love & purity—should* be the experience of the soul.— Yours very truly Elizabeth P. Peabody

MS, PHi

The fragile state of Peabody's finances are the subject of this letter to her relative Rawlins Pickman.

✄ To Rawlins Pickman

My dear Miss Pickman   *Nov. 12th* [1858][1]
You take such a genuine interest and are so truly kin to me, that I never have any good turn done me by fortune that I do not feel at once that I must tell you—And I know you will think of me often in respect of the effect that these bad times may have on my fortunes—I believe you know that besides the debt I owed to Mr Mills—from the time I commenced my life in West Street, I owed another accumulated by the loans from time to time *offered* me (for I never solicited a single one) in order to further the publication of Bem's charts and Manual—which in all came to 1200—These sums I considered my self bound to pay—for they were advanced in confidence that I should ultimately succeed—and on 600 dollars I paid interest—besides the

[1] Date is provided by the Massachusetts Historical Society and given in another hand.

premium I paid to the insurance office to secure $1000—This made more than an $100 to pay every year besides the $35 I paid on the old debt to Mr Mills—& for the last ⟨half⟩ seven years I have had this burden to carry and so though I have lived & for four years supported father & mother & paid for 200 charts & 5000 copies of the manual— I did not gain any thing ⟨upon⟩ to pay the principal of these debts—

Well! I did not know that any one of my creditors to this debt of honour $1200 knew of the rest—but a week or two ago I received from Marcus Spring a note most kindly & affectionately begging me to consider his debt of 210 *cancelled*—and in a few days afterward a letter from Mr S. G. Ward signed by himself & the other five gentlemen— two being in New York—cancelling *theirs*—and he wrote me an additional note saying that Mr Mills had authorized him some time since to add his name—but that on account of the failure of the firm—Mr Ward had thought it best not to go to him for a signature—The letter of Mr Ward was as flattering as you can conceive in the name of the rest—and in his private note he expressed that he hoped I would not hesitate to *accept* what was so hearily offered—& so "entirely unsought an expression of esteem"

So you see, at once in this dark time is my burden lightened—and I have only the debt to Mr Mills to see to—& if he authorized his name to be put I think that *at least* the note has been withdrawn from *the firm* & will not fall into other hands but I shall have the pleasure of paying to him in his need what he lent me in his prosperity—so that next August I shall send him the $35—for I have no hope of doing more—seeing no chance of selling my library which would pay it all off.—But my good fortune has not stopped here—but my old friend Mr Jonathan Phillips[2] the other day sent me an $100 saying that he was sure *in this time* I should have small chance of introducing my US History into this town or any where else—& *that is true enough*— I put it at once into the Savings bank & in no case shall draw out $35 of it so as to be sure to pay my interest in August.—And perhaps I may not draw any of it out—for I have just had an article accepted in the Christian Examiner and Mr. Emerson has another article of mine which he is going to present to the Atlantic Journal[3]—and these articles if paid for—together with the pay for "The Last Evening with Allston" in the October number of "Emerson & Putnam" will pay all

2 This is the same Phillips who befriended Horace Mann in the mid-1830s and who attended Channing's adult Sunday School discussions.
3 No such articles by Peabody in either journal appeared at this time.

my personal expenses this winter & spring[4]—& very like next summer—And then besides, I can now feel free to do some thing which
may prove of more benefit ultimately—I shall write my new manual
slowly, & think that there is no doubt I may print it bye & bye, & *that*
will give a new impulse to the Charts. Dr. Raymond of the Polytech-
nick School in Brooklyn writes me that he likes the U.S. History more
& more & by the time my new manual is ready will be all ready to introduce it into his school of 400 scholars—& his name carries with it
great prestige.—So you see "hope springs undying in the human
breast"—I by no means despair of one day being rich enough to pay
these very debts of which I am now discharged—I shall drop my Life
policy at once—& have no yearly burden (beyond my own support—
which never costs me much—) except that $35 interest to Mr Mills—
There is one thing I have gained in the experience of my life & that is
a certain sense of *power* which I have sometimes seen [in] those who
were rich [yet] so destitute of that I have felt that I was richer in the
possession,—in my sensations, than they with the *fear of want* which
every crisis produces—I had a letter from Sophia mailed Leaming-
ton—October 23rd—which shows them to be still in England & Mr
Hawthorne reposing in his release from business. She says that as soon
as the Consulate accounts are made up they shall *go to Paris*.[5] The
Paris letters will probably be sent back to England—as Miss Shepard
has gone there & put Una into a "Paradise of hard study" as Sophia
says. Sophia's letter is not one to be sent about—but I had one from
Una which has gone to Mary & may be returned to *you*.—*Mary* seems
to be in a "Paradise of hard teaching"—She says that Article in Mr
Foote's paper about Antioch College had a mistake in it[6]—the name
of Eli Thayer instead of Eli Fay—which was a very great pity.—I wish
the article might be copied into some other paper & the correction be
made—because the article otherwise is quite a nice one.—Mr Foote
did not send me any copy of the paper but sent one to Mary

Goodbye my dear friend—I know you will take kindly this egotistical letter & that Aunt & Mary will also be glad to read it—When
I come to Salem I shall bring Mr Wards letter—Perhaps will send it

---

[4] "Last Evening with Allston" appeared in *Emerson's Magazine* 5 (October
1857):498-503.

[5] After the election of James Buchanan, Hawthorne resigned his post as United
States consul in Liverpool, and left the post in October 1857. On January 5, 1858, the
Hawthorne family crossed the English Channel and the next day arrived in Paris,
where they stayed a week.

[6] Eli Fay was the Ohio "Christian Connexion" clergyman who first proposed
that Horace Mann serve as president of Antioch College.

by Mr Johnson   In sending to me by Mr Johnson—you must send to him Saturday morning   He comes to Dorchester twice more—Yours most truly Elizabeth P. Peabody

MS, MHi

Peabody's continuing scholarly work, especially her historical and linguistic interests, are evident in this request to use the Boston Athenaeum. Charles Folsom was librarian there until 1856, but in 1858 he apparently still had some official function.

✖ To Charles Folsom

My dear Sir—   November 1858
   I am preparing a work for the press on chronology—and I want very much the privilege of consulting the Art of Verifying Plates—
   Would it be possible for me to have the volumes containing the observations on the centuries from the 25th before Christ *forward toward* the time of Christ—*here*? And if not—can I go to the Athenaeum & take some notes in the evening? I want the volume that has the 25th century first—because I want to know their sources of Chinese History as they give a date there & John Müller says *positively* that the *historic* period of the Chinese begins according to themselves—about the times of the Trojan war—altho' the mythical period goes back 800 centuries!—
   I also want that volume of [Prinsens? Brinsins?] Egypt which gives his view of the chronology of *Menes*—& Thutmosis.[1] I shall carry this note up myself to you—to leave if I do not find you—and then I will get father to go & get that volume if I may be allowed it—
   I have a Polish library of books sent to me by the Princess Orestoryoka who heard that I was going to publish a history of Poland—It consists of Polish & French books on Polish history—Lelewel's great work on coins[2] &c—it has occurred to me to make a present of the whole lot to the Athenaeum—if they will return the compliment by

[1] John Müller, *The Art of Verifying Plates* and Brinsen's *Egypt,* cannot be identified.
[2] Lelewel's work on coins is Joachim Lelewel, *Observations sur le type du moyen-age de la monnaie des Pays-Bas* (Brussels, 1835).

giving me a right to take out books.—This right has been several times voted to me for a year at a time—once when I was writing my key to the History of Greece[3]—and now I want to write and publish several historical works—what do you think about the feasibility of my getting this right for at least several years—by handing over these books which I do not want to have separated from each other?

Yours Respectfully, E. P. PEABODY

MS, MB

3 Elizabeth Peabody, *Key to History, Part III, The Greeks* (Boston, 1833).

The Athenaeum's refusal of membership to women was a frustrating experience, and having to get Folsom to intercede must have been humiliating.

✄ To Charles Folsom

22 Bedford Street

Mr. Folsom Boston,
My dear Sir Nov 27th [1858]

You know that when I presented to the Atheneum that Polish Library which the Princess Orestoryska sent me, my *first idea was* to make a *regular bargain*, & have a perennial right, if possible, to take out a book when I wanted to—& you advised me to say nothing about that in giving it, & I took the idea that I should get this privilege *all the same*—But I have always been a pensioner on *your* bounty in this respect & got out books whenever I have done so—upon *your right*—. Now I want to know if my first plan is to be forever despaired of—for I want to get from the Atheneum a book now & then I cannot get elsewhere especially since it seems as if the Public Library was not to be opened for an indefinite time—I at least have been expecting it for three months & still they say *"six weeks time"*!

Since beginning this letter a friend at my side *has said*—that perhaps I can get the books I want just now from the *Wales* Library—at Cambridge—It is Wilson's Sanskrit Grammar[1] & some *first book* in

1 Horace Hayman Wilson, *An Introduction to the Grammar of the Sanskrit Language* (London, 1841).

Sanskrit that I want—as I have a chance of studying that old tongue a little—

Now I will call some time next week at Little & Brown's where I see your name—to get a line in reply to this letter—if you will be so kind as to help me in my present quest—it will be just like the other kindnesses of the kind which I have all my life received from you—& which perhaps makes me too free to *keep asking.*

Yours truly

ELIZABETH P. PEABODY

MS, MB

A livid letter to Caroline Dall, defending Horace Mann's reputation and excoriating Dall for her public discussions of matters best left discreetly alone or expressed in private.

✄ To Caroline Healey Dall

[Concord][1]

My dear Mrs. Dall—   February 21st 1859

I am preparing to go to Pennsylvania for some months—& do not think I shall have time to go up to Bradford Street *before*—as many things are crowded into a small space of time.—I do not suppose Wm's statement to *you* can be essentially different from that made to *me* which was probably the *first* made & covers eight sheets—but I saw an extract he made from the one to you in a letter to another friend which made me think that the one to you had fructified on the comments made to him by several letters that have been written to him since he wrote to me. I am naturally asked about him a good deal & I wish to do him the justice of speaking of him according to his *best statement*—I do not doubt that he wishes to speak act & think according to the highest truth—& I hope he will think himself out of what I cannot but consider a serious error. I answered his first letter with a complete statement of my views on the several points that came up—& his second letter convinced me that nothing was gained by controversy—He needed a "terrible letting alone" which I am afraid he does not get—I said in my second letter that I thought it better we should

---

[1] In 1859, Peabody was living in Concord with her newly widowed sister Mary.

drop the subject of what he had done or was doing personally—& let
our communications be on general principles. The truth is that marriage & its troubles are rather too delicate a subject to admit of a great
deal of talk.² And now of another matter on which I trust you will
bear with a little frankness. I heard at Miss Clapp's in Dorchester that
you said to Mrs. Hall that I could not & *did* not deny what you said
about Mr. Mann's not permitting the young ladies at Antioch College
to read their parts! On the contrary I said *that evening that you asserted it* in your lecture *that it was not the fact*—as the young ladies
did all read their parts at the Antioch Commencement which you
could have ascertained had you asked *any* person who was present.—
Moreover Miss Adeline Shephard declaimed one of her compositions
in a literary society but she said she never would do it again—as Mr.
Mann did not think it good taste—He is perhaps a little fastidious
about what is ladylike—but I have very little patience with any
woman who has any thing but gratitude to express to or of Mr. Mann
in regard to the woman question. I think *nobody* is doing so much for
woman's education and advancement as he—and *so little to be regretted.* I can forgive him for the fears he expresses of excess and indelicacy—because there is so much excess and indelicacy which puts
the whole cause at disadvantage.—He is perfectly willing that a
woman should when occasion calls do what Miss Dix—what Florence
Nightingale—what Mary Patton³ did—But he thinks that it requires
occasions to call forth this kind of action. When women go into public
on the impulse of personal ambition and display—he is more disgusted
than when *men* do so—precisely because his ideal of woman is high
not low.—He justifies woman on occasion going to grogshops & breaking up the rumbarrels—but he does not think *that* is the most beautiful action for woman—the kind of action which is her highest destiny—He thinks a woman is doing a *higher* & nobler & finer duty when
she is educating her own children than when she is addressing public
audiences; when her left hand does not know what her right hand is

2 William Francis Channing was the nephew of William Ellery Channing, and
a prominent Boston doctor, reformer, and feminist. In 1859, he divorced his wife,
Nancy, after a five-year separation, on grounds of moral and mental incompatibility.
The press pounced on the story, revelling in all the details, claiming that Channing
advocated easy divorce and sexual license. He finally broke his silence in 1859 with
a long letter of defense to the *New York Post,* which hardly deflected his attackers.
Bitterly, Channing left his profession and Boston, railing against Puritan hypocrisy
(Leach, *True Love,* 59–60).
3 Mary (Ann) Paton, not Patton, a Scots singer, began her vocal career in 1820.
In 1840, she toured the United States and was a sensational success.

doing—and in this I recognize a high ideal of woman—The *inward* scope is the *highest* scope of human action—he believes it to be the woman's prerogative & when it is renounced for more external action he feels that she foregoes finer faculties than she uses—Still I know he would rather woman did *coarse* work than no work at all. My mind & Mr. Mann's are different in natural tendencies—I am not *identical* with him on any subject & so not on *this*—but I consider him one of the greatest Reformers of the day—on the woman question as well as on most others pertaining to our common humanity, & I think it wrong that any one should assert without absolute knowledge anything invidious about him as President of Antioch College—especially at its present crisis—for I do not believe that in another century there will be anything organized so important for woman's benefit as that college to whose success he is giving his *substance* & his *life*—And yet I must confess that I was not sorry to have you separate yourself so wholly as your attack did separate you from Mr. Mann—I thought the lecture in which you spoke of him in so bad taste that it would be an argument against women's education.[4] I must say I could hardly believe you had *read* Aristophanes your statement of his influence was so exaggerated[5]—I do not think that in all classical literature there is any thing so indelicate as your broad allusion to Madame Chevreuse's *menses* in your lecture upon her[6]—When I heard *that* I felt that it was a special providence that I was not in company with any gentlemen— I wrote you a note about it—which I did not send—because I suppose you would hear of it from others—It was cowardly to shirk my own responsibility in the matter—But since your second course of lectures I have heard so much animadversion upon this want of womanly delicacy that I am determined to keep silence no longer—I must tell *you*—since I cannot disagree with others who say to me that you inflict more injury on the cause of woman by this bad taste than you can remedy by all your learning and talents—I heard you are going to write lectures upon *labour* & are going to make *painful statements*—I beg you will consider what I say—I do not think I am squeamish—but I would not go to hear your lectures with a gentleman by my side.—I do feel that the natural sphere of woman is above the slough of human nature. I would go to a Magdalene Refuge to *work in the reform of*

---

[4] I have been unable to locate the lecture to which Peabody refers.

[5] A reference to Aristophanes' *Lysistrata*.

[6] Marie de Rohan, Duchesse de Chevreuse, a woman of great beauty and restless energy, was famous for her sexual adventures and her political intrigues. She conspired against both Richelieu and Mazarin, and was exiled repeatedly.

the inmates—but I would not talk to men about prostitution—in a public assembly. I think there is a more eloquent lesson given by woman's silence on such a subject than by anything she could say—I do not like conventions of women for Women's Rights—as you know—I did not when I first heard of them & would not sign the first call that was made—I like them still less in practice—but the one held here over which you presided I thought *the best* that I had known of[7]—and I liked your action & speech in that (only there was one sentence you spoke then which I wish you had left men to say—if said it must be) still *that* was deformed by Mrs. Oakes Smiths foolish poem—and still more foolish theatrical display of herself[8]—women do not seem to be able to divest themselves of a certain consciousness of their own personality—bodily or mental—and so make fools of themselves in public by thrusting *their own personality* before the audience. Of course there are exceptions—I suppose that when the subject matter that they have to speak of so absorbs them that they forget the Ego—*they will not do this*—But where they go into public to make an impression of the talents & power they always betray it in this way—& become the object of the pity of the audience—

I do not altogether like to be saying all this—and I feel I have no right to call you to account because your action does not suit my taste—but I am impelled to it because from what I hear that you say of me—I think you may consider my not saying it a proof that I think the contrary—You speak of me as an intimate friend and counsellor—If I am your counsellor & you believe me to be your friend—it becomes my duty to act in those capacities to the best of my ability—You told me once that I did you good in your youth by withholding my sympathy—Perhaps to know that I do not give it now—may be useful—and if it is I shall be compensated for the pain & embarassment it has been to me to write this letter.—Yours truly E. P. Peabody

MS, MHi

7 In 1859, Caroline Dall delivered the principal address at the New England Women's Rights Convention in Boston.

8 Elizabeth Oakes Prince Smith, author and reformer, was an active campaigner for women's rights and spoke widely on that topic. Susan B. Anthony had denied Mrs. Smith the presidency of the Second National Women's Rights Convention because of her fancy New York clothing.

A summary of Peabody's involvement with Delia Bacon, and a (never-granted) request to see her papers and write her memoir.

✄ To Leonard Bacon

Dr. Bacon,   Concord, Massachusetts
    My dear Sir,   October 23 [1859]
    You perhaps remember a year or more ago that I—Miss Peabody
of Boston called on you to inquire something about your sister's Miss
Delia Bacon's health—I have just learned of her death[1]—and at the
risk of awakening the sad feelings which so sad a catastrophe of so
gifted a person must awaken in your mind—& that person a beloved
sister, I feel compelled to address you.—
    You told me you thought her theory about the authorship of
Shakespeare's plays, and her views of Lord Bacon were a part of her
insanity—Undoubtedly her insanity at best centered on that subject
& influenced her views—But my dear Sir, I was made the confidante
of her mind, long before any insanity developed itself, and in the early
stages of her inquiring upon the subject. She read to me a long part
of Lord Bacon's works; she told me a great deal of Sir Walter Raleigh's
life which she had [word illegible] out, she read to me with commentaries the tragedy of Hamlet, & at one time it was a plan that I should
write at her direction a commentary on Hamlet, as she found writing
very irksome—
    But one proof of a disposition to morbidness—which grew out of
the abominable manner in which her faith & delicacy had been outraged by Mr McW[2]—was the want of faith and the jealousy she was

1 Bacon's brother Leonard was pastor of the Congregational First Church in
New Haven, Connecticut, a professor at Yale Divinity School, and a leader in the
Connecticut antislavery movement. Although his response to Peabody's overtures
were less paranoid than his sister's, he too put off any attempt to allow Peabody to
publicize Delia Bacon's work. In his response of February 11, 1860, he noted that any
disposition of his sister's papers could be accomplished only with full consultation
of the remaining family members, which, he implied, would take a very long time
(MS, CtY).
    2 In 1845, Delia Bacon formed a friendship with Yale Divinity graduate Alex-
ander McWhorter. After two years of courtship, McWhorter showed no interest in
marriage, whereupon Leonard Bacon brought misconduct and breach of contract
charges against him in the New Haven Ministerial Association. In 1847, McWhorter

too apt to have *of others*. I entered into her investigation &c with a great deal of interest; & even pointed out to her some coincidences & made some suggestions that *helped* her—But although the whole affair was under a solemn promise on my part that I would never anticipate her, by even suggesting the discovery, but allow to her the whole glory of this remarkable piece of historical criticism which really belonged to her—for her to bring out in her own time—Yet I saw that it worried her to see how completely I did get possession of her idea;—and in order not to worry her I gave the whole up & promised her I would—as far as in me lay—not think of it until after she had given it to the public. When she was injuring her health, by her efforts in Brooklyn and New York, to get means to go to England, I came to her help again & obtained partly by means of Mr. Emerson's cooperation who had seen one manuscript of hers a promise from my cousin George P. Putnam that he would pay her expenses out to England.— He provided however that as there was risk of accidents that she should put into my hands the whole proof—*external*—as well as internal—that she had of the facts of Shakespeare's not being the author.— I then had some other interviews with her that she might do this—& she began to give me the key to the cipher.—But she suffered so much from *the fear that I would steal her secret* & publish it myself that as soon as her Brother offered her $1000 to go—I even proposed that she should not tell me anything & so she went to England—with letters from me to Mrs. Hawthorne I think—or else I wrote to Mrs. H independantly—though *he* had all an English scholar's *fascinating* prejudice against disturbing the time-honoured myth,—he was very much struck with what Miss Bacon said to him,—& you know her hope that he really published her book for her—which he wrote a preface to—& still thinks a very remarkable production to which people in time will *grow* sensible. But she never gave him the key to the cipher—In fact she never told any body so much as she did to me;—now I think that if I could have all her papers—I might ferret out the whole matter with the hints she gave me, and in the course of time—& bring it out at last in an intelligible manner—giving her the whole credit.—Perhaps in a kind of *memorial* of her *as a scholar.*—I never was *in the least offended* by her jealousy & suspicions of me.—I fully account for this morbid sensitiveness by her cruel experience.—She was to me a

---

was acquitted by a narrow margin. The entire situation was revived when Catherine Beecher published a sensational account of the affair in 1850, entitled *Truth Stranger Than Fiction,* an attempt to vindicate Delia Bacon.

most interesting & beautiful being—a glorious & wonderful work of nature;—most unhappily environed by uncongenial circumstances in many respects.—And I never felt so sadly as when I saw her go off to England *alone*—so wholly unprepared & unsuited to rough & tumble it.—Majestic as she was in person & mind her entire unworldliness— her childlike character—inspired me with a tenderness without bounds—& had I had the means I would have gone with her to take care of her.—She seemed to me an inspired child of genius—who needed a motherly—sisterly nurse & friend.—

Once after she arrived she wrote to me—once only. Soon her morbidness on the subject of my knowing as much as I did of her thoughts grew extreme—and her extreme unwillingness to have any thing said about her—did for several years seal my sister and brother Hawthorne's lips from saying a word about her—When at last the tragedy had its final denouement, they wrote me how much they had had to do with her for they knew of my interest for her—I do not say that I think the demonstration of her theory is complete—I think neither Mr Hawthorne nor Mr Emerson thought so—But they both thought & *I think* that her criticism of those times is the most profound that has ever been written—& that the question can never sleep again.— The more we think about it—the more proofs accumulate that she was right in the main—

Finally—I ask—may I see all her papers?-& perhaps have the satisfaction of doing justice to this wonderful critic & scholar in a memoir? If so will you please to let me know in a line addressed to me—Care of my sister Mrs. Horace Mann Concord Massachusetts (with whom I am living at present).

Yours respectfully
Elizabeth P. Peabody

MS, CtY

In March and April 1853, Elizabeth Peabody had approached author and lecturer Delia Bacon with the proposition of editing her papers, particularly those that sought to establish Sir Francis Bacon as the author of the plays attributed to Shakespeare. As this letter indicates, Peabody received a cold response. In 1853, Bacon went to England to research her claims regarding the Shakespeare plays, and published her findings in 1857 as The Philosophy of the Plays of Shakespeare Unfolded. *Her views were ridiculed or ignored, and Bacon slipped into insanity soon after her return to Connecticut. She died on September 2, 1859.*

Evidently, one of Peabody's complaints against Caroline Dall had to do with Dall's self-assurance, which Peabody interpreted as egocentrism. Indirectly, this rebuke to Dall was also a criticism of Margaret Fuller.

✖ To Caroline Healey Dall

My dear Mrs. Dall—   New York—Friday Evening [1859][1]
    I do not know whether I put it clearly that Eliza Clapp did not want to enter into any controversy on the subject of her letter—and that was the reason she was so unwilling to send it to you—But I told her *I* wanted you to have it because it was what I wanted to say—& I would therefore send it as *my letter* in which case you could not understand her as challenging you to a controversy.—*She* thought you would not take any thing from *another* but I could not quite think *that* though I know you are pretty pertenacious—but you have taken so much *from me* that I am bound to testify to it practically by acting on the ground that you love *the truth* better than yourself—& the cause of woman better than your personal success as a lecturer—or your *personal feelings.*—We cannot enter into the work of redemption except through the path of self-crucifixion—& the more there is to crucify— *the great the power acquired by the sacrifice*—"He scourgeth whom he would bring to glory"—If like great Margaret *your Me* is *"mountainous"*—it may become for you the Pisgah on which you shall mount to see the promised land—nay more—the Mt of Transfiguration—He that would *gain* his life must *lose* it. I do not know *one* ⟨acquaintance⟩ *friend* of yours who does not pray that you may *experience this*—as does yr friend Elizabeth P. Peabody

MS, MHi

    1 Letter is dated by MHi in an unknown hand.

To Samuel Johnson, an expert on Asian religions, Peabody writes this letter of congratulation. Could it be, she wonders, that he might offend his audiences by being too critical of Christianity?

✺ To Samuel Johnson[1]

Roxbury Centre Street

My dear Mr. Johnson—   [late 1850s?]
    I could not say to you when I saw you all that I felt of the very great value of your lectures on the Eastern Religions—They seem to me to be the most adequate & useful statements that have been made— They carry an inward evidence of their justness & profoundness & the object which you had in view (to prove man—man taken as a whole— wherever he has had any opportunity to develop himself through ages—& man's accessibility to the influence of GOD—wherever & however he is circumstanced) has given you a point of view which announced your subject & made all that was most important & essential appear to you—& of course to your hearers—for I assure you that whatever you see you make appear to your hearers—. I always hear those who love to hear you, dwell on the perfect clearness & intelligibleness of your statements. In fact it is because you are so *perfectly intelligible* with such force as your simple earnestness adds—that *all do not* love to hear you.—You are not to be escaped by drowsiness, or frivolity, or worldlimindedness, but for a time you make them *confess*—& cry—like the devils to Jesus—*why* wilt thou torment us before our time—oh Son of GOD!—
    These statements of the Eastern Religions are profoundly religious in their effect—I think I never had such an impression made

---

1 Samuel Johnson was a liberal clergyman and author. He began his ministry at the Unitarian church in Dorchester, where he stayed only one year. His views on politics and religion were too liberal for his congregation. From 1853 to 1870, he served a liberal free church in Lynn, living in nearby Salem until 1876. With his friend Samuel Longfellow he wrote a collection called *Hymns of the Spirit* (Boston: Osgood, 1864). Perhaps the most famous of Johnson's hymns is the memorable "Life of Ages Richly Poured." Too radical for any denomination or reform society, Johnson was an extreme individualist in temper, a Transcendentalist in philosophy, and an advocate of natural religion. One of his major topics of interest and research was Asian religions (the subject of a lecture series in Boston in the late 1850s and the topic of this letter); he published three volumes, one posthumously, on the connections between Asian faiths and universal religious expression.

upon me of the everpressing *presence of* GOD as *Father* to the soul of man—& to this modern world of *scepticism* which *includes* almost all the Churches— (for what is the *faith* of these churchgoing slaveholders north & south but a wilful violence ⟨produced by⟩—the reaction of the gaping ghastly unbelief they are half-conscious of?) I do not know what could be offered *so expressive* as these statements of the Heathen religions—I do not know but I am *peculiarly jealous* of exalting these *blind religions* above Christianity—which seems to me by combining the brain, the muscles—& the nerve, to have *an Eye* the others have not—However, I liked your lecture on Christianity too very much—I feel that it is elevated by being shown to have relations to the past—& that you can fairly state that these religions themselves are the proof of the "Lamb *slain,* from the foundation of the world" (the human soul suffering under the knife of *inadequate* circumstance)—but Jesus of Nazareth appears the harmonising, rejoicing Conqueror, not conquering by *fasting* & *penance,* but by *loving & doing what he would*— Still more important—if possible—is your other proposition that the human soul is not merely the product of the past—but contains within it the germ of the "open vision"—Do you not think that Christ's greatest & peculiar work is to nourish this germ by having been what he was?—I rather doubt whether Jesus of Nazareth is done so much justice to in your mind propositionally as Confucius & [word illegible]—but this I can understand too as but the excess of a true & righteous tendency.—The Protest which is your religion reacts a little perhaps—It is hard to separate Jesus from the Church which does his doctrine so much injustice or at least his Spirit of love—But I think that to dwell with the same overflowing love on him as on the Oriental Saints will but increase the impression you make of their unquestionably legitimate inspiration—To me they seem to represent the heat & force & he the embracing and explaining Light—

But do publish them & *soon*—before you begin to criticise them yourself—for if you do not you will destroy their perfection as works of Art—& by no greater accuracy in details could you compensate for injuring that poetic wholeness which gives the *greater truth*—They seem to me as truly so many floods of inspiration—didactic though they are in form—as any poems—& I am clearly of opinion that one must respect the Holy Ghost's first word—There is at the present time I am confident mingled up or existing contemporary with our worldliness, & expediencies, & general humbuggery, a more clearly defined sense of *want* than probably ever before was felt in our western world for something in religion which has the stamp of Universality about it—Depend upon it that everywhere there is a great interest to under-stand what GOD was doing before Christ came & elsewhere than in Palestine & Christendom—The book would *sell* & if you give your name to it, would open to you audiences & spheres of influence all over the land.—Do not then delay longer than you can possibly help. Could you not print it early in the spring—before people disperse? I know so many people that would be so much wiser & happier to read it! & I have in view some believers in Positive Philosophy as the last word of the human mind who deserve a better fate than to fall into that pit.—

I have read through Alger's book which is very beautiful but I wish he had more distinctly given us the authorship and chronology of his gems—I find the Atheneum has not Bunsen's Universal His-tory—which is a very great disappointment to me as I want to read about those languages immensely—but they have a translation of Boff's Comparative grammar—not yet put into circulation.—[2]

Your friend Wasson gave us a good lecture but his want of taste &c were thrown out into rather too strong relief[3]—by the *prophetic* anthems we had been hearing in the day—On the whole I think that when you want to show him up again—of an evening—you must not preach all along yourself—I do not know but that blast of your trum-pet will shut you out of the North Church *for some years*—but never-theless it was *worth while*—I think it will echo & recho within the spiritual courses some years also—Better *say something* once in a great many years than to keep saying & doing nothing   Very truly your friend Elizabeth P. Peabody

MS, MSaE

[2] The books referred to here are William Rounseville Alger, *The Poetry of the East* (Boston: Whittemore, Niles, and Hall, 1856), and Christian Karl Josias von Bunsen, *Outlines of the Philosophy of Universal History* (London, 1854). The Boff volume cannot be identified.

[3] David Wasson, poet and clergyman, studied law and went to sea before de-ciding on a theological career; he was graduated from Bangor Theological Seminary in 1851 and began to serve an orthodox congregation in Gardner, Massachusetts, but soon left because of his liberal views. He ministered to several free churches until the 1870s, then retired and devoted himself to writing poetry and essays.

5

1860s

Europe, Froebel, and Early Childhood Education

THE ANTEBELLUM MOVEMENT for educational reform, which sought to make learning practical, moral, and democratic, swept across the United States in the late 1830s and the 1840s. The travel of Americans abroad, the emigration of Germans who contributed much to the intellectual life of New England, the circulation of German publications, and the establishment of private German-American schools served to stimulate interest in German educational practice and dissatisfaction with American backwardness. As early as 1836, Calvin Stowe of Lane Seminary addressed the topic in a speech entitled "The Prussian System of Public Instruction and Its Applicability to the United States." In May 1840, the educator and editor Henry Barnard carried a lengthy article on German primary education in his *Connecticut Common School Journal.* The term "kindergarten" appeared in 1856 for the first time in an American publication in an article by Barnard in his *American Journal of Education.* In 1859 Anna Parson and Ednah Dow Cheney reviewed a French kindergarten manual, *Le jardin des infants* for the *Christian Examiner.*[1]

In 1859, Elizabeth Peabody encountered Margarethe Schurz, wife of the Republican politician Carl Schurz, and their daughter Agathe, whom Margarethe had educated in her own kindergarten patterned after the philosophy and methods of German educational reformer Friedrich Froebel. On the basis of these conversations and a reading of the preface to Froebel's *The Education of Man,* Peabody opened a kindergarten at 15 Pinckney Street on Boston's Beacon Hill in 1860. Peabody soon had thirty pupils, two assistants, a French teacher, and a gymnastics instructor.[2] With her sister Mary, who had returned to Massachusetts after the death of her husband, Horace Mann, in 1859, she wrote *The Moral Culture of Infancy and Kindergarten Guide,* a manual for early childhood education and a description of Peabody's pedagogical principles.[3]

Peabody's involvement in the political issues of the time led her to champion a school for black orphans in the Georgetown section of Washington, D.C., at which Mary Mann's niece Maria taught. This school struggled against the racism and fear of its neighbors, who were

[1] Ruth Baylor, *Elizabeth Palmer Peabody: Kindergarten Pioneer* (Philadelphia: University of Pennsylvania Press, 1965), 30.

[2] Ibid., 85.

[3] Elizabeth Peabody, "The Kindergarten—What is It?" *Atlantic Monthly,* November 1862, 586; Elizabeth Peabody and Mary P. Mann, *The Moral Culture of Infancy and Kindergarten Guide* (Boston: H. E. O. P. Burnham, 1863).

hostile to the thousands of freedmen pouring into the District throughout the Civil War. Her 1865 letter to Emily Howland is typical of the many she wrote to gather support for this venture.

Like so many other members of her class and circle, Peabody viewed the Civil War as a divinely ordained crusade against a national sin, the curse of slavery. With William Henry Channing, who said in a sermon following Lincoln's second inauguration, "the Christ of *to-day* was the American nation," Peabody believed that "there are those who find the history of these United States a Revelation of God, which he who runs can read . . . we have read our Bible in the American newspapers for the last seven years."[4] She wrote to her nephew Horace Mann, Jr., in a letter of February 25, 1865, that the passage of the Thirteenth Amendment was a seal on the godliness of the nation.

Her nephew was also the recipient of a letter describing Elizabeth Peabody's two interviews with Abraham Lincoln in February 1865. She had probably been invited to Washington by Ethan Allen Hitchcock, Lincoln's military advisor, who had spent a week in 1862 visiting in Concord and had stayed in Mary Mann's house. In 1864, Mary Mann noted in a letter to her son Horace that General Hitchcock was keeping them informed of war matters. Hitchcock, Elizabeth Peabody wrote to her nephew, had arranged the private interview with Lincoln that constituted the first of her two encounters with him. Lincoln recalled serving in Congress with Horace Mann, both of them deeply troubled by the extension of slavery. After conversations on peace negotiations and their relation to the passage of the Thirteenth Amendment, and on the transfer of prisoners, the interview ended. "I realized," wrote Peabody, "that I had been very much interested indeed and surprised—the naturalness was like that of a child—& had a touch of pathos in it—He seemed to be full of feeling—." Peabody's second interview came during a presidential reception. Again they spoke of Wendell Phillips, whose speech of January 26 before the Massachusetts Anti-Slavery Society had criticized Lincoln's emerging Reconstruction policy. In answer to Peabody's reservations about the Phillips speech—"He says he does not *trust you* on Reconstruction"— Lincoln replied, "Oh *that* is no matter. . . . Give it to me. I *like to read his sharp things.*" Again Peabody was impressed. "And so at last I went away—

4 To the Editor, *The Radical* 2 (1866–67): 746–47.

but I felt I should go again soon—I am astonished to see how I *love* him—*trust him*—feel as if he were a father."[5]

Peabody was becoming gradually dissatisfied with her kindergarten, and by 1866 she was ready to close it temporarily. "Seven years of experience with my so-called kindergarten, though it had a pecuniary success and a very considerable popularity,—stimulating to other attempts,—convinced me that we were not practicing Froebel's Fine Art, inasmuch as the quiet, certain, unexcited growth of Self-activity into artistic self-relying ability, which he promised, did not come of our efforts; but there was on the contrary, precocious knowledge, and the consequent morbid intellectual excitement quite out of harmonious relation with moral and aesthetic growth."[6] In short, her school was looking too much like Alcott's Temple School, with its stress on introspection and intellectual precocity, even though Mary Mann had introduced nature walks. Peabody may also have been feeling the lure of European travel; both her sisters had been abroad. She determined to travel to the Continent and observe firsthand both the kindergartens themselves and the training of kindergartners. To raise the $1,100 needed, she delivered a series of lectures in Boston and Concord entitled "Great Civilizations of Antiquity." On June 8, 1867, she sailed for England on the *Bellone,* and traveled for fifteen months on the European continent, visiting kindergartners in Berlin, Dresden, and Hamburg.[7] One of her acquaintances from Boston, Thomas Wentworth Higginson, who encountered her at a railroad station, provided an unforgettable impression of Peabody at age sixty-three or sixty-four:

Mr. [Higginson] saw once at Neuchatel, emerging from the railway train, a pair or three ladies with the most villanous-looking courier he ever saw. One lady advanced toward him. She had a long and dusty black silk shirt, a short black sack, with something like a short white nightgown emerging between, very tumbled; bonnet all smashed, having been slept in, spectacles on *chin,* and a

5 To Horace Mann Jr., [February 1865], in Arlin Turner, "Elizabeth Peabody Visits Lincoln, February 1865," *New England Quarterly* 48 (March 1975): 116–24; in this volume 326–331.

6 Elizabeth Peabody, "Our Reason for Being," *Kindergarten Messenger* 1 (May 1873): 1.

7 Baylor, *Elizabeth Palmer Peabody,* 93.

great deal of dishevelled white hair. She was of great size and held her head inquiringly. It was Miss Elizabeth Peabody.[8]

Upon her return in 1868, Peabody plunged into her new work of disseminating the kindergarten gospel according to Froebel. She repudiated her 1863 *Kindergarten Guide* and replaced it with a "corrected" new edition.[9] This sense of apology and even remorse over her premature kindergarten efforts dominated a December 1868 address to the New England Women's Club. Her earlier attempt, she confessed, had been too intellectualist. Froebel's attention to play, properly guided, on the other hand, served as the basis for true learning and led to moral and spiritual development.[10]

Peabody also embraced the cause of redressing the financial plight of her sister Sophia Hawthorne, now a widow. Since 1850, Ticknor and Fields had acted both as publishers and bankers for the Hawthornes, and Hawthorne had placed the greatest confidence in their integrity, never asking to see a rendering of his account. After Hawthorne's death in 1864, Sophia became more and more uneasy about the casualness of this relationship, especially because her livelihood was dependent on the payment of royalties. On May 2, 1868, she asked James Fields for a full statement of her account, but was apparently displeased with his response and wrote again on May 20; on June 12, she inquired about the royalty rate for *Passages from the American Note-Books* and was apparently told that a reduction from 15 percent to 12 percent was planned. In an angry response on August 2 she described herself as "a lioness over her cubs—when their lives are in danger." In 1870, Gail Hamilton, a friend of Sophia, entered the fray with the publication of *A Battle of the Books* in which she attacked Fields for his dealings both with Sophia and with her.

In October 1868, when Sophia sailed for Europe, Elizabeth Peabody picked up the family standard. Peabody had written Fields, trying to bring about a reconciliation, explaining how each side had come to be suspicious of the other; she appealed to Fields's sense of honor. On November 20, she wrote him again, strongly implying that Hawthorne had been cheated out of royalties and informing him that

8 Mary Thatcher Higginson, ed., *Letters and Journals of Thomas Wentworth Higginson, 1841–1906* (Boston: Houghton Mifflin, 1921), 240–41.
9 Elizabeth Peabody and Mary P. Mann, *The Moral Culture of Infancy and Kindergarten Guide* (Cambridge, 1869; New York: J. W. Schermerhorn, 1876).
10 "New England Women's Club—Record Book of Weekly Social Meetings, Monday 21 December 1868," MS, MCR-S.

Sophia would certainly ask another publisher, Putnam's, to publish the English and Italian notebooks. She sent him her worksheets on December 14, which, she said, indicated the arithmetical errors made in calculating the royalties. Eventually, Peabody was convinced that some of her own figuring was in error, as she admitted in a letter of January 4, 1869. She was sure, nonetheless, that the publishers had taken advantage of the Hawthornes, and in any event, the whole imbroglio had destroyed Sophia's friendship with the publisher.[11] Sophia Hawthorne spent the last years of her life in Europe and England, dying in London in March 1871 at age sixty-one. Throughout the 1870s and even later, Elizabeth Peabody would be drawn back into family quarrels. In the mid-1880s, she was still trying to mediate among the Hawthorne children, to protect Hawthorne's reputation, and to fend off a rumor that she and Hawthorne had once been secretly engaged. The Hawthorne connection haunted her for the better part of fifty years.

11 This summary of the Hawthorne-Fields conflict is based on Randall Stewart, "Mrs. Hawthorne's Quarrel with James T. Fields," *More Books: Bulletin of the Boston Public Library* 21 (1946): 254–63.

Caroline Dall's unremitting public advocacy of women's rights caused Elizabeth Peabody discomfort, and she responded in several critical letters like this one.

✄ To Caroline Dall

Dear Mrs. Dall—   Jan. 4, 1860
    I have read your book with much interest & see nothing in it to which I should not have *listened* with interest[1]—though I do greatly prefer to *read* any thing rather than listen to it—(unless it be an oratorical genius who speaks—).
    I agree with you that something ought to be done *at once.*—I have just been to Concord, & found that Mrs. Alcott was not only willing but very desirous of undertaking a position of immense importance

1 Dall's book was *"Woman's Right to Labor;" or, Low Wages and Hard Work; In Three Lectures, Delivered in Boston November 1859* (Boston: Walker, Wise, 1860).

and only attractive to a person of the most disinterested benevolence & selfsacrificing temper—I mean the matronship of the Female part of the Boston jail. She says she has talked with you about it already—and she asked *me* to aid which I shall do most cordially—For I believe that she is the woman to do the most difficult duties best. I never saw such humane sentiments united with so practical a mind—& such singular extent of information in regard to the "perishing classes."—While she is in office she might also train a successor—though no training could ever make a second Mrs Alcott.[2]

I cannot but think that your book, with its statistics & array of facts, will prove eminently suggestive to all its readers,—& prepare the way for an effort to put her immediately into this place which I am going to try & could be done at once by applying to the proper authorities—I was sorry that circumstances seemed to conspire against your getting good audiences—But this *book* is better than lectures—It will penetrate beyond the reach of a single voice & be read & reread & cannot fail to awaken attention. I was sorry that the statistics were so much rather English than American—though I saw you had reasons for that—

but it is of no consequence—

I rather think [that] you misunderstand *me* somewhat respecting the duty of women's meeting this question of "Death & Dishonor" face to face & dealing with it simply & earnestly. I have no respect for the squeamishness that would blink our duty to the fallen in order to make an impression of our own beauty and delicacy. There is a way to do every thing—if we can forget our private selves for a principle.— For virtue in woman will have the manners of Love & modesty even in a brothel where it shall go to seek & save that which was lost—In haste   yours &c **E P Peabody**

MS, MHi

2 Abigail Alcott never took on such a post at the Boston jail.

About to leave for Boston and then Richmond, Peabody asks Frank Sanborn's advice about a companion.

To Franklin Benjamin Sanborn[1]

Concord,
My dear Mr. Sanborn, March 1860

I have just got reason to think that I can be instrumental in saving Stevens life—[2]

I cannot explain for I am in a hurry going to Boston at 1½ o clock—& *to Virginia* perhaps tonight—I want to see you very much *on one point*—Will you come up? I am very sorry to give you the trouble but I must—Perhaps I had better tell you—what I mean to ask It is whether under any circumstances Anna Brovis *could* go with me to Virginia if you think on hearing what I have to say it were best—

Yours truly
E P Peabody
at Mrs. Mann's

MS, NcD

1 Franklin Benjamin Sanborn, biographer of many leading Transcendentalist figures, was involved in the John Brown episode. He toured the West in the summer of 1856, and met John Brown the following January. He became Brown's New England agent. Sanborn tried in vain to dissuade Brown from his planned assault on Harper's Ferry, then helped supply him with men and material. After the failure of the raid, Sanborn was ordered to testify before the U.S. Senate, but fled twice to Canada to avoid arrest after refusing to appear. Arrested on April 3, 1860, he was quickly freed, and the Senate's agents were chased from Concord by a crowd of citizens.

2 Among John Brown's raiders was Aaron Stevens, a native of Connecticut; he had served in the U.S. Army, escaped from military prison after serving one year of a three-year sentence for assaulting an officer he had seen abusing a soldier. He reappeared in Kansas working for antislavery groups and was recruited there by John Brown. In March 1860, Peabody traveled to Richmond to appeal to Governor John Letcher for a reprieve for Stevens. Letcher rejected her appeal. Louise Tharp speculates that "Miss Peabody looked to him like a typical antislavery agitator, and he hated them all" (*Peabody Sisters of Salem,* 285). Stevens was hanged on March 16, 1860.

A letter of thanks to a supporter of one of Peabody's many causes, a comment on her own poverty, and a question on the intensifying sectional conflict.

✎ To [Gerrit Smith]¹

My dear Sir,   Concord Mass 1861

Your membership and $20 is a godsend to our *subrosa* society—which was not before quite complete & was just looking round for the member who might pay for the fourth quarter which ends April 1st. I was sorry of course that it was not in your power to set up Mrs. Slaterly² (Mattie Griffiths sister) in business because it must be done & I am at a loss how to gather together in small sums so large a sum without doing what her delicacy so shrinks from—But your cordial words give me courage—I am convinced that the best way to aid such cases, is to set the needy ones in the way to support themselves.—The money that has been sent to these ladies anonymously in the past in small sums which had to be used at once if put together would have enabled them to be supporting themselves now—the children's education & all—and even repaying the obligation with all the cheering results upon themselves of *selfsupport*. But I know you give away all your income—and do an immense deal of good, and are the only & a most adequate judge of the mode of distribution—I recognise the principle Mr Emerson set forth in his Essay on Gifts—each person has his own poor drawn toward him by affinity—and thus all are provided for at last—So I thank you for telling me my letter was eloquent & touching—it gives me confidence in myself & my pen (*my* only instrument for digging gold)—would to heaven it were guided by a genius that would make some *bookseller* engage it! If I could but coin *my time* into the wherewithal to aid these noble creatures!—I always see that

---

1 On February 9, 1861, Peabody wrote to Gerrit Smith describing her attempts to solicit members for a committee to aid Mattie Griffith, author of *The Autobiography of a Female Slave,* and thanking Smith for his letter and membership. Peabody spoke favorably in the February 9 letter of plans to compensate slaveowners for emancipation: "I have been trying to get Mr. Garrison & Mr. S. T. May to personally set agoing the plan to rouse the north to demanding of the government to adjust matters with the Border States by appropriating *U.S. Revenue* to compensate the Emancipators for loss. . . . It seems to me *all parties* in the north might unite in this—" (MS, NSyU).

2 Mrs. Slattery, not Slaterly, was Mattie Griffith's sister.

it is best for *my mind* & *character* that *I* should have been born poor—
Iron Necessity has taught me & blessed me as Prosperity would not
have done   But I do not see exactly how it had been best for *others*
with whom I have been in relation. There are several instances within
my circle of acquaintance in which it has seemed to me *want of means*
has been a terrible cause of moral & intellectual ruin—if not of spiritual also—

But I know the final curse of poverty *anywhere* is that the Earth
is not yet developed by the genius & labour of men, that there are
riches enough in *nature*—& consequently that to stimulate & educate
the human faculties is the highest charity—and this can be done sometimes by those who have no money—And by the want which *drives*—
ah would that it never [be?] crushed or *discouraged*

Which do you think is nearest right—Wendall Phillips, who in
his 'Lesson of the Hour' shows how the Union must be broken in order to free the Slave[3]—& that the slave holders in their final blindness
are cutting their own throats?—*or Mr Adams* in his last speech?[4]

How strange it is—that among all the things said—some one set
forth with *power* the simple plan *of paying the slave wages* & making
free labourers of them at once.—Mrs. Childs "Right Way & Safe
Way"[5]—sets forth the West Indian experiment as *successful*—*proves it*
beyond all cavil—*have you seen it?*[6] I will not trouble you with another sheet—with dear love to your beloved family I am yours E P
Peabody

If you have a pamphlet or copy of the debates of the Cleveland Convention[7] to spare I wish you would send me one—

MS, NSyU

3 Wendell Phillips's speech, "Lesson of the Hour," was delivered in Boston in
January 1861.
4 Peabody might be referring to Charles Francis Adams's speech "The Republican Party a Necessity," May 31, 1860, or to his speech on January 1861, as chair of
the House Committee on the State of the Union.
5 Lydia Maria Child, *The Right Way the Safe Way, Proved by Emancipation in
the British West Indies* (New York, 1860).
6 "Have you seen it?" is underlined twice.
7 Possibly she meant the Chicago convention of the Republican party, May
1860, or the Charleston convention of the Democratic party, April 1860.

Peabody attempts to persuade the governor of Massachusetts to become interim president of Antioch College (Horace Mann had been president until his death in 1859) and then yield the post to William Henry Channing.

✶ To John A. Andrew[1]

Private   Concord Mass.

My dear Governor,   Sept 8 [1861]

I have a letter from Anna Q. T. Parsons,[2] who says "What a opportunity Gov. Andrew has let pass by—of opening a function for women by granting them or inducing the Goverment of Oregon to grant *pieces of land to women* inducing them to emigrate by proposing horticulture; for how can any really selfrespecting women go out on the plan proposed?—and it is only such who are desirable to people a new country—could a fair inducement of this kind be offered to women who overflow in our rural districts, it would be a blessing to them and to the territory. A plan comprising elderly, or at least middle aged women, with young marriageable girls, could thus be able to go without sacrifice of modesty & selfrespect." Is not this worth your serious consideration, my dear Governor; & should you initiate such a thing, would it not be a *new* glory of your term of office:—

I heard from a friend of yours, whose wish was perhaps partly a father to the thought, that you seemed less & less inclined to sacrifice your splendid position & prospects in Massachusetts to go out to Antioch College. On the other hand, Mr Hale & Mr Clarke & others feel that *the prestige* of Antioch College all over the West, would be infinitely increased, if so well known & deservedly popular man as yourself should identify yourself with it. I sympathise with both parties; and I am going to take the liberty of suggesting a *compromise*!

It will make no essential difference to your future in Massachusetts, if you should defer returning to your profession for *one year*—

1 John A. Andrew, governor of Massachusetts and antislavery advocate, was one of Lincoln's earliest supporters, mobilizing Massachusetts immediately after Lincoln's call for troops. Neither Andrew nor William Henry Channing took up Peabody's suggestions about Antioch.

2 Anne Q. T. Parsons was an educator, reformer, and psychic, a frequent visitor at Brook Farm, one of the founders of the Boston Religious Union of Associationists, and founder of the Boston Women's Union.

while *one year*—& that the first year at Antioch College[—]will do all for it that said identification merely would do.—Now I think, & my sister too (which is more to the purpose, since she had seven years experience there & knows all about it)—that William Henry Channing, uniting the prestige of his uncle's name, & his own as his biographer, with years of thought about Education, and about the interests of woman *in this country* (which, in the length & breadth of its great extent, has taken the place of the narrower phalanstery of his earlier enthusiasm, when he despaired of the country in its benighted condition), is almost an ideal person for the Presidency of Antioch College—& nothing intervenes except a *notion* that he is not *practical*— which is a *very false notion* as he is peculiar among persons of his class of mind, for his *strong turn* to put into social forms the principles of Christianity—which he believes in so broad a manner—& with such universality of human sympathy—as to appreciate all its forms from Catholicism to the extemest left of Unitarianism. Sympathy & comprehension of *every form* of Spiritual experience is his speciality—& then he sympathises with youth, and with young women, in the most delicate manner; while he would stimulate them to the widest & noblest life. Hitherto he has had no adequate practical sphere. He has always repudiated *mere* preaching—he wants to *practice* as well as *preach*. Now I understand that he *also* has been offered a professorship—What if you should write to him & tell him how you are drawn to be the President of Antioch College—only by not knowing whom to recommend—& propose to him that you should go for *one year* provided *he* will lay out to be your successor—& inviting him to write out to you *his views* so that you may have some adequate ground on which to base your recommendation to them—saying to him *what you can say with truth*—that—it is only *the want* of a *reputation for practical affairs* that any one to whom his name has been mentioned has *hesitated* to choose him for *President*—But that if he is conscious of a practical power that some of his friends ascribe to him you will take *his* word for it—as of course he would not wish to put himself into a place to which he did not feel himself fitted.

You then can say to those who urge you to go, that you are willing to go for a year—and state the thing fairly—to yield it up into *his* hands afterwards—

His address in England is care of Isaac B. Cooke Esq.

    Claughton
    Birkenhead
    England—

since you have some months *to decide,* you will have time for a full interchange with him on the subject; & meanwhile Anticoch College will be making more & more impression of its importance—by having the impression diffused of your probable connection with it for a time. Very truly yours,

Eliz. P. Peabody

What a good meeting at Worcester!

MS, MHi

In this letter to her nephew, Peabody demonstrates both the range and the limitations of her organic view of nature.

✖ To Horace Mann, Jr.

Jan 1st 1862

My dear Horace

Mr Emerson says the highest office which nature (studied scientifically) has—is to lead the mind into those spiritual facts which are of essential importance to its own growth. You have sometimes expressed that there was a *something* in every organization which the naturalists did not get at—Every phenomenon refers to some phenomenon back of it—or to some law which one wants to find is *the cause* of it—Whenever one shall find the final cause one feels that he shall be endowed with some new power—a power to produce the thing. When you were studying chemistry—you not only wanted to know what things composed it—but to decompose it into those constituents & you felt it to be a high delight when you could so do it that not any thing should escape & in such a way that you would see how to recompose it—& actually recompose it.

I once studied chemistry with a great enthusiasm in Dr Thompson's large work in which experiments are described—and I went over these in my imagination & enjoyed it infinitely. For years after I knew the proportions of everything to the very decimal expression of the facts—But as it was *words* not things which I saw, & it was by my sensuous imagination I saw them & not my senses—it faded away—

But whenever any natural fact symbolized to me a fact of my internal being—or a law of life—it became immortal in my mind. Such facts in nature as that plants which unfolded themselves in richest flowering in the tropics—in the more northern regions expended their substance in *sheathe* for the bud & flower—which left little comparatively for the magnificent petals,—& that therefore the blooms were always smaller and more scarce—Such facts suggesting that the law of. *all life* was expression of the inmost under the warmth of Love—I saw that so when this failed the inmost heart was chilled & hastened to fold itself up in sheathes—A large part of that force which has been given for expression was expended in making defences—& never after could I see a confiding outpouring character, making itself into a symbol of love & every inward beauty of soul but I thought of the tropical flower—And on the other hand when I have seen the delicate soul wrapping itself up in reserves lest it should be frost bitten by the ungenial society in whose cold atmosphere it lives, I have thought of the transformation of the tropical flower into the northern form—And the spiritual meaning made the fact a perpetual possession of the memory. Moreover this reciprocal light which the natural & spiritual throw on each other enables one often to make a new *dive* into the *natural* fact.—Mr Agassiz told Mr Emerson once that when he got puzzled about his zoological classification he went to Mr Lovering once and talked with him about the stars—& differing as seem the phenomena of the heavens & the earth, he often got the clue he wanted. This I could understand for I know that the law of life is *one* & the same in whatever sphere manifested—It follows then

'as night the day'

that in the Science of Sciences—that is—in the Science of the Spirit— must be found the key to unlock nature.[1]

But in this science we are often less instructed than in any other— We are less acquainted with our own highest consciousness often— than we are with the whole phenomenal life of some insect or bird.

Such was the case with Chantry—who represents a whole generation of men in France during the last century—[2]

1 This letter indicates Peabody's difficulty, along with that of other members of her Transcendental circle, in understanding the empirical and hypothetical method of modern science, typified in the work of Darwin. Like Alcott and Emerson, she was firmly wedded to an idealist philosophy.

2 A search of the literature on the French Enlightenment has turned up no references to a scientist named Chantry or to a work (or assistant) called Picceola. It is possible, of course, that Peabody mistook a French name, but "Chantry" is not close in sound to any prominent French scientist or philosopher of the eighteenth century. Nonetheless, the intent of the letter, to connect science to the outlook of idealist philosophy, still seems clear.

But he was shut up to a solitude so awful and lifeless—with a mind so destitute of the habit of that faith which is the *evidence* of things unseen—& the substance of things hoped for—that a manifestation of life—because it was a manifestation of life—*Cause* or that which is self-moved—became to him a veritable revelation of God—& teacher of the *Final Truth*—which is that something which you said was always *left out* in all natural histories & systems of science—that some thing which draws you on so all prevailingly to hunt through all the kingdom of nature—It is nothing less than *God* who invites you to enter into his counsels & sit down with him on his throne—

Picceola is a great study of the human soul whose deepest laws & innermost being is made manifest in this wonderful relation established between the soul of Chantry & the little *Picceola*—who in her transient existence realized *a value* beyond that of diamonds—Wherever there is life—organizing life—there is God—inviting us with forms & colours more or less alluring—to *live with Him*—communicating joy or good.

In that beautiful photograph of yours I am sure I see the *very soul* that goes forth into nature, seeking that which cannot be found in books—That going forth is truly a prayer I see by the deep seriousness of the expression. Cultivate this mood of mind & bye & bye in this world or the next, you will realize that God is always found by those that seek Him simply.

Yr affectionate
AUNT LIZZY

TS copy, OYesA

Peabody tries to interest the editor of the North American Review *in Ethan Allen Hitchcock's analysis of Shakespeare's sonnets, and describes a conversation with Harriet Tubman.*

✕ To Charles Eliot Norton[1]

Concord.

My dear Sir,   30 August 1864

I wish you would mark what discrepancies you observe in that article. Perhaps, with omissions of some passages, it might still serve to introduce the sonnets under Gen. Hitchcocks idea.[2]—It was not supposed to be an exhaustive treatment of the subject, as I remarked in the N.B. at the end.—it was compiled from letters written during three months. I think the definition on page 18th of the 'Master Mistress' might be omitted.—I wish—that—if with a few such alterations—the article should seem to you would make them with a pencil, & I would then see if I found it at all unjust to the General to insert what you think would be admissible—& no more.

He is engaged in a more elaborate commentary, which bye & bye he wishes to print—But publishers are more likely to meet his wish in this respect if the periodical press seems to invite such a disposition— He was so much pleased to have me do this [thing ?] & left to my judgment to put in as much as I pleased—I doubted about that very sentence because it seemed to me not so clearly expressed as was possible.—Shakespeares genius he supposed to be as I thought a love of God & nature so conceived that the latter is a mirror of the former— Nature only being interesting because it is the garment of God—& God only intelligible through the medium of nature which is his *word,* including as it does *Man*—the Special word.—The third time he defined 'Master Mistress', or the purpose of these sonnets, he did it still more felicitously. I put in *all* the statements, because an idea that can only

---

1 Charles Eliot Norton, the son of Andrews Norton, and an editor and author, in 1864 became co-editor of the *North American Review* along with James Russell Lowell. In the following year he joined E. L. Godkin, Frederick Law Olmstead, and J. M. McKim in founding the *Nation.*

2 Ethan Allen Hitchcock, grandson of Ethan Allen, graduated from West Point in 1817 and held various military assignments, including that of military advisor to President Lincoln. Hitchcock wrote several books and articles arguing that various authors, including Dante, Spenser, and Shakespeare, were part of a secret society espousing a kind of radical pantheism.

be approximate at best by expression—I thought would be more easily
apprehended if there were several definitions; & in different letters he
had defined in these several ways,—But if you prefer to give it up entirely—I will take it & revise it & offer it to the Ch. Examiner which
had however a less wide circulation than the North American.—

I am glad to have this opportunity to express how very interesting
you have made the N. American. It seems to me now full of life and
riches. I have just been reading the July number.—I was very much interested in the article on the Constitution—though I think the author
does not quite do justice to the negroes' *quietness,* in supposing it the
result of want of appreciation of freedom & a proper indignation
against oppressors! I was lately talking with the woman whom you
may have heard of some years since—as having first escaped herself
from Maryland or Virginia, & afterwards *gone back eight times,* each
time bringing off relatives & friends, & showing prodigious courage &
ability, as well as heart—in her heroic efforts—This is a negro without
cross—with wooly hair & *no beauty.*—She had been in Port Royal for
two years, in the employ of Gen. Saxton, with great results.[3] She told
me that it was curious to see how the negroes received freedom entirely
as the gift of the Lord, for which they had *waited* & which they believed would surely come—& ever the *more* in proportion as slavery became more outrageous and cruel. I would give the world to repeat an
account a very old negro gave *her* of the entrance of the *Wabash*
(wasn't it) into Port Royal Harbour.[4]—It is truly a great revelation of
this world how He was *revealed* to the naked need of the nature A
worship of God with the *heart & will*—if not with the mind.—This
woman said the negroes were satisfied when they could get *guns* &
therefore they were not rampant about pay.—They were determined
never to give these up—They waited to see if *constitutionally* & without *mutiny* they should get and retain their freedom.—If they were at
last *cheated*—we should see that this anger so slow to rise was not
ready to abate. She said whites had no idea of the reserved power—intellectual & moral—that lay hidden behind faces that looked stupid

[3] This is probably Harriet Tubman, important conductor on the underground
railroad, who left her hiding place in Canada many times to lead groups of slaves to
freedom.

[4] On November 7, 1861, Federal naval vessels and troops began their conquest
of the sea islands along the coast of South Carolina. Union private E. O. Hill wrote
to his family: "I have seen a big battle, but did not take any part in it. It looked kind
of careless to see the old frigate Wabash pour in broad side after broad side into that
little fort" (quoted in Willie Lee Rose, *Rehearsal for Reconstruction* [New York:
Bobbs-Merrill, 1964], 11–12).

as brutes. It was the tradition of years with them to *feign death*—They grew up with it. Not even friendly whites could beguile them of their confidence,—but *She knew* moreover *the pity* they had for their masters when they thought of the justice of God, and knowing their deficiency of the power to labour was wonderfully prevalent. And this I had known before from personal observation & a great deal of report.

Yours respectfully

ELIZABETH P. PEABODY

MS, MH

Peabody describes the U.S. House of Representatives' passage of the amendment to abolish slavery.

✒ To Horace Mann, Jr.

My dear Horace   25th of February 1865
        Today you are 21—and your mother and other friends are dining in Concord in honour of the day—but I, far away in Washington, am not able to make merry with them, and so will answer your letter, which I have but lately received.
        I will congratulate you first that you do not come to the age to vote, until the Constitution of your country has become freed from its blots, and is indeed the Charter of humanity, and for the first time since Christ came into the world, there is a nation, & that is *your own,* in whose public action it is possible for Christ to be manifested. Kossuth's "Future of Nations" is realized—even in *his* life-time. America is *now* truly the Land of the brave and the home of the free—I wish you could have heard a sermon Mr Channing preached in the Capitol the Sunday after the amendment passed the House—It was such an opening into *our* Future! But it was something to see the Amendment pass the House which I did! I went the day Col. Ashley introduced the bill[1]—& some noble speeches were made by Scofield of Pennsylvania & others—and also some speeches on the other side by James Brooks & others—The day the bill passed was a fortnight after during which time several new converts were made—& Col Ashley was so sure it

---

[1] James Mitchell Ashley, representative from Ohio (1858–68), introduced the amendment to abolish slavery.

would pass he courteously yielded the floor to the opposition to relieve themselves for three hours—when Mallory of Kentucky & others said their say against it—There was an attempt at the last moment to rush in other business—to postpone it &c, but the question prevailed—& the yeas & nays were called—Every one was said with its own expression—& when a democrat wheeled in a murmur & clapp of applause tried to burst out but was repressed by the Speaker—who was Mr Colfax—The Speaker does not generally vote, but may do so—Mr Colfax ordered himself to be recorded as an *aye*—When the vote was declared it was found to be 7 above the majority of ⅔rds and then such a shout—while the floor on the right side of the house seemed to *blaze* with excitement—& the galleries wholly sympathized—On the *opposition* side the members threw themselves back and bore it as quietly as they could—I only wished I had an opera glass to see *their faces*— But the eyes on the right side somehow showed out like stars—Some embraced—most shook hands—So we did in the gallery—Tears & smiles contended for mastery. Mr Channing said Mr Colfax's eyes were full of tears—Mary said to Mr Channing "You helped to do this" and indeed such preaching as his must have had effect for *it is the gospel of freedom* in the full sense of all the words—Then *all hail* young citizen of the only perfect Republic!—

TS copy (incomplete), OYesA

Peabody vividly recalls two encounters with Lincoln; her ability to convey human personality is nowhere better demonstrated.

✖ To Horace Mann, Jr.

[Washington, D.C.]
[February 1865]

My dear Horace, Before I send of[f] this letter I wish to tell you of my two visits to Mr. Lincoln. Gen Hitchcock[1] wanted me to have a real chance to see him & so I did not go to the Receptions till I should have had my first interview—& one day last week he came for me. —We

[1] Ethan Allen Hitchcock was Lincoln's military advisor and, as previously mentioned, author of several studies of literature, in which he sought to demonstrate the existence of a radical and conspiratorial tradition of pantheism; see letters in this section to Charles Eliot Norton and Henry Wadsworth Longfellow.

were sandwiched in between others who were waiting in the anteroom, & the moment we went in & I was in the act of being introduced & he had hold of my hand with the most courteous & kind look, a servant spoke over my head another name, which struck his ear & he said "Yes—yes"—looking over my head "I must see him, directly—tell him to come in"—& he motioned with his head toward the corner of the room & saying "excuse me" dropped my hand and darted off to the same corner with another man—There was such naturalness & such eagerness and such confidence in my kind understanding of the case that I was not disturbed but followed him with my eyes—& saw him as he sat down with the visitor before him & watched his mobile countenance as he spoke low & fast with him—His face was very pale—his eyes very dark & bright—his countenance very mobile—& a certain fineness of fibre wholly took off the clownish effect of his g[au]nt figure, which was carelessly though cleanly drest—with black cravat & buff waistcoat.—Meanwhile the Gen. had got me a chair & begged me to sit down;—& immediately after—Mr. Lincoln darted back again—& threw himself into a large chair & drawing it up to the fire—motioned to us to do the same. He then turned to me & said—:"And Horace Mann was your brother in law?"—"Yes" said I—"I knew Mr. Mann in Congress—I was there when he came—early in 1848—when John Quincy Adams died[2]— We were all greatly interested to see the one who was to succeed the 'old man eloquent'—and gathered round him—(it was in the old hall) to hear his first speech—And a very remarkable speech it was—It was upon secession!—the United States North & the United States South contrasted"—I said, "Yes—he was very much interested in antislavery—He went into Congress because he feared the Extension of Slavery." "I remember (said he)—he never spoke of any other subject in Congress—and he was reasonable. He was not so extreme as some—As Wendell Phillips for instance— (and he looked up with the sweetest smile as if he did not hate W. P. for being extreme on this subject)"—I said—"He took a different view— He once had a controversy in the Liberator with W. P. on the question of whether an Antislavery man could conscientiously take office under the U.S. Constitution." "I did not know it," said he, I continued— "His affirmative to this was ably stated & argued in a letter to Mr. Gar-

[2] Lincoln served one term in the House of Representatives, 1847–49. Horace Mann was chosen to succeed John Quincy Adams, who had served from 1831 to 1848, the year of his death. He served two terms; his speech in the House attacked the extension of slavery into the frontier territories, thus establishing himself as an anti-slavery man but not an abolitionist.

rison which closed the controversy"[3] His countenance grew very sweet—as he said "Mr. Mann was very kind to me—and it was something to me at that time to have him so—for he was a distinguished man in his way—and I was nobody"—This was said with expression—as if he was remembering some interview that was pleasant. Then looking up to the General he said—"He had a most benignant countenance. And the benovolence of his character (and he was a very benovolent man)—beamed through his features,"—He said this eagerly—& emphatically—as I have marked it—& again his eyes dropped as if remembering.

This was very pleasant to me because I knew that your father must have liked him—as his smile was always intentional—and he evidently had always looked at Mr. Lincoln with pleasure & sympathy.

I said—"I do not think he is so far off—Mr. Lincoln—that he is not rejoicing with us over the Amendment—You ought to have been in the House that day—Sir!—" He looked up suddenly & eagerly—& very brightly—and said—"What do you think I was doing that day? I was writing my instructions to Seward—!! There is a little secret piece of history connected with that.—I had dismissed—some time before—all anxiety about that voting—I knew the bill would pass—the day he introduced it—But you know Ashley wanted to get a larger majority & so put off putting the question for a fortnight[4]—and meantime that Peace Commissioner business came on—You look at the date of that correspondence.—I eased it along—and concluded to send Seward down. Twice while the talk in Congress was going on that morning—& I was writing to Seward—notes came from the House asking me if there were any Commissioners of Peace in Washington—or whether I thought they would come—Those converts of Ashley's would have gone off in a tangent at the last moment had they smelt Peace. I left off writing each time—& took sheets of paper—& elaborately wrote that as far as I knew there were no Commissioners of peace in Washington—nor did I think they would come." Here he laughed—

[3] In May 1844, the American Anti-Slavery Society resolved "that secession from the present United States Government is the duty of every abolitionist." The printed version of this resolution, published in the *Anti-Slavery Examiner,* contained an introduction by Wendell Phillips.

[4] James Mitchell Ashley, representative from Ohio, first introduced the amendment to abolish slavery on December 14, 1863, but it failed to pass the House. He introduced the amendment again in early 1865, and it passed on January 31, 1865. The amendment was passed by the Senate on April 8, 1865, and was ratified by the states by December 13, 1865, whereupon it became the Thirteenth Amendment.

& repeated again in the same words & with the same emphasis "as far I knew &c—"

But just then his countenance changed & dropping his voice he said to the General—"have Waller & ———— gone?" "Yes," said the General, "they were exchanged yesterday"[5]—He made another remark to which the Gen. replied & then he said—loud & eager—with bright look—"How is it with the prisoners generally—What proportion will not go back?"—"About one sixth I should think in general would not be exchanged." "But five sixths of the Indiana prisoners would not go back" said he to me exultingly—"Five sixths!" & he rubbed his hands —At this moment the door opened & the word "telegram"—We all rose—he took it saying "You see how it is!" and we took our leave— He opened the telegram, glanced at it—& then said to me with kind shining eyes—as he shook hands, "I am glad to have made your acquaintance."

After I came out I realised that I had been very much interested indeed and surprised—The naturalness was like that of a child—& had a touch of pathos in it—He seemed to be full of feeling—I asked the General about Waller—& he told me that he and his companion had been condemned to death for treason in the beginning of the War for going from the free States to raise a rebel company in Kentucky—but Mr. Lincoln had commuted the sentence to imprisonment & they had been imprisoned three years in the Capitol Prison—He is full of the milk of human kindness—It is hard for him to sign a death warrant. He would not kill anybody—especially young men. He ordered them to be exchanged lately & yesterday they went—His mother has long been soliciting the pardon of Waller—On Thursday noon Mr. L.'s reception came off & I went—for I wanted to see him again. He stood near the door of the green & gold room—looking at the door—He was nicely dressed in black—with white kid gloves & as I approached I marked his eyes—so sweet and melancholy—& his composed features struck me as very small & refined—& his cheeks looked patient—Truly as Mr. Everett said, I did not see but that he was the peer of any gentleman—When we were near enough to be recognised his eyes & face lightened—and he said as he held out his hand, "Miss Peabody I am glad to see you, I was with Mrs. Johnson & Miss Donaldson whom he then greeted by name—& we stopped—There was a band in the East

---

[5] The reference here is to William E. Waller, a Confederate recruiter, whose death sentence had been earlier commuted and who, along with Confederate Captain Shultz Leach, was being exchanged for a Union officer, Captain Ives.

room—"Is not that music beautiful?" said he—I assented & spoke of the flowers which in vases & flowerpots stood in all the hall & rooms—"Yes—the Greenhouse is in fine order"—Another squad of visitors approached as I saw & we stood back on a level & people came in. It was delightful to watch his countenance—His face reflected the expression of each—grave & patient when anybody came who evidently had no heart or interest in him—full of feeling to reflect feeling—Every child was noticed. When one was running by without speaking he stopped him—saying, Here—here—I always speak to little boys—Sometimes mothers offered the children—he always said some kind thing—it was evident he was genuinely fond of children—One beautiful boy of 14 looked up with fair forehead & soft sweet eyes—He bent over him and said some thing—& when he stepped back I said, "It is not often I guess that this ceremony calls out so much feeling all round," He said Yes—they feel cheerful! As we stood a moment more I said "Do you see the Liberator?" "Not often," said he—"There was an interesting number Feb. 10th with an account of the Jubilee over the Amendment—Fred Douglass made a speech & Mr. Garrison"—"Oh I should be glad to see Mr. Garrison's speech," said he. "Have you got it?" I pulled the Liberator from my pocket & said, "—But here is Wendell Phillips speech on Reconstruction. This is not so respectful—He says he does not trust you on Reconstruction."[6] "Oh that is no matter!" said he "Give it to me. I like to read his sharp things" I said there is very much you will like—I think you will agree with almost all his views—" "Oh yes I dare say" & he very eagerly took the paper & put it into his pocket More people came in—all of whom were received with great feeling & attention—Sometimes sailors in crutches. Sometimes elegantly dressed ladies—sometimes very plain common women—I saw some girls with hoods on—After an interval the band suddenly struck up Hail to the Chief—very brilliantly—Oh is not that beautiful—said he—& it seemed to me that the music pervaded every fibre—At last we had to move on to make room for the thickening crowd & after going round the East room—we went to see the Conservatory & as I returned to go out at the door I could look in & see him standing there with his eyes always on the door—& receiving—Evidently giving himself up to an interesting duty.

And so at last I went away—but I felt I should go again soon—

6 The *Liberator* of February 10, 1865, reported on the Grand Jubilee at the Boston Music Hall; the same issue reported a January 26 speech by Phillips denouncing Lincoln's lenient Reconstruction plans.

I am astonished to see how I love him—trust him—feel as if he were a father—

The General is delighted that I like him so much for he is a very great favourite with him. He told me that when he saw him—the second time—the first after his introduction—he came into the War Office—a back room of it where the General used to sit in the first years of the war—As he came in lost in thought he gravely bowed—& sat down & seemed to think—The General observed him & was realising the impression he made—when he suddenly looked up & met the Generals eyes—The General said he made the trite remark but it was called out by his observation of him: You have a very trying position, Sir—Yes said Mr. Lincoln & did I not see the hand of God in the crisis—I could not sustain it—The General said the tone & manner were so simple & earnest that he felt the intelligent devotion—the devout responsibility. It is an infinite comfort to think such a man is guiding us—The General thinks his abilities are very great—& his integrity & love of country most profound—& that we have had no greater President—& depend upon it he says bye and bye this will be seen & acknowledged. The General also has entire faith & hope that the spring will see the close of the War—Sherman—Sheridan & Grant are perfectly competent—have forces—& means enough—The War means of the Confederacy are exhausted—Lee has military ability— but he must succumb.—Before you get home we may have peace—God grant it!

Ever yours

Elizabeth P. Peabody

MS, in the private collection of Mary and Harry Dalton, Charlotte, North Carolina; reprinted in *New England Quarterly* 48 (March 1975): 117–24.

Peabody's concern for freedmen's education is evident in this letter describing the racial hostility directed toward a school for black orphans in the nation's capital.

✎ To Emily Howland[1]

My dear Miss Howland,   March 9th, 1865

Everything about the School for Miss Mann has been at a *standstill*,[2] because of the want of a place to put down the house which is upon the way & may arrive at any moment. I am entirely satisfied that the Miner Estate is to be despaired of.[3] Mr. Channing & Mrs. Johnson are the only ones upon the corporation that is to be—who desire it. The rest not only do not desire it but are in deadly opposition to it. Mr *Baker* (though believing he says that she is entirely wronged in the affair of the Home) avers that he never could *advise* & I think he said *consent* to having her mixed up with the interests of the Miner school when she has such active enemies who will thereby become enemies of the Miner school. I told him (& brought proofs) that the coloured people of Georgetown & Washington did not share the enmity—or prejudice—& they preferred her.—I was greatly disgusted with Mr Bakers taking such a mean view of what was the duty in the premises. But every thing was said that could be said & he was inexorable. But more formidable than this one obstinate man is the fact that a month before you wrote to Mr Tatem—a *Mr Leigh* had written & offered on behalf of the New York Freedman's Society to build a house & remove Mr Pond's school there. He says this plan originated *last summer* before Miss Miner came back—That it is an old plan of the Freedman's So-

1 Emily Howland was a Quaker educator and reformer who taught at a school for free blacks in Washington, D.C. in 1856; she settled freed slaves on a tract of land near the mouth of the Potomac in 1867, and was an active supporter of black education and women's suffrage.

2 Maria Mann, Mary's niece, taught since October 1864 at this school for orphaned black children who had come into Northern lines as contraband. From the very start of her work, as Peabody described the situation to William Cullen Bryant (October 1864, MS, NN), she encountered great resistance and racial enmity.

3 Peabody hoped that Maria Mann's school would be taken up by the Miner estate. Myrtilla Miner, advocate of black education, purchased property in Georgetown for a school for free black children. This school too occasioned great hostility in the white community; it was open only intermittently during the war. From 1871 to 1876, the school was part of Howard University and in 1879 became Miner Normal School and eventually a part of the Washington public school system.

ciety to get this Estate into their system of operations. Only he & Mrs. Johnson can stand for Maria against this formidable society. I therefore feel as if the only thing to be done is, to get the War Department to give us a piece of Land whereon to set this house—If *that* cannot be done, she must give up, & go elsewhere—*selling this house.*—And if it goes into operation she must have more than 12 scholars. She feels *discouraged* both because of the *College* whose preparatory school will take off so many boys—& because this school of Mr Pond's on the Miner Estate will come across hers—& *12 scholars* for three quarters in the year will not bring $150—She means to take some *free scholars* in consideration of the gift of the Schoolhouse &c.—but she ought to have 40 scholars to pay her board—clothes—& vacation journey. What do you think about this. I wish you could come up on Saturday. She is staying at Mrs. Johnsons's & I could meet you there Saturday forenoon.

The enmity against her does not *sleep* but has new manifestations continually.

She feels that nothing can baffle or *lay* this evil spirit but her success in a school in this District—& so resists the advice of myself & Mr Channing to leave *the ground* in scorn & go to some place to work for humanity under more generous auspices.[4]

Yours very truly
Eliz. P. Peabody

Mrs Bliss seems one of the greatest enemies of Miss Mann. Her prejudice rises to malignancy. She wont open her mind to know any thing in her favour.

MS, NIC

4 Peabody followed up this letter with another to Emily Howland on June 11, describing Maria Mann's work at Harpers Ferry after her orphanage position became untenable. She suggested that the Miner estate board might yet find a place for Mann at its school (MS, NIC).

A request for Longfellow's autograph for an auction, and a reflection upon their mutual sorrows; Hawthorne had been dead just one year, and Longfellow's wife Fanny, Peabody's student almost forty years earlier, had died in 1861.

✺ To Henry Wadsworth Longfellow

Dear Mr. Longfellow,   Concord Mass. May 19 [1865]

You are so kind that I dare say you have been asked for & sent autographs to the Chicago fair—But there is a raffle whose highest prize is Mr Emerson's manuscript of his Remarks at Concord Mass on the day of the funeral[1] But there are a hundred shares and we want a prize for every subscriber—I have ten of Carlyle's—25 of Horace Mann's sentences attested by his wife—some of Hawthorne's & I have written out some verses of your own if you will put your name to each & return them to me I should be very grateful. Of course if you have the manuscript of some published piece & would put your name to each verse—& put it in the envelope & ⟨return⟩ send it to me—it would make many beautiful prizes—I dare say you will be willing to make so much effort—for the still suffering soldiers—

Let me take this opportunity to express to you how beautiful we all felt your beautiful verses to be upon Hawthorne's funeral[2]—Today is the anniversary of his death—I hope he is not so far off but that he is rejoicing over the rescued country for which he died despairing—*Of* which he died—as I feel.

I have thought of you a great deal this last year in connection with my sister Sophia's letters to me—which I have sometimes almost thought I would send to you to read—feeling as if the blessing upon

---

1 On April 19, Concord's citizens gathered in the Unitarian First Parish Church to hold a memorial service for Lincoln. Included on the program was an address from Emerson, who acknowledged all of Lincoln's qualities as a leader and a wise, compassionate person. "Rarely was man so filled to the event. . . . Only Washington can compare with him in fortune."

2 On June 23, 1864, Longfellow wrote to Sophia Hawthorne, "I have written a few lines trying to express the impressions of May 23, and I venture to send you a copy of them. . . . I feel how imperfect and inadequate they are; but I trust you will pardon their deficiencies for the love I bear his memory" (*The Life of Henry Wadsworth Longfellow*, 3 vols., ed. Samuel Longfellow [Boston: Houghton Mifflin, 1893], 3:38–39). The poem was called "Hawthorne," and was first published in *Flowers-de-Luce* in 1867.

her spirit perpetually shed by departed love—& wh. she does *not* depart might be consoling to your own bereaved heart for it seems so reasonable as well as so sweet—There cannot be any parting of those who go within [?] the veil as it seems to us—It is we who feel & see a veil— they *cannot*—They get nearer their beloved ones—for to them the veil is lifted—And they would not be identical if they ceased to love—[3]

But pardon me—I have no right to touch such sacred things to you though I cannot but feel that I comprehend because I watched the opening of the bud of the flower you had in its full & I appreciated it *rarity* always—most Respectfully

Elizabeth P. Peabody

MS, MH

[3] Peabody's reference is to Longfellow's grief over the death of his wife, Fanny, on July 10, 1861.

Much like Elizabeth Peabody's, Henry Wadsworth Longfellow's life spanned nearly the entire nineteenth century, from 1807 to 1882. After graduating from Bowdoin College in 1826, he traveled to Europe for further study. Longfellow was deeply and permanently impressed by European culture and returned to the United States in order to teach modern languages at Harvard College and translate French, Italian, and Spanish literature. From 1843 to 1860, Longfellow also wrote many of his best poems. In 1861, his second wife, Fanny Appleton, died from burns received when her dress caught fire from hot sealing wax. Plunged into despair, Longfellow forced himself to keep writing, but his later work never achieved the power of his antebellum verse.

In this letter to Garrison, Peabody makes an effort to preserve and protect Horace Mann's posthumous reputation.

✸ To William Lloyd Garrison

My dear Mr Garrison   July 20, 1865

Will it be possible for you, or for any body, to procure those two letters of Mr. Mann's addressed to yourself which were written just after the controversy with Mr Phillips which proved so unsatisfactory.[1]

[1] Between February and June 1853, Wendell Phillips and Horace Mann engaged in an increasingly bitter correspondence in the *Liberator*. Phillips, who bore Mann no personal animosity, felt obliged because of his own abolitionist and antipolitical position to accuse Mann of putting the Constitution above higher law in seeking a political solution to the slavery question.

Those letters we think were a most admirable statement of the argument for antislavery men's acting under the Constitution of the United States against slavery & Mrs. Mann wishes them to form a part of the volume of Antislavery papers which she means to publish as soon as possible.[2] She had the two letters which were given under every promise of carefulness to a friend but which were lost. The date of the letters of which there were *two* in consecutive papers was[3]

I do not know what you thought of the letters then but perhaps now you will yourself endorse them as possibly earnest antislavery sentiment. I hope you will have interest enough to read Mr Mann's life[4] & then I am sure you will not fail to see how entirely earnest & sincere he was in this cause, altho *his method* was his own, & it was his instinct not to complicate his life work. I think none will greet Mr Lincoln in the next life with more fellow feeling than Mr Mann, who we have good reason to believe, very much liked & valued him when they were in Congress together. I have had curiosity to look out Mr Lincoln's old speeches there in the Globe, & I find the same man, especially in certain resolutions of enquiry into Mr Polks message about the Mexican War, & a speech on these Resolutions some time after.

Mattie Griffith and her sister are in Concord this summer, having rented a small furnished house till October. Don't you want to come up & see them & me? The cars from the Fitchburg Depot leave at 10 minutes before 7, & also at 11, every morning, & return at 1½ past 1, and ½ past 6 every evening. It is an hours ride—would it not be a very pleasant excursion? You could at least have a six hours visit & you can go to & from the Fitchburg Depot in cars.

Mrs. Mann lives near the Depot, & any body will tell you how to get to it & I will take you to Mrs. Slattery's

I should delight to see you in this *good time* [;] *come.*

I hope you will feel willing to tell Mr. Owen, for his book, about that conversation you & Mr Thompson had with Mr. Lincoln that so completely won your confidence & which I believe you never have published

Yrs truly
Eliz. P. Peabody

2 Mary Mann, ed., *Life and Works of Horace Mann,* 5 vols. (Boston: Walker, Fuller and Company, 1865–68), is most likely the "Antislavery papers" Peabody refers to.

3 Peabody inserted the newspaper citations at the end of the letter. She obviously discovered more than two letters that she was interesed in.

4 Mann's first biography was Mary Mann, *Life of Horace Mann, by His Wife* (Boston: Walker, Fuller and Company, 1865).

I do not know how to direct to Mr. Phillips. Will you please direct this note which I enclose.

Mann on Wendell Phillips, Feb. 21, 1853; pub. in *Liberator,*
    March 4
Man's Reply to Phillips, Mar. 14, 1853; pub. in *Liberator,*
    March 18
Mann's Reply to Phillips, Apr. 4, 1853; pub. in *Liberator,* April 8
Mann's Reply to Phillips, Apr. 19, 1853; pub. in *Liberator,* May 13
Mann's Defense of position, May 20, 1853; pub. in *Liberator,* June 3

MS, MB

As Peabody's acquaintances die, she feels surrounded by their spirits, a theme she will return to increasingly in the following years. Here she shares some thoughts with the father of Foster Haven, the child the Peabodys looked after in the 1830s.

✄ To Samuel Foster Haven

My dear friend,—   [1865]
    I have just returned from looking at the portrait of Foster by Ames; and I should think there was a great deal of likeness in it.—My own image of his childhood is so very vivid—& always occurs to me— that perhaps I should not appreciate the likeness as well as some others:—Then my next strongest image is of him as he lay at last[1]—& *that* it is—perhaps which makes me feel as if this was rather too high toned in *colour*—which is Ames's tendency—But the *expression* is very fine & I should judge *characteristic* from all his cousins have told me.—Ah I never shall cease to regret that I did not make more strenuous efforts to keep up that acquaintance which was so rarely intimate—& which never ought to have been so much dropped. Last summer I wrote out some of my recollections of that blessed season of his childhood— (indeed *all* my *clear* reminiscences) & I shall always hope that the time may come when these papers I gave you will be found again[2]—For I know I miss many exquisite touches.—I will some time

[1] Foster Haven, son of Peabody's student Lydia Sears Haven, who served as a doctor in the Union Army, was killed at Fredericksburg, December 1862.
[2] The relationship of the reminiscences she was writing in 1865 to the ones published in *Lectures in the Training Schools for Kindergartners* (Boston: D. C. Heath,

show you these sketches—and get your leave to print them in some form—with perhaps your own supplement of another period of his life—or they might go as they are into "the little Pilgrim" perhaps?— They have already quickened the spirits of many children—to whom I have described his first acquaintance with his Heavenly Father— There is no mistake about that;—he had the vision: & it informed heart soul & mind—& I believe that *in the Spirit* as he is now—he is individualized by that very experience for recognition—I hope you have enough of the Swedenborgian cast to your imagination from the influences on your childhood to indulge yourself with following the spirits of the Mother and son—in their reunion.—The very loveliest thing in Swedenborg's works is the relation of an interview he was having with some spirits—when he saw there appeared in the group occasionally—& ever & anon disappeared—a figure with thoughtful brow & folded arms—who walked amidst them as they were talking, intently listening! Swedenborg asked who this was—and was told that it was "a still embodied Spirit who, in seasons of lofty contemplation, became visible to them, though himself unconscious of their communion."—

It seemed to me, whether it was a parable or an experience, a beautiful expression of the great spiritual law by which all who love one another are united, who are at one on any high theme of thought— It was delightful to think that only when worthy of our departed friends did we become visible to them—& on the other hand—that to *heaven* we mounted on the wings of universal truth—We were surely in their presence.—

But nature requires solace also—and I am thankful to think of you as a part of Catherine's family, where you can have around you the young people who were associated with Foster's pleasures—who loved him—& love you—and will always be attentive to you—

Did you happen to see by the papers, that old Mr Pickens, in dying, left both to Mary & myself each a thousand dollars? This will was made in 1858 and I had hardly seen him for twenty years. It reminded me so strongly of Lydia;—for I think his interest in *us* was but the postscript of his interest *in her,* of whom he had always known—& whose beauty & orphanhood very deeply touched his heart.—He had

---

1888) is unclear. It may be that the manuscript she showed to Mann in January 1838 is the same one Samuel Haven misplaced, and that the rewritten manuscript eventually found its way into print in the 1888 *Lectures.*

outlived his consciousness of identity & died in the Asylum but in every luxury, cared for by his friend James Read—and he was the only man to whom he left any thing in his will! All the rest was to *women*—many of whom were daughters of his friends—It is wonderful how many widows and old maids he has left *comfortable;* & he seemed never to have forgotten a kindness.—

A few years ago I had a present of a $1000 from some nameless friend who put the money with Wm Hull Clarke to be invested—& it has always brought me a hundred dollars a year—These two *legacies* of Foster's & Mr. Pickens's which I feel to have come as it were from Lydia, make me quite rich—while I keep this kindergarten I have a little more—But I think I shall not keep another year but *retire upon my fortune*—a part of which is my home in Mary's house—as long as she lives.

Mr Pickens made it a provision of his bequests to all ladies—that no husbands—present—past—or to come—should have any interest in them! I hope I shall see you when you come to Boston. I am always to be seen at ½ past 1, & on Saturdays at 12 o'clock (my closing hours)—

Yours truly ELIZ. P. PEABODY

MS, MWA

Another attempt to interest the literary establishment in the work of Hitchcock, and an indication of the curious byways that Peabody's philosophical idealism would lead her down.

✳ To Henry Wadsworth Longfellow

Follen Street

My dear Sir,   January 20, 1867

I send you herewith a copy of the last work of Gen. Hitchcock[1] which he sent as a new Year's gift to Mrs. Mann, because I want some-body to read it who will be interested in it & think you can hardly fail to be so—It is probably the last thing the dear old man will write—He thinks it is so—for within the year he had had a fall which has very

[1] Ethan Allen Hitchcock, *Notes on the Vita Nuova and Minor Poems* (New York, 1866).

seriously jarred his nervous system. But I think it is the book that has done *best* justice to his theory of interpretation of some of the greatest poets as well as of the authors of mystic books—And if he had published this before he did the work on Shakespear[e]'s Sonnets and the one on Spenser's Colin Clout &c[2] I think those volumes would have attracted more attention—I think there is a great deal of most interesting suggestion in all *three* books and I think he adduces a great deal of good arguments for his general idea—I was very much struck with the book on the Alchemists—you know probably that he believes Alchemy was a symbolic language by which *philosophers of* the Spirit hid from profane Jupiters, working by strength & Force merely & Vulcan, the prophecies of Prometheus painfully uttered through the cycles of earthly life—

But do read this book and *if* you do like it I wish you would write & tell *him* so—if you cannot write & tell the *Public* so—

It seems to me a most interesting fact that all three of these books on Shakespeare, Spenser, & Dante have been written there at Washington in the midst of all the political & military turmoil of the last six years. Gen H was there first as private counsellor of Mr. Lincoln & Mr. Stanton—though with no official power—or we should not have had the disastrous campaign on the Peninsula—which was only not *fatal* because he was there (as I should like to prove to you by telling you what I know of the secret history, if you should like to hear)—during the nervous strain of that time—and later during the agony of his official term (being Commissioner of prisoners) he could with difficulty sleep—& rested only by having *in the night* these Poetic Studies—for he kept his books & notebooks on a table beside him—& thus escaped the miseries of the *nightwatches*—

This Philosophy which he believes did voluntary move harmonious numbers in the three poets—is *his philosophy*—which he feeds upon—And is it not almost peculiarly American—that there should be a union of Apollos lute with the military trumpet—& of Platonic lore with the military science in which he is an adept[?]—For his strong Yankee commonsense inherited from his grandfather Ethan Allen is no less marked in his very highly respectable military career—than his love for these still studies—

I write this note in a hurry for Mrs. Ames to take—& so please

2 Ethan Allen Hitchcock, *Remarks on the Sonnets of Shakespeare* (New York: J. Miller, 1865); idem, *Spenser's Poem; Entitled Colin Clout Come Home Againe, Explained* (New York: J. Miller, 1865).

excuse its *incondita carmina*—I wish you would *yourself* bring it back when you have read it

Yours truly

ELIZABETH P. PEABODY

MS, MH

✖ To [Rebecca Amory] Lowell

New York City,

My dear Miss Lowell,— June 2 [1867]

I was unexpectedly detained a day longer in Boston by the mistake of a mantua maker; and I grieve to say I did forget that I had as it were appointed a meeting with you—But I did not probably think you would go—& so I did not think to countersay it—as in one or two other instances—I can only say for excuse that I was very much confused at the last moment. But I am very glad to get the *letters* & very much obliged—

I found here when I arrived last night a letter from you—from Mr. Snelling—& from poor Mad. Solger herself.[1]—I cannot think there can be *law anywhere* for a person to forfeit a house for which they have paid as she has ever since Dr S died or was disabled. No notice was ever served to her those two years—that she ever knew of—& of course she did not know of the advertisements. Dr Solger had his life insured & the $2000 was paid her & she went straight to Mr. Hooper & paid what he had advanced who had paid the bill before it was due in order to deliver her from prison who had sold the house & wanted to get it back again. This is a clear case of a swindling trick by some desperate rascal who takes advantage of her helplessness. I have already written the whole account of the matter to a noble & gifted young lawyer of Washington—Marcellus Bailey—& begged him to go to her at once & see all about it—telling him how entirely every cent has been honorably paid that she knew was due & I feel sure she will be righted—

I do not know whether you know that the first $1000 paid on

---

[1] Madame Solger was the widow of German émigré Reinhold Solger, scholar, author, and politician, who died in 1866. Madame Solger was subject to mental depression, and her ability to discipline her children after her husband's death declined rapidly.

that house was borrowed from some men—Germans I believe principally—for whom Dr. Solger obtained places as treasury clerks—& who immediately when he was sick came to dun him—& whom she kept at bay by paying monthly *all the salary* which she received (getting the rest of her living by the boarders & her french scholars) & she *promised them* she would pay all if they would not torment him. She has continued to pay ever *since* by these [word obscured] statements & lately told me she had still three hundred dollars to pay.—She is therefore without means to buy off these men & they would not to be bought off.—She says now her french lessons stop & her boarders diminish for the summer.—But she has just received a letter from me in which I spoke as usual a great deal of her husband & she says that has comforted her so much (the sympathy) that she feels calmer—& has sent to the lawyer to see if he would not adjust it. I do not know his name or character & so I have asked Mr Bailey to go & see about it. She will do all that can be done & I have written to her that I have done so.—

Mrs. Dana is perfectly friendly to Mrs. Solger—& perfectly sincere subjectively—but I must tell you that she is not *reliable* being a victim of epileptic fits & always in a state of *insanity*—though not perhaps of *derangement*—Should you ever see & talk with her you would perceive that this is so—& I happen to know it & so does Mrs. Solger—who discovered her insanity by her own observation before she was told of it by me *with its cause.* I do not doubt however that there is something very important in her report of *Julius.*[2] I know he is utterly uncontrollable by his mother—and by *himself.* So powerful is his temperament & so wholly undisciplined as he has always been Dr. Solger has very false theories with respect to his duties as husband and father though the most & proper *feelings*—& he trusted too implicitly to circumstances to instruct the mind—& was too jealous of using her personal influence over their thinking. Hence Mrs. Solger never knew the grounds of her Protestant faith but only her anti-catholicism & the children had no clear ideas of duty given to them. Julius needed this especially being passionate rather than intellectual & poor Mrs. Solger has neither the comforts of Protestant or Catholic religion & realises nothing in the universe greater than her own broken heart—which is to me such a testimony to the reality of the GOD who is Love. I have written to Mrs. Solger that we have all—you—Mrs. Snelling & I—all

2 That is, Julius Solger, son of Madame Solger.

her friends—heard rumours of his dangerous condition—& we think that someplace must be found where he can go & be educated—feeling the control over him of a strong will—& having his mind trained to self discipline or he will be ruined, and that no money he can earn now should be put in competition with it. I have therefore prepared her for any suggestion her friends may make—& I shall speak to Mr Kapp about it—Dr Solger's German friend in New York—Mrs Solger will not be surprised at my advice to her about Julius because his faults are a common subject between us—He has a good heart & loved her as many another undutiful son loves his mother—but having no self control constantly distresses her. Mrs. Ripley is all but dead & Mrs. Simmons can do nothing but nurse her—& does not attempt it— having taken her to her house—while Elizabeth keeps the old manse & has a family to board with her in which she is much interested— Julius needs a man to take care of him—I wish there were a Schnop- penthal here—I suppose you have read that delightful life of Carl Ritter—by Gage Published by Scorbener—as well as Lessings Life— If not you have a great treat in both.[3]

I have just got another heartbreaking note from Mrs. Solger—& now she has got $500 to earn and pay—for she still has 300 of those other debts. I trust she will not die. But such shocks as these are kill- ing—I will enclose her note—When you see Mr Snelling show it to him—& keep it for me if it should prove the last—Well—GOD reigns!
Yours truly E. P. PEABODY

MS, VtMiM

[3] The books referred to are William Leonard Gage, *The Life of Carl Ritter* (London, 1867) and Karl Gotthelf Lessing, *G. E. Lessings Leben* (Berlin, 1793–95).

Peabody confides in Conway her belief, which Sophia shared, that Hawthorne's publishers had been cheating him and his widow out of legitimate royalties.

✄ To Moncure Conway[1]

Cambridge
[1868]

They should have given but £100 for this new book—They gave at least £250 for the Old Home which has *all* been printed in the Atlantic Monthly—while only a small part of this had been.—Could you believe that in the last 17 years during which *all* Hawthornes novels have been written,—he should have got *less* than 17000 dollars;—when Washington Irving's family have received for his, including only one new one (Washington's Life which was not very saleable) $150,000 dollars? Some years when the novels were first published—they received 3 or 4000 dollars—in others *not a hundred* For 14 years they did not *once* have an account of sales—though Sophia begged for it a great deal—and it was always promised—She got startled by hearing from Fields that though he was not *quite sure* he believed Fields & Elder gave £100 for the Old Home—because she did have in her possession the letter that enclosed £250 for *that* in the handwriting of either Ticknor or Fields—& by two other circumstances—and this was the reason she wished to know about that fact & wrote to me but I did not get the letter till I was at Liverpool & so delegated the errand to W.[illiam] H.[enry] C.[hanning]—I wish you would find out and also ask them what terms they will offer for the English & Italian journals—For Sophia is very much inclined to break with Fields entirely and in that case—Smith & Elder might make their bargain with Ticknor & Fields or perhaps Putnam & Co to publish them in America at the same time. I am not empowered to make any bargain with them— But Sophia has now for the first time taken me as her business advisor and wants to know what I think. I cannot tell unless I can know what

1 Moncure Conway, who was born into a southern Methodist slave-holding family, changed both his politics and his theology after a Harvard Divinity School education. From 1863 to 1884, he served South Place Chapel in London, a liberal congregation. In 1884, he returned to the United States, but took up the South Place Chapel post again from 1892 to 1897.

Smith & Elder have done in the past & will do in the future   You may consult them if you can make them say they will not consult Fields—in whom Sophia has lost all her confidence. This is a delicate business but I think you can use your genius to do it—Sophia has no dependance for her future except on the income of these books and the house in Concord which she has not yet been able to rent or sell—& it is *five* years before Julian will be educated to his profession at the Polytechnik school in Dresden[2]—*People say* that Ticknor & Fields have grown rich on Hawthorne's books—This is probably an exaggeration   *They say* they have made less than they have credited to Sophia   This is poor encouragement for first class literary Art!—if *all* Hawthorne's works will not bring to both publisher & author but three fifths of what Charles Reade[3] gets for *one novel* before a copy is sold! Give my love to Dear Mrs. Conway who procured me the greatest pleasure I had in Europe in my interviews with Mazzini—yours truly E. P. Peabody

MS (incomplete), NNC

2 Julian Hawthorne had a difficult time deciding on a career. In 1866, he was asked to leave Harvard because of his poor record, enrolled in the Lawrence Scientific School to pursue a career in engineering, but found the courses there primarily on geology and zoology. Julian proposed going to the Dresden Realschule, and his mother agreed. The Hawthornes sailed in October 1868. He spent a year learning German technical vocabulary (in considerably less time than his aunt Elizabeth had predicted), and returned to New York. In November 1870, he married May Amelung, whom he had met in Dresden.

3 Charles Reade was a popular English dramatist and novelist, author of *The Cloister and the Hearth* (1861).

Peabody refers again to Sophia's battle with her late husband's publishers and hints at her own self-imposed assignment as defender of the reputations of her Transcendental colleagues.

✺ To Moncure Conway

My dear Mr Conway   May 18th 1869

I am afraid that I did not say to you what I did to every body else with whom I spoke of the little errors—or rather of your preface about Mr Hawthorne & Brook farm[1] viz—that the article did more justice to the idea &c of the latter than any thing else I ever saw written about it—And also that I felt it to be a great tribute to Mr Hawthorne's genius—though I *did to you* [word illegible] against your associating that monstrous deformity of Lord Byron with the merely possible furry ears of that exquisite creation Donatello—And my sister Sophia felt so too *about this point*—& told me how horrified Mr Hawthorne was with Trelawny's treachery[2] & the painful *fact*—while Donatello was a darling fancy of his—playing on the border land of humanity & nature—

My sister spoke gratefully of your letter & kind offers—& ought to have written to you but she had had a wretched winter—*in health* & always speaks of weary hand & brain *in copying*—for she says nobody but herself can ever go to Hawthorne's journals & she feels it a duty to the world to copy all that can be made public at any future time— It is *all* exquisite, she says—She speaks of this as a reason for not writing even *to us* as she would like to do—

Mr Hillard advises her to have all her transactions with Smith & Elder privately & by her own correspondence   Please do not speak of her plans—or name her if you can help it to *Fields*—who is in England—I hear Mazzini has returned to England and I suppose you see

1 Peabody refers to Conway's "Concerning Hawthorne and Brook Farm," *Every Saturday,* 2 January 1869, 13–18. A sympathetic account of Hawthorne's life, especially focusing on his association with Brook Farm, Conway's essay includes a quotation from Trelawny's recollections of Byron and Shelley about examining the body of Byron, and discovering that "both his feet were clubbed, and the legs withered to the knee: the form and face of an Apollo, with the feet and legs of a Sylvan Satyr." Conway adds: "I am as certain as if he told me so, that in this sentence lay the germ of the character of Donatello, 'the Marble Faun,' in Transformation" (p. 17).

2 The English illustrator Trelawny had apparently taken some liberties in his drawings for *Transformation,* the 1860 London version of *Marble Faun.*

him—Give him my reverent remembrance—We had in the Anti-Slavery Standard his letter in reply to the slanders of him—beautiful as ever.—Don't you think we are going on nicely in America? Do you have all our papers? I hear our new President Elliot of Harvard U is going to organize lectures on great subjects to post graduates—to which women are admitted—

Give my love to dear Mrs Conway to whom I suppose Mary will write. Mrs R. Apthorp is going to spend the supper with Mrs Cobbe.

Yours ever E.P.P.

MS, NNC

An introduction to German educator Emma Marwedel, and an early expression of what Peabody had learned on her tour of German kindergartens.

✹ To Gerrit Smith

My dear Mr. Smith—   Cambridge July 12th [1869]

Mr. May, who has become my neighbour in Cambridge was here the other day and introduced to a German lady[1]—who is at present staying with us, & who interested him extremely, in speaking to him of her ideas of the reform of female education—and showed him a plan she has made out of an institution for the horticultural Education of Women to be selfsupporting. He asked her for a copy of this plan & its preamble which she gave to him and which he said he should send to you—

Now I want to say a word about this lady to whom I was introduced in Germany as one of the very foremost & wisest & most practical of the Reformers—having spent many years in studying the best

[1] Emma Marwedel was born in Munden, near Göttingen, Germany. By the time Peabody met her in Hamburg in 1867 she was a disciple of Froebel and a crusader for new forms of education. She emigrated to the United States at Peabody's urging, tried unsuccessfully to establish a training school for kindergartners in New York. In 1870, Marwedel set up a cooperative industrial school near Brentwood, Long Island; that, too, failed. In 1871, she established a private school, which included a kindergarten training program in Washington, D.C., and in 1876 opened a model kindergarten and training school in California. She retired from teaching in 1885, and died in 1893 of "senile gangrene," brought on by malnutrition caused by poverty and her total absorption in the kindergarten movement.

methods of ameliorating and elevating women in Germany England Belgium and France—And who was strongly advised to come to America—by Mr Adolph Meier brother of Carl Schurz' wife who had been in America and thought it was the only place where there was opportunity & scope to do justice to her ideas.

She is a very remarkable person—her heart absolutely *inflamed* with love—& her head as clear and reasonable as if she were of coolest temperament—very variously & highly cultivated. Her desire is to go into the work herself & she feels sure that she could make the plan succeed through her great moral power over people to make them work— wh[ich] I *saw* in Europe when she was at Hamburgh—

She lost one of her trunks on her arrival which has embarrassed her—But her ability to teach German &c prevented her from despair & she went into the family of Mrs. Severance for a few months by invitation, where she became at once the Providence of the house—by the sympathy & practical help which she gave to each & every member of the family—And Mrs. Severence thinks it very much of a pity that she should be hindered by teaching German from going on with her work   She was then a guest for some weeks of the daughter of Ellis G. Loring, who went just now to Germany to join her husband, & wanted to be able to talk German—And since then she has been with us—& certainly there never came into a house such a universal helper & sympathiser—And she proved herself to all of us a most womanly woman— & capable of being the inspirer and Providence of a *home*—I do think she is a woman whom you would wholly sympathise with and like— And I want you to know her *personally*—She is invited to take the Editorship of a German woman's paper in New York for $10 a week!! & will go there in September if she cannot immediately do anything more effective for the carrying out of her plans & Mrs. Livermore in Chicago thinks it would be a great thing for her to go & lecture to the German women of the west, whose prejudices are a great stumbling block of the woman's cause there. This she is willing to do—But the selfsupporting Horticultural School somewhere she thinks would be the most useful thing to get agoing—I have thought it might be made an appendage to the Ithaca (Cornell) University where the women could have the advantage of the lectures & classes of the University. One of the difficulties of having women at the university is I believe the difficulty of providing them with suitable domicile. Such an institution might become the boarding house of the women students and they might support themselves wholly or in part by cooperating in the housekeeping & garden—If ever there was a person who could make such a thing *go,* it is *she*—with her great tender heart, and large liberal ideas, and practical ability—& varied talents—

My year in Europe gave me great opportunities to see plans of social origination of various kinds, & all the time I was there my feeling *grew* deeper & my thought more comprehensive of the American opportunity—I directed my attention especially to Froebels Reform of Primary Education & came home determined to devote the remainder of my life to getting it agoing in America everywhere that I could—Its great idea is to educate children by employing the physical activities *in production*—not mechanically—but by a constant supervision—giving rules that become ideas—which inspire them to invention in the most gentle and genial way—by *doing*—they learn the laws of action—& become intellectual in their habits of mind while they become expert in every species of manipulation. They begin to produce & even invent at three years old—& what things they produce are in the sphere of childish fancy and affection so they are not taken out of the radiant mist of childhood, while they are made able & intelligent workers—& always work with reference to giving pleasure or being useful to others.—This work employs them till they are seven, & the materials they use become objects of instruction opening their minds into every field of knowledge from their own stand-point. I should admire to tell you of the beauty of these well taught kindergartens whose teachers have to go through a preliminary training of a really profound character—which is the very education for mothers and for *all women*—for women[,] actually mothers or not[,] are always in the maternal relation to society—

The primary education of Froebels is the first step in both industrial & literary education—which *last* never begins in Germany till children are seven years of age—And when it begins they have been prepared by kindergarten to do every thing intelligently—knowing how to apply mean to ends & to reason, and produce by the application of laws. *I have seen* it all *done*—And now it is my first object to fill with students the normal school for kindergartners kept by Mrs Kriege in Boston, whose daughter—thoroughly trained in the training school of Berlin—keeps the kindergarten.[2]—I have some faint hope

---

2 Peabody met Matilda and Alma Kriege on her first European trip. Impressed with their work as students of the Baroness Marenholtz-Bülow academy for kindergartners, she invited them to Boston to work in her Pinckney Street school. Preceding Peabody back to the United States, the Krieges soon became the dominant elements in the school. They added a training school in 1868, and moved the establishment to 127 Charles Street.

too that some of the Peabody fund for Southern Education may be used to make another of these training schools in Baltimore for Dr Barnard[3] says it is a great pity that the schools of the South & South-West to be established should repeat the mistake of the one sided schools of New England that practically sharpen the wits without elevating the moral tone, or educating the activities to any thing worthy the name of *men's work*. But a true education will keep all the powers of man in harmony & issue in *production*—If it begins on artistic principle it will go on so—and at length give labour its true dignity by identifying the artisan & artist as they were identified in the great ages of classic & mediaeval Art—

But I must ask your pardon for lengthening out my letter which I began only to interest you to make Miss Marwedel's acquaintance personally—yours with affectionate reverence Eliz. P. Peabody

One word more: I am getting printed with a preface of my own—a remarkable paper of Cardinal Wiseman's on the connection of the Arts of design with the Arts of production—[4]

I am getting one of the Labor reform printers to publish an edition of 5000—so that it may be a cheap tract which people will buy by the hundred & spread among the work people—& the work people themselves *will buy*—It strikes me that labour is not to be elevated by making the hours of labour few—or increasing its wages so much as by making the labour itself *Art* as it becomes when it is done by *attraction* & according to the principles of Eternal order & Beauty for the glorification of the labourer—Cardinal Wiseman proves this I think by historical & biographical illustration.

MS, NSyU

[3] Henry Barnard, as noted earlier, was an advocate of public education and founder of the *American Journal of Education,* excerpts of which he collected into the fifty-two volume *Library of Education.*
[4] That is, "The Identification of the Artisan and the Artist a Proper Object of American Education, with a Plea for Froebel's Kindergarten as the First Grade of Primary Education, by Elizabeth P. Peabody," Boston, 1869.

West Street, Boston, looking up toward Bedford Street,
away from the Common. Elizabeth Palmer Peabody ran her
West Street bookshop, which became an intellectual center,
in the front parlor of her family's house at No. 13 West
Street, on a narrow block between Tremont and Washington
Streets.
(*Courtesy of the Bostonian Society, Old State House*)

Margaret Fuller, who held conversations in the West Street
bookshop.
(*Concord Free Public Library*)

Ralph Waldo Emerson
(*Sophia Smith Collection, Smith College*)

"THE NEST."

The Nest, one of the Brook Farm buildings.
(*Concord Free Public Library*)

BROOK FARM BUILDINGS.   *Copyright, 1910, by M. G. Cutter.*

Brook Farm buildings,
after a contemporary drawing by Mary Caroline Crawford.
(*Concord Free Public Library*)

Portrait of George Ripley,
Unitarian minister, and friend
of Elizabeth Peabody.
(*Courtesy of the Boston Athenaeum*)

William Torrey Harris, an educator
and idealist philosopher with whom
Elizabeth Peabody corresponded.
(*Concord Free Public Library*)

Elizabeth Palmer Peabody with William Torrey Harris.
(*Concord Free Public Library*)

Engravings showing the experimental movement with which Elizabeth Peabody is identified: (*top*) "Group in a New York Free Kindergarten" and (*bottom*) "Making Cylinders in Clay" (From Talcott Williams, "The Kindergarten Movement," *The Century Magazine* [January 1883].)

Elizabeth Palmer Peabody with Mr. and Mrs.
Daniel Lothrop and Margaret Lothrop.
(*Concord Free Public Library*)

Elizabeth Palmer Peabody
(*Concord Free Public Library*)

6

1870s

The Kindergarten

IN JULY 1870, Elizabeth Peabody gave an address to the Principals' Association in Chicago entitled "Genuine Kindergartens Versus Ignorant Attempts at It," and in that same year described her earlier Pinckney Street school as "an ignorant therefore—as *to the end* proposed—*unsuccessful* attempt."[1] Peabody took very personally the spread of "pseudokindergartens," as she described them, in the United States. Having seen the authentic school, those established by Friedrich Froebel and his followers, "she felt that she must give the rest of her life to the work of abolishing the mischief she had done, and of spreading the true thing in her native land. For the popularity and some good points of her school, together with her book, [*Moral Culture of Infancy and Kindergarten Guide*]—of which the publisher who owned it had sold 4,000 copies,—had multiplied imitations more or less happy all over the land."[2] Peabody repeated her Chicago address in Watertown, Wisconsin, home of the Schurzes, but regretted missing William Torrey Harris, superintendent of the St. Louis public schools, whom she hoped to persuade to establish a kindergarten program within the St. Louis system.[3] Later she wrote him an astonishing barrage of letters, most of them on kindergartening.

Peabody more than matched her tours with a prodigious output of publications. Her articles on the kindergarten were carried in many periodicals; pamphlets and tracts carried her gospel; the federel government even had a hand in the production of two. Her essay "Kindergarten Culture" appeared as part of the *Annual Report for 1870* of the U.S. Commissioner of Education. Peabody spent from January to March 1871 in Washington, D.C., "at the invitation of Com[missioner] Eaton, in order to be a general *Referee* on the subject of: Froebel's kindergartening; whose great claims upon thinking people have begun to appear," as she wrote to Gerrit Smith.[4] Her work, she thought, was not in vain. The Senate ordered 20,000 copies of the 1870

1 Elizabeth Peabody to Anna Ward, [ca. 1870], MS, MH.
2 Elizabeth Peabody, "The Origin and Growth of the Kindergarten," *Education* (May 1882): 524.
3 Elizabeth Peabody to William Torrey Harris, 25 August 1870, MS, MoSHI.
4 Elizabeth Peabody to Gerrit Smith, 8 February 1871, MS, NSyU. On the rise of kindergartening in America, see Baylor, *Elizabeth Palmer Peabody*, 95–118; *Kindergarten and Child Culture Papers: Pioneers of the Kindergarten in America*, ed. by the Committee of Nineteen, International Kindergarten Union (New York: Century Co., 1924); Snyder, *Dauntless Women*, 19–181; Evelyn Weber, *The Kindergarten: Its Encounter with Educational Thought in America* (New York: Teachers College Press, 1969), 18–92.

annual report.[5] Her stay in Washington also led to an essay, "The Kindergarten," which the Bureau of Education published in July 1872. In the private sector, businessmen such as the games manufacturer Milton Bradley and publishers such as Ernst Steiger made available the teaching devices and instructional material needed for kindergartens. The arrival of Froebellians from Germany was a further boost, among them Matilde and Alma Kriege, who had taken over the Pinckney Street school in 1868 and established a training school for teachers there; Emma Marwedel, an utterly devoted and single-minded advocate of Froebel's method; and Maria Boelte, with whose niece Amelia Boelte Peabody later corresponded. By the mid-1870s, a network of kindergarten training schools had sprung up, with Peabody as a genial guardian of the purity of instruction. The kindergarten also flourished in the Midwest, principally under the leadership of Susan Blow in St. Louis and William Hailmann in Milwaukee.[6]

Peabody's description of Froebel's system in her May 1882 article in *Education* provides a useful summary of the many such descriptions in other publications. She began with the standard Romantic division of the self into Reason and Understanding, Reason (or imagination, as she called it), being spontaneous, Understanding developing through education. The notion that imagination is prior to understanding is not original with Froebel, she noted. What his followers "do claim for him [is] the exceptional practical ability of so applying those [philosophical and spiritual] truths as to guide children to grow into an equipoise of heart and mind that shall produce productive activity in individuals, and harmonious progressive society."[7]

Balancing the child's inner truth with the requirements of outer growth demands an unusual teacher, one who subsumes her own personality to that of the divine. "Hence the preparation of the kindergartner comprises religious and moral, as well as intellectual, exercise on her own part." Peabody insisted, here and elsewhere, that education, especially on the kindergarten level, was spiritual and moral at root. Indeed, echoing her Romantic colleagues, she likened educating the child to the Second Coming: "Is not this method of developing the human being, perhaps the second coming of Christ, whose triumphs, the prophet says 'a little child shall lead'? Is the Christ-child anything but *childhood received* in the name of Christ?" What distin-

---

5 Elizabeth Peabody to William Torrey Harris, 28 March 1871, MS, MoSHI.
6 Peabody, "Origin and Growth," 507–8.
7 Ibid., 511.

guishes Froebel is his method, his use of shapes, games, music, and dance to awaken the intuitive elements of consciousness. "In virtue of the fact that the mind is generated by the Creator of the Universe, it is of the same essence, and has, in germs of thought, all the variety of the Universe; these germs are to be vivified by being touched into life when the things are presented to the senses."[8] Thus the kindergarten movement represents an important form through which philosophical idealism was sustained in the postwar period and disseminated to the population. Eventually, the spiritual emphasis in the movement was challenged and discarded, but in the 1870s and 1880s the spread of Froebellian kindergartens acted as a countertrend to the naturalism of Darwinism and material abundance.

The kindergarten movement sustained the antebellum stress on women's nurturing and educative identity. Kindergartners, it was universally assumed, were women whose service to the culture involved tending like votaries the divine flame in the young. As Berthe Marenholtz-Bülow, Froebel's disciple and European protégée, put it, "with the knowledge that a divine spark slumbers in the little being on her lap, there must kindle in her a holy zeal and desire to fan this spark into a flame, and to educate for humanity a worthy citizen. With this vocation of educator of mankind is bound up everything needful to place women in possession of the full rights of a worthy humanity."[9]

Peabody left for Europe again in September 1871 and talked with English kindergartners. As she wrote to her friend Susan Cole upon her return, she was ill for several months in London "but thought by going to Rome I escaped the worst month as it proved in England. I was too much run down to be better for the journey (tho I did not lose the main object of it which was to see the Baronness Marenholtz . . .)—and when I came back I was so prostrated that my physician gave me no encouragement that I should be better there in time to enjoy the summer, & joined with my nephew George [Mann] in persuading me to come home with him."[10]

The Froebellians desired to defend their system and the name "kindergarten" against competitors, to establish and preserve, in other words, an educational orthodoxy. Peabody was at the center of such efforts. She had, of course, already been involved in earlier educational experimenting—in the 1830s with Bronson Alcott and in the early

8 Ibid., 518.
9 Berthe Marenholtz-Bülow, "Froebel's Educational Views," in *Kindergarten and Child Culture Papers*, 169.
10Elizabeth Peabody to Susan Cole, 10 July [1872], MS, MSaE.

1860s with the "false kindergarten." In 1871 she wrote to Alcott several times about a third edition of *Record of a School*, wishing to establish some distance between Alcott's introspective method and Froebel's approach. She insisted on a new preface and appendix to explain her own evolution, but the publisher Roberts Brothers refused, prompting Peabody to write angrily from London: "The Record of a School in its day was a genuine part of my life—whose latter development is my view of Froebel's kindergarten—which starts from the *same ground*—but—that the most important study for the educator is the *nature of the child*—which is looked at in other relations by Froebel than Mr Alcott looked at it in 1836—"[11]

In December 1874, unable to maintain her magazine *Kindergarten Messenger*, she allowed it to become a department of the *New England Journal of Education*. But the editor of this journal permitted competing teachers to advertise in his pages, and within a year Peabody withdrew in protest. As she explained to Harris, "You see that I have left the Journal of Education and am going to set up by myself again. It was not that Mr. Bicknell took into his advertising column Miss Coe's boastful & deceptive advertisement—but that he gave it the puff editorial & would not let me clear myself by allowing *my counter* advice about training to go into the columns of which I had the editorial responsibility."[12] In January, she began her *Kindergarten Messenger* again, repeating in the first number her quarrel with the *Journal of Education*, and in 1878 she joined with William Hailmann to form the *Kindergarten Messenger and the New Education*.

This unfortunate association with "unauthorized teachers" was not Peabody's first encounter with the competition. In 1870 or thereabouts, she wrote to Anna Ward that "pseudokindergartens have prejudiced some & misled others into what was mere trifling," among which she had to count her own Pinckney Street school. But stern measures were called for now that the Froebellian truth was known: "The practical point for the moment is to have 24 children . . . be offered for the kindergarten in 5th Avenue—right in the vicinity of Miss Coe's pseudokindergarten."[13] After her brief alliance with the *Journal of Education*, Peabody realized how rapidly other kindergarten efforts had spread. At the Centennial Exposition in Philadelphia in 1876, a rival system calling itself the American kindergarten was ad-

11 Elizabeth Peabody to Mr. Roberts, 28 September [1871], MS, MH.
12 Elizabeth Peabody to William Torrey Harris, 10 January [1877], MS, MoSHI.
13 Elizabeth Peabody to Anna Ward, [1870], MS, MH.

vertised, and Peabody was appalled that Harris himself "spoke of the adoption of the method into the American public schools—as *Americanizing it*—& I hope before you drop the subject you will distinctly say that by *Americanizing* it *you* do not mean departing from Froebel's principle." Kindergartening "cannot be a different thing in Germany & America." Indeed, Froebel believed his method was more suited to American conditions than to German.[14]

As a further attempt at establishing some accountability in kindergartening (remembering that it was a part of public, private, and charity systems), Peabody and her colleagues founded the American Froebel Union in 1878. As she explained to Harris, "the great object of the Society is first to raise the standard of *qualification*." Equally, the Froebellians wished to give their imprimatur to a "Standard Library for the profession. . . . These are the Holy Scriptures—everything else comes in as commentary & development."[15] Such attempts at establishing and defending an orthodoxy prompted criticism, which Peabody promptly refuted. To her long-suffering correspondent Harris, she wrote, "You say you think that I never ought to commend any lady or school because it excites jealousy—But here I must differ—what are the reliable kindergartens & who are the reliable trainers—are the practical questions it is most important to answer—and no fair-minded decent person will be other than nobly stimulated, by just praise bestowed on others."[16] The Froebel Union likewise was a necessary arrangement whereby properly trained teachers could be certified and Froebellian books distributed. "We do not mean to be an impertinent meddling body—but merely *be* what we are[—]*a light of intelligence* pointing out the *sources* of knowledge & skill in this preparation of children for school, to those who ask."[17]

A glimpse of Elizabeth Peabody's appearance and manner in the 1870s comes from a memoir by Miss R. J. Weston published after Peabody's death in 1894. The writer recalled a gathering at Peabody's home on Follen Street in Cambridge to honor Peabody on her birthday. Her flaxen hair was turning silver, but her manner was youthful. Mary Mann was dressed, as usual, severely and in spotless daintiness, and Sophia Hawthorne's portrait looked down from the wall. "Miss Peabody always liked to express her indebtedness to Hawthorne for the help he gave her in her writing. He kept her from printing too

14 Elizabeth Peabody to William Torrey Harris, 19 January 1877, MS, MoSHi.
15 Elizabeth Peabody to William Torrey Harris, 19 February 1878, MS, MoSHi.
16 Elizabeth Peabody to William Torrey Harris, 5 February 1879, MS, MoSHi.
17 Elizabeth Peabody to William Torrey Harris, 19 April [1880], MS, MoSHi.

much, she was wont to say. . . . There was always a feeling of comradeship between them, which began in youth."[18] "Comradeship,"
however, hardly describes the relationship between Peabody and Hawthorne that existed while he was still living. But as the letters of this
section indicate, Peabody continued to work hard as in the 1860s to
preserve and defend Hawthorne's posthumous reputation. In the
1870s, Peabody launched yet another career, that of chronicler and in-
terpreter of her antebellum colleagues and acquaintances. Her version
of them, as the letters about Emerson and Hawthorne especially reveal, blurred their radical and critical edges, presenting their vision as
Peabody saw it—consonant with Victorian Christianity and social
values.

18 R. J. Weston, "A Birthday Visit," *Kindergarten News* (Springfield, Mass.) 4
(February 1894): 42.

Peabody requests a meeting with William Torrey Harris. She connects
Froebel's early childhood-education theories with Emerson's outlook
and with the work of the Spencerian E. L. Youmans.

✖ To William Torrey Harris[1]

Mr Harris—   Cambridge, Follen Str.
  My dear Sir—   May 18—1870
    I have often intended to write to you since I learned you were su-
perintendant of St Louis schools upon the subject of making Froebels
kindergarten a part of yr public school system—And now having
[been] persuaded by my explanations of the System & showing the
work I brought from Europe done by children in the kindergarten
under or *not over* seven years of age, our Boston Committee to decree

1 William Torrey Harris was born in Connecticut and attended Yale College.
In 1857, he began teaching in the St. Louis public schools and became superintendent
of schools in 1868. Harris became deeply involved in the study of German philosophy,
especially the work of Hegel, and saw in the application of Hegel's thought to all
areas of life, especially education, his lifework. In 1867, he founded the *Journal of
Speculative Philosophy*, which carried the first American translations of important
works of Hegel, Fichte, and Schelling. In 1880, he moved to Concord and assisted in
the running of the Concord School of Philosophy. Harris saw himself as Emerson's
successor and leader of a great idealist movement, but clearly philosophical idealism
was at an end. From 1889 to 1906, he served as U.S. Commissioner of Education.

the Experiment of one kindergarten of 25 children under a teacher trained by Mrs Kriege, I feel a great point is gained, & shall [should?] preach this gospel of the Second Advent elsewhere—Indeed I have effected that private kindergarten should be established in Baltimore Philadelphia New York New Bedford, Milton & Roxbury—You have in the Eliot school a Mrs Widdigan who was educated for it regularly in Germany I hear—& I wonder if you cannot begin in St. Louis—with one public one under Mrs. Widdigen—She must have an adequate salary & some appropriation for material—It is all covered in Boston— The teacher has $700 dollars—& another hundred is given for the materials—Perhaps it is only so much the first year because school furniture is to be provided—I am invited to the School Teachers' Convention in Chicago & to Watertown Wisconsin, in the first half of July to speak upon "Kindergarten versus ignorant attempts at it" I wish I could meet you at one of the places—I want to confer with you amazingly.

I am just now listening to Mr Emersons university course on the Natural history of the Intellect[2]—It is also Froebels doctrine that the Will & heart are given blind but infinite scope in the instance of every child but the intellect is born in time by meeting the Infinite Intelligence at what is called matter—not without human intervention by sympathy and *advice* given with strict regard to the Eternal Laws of Order—

I was struck in the Essay on education appended to Youman's first book on Botany, just published by Appleton for children who know how to read and write by Miss Youmans making the same criticism on Pestalozzi's object teaching that Froebel does[3]—& which his method *avoids*—because there is no *development* of mind made by detached information—but things must be taught in *connections*—you will like the book & I hope it may supersede the present superficial object teaching. But Froebel has a deeper secret still in letting action precede thinking & then *thinking* go back to appreciate action, which prepares the mind to analyze Nature truly. Yours respectfully

Elizabeth P. Peabody

MS, MoSHI

2 Between April 26 and June 3, 1870, Emerson gave a series of lectures called "Natural History of the Intellect" as part of the University Lectures at Harvard. Emerson was very unhappy with this assignment, since it required organizing his essentially unsystematic thought.

3 Peabody's reference is to Eliza Ann Youmans, *The First Book of Botany: Designed to Cultivate the Observing Powers of Children* (New York, 1870).

An early, but typical Peabody letter, explaining Froebel, urging Harris to adopt kindergartens into the St. Louis system, and adding a recommendation for a German emigré scholar.

✎ To William Torrey Harris

Mr Harris   Cambridge Follen Str.
My dear Sir,   August 25th [1870]
    I was disappointed not to see you at Chicago nor Watertown, where I met excellent conventions, and a glad reception of my doctrine of primary education, which is just Froebel's reform of Primary Education—for which I make a plea at the end of Cardinal Wiseman's lecture "on the relations of the arts of Production with the Arts of Design"—Mr Crowe promised me he would give you that pamphlet, but I think you cannot have read it, or you would not say, as you do, in your letter to me, that St. Louis is too *hot* for the kindergarten culture of children!—If St. Louis is not too hot for children to be born there, it cannot be too hot for the mind as well as the body to grow on nature's plan of development, which is just Froebel's kindergarten plan—Miss Youmans in an essay at the end of her lately published book (by the Appleton's) called First Book of Botany describes Natures plan of simultaneous development of body and mind which she implies is *spontaneous* in both cases—but she does not seem to observe that neither in the case of the body or the mind does that earliest development take place except very fitfully & irregularly & sometimes so inadequately as to leave the child feebleminded, unless careful adult intervention assists—The child does not even walk of itself, like the little chicken & other inferior natures, but depends on the parental teaching, and certainly the mind never develops except in intercourse with more advanced minds—indicating that there is in the human race a certain solidarity—not inconsistent certainly with individuality—but whose evolution is necessary for the perfection of the individuality as well as of the race. I believe that your philosophy like mine conceives of *Nature*—not as an entity but as an *expression* of the Infinite Spirit building up the human understanding by positing its ideas in "the beauteous forms of things" whose totality point by point corresponds with the Infinite Consciousness with which it is the destiny of man to commune progressively forever—

Now the kindergarten culture comes in, as the first Human intervention, with the child,—and by so guiding its playful activity—in the production of forms—at first transient—and afterwards permanent as child's toys, as to lead it into artistic work as well as aesthetic enjoyment and prevent this prodigious force of blind will making disorder & originating evil—(as it must needs to before it *knows* any thing individual or sees any gradations or connection enabling to use material to produce effects)—it makes him a principle of order conscious at last of being an *intelligent cause*—not absorbed but in a mutually rejoicing communion with the First Cause.

Now it seems to me that *whatever the climate* this kind of culture must be indispensable to a perfect human development—and cannot begin too early It does begin in the thoughtful tender Mother's arms and is generally carried on with tolerable perfection for two or three months while she takes care of her own baby—but it needs to go on under all the nursery supervision—and as soon as the child craves the company of other children (that is certainly as early as three years old) it should have a gardener of the mind to help it to take possession of nature & a larger social environment,—and this is just kindergarten culture. I think you have let quite a prize slip thro your fingers in letting Mrs. Widdigen who was an expert in the art and something of an adept in the philosophy of Froebel—slip through your fingers though I am glad she is in California where I have friends who wish to get up a true kindergarten.

But still I hope to make you a convert to my system If you will read it—I will send to you a german pamphlet containing the Report of "The Philosophers Congress" which met at Frankfort-on-the-Main last September, and which after devoting four of its sessions to listening to Baroness Marenholtz-Bülow developing a whole system in its philosophic scientific artistic & humane bearings accepted it as the most advanced because the most radical word that had been pronounced on Educational method The Report was made by Professor von Fichte of Stutgaard, who is a son of the great philosopher.—Of all the Superintendents of Education you are the one I counted upon most certainly as an acceptor of this Idea. For two years I have been working to beat it into the brains of our Boston School Committee who have at length ordered one to be taught (a kindergarten I mean) by the teacher I chose for the crucial experiment out of a whole class that Mrs. Kriege had been teaching. I felt that was a great step taken, because this kindergarten would be a practical argument, and school committees in general cannot enter into the *a priori* philosophical argument.—But when out at the West I was agreeably surprised to find a large number of men who did enter into *the idea* and saw that if the adult did his duty to the child, it might be as perfect in its evolution from the first—as any of the unconscious forms of nature. It has been for ages accepted that the human being alone in the universe must needs be a developed conscious *disorder*—a depraved being—before it could see to choose between good & evil—or order & disorder—& begin a life in harmony with the Infinite Spirit,—it was amusing to see with what naively expressed delight the idea was accepted that children become causes of evil to themselves & others by the very nature that would make them causes of good if they were treated as living organisms instead of dead clay to be modelled by the will & according to the notions of others—

Now please do not throw this letter into your wastebasket as an idle dream but consider it seriously in the scientific point of view—when you will see, as I do, that a new Primary Education is necessary, as the underpinning of our Public school System—and that this will require a new special normal training—

There is one school for this in Boston—and I hope before long there will be another in the District of Columbia kept by the teacher from Lubec of which I speak in my Plea For I am glad to tell you that I am in a cordial correspondence on the subject with General Eaton and the Chairman of the Congressional Committee of Education who called on me when I was in Washington last winter to ask me if I could help them to some kindergarten teacher, for my Plea had made an impression on him and others.

But I will not write an interminable letter. I do not want to bore you on a subject on which I crave your sympathy & cooperation especially—

To change the subject—

You know perhaps that Dr. Eliot has invited to the Professorship of languages in Washington University Mr. Leopold Noa from London an exile from Berlin since 1848—though not a politician, and also his sister to teach in the Mary Institute. I hope you will make the acquaintance of Mr. Noa. He is an eminent scholar in ancient as well as modern languages—in science Mathematical & Natural and Musical—and a very superior & faithful teacher with a rare dignity of moral character—His sister is not only well educated but *original* and ideal— I think they are a great & valuable addition to the teaching force of St. Louis, and Mrs. Noa, who is an English lady, is a lovely artist in

pastells who is named as sometimes superior to Winterhalter in por-
traiture, and a very pleasing woman besides.
    I am very respectfully yours

ELIZABETH P. PEABODY

MS, MoSHI

---

*On her return from the first European tour, Peabody began to discrimi-
nate between those who taught according to the Froebellian method
and those who claimed the name of kindergarten illegitimately.*

✄ To Anna Hazard Barker Ward

My dearest Anna,   [1871?]
    I enclose to you some papers which I want you to look over and
be interested in—you have I suppose read Cardinal Wiseman's lecture
that I republished summer before last with my plea at the end for
Froebel's kindergarten[1] as the desirable indispensable *first step* to an
education artistic in scope & profoundly moral & religious in character
to be effected before the speculative intellect—is developed.—I have
been working to get this recognized for the last three years & not without effect—It has been initiated in the Boston Public system this fall
& I am here on the errand of getting it agoing in New York—where *it
is to be* properly stated through the Normal School next fall—But the
desideratum is one genuine private kindergarten under a trained
teacher as a visible argument & I have got the Principal of Rutger's
Institute to advertise one to begin in a week or so at 5th Avenue near
42nd Street—having engaged a thoroughly trained young girl for the
purpose (a niece of Mattie Griffith that *was*—Mrs Browne now). But
it is late in the season to begin—& pseudo kindergartens have prejudiced some & misled others into what was mere trifling (my own attempt in Pinckney Street was an ignorant & therefore—as to *the end
proposed—unsuccessful* attempt) & so I want every body I can influence to see the discrimination. I have not had a moment to go and see

1 *The Identification of the Artizan and the Artist: Contains a Plea for Froebel's
Kindergarten, by Elizabeth P. Peabody* (Boston: E. P. Peabody, 1869). The speculative
dating of this letter as 1871 comes from Peabody's comment regarding this pamphlet
which she republished "summer before last."

you—who have grandchildren & I know must have influence with many mothers—& I must go back to Boston *tomorrow*—So I send you these newspaper slips one of which will show you that eminent Catholics do not consider it *anticatholic* & that you can work for this cause with all your heart which as I believe will be found to be the unity of humanity and in the course of time compose all controversies. It is a *sine qua non* that this first kindergarten be at once filled up—*&* for the *Principal* of Rutgers Institute to be encouraged to make all liberal arrangements *for its being* done right. I write this because I shall miss seeing you I dare say.—If you have not seen Cardinal Wisemans lecture I will send it. But I sent Sam a little bundle of them—as soon as they were reprinted—If you have not read it this may sound abrupt & be unintelligible—but the within papers will explain—

The practical point for the moment is to have 24 children (little boys & girls between three & six nearer to three the better) be offered for the kindergarten in 5th Avenue—right in the vicinity of Miss Coe's pseudokindergarten—I hardly know but I am as much interested for the sake of little Miss Sattene as for the other reason[2]—for she has been trained on money I realised for the purpose—being Trustee for a *loan fund* to enable the right sort to get the special preparation necessary—& she is really the only person left of Miss Knight's class—for the New York experiment. I wish you could know her & her interesting mother & sister and little brother—

But it is the general & not a private interest which is the main thing—the *regeneration of humanity* by the second coming of the Christ-child—

Yours ever truly
ELIZABETH P. PEABODY

MS, MH

---

[2] Miss Coe was one of Peabody's competitors in the establishing of kindergartens, while Miss Sattene was one of the authentically trained kindergartners.

Peabody writes to Bronson Alcott, detailing her desired changes for a new edition of Record of a School.

✎ To A. Bronson Alcott

My dear Mr Alcott,   July 29th, 1871
    I was glad you were pleased with the new preface proposed—incorporating Louisa's sentences as a quotation from a letter, as it were.—[1]
    And I hope you will also sympathize with my exercise of my prerogative respecting my own book—*otherwise*—I have arranged to put it at the end of the Journal which makes the III chapter of the book,—the Conversation on Krummacher's Parable of the Caterpillar; & the reading lesson that follows.—
    And I want the Analysis to go in as the IVth Chapter I think it makes a most valuable part of the book—& that there is nothing objectionable in it. I put, in another place, your own subsequent expression of doubt as to its being a model for other teachers, but as your experiment it was legitimate & fair—& it is a most interesting psychological study from nature. It is perfectly in harmony with yourself—& shows the buds—of what has blossomed since;—& the expanded flower must not be ashamed of the crude bud. I retain too the sentences about Jesus Christ & the Bible,—& am only sorry that the fact of its being presented ⟨printed⟩ stereotyped, up to the 80th page makes it impossible to restore some passages which you had left out especially a part of the conversation on Elijah. In reading the book over again, I find it more interesting & valuable than I thought it was & I only would leave you

[1] None of the proposed changes went into the new edition of *Record of a School,* except for the preface to which Peabody refers. It begins with a letter from Louisa May Alcott, in which she points out that any praise of the pedagogy of Plumfield in *Little Men* should actually go to her father. Then Peabody goes on: "I find myself, however, in the somewhat embarrassing position of seeming to affirm some crude ideas of my own, inevitably mingled with the narrative, and which in thirty-six years have given place to clearer ones. While my maturer age endorses the instinct which led me to set forth so lovingly this actual and most genuine outgrowth of Mr. Alcott's mind, and I believe with him—now as then—that education must be moral, intellectual, and spiritual as well as physical, from the very beginning of life, I have come to doubt the details of his method of procedure; and I think he will not disagree with me that Froebel's method of cultivating children . . . is a healthier and more effective way than self-inspection." (*Record of Mr. Alcott's School,* 3rd ed. rev. [Boston: Roberts Brothers, 1874], 4).

some of *my own* which I think adds nothing of value—All that you & the children say is very good—is *invaluable* in its place even if it be sometimes not the best thing in itself

And then I propose to put into the Appendix such passages of the Explanatory preface as relate to your school—leaving out some reminiscences of my own school which are of no value—But I think even this Appendix had better all be left out—than to leave out the Analysis. I have taken an old *first* Edition that I have found in the house, and taken the chapter of the Analysis & struck out here & there a paragraph (for instance the one in which capital punishment was mentioned & one or two others & the N.B. which ⟨you have⟩ in the 2nd Ed. was incorporated into the 2nd chapter, speaking of discipline—& I find it makes 50 pages—I see by looking at the 2nd Edition that the analysis and the Chapter conclusion only make 54 pages of that larger print & I think it might all go in if printed directly from that & it would not make the whole book thus far *200 pages* or more than 200 pages even in this large print   I want to add an N.B. of about a page to that concluding chapter or perhaps it would be better to put it in the Appendix at the end of the Explanatory Ch.²

Then we might have an 100 pages of Appendix if we needed to—but I do not think that my Explanatory Preface so far as I want to print it & the Extract from the Conversations—on the Gospels—will make an 100 pages—& the smaller the book is—the better

I want you to consider however whether—if there is a chance of your printing a volume of those Conversations—it is not a pity to *anticipate* it by putting into *this book* your most brilliant chapter? I think this book may call for that—just as Louisa's book calls for this.

One word more. If you have the certificate of the copyright will you endorse on it these words & send it to me—as soon as possible for fear of accidents "Transferred to Eliz. P. Peabody—the Author. August—1871 A. B. Alcott." Truly your friend E. P. Peabody

MS, MH

2 Such an appendix never appeared.

Peabody expresses her growing anxiety that the new edition of Record of Mr. Alcott's School *will not reflect her changed philosophy of education.*

✦ To A. Bronson Alcott

Dear Mr Alcott   August 22 [1871]

I have heard you were in Cambridge and did not come & see me tho you went to Wilson's—I hope this does not mean that you feel hurt with me—He sent me the proof of the Preface & Concluding Chapter—But did I not send you an Appendix—& have you any objection to that? I hope there has been nothing that I have said about assuming my book which has seemed to you disrespectful or unkind— If you will tell me what you paid for taking out the copyright I will send you the money—I do not recollect what is the fee—

I gave Mary Peabody[1] that essay of Wiebe's[2] to read herself—for her own instruction & then to give you to read—But if you have read it will you please to return it to me—for it is the only one I have—and I am obliged to refer to it in writing some new ⟨letters⟩ lectures to deliver next month—

In the last Atlantic there is an article called American Life in Paris by Mrs. M. L. Putnam[3] in which she speaks of maternal education beautifully—But it is only the favored few who can give such education to their children & hence the necessity of kindergarten in that same Spirit—

It is to be observed that the bulk of your scholars were always older than kindergarten children whom Froebel meant should be under seven—so that his rule of not letting children go into the abstract— does not apply to your children—He was [number illegible] years old at the time the Record of a school was written & had not yet elaborated the kindergarten—or entirely devoted himself to children under seven— but his psychology & yours were identical—if the ideas expressed in my concluding chapter were yours—If you & he had met then—what

---

[1] Mary Peabody was brother Nathaniel's daughter.

[2] Edward Wiebe, *The Paradise of Children: A Manual for Self-Instruction in Friedrich Froebel's Educational Principles, and a Practical Guide to Kindergartners* (Springfield, Massachusetts, 1869).

[3] M. L. Putnam, series of articles on European Travel, *Atlantic* 27: 92–101, 232–40, 468–77, 715–25; 28: 276–87.

friends you would have been—Your doctrine about studying children
was his practice

In haste yours

ELIZABETH P. PEABODY

Excuse this ink—Is not the modern *ink* fatally evanescent?

MS, MH

Peabody's anger at Alcott for his role in the new edition of Record of
a School, *which seemed to imply her continued agreement with his
outlook, is evident here; she is quickly assuming leadership of a new
kind of reform and is loath to be connected with a failed prewar venture.*

✦ To A. Bronson Alcott

New York—Aug. 30 [1871]

Dear Mr Alcott, as Louisa's letter makes a part of my preface it
can serve as an advertisement exactly as well as if it stood alone. When
Roberts advertises the book he can just extract her letter from the
preface & put it into the paper—and I must insist on the thing being
just as I left it with Wilson.—There is nothing disrespectful of you or
your school in it—and it is due to myself to put my views before the
public in the right way that I may not appear selfcontradictory

My sister writes me that you said there cannot be any copyright at
this late day; but that you thought Mr Roberts would pay something
if the book succeeds. Of course I shall be very glad to get something—
but I would rather have it *my way* than to get any money—and I am
clear that I have a right to have it *my way*—with the new preface &
appendix as I have finished it and I am sure the law would give me an
injunction against the publication at all unless it shall be according to
my will. A book is with me an earnest thing, & Mr Roberts will find it
all the *more* saleable I am confident for its publication being made consistent with my present purposes—[1]

[1] In an angry letter to Roberts, Peabody admitted that no law protected her
from the republication of her original *Record of a School* after the copyright expired;
"but I did not know that when the author was *alive*—that it was considered *courteous*
to publish his or her book without consultation—and it seems to me a *great injustice*
and needing the protection of a new law—that this should be done." Peabody threat-

I am sorry to be obliged to use so peremptory a tone—and I hope you will forgive me for what appears to you perhaps as my obstinacy— as freely as I forgive you for taking the liberty to republish my book without consulting me—

You can show this note if you please to Mr Roberts—or tell him— that you found to your surprise that I had something to say when I found the book was being published without my knowledge   I have expressed very fully that the only mistake about this introverted method was in applying it too early. I have distinctly recognized however that only a few of your scholars were of the kindergarten age—you learned from my sister, I suppose, that I am going to Europe & why— I suppose Roberts may possibly send some copies to Europe—I shall like to know where they will be & perhaps can promote their sale there. My direction will be 5 Shaftsbury Terrace Allen Street Kensington London West—

I will enclose a letter to Mr Roberts which you can give him & which will release you from any embarrassment in the premises—

Your friend
E. P. PEABODY

MS, MH

---

ened to publish "The Rejected Preface and Appendix" with "some remarks upon this outrage to which an Author is subjected by the existing laws" but she never did (28 September [1871], MS, MH).

Peabody provides a brief but pungent description of her second European visit.

✎ To Susan Cole

My dear Mrs. Cole,   Cambridge, July 10th [1872]

Ever since I returned home the 20th of May, I have been wishing to go down and see you.—I believe in very feeble phrase I wrote & thanked you dear Susan for your token of thoughtful love—by which I was enabled to go to Rome as I very much desired to do in March,— & which would have enabled me to remain until August in England, as I also very much desired to do—for the horrible winter had so prevented my getting over the cold I took in December, had kept me greatly confined in the house—and unable to avail myself of many pleasant invitations &c that I hoped to but thought by going to Rome I escaped the worst month as it proved in England. I was too much run down to be better for the journey tho I did not lose the main object of it which was to see the Baronness Marenholtz-Bülow & give the cheer of my sympathy to Mrs. Gould's noble work in Rome that she craved more than its worth as it seemed to me—and when I came back I was so prostrated that my physician gave me no encouragement that I should be better there in time to enjoy the summer, & joined with my nephew George in persuading me to come home with him— The voyage cured me—though there was a little reaction again on getting upon land out of the ocean breezes which I so love.—and since I came home, there has been quite a pressure of things to do & persons to see;—but just now I receive an invitation from the committee of South Church to the Anniversary on the 19th—and before I have any other invitation to a private house I want to know if *you* would like me to come & pass the night before or night after with *you*.—I know the occasion may fill your house with guests, but nevertheless I will venture to write,—for I want to tell you of the many satisfactions that crowned my visit to Europe—notwithstanding its distressing occasion—

Yours very affectionately

ELIZ. P. PEABODY

MS, MSaE

An invitation to Hawthorne's friend Horatio Bridge to visit her in Cambridge and learn the unhappy circumstances of the Hawthorne family.

✆ To Horatio Bridge[1]

19 Follen Street   Cambridge

My dear Mr Bridge   Oct. 15 [1872?]

Mary has just bro't me your letter which she wants me to answer— I live with her here—& shall be very glad to see you & tell you much of

---

[1] Horatio Bridge was a classmate of Hawthorne and Longfellow at Bowdoin College, class of 1825. In 1838 he joined the U.S. Navy; he served for thirty-five years, retiring in February 1873.

the last terrible year—or rather *nearly two years* since I saw you—You seem not to know of the tragedies that we have lived through—my nearly year in Europe—Una's insanity & recovery[2]—Rose's marriage &c. Una is in England permanently—& I think in a very favourable position for her happiness & health on the whole—Rose is boarding in my neighbourhood here with her young Husband—who is gifted—you may see a little the quality of his mind by his article in the last Atlantic on Hawthorne's Septimus Felton[3]—Julian has gone to live in Dresden with his wife & child & mother-in-law—this is all I need to say till I see you—I have often thought of writing to you and did not *because* I had so very much to say—

Yours truly in haste

Elizabeth P. Peabody

To come to us in Cambridge take the Garden Street car to the State Arsenal which makes the corner of Follen Street—our house is the *7th* in the Street in the corner for Follen Street is a right angle   The Garden Street car leaves the Revere House twice every hour   Also three North Avenue cars leave the same place one having Arlington on it three times in the hour—I will draw you a map on the other side— Do not come on a Wednesday afternoon—I am engaged at 2 in the afternoon & evening & if you can you can let me know beforehand but I am generally at home—I would not like to meet you[4] If you come in the N. Avenue cars tell the conductor to stop at Waterhouse Street & go down the lane to our house—there is one large house that you pass—

MS, MeB

[2] Una and Rose's attendance on their mother in her last painful illness was an emotional upheaval for Una, made worse by Rose's hasty marriage to George Parsons Lathrop in September 1871. Lathrop confirmed the gossip about Una's insanity in a letter to the *New York Tribune* on June 25, 1879, referring to Una's attack of insanity at the time of his and Rose's engagement and to another attack ten years earlier.

[3] Peabody's reference is to Lathrop's "Hawthorne's Last Novel," *Atlantic Monthly* 30 (October 1872): 452–60.

[4] Probably she meant "I would not like to miss you."

Peabody continues her effort to protect the reputation of Hawthorne, here from the charge that he took his characters from real-life people.

✄ To the Editor, *The Commonwealth*

February 7, 1874

Mr Editor:—I observed, in a reference to Mrs. Badger[1] in one of the speeches at the indignation meeting, Monday, that a gentleman spoke very authoritatively of her having been the original from which Mr. Hawthorne painted his "Hilda," of the "Marble Faun." Mrs. Badger needs no adventitious interest, derived from romantic associations, to make her memory precious and her character and gifts held in profoundest respect; but I think it but truth to say that I know from personal conversation with my brother-in-law on the subject that neither of the women in the "Marble Faun" were portraits, and that Mr. Hawthorne never drew portraits in his novels, not being intent on character-drawing, but only upon illustration of great spiritual laws, as both Mr. Edwin Whipple and the Rev. Mr Mayo have suggested in reviews of him, of which I heard Mr. Hawthorne speak, saying that they had discovered his secret.[2] When the "Blithedale Romance" came out the same suggestion was made that the characters were portraits, or intended to be such. He distinctly said then to me that whenever he referred to any real person he gave the name, as in saying that "Zenobia" in one particular reminded him of Margaret Fuller, though in all else she was so different. In the same way he acknowledged that he had taken one trait of "Hilda's" genius and one of her characters from a mutual friend of ours, whom she resembled in no other respect. As this statement of the speaker had been previously made in a Boston paper that may be read abroad, I have felt it should not go uncontradicted; and I hope that the *Globe,* and any other paper that copied its article, may also copy this note

Elizabeth P. Peabody

TS, *Commonwealth*, 7 February 1874, 597.

1 Ada Shepard, Antioch College graduate, joined the Hawthornes in England in autumn 1857, to be a companion and tutor of the children. She married a Mr. Badger in 1864.
2 The reviews to which she makes reference are Edwin Whipple, review of *Marble Faun,* by N. Hawthorne, *Atlantic Monthly* 5 (May 1860): 614–22 and Amory Dwight Mayo, probably "The Writings of Nathaniel Hawthorne," *Universalist Quarterly Review* 8 (1860?): 272.

Peabody's letter to an unnamed correspondent is devoted to raising interest in and funds for an edition of the works of liberal theologian F. D. Maurice—an example of Peabody's efforts to bring together her long-standing interest in history with the new emphasis on science.

To [?]

You will call on Dr. Barnard will you not? I enclose his letter received yesterday.

Boston, November 1st
1874

My dear Sir,

I believe I wrote to you my idea that it was best to undertake to print at first only the two books which are the *keystone* to that arch of Scripture Studies—I mean the two that have never been reprinted in England but which are the most important of all—because they show in what consists the unity of the Bible which involves the important answer to the questions of the hour. The commentary on the Epistle to the Hebrews[1] does not touch the question of whether or not Paul was the author—Whoever was the author it sets forth the Pauline doctrine of the unity & progress of Revelation from the symbols of *history* & ritual to the deepest *spiritual truth* which pervades time because it is Eternal & cannot be outgrown—

The Unity of the New Testament[2] entirely disposes—not by controverting but by foreclosing Mr Martineau's argument[3] & that unity

1 That is, Frederick Denison Maurice, *The Epistle to the Hebrews* (London, 1846). Maurice was an English clergyman, lawyer, and author. Brought up in a Unitarian household, Maurice rebelled against the narrowness and didacticism of dissenting culture and turned to the law. He received his L.L.B. in 1827 from Trinity Hall. Becoming known as an intellectual leader, Maurice published several articles praising Romantic writers; his study of the Romantics opened him to the emotional and sensory aspects of the liturgical tradition, and in 1830 he resolved to become an Anglican. He was ordained in 1834. In the late 1830s, Maurice's publications brought serious charges of unorthodoxy from his Anglican peers. By 1844, he was emerging as the leader of a group of Christian Socialists who saw in the reconstruction of society around genuinely Christian principles the only hope for society. Such views brought increasing charges of infidelity and eventually the Christian Socialist movement collapsed. In 1866, Maurice was elected professor of moral theology at Cambridge. He died in 1872 at age sixty-seven.

2 F. D. Maurice, *The Unity of the New Testament* (London, 1854).

3 Probably James Martineau, *The Rationale of Religious Enquiry* (London, 1836).

of the biography of Jesus so laboriously worked out by Carpenter & which leads the mind *out of the way*—

As the book is in our Theological Library at Cambridge you probably read it there—but may have forgotten its value after so many years. Maurice wrote so voluminously (though to be sure his works are collections of sermons in many cases of the more important ones) that we are in some danger of losing sight of the *peculiar* intellectual contribution that he made to his age—& I think we get this especially in these two books—the *preservation of the old & its reconsecration in the generous and reverent acceptance of the new*—Revelation in his eyes is *instant* & from *unconscious nature* as well as from the Higher Consciousness of *Man*—I think the naturalists themselves are not *so*[4] reverent as he is of the revelation (or *unveiling* of Science) but he does not on that account look with less awful reverence to *the Revelation* from the worshipping Soul of Man—whose *most wonderful* chapters are the Hebrew Scriptures

The Commentary on the Epistle to the Hebrews is a small book— I wish it might be published as the 1st volume of Maurice's "Studies in the Hebrew and Christian Scriptures" which might be the *general name* for our American Memorial Edition—

The objection will be that the title—"the Commentary on the Epistle to the Hebrews" is not a taking title for the bookbuying public. I think that perhaps it might be as well to say "Epistle to the Hebrews"—and then trust to *Reviews* of it—to make people read it as a work showing the Unity of the Bible   I want to write a Review of it. You perhaps would write another. And other dear lovers of Maurice might write others—This could be followed by *the unity of the New Testament* ⟨perhaps⟩ & in our memorial preface (of which I have conceived another form) it might be said that this showed the Unity of Revelation

You know that "the Prophets & Kings"[5] were once published in Boston—The plates can be bought for a very low figure as I happen to know—and if not bought will be melted up by the stupid owner. Now I think if some money could be got to buy those plates they had better be secured & then some money to be able to own this *first volume* of "The Unity of the New Testament" or "The Unity of the Bibl[e"]— shown in Maurices "Epistle to the Hebrews" we might get some pub-

[4] "So" is underlined three times in the MS.
[5] F. D. Maurice, *The Prophets and Kings of the Old Testament* (London, 1853).

lisher *agoing* on the work—& in the end all the volumes I have indicated be made the interest of the publisher to complete.

But what I especially write for today is to say that Dr. F. A. P. Barnard of Columbia College[6] is interested about this & written to me more than once & *wants to see you*—& I wish you would see him & Drs. Potter & Washburn[7] & see if we cannot do something at once—Only see what sum of money two or three persons will pay down & the rest is easy.

E. P. Peabody

MS, MSaE

[6] Frederick Augustus Porter Barnard was president of Columbia University from 1864 to 1889.
[7] Eliphalet Nott Potter was an Episcopal clergyman and president of Union College from 1871 to 1884. Edward Abiel Washburn was an Episcopal clergyman, author, and editor.

Peabody tries once again to distance herself from Alcott, even proposing that he write an account of his intellectual pilgrimage.

✄ To A. Bronson Alcott

Post Script
Dear Mr Alcott   [1874]
    I have been looking at Mr. Russell's article which is interesting in itself—& portrays as you said a scene of real life—
    But I cannot think it desirable to present it as a specimen of the best way to manage little children—I think the words *bad & good* are applied in it to perfectly innocent action & so would puzzle the conscience—It is a specimen of the old method of *repression* a little ameliorated though because the instrumentality of repression is words & kind words instead of blows & hard words—& the childs free will is certainly respected (or is it not circumvented rather)   But instead of repression of activity the true way at this early age is to *direct the activity* into legitimate channels. The attention of the child is to be attracted to doing something & not required as an act of pure strength at so early an age—Some of these children seem to have been too young for even Froebels kindergarten but rather subjects of the individual

care of the nursery where the rule is ⟨to take⟩ for the nurse to obey the playful instincts of the child not to antagonise them. I do not want to put it into my appendix without accompanying it with my protest. It is one of those things that prove how much Froebels philosophy & art are *needed*.

When you publish the volume of Conversations on the Gospels which Roberts will doubtless like to do if *the Rec.* sells well, I wish you would write a kind of autobiographical Appendix, telling of the progress of your mind from one phase of practical method to another— Then you could insert this as a specimen of the Salem Str. School; and tell other things of your earlier & later methods, & then refer to the Record of a School in Boston, & then add your present criticism of what you did then, and the conclusions of your maturest mind with regard to the education of children. It seems to me this would be admirable. You began with Pestalozzi—will you not end with Froebel? Yours truly E.P.P. Would it not be a good plan to write this autobiographical letter *now* & make *that* the appendix to *this book* [several words illegible.]

MS, MH

Memories of Samuel Gridley Howe, shared with his widow shortly after his death.

✎ To Julia Ward Howe

My dear friend,   Cambridge Feb 9th 1876

There was one great ⟨mistake⟩ omission made, in the Reminiscences of your noble husband (which so glorified his name at the beautiful memorial service yesterday afternoon)[1] and that was ⟨made⟩ the mistake of Mr. Bullock, in ascribing or giving the initiative to Col. Perkins—of the Asylum for the Blind.—This of course you know, and I only write ⟨this⟩ to you, because I want to get into print the *facts*.

When we first became acquainted with Mr. Mann—(all boarding

1 Samuel Gridley Howe died January 9, 1876; shortly afterward a memorial service was held in Boston's Music Hall, presided over by Alexander Rice, governor of Massachusetts. Oliver Wendell Holmes, Ellery Channing, and Charles T. Brooks read eulogies.

together at Mr[s]. Clarke's he took Mary & me to a small wooden house, then in a court in Hollis Street, where, in the simplest surroundings, we found Dr. Howe with the half dozen first pupils that he picked up in the highways & byeways—to open their blind eyes.—he had then been about six months at work, and had invented & laboriously *executed* some books with raised letters, to teach them to read; & some geographical maps—and the geometrical ⟨outlines⟩ diagrams for mathematics.—He had gummed *twine,* I think, an enormous labour—upon cardboard forming the printed letters!

I shall not [for?] all time & eternity, forget the impression made on me, by seeing the hero of the Greek Revolution (& who *would* have been so of the Polish had he been able to get to Poland [line illegible] in *time*—with the flags he carried over from the American sympathizers,—but was obliged to deposit with Lafayette—because (God save the Mark!) Order reigned in Warsaw!—to see this hero—I say—wholly absorbed & applying all the energies of his genius to this—I do not like to call a *humble work*! and doing it as Christ did without any money and without price—(for his own resources would not have paid the expenses—with all the economy & self denial he used—but for the fuller purse of his friend & *brother* Dr Lister)—

Very soon after our visit to him—he brought out his class for exhibition in order to interest people—and get the money sufficient to do the work on a larger scale,—The many exhibitions created a furor of holy enthusiasm—& Colonel Perkins' great heart *responded* to the touch of Dr. Howe's—& *then* he offered his fine estate in Pearl Street—with the beautiful large house & grounds—provided the City of Boston would raise $50,000—And to this appeal *the ladies of Boston responded,* with the *first fair* that ever was known in Boston—It was at Fanueil Hall, & every body contributed if not ⟨with⟩ money—⟨with⟩ the works of their hands—& more than 49 thousand dollars was the net result.

I am too sorry Mr Bullock did not know these facts;—but could not they be, in some manner appended, as a postscript to his oration,—in the printed Report which of course we must have—

My dear friend—You do not know how constantly you have been on my heart & in my thoughts, since the gates of glory swung wide to receive this true brother of Christ whose selfforgetting [word illegible] modesty will make the welcome home *such a surprise*! I think you must be quite exhausted with conflict of emotions, in which joy can only be discriminated from pain because you would not be without it, as

George Eliot has somewhere said "dark with expressive bright" are the joys of grief in such a sorrow! always your friend Eliz. P. Peabody

MS, MH

In the midst of her furious efforts on behalf of the Froebellian kindergarten, Peabody is tormented by a particularly nasty family quarrel, recounted here for Mrs. Moncure Conway.

✖ To Ellen D. Conway

Dear Mrs. Conway—   Nov 21st [1876]
    In the whirl of the centennial, though I took an hour to answer your letter, I find I did not send it—and now I will write another sheet. Rose did get her baby—and it ⟨was⟩ is a nice one.[1] It seemed as if the curse was lifted—but alas—she has not got up well—and in fact is raving mad at this present moment—going over all the mental agonies that attended that fearful night when that *fatal letter* came by which she found her husband was so fearfully *misunderstood.*—And all the Sufferings they have had since—have come rushing back on her in her weakness![2]

[1] This was George and Rose's child, Francis Lathrop.
[2] George Lathrop's *A Study of Hawthorne* (1876) was the first major critical assessment of Hawthorne. Julian was irritated by its publication, which established Lathrop as a Hawthorne expert so that he was asked to write the introductions to the Riverside edition of Hawthorne's work.
    On July 8, 1876, the *New York Tribune* printed a long bitter letter from Julian Hawthorne, in which he claimed that since 1872 he and Una had been trying to get Lathrop to return papers which had come to Lathrop because of his marriage. The publication of *A Study* revealed that these papers had been used, and Julian saw it as an invasion of family privacy. To Julian, Lathrop had forced himself "into prominence by attaching himself to a famous name" and had "composed and published [his book] in violation of a trust and in the face of repeated warning and opposition; and after all it conveys no just & truthful representation of its subject."
    Lathrop's letter of response appeared in the *Tribune* on July 13, 1876. He denied knowing that the family papers in question belonged exclusively to Julian and stressed that the biographical aspects of his book were subordinate to the critical and evaluative portions. *A Study,* he wrote, "was not undertaken with any expectation of injuring any one, least of all any member of Nathaniel Hawthorne's family, but with a sincere love and reverence for his memory." Much of this information comes from Maurice Bassan, *Hawthorne's Son: The Life and Literary Career of Julian Hawthorne* (Columbus: Ohio State University Press, 1970), 113–18, 158–60.

The child was born on the 10th and I came back on the 12th—& rushed up to see her   But the nurse & doctor were inexorable—they said she was very nervous & must only see *them*—So I was obliged to be satisfied with seeing the child & George—I asked G. if he did not mean to name it Nathaniel Hawthorne & call him Hawthorne—and he said no—neither he or Rose wanted to put the *curse* of that name on their child—while [two underlined words illegible] all of the named (Julian Una & their aunt Elizabeth H) [two words illegible] did not retract their public accusation of *him*—*before the world.*—He had begun his life worshipping Hawthorne in his books—he had [word illegible] said he should grow up knowing himself as only [word illegible] as a Lathrop—& he & Rose would commence a new life entirely separate from the ⟨family⟩ blood of Hawthorne. And he said Rose felt this too—and that only in another world could that Ideal which he had worshipped & sacrificed to be *realized* & enjoyed—

I was really *appalled* to see how deep & incurable the wound had become and I had a foreboding that Rose's "nervousness" might have serious relations—and so it has *proved*. She believed herself in the midst of enemies—& to day her frenzy has fixed on G himself—this was very temporary—when George is with her she seems tranquillized—But will not take a mouthful except he takes it too—thinking everybody wants to poison her & him too

The Dr. will not let *me* go near her—as I should do—though I have been nearly ill in bed since I returned having a fearful cold & cough—and Mary though better than she was is only able to get along by being half the time horizontal on the bed—Rose has never been so well & tranquil as in her pregnancy—and even Julian's conduct did not overcome her. She felt so happy at George's success & the defence of him that hers burst out on all sides—and the Dr tells us that this condition of mind will not last—It is a consequence of puerperal fever which is often temporary though it may last *six months*! It came the crisis ten days after the child was born—We had a letter from Una today rejoicing in the news of the baby's arrival & the "completion of the little family." I do not know whether *you* know of her engagement to a gentleman—one of George Lathrop's friends—who became interested in her at the time of her illness when she was last here—that is he seems to have fallen in love *then* having admired her before.   He knows all about the past physical history but believes if he has the care of her he can keep her well & happy—and I trust it will be a happy union[3]—Nothing breaks the tender affection of the *sisters* for each other—Rose does not think Una responsible for the part she has taken lately with Julian because *she can never know* the ⟨claim⟩ debt of gratitude owing to Lathrop—& her own tragic influence upon their life!— though he is at present in the Sandwich Island for his health! [Two words illegible] too a Literary Art like Lathrop's

You will see I suppose the deplorable letter that Julian has written in the Tribune concerning Lathrop's Lovely "Study of Hawthorne"

I trace this warping of Julian's mind with respect to Lathrop that makes him see everything in a false light—to the sad fact that Mr Channing *in his fit of insanity* (some of which has become chronic) *wrote to him* under the excitement you [word illegible]—& got a letter to him before my truthful account arrived in which he spoke of Lathrops stealing into the family disreputably—and so forth & so forth—and at least made him think that L & R had neglected Una culpably after they had driven her mad![4]

When Julian told me—just as I was going to sail—the engagement of Lathrop to Rose & I asked him how he ⟨left⟩ liked it he said it was splendid—that Lathrop had the finest moral nature he had ever known in a man—& it was by such words he first introduced him to Sophia in Dresden—who took him as she said into her heart *next to Julian*—and wrote to him—⟨& by man⟩ after he returned to America as a counselling friend—and by several tokens showed she had a presentiment of the future union with Rose (betrayed in letters to us from England)—

When my letter arrived he did write and say he "took back" what he had written to Lathrop under the impression Mr Channing gave him—

But such things cannot be taken back quite—Lathrop could forgive but the sore place was left and it has never been as it was before—

Julian doubtless believes he tells the truth but the facts are not quite as would be inferred—Rose never heard that her father's letters were given to Julian exclusively & having them in her possession she retained them to read & nobody hindered or gainsaid till Julian heard of "the Study"—Then he sent for the letters peremptorily & as Rose had read them—she sent them back for Julian & Una whom she recog-

---

3 Una Hawthorne met the young, ambitious writer Albert Webster in 1874. Una visited Julian in London in March 1875, and returned to the United States in 1876 to visit Webster, who was in the last stages of tuberculosis. Lathrop recommended the climate of the Hawaiian Islands; Webster died enroute there. On September 10, 1877, Una died at a Protestant convent in England and was buried beside her mother in London's Kensal Green Cemetery.

4 This letter from Ellery Channing has not been located.

nized as having equal but *not superior* right to hers—Lathrop had not had time to read them—& having the materials for his study in printed things he did not need to explore them—But Rose took out the letters *to* her father & his reply to one (Motleys) with no consciousness or idea of violating the intended privacy—& he read & used *them*—Rose who is more like her father in all respects than either of the children— is greatly afflicted—She feels Julian has done more harm to his own than her husband's reputation—for the letter is very completely established here—& *she sees* that it is he who has violated sacred privacies— & her "heart aches for him" as she says—I hope it will not affect her health—She never will lose the effect on her imagination of the shock given her by Mr Channing's *insane* letter to Lathrop received the evening I arrived in London—But the effect on her *body* seems at last healed—and she has the sweet expectation of which she has been hitherto deprived—I had thought if a child was born I could forgive Mr C because it would seem that GOD had—But he has never come up to the hope which I expressed to R & L that night as a faith—that he would *retract* and apologize for his *monstrous charges* against them both made under his first impression taken from Una in her derangement & which Rose admitted it was difficult for any one to escape. She had herself been made to believe what was [word illegible] of all their best friends—before she knew that it was *insanity*—ah me! how can mortals act violently & impetuously amid the confusion of life—there is no safety but *in humility*   EPP

MS, NNC

A sympathy letter and reminiscence upon the death of Abigail Alcott, Louisa May Alcott's mother.

To Louisa May Alcott

Please excuse this blot I have kept the letter a week to copy it, but have not time

My dear Louisa— [December ?, 1877]

It would do as little justice to myself as to the venerated Mother whom you have lost to mortal vision;[1] but with whom I think you must feel *identified* for ever more, did I not express to you my feelings of intense sympathy—before the privileged days of seclusion are passed by.

I lived with your mother in perhaps the most intense period of her suffering experience of life—and feel as if I knew the heights & depths of her great heart as perhaps only you & Anna can do For a few months we were separated by stress of feeling in most tragic circumstances—and she doubted my friendship—truth & honor—in strict consequence only because of the depth of my loyalty to her! But God gave me an opportunity to withdraw the veil & I have under her own hand her written expression of her conviction that I was *true to her* & her deepest worth *at that very time*. I have never known a great, more devoted, more tender, more selfsacrificing human being; & it was all pure moral force & *character* for she owed nothing to the *Imagination*. It was the tragic element in her that she could not *escape* on *that wing* the full painfulness of *experience*—There was no froth on the cup of life for her—It was all the reality down to its very dregs—the [word illegible] uprightness & downrightness and plain speech—*but an infinitely tenderer heart*—such a heart as needs *the winged horse* which for fresh air takes daily excursions into the Ideal—"Ah, me!" said Mr Emerson once, in one of his earlier lectures (which were *poems*) "it is wonderful how painful is Experience! Infinite compunctions cover every beloved name! with the Ideal only is the Rose of Joy!" In all the time & especially the many years of the first part of the time I knew her she was too much without the "Rose of Joy"—It was for you, dear Louisa, in these later years—indeed ever since you grew up, to gather these roses for her & crown her old age with them. You *understood*

[1] Abigail Alcott died on November 25, 1877.

her—the first person perhaps who ever did sufficiently to do justice to her—Let me congratulate you "Many daughters have done virtu-ously—but thou excellest them all" Gifted by God with your mothers heart and your father's ideality you united them in yourself, & saw them both in God's idea of them.—I do not think I ever enjoyed any-body's fictions as I have enjoyed *yours*. I have enjoyed it in imagina-tive sympathy with both your father and your mother,—but especially with the *latter* because she did not forecast the "all is well!" as your more imaginative father could do—But I think you have been & are no less a blessing to *him*—whose last days are his best days—When we sit down together on the banks of the River of Life (or the fields of asphodel—not before—we will talk of—what we cannot speak among the shadows & cross lights & confused echoes of time. Express my sym-pathy to Anna & your Father—Abby is I believe in Europe & I hope in prosperity Yours truly Elizabeth P. Peabody

MS, ViU

A quiet, reflective letter, as if seeking to do justice to other aspects of her crowded life besides the ever-present kindergartening.

✄ To Ellen D. Conway

My dearest Mrs. Conway   April 27 [1878]
        I was delighted to see yr handwriting again though very sorry to hear of your illness—My sister received your letter while I was away—from March 1st to April 13th in Florence Mass. New York & Phila-delphia engaged in the kindergarten propaganda during which time I gave 12 parlour lectures, and visited kindergartens new & old & other educational institutions & was so perfectly busy that she retained the letter till I came home—ill—& have been in my chamber ever since—Yet busy with preparation for an important meeting of our American Froebel Union[1] which has had to be deferred but will come off on the 27th.
        I will however take my *first* hour of leisure to night to write to

[1] In a letter to William Torrey Harris (19 February 1878, MS, MoSHi), Peabody described the formation of a Froebel Society "for the express purpose of keeping the standard of kindergarten up to the mark of Froebel."

you—and to beg you to let me soon hear again how you are—I do not like to hear of that tumor on your breast & it seems to me the treatment you are undergoing is not homeopathic—You do not say who is your doctor. I suppose it was old Mr & Mrs Howes with whom you spent that week—I wish Mrs. Howes could hear these lectures Emerson is giving at the old South now & then. All that is really intellectual in him seems as bright as ever though he has utterly lost his memory of proper names—and of some other objects[2]—Ellen is his right hand man—goes every where with him—fixes his manuscripts—&c &c &c— you don't know the change that has come over us—Perhaps you do know that last August my nephew George Mann married Esther Lombard—they went out to St Paul for a year for George to be second teacher in a high school—in practical preparation for taking the principalship of some Eastern school & they return this summer & take Mary—who has been such an invalid these last years that she wants to give up housekeeping—& besides cannot afford to keep this expensive house in Cambridge—and I am going to return to Concord next week to live with my brother N.[athaniel.] Concord has immensely *improved*—the public library built & given by Mr Monroe occupies the Brooks house lot—& all the old houses are moved off and elegant edifices taken their place on both streets—

But there is another more melancholy change—Mrs. Alcott—Miss Thoreau Mrs Brooks old Mrs. Goodman—and Elizabeth Hoar are dead[3]—Elizabeth died of a cancer or rather was visibly translated for never was such a triumph of mind over body seen—The last fortnight she lived by breathing ether every *ten minutes*—that gave her breath & strength to talk. She could not lie down & only slept for a few minutes at a time leaning on some body's hands—But she declared it "was not so bad as it seemed" She saw friends and talked all the time till at last she said she has said *all* she had to say & done all she had to do—& asked to be laid down & to have ether still administered so that she should not suffer She then fell asleep & never waked again—She died at Mrs Howes [?] in Cambridge—

I write to poor dear Mrs Travers by this mail—I suppose she is

2 Ralph Rusk writes, "He appeared at the Old South Church more than once in these years, with worn wares of his, in obedience to the call of the Committee for the preservation of the church. In February of 1878, he practiced faithfully his reading of his lecture on education for a Concord audience, but could not even remember the subject and continually asked what it was" (*The Life of Ralph Waldo Emerson* [New York: Charles Scribner's Sons, 1949], 498).

3 As noted earlier Abigail May Alcott died November 25, 1877. Elizabeth Hoar was Charles Emerson's fiancée and a virtual member of the Emerson family.

still in Colwell Gardens & I do not know where you are—whether at Pembroke Gardens no 2 or Hamlet House Hammersmith   May Alcott is married I find—to a Swiss Artist in London[4]—Louisa who has bought the Thoreau House for Anna & has been living there this winter—says she & Mr Alcott will go out & make her a house [?] soon— They do not seem to [word illegible] like the marriage—I hope it is a good one in all respects—

MS (incomplete), NNC

4 May Alcott went to Europe in 1876 to study painting and while in Paris met a Swiss banker, Ernest Nieriker. They were married on March 22, 1878. In November 1879, their daughter Louisa May ("Lulu") was born, and in the following month May died.

Peabody as memoirist; an account of Emerson's "Divinity School Address" and its reception.

✏ To James Elliot Cabot

Concord Mass
My dear Mr. Cabot,   June 30, 1879
     For the same reason that you wanted me to tell you my recollections of Mr. Emerson's conversation & that led me to expose to you one book of my private journal—you will like to have this letter in which I will make an extract from another volume of it[1]—which I cannot so well show you, as it is more about my own poor personality than his!—It is at the date of July 1839 when I was spending a week or two in his house—and is I think very interesting, because it does better justice to his attitude towards Christianity than is done especially by the free Religionists who claim him incontinently—You know I told you that there was a passage in his manuscript of the Di-

1 Emerson became acquainted with James Cabot in 1844 when Cabot gave him a translation of the *Bhagavadgita*. In the last thirty years of his life, Emerson relied more and more on Cabot, first as friend, increasingly as secretary, and finally as editor and compiler of his last works. Between 1872 and 1875, Cabot helped Emerson and his children Edward and Ellen collect fragments from the journals and old lectures for publication as *Letters and Social Aims*. The volume came out in 1876. In 1877, Cabot began collecting materials for a life of Emerson which, he said, someone else should probably write.

vinity Hall Sermon,[2] which he did not *read* merely because he found
it would stretch out the time beyond the hour (as he said), which was
a *caveat* against just that irreverent handling of the name of Jesus "the
head of human culture" as he ⟨called⟩ named him—which has taken
place & which he characterised then as "a *puppyism*" which would be
presently developed because every *step* of *human culture* was immediately exaggerated in its last word—& so made false—by *human vanity patronising* it—

    But I will proceed to my extract—"I was speaking today of what
Eckermann[3] says of Goethe's saying that Jesus was not quite universal—⟨He⟩ Goethe said 'the God of Jesus was only the infinite of a perfect humanity—But besides Humanity there is Eternal *Nature* which
doubtless has elements not included in Humanity'— And I said to
Mr. Emerson This gives me an *a priori reason* for Jesus' *miracles*
which as Dr. Channing says, are never violations of nature but fulfil-
ments of laws broken by historical humanity[4]—If they were external
facts, they would answer Goethe's cavil—Jesus not only 'knew what
was in man' but he had the secret *of nature* also, as ⟨they⟩ miracles
make evident, & that this was a less thing than the first seems to be implied by the very slight account he seemed to make of it himself—Does
it not prove that *GOD* whom he always speaks of as *Father of himself*
(by *himself* he always means *humanity*—as Montaigne does by his
I—) is none the less so because He creates the Infinite universe—which

    2 As mentioned earlier, Emerson delivered this address on July 15, 1838, at the
invitation of several members of the graduating class of Harvard Divinity School. The
omitted passage has never been found, and it is likely that Peabody's memory of
seeing it was in error.
    3 Johann Peter Eckermann was Goethe's companion and secretary during the
last years of Goethe's life. He assisted Goethe in the preparation of the definitive
edition of Goethe's work, *Ausgabe letzter Hand.* In 1837, Eckermann published the
first two volumes of *Gespräche mit Goethe in den letzter Jahren seines Lebens.* In 1848,
the third volume appeared.
    4 Here again, Peabody either suffered from a lapse of memory or she reinter-
preted Channing. Channing argued in his sermon "Evidences of Christianity" that
in fact miracles *are* violations of nature and thereby evidence of God's power over
His creation. "When I examine nature, I see reasons for believing that it was not intended by God to be the only method of instructing and improving humanity. I see
reasons, as I think, why its order or regular course should be occasionally suspended,
and why revelation should be joined to it in the work of carrying forward the race."
In "Evidences of Revealed Religion," Channing argues, contrary to Peabody's statements about miracles as fulfilment of law, that natural law does not confine and re-
strict the Maker. "If, then, the great purposes of the universe can best be accomplished by departing from its established laws, these laws will undoubtedly be suspended" though not lightly or frequently (*The Works of William E. Channing, D. D.*
[Boston: American Unitarian Association, 1882], 212, 223).

is the House man dwells in & must enlarge forever to give scope to his unfolding being?"

Mr Emerson did not reply to this *directly,* but said

"The mission of the present time is to re-proclaim the Living GOD, and, in order to do this, Christianity—and especially the person Jesus—must be set aside for the time—as if they were not—It would be doing injustice to Jesus to suppose that so pure a name would not clear itself from the consequent misunderstandings which undoubtedly will come to superficial *thinkers* These will not do injustice to Jesus & His truth he preached so much as the popular worship of him does—for that veils instead of unveils GOD"—My Journal goes on to say "This explains Mr Emerson's course with respect to Christianity & Jesus's name—& is consistent with what he says in his Divinity Hall Sermon—He *believes* as much as any Christian who attacks him does *and ever so much more* He does Christianity the justice to believe that it will renew its life in the revival of a profounder *Theism* than at the present obtains in the Church—and he thinks the only way he can do full justice to it—is to cease to mention it more & more, that he may not be guilty of keeping up *false* thought concerning it in the minds of men—

"We may differ from him in *our course,* but have no right to condemn him in his, for he omits talk about Christ⟨ian⟩ from precisely the same reverence—only perhaps that makes us dwell upon Him"—I wish he had *printed* what he left out of the reading of his Divinity Sermon—but he did not from a gentlemanly feeling towards Mr Norton & Mr. Ware who had committed themselves in *print* against the sermon as it was delivered.[5] "It would be shabby" said he "to show them up the world as having misunderstood me *in their heat for* God" Yours truly E. P. Peabody   over   Mr Emerson in his extreme modesty did not realise that he was to become the leader of thought in his day and generation—& so did not feel the responsibility *as such* which he must do *now*—or he would have seen that he ⟨must⟩ should not postpone himself to an *elegancy of behaviour*—as a gentleman— but one cannot but love him better for this *nicety*—You may keep this

[5] Henry Ware, Jr., preached a rebuttal to Emerson, "The Personality of the Deity" on September 23, and sent it to Emerson, hoping to stimulate an argument. Emerson however refused to be drawn in. Andrews Norton added to the criticism with "The New School in Literature and Religion" published in *The Boston Daily Advertiser* of August 27, and followed up with "A Discourse on the Latest Form of Infidelity," an address delivered "at the request of the Association of the Alumni of the Cambridge Theological School."

for your memoir—or use it in any way you please—but I hope will not curtail it   Both his wife & I *care* a great deal for the fact that he is a *Christian* par excellence beyond the reach of words to do justice to—because *words* are bereft of their deeper meaning by the *inadequate ear* that hears them—I one day was reproaching him for not *printing* more & he said "You think too much of many words—the one word *GOD* expresses all that can be *said*—to any who can understand—"   This was a *sophism* I think but it was not the sophism of an *atheist*—but of a sublime worshipper of GOD—if not *teacher of man*

MS, MH (incorrectly catalogued as letter to Emerson)

A letter on the Concord School of Philosophy, gathering up the fragments of the past.

✂ To Mary Peabody Mann

My dear Mary   August [18]79
   I am very glad to get your letter this morning which Rose has read to me—& learn that dear Louise is not *in danger* of losing her life—Rose says she wrote to tell you I did not *fail*—In fact I had the success I almost always do have when I say any thing to people who have faith in me for it gives me *courage*—I take part in the discussions and when I read they all say I can be heard all over the house, & I feel that I do say what I want to. I have said from the beginning that I never felt so completely *at home* as I do in this School of Philosophy[1] the spirit of which is to listen to & appreciate whatever may be said on the themes whose discussion "makes the soul"—But I have been too busy to write letters because I have been writing something I expect to read tomorrow evening in the quarter of an hour preceding Mr. Al-

[1] The first session of the Concord School of Philosophy met for six weeks beginning July 15, 1879. The five chief lecturers were Alcott, Harris, Ednah Dow Cheney, H. K. Jones, and David Wasson. Seven other lecturers spoke on Saturdays and at other times during the session: Emerson, Charles Saunders Peirce, Cyrus Bartol, Thomas Wentworth Higginson, Thomas Davidson, Harrison Blake, and Franklin B. Sanborn. Sanborn, who gives a full account of the school's nine years of operation in *Recollections of Seventy Years*, 2 vols. (Boston: Richard G. Badger, 1909), 2:485–513, does not list John Albee as speaking in 1879, but does quote from Raymond Bridgeman's account of the 1881 session, that "Mr. Albee's [lectures] were on language and style, under the quaint title of 'Faded Metaphors' " (p. 506).

cott's lecture—& also a little paper on Milton's Paradise Lost struck out by the astonishingly unappreciative words of Mr. Albee and others about that magnificent poem. But Mr Albee's lecture on poetry was very beautiful & Mr Sanborn gave two *very beautiful* lectures on Oracles—ancient & modern—closing with Mr Emerson's poetry as the most oracular of all—Indeed all the lectures are superb & Mr Alcott says better things than I ever heard him say before—though once I have disputed him—or rather his *words*—for what he meant was all right. He acts his part as Dean and Originator of the School excellently. I take tea & spend the Sunday Evenings with Miss Emerson—& this morning I went there to breakfast & to finish & send off an article on the kindergarten that I read to her last evening & which Lyman Abbot—Ed of the Christian Union sent to me to write & promised to pay for. It will come out the middle of August—I have just now answered a letter of Anna Russells telling her I would go to Lancaster next Saturday at 12 o'clock & stay till Wednesday the 16th, and another to Mrs. Aldrich who is wild to get me these days. I will go there Wednesday. It is only nine miles from Lancaster.

Mr. Harris's son Theodore has a type writer and is copying my lecture and the little paper on Milton. It is a delightful thing to have if one always knows how to write on it. I shall pay him for making the copy—As I am paid for the article in the CU—& my lectures—it will pay all my expenses—They are only $5 a week—bed food sundries—but I do not know what he will ask for the copy—Let me find a letter to me from you at Lancaster next Saturday or Monday if you do not write before.

Yours ever
ELIZ. P P—

TS copy, OYesA

An invitation to a Wisconsin friend to attend the Concord School, and a reference to a fall that nearly took Peabody's life.

✹ To Aubertine Woodward[1]

Concord Mass Dec 23 [18]79

My dear Miss Woodward,

The best way to show you that I am recovering is to write myself & thank you for the pretty Christmas card & the valuable Christmas gift which will arrive in due time. I have today the publisher's card saying he should mail it, & I thank you for the slip of newspaper with all these interesting northern works noticed on them I shall send that to the committee of the Concord Public Library which should have them all—I have never sufficiently thanked you for your own book which I lend to my grand nephews to read—& shall leave in my will to my little splendor Francis Hawthorne Lathrop—His mother my darling Rose is here in Concord in the old Hawthorne home-stead—"the Wayside" which is an very lovely place—I wish you could see it—& why cannot you? I will enclose the Circular of the Concord School which will tell you what had this last summer—no! the [word illegible] will give you no idea—& [?] what is to be done next summer when I think you & Prof Andersen might come. Every body takes boarders during the five weeks & Rose had a lovely housefull last year, living as she does next door to the "Orchard House"—& you & the Professor might both come & board at Mrs. Anderson if you cure her of her present sickness—now this is worth thinking of! I am glad if you find the climate of Madison good for you in the winter but you will want a change next summer[.]

I hope to have my "Reminiscences of Dr Channing" done before his centennial comes off in April[2]—but I have been dreadfully hindered by my fall—I had a nurse & doctor *seven weeks*—it was a mirac-

---

1 Annie Aubertine Woodward Moore was an author, musician, and translator, who studied music in Philadelphia and gave private recitals in Boston, New York, and Philadelphia. She translated several German novels and eventually began work on Norse mythology. As a result, she befriended the linguist Rasmus Anderson of the University of Wisconsin, with whom she was evidently planning a trip to Concord. In 1887, Woodward married Samuel Moore, a contractor. She died in Madison at age eighty-seven.

2 Peabody refers to her *Reminiscences of the Rev. William E. Channing* (Boston: Roberts Brothers, 1880).

ulous escape from instant death—But it has not been at all an unhappy experience, it has brought out so much love and kindness from
my friends   truly yours

Eliz. P. Peabody

MS, WHi

≋7
1880s

Reminiscence and Farewell

I T WAS INEVITABLE that Elizabeth Peabody would play a central role in the Concord School of Philosophy, which Bronson Alcott began in the summer of 1879. Much as Froebellianism acted as a counter-trend to naturalism and secularism in education, so the Concord School represented a desire on the part of amateurs to resist the secular tendencies in philosophy. As Bruce Kuklick has pointed out, post-war philosophy was rapidly becoming more professionalized and more scientific in assumptions and methods. Seeking to "rejuvenate Transcendental ideals," the school's lecturers expressed deep hostility to contemporary science and manifested a fatal fondness for reminiscence. Transcendentalism was to be left behind in the process of rebuilding a world view in the wake of war and Darwinism, and the Concord School registered a final protest against this abandonment.[1]

Though not part of the program the first year, Peabody had enjoyed the first session immensely, walking and reminiscing with Alcott, Emerson, and Ellery Channing. In the 1882 session, she lectured on Milton and the philosophy of education. In a letter to Mary Mann, she referred to the philosophical idealism that underlay the school: "in the evening Dr. Holland gave a most brilliant lecture—demolishing atomism," and described her own role: "My success has been complete—& next year I am booked for a lecture on Paradise Lost—perhaps one on the Philosophy of Education besides—which I shall write at my leisure in the course of the year."[2]

In keeping with the retrospective and elegiac mood of the school, Peabody turned increasingly to the memoir and the reminiscence during the 1880s. In the first year of the decade, Roberts Brothers issued her *Reminiscences of the Rev. William Ellery Channing*. She was dissatisfied with it in some ways, she confided to her old friend James Freeman Clarke: "So little of that great range of thought that I had record of in my Journals and letters returned to me by friends—& in my memory—*did I attempt to put down* (I had to fight with Roberts for the space I did fill)—and so much did I fear that the narrow window of my individuality through which I must necessarily look would *curtail* the view—that you will believe me when I tell you that it was in a kind of agony of apprehension I left Boston,—when it was just printed & not bound."[3] No letters of Peabody's to Channing, if any

1 Bruce Kuklick, *The Rise of American Philosophy* (New Haven: Yale University Press, 1977), 57–59.

2 Elizabeth Peabody to Mary P. Mann, 12 August [1882], TS copy, OYesA.

3 Elizabeth Peabody to James Freeman Clarke, 14 April [1880], MS, MH.

were written, have been located. Others of her published reminis-cences were "Emerson as Preacher" in Franklin Sanborn's *Genius and Character of Emerson* and *Last Evening with Allston and Other Papers*.[4] Her manuscript accounts include her own early life and first en-counters with Hawthorne, written for her nephew Julian in 1882 to aid him in writing his biography of his father,[5] and the letters con-tained in this section. The student of Peabody comes quickly to sus-pect, however, that even this much written material hardly touched her vast reservoir of anecdote and interpretation. Possibly only those who listened to her monologues could appreciate her stature as living oral history. Jane Marsh Parker was just such a fortunate listener; she provided an amusing and moving account of several unforgettable days with Peabody in 1885. The first *Century* installment of Henry James's *The Bostonians* had appeared while Parker was visiting a per-sonal friend of Peabody, who declared that "Miss Birdseye (we were reading the story aloud) was surely drawn from Miss Peabody," and, wrote Parker, "my desire to see her was greater than ever, severe as was our censure of Mr. James all in all." Shortly thereafter, Peabody did visit the home of the mutual friend, gathering "a circle of lis-teners on either hand," discoursing on "the wrongs of the Piute In-dians, in whose behalf she was going to Washington to see President Cleveland. . . . The Piute Indians went out to dinner with us, and while the rest of us feasted on many courses Miss Peabody ate frugally of the simplest fare, discoursing eloquently yet with marvelous concise-ness and directness, considering all she had to tell and told, upon what seemed to be her absorbing hobby." For Jane Parker, listening to Pea-body "surpassed anything in my experience":

She had an original, spicy, terse way of saying things that stimulated attention, kept up an expectancy for something better yet. She held to her thread no matter what its length; never dropped a stitch; and her sequences were so simple and clear that following her was seldom baffling or fatiguing. . . . Some-body led to the turning on of the Channing faucet just as we sat down at dinner last night. There was biography for you! Why didn't she put all those delicious memories into her Channing Reminiscences? . . . "The hardest work I ever did in my life," she said, "the very hardest"—and we knew she had done a great deal of it—"was copying Channing's sermons from rough notes while he read

4 Franklin Sanborn, *Genius and Character of Emerson* (Boston: Osgood and Co., 1886); Elizabeth Peabody, *Last Evening with Allston and Other Papers* (Boston: D. Lothrop and Co., 1886).

5 Julian Hawthorne, *Nathaniel Hawthorne and His Wife*, 2 vols. (Boston: Houghton Mifflin, 1884).

aloud to me a translation of Plato." That was a test of her brain's duality that she had reason to be proud of. . . . Such a pile of letters as she wrote while we were taking our naps—the rain shutting us all within doors! She seemed a little weary when we gathered around her, intent upon getting her story of Brook Farm, until, some one making an allusion to Spiritualism, she turned on her faucet of reminiscences in that field of wonderful manifestations: her investigation of the subject; her conviction that Spiritualism was not a delusion . . . her own communications with the unseen world; her conversation through a medium with Dr. Channing.[6]

The Piute Indians whom Parker mentioned were the tribal people of Sarah Winnemucca, who had come East in 1883 to rally support among the reform community. The Indian agents in Nevada, or "Indian Ring," as Peabody called them, had been systematically exploiting the Piutes, cheating them out of their treaty-guaranteed land. Peabody worked vigorously to publicize the situation, even writing to President Grover Cleveland's sister Rose Elizabeth, asking her to intercede with him: "Miss Peabody, an old lady of 80 years, sister in law to the late Horace Mann,—craves a private interview with Miss Cleveland. She has received from the Princess Winnemucca of the Piute tribe, a letter addressed to President Cleveland which she wishes Miss P to *deliver* & which certainly does require a little explanation. . . . But let me *see you* and I will say *viva voce* what I want to[—]I have been interested to the point of absorption in the affairs of these three thousand people & their brave champion—& for the last two years I feel sure I can interest you in them."[7]

Besides the appeal of a desperate cause, Sarah Winnemucca touched Peabody because both were teachers. Winnemucca's school in Nevada was unusual in its bilingual instruction. "The expected superiority of *her* school is and must always be that as she knows both languages as *vernacular* (thinks in both) she can teach English *perfectly*; so that her scholars can grow up to be *teachers of English* also *perfectly*, and this will rend the veil that has been hanging between the two races from the beginning; a veil as impenetrable as that dividing the castes of Eastern India from each other!"[8] Unlike many reformers of the time, particularly the backers of the Dawes Severalty Act, Peabody did not believe that Native Americans should be required to give up traditional ways. "In civilizing the Indians, we do not want to have

6 Jane Marsh Parker, "Elizabeth Peabody: A Reminiscence," *The Outlook,* 49 (February 1894): 214–15.

7 Elizabeth Peabody to Rose Elizabeth Cleveland, [1885], MS, NRU.

8 Elizabeth Peabody to Rose Elizabeth Cleveland, 22 December [1885], MS, MnHi.

them exchange their *characteristic* virtues for the characteristic *vices* of civilization—which tend to reduce ⟨men⟩ humanity to *atoms* repulsive to each other instead of assimilating organically . . . & which the *natural* religion of the Indians ensures within the circle of natural relationship."[9] Ednah Dow Cheney recalled that Peabody "did not object to his [the Native American] being required to live in houses and adopt our methods so much because she considered it wrong as because she believed that he had a mission on this earth which was being interfered with. She believed that he had received inspiration from the Great Spirit, handed down through traditions, and she was not willing that any of these traditions should be lost."[10] Given the immense power of the Bureau of Indian Affairs and the influence of the "Friends of the Indian" reform group, it is not surprising that many dismissed Sarah Winnemucca as an angler for poor Miss Peabody's sympathies. The secretary of the Indian Rights Association, on the other hand, warned his group against Peabody "whom he considers her [Winnemucca's] dupe."[11]

Around 1885, Peabody began a long correspondence with Harriet Lothrop, wife of the publisher Daniel Lothrop and author of *The Five Little Peppers* series. This correspondence, like so many others Peabody undertook, covered much territory, but centered on the twin issues of writing and education. Peabody wanted Daniel Lothrop to publish the work of German emigré kindergartner Emma Marwedel, and her own as well, and submitted several lists of possible essays to be included in an edition of her writing.

On February 11, 1887, Mary Mann died. Peabody invited Josephine Jarvis, a kindergarten colleague, to live with her, but apparently this did not come about. In 1888, she moved from Boston's Lamartine Place to the Gordon, a residential hotel. In the last years of the decade she worked on her papers, having in mind the writing of her own memoirs, a task she never accomplished. She died on January 3, 1894.

Elizabeth Peabody's funeral was held on Saturday morning, January 6, 1894, at the Church of the Disciples in Boston. The casket, covered with flowers, rested at the front of the sanctuary, and on the platform slightly above it sat Franklin Sanborn, Julia Ward Howe, Ednah Dow Cheney, and the church's minister, Charles G. Ames. After a

9 Ibid.

10 Ednah Dow Cheney, "Funeral Service," *Kindergarten News* (Springfield, Mass.), 4 (February 1894): 60.

11 Elizabeth Peabody to [?], 26 May [1886], MS, NCaS.

Scripture reading, the kindergarten teachers sang "Lead Kindly Light." Then came the eulogies. Ednah Cheney recalled anecdotes from Peabody's childhood and connected them to her advocacy of early childhood education. Cheney reminded her audience that Peabody lived during revolutionary times, and always sympathized with the oppressed, whether Hungarians, Poles, Italians, or Afro-Americans. Peabody could never understand Boston's deep-rooted racial prejudice. "When she walked down the street arm in arm with a colored man the whole town was aflame with indignation while she was calm, dignified, and unimpassioned." Frank Sanborn described Peabody as "an eager and sympathetic spirit to whom age seemed foreign and activity the only mode of life." While others had fallen away from the Transcendentalist outlook, she had not. "She forgot not the shrine of her youth and hope; the garden never ceased to bloom for her, however sterile and deserted others might deem it; the fountains still flowed from its concealed perennial source, and where its waters went they fed the roots of undying flowers."[12] Elizabeth Palmer Peabody was buried in Concord's Sleepy Hollow Cemetery.

12 Cheney, "Funeral Service," 60.

Almost fifty years after seeking a patronage appointment for Nathaniel Hawthorne, Peabody writes to the wife of President Hayes seeking an appointment for Hawthorne's son.

✄ To Lucy Webb Hayes[1]

Mrs Hayes   Concord,
  My dear Madame   June 10th [1880]
    I cannot hope that you will remember me though when I was in Cambridge, I had the pleasure of nearly half an hour's interview—with a very few others present—But my friend—Mrs. Elizabeth Thompson—who has been with me for a week—tells me that if I send a letter to you *through Mrs. Rogers, she* will put it into your *own* hands and thus I may reach Mr Hayes *directly*—

1 Lucy Ware Webb Hayes was the first female student to attend Ohio Wesleyan University, graduating from Wesleyan Female College in 1850. A child of strongly abolitionist parents, she was instrumental in persuading her husband, attorney

The number of persons of a literary character that Mr Hayes has favoured with appointments, especially the case of Mr Bret Harte,[2] have stirred up some friends of Mr Hawthorne's *only son* to write to me and ask me if it is not possible that he be appointed to some place in Europe of a similar character. He is living at present at "the Crofts" Hastings England.

He is a literary artist of a great deal of talent & quite devoted to his Art—& has engagements to write that bring his daily bread—But he is a *slow writer*, because not a hack writer,—& the sickness & death of his sister Una, two years since, involved him *in debt,* & this presses on him fearfully. He has a delicate wife & *five* children, who practice the most rigid economy, & he is diligent even to the injury of his splendid constitution—He has never thought of asking for office—& feels as if he has no friends *at court*—but *if* he could have some consul-ship—or secretaryship—which would give him the necessaries of life, he could use his pen exclusively to clear off his debts, which did not come upon him by any fault or extravagance of his own,—but by his sister's having pledged her income to an *orphanage* in which she ex-pected to make her own home at the time—but was obliged on ac-count of her own failing strength to leave—And she could not recall her pledge—which was *for five years* & had to go to her brother & live at *his* expense—& *died* before the pledge had expired—to redeem which she had used her principal which was diminished by the *Boston fire*—

I know that personal wants are not qualification for office!!—but this young man has great capacity & his pen work would be better—if he had other work—& his father's contributions to American literature which never brought him on an average $1000 a year from the day he

---

Rutherford B. Hayes, whom she married in 1852, to oppose the further extension of slavery. After her husband's election to the presidency in 1876, Lucy Hayes was more prominent in setting a tone for the White House than many of her predecessors had been, "setting with Hayes an example of wholesome, religious, family-oriented re-spectability comparable to that of the English Queen and her husband" (Francis P. Weisenburger, "Lucy Ware Webb Hayes," *Notable American Women,* 2: 167). Her ban on liquor at White House functions earned her the nickname "Lemonade Lucy." After her husband's term of office, the Hayeses returned to Fremont, Ohio, where Lucy Hayes was active in community, church, and charity organizations until her death.

Nothing ever came of this attempt by Elizabeth Peabody to gain a patronage post for her nephew Julian.

2 In 1878, the California author Bret Harte became U.S. consul at Crefeld, Rhenish Prussia, and from 1880 to 1885 served as U.S. consul at Glasgow.

published the Scarlet letter,—and the fidelity with which he discharged *official duties* to which he was appointed for many years of his life—constitute some claim perhaps for the son—

At all events, I on my own responsibility without my nephew's knowledge—venture to make this confidence to you—of *his private affairs,* to present the case to Mr Hayes—Mr Hawthorne is so much the *pride of the country* that I think his appointment of Hawthorne's *son* would not be found fault with to say the least—

Believe me with the highest respect for yourself & your noble husband—

Yrs in confidence
Elizabeth P. Peabody

MS, OFH

Peabody writes an intense letter begging for details of the relationship between novelist George Eliot and George Henry Lewes, reflecting a devotion to conventional morality despite all her personal idiosyncrasies.

To Ellen D. Conway

My dear Mrs. Conway June 28th 1880

I have just seen your address by an article of Mr Conway's—and I hasten to write to you though I have had no reply to my last—This time I have some questions to ask which I wish you would answer categorically, because in everything that George Eliot has written there seems to me the purest spirit of *chastity* and consecration of marriage. What was *the fact* in regard to her living with Mr Lewes?[1] The story is that she went to him when his wife left him—to nurse him when he was ill unto death apparently and that the friendship—*or* love be-

1 In July 1854, the English novelist George Eliot (Mary Ann Evans) entered into a nonmarital relationship with George Henry Lewes, while she was working as an assistant editor for the *Westminster Review*. Lewes, who had married Agnes Jervis in 1840, left his wife and family for George Eliot. Divorce was apparently not an option, and Lewes continued to support his family, but after 1854 considered himself married to George Eliot. Despite the social disapprobation, their devotion to each other was complete, and Lewes was particularly supportive of George Eliot's writing. Lewes died in 1878, and George Eliot married J. W. Cross on May 6, 1880. She died on December 22, 1880.

tween them recalled him to life. Now—*was* this friendship—or the specific love that makes *two* one body—sacred from all outward violation & separation? As [in?] her late marriage she called herself "spinster" and Marian Evans—it makes me think that she has preserved her maidenhood inviolate and lived with him in the house, keeping it for him in his forlorn widowhood and letting the world say what it would—*trusting in her own character & written word* to answer all the disagreeable deductions & reports of spectators—It was said in a late newspaper that she went there to take care of or educate his children—& not as a nurse to himself—*which is the fact?*—I can conceive that a pure, chaste woman could so disregard the conventions of our social life as to do this thing—tho I do not think it would be possible for one to do it—*so much* do I feel that it is worth while to sacrifice even to *on dit*—in honour of the moral sa[nctity?] of life—than to have the profaning breath of *a question* come near it. But *she* may think otherwise—and undervalued the worth of a *rite* which is so often as so generally profaned & which covers as much brutal selfindulgence so much cruel violation of the personal rights of women—this recent *marriage* of hers seems to me to prove that nothing like *real marriage* took place with Mr. Lewes—I do not say a woman should *never* marry *twice* but if the first marriage of a woman has been a soul-consecrated bodily Union—I should think it would be worse than to be burned alive like the Brahmins wife—I do not say that a man may not marry again righteously & purely—and when the first wife was good and true & for the time wholly lifeabsorbing—nor that a woman whose first marriage was a tragic mistake—may not find her true husband by & bye. But if George Eliot loved Mr Lewes & thought to risk [three words illegible] being an *adulteress* & the world's judgment on the daring act—& the social exclusion it wrought—it seems incredible she should have married *again*—Perhaps—as it is said that the last husband is her man of business—this case ⟨was⟩ is too a case of friendship—but that after what has been said of her living with Mr Lewes she may have [this?] time concluded to shut up men's mouths by going through the ceremony—& that she is virgin still.—I am driven to conjectures of this kind—*because* the creator of *Dorothea* & D[aniel] D[eronda] does seem to me to be entitled to every reverent doubt.—In both cases—*if I am right*—there seems to me *quite sufficient* reason to doubt her judgment but to make a mistake of social doctrine is quite a different thing from *personal degradation* which it would be to give herself to another woman's husband in body—or to marry for *convenience not love* & *a boy* in respect to comparative age—though it is true Mad. de Stael did

the last thing. I know you must know something about the real facts—
& I ask for them in no mean or idle gossiping spirit—I think there is
a world wide difference between *mistaken false theories* & the violation
of the highest law—of personal chastity—though I am in favour of
the time honoured law of marriage, as the one most wonderfully calculated to protect the purity of human generation, & give *adequate*
parentage to the succeeding generations—as well as to *sound* the infinite depths of human relation & of individual souls.—

I lately heard one of the very truest of wives—in a marriage which
reveals the *ineffableness of the love of GOD*—in its mutual self-
emptying devotion of the married pair—*say*—that George Eliot has
said things in her novels which had been of the greatest help to *her*—
but if she was not a truly chaste woman in her life—she could *no
longer be any thing to her*—and that a doubt of it—borne into her
mind when she was sorrowing and *ill*, had nearly cost her *her life*—
for *moral purity in consistency* seemed to her the *axis of the earth*—&
the surest revelation of GOD—the GOD who is Love & Wisdom as well
as Power—in fact those three *in one*—

Have you read my Reminiscences of Dr. Channing? If my publisher had had faith they would succeed he would have printed a thousand copies & given some to give away, or send some himself out of the
country—But he gave me only *five,* and my nieces & nephews want
these—& ought to have them. He has refused to send *one* abroad—I
sent one to the [MS torn] to Captain Maurice with the *selfish* aim of
getting in return the forthcoming volume of *Maurice's life*[2]—when it
shall come out. It will take all the small editions they ⟨I⟩ have printed
to pay the expenses—since the publishers have given an hundred away
to Editors to ensure if possible the sale of the rest—But I know 500
have been sold so I hope they may think it worth while to give another
edition—when I shall get my royalty of ten percent & perhaps more if
I take any part of it in books—as I shall do—for I find I have put so
much of *myself* into the book—that it serves the purpose of a confidential letter to a friend—

I hope you will write me right away about George Eliot & *yourself* & *your dear ones* & tell me something of dear Mrs Travers & what
you hear about Julian Hawthorne & his lovely wife & children. He is
beginning to succeed [one word illegible] a year in earning as income
by his art (literary art)——yrs E. P. Peabody

Give my love to your husband—I would think he *would* be tempted

2 Frederick Maurice, *The Life of Frederick Denison Maurice,* 1884.

to come to a [word illegible] the 12th of July and report the sessions of the Concord School, which very likely equal those of last year would give him a brilliant set of articles for some periodical—or even a book   Give my cordial regards to him & believe me dear Mrs. Conway always your grateful friend, Eliz. P. Peabody

MS, DLC

A long and justly famous letter, chronicling Peabody's relationship with Jones Very more than forty years previous, powerful in its vivid detail and evocation of character.

✼ To William P. Andrews[1]

Nov 12th 1880
Concord Mass

My dear Sir,

You speak of enclosing two *poems* to me, but you forgot to put them into the envelope. Perhaps the only article which I have as yet seen written on Mr. Very, since his death, & which was sent me by Mr Edward Silsbee, was written by you. It appeared in the Sunday Herald, May 16th—In reading it, I changed the chronology of some of the things stated—but I will just give you my reminiscences, & let them criticise this very good article in its trifling inaccuracies.

The first time I saw Mr. Very was in the Salem Lyceum when he read a lecture whose title had attracted me to go and hear him "Why there cannot be another Epic Poem?" which is I believe in print[2]—He was alone on the platform and when his lecture was finished stood for a moment—uncertain, shy, and embarrassed.—Being on the front seat with my father, I said, "Let us ask him to go home with us"—and stepped up to him—to do so—He grasped my outstretched hand like a drowning man, a [word illegible], and accepted the invitation.—As I walked home with him, I expressed my delight in the lecture, & my desire to hear his thoughts on all the current subjects of the day, which were mainly the transcendental topics—I found that he was an enthu-

---

[1] William P. Andrews was one of Very's earliest biographers and editor of *Poems by Jones Very* (Boston: Houghton Mifflin, 1883).

[2] "Epic Poetry" appears in *Essays and Poems by Jones Very* (Boston: Little and Brown, 1839). Peabody's recollection of the events of 1834–38 is remarkably accurate, given the intervening time, and should be compared to the letters written at the time.

siastic listener to Mr. Emerson, and he told me he was writing upon Shakespeare, who had, he thought, betrayed his individual spiritual experience in Hamlet,—which was the utterance of a man who had looked through all human knowledge yet without being sure of the divine knowledge which complements it in order to give the mind peace—and the highest power He was the consciousness of Nature but not the full consciousness of *man* who was created to have dominion over nature—He was possessed by the Universe—perfectly—but did not possess it—This was his difference from Christ—To the perfect impartiality of Shakespeare, to whom all things were equally interesting because they existed, and who painted the fool & the villain with equal interest because they existed, *Christ* adds love of a morally discriminating yet spiritually redemptive character—He seemed to me to say that every Christian was bound to ⟨be⟩ have, or *could* ⟨be⟩ have if he were sincere, this impartial appreciation of his fellow creatures. Mr. Very, that evening, did not seem at all excited or mystical.—

As soon as he was gone I wrote to Mr. Emerson, who at that time was the Chief Curator of the Concord Lyceum.—The little town was then so poor it only paid $10 for a lecture; but the lecturer was invited to the hospitality of Mr. Emerson's house.—I begged him to send for Mr Very at once and make his personal acquaintance and have him lecture. He took my advice and warmly thanked me for giving him the pleasure of so remarkable an acquaintance—

Soon after I heard ⟨what⟩ the circumstances of his family history— his early voyages with his father—his rapid fitting for College and remarkable Career there—and that to his Greek class he was in the habit of preaching—in so interesting a manner that the students felt it a great privilege that he always invited two or three to walk with him every day to "Sweet Auburn."[3]—for he always spoke of the deepest spiritual subjects and in the most devout tone—yet so free from cant as to command their reverence   This was a wonderful proof of power I think—for young men in college will not stand any sanctimony.—He came to our house (we lived then in Charter Street) whenever he came to town, and talked of his Shakespearian Essay and how difficult it was by a moral and spiritual effort to see with the impartiality of Shakespeare—But Shakespeares insight he said was *natural* not spiritual— He did not realize personally that he saw with Him who sends his rain on just and injust—But *we* were *called* to do this!—to do it would be

[3] A reference to Mt. Auburn Cemetery in Cambridge, a favorite retreat for the reclusive Very.

to be hidden in Christ—This identification with Christ seemed to be his aim—It was a spiritual act which would enable us to see what was in man as Christ did.—

One morning I answered ⟨the⟩ a ring at a door, and ⟨found⟩ Mr. Very walked in—He looked much flushed and his eyes very brilliant, and unwinking—It struck me at once that there was something un-natural—and dangerous in his air—As soon as we were within the parlor door he laid his hand on my head,—and said "I come to baptize you with the Holy Ghost & with fire"—and then he prayed—I cannot remember his words but they were thrilling—and as I stood under his hand, I trembled to the centre—But it was my instinct—not to antago-nize but to be perfectly quiet—I felt he was beside himself and I was alone in the lower story of the house.—When he had done I sat down and he at a little distance, did the same—and there was a dead si-lence.—Soon he said,—with a slightly uneasy misgiving said, How do you feel? I replied gently, "I feel no change"—"But you will"—said he hurriedly—"I am the Second Coming—Give me a Bible"—There was one in the room to which I pointed. He went to the table where it was and turned to Christ's prophecy of the Second Coming—and read it ending with the words, "This day is this fulfilled in your hear-ing"—I was silent but respectful even tenderly so—I thought this was perhaps a passing frenzy caused by overtaxing his brain in the attempt to look from the standpoint of Absolute Spirit. He then left me, and after a little while I went to see my friend Mrs. Foote.—and there I learned that Mr. Very before he came to see me went to see several of the ministers of the town to baptize *them*—Two had resisted him *bodily*—The Baptist minister had actually put him bodily out of the house, and Mr. Upham, who at that time was a good deal excited against the transcendentalists, calling Mr. Emerson an Atheist—and declaring that it was wrong to listen to him,—had told ⟨him⟩ Mr. Very that he should see that he be sent to the Insane Asylum—Hearing this I walked directly up to his mother's house—She was a person of great energy—was said to have more than doubts of another world and of the existence of God—having had a severe experience of life, and being at odds with the existing state of society—a disciple of Fanny Wright—She did not receive me graciously at first, but I persevered till she recognized that I was opposed to all violent methods—and had the greatest reverence for her son. When she told me she was sure he was not insane, but more sane than others, that he was an *angel* whom God had inspired—and a *proof* that there *was* a God above us who was Infinite Love—, I cannot remember her exact words but I know that I was so struck with what she said, that it seemed to me that to produce such a result in her mind was reason sufficient for Providence giving her the wondrous sign—She had had a stormy interview with Mr. Upham I found—and declared that Mr. Very should *not* be carried to the Insane Hospital. She said that if there was anything in him that seemed insane it was caused by the brutal manner in which he had been treated.—I left the house about twelve o'clock and understood from her that he was resting in his chamber—

That evening he again appeared at my door. He came in very quietly and said, "I misunderstood the Holy Ghost—the time is not yet for the baptism of fire—Nothing can be done with violence in the Second Coming—You are all in the baptism of John—I only am in the son—and I must speak as the Son"—

With these words (or to this effect) he unfolded a monstrous folio sheet of paper, on which were four double columns of sonnets—which he said "the Spirit had enabled" him to write and these he left with me to read as the utterances of the Holy Ghost.—

They were the very sonnets afterwards published by Mr. Emerson—I read them with wonder—and wrote at once to Mr. Emerson and told him all these phenomena—and Mr. Emerson, as soon as possible got him again to his house.—

But I think there was a little time elapsed first. His brother Washington saw & agreed with me—that there was some disease about his brain—an intensity of action of the higher intuitive powers suspending those of the common sense—He went with him to Cambridge to see Mr. Edward Channing, then Professor of Rhetoric there—with whom Mr. Very had left the papers on Shakespeare—and Mr. Very was persuaded to go to Somerville—and under the medical discipline of Dr. Wyman, he finished the essay there—The considerate and tender manner in which everything was done, took down the excitement—but still Mr. Very retained his point of view—He believed himself to have made the sacrifice of self necessary to identification with the *hiding in Christ* which made him the voice of the Holy Ghost, pure and simple—He said every man would attain to this when he made the final sacrifice, which took different forms in different individuals—the bosom Idol he had had to sacrifice was Beauty—In one of our conversations I asked him what *I* had to sacrifice in order to be *a filial obedience* (which he said was the highest attitude for a finite spirit to attain) and he said, "Spiritual Curiosity"—Of a well known person much talked of at that time for his transcendentalism he said, "he was a spiritual dandy"—He went to see Dr. Channing—I think the Dr. did *not* send for *him* but he went of his own accord & called on him. Dr. Channing told me of his visit, and was immensely impressed and touched with his union of gentleness, modesty, and yet complete sense of his word being the utterance of the Holy Spirit.—I remember Dr. Channing said—Yes, he had lost his *senses,* but only that part of his mind which was connected therewith—there was an iron sequence of thought—Men in general said he—have lost or never found this higher mind—*Their* insanity is profound,—his is only superficial.—To hear him talk was like looking into the purely spiritual world—into truth itself—He had nothing of self-exaggeration—He seemed ⟨only⟩ rather to have obtained self annihilation & become an oracle of God. He quoted some of his sayings— (identical with many parts of his sonnets)—as proofs of the 'iron sequence' of his thought   I remember his repeating "He had not lost his *Reason*   He has only lost his *Senses.*"

The tender reverence of Dr. Channing's manner to him—as described by Mr Phillips who was present, accounted for the impression he made on Mr Very—who came immediately to see me, and declared that Dr. Channing was nearer to the kingdom of heaven than any body he had yet seen—"What has he to sacrifice to be in it?" I asked—He replied, *"his love of rectitude."*

I was greatly struck with his answer—It expressed Dr. Channing's perhaps *extreme* sense of moral responsibility—I thought—or *personal* responsibility perhaps I should say.

The extreme tension of Mr. Very's mind seemed gradually to subside—and especially when talking with me. In stating his thought he would often smile, as if recognizing that from *my* point of view it must seem absurd & he made allowance for me.—I especially remember this most beautiful, *considerate* tender smile—with which he silently answered me when once I said, "Mr Very—I feel as if I *could* take your point of view—but I do not dare to—because if I did I am afraid I should lose my senses and could never recover ⟨them⟩ myself again." He entirely repudiated the role of a proselytizer—His whole duty was to utter the words given him by the Holy Spirit—he was not responsible for their effect or non-effect upon others—I think sometimes Mr. Hawthorne was present when he was calling on me—At all events I know Mr. Hawthorne was greatly interested in these remarkable mental phenomena—and said one day that he more than realised the conception of entire subjectiveness he had tried to describe in the preacher of "the Story teller"—But the intellectual development of Mr. Very was previously so great, that it made his *ecstasy* altogether *sui generis—*

I was attending Margaret Fuller's Conversations at the time—and one evening I told him that the subject next time was the difference between Wisdom & Genius—What is the difference, Mr. Very? He looked at me then with that wonderfully sweet smile and replied—"To the preexistent Shakespeare wisdom was offered—but he refused it and *fell* into genius"—and I thought I discerned in this sentence what he meant when he spoke of the different nature of the universality of Shakespeare and of Christ—

I cannot tell the precise date of the visit to Mr. Emerson in which they together ⟨arranged⟩ selected the sonnets for the volume. I think it was very soon after they were written *impromptu*. Now and then a metaphor would not be fully carried out, but a slight verbal connection was necessary.—I remember Mr. Emerson said Mr. Very was very averse to correction—declaring that it was the utterance of the Holy Ghost. But Mr. Emerson said he said to him,—but we cannot permit the Holy Ghost to be careless (& in one instance) to talk bad grammar.

Our family's leaving Salem to live in Boston in 1840 brought my acquaintance with Mr. Very to an abrupt close—He never came to see me in Boston—As the preternatural excitement of his nerves subsided—I was told that he shunned society. It was not easy for me to do anything about it—But now that he is gone I marvel that in 40 years I did not do something to ⟨keep⟩ reopen intercourse with a Spirit so rare—I think I got the impression from someone—that it was painful to Mr. Very himself to recur to a season—in which he certainly was in a degree *beside himself*. I was afraid I might wound him by alluding to it or I do think I should have written to him—It is most painful to think he might have pined for intercourse which was so sympathetic and respectful as mine was—Ah—as Mr. Emerson once exclaimed in a lecture, "It is wonderful how painful is experience—Infinite Compensations cover every beloved name!"

We might have more of heaven upon earth than we do were we only faithful to the opportunities—and took counsel of our *hearts*. I can forgive the Misses Very for being unforgiving of what seemed to them *willful neglect*. But nature was faithful, doubtless to the heart that loved her—and surely *God was*—to such enthusiastic *obedience*. I hope in the projected volume there will be a wise selection of all *that is best*—leaving out what is only cousin to it   But I wish I could see *all* his manuscripts! If you ever come near Concord come & see me I pray—yours truly E. P. Peabody.

MS, MWelC

Peabody's letter of sympathy to Emerson's widow, that same Miss Jackson whom she had interrogated in the 1830s.

✸ To [Lidian Emerson]

My very dear friend   Boston Monday Evening, May 2nd [1882]

I remained in Concord till ¼ of 1 today—but neither yesterday or today did I feel it right to attempt to see you—for I thought you probably could not hear one emotion more & perhaps the association with those early days when I was so much with you would excite some— With your faith I know you do not feel separated but more than ever united and are rejoicing that he no longer "Sees through a glass darkly—but *face to face*"[1]—I have heard with great pleasure of your being together so much with friends in the evenings this winter—Of his occasional expressions of weariness with his interrupted utterance and oblivious memory—Of his not painful illness—& of the relief of the pain of his last hours by the ether your brother's genius discovered[2]—and can believe that he was among "the cloud of witnesses" that always hovers over the beloved *life* by those who pass on into glory—compensated for all the vexations of his earthly life connected with that discovery in beholding the mortal pains it has removed and is all the time removing from the children of men—*Of course* it is impossible that human nature should not grieve for the loss to sight of *the beloved*—but is it not delightful to [sense?] that those within the veil do not experience the separation because their larger life must needs comprehend ours—And those in the higher mansions must love the freedom of those in the lower—As Milton says

> Millions of spiritual creatures
> walk the earth
> Both when we wake and
> when we sleep[3]

I was most grateful that you remembered me to have me asked to come to the house—and whenever you are rested enough from other

1 "For now we see through a glass darkly, but then face to face," 1 Cor. 13:12. Emerson died April 17, 1882.
2 Charles T. Jackson is credited with the discovery of the anesthetic properties of ether.
3 *Paradise Lost*, book 4, line 677.

friends to be able to see me I will go up in the eleven oclock train if a letter or postal card can be dropped to me—at my new residence 54 Bowdoin Street Boston

When Christ said to his disciples "Lo I am ever with you to the end of the world" did he not announce the general law that governs the intercourse of the ascended with their beloved ones here below?— I was glad to hear that you were willing to live a little longer with your children—My sister Mary was not able to go to Concord—but if she keeps still she is wonderfully well—and sends you her most affectionate sympathy & congratulations

Yours always
Elizabeth P. Peabody

MS, MH

More family quarreling, this time over restoring the Wayside as a Hawthorne memorial and over Dr. Grimshawe's Secret.

✎ To Horatio Bridge

Boston, 54 Bowdoin
[January 1883][1]

Dear Sir,—

The plan of making "The Wayside" into a memorial of Hawthorne was planned by a lady of Concord, who knew that people often came to Concord—*& were disappointed* at not being permitted to go into the study tower, & also that the chairs & desk he used were not there, & that the little library where ⟨his⟩ that beautiful photo was taken in London, without his being aware, by the tact of Motley, was also *shut up*[2]—for Lathrop was very nervous—& Rose always immensely anxious to keep him unannoyed. This lady knew that it was very hard for Lathrop to *pay* the yearly installments on the house—& at the moment the plan was conceived, both Rose & Lathrop were away from the house & the impression was that the death of the child had made it a too painful residence for them[3]—& Julian with his wife

[1] This letter has been dated "January 1883" by Bowdoin College Library.

[2] For Peabody's role in perpetuating a curious story about this picture, called the "Lothrop Motley" photo of Hawthorne, see her letter to the Salem *Gazette*, August 21, 1886.

[3] Rose and George's son Francis died February 6, 1881, of diphtheria.

& children were there—*They* were spoken to and did say they thought that Lathrop would be glad to sell it to the nation if the money could be raised by dollar subscriptions, as had been proposed for Longfellow's monument. Mrs. Julian Hawthorne said Julian would put his father's chair & desk in the room in the tower, & there might be a Mark Twain scrapbook there for the autographs of all who sent their dollars—which in the end would make a curious thing to be seen.

I was then consulted & asked to speak to Lathrop—who said he had undertaken to purchase the place—precisely because it was *Hawthorne's*—& a clear object with [word illegible] Hawthorne to have a place in America that was *his own* & he had been at much expense to send home pieces[?] from abroad to ornament it—It seemed to Lathrop an act of *impiety* to sell it,—& precisely because it was such a pecuniary burden to pay for it—he was sure the uncharitable world would believe that it was a mean speculation *on his part* to get the house paid for.—He said if he could afford it he would make another entrance to the house between the two parlours & let the door under the tower be the one into which the people could come & go up to the tower, & would keep a servant to attend to it. For a time however, he did not quite decide, and meanwhile he wanted it kept a secret that the subject had been raised to him—& thought *I* was too near a relative to be known as saying anything about it to the public.

Hence my caution to you not to mention it;—and meanwhile he and Rose have returned to the house in July after Julian had left it. Julian's family had been in it for the winter at Rose & Lathrop's invitation. The death of the child had so touched Julian that he wrote a letter to Rose in which he said such lovely things to Lathrop—that it healed the breach & they went to see him in London[4]—You have read of the cross purposes in the bringing out of Dr Grimshawe's se-

---

[4] On the death of Francis Lathrop, Julian Hawthorne wrote a letter of condolence, dated March 15, 1881. This act brought about a measure of reconciliation, and the two families visited in England during the summer of 1881. This truce came to an end in 1886 when Julian announced that he was publishing a new and complete novel by his father, *Dr. Grimshawe's Secret*. The Lathrops were sure they had seen all of Nathaniel Hawthorne's writing, and Rose went so far as to write the *New York Tribune* on August 16, 1882, that "no such unprinted work has been in existence. . . . It cannot be truthfully printed as anything more than an experimental fragment." The Lathrops' contention that Julian had assembled a novel from fragments and was passing it off as an authentic Hawthorne novel is corroborated by Edward Davidson, who has shown how Julian patched together drafts and passages into a novel (*Dr. Grimshawe's Secret,* ed. Edward Davidson [Cambridge: Harvard University Press, 1954]). For a full account of the Lathrop-Hawthorne quarrel, see Bassan, *Hawthorne's Son,* 119, 158–60.

cret—But this has not again broken their intercourse—Neither party meant to wrong the other—Rose did not know of the manuscript Una had & had assured Houghton & Mifflin there was nothing more ever to be printed & Houghton & Mifflin who had paid for the right to publish all & had told the public their edition comprised all—*required* her to justify them.—Julian thought that to dedicate the book to Rose and Lathrop would show the public they were friends & was not prepared for the uncharitable public's taking the act as an ironical insult—But they concluded on both sides to say nothing more to the public on their private relations which are entirely friendly. Julian was at Staten I[sland]   I mean near that post office in New York—at the Russian consul's house which he gets for the taxes   So is well situated & seems to do very well with his pen   He has a splendid wife and children & looks like his father more & more.—But to return to the memorial plan Rose & Lathrop have been in their house again since July last & have come to feel that their child's life give it a new consecration & will not part with it—but are working to pay for it.—I hope that it may come some day into the hands of *Hawthorne*—the name does not seem to be in any danger of dying out for Julian has *three sons*   The original projector of the memorial is trying to work out some plan of getting that *tower chamber* into the possession of the nation—She says why cannot the dollar subscription be proposed without saying what is the nature of the monument proposed—& when a sufficient sum is found to be subscribed—go to Lathrop & propose to buy the tower chamber paying sufficient to enable him to keep a servant to *tend the door,* & securing the ultimate possession of the house as has been suggested in the case of Longfellow's house—& if money enough should be subscribed why not have a statue of Hawthorne—a reproduction in marble of the sitting figure of the photograph above mentioned—which is quite a wonderful likeness—the monument to be erected in the beautiful lawn on the west of the house—To have it there would ensure that the property should never pass out of the hands of the descendants   What do you think of this— would you like to be named as the treasurer of such a fund?—

I think perhaps we had better wait till the Longfellow Memorial is made—But then when we delay to execute *our thought*   Death is likely to mock our show of [word illegible]—If you come north next summer I hope we may meet & talk over some plan—& you become the President of a memorial society like the Longfellow one—

I especially like the idea of a dollar subscription to a memorial of a great American because it is completely *American* & *democratic*

Were you not very interested in those passages of Grimshaw's Secret in which Hawthorne compares the English & American & give his ideal of true American selfrespect—?

> Yours truly
> ELIZABETH P. PEABODY

MS, MeB

Peabody hopes that the editor of a Boston newspaper will not unfairly represent the situation of the Piutes.

✎ To Edwin Munroe Bacon[1]

Mr. Bacon   Boston,
    My dear Sir,—   [1883]
    I wish I could have a half hour's talk with you. Could you come to see me [at] 54 Bowdoin Street or appoint a time for me to come & see you?
    I heard that there was an unfavorable notice of Sarah Winnemucca Hopkins' book in the Advertiser ("Life among the Piutes") when it first come out;[2] and I was away with her on a journey which included a visit by invitation to Senator Dawes' house who was interested in her by a letter she wrote to him, *criticising* the Senatorial bill.[3] He met us at the cars at the time appointed & took us home and gave us the most affectionate hospitality telling us that his daughter had a meeting already organized for her. After dinner when *he* heard her speak & shared in the great interest she excited—and in the evening after tea—he took her into his study & had a long talk with her—and said he should bring her before the Indian Committee of which he is chairman—& he told me to multiply occasions for her *to speak* as it

---

1 Edwin Munroe Bacon, journalist and author, was editor of the *Boston Daily Advertiser* in 1883.
    2 Sarah Winnemucca Hopkins, *Life Among the Piutes,* privately printed in 1883.
    3 Henry Laurens Dawes was a Massachusetts congressman and senator. In 1884, Dawes sponsored successful legislation to grant to the Piutes land out of which they had been cheated, but this legislation was never implemented. In 1887, Dawes sponsored the act bearing his name that granted to each male Native American head-of-household 160 acres in severalty, thus breaking up tribally held lands.

was desirable that she should *stir hearts* as she did that day (& always
does) to press in Congress the consideration of the Indian question—
which like other moral and philanthropic questions were all to be
postponed for merely political ones. Since then she has spoken in my
hearing in Providence Hartford New York Newburgh Poughkeepsie
Dorset in Vermont Salem Cambridge Boston again and in Philadelphia—& already more than 3000 names to her petitions which three
of our Representatives are about to present. Now in Mr Goddard's
time the Indian question was best supported in the Advertiser—but
since she has been here—it has seemed especially to avoid speaking of
her. Now I want to tell you how she has been misrepresented in some
quarters—& how every thing has been thoroughly investigated & every
thing is perfectly right about her. She has shared our bed & board for
months this last summer and fall. I want the Daily Advertiser to recognize her & her cause—& think you will agree.

Truly yours
ELIZ. P. PEABODY

TS copy, OYesA

---

*A Hawthorne reminiscence, written by Peabody for (probably) Francis
Henry Lee, a Salem antiquarian.*

✄ To [Francis Henry Lee][1]

54 Bowdoin Street Boston
Feb 3 [ca. 1885][2]

My dear Sir
    I wish I were in my usual health & vigor,—but perhaps it is for-
tunate for you that I am not able to write out all my associations with
Chestnut Street—from youth to age—
    Mr. Hawthorne lived there in 1847,—in which year his son Julian
was born in Boston,[3]—and it was decided not to return to Herbert

---

[1] This letter bears no name of correspondent, but is probably addressed to
Francis Henry Lee, a Salem philanthropist and local historian, who corresponded
with a number of Salem residents with a view to publishing a book of reminiscences
about Salem houses and people. He never published this book.

[2] According to the staff of the Essex Institute, Salem, this letter and another to
Lee date from around 1885, judging from other Lee correspondence and notes.

[3] Julian was actually born on June 22, 1846.

Street. You cannot remember Una & Rose running into your mother's house as Rose was not born till 1851, when they were living in Lenox.—As there was not a bit of a yard to the house near Boots Court (or in it) Una could never play outside, & I dare say your mother was very kind in inviting her in there—She was about three years old at the time—And I remember my sister said she had to pass much time dragging the baby in his basket carriage on the side walk with Una as attendant. There was no room in the house for a study for Mr. Haw-thorne—of less consequence *then* because, while he had business cares, he could not compose stories. He had proved at Brook Farm that it was too late for *him* to combine imaginative creation with external ac-tivity, though he agreed with Dr. Franklin that it would be best for society, and more healthy—in the long run for mind as well as body—to give some hours of the day to one & some to the other kind of labour.

But the habits of forty years cannot be changed.—He enjoyed his life in Chestnut Street—however perusing the living books his chil-dren opened to him. He would get home from the Custom house at 5 o'clock—& have some hours delightful intercourse with the children of which my sister would write to our mother, & when they were out to bed he would read to his wife—From Chestnut Street they removed to Mall Street, his mother & sisters taking part of the house, and there his mother died—Soon after came the loss of his office—& his return to his pen—and the Scarlet letter was published while he was there[4]—his first pecuniary success as an author, & his removal to Lenox which he left in the fall of 1851, having first published while there the House of Seven Gables, The Wonderbook & Tanglewood Tales.[5] The winter of 1851–2 he lived in Mr. Mann's house in West Newton, while ⟨he⟩ Mr. M was in Congress the second year.

But all this is irrelevant to your purpose which involves only the short period of his residence in Chestnut Street Salem—My acquain-tance with Chestnut Street began about 1812, when we moved from Union Street to the corner of Cambridge & Essex—I became playmate with Hannah and Horatio Robinson who lived at the corner of Cam-bridge & Chestnut. There was then a private School for boys in Chest-nut Street which was very aristocratic—This was broken up after the peace of 1815–16 when there was an attempt to unite democrats &

[4] *The Scarlet Letter* was published in March 1850.

[5] *The House of Seven Gables* was published in April 1851, *The Wonder-Book* in July 1851, and *Tanglewood Tales* early in 1852.

federalists in the municipal government & a great movement was made to have adequate public education for boys—The school committee consisting of 6 of each party, and the new school house was built on Broad Street—

If you will come and see me I will be very happy to answer any questions you may like to ask—I have very strong & interesting associations with the names of all the families the Pickerings, Saltonstalls, Mrs. Tom Saunders, the Peirces, the Dodges, the Phillipses—and when I returned in 1836 to Salem (which I left in 1820 as a resident) I renewed associations with Mrs. Cole, the Misses Hodges &c. I remember when your father first came to Salem the ward of Mr. Pickering, & finding him married when I returned 17 years after.

The latest interesting inhabitant who came into the Street was Mrs. [?] Samuel Johnson, recently deceased—I have taken up a good deal of space saying nothing but perhaps *viva voce* I might be more interesting than with the pen—

If you see my dear and respected friend Mrs. Cole please say to her I send my most respectful regards and also remember me to your mother—

I am, dear Sir yours—kindly—
ELIZABETH P. PEABODY

I should like much to hear your reminiscences & see your illustrations

MS, MSaE

An early memory of the Hathornes, and Peabody's "discovery" of the mysterious author who turned out to be Nathaniel Hawthorne.

To Francis Henry Lee

Dear Mr. Lee,   [1885]
I am writing Reminiscences of my Life & times for posthumous publication but I think I can make a few extracts from the part which tells of my earliest recollections of Salem of which I was not a native but went there in 1808 on my 4th birthday, for it is one of my earliest recollections that my father told me when we were driving thither from Lynn in a carriage to remember that I went to live in Salem on my 4th birthday. My sister Sophia who married Mr. Hawthorne was

born in Salem, in a house in Summer Street in September 1809, and when she was two years old it is a curious coincidence that we lived in the Fontein building in Union Street very near the house in which Hawthorne was born.[1] But his mother in her widowhood moved into a house belonging to her brother in Herbert Street the next street east.[2]—My sister Mary who used to play out doors with the neighbor's children remembers playing with Hawthorne, and his sisters, for there was communication through the ⟨back⟩ yards of the houses of both streets—But I was a less playful child and I only remember his eldest sister Elizabeth who was a year older than I and he, who were of the same age within six weeks, he having been born July 4th & I May 16th 1804. The circumstances were these My mother had given up keeping school to her sister Amelia who with her adopted mother Mrs. Cranch had taken it into Mall Street, that my mother might devote herself to the care of Sophia who had a terrible time in getting her teeth, aggravated undoubtedly by the medication in the heroic method which was at its height, at that time mercury being given even to babies for every little ail, & my poor sister who was made a sufferer for life by ⟨the⟩ her loss of blood ⟨she lost⟩ in a most frightful [salvation?].—I remember mother always sitting with Sophia on a pillow in her lap—and she had me there endeavouring to teach me who at six years old could hardly read intelligibly though I had been taught for two years.—⟨and⟩ But though ⟨so stupid in that⟩ backward in perception I was precocious in ⟨some ways⟩ reflection & remember how warmly used to be discussed the peculiarity of the widow Hawthorne who had shut herself up after her husbands death & made it the habit of her life never to sit down at a table but always eat her meals above in the chamber she never left. For this, she was constantly criticized & ⟨blamed⟩ condemned by the neighbours, including connections of the family, whom she would not see but my mother's sensibility & imagination were touched by what she heard; and being told ⟨of⟩ that the smart little Elizabeth, ⟨who⟩ was a bookworm, she took the occasion to write to Mrs. Hawthorne a note, to ask her if she would allow Elizabeth to come to ⟨her⟩ our house to be taught an hour or two a day, be-

---

1 The name of this building apparently comes from its owner or resident. It was, as Peabody says, on Union Street and its backyard probably touched that of Hawthorne's boyhood home at 10½ Herbert Street. I am grateful to Ellen Mark for this information, as well as for data on Francis Lee and on the approximate date of this letter.

2 Nathaniel Hawthorne's father, also named Nathaniel, was a sailor. He died in Surinam in 1808, aged thirty-two.

cause she wanted a companion to stimulate a dull little girl of her own by example—My mother had a wonderful epistolary power, & I dare say she made Mrs. Hawthorne feel her respect & sympathy. At all events Mrs. Hawthorne was so much touched by the note, that she not only complied with her request, but sent through Elizabeth an invitation to mother to call & see her, which she did, and found her a most intelligent, well read, and lively woman. (But my youthful admiration for the astonishing learning of Elizabeth reacted to discourage me who had no power of utterancy at all—at that time)

We soon moved away to the corner of Cambridge & Essex St to a house owned by Miss Susy Hawthorne (or Hathorne, as it was spelled & pronounced then), and the other acquaintance was dropped. Some eight or ten years after when Mrs. Hawthorne was living at Sebago Pond in Maine[3] (where she had gone with her children upon a farm of one of her brothers) I saw a letter written by Elizabeth Hawthorne to one of her schoolmates in the beauty of whose composition was so great and the subject matter so interesting, that I obtained permission to copy it off—and planned to write & ask her for correspondence, on the pretext of our ⟨youthful⟩ childish intimacy. But I had not quite courage to do this & in 1820 left Salem for residence in Lancaster Massachusetts. When however some 15 years later, I heard after years of wondering who was the author of certain tales in the Tokens & New England Magazine among the rest "the Gentle Boy" I learned on returning to Salem to live in 1836, that they attributed to a son of the widow ⟨s' son⟩ Hawthorne.[4] Now I did not remember any son only Elizabeth, & I concluded at once that the stories were written by Elizabeth for I argued that a man who could write so would be very distinguished, & of this man I had never heard & nobody in Salem seemed to know any thing about him.

And so I determined to call on her and attempt to renew our intimacy, altho I heard that ever since Mrs. Hawthornes return to Herbert Street about 15 years before, Elizabeth had shut herself up; & refused to see any body, lying in bed all day and reading, and like her mother refusing to see any visitors whatever.

Nevertheless I called, and was told, by an old aunt who also had a domicile of her own in the house that though Mrs. Hawthorne &

---

[3] Madame Hawthorne moved her family to the shore of Sebago Pond near Raymond, Maine in the fall of 1818 when Nathaniel was fourteen.

[4] *New England Magazine* was published in Boston from 1831 to 1835. *Tokens* was begun in 1825 by Samuel Griswold Goodrich and merged with the *Atlantic Souvenir*.

Elizabeth never saw visitors—there was another sister Louisa who was more like ordinary people. I was ushered by her into a neat little parlour on the second floor where Miss Louisa received me. When I told her of my early acquaintance with Elizabeth, and my desire to renew the acquaintance she said, But Lizzie never sees any body; ⟨she said⟩ I know it but ⟨I thot⟩ thought she might make an exception of me, who never had forgotten her, and who felt acquainted with her from the Gentle Boy & other tales that I named—

She replied—But it was not Lizzie but my brother who wrote those tales—

I had been so certain & had maintained to Miss Susan Burley[5] & others who like me had long wondered after the author, that I was silenced—All right I said—If your brother wrote those stories he has no right to be idle—He never is idle, she said; then rising, added I will go & tell Lizzie of yr call—she soon came back laughing and said Lizzie says that if you will come some evening she will come out and see you—

But she did not say *what* evening, and in vain waited for weeks for the special invitation I expected. ⟨At length I met Louisa in the street⟩ But not long after this the first edition of the Twice Told Tales was printed,[6] and a copy was sent to me "With the respects of Nathaniel Hawthorne" and soon after I wrote a note to Miss Elizabeth & told her I wanted to ask of her brother what were the steps to take to get an article into the Democratic Review (for I had heard that Mr. O'Sullivan had been in Salem to engage her brother as a contributor to it;[7] and ⟨why not⟩ won't all three of you put aside ceremony & come & pass *this* evening with me? It was Saturday noon & my idea was that this invitation which I knew would be a most unexpected surprise might succeed—if there was not too much time given for them to deliberate, and my device succeeded, as I will proceed to tell.

But this [is] a long enough article for your little paper, and I will defer the account of my first meeting with Hawthorne himself to your next issue, if you are to have one, and care to have it. He often ⟨E. P.

5 A prominent Salem socialite, Susan Burley encouraged Sophia Peabody in her artistic endeavors. Miss Burley was famous for her parties, and was delighted when Elizabeth brought Nathaniel Hawthorne to her house for a literary evening in 1839.
6 The first edition of *Twice-Told Tales* appeared in March 1837 under the imprint of the Boston American Stationers Company. The second edition was issued in 1842. Elizabeth Peabody went to see Hawthorne at his family's Herbert Street house in March 1837.
7 John Louis O'Sullivan was cofounder, with S. D. Langtree, of the *United States Magazine and Democratic Review* and was coeditor from 1837 to 1846.

Peabody⟩ told me that that invitation of mine made an era in his life.

ELIZABETH P. PEABODY

and she said "I thought you were coming to see Lizzie some evening—" I replied "I did not know what evening she would like to have me come. Oh any evening! she replied.—So again I was nonplussed. But just then the Twice Told Tales was published and a volume was sent to me with the respects of the author, which gave me opportunity if I had not been stupid to write to him & invite him to come & see me—

Soon after the Democratic Review was got up, and O'Sullivan came to Salem to find Hawthorne and engage him for a contribution, which I did not know till a little time after, when wanting to print an article of my own[8] I enquired of a friend in Boston, how I should proceed, & he told me to ask my townsman Hawthorne—whom O'Sullivan had just been to see. Then I wrote a note to Elizabeth & told her I wanted to see her brother on some literary business—And why will you not all three come & pass this evening with me—

It was Saturday noon when I sent this note, and all my family laughed at me for thinking they might come

MS, MSaE

8 "And she said . . . of my own" is written on separate sheets after the signature, and may come from another letter, or from a draft or copy of this letter.

Peabody writes to President Grover Cleveland's sister on the Indian question, and reveals her astute knowledge of political corruption.

✕ To Rose Elizabeth Cleveland

Dear Miss Cleveland,   [1885]

I saw by the newspaper yesterday, that the new Commissioner,[1] who, I understand, was in Congress once with Mr. Price[2]—expresses great respect for him and keeps him in office, as it were, for a time, *in order to join on* his administration to the old one—& I am in dis-

1 The new commissioner was J. D. C. Atkins, Commissioner of Indian Affairs from 1885 to 1888.
2 Hiram Price was Commissioner of Indian Affairs from 1880 to 1884.

may. I think perhaps your brother will simply put Sarah's letter into *his* hands, and ask him to see to the matter, & He will consult *Mr. Price*—who authorised a statement in the Baltimore Sun which brought me on from Boston to see into—Had I had time to get to the end of my talk with you & tell you the *last six months* of *martyrdom* of Sarah— & the way in which the Indian Ring has operated; you would have seen that in doing the right thing now—not only this maltreated tribe would be relieved—but a great light thrown on the *whole Indian problem*—for no tribe had the advantage of *this one* in having one of *themselves* civilized with *the language*—so as to be able to deal first hand with the government and dispense altogether with the corrupt *agency*. For the difficulty is *not* in the legislation of Congress so much as in the *maladministration of the Indian Office* (that one by its very nature liable to the greatest temptations to corruption & which *in the last 25 years*, without change of *party* (though *six changes of personalle* has become the most *gigantic mass* of corruption) after seeing Mr. Price may only hope [word illegible] in this *radical change* & a possible *return* to first principles—

I think your brother may simply refer Sarah's letter, or put it into the hands of the new Commissioner & ask him to look into the matter *he* will carry it to *Mr Price*—& Mr. Price is just the mouthpiece of the Indian ring (perhaps unconsciously) & will fill Mr. Atkins with the falsehood of 25 years growth.

Now—seeing that Sarah [refers ?] to *me,* first of all her references— *if*—your brother does do that I wish he would ask Mr. Atkins to *send for me* & have a conversation in which I can show him documents that have accumulated in my hands these last two years—(& I have had copied in Calligraph so that they can be perused within half an hour)—

I had these in my pack at each time I saw you & meant to *end* by showing them to you—& thought perhaps you would wish to show them to your brother,—

I shall take this note [around?] to you *to day* & put it into your hands at your today's reception,—& hope I shall not be *too late*!

One important reason for a radical change in party every now & then—is, that as soon as a party becomes paramount—all the rascals *rush into it* & the *administration* necessarily becomes corrupt—& needs a thorough ventilation & breaking up of *rings* which in a free country are an *inevitable growth*—& of all rings this *Indian* Ring has in it the greatest element of evil—the Indians being *men* who are virtually deaf & dumb & cannot speak for themselves as the other interests can (Rail roads—Bonds—&c—&c)—

The fact that one of themselves is raised up by Providence to be *tongue* is, I think, "the little stone cut out of the mountain without hands" "which shall *smite* the image clay and stone & brass that looks so unconquerable, & overthrow it—& fill the whole earth" as *of old!*

You & I must have *another* hour of conference on this matter & who knows but we may begin a new era? Woman's *wit* is needed in *administration*—The only good thing that has been done in the Indian matters is "the giving lands in severalty & other [water?] rights to the *Omahas* & that has been done *wholly* through the instrumentality of Alice Fletcher, who first *studied* the Indian side, so as to be their representative,[3]—going to their wigwams & *living with them*—& surprising their secrets out of them, by this proof of sympathy. I should like to show you a letter I have from her. In this work she has made herself a cripple *for life*—her beautiful black hair has turned *white* in the hardships she has endured—*but the work was accomplished* in every *detail by her solely.*—Sarah Winnemucca was *born* to the knowledge—ability & disinterested love Alice Fletcher *acquired.*—But enough—too much perhaps—*with my pen* yours *affectionately*

E. P. Peabody

MS, NRU

[3] Alice Fletcher, privately educated, studied archeology and ethnology in the 1870s. In the late 1870s and the 1880s, she became interested in Indian reform; she traveled west and lived among the Omahas, absorbing their culture, and becoming convinced of their desperate situation. She believed that a severalty bill for the Omahas would best preserve their land, and successfully lobbied such a bill through Congress in 1882. Fletcher was also instrumental in gaining passage of the Dawes Severalty Act in 1887, widely hailed as a liberal victory.

A frank letter to the niece of a fellow kindergartner, commenting on the failings of Julian Hawthorne's biography of his parents and expressing Peabody's hope that a book doing justice to Hawthorne could be written.

✼ To Amelia Boelte[1]

Jamaica Plain
Massachusetts, U.S.A.

My dear Miss Boelte,   May 2nd, 1886

I hope you got my postal card announcing this letter and the books. I have been sick and crowded with inevitable business, and this is my first hour to write, and I hope I am not too late, and that your friend who is going to write a book about Hawthorne has not hurried through the work. It is a great opportunity to do a thing that I hope greatly at heart, and that is that Hawthornes life should be properly presented to the continent of Europe and not under the shadow of some mistakes that have been made by his principal and greatest biographer, his son Julian.

Hawthorne expressed in his lifetime that he hoped his biography would not be written. He thought what he had maturely decided to publish would give what was alone valuable in his life. But of course people wrote about him and finally his son-in-law Lathrop, who had been brought up as it were on his books, of which he was personally fond, but who had never seen the man being only eleven years old when he died and living away in the Sandwich Islands, but who met his youngest daughter in Boston in 1868 and married her in 1871, published 'a Study of Hawthorne' collecting all that was extant about him from his friends and myself, of which he made good sale and produced a lovely little book. A year or two ago a Boston publisher wanted to publish a Life of Hawthorne and engaged Julian to write it. But the circumstances were peculiar and unfavourable. Julian, who had married at 21 (in 1870), had been driving the quill like mad *ever since* for

---

1 In 1852, the German novelist Amelia Boelte wrote to Hawthorne asking for galleys of *The Scarlet Letter*. More than thirty years later, Elizabeth Peabody corresponded with Boelte, who had apparently informed her that a friend of hers would be writing a biography of Hawthorne for European audiences. The manuscripts of these Peabody letters were passed on to the unnamed author of "Drei Briefe" by Boelte's sister Fanny.

daily bread for himself and growing family and had had eight children losing only a baby in 12 years, and was utterly run down in health and in means and was paid beforehand for his work on the condition of its being written at once. He was at the time with his large family in a cheap town to live in on the extremity of Long-Island away from all Hawthornes localities, relations and friends. I knew nothing but that the book was written—none of the unfavourable conditions—he did not tell me his plan or ask for my help, who had all his mothers early journals, had been the confidante of my sister from her babyhood and of Hawthorne for nearly a year before he became intimate with Sophia except [?] through my acquaintance with him. At the time he first saw her we all and she herself considered her a hopeless invalid and not a subject for marriage. I sent to Julian her letters to me during the summer that she became intimate with him with no tho't on her part of marriage to any body, and when he thought, as he once expressed it to me, that she was "a flower not (never) to be worn in any man's bosom but lent from Heaven." I knew the history of the three years engagement when it was kept secret from almost everybody else, even in the two families. But he never came and asked me anything.[2] His sister Rose was in New York, he never asked her anything or showed her the book. We saw it first when it was printed. He was especially intent on showing what his father was in his own family, what the marriage was. He calls it in his preface the annals of a happy marriage. But it speaks of other people in the most careless and reckless manner, on stating the hospitalities the family received in England, and misrepresenting Hawthorne with respect to others.

There never was a person more careful of others feelings and personalities in what he put noted, he never put noted anything except after looking at it in all moods, and his genius led him to look at things in their eternal relations as it were, and to let the circumstantial go after it had done its work. In his private journals however he as far as possible put down in all its rare ugliness the mere fact—or the passing mood—not for other people who he never expected would see it,

2 Despite this claim, Peabody had in fact been of immense help to Julian during the preparation of his *Nathaniel Hawthorne and His Wife* (1884). In 1882, Julian asked his aunt for information and recollections, and she wrote out for him or told him about the Peabody family, her "discovery" of Hawthorne, his courtship of Sophia, and Hawthorne's challenge to a duel. These accounts, found in a notebook now in the Pierpont Morgan Library, New York City, are published in Norman Holmes Pearson, "Elizabeth Peabody on Hawthorne," *Essex Institute Historical Collections* 94 (1958): 256–76, and idem, "Hawthorne's Duel," *Essex Institute Historical Collections* 94 (1958): 229–42.

but for his own cool consideration, for he did not want to be the fool of his own ideality. Well! Julian has violated these private papers and published some things especially about persons that Hawthorne would never have let any mortal eye see. He destroyed quantities of these private journals in which all the ups and downs of his early and earlier life were written down. And I think it was only the accident of his death away from home that caused any to be left. We cannot regret that they were left. My sister called one of them the American, the English and the Italian note-books. He had to make up for his publisher two large volumes and I could have given him most precious matter, but he filled up by putting in other people's letters to his father without their leave, and which were mostly not worth publishing, and which involved a good deal of false statement. So that when it came out, there was quite a burst of resentment by friends of persons spoken of, and Julian who was all worn out nervous with his dozen years of book work, and full of neuralgia, replied angrily and made bad worse by insulting all the best friends of his father and both families.

Well, now I am going to send the book by mail in sheets and mark on the margin all that I do hope his German biographer will *leave out*, and which, if all of it is left out, will give a much more just and truthful picture of the man. Then I shall send to Lathrop and ask him to send his 'Study' and also another thing he has lately written, and to a certain Dr Loring who will send a copy of a lecture in which he does justice to other aspects of Hawthorne touched on neither by Julian or Lathrop. I should not wonder, if such a book were written in Germany, it would be translated into English, there are so many people who feel so much regret at Julians mistakes, which seem likely to be immortalised with those parts of the book which are most exquisitely done, and which show what some people doubt, that genius and culture in *both* parties to a marriage do not spoil but may make perfect a marriage. I think his German biographer has a great opportunity to do a most beautiful and truthful thing.—I think you will enjoy the picture my mother's letters give of our family and of herself, written as they are so unconsciously.

I will not prolong this letter now.

You will observe, my dear Miss Boelte, that I have been very frank with respect to my nephew's faults which however I consider superficial and largely the effect of an overwrought nervous system, and it is quite friendly confidential and I beg you will never speak of it to anybody and *destroy this letter* after it has served its purpose, though of

course you may *read it* to the lady who is to be the biographer, putting
her under bonds to be also reticent. Julian is a splendid fellow but
could not understand how I should say what I have.
  Affectionately yours

Eliz. P. Peabody

"Drei Briefe von Elizabeth P. Peabody über Nathaniel Hawthorne u.a.," *Archiv für
das Studium der Neueren Sprachen und Literatur,* 133 Band, der neuen Serie 33 Band
(Februar 1915), 321–23.

---

*Peabody's further comments on Julian's biography and an observation
on Hawthorne's use of his journals.*

✦ To Amelia Boelte

4 Cheshire Street, Jamaica Plain
Massachusetts, U.S.A.

My dear Miss Boelte.   [May or June 1886]
  I mail to you to day the sheets of Julian Hawthorne's Life of his
father and mother which I have detained in order to mark with a line
on the side all that I do hope you will *leave out* or rather that 'the lady
of future' who you say is to write the Life of Hawthorne for continental Europe had best *leave out,* because it is erroneous as matter of
fact, or censurable because wounding to the feelings of others—and has
excited angry controversies of a personal nature and having nothing of
interest legitimate to the subject. In my last I told you of the unfavourable condition of Julian as to health of body and mind, under which
it was written. But *what is left* after all that should be left out, does
real justice to both his subject and himself, and you will see that he is
no ordinary person. I do not think he exaggerates the beautiful and
grand traits of his father and mother.
  But Hawthorne in his journals and private correspondence and
casual talk in the bosom of his family was the other pole of Hawthorne
as a finished author. In the last role you have his matured judgment,
his highest intuitions and most spiritual attainments. He never published without maturest reflection and severest selfcriticism. I heard
him say once with great emotion that whenever he found that he had
published a transient mood of his mind, his conscience accused him of

lying. And once he begged me never to publish anything until I had read it in all moods of mind and taken *time,* and made it as perfect as I was capable of. On the other hand he liked to set down on paper transient moods, impressions of other people's minds with whom he conversed, the hardest and barest of facts without their spiritual atmosphere—for future reflection—in order to deduce from them on the one side and from his Ideal on the other, the Science and poetry of life.

I interpret the paragraph about Margaret Fuller from his journal as *Mozier's* malicious and mendacious conversation with him intentionally given, though in one point it played into Hawthorne's preference for wild flowers rather than cultivate flowers, and Margaret partook largely of a current fault of that time, a too conscious attempt at individual self-culture versus the universal culture of that which is alike in all men. And it was unjust to one of Hawthorne's highest characteristics, a profound obedience to the ninth commandment both in spirit and form, to report his transient feelings of annoyance, as expressed in the confidentialness of home with respect to persons who had been hospitable and meant to be gratefully kind to him, but who embarassed him with their expressions of admiration, or amused him with their infirmities. I think his letter to Margaret refusing to take into their family Ellery and Ellen Channing shows how carefully he avoided wounding even when himself most embarassed and annoyed. Delicacy Degerando defines as 'the flower of justice', and Hawthorne had it, and he shows it in his expressed *respect* for the amiable character of Tupper, and it was most cruel [?] to both and to Tupper's family for Julian to have printed his keen perceptions of Tupper's weaknesses and lionization of *him.*

But I have not marked out that, for it shows Hawthorne's paramount respect for kindness of heart and intent, that he recognised it so fully when it was foiled by such vanity and egotism as Hawthorne had not a shade of.

What he leaves to be understood of my brothers and father by printing a letter of my mothers and other remarks, is wholly opposite to the fact. My father was most indulgent, not a particle of the disciplinarian in him, and Wellington, who was his youngest son, a darling pet, though he was occasionally thoughtless, and we all at the moment were frightened lest he should be led into dangerous and expensive habits, in consequence of his popularity with some rich fellows, of whom he was tempted to borrow money. But he died at 21 after a heroic and brilliant career as physician of a marine Hospital in New

Orleans during an exceptionally terrible season of Yellow-fever, when all the physicians fled, and left him to be nurse, servant, and physician to 120 patients, of whom only 20 died, and he had no nurses but black men (slaves). Seldom is such a noble story to be told of young men as of them both, the other died at 25, and both before Hawthorne and Sophia were even engaged to be married.

In nothing is Julian more diametrically in contrast to his father than in this reckless way in which he deals with persons he did not know, but only had heard a little of them.

A great deal of the letters of other people that he prints was also very wrong and erroneous, and he used the letters of other people without their leave. Now Ellery Chaning is shown up on his weakest side. Those letters must have been written when he was drunk, and the worst of it is that these ugly things are likely to share the immortality of that part of the book which is so very beautiful and I think no more beautiful than the subject demanded. But a European life might cast out all this ugly matter and leave a true—a truer view of Hawthorne and his wife, and I hope this will be done. 'A Life of Hawthorne translated from the biographies of his son, son-in-law and friend Dr. Loring with omissions of irrelevant matter' would be a splendid book.

I have asked Lathrop to send you his studies of Hawthorne, and Dr. Loring to send you a lecture he wrote which does more special justice to Hawthorne's commonsense and practical efficiency. . . .[1]

I do not think Holmes's Life of Emerson at all worthy of the subject. He did not begin to admire Emerson till after Emerson was acknowledged. He was among the scoffers at first. Bye and bye there is to be a worthy life written by his literary residuary legatee J. Eliot Cabot, a rare person.

I shall see that none of the books sent you cost you anything but the postage and if possible shall send my own works by private hand that they may cost you nothing at all.

The 'Mosses from an old Manse' are a collection of tales of his solo, *twice told,* that he so named because he was then living at the Old Manse. I will try to send them to you. I wish I could afford to send all his collected works now published by Houghton Mifflin and Co., Boston.

I am sorry to hear that the Baronness is failing. But she has done

---

[1] According to the *Archiv* editor of these letters, several passages concerning Peabody's kindergarten interests have been left out. These omissions are indicated by ellipses.

a good work. I consider that Froebel's system of Education is the second coming of Christ. Childhood is the Redeemer of the race that is—childhood *understood* as Froebel understood it. . . .

Yours, affectionately   Elizabeth P. Peabody

P.S. Dr. Holmes is in Europe, in England now, and I have asked his wife to send your letter to him, and I think he may *go and see you,* for he is going upon the continent. He is a very bright man and grown more and more popular as he has grown older and wiser. He married a favourite pupil of mine, to whom he owes I think as *Hawthorne* owed to Sophia (though there was never anything more different than the two couples).

"Drei Briefe von Elizabeth P. Peabody über Nathaniel Hawthorne u.a.," *Archiv für das Studium der Neueren Sprachen und Literatur,* 133 Band, der neuen Serie 33 Band (Februar 1915), 323–25.

Another letter to her German correspondent, this one a strenuous denial of an engagement or romantic attachment between Elizabeth Peabody and Hawthorne.

✖ To Amelia Boelte

Dear Miss Boelte.   June 30th, 1886

Today I received a card from you on which was written what I hope has not been read at any post office, especially the one in Jamaica Plain—that *some*body has told you that Hawthorne was first engaged to be married to *me!* and that I magnanimously gave him up to my sister Sophia, because I found she had given her heart to him, and that you have told this story to sundry other persons!—

I must hasten to tell you that it is all a mistake.—It is true that for the first three years after Hawthorne became known to and a *visitor* in our family, it was *rumoured,* that there was *probably* an engagement between him and *me* for we were manifestly very intimate *friends* and Sophia was considered so much of an invalid as not to be marriage-able by any of us, including *herself* and Hawthorne, and as my sister Mary for two years of this time was living in Boston and keeping school there, *I* seemed to be the only one of the three to whom he *could* be engaged.

But *I* was aware, from the first week of our acquaintance with Hawthorne, that *he* was so much in love with Sophia—at first sight—that he would probably never marry any *other* woman.

At that time (from 1837 to 1840) a great change took place in Sophia,—which we all (myself, Sophia, and Hawthorne) did ascribe to his intimacy with her, which worked like animal magnetism upon her, suspending, when he was *walking* with her, the chronic pain in her head, that she had had, from the time she was 12 years old to thirty, and for the *next* three years 1839 to 1842 she *was* engaged to him, which was not made known however even to his own sister, nor to our acquaintance, till they concluded to be married and go to the old Manse in Concord *to live* in July 1842.—And by that time the rumour had (*I* thought) entirely died out,—for during those three years (when I was keeping my circulating foreign library and importing book-store in West Street—Boston, he came to spend the evening whenever he was in Boston, and saw her in her own parlour, to which was never admitted any other of our guests.—She had made her marriage conditional on her perfect recovery,—and besides, not until that date had he the pecuniary where withal to be married. You can easily understand that under such exceptional circumstances of our acquaintance, there *might* be a misunderstanding, and *false impressions* and also that the *imagination* of people would be *piqued* to *create stories.*— But the truth is that Hawthorne *never* had the idea of marrying any other woman than my sister Sophia.[1]

But I was the *confidante* of this determination of his, even before Sophia was;—and, while he still thought (to use his own exquisite words in a letter to me), "She was a flower never destined to be worn in any man's bosom, but lent from Heaven for a *season* to mortals, to

[1] Peabody possibly protests a bit too much here. James Mellow has assembled a circumstantial case for a personal attachment between Hawthorne and Elizabeth Peabody in the spring of 1838. Mellow speculates that Hawthorne may even have proposed to her. In 1894, Caroline Dall added to the rumor when she wrote to Thomas Niles that there had indeed been such an engagement: "Sophia never knew of her sister's engagement to N.H., but Hawthorne lived in terror lest E. P. P. should tell her. Many an hour of bitter weeping has she passed in my house because of his insulting letters about it—after he was married" (Caroline Dall to Thomas Niles, quoted in Mellow, *Nathaniel Hawthorne in His Times,* 146). Mellow sensibly adds that Dall was not exactly a trustworthy witness.

The close-quarters living of the Transcendental circle gave rise to many such rumors of romance; Hawthorne's *The Blithedale Romance* (1852) explores the possibilities for unconventional and freer relations between men and women. It is not necessary to assume a romantic attachment between Peabody and Hawthorne to see that she at least was trying to break away from a couple-dominated social life and imagine other kinds of friendship and intimacy.

show the possibilities of human purity and womanliness." In a subsequent letter, he said, (referring to her *conditions*)—"Far be it from me to snatch the boon from Providence before it is granted." She, in her perfect piety having said that "if God willed to grant them the *boon,* He would make her well." And she believed He would.

An engagement like *this* was too sacred a thing to be exposed to the pitiless gossip of society and *hence* the secrecy of it, and *you know* when society's curiosity is excited and not gratified,—it will *make up* and then believe its *own* conjectures.—

There is *generally* conjured up some romantic story about any woman who is never married. But I have escaped rumours of being engaged pretty well—especially considering that in the case of the husbands of both my sisters, it was manifest that they were very intimate and cherished *friends of mine,* before they were engaged to my sisters. And to have known two such men intimately as friends might very well account for *my* not marrying *at all,* for a third—equal to either—was not likely to turn up.—But I was endowed by Heavenly Grace with such a power of imaginative sympathy, that I have known and understood married love in the persons of my sisters, and also of several other friends. I believe *matches* are made in Heaven, but I think, that in this world, it is more often true, than otherwise perhaps, what Klopstock says: "They find not one the other, they who for each other and *love* were made." And it is from the *mismatched* that most of the social evils of life arise,—and the Millenium will not come til there is a reform of this matter. It is *because* I believe marriage is a sacrament, and nothing *less,* that I am dying as an old Maid.—I have had too much respect for marriage to make a conventional one in my own case.—I am free to say that had Hawthorne wanted to marry me he would probably not have found much difficulty in getting my consent;—but it is very clear to me now, that I was not the person to make *him* happy or to be made happy *by* him, and Sophia *was.*—If there was ever a "match made in Heaven" it was *that,* as I think you will agree after you have read the life of his father and mother by *Julian.* . . .

In the ensuing autumn I am going to publish a *volume* collecting all my book literary work which has the merit of being an expression of *the life* of *my life,* which has been spent in relations of intellectual intimacy with the elite of my time and in *earnest* work. I should like to have an idea of what your own work has been in *life.* I think it must have been exceptional among women. How came you to be such a polyglot? Could you make a catalogue of your literary works for me?

. . . [I] for the rest of *my* life shall probably devote myself to the solution of the Indian problem, which offers 'pastimes new' and *very rich* for the heart and soul.*

Affectionately yours
ELIZABETH P. PEABODY

*[The following material is placed in a footnote following "heart and soul." Its actual placement in the manuscript cannot be determined without recourse to the originals.]

For which all my past studies have prepared me and especially those I have made in *infancy*. The customs etc of the Pinto's[2] the tribe of Indians who never knew of Whites till 1848 confirms wonderfully Froebel's ideas of the primitive men.

In looking at your note again I see you speak of Mrs. Godwin as the source of your notion about the engagement. It surprises me to find that one so far off from Salem as New York should have heard of this story, and perhaps incidentally you might really do a service to the truth of facts if you were to say that at the time Hawthorne for the first time in his life made acquaintance with women in society, there was a story current that he was engaged to Elizabeth Peabody, who was the first lady-friend he became intimate with, and when six years after, he married her youngest sister Sophia it was conjectured that she had magnanimously given him up in her favour, but that you had learnt from Elizabeth herself that it was all a mistake and that in the very first week of the acquaintance with the family, the impression was made on his heart by the younger sister whose flowering and fruitage are so beautifully set forth in Julians Life of his father and mother.— But the facts were very peculiar. Sophia in 1837 when Hawthorne first saw her was considered a hopeless invalid by her own family and not marriagable. As Hawthorne himself exquisitely expressed it in a letter to Elizabeth as she has told me herself he regarded her as "a flower not destined to be worn in any mans bosom, but lent by Heaven to mortals to show the possibilities of human purity and womanliness" and he congratulated himself on having her for a *friend* since *he* should *never* marry." But as she gradually recovered her health, another view of the subject took possession of him. And at last there was a conditional engagement. She said that if God willed that they should be married sometime, he would make *her well*. Elizabeth was the sole confidante of both these remarkable lovers, who did not meet till they had both been *disciplined* by suffering of opposite kind, and yet left open to the

[2] This is probably a misreading of Piutes, a Native American people in whom Peabody became interested in the 1880s.

inspiration of *first love.* As the surrounding world was not gratified with polite explanation of the phenomena of the case it as usual *created* this story, which Elizabeth's peculiar reputation made credible.— But I do not mean to dictate the *form* but only the important substance of what you shall say. If you had not the means as you say of propagating the mistake, it would be best I think not to even mention so delicate a matter.

"Drei Briefe von Elizabeth P. Peabody über Nathaniel Hawthorne u.a.," *Archiv für das Studium der Neueren Sprachen und Literatur,* 133 Band, der neuen Serie 33 Band (Februar 1915), 326–28.

Peabody takes upon herself the responsibility for a story about some Hawthorne photographs, levels some serious charges at her nephew, and perpetuates a Hawthorne legend.

✎ To Caleb Foote, editor of the Salem *Gazette*

Jamaica Plain, Mass.

Dear Mr. Foote: August 21, 1886

I have only just been shown an article of Julian Hawthorne's in the New York World of June 26th which I feel bound in conscience and honor to Mr. Holden to answer publicly, because I am responsible for assertions made by Mr. Holden respecting the Lothrop Motley photograph, so called, having myself had the whole story from Mr. Motley's own lips, as you will presently see.

To begin at the beginning, I will say that very soon after Mrs. Hawthorne's return from Europe in 1860, she told me that Una, on board the steamer coming home, said that when she was at Mr. Bright's in Liverpool just before sailing, she saw a photograph of her father that was ever so much better than any other. The description which Una gave of the photograph was a description of the Lothrop Motley photograph now in the possession of Mrs. Rose Hawthorne Lathrop. Sophia told me that Hawthorne, who heard Una describe it, declared that he had never sat for such a photograph; and when she persisted and frequently afterwards reasserted it, the matter became very painful to him, for he thought it one of the illusions of the delirium of her Roman fever. But after his death, when Mr. Bright wrote to Mrs. Hawthorne begging to know if he could do her any service, she wrote to him telling what Una had persisted in declaring, and that she would like to have that photograph. He then sent it; and one day after it came, and Sophia had hung it up in the library, and I went to Wayside to see her, she took me into the library, without saying a word. I saw it and exclaimed, "I never saw so wonderful a likeness—he seems to be alive!" She said. This is the photograph Una saw at Mr. Bright's, and which I asked him to send to me, if it really existed. And when I opened the box that contained it, it nearly knocked me backwards, it looked so alive."

Some years subsequently, I think it was after Sophia's death, Mr. Motley was talking with me about Hawthorne, and I spoke of this wonderful photograph. He then told me the story, which I told to Mr. Holden, and have told to many others. He said: "That photograph I gave to Mr. Bright. I got it without Hawthorne's knowing it, during the week in which he was visiting me in London. I had succeeded in showing him the lions and even in lionizing him somewhat without his being aware of it." He told me how, and continued, "We were walking down Oxford street together one day and I said, 'what a bore it is to sit for a photograph, (to which he heartily assented) but nevertheless I have yielded to Mary's importunity, and have been sitting for mine, and I wish you would go in with me and help and decide which is the least bad.' And he assenting, we went into the photographer's."

Mr. Motley did not give the photographer's name, and probably it was not Mayall though it may have been during the same week that Mr. Bright persuaded Hawthorne to go to Mayall's and sit for the photograph which Mr. Bright wrote Julian about, (see frontispiece in Harper's for July) and which is not identical, as is plain, with the one which Rose has—and which, curiously enough, has not the name of the photographer upon it, as is usual.

Both of these photographs are good, but the one that Motley obtained in his most innocent way that he might save Hawthorne from being bored, bears internal evidence of the unconsciousness of the subject, and is in an attitude which Hawthorne might easily have retained a half a minute or more, and Mr. Holden has proof that at that date photographs were sometimes taken nearly instantaneously. Mr. Motley had made previous preparation with the photographer whose instrument commanded the chair in which Motley, with a careless air, asked Hawthorne to sit while he went into the operating room, to get proofs of his own likeness; from these they agreed upon the best and went out. I remember that Mr. Motley added that only four copies were made, when the negative was accidentally broken; and that he kept two himself, gave one to Bright, and I think he said the fourth was given to Bennoch, but I am not quite clear in my recollection as to what was done with the latter copy.

All the above story that I have put in quotation marks, is nearly, if not quite verbally correct; and I wrote it to Julian when he first accused Mr. Holden of consciously making it up; but he replied to me that he was sure I was deluded by my imagination, and that old age had weakened my memory.

I am now very much surprised and pained that by reason of this new elaboration of the matter in the World, I feel constrained to come out with this public statement. But is is only fair to observe that he was misled by Mr. Bright's having forgotten the photograph he had sent to Mrs. Hawthorne twenty years before, and which, naturally enough, had not made such an impression upon his mind as the one he had taken so much pains to get, as he tells in his own letter to Julian. Had he not died immediately after, I should have written to him and recalled the circumstances of his having had another which Motley gave him, and which he in turn had sent to Sophia.

Julian's error, I think, was mainly due to his most unfortunate characteristic, namely, an abnormal impetuosity of temperament, preventing all reflective self-criticism; a fault that has led him into all the mistakes of his literary and practical life. These peculiarities are in strange contrast with the moral delicacy and broad intellectual comprehension that he generally displays in the analysis of character in his books. And to these peculiarities, also, he is the exact opposite of his father, who, as he once told me, never gave to the world anything that he wrote, till he had read it in all moods of mind and had reflected upon it in all lights. I have a letter from him begging me never to publish anything till I had done so. He said to me once, "When I find that any story of mine betrays a morbid state of mind, I feel as if I had told a lie."

The reason he gave for requiring that nobody should ever show a letter of his, and for burning up so much of his writings and private journals was that in those he wrote on an entirely different principle than when writing for the public and posterity; putting down his present moods and the barest aspects of facts as they actually took place in all the ugliness of their outward literalness, to be reflected upon as a balance to his creative imagination, which considered facts and characters in their remote spiritual relations.

I can never sufficiently lament that this impetuous self-confidence led Julian into writing and publishing the life of his father and mother without showing it to anybody—not even to his aunt Elizabeth Hawthorne, to myself, or to his own sister, who was close by him in New York; for thus he missed knowing of the existence of much rich material in our possession, and had he done so, he might have been saved from every mistake that deforms a work in which his genius will immortalize not only much beautiful truth, but some passages that do injustice to both his parents, who were more scrupulous than is ordinary in what they made public of their thoughts, especially respecting persons, in which they always realized their liability to err, precisely because they knew themselves to be so impressionable, and to need the perspective of time for a final judgement.

Yours truly,
ELIZABETH P. PEABODY

Salem *Gazette*, 27 August 1886, copy, MSaE.

Peabody's two criticisms of her nephew Julian, that he was wrong in attacking Holden's account of some Hawthorne photographs, and that his biography of his parents was written without consulting other members of the family, are both in error. As mentioned earlier, Peabody herself contributed much to the writing of the biography by providing Julian with lengthy written accounts of her early years and her "discovery" of Hawthorne. On the question of the Hawthorne photographs, George Parsons Lathrop, Hawthorne's son-in-law, himself often at odds with Julian came to Julian's defense in an article, "Some Portraits of Hawthorne," Century Magazine, 11 (April 1887): 895–99.

George Holden's letter of June 15, 1886 to the Salem Gazette essentially gives the story of the Hawthorne-photograph incident as Peabody repeats it here. The historian John Lothrop Motley lured Hawthorne into the studio of London photographer Mayall one day in May 1860 and on the pretext of having business there, Mayall took Hawthorne's picture without his knowledge. Peabody told this story to Holden, identifying the picture as the one in the possession of Rose Hawthorne Lathrop, and identifying her source of the story as Motley himself. Since in Peabody's eyes, Motley, who claimed to be with Hawthorne at the time the photograph was taken, was obviously an authority on the incident, Julian Hawthorne's derogation of the incident as a "fabrication" served only as further evidence of his "impetuosity of temperament."

Lathrop reconstructed the incident in this manner. Assuming that Bright not Motley had accompanied Hawthorne to Mayall's studio,

Lathrop dismissed the notion that Hawthorne's appearance at the studio was accidental; Bright's letter to Julian, which Julian quoted in his biography of his parents (Nathaniel Hawthorne and his Wife, *2: 257) indicates clearly that this was a prearranged visit. Since, after some sleuthing, Lathrop determined that there were three photographs of Hawthorne in very similar poses, he concluded that Mayall had taken three pictures of Hawthorne, one of the agreed-upon one for Bright; another a photograph chosen by another English friend, Francis Bennoch, and a third, taken surreptitiously. This one, speculated Lathrop, was obtained by Motley upon hearing that Hawthorne had sat for a portrait: "In speaking of the affair afterwards, Motley—if the circumstances were such as I have suggested—would of course say to his friends that the photograph had been made without Hawthorne's knowledge; and in this way the tradition, with the facility of transformation belonging to all tradition, would become established, that Motley himself had arranged a little plot for obtaining a photograph of Hawthorne unawares" (Lathrop, "Some Portraits of Hawthorne," p. 899).*

To [Anna Cabot] Lowell[1]

Boston,
My dear Miss Lowell, December 26, 1886

I have been intending to write you a note ever since the 1st of October, when we moved to this lovely residence and tell you that No *1* Lamartine St is just opposite your cottage, and so to 298, where we live, is not a mile off in a straight line.—I thought when I came here, that it would not be too long a walk for me to call on you, but *Time* is a potent mortifier of the pride of Life The fatigue of the removal and rearrangement—though the latter was immensely satisfactory—and especially my sisters alarming feebleness lasted to the middle of November, when occured her her 80th birthday, stole away the fair weather.—And within the last three weeks, it has seemed as if a removal to a still more *lively* residence were impending—first, for her—then for me,—so that we surrendered ourselves successively into the hand of a physician who has put me again into the way of recovery—

1 Anna Cabot Lowell was one of two unmarried daughters (the other was Rebecca Amory Lowell) of John Lowell.

which I must confess I crave for another, yes—for Sarah Winnemucca's sake. I sent you *My Report* which I trust you have read[2]—I think that "dreadful fortnight of silence" of which I spoke gave me my first death blow. —But finding those 200 books, & hearing from her that she had not lost her *noble self* revived me, and I wrote to her of the recovery of the books, the sales of which would just support her without compelling her to menial druggery (whose vocation is evidently [nation?] *saving*) and was able to tell her that the first copy I offered for sale the purchaser insisted on Paying $5 instead on $1—& I enclosed the $5 in my registered letter. [Illegible], as I thought, it might be I touched her faith into life again & she called all her scholars together again (whose parents would afford their lunches), and who, as she rightly judged, would return to their common sense again when they saw she had retained no "money meant for them" but for the first time in her life went into service in white women's kitchens, rather than not be self-supporting—The *temporary* despair & relinquishment of her great work *proved* reactionary—and *rested* the long overstrained nerves. She felt better in health than for nearly two years. 21 Scholars assembled within a week & she found they had lost nothing & were enthusiastic to go on with all their studies & work. [They?] were ready to become her efficient *assistants*: 12 of the last "boarders" waited to come, but could not because their parents necessarily lived 15 miles off & it would cost a dollar a week to feed each—the 200 books if they were all sold at a dollar a piece—could not do more than support *her* till the next harvest. I sent her letter to Mr Potter of New Bedford, who read it to their Indian society—who had heard & believed in Sarah.—& they contributed on the spot enough to board *one scholar* from Jan 1st to July 1st—and another friend of hers, who insists on being nameless, sends me 50 dollars to board the whole 12 through the month of January & suggests that ten Sunday Schools, might be interested to furnish $50 I don't know whether this can be done—Now would it be with your Roxbury Sunday School   I shall immediately write round & see about this, & at all events, I think "The Spirit Father's" voice will be heard in the hearts of enough of his people. as Sarah herself says, "if it really is *His will*." She thinks it was "crazy" in her to doubt—But only *I* know what a weight of woe brought her down for once—but of this I cannot *write to say the least.*

2 Peabody's reference is to her *Sarah Winnemucca's Practical Solution of the Indian Problem: A Letter to Dr. Lyman Abbott* (Cambridge: John Wilson and Son, 1886).

But I want to see you for other things than to get your sympathy for Sarah   I have not seen you since the Life of Maurice came out.[3]— It seems to me that never before did so many *great subjects* solicit our attention.—Sometimes I feel as if all mysteries were solved. They *are* solved by & by—I have to use the words they are so emasculated by a deadening [controversy?]   [Several words illegible] by the trinity of *Faith, Hope* and *Love,—none* of which are essentially intellectual operations of *the soul*—but spiritual *aspirations*—which are as opposite as *fire* and *ice* in their effects on the plan of practical life.

But a truce to metaphysics—not but that metaphysics are the *only science* in the highest sense of the word science—

What do you make of Mr Frothinghams Memorial of Wm Henry Channing?[4] and of Mr Frothingham himself?

But I will not prolong my note *ad infinitum—hoping you will come to see me*—I will only say with Christmas greetings and New Years good wishes—I am yours truly

E. P. PEABODY
With Love to Lucy Solger

MS, NNBa

[3] That is, *The Life of Frederick Denison Maurice, Chiefly Told in His Own Letters Edited by His Son, Frederick Maurice* (New York: Scribners, 1884).

[4] Frothingham's book was *Memoir of William Henry Channing* (Boston: Houghton, Mifflin, 1886).

Peabody describes the last days and the death of her long-time companion, her sister Mary, with whom she had such a troubled relationship.

✖ To Eleanor Lewis

[Boston]

My dear Miss Lewis   March 27 [1887]

Your letter to Mary and me arrived this morning, & was brought and read to me by my nephew;—but Mary is no longer *here*! She ascended into heaven the *11th of February*, after weeks of pain & weakness of *body* that made those that loved her *rejoice* that she has not to draw another breath on this scene of things,—that she so ardently desired to be freed from—to enjoy unhindered the manifold activities of her spirit in relation to persons & things *common* to "the choir invisible," into which she felt herself going. She died just at 3 o'clock on a *Friday.* The Monday *before* she wrote a letter to Ben[1]—rather putting him off from coming to see her, because he could only be absent from his office *one week*—& the Dr. had told her *that day*—that tho' she might go any day, as her heart was in such good order, that she might last *some weeks.* After she had finished her letter she said that she should never write another letter, for her fingers were so stiff she could not easily wield a pen. The next day (Tuesday) I had a letter from a friend, who had within a year, lost her only son, & lately a brother, a fine fellow, with fine prospects,—had hanged himself—doubtless in a fit of insanity—for she said there was no cause they could divine—inward or outward—to prompt the desperate deed. In the letter she said, though it was impossible for *any body* to dogmatically assert that there was *not* individual immortality, she saw more reasons to *doubt* than believe it—the principal one being that people—the majority—were so absorbed in objects of a transient nature, *they were dead* already—in a spiritual sense. She added that the only striking exception *she knew* (!) was *Mary & me*—& *our* youthful ardor engaged in works of love, *not transient* in their *nature!* When we read this letter—as we did *aloud*—Mary said, "I will answer that *letter*" and immediately got up out of the chair she had been sitting in—without help—not having been able to do so *for more than a fortnight* (for all her lower limbs—up to the hips inclusive were frightfully *swollen*) and she went into her own chamber—that opens out of mine,—sat down at the table—& wrote a long letter with flying pen,—sealed & stamped it & gave it to me for the post office. I said "Aint I to see this letter?" "No,—said she, there is a secret of *hers* alluded to in it that I have no right to tell you. But since she acknow[ledges] us at eighty to be presumptive proofs of immortality—I thought my dying testimony might prevail with her!"

I tell you this to prove how completely she was herself— (an eternal self)—so late. That was the last letter she wrote & I am going to write to my friend to send me a copy of what in the letter was not strictly private. I do not doubt it was what she had been saying for the several weeks in which she thought every breath she drew *might* be the last—& wondered why it was *not.*

So I have not felt separated—rather *nearer* than ever—feeling she could understand just what I thought & felt better than my words

---

1 That is, Benjamin Pickman Mann, Mary's son.

could tell it. Ben arrived the next day from Washington, & already her features had recovered their youthful beauty—& the expression that the ascending spirit had imparted on them before abandoning the clay forever.—I wish you could have seen her—looking so comfortable & sweet in the casket—Her funeral was on Monday the 14th from George's house,[2] where Mr. DeNormandie spoke beautifully of her influence at Antioch & the help she gave her husband & of his deathbed where he said he stood *with Mary*, & which he said was sublimer than the death of Socrates. There were services at the same hour at Yellow Springs—*Pres Long*—having telegraphed for the hour—& many friends gathered—Ben stayed with me for ten days arranging & classifying her voluminous papers—which with his father's are now deposited at George's house and letters of sympathy began to pour in upon me at every post which it was a great comfort for the boys to get—and see in how many souls the memory of their mother was immortalized. Since he went away I have been engaged in correcting the proofs of her Romance in Cuban life which Lothrop is publishing—It will be out next week. The title is "Juanita—a Romance of real life in Cuba"—He also has in press the sequel to "A Wooing o't"—by Mrs. Alexander.

I continue here at 298 Lamartine Street & trust to continue during my natural life—for I am even luxuriously situated. Since Mary went my Indian work has been successfully finished—by which Sarah Winnemucca has become independent on her brother's own farm & in her own model school—This was already foreshown before Mary went & she contributed means for it—& was very happy in it. As Mr. Stearns advanced the 200 dollars—Miss Francis left her—she could give $50 to S.   Sarah feels as if she was hovering over her & had brought about the consummation since she was translated—for the last contribution was a 100 dollars from *Japan*.

I believe all things have been happily settled concerning Miss Francis estate, and what she proposed should be given *you*—will be reserved for you—Only *the money*, 27,000 was divided to the heirs & they relinquished all things else. The administrator was the relative who has been her business agent, and sympathized in her charities.

You will not expect me to write of any thing else this time. Your letter today was very interesting—I hope you will continue them to me—& with great respect to your Aunt am yours truly

Elizabeth P. Peabody

TS copy, OYesA

2 George Combe Mann, another son of the Manns.

Peabody writes a kind of summing-up statement; the body is failing but the spirit is triumphant.

✖ To Ednah Dow Cheney[1]

My dear Mrs. Cheney   [May 1887]

I went into town Monday—to get a demonstration that my day for social intercourse beyond a virtual tete a tete & out of reach of my own chamber—is past & gone for the forever of this world & so I cannot go and hear you on Monday—on which day I shall be 83 years old—

But I do not complain—within ten days I have had the pleasure of knowing that my kindergarten work is *done*—& the great aim been accomplished by abler & younger hands than mine—and also that Sarah Winnemucca's great experiment is so far *accomplished* that it needs no further bolstering up—all the conditions of independance of self support & the education of their children *within themselves* attained—on a small scale as to numbers indeed—but making a *vital seed* of an *ideal future*!

As I realized all this—at a moment when I seemed to be entirely exhausted of bodily energy—I was perfectly acquiescent—& said "Now Lord—let thy servant depart in peace for mine eyes have seen thy Salvation"—But since May came in I have taken a turn upward physically—& think I shall have a season for solitude & Reminiscence—*which may last some time*—and bear fruit of another kind—than the past has ripened—

I am *quite* blind—deaf—and dumb—yet—though nearly so from dim eyes, dull ears, and voice-repressing bronchial organs. But "silence is golden" & the eyes of the spirit and its ears too open all the more as the sensuous organs close. I hope the writing of the Reminiscences of my life may prove of value—A life as long as mine & having such [rare?] relations with the best of my contemporaries *ought* to teach lessons worth recording—

I write to assure you that my absence on Monday is inevitable &

1 Ednah Dow Cheney, as noted earlier, was involved in many reform movements, including education, antislavery, and women's rights. As a younger woman she was influenced by Margaret Fuller; later she taught at all nine sessions of the Concord School of Philosophy.

not from want of interest—I hope you may have time to come now &
then for a tete a tete—

Truly yours
Eliz P Peabody

MS, MNS

---

*A recollection of Hawthorne's detached and even critical attitude to-
ward the Northern cause during the Civil War.*

✹ To Horatio Bridge

[Boston]

Dear Mr Bridge   June 4th 1887
    Yes that letter was written to me & ought to have been destroyed
as soon as read as he always wanted his letters to be, for, like his private journal, they were always written from the mood of the moment
& were really never to be considered as expressing his mature thought—
& it was only his *mature* thoughts, his *final* conclusions after surveying
the appearance of the moment in the light of *the great Whole* that he
meant to print & give to the *human race.* In that particular letter he
himself suggests that his mind [was?] in a *gaseous* state—& that things
may seem to him *different*—& it was in fact not a week after that the
publication of Frank Pierce's letter to Jefferson Davis found among
the latter's papers when his house was ransacked *came out in the Evening Post (Bryant's)* & showed under Pierce's own hand that he had
encouraged Davis *to secede* & trust that War would at once be transferred to the streets of the North where the Democrats would fight on
the *Southern side.* We took Bryant's paper and when this copy arrived
it happened Sophia was calling at our house & Mary pointed out this
letter to her—& offered to let her take it home to Mr. Hawthorne. But
Sophia exclaimed that it was "a forgery *of course*" & she wondered
Mr. Bryant could give it a place in his paper—
    About an hour after she returned home, however, she sent down
for it saying "Mr. Hawthorne wanted to see the paper" & we went up
& from that day to the end of his life Mr. Hawthorne never named
Franklin Pierce to either Mary or me.[1]

1 During the spring of 1863, Hawthorne was writing reminiscences of his English
experiences, to be published as *Our Old Home,* and pondering to whom to dedicate

But in regard to the publication of that letter—never in my life was I [more?] amazed as to see it in print. I never showed it to *any body but* to Ellery Channing who had asked me to write the letter that called it forth—& I should have sworn I did not give it into his hands. [so?] that he might have taken a copy—for I did not want any body to see what he said about the want of any sincere Union sentiment in the North—& his ⟨conviction⟩ impression that, at bottom, there was no earnest anti-slavery sentiment here *at all*—but that they would be willing to see slavery last "a hundred years longer"—as he apparently did himself—and I felt that that sentence did great injustice to his character & sense of human justice. *I* know that *he* knew *nothing* about slavery—He had never been at the South. He never saw a slave or fugitive slave. He looked at all antislavery literature as beneath the consideration of a reasonable man—It was perfectly true what he often said—that he knew nothing about contemporaneous history, that he could not understand history until it was at least a *hundred years old!*—

I am writing the Reminiscences of My Contemporaries during my lifetime which I shall have for posthumous publication—of they are thought worth it—& in it I shall give my whole acquaintance & intimacy with Hawthorne—& in them I look forward to giving what I believe will be the most true psychological biography of him as I got it from his own account to me in 1838–39 of the growth of his mind—& I fondly think that my account will explain all the apparent inconsistencies that have arisen from unscrupulous biographers.—The only thing I have seen written about him, that I agreed with & thought was

---

the book. In July he had decided on Franklin Pierce, his old college classmate, whom Emerson described as "either the worst, or . . . the weakest, of all our Presidents." Pierce's criticism of the Lincoln administration and the war effort cast doubt on his patriotism, especially in context of the bruising defeats the North had suffered during 1861 and 1862. Hawthorne's association with Pierce worried his publisher Fields, but an attempt to dissuade the author met with a firm rejection. To his sister-in-law Elizabeth, Hawthorne was more outspoken. When Fields tried to get Ellery Channing to reason with Hawthorne, Channing contacted Peabody. She wrote Hawthorne directly, and in response, Hawthorne expressed his irritation at her intrusiveness and crusading zeal. "I admire the valor and generous pertinacity with which you come again to the scratch, offering me the same kind of advice as when I was going to write the Life of Cilley, and the Life of Pierce, and which availed nothing, then as now, because I trusted to my own instinct to guide me into my own right way. I do not write (if you will please observe) for my letter to be read to others" (20 July 1863, MS, MH). In this letter to Bridge, Peabody puts the date of the publication of Pierce's letter at a week after Hawthorne's letter to her, when in fact Pierce's letter to Jefferson Davis appeared September 19, the day *Our Old Home* appeared.

written with sufficient conscientiousness is George P Lathrop's "Study of Hawthorne"—on which I have no criticism to make—there are some splendid things that Julian says in his book, but it [does] infinite injustice to his father's character in a [conscientious?] point of view by its extract from his journal & report of his observations about people—in the privacy of Home—when every momentary impression on his sensitive nature was expressed in the most exaggerated way—& *jocosely* his *final* judgement of persons ⟨as well as⟩ as well as *subjects* were generally the absolute truth—the *passing* impressions which he *recorded* precisely because they were so transient that he was afraid he should lose sight of things as they [two words illegible] are to the common observation—& so made him seem ⟨exquisite⟩ *visionary* to the common sense reader.[2]

But I cannot on paper say just where I wrote about that double action of mind—which in Hawthorne were in such [word illegible] sharp contrast—"the thinking in eternity and in time" *at once,* as Liebnitz says every one does—more or less—

I mean to write to Ellery Channing & ask him if he *did* take a copy of that letter—to show to Fields perhaps—who had asked *him* to remonstrate with Hawthorne about printing the preface to "The Old Home" & which he did not elect [?] to do & so asked me   For I have kept it always with my most secret [papers?] wrapt up with the endorsement—"to be burnt—unread—if I do not burn them myself before I die"—

I have many such papers that I have kept—because I might want to refer to them when I write my *Reminiscences* which I have put off to my old age when I could do nothing else—

I have been so miserably prostrate *bodily* since my sister died—last February—that I have come to fear that I have put it off *too long.* But I am reviving somewhat in this late Spring. If I write to Ellery Channing he may not answer me—you know how [word illegible] he is—& he may feel outraged by being shown up in Julian's life of his Father & Mother as he has been—

Ah me! GOD knows I am not responsible for any part of Julian's Life of his Father & Mother—

I wish I could *see you* & talk over this subject. Cannot you come & see me this summer when you come North   I am living at the corner of Lamartine Street & Cedar Avenue—at Jamaica Plain near the

2 See Elizabeth Peabody to Amelia Boelte, [May or June 1886], for another statement of this point.

station on the Providence Rail Road—which is only [word illegible] & twelve minutes from the Providence Depot in Boston—

I have pleasant rooms—where we can talk for hours & I wish you and Mrs. Bridge would come—.

The calligraphy & composition of this scrawl will show you that just now I am indeed infirm. But my head is clear though my body is for the time almost useless—eyes ears voice
Elizabeth P Peabody

I wish I could see those notices of the letter of which you speak

MS, MeB

Peabody hopes to encourage Daniel Lothrop to publish her late sister's novel based on her Cuban experiences of the early 1830s. Peabody approaches Mrs. Lothrop, with whom she had already been corresponding.

✲ To Harriet Mulford Stone Lothrop[1]

Dear Mrs. Lothrop   [ca. 1887]
I have ordered a manuscript novel written by my sister Mrs. Mann[2] to be sent to Mr. Lothrop today, which he said he would publish probably but as we were in the street I could not tell him about the circumstances of its composition which makes its publication just now (when Cuba is nearing its emancipation this [?] will naturally fix attention on it)—I see Christina has signed the order for Emancipation though it is more than a year before 1888—[3]

My sister was in Cuba in 1833—when first slavery with all its existing [?] ⟨horrors⟩ contrasts first burst upon a New Englander for it was before Abolition excitement *began* here; & Cuba was then in a *treaty* with England to forbid slave *importation*—But as the cholera

[1] Harriet Mulford Stone Lothrop, the author, under the pen name Margaret Sidney, of *The Five Little Peppers* series, married publisher Daniel Lothrop in 1880; in 1883, they purchased the Hawthorne house, the Wayside, in Concord. In 1885, their only child, Margaret Mulford Lothrop was born; seven years later Daniel Lothrop died.

[2] Mary Peabody Mann, *Juanita: A Romance of Real Life in Cuba* (Boston: Lothrop, 1887).

[3] During the reign of Maria Christina II, Spain granted gradual abolition of slavery in 1880 and definitive abolition in 1887.

had just decimated the plantations—there was a great *smuggling* of slaves into Cuba by a conspiracy of the great slaveholders, some of whom themselves went to Africa after them! & the Planter at whose place she *was*—though a New Englander!—received a large number on his plantation, many of whom were not the usual cargoes [?] but of superior tribes,—affording heroes & heroines of various little *novelletes* which she gave us in her letters,—together with an inside view of Cuban society—composed of old Spanish grandees—and gentlemen & ladies of different nationalities—who—like her host—had gone there & made fortunes bringing their ideas of society so different from old Spaniards—she was so situated as to get interested in these *various* slaveholders—some of whose wives were *tortured* in various ways by the inevitable play of all the contradictory social principles—Her letters were full of the picturesque life about her in the gorgeous tropical climate & she has also [two words illegible] not a little dramatic genius—But her letters could not have a very wide circulation—because they necessarily involved details of family history of which she was part for the time being.—But it was an intense experience for *herself* & when she came home she was so full of it—& it was in its features so different from American slaveholding we were learning about that she could not get away from it—& so wove it into a fictitious story that she thought might be published—But when it was done, there were so many *portraits* of real people & so many *real incidents* that she felt it would be a violation of social honour for her to ⟨print⟩ publish it—& so it has only been read privately—

But *now all these persons are dead,* & there is no individual to be pained;—& everybody who has read it urges her to print it—for it is a tale of moral beauty as well as of moral evil & showing how God makes even Satan do his will in the long run   I tell you this because if Mr L gets anybody to read the manuscript I hope it may be *you* for then I am pretty sure he *will* print it & I do not mean to say—M has as much genius as H. H.[4] & Mrs. Stowe—But she has a great deal   yrs ever E.P.P.

MS, MCR-S

4 That is, Helen Hunt Jackson, American poet and novelist, best known for her advocacy of Native Americans and author of *Century of Dishonor* (1881) and *Ramona* (1884).

Peabody composes a sympathy letter to Bronson Alcott's eldest daughter.

✖ To Anna Alcott Pratt

Boston,
My dear Anna   March 8 [1888]
    I have been utterly housebound *for months* and do not know as I
shall ever get out again—or I should have been to see your father—&
now should fly to you in your grief at the death of Louisa—that seems
so untimely & must leave you so desolate.[1] But it is not what it seems—
In her case as well as in his it is not *loss* of life but *more life,* and if
you cannot see her she sees you and knows you better than ever since
"Death with the *Might* of his *Sunbeam* touching the clay," the Soul
has awaked to *"the fullness of life"* *Faith* is the souls *supreme* power
& the like & value of *bereavement* is to call it into the consciousness so
that it may indeed be realized as *"the evidence* of things *unseen* the
substance of things hoped for." Since my sister Mary's death, it seems
to me that for the first time I have really opened the spiritual eye &
entered into Full communion with her. I do wish, dear Anna, that you
would come & see *me* I have so much to say about your father, and
about our possible communion with the Choir Invisible, to whose
number the handful of persons *living* in the first stage of our existence
is but a handful—what are you going to do with Mays child?[2] Shall
you not send her back to her father in Europe?
    With inexpressible sympathy I am your E. P. Peabody
    290 Lamartine Street Jamaica Plain near the steamcar station.

MS, ViU

    [1] Bronson Alcott died on March 4, 1888, and Louisa May Alcott died on March
6, 1888.
    [2] Peabody's reference is to Louisa May (Lulu) Nieriker, daughter of May Alcott
and Ernest Nieriker, born November 8, 1879. May Alcott Nieriker died shortly after
the child was born, and Lulu was brought to the United States, arriving in August
1880, to be raised by her aunts.

A note written by Peabody in a very bad hand because of her cataracts, after the death of Bronson Alcott and the closing of the Concord School.

✄ To Franklin Benjamin Sanborn

Jamaica Plain
Dear Mr Sanborn   June 25th [18]88
    Your biographical sketch of Mr Alcott[1] was most entertaining & instructive a real apotheosis—and I hope you will have it printed ver-bal[ly] with report of all the other [word obscured] and
    I have written to Mr Harris but as he may have left for the west I enclose my note for you to *address*
    I hope I [several words obscured]   If this memorial day should be the last of the Concord School it would make a beautiful whole—& you might add a postscript telling of the various schools &c that have grown out of it & justify its existence

Truly yours
ELIZABETH P. PEABODY
(*oldest* member of the School)

MS, MCo

    1 Sanborn's "biographical sketch of Mr Alcott" was probably shared with Peabody in draft form as he did not publish it until 1893.

Peabody repeats the story that their neighbors at her childhood home in Salem turn out to be the Hawthornes.

✄ To Thomas Wentworth Higginson   (*incomplete*)

Dear Mr. Higginson   [ca. 1880s]
    It may interest you to know a fact I have found—a genealogical register of the Hatwhornes, viz. that the great grandfather of Haw-thorne (my brother in law) married Sarah Higginson a granddaughter of the Rev. Francis Higginson of Salem—He was named Nathaniel,

and was the son of Judge John Hathorne who was one of those who condemned the witches (Hawthorne used to say that this deed was *a curse* upon the family—which he had inherited!) Hawthorne's Grandfather was Daniel Hawthorne "the bold" of Revolutionary memory. His father Nathaniel was born in May 1775 and he himself July 4th 1804—having a sister (Elizabeth) 2 years older than himself & another Marie Louisa two years younger, His mothers name was Elizabeth C Manning She married his father in 1801 & inherited [word illegible] activities She was poetical [by?] temperament with great good sense and highly cultivated by reading. But losing her husband who died in the West Indies of yellow fever in 1807 she shut herself up in a passionate devotion to his memory in a most remarkable seclusion even from her husbands family. She was lovely in person even to her dying day & I used to think she looked as if she had walked out of an old picture as she preserved the ancient costume—

When my sister Sophia was an infant in arms we moved into the neighborhood—an uncle of mine Married a Manning—who was cousin to Mrs Hawthorne from whom my mother learned of Mrs Hawthornes peculiar life (wh. of course subjected her to much gossiping untrue). But there was something about what she heard that interested my mother's imagination—and she wrote her a note & asked her to let her little daughter E who was two years older than I—come into our house & be taught to read & write with me   Mrs H was touched with my mother's note & asked her to come & see her in her chamber which my mother did & liked her—I have a dim remembrance of Nathel just my age—but only recollect his back & curls—of which I was reminded by Julian when he was of the same age. I looked up with great veneration to Elizabeth who seemed to me quite a wonder—she could read & write—and I was very dull about it—Hawthorne once told me he did not remember when he did not read Shakespeare & my mother also had the same experience)—We moved out of their neighborhood in 1808—& I never had any intercourse again till 1838 when I went back to live in Salem & discovered that Hawthorne was the author of those tales after wards published as Twicetold Tales—I made a move to renew my acquaintance with Elizabeth believing her to be their author—Elizabeth had lived for twenty years in as great seclusion as their mother but she responded to my call—by an invitation to me to come & see her which was however so indefinite I did not go. When the volume of Twice Told Tales was published he sent me a copy, and afterwards at my invitation came with his two sisters & passed an informal evening—when our acquaintance was propitiously begun in looking over the volumes of Flaxmans which I happened to have on my table & they had never seen—

My sister Sophia being an invalid had gone to bed not believing they would come & I could not induce her to get up though I told her he was splendid & looked just like Lord Byron. She said if he has come once he will come again—a few days after he called & she came down stairs while he was there—He was evidently much taken with her *then* [letter incomplete]

MS, NN-B

Quite possibly this letter, dated 1890 by Houghton Library, is the last one Peabody ever wrote.

✖ To [Samuel Gray Ward?]

Boston
19–20 June [1890]

My dear friend I received (fifty) dollars which I understand to be the dividend on my money invested with you for the whole year beginning July 1st. I am deeply grieved to hear that Anna is suffering as much as ever in body—I had no idea that as time wore on her pain was [accentuated?] & should like to know the spiritual exercises into which she is uplifted but I do not suppose she could write them out for me who, without any *acute* pain am not so patient as I ought to be with the tediousness of this borderland between the two worlds—

But how is it with you? What are the thoughts which cheer or sadden you? I wish we could have some talk together—for you seem less inclined than ever to write—In the world to come we shall understand one another without words which at best only *point* to what we want to say—this *yearning* is not so healthy a state as *tranquillity* which I only occasionally feel but perhaps you feel it all the time—I am content to *muse* His praise—while the fire burns. You have a resource that lifts you out of egotism that I have not in your children & grandchildren who are with you in fact or imagination but I am the last of my generation   I will not bore you any longer with dear love to Anna am yours as ever   Eliz P Peabody

MS, MH

An undated letter of consolation, which could have easily been intended for her own mourners.

✄ To Elizabeth Curson Hoxie

East Hampton, Long Island

My dearest Libby—   [n.d.]

I have heard from Margaret D C—of your *immense loss*—that lovely who seemed to be such a blessing from first to last—the youngling of the flock; truly, the flower of the family! and *the one*—was he not? & is not this a soothing thought who has enjoyed his life more uninterruptedly than either. I trust, dearest, that you have so far kept the faith of your childhood as to feel a full assurance that he is lost *only* to your senses—& that you are not lost *even to his senses*—but that from his inner point of view he is nearer to you than ever had more intimate cognizance of all you feel & thirst & are!—The next mansion of the Father's house must needs *include* to those who go into it *this one*.—So sure am I that our affections are our tenure of immortality that it seems to be a corollary of *Reason* that those within the veil find it a perfect transparancy—*Identity* could not be without memory—& memory must be *sight*—when this finite body ceases to shadow the blessed reality of the union of spirits the *communion* of the past made perfect! Early death is so plainly a *disorder* & disorder must needs be superficial—the *contrivance* of the dear God to give us *freedom and faith*—the self possibility of love which in its essence is an *act of faith*—the self emptying impulse which we share of God's creativeness—Do let me hear from you—dear—Your natural *utterancy* will here come into a blessing if you give it free scope—& you know I cannot be weary of the expanses of your heartthought—or what is so near your *life fountains*. I think of poor John—with his *less* degree of salient imagination to clear the apparent gulf.—I hope he will trust himself fully to *you* to carry him across on your strong wings—I am going to mail to him today a Circular which will interest you & him—This race interest is I know in both of you as in few—*In you* I know it is deep as life & *the more* you cling to your child the more full of life is the bond that unites you to all who share your nature, It is because of the strength of your individual affections that you have kept so strong lively & tender your social deeds—Perhaps John can solace talking to his neighbours or even going about a little to induce people

to enter into this colony—His grave—quiet—advocacy of it—would
go far to persuade substantial people who are prone to turn away from
visionary schemes. My friend Mr. Newton who takes time out of a life
of work for humanity in the midst of New York Society (He is Rector
of a Church which is a *worker*—not a Dreamer—[in?] beneficent
ways)—says *what the Earth needs* is a ministry of explanation for
which he has no time at all—& he appealed to me to know if some of
the old Brook farmers perhaps—would not like to lend a *tongue* if not
a hand.—You know *Dana & Ripley* have *not kept the faith*—Did they
really have it? or was it not a dream of their fancy? They did not have
it as you & John did Frank Shaw & George William Curtis—Don't
you think *they have kept the faith*? Devoted as they have been to their
families—it has not turned them from *the great family interest of
mankind*—but deepened & enriched it—and I feel sure that you will
find your dearest consolation for private loss in working *for the
whole*—in which the list will again reappear in their individuality—
for "Eternal form shall still divide the Eternal soul from all desire"
and *Reunion* heal the wound of *Bereavement*—with boundless over-
payment—. It seems to me that one thing we shall find when we are
reunited—that the apparent separation so grieving to *us*—was an *accession* of enjoyment to *them*—that they enjoy us more than they possibly could have done had they remained in this discordant state
which our best earthly life is—that they suffer less from our sufferings
& even from our faults than they would have done here because they
see their limitations—Just as we suffer less than children do who are
suffering—when we see that though it seems interminable to them—
the limitations are wholly within our sight—& the *advantages* of their
trials are also patent to us.—The greater our *sympathy* the more we
are thus consoled—if we will give our sympathy the wings of imagination to transcend space & time & get into that intensity of life which
has no here or there or now & then.—Remembering your mother I feel
as if *you* had observation as well as experience—(in your likeness of
character to her) of the *annulling* of pain and perplexity—by completeness of life—& this completeness of life the good dead *have*. In
communing together, I think you will find that he has been enjoying
you as he could not have done on earth.—My sister Sophia in her loss
of Hawthorne had such consolation. She often would say that in the
greatest trials she had after his death (& one was that he had been
cheated all his literary life by his publishers—& kept unnecessarily
anxious by their never giving him *an account*—so that he never knew
what he had a right to spend,—) she would rejoice sometimes that he

did not know their selfish rascality till he was in a point of vision where magnanimous forgiveness would not be made difficult by an imagination so afraid of self delusion that it always instinctively disarmed *disappointment* by imagining the worst possible issues to be the probable ones.—In remembering the last months when the fear of paralysis (as we now believe) overshadowed him with what he conceived to be a living death of unutterable horror—to him—She would often say, "I did every thing for him that human love could do on earth and he knew it—& my Father took him in order to do what my heart *desired—banish* the cloud a too sensitive temperament drew over his sky—He required *finer conditions*—He no longer is anxious about the children or me—He sees that all we have to suffer is Revelation which we should realise as blessings—"I must go home to my husband & get strength for my work (as she sometimes said to us after counselling us how to meet some present difficulty of life)—When she was dying—her children said to her "We are consoled because you are going to Papa,"—"Yes,"—she said "I see them together—beyond the shadow—with a sense of peace *for them*—that balances—even banishes—the pain of *present loss*—which I know is *no loss* in reality. I find myself at the end of my paper & so much to say—Good Night—Anson I believe hovers over you & feeds on your love by the grace of GOD, who does for us *more* than we know how to desire
EPP

MS, MH

Index

Elizabeth Palmer Peabody's letters are indexed in **boldface** numbers under the names of their recipients.

About the Author

Bruce Allen Ronda worked for six years tracking down and deciphering the *Letters of Elizabeth Palmer Peabody*. He was graduated from Hope College (A.B., 1969) and earned his M.A. (1974) and Ph.D. (1975) from Yale University, where he was a Woodrow Wilson fellow. He has been Associate Professor of American Studies at Skidmore College and has received a Mellon Grant and a Fulbright fellowship. His home is in Scotia, New York.

About the Book

Text set in Linotype Baskerville by Yankee Typesetters, Concord, New Hampshire.

Printed and bound by Braun-Brumfield, Inc., Ann Arbor, Michigan, on 60 lb. Glatfelter.

Designed by Joyce Kachergis Book Design and Production, Bynum, North Carolina.